# BODIES IN DISSENT

# BODIES IN DISSENT

*Spectacular Performances of Race and Freedom, 1850–1910*

**Daphne A. Brooks**

Duke University Press    *Durham and London*    2006

2nd printing, 2007

© 2006 Duke University Press

All rights reserved

Printed in the United States

of America on acid-free paper ∞

Designed by Amy Ruth Buchanan

Typeset in Minion by Keystone

Typesetting, Inc.

Library of Congress Cataloging-in-

Publication Data and republication

acknowledgments appear on the last

printed page of this book.

Duke University Press gratefully

acknowledges the support of

Princeton University, which

provided funds toward the

production of this book.

*For*

**Juanita Kathryn Watson Brooks**

*and in memory of*

**Nathaniel Hawthorne Brooks, Sr.**

# CONTENTS

# ACKNOWLEDGMENTS

This project would have never been completed without the financial support of several institutions and the counsel and encouragement of advisers, mentors, friends, and family during what, at times, seemed like an epic gestation period. As a dissertation, the project was funded generously by the Mellon Foundation, the University of California, Los Angeles, the Ford Foundation, and the W. E. B. Du Bois Institute for Afro-American Studies Research at Harvard University. Princeton University, the University of California, San Diego, the President's Postdoctoral Fellowship from the University of California, Berkeley, and the Woodrow Wilson Foundation each financed my time away from teaching so that I could complete revisions of the manuscript. I am particularly grateful to the late Richard Newman, Lisa Thompson, the staff of the Du Bois Institute and the entire "Couch" writing collective (Farah Griffin, Guy Ramsey, Bill Lowe, and Salim Washington) for allowing me the opportunity to spend time cultivating this project in its earliest stages and in the midst of an energetic and supportive scholarly community. Jane Gonzalez and the U.C. President's Postdoctoral Fellowship staff provided helpful assistance to me during my two years of sabbatical research at the University of California, Berkeley. Many thanks as well to Richard Hope, Sylvia Sheridan, and Bill Mitchell for organizing and overseeing the Woodrow Wilson's vibrant and nurturing Career Enhancement Program for junior faculty which provided me with the necessary time to complete research on this project. A very special thanks to Ken Wissoker for his patience, steady support, and editorial vision and to Courtney Berger and the entire Duke University Press staff for overseeing the development of this project.

Over the years, it has become apparent to me that an archivist's best friend is her librarian. For their generous time and diligent resourcefulness, I would like to thank the wonderful library staffs at the University of California, Berkeley's Bancroft Library, Yale University's Beinecke Rare Book and Manuscript Library, the New York Public Library's Billy Rose Theatre Collection, the Victoria and Albert Museum's Gabrielle Enthoven Theatre Collection, Irena Tarsis and the Harvard Theatre Collection, Brown University's John Hay Library, the British Library, the Library of Congress, Stuart Walker and Boston Public Library's Rare Books and Manuscript Reading Room, Oxford University's Rhodes Library, the San Francisco Performing Arts Library, the San Francisco Public Library, the Schomburg Library, the Smithsonian Museum, UCLA's Special Collections Library, and Emily Belcher, Anna Lee Pauls, Meg Rich, and Princeton University's Special Collections Library.

Staff and research assistants helped make the completion of this project a reality. Abundant thanks to Princeton University's Chris Faltum, Pat Guglielmi, Karen Mink, Marcia Rosh, Nancy Shillingford, and Jean Washington, and to UCSD's Christa Beran, Gretchin Hills, Nancy Ho-Wu, Lucinda Rubio-Barrick, Debbie Morrow, and Diane Lucette Wells. Thanks to Jonathan Walton, Simeon Bannister, and especially to Jeff Gonda for his brilliant and meticulous research assistance and to Kevin Mensch, Laurie Prendergast, and Matthew Stavros for their helpful technical support. For stepping in during the eleventh hour and reading drafts of this project, for providing sharp and illuminating editorial advice, and for his generous intellectual support and friendship, I thank Ed Blum.

Mentors, teachers, advisors, and sage counselors paved the way for me, read drafts of this project, created opportunities for me, and provided guidance, advice, and critical wisdom at every turn during the writing of this manuscript: I extend deep thanks to Lindon Barrett, Jennifer Brody, Ann duCille, William Gleason, Farah Jasmine Griffin, Robin Kelley, George Lipsitz, Lisa Lowe, Carla Peterson, Joseph Roach, Eric Sundquist, Mary Helen Washington, Cornel West, and Richard Yarborough. For her steadfast friendship and for encouraging me to open the door to the archive with an eye toward activism, I thank P. Gabrielle Foreman. This book was nurtured into being by the intellectual passion and creativity of the late Gillian Brown, the late Sherley Anne Williams, and especially the late Barbara Christian, and it is dedicated to their enduring legacies.

I am enormously grateful to my colleagues in Princeton University's Department of English and Program in African-American Studies as well as to those at the University of California, San Diego, for having provided me with nurturing scholarly communities in which to produce and complete this work.

Friends and loved ones, colleagues, teachers, students, acquaintances, and creative partners taught me, challenged me, encouraged me, and accompanied me on the journey. Endless thanks to Oliver Arnold, Bertram Ashe, Katherine

Bassard, Herman Beavers, Deborah Blanks, Dan Blanton, Sara Boyd, Thomas Breidenthal, Rochelle Brocks, Barbara Browning, D. Crystal Byndloss, Eduardo Cadava, Veronica Chambers, John Chardos, Matthew Christensen, Kamari Clarke, Lauren Collins, Kandia Crazyhorse, Angela Crenshaw, Katie Czukas, Lawrence Danson, Cathy Davidson, Michael Davidson, Madhu Dubey, Kathleen Davis, Jeff Dolven, Brent Edwards, Emory Elliott, Safura Fadavi, Rod Ferguson, Ellen Fernandez-Sacco, Diana Fuss, Rachel Gabara, Sophie Gee, Rosemary George, Alison Gibbons, Simon Gikandi, Eddie Glaude, Herman Gray, Jennifer Greeson, Bill Handley, Michele Habell-Pallan, Marta Hanson, Saidiya Hartman, Briallen Hopper, Brandon Jacobs-Jenkins, E. Patrick Johnson, Kimberleigh Jordan, Ralina Joseph, Claudia Johnson, Josh Kun, the late Karl Lange, Shirley Lim, Arthur Little, Roger Q. Mason, Dwight McBride, Sarah Meer, Elizabeth McHenry, Jesse Mills, Carlos Miranda, Dave Morris, Sue Anne Steffy Morrow, Megan Mullarkey, Mark Anthony Neal, Katy Niner, Jeff Nunokawa, Nell Painter, Ruby Pan, Diana Paulin, Heather Polley, Eric Porter, Ann Powers, Albert Raboteau, Catherine Ramirez, Guthrie Ramsey, Paul Raushenbush, Chandan Reddy, Jane Rhodes, Glenn Robertson, Amada Sandoval, Janet Sarbanes, Nayan Shah, Nigel Smith, Vance Smith, Shelley Streeby, Stephanie Smallwood, Eric Sundquist, Meghan Sutherland, Eileen and Steven Swerdlick, Simone White, Michael Tan, Cristal Truscott, Eric Weisbard, Tim Watson, Michael Wood, Patricia Yeager, Lisa Yoneyama, and many others.

A handful of people carried me the length of the way. For reading drafts of this project, offering wise counsel, for processing the challenges of this work with me, supporting me as it continued to take shape, and for their lasting friendship, I am especially grateful to Angela Ards, Gisele Fong and Dean Toji, Allegra and James Gibbons-Shapiro, Elisabeth Guzman, Judith Halberstam and Gayatri Gopinath, Reggie Jackson, Nicole King, Rachel Lee and Gabe Spera, Maureen Mahon, Sayuri Oyama and Kenji Tierney, Imani Perry, Sonnet Retman and Curtis Bonney, Noliwe Rooks and Bill Gaskins, Dave Swerdlick and Asila Calhoun, Lisa B. Thompson, Gayle Wald, LeNaye Willis, Tamsen Wolff, and Sandra Yarock.

For a decade and a half, I have been lucky enough to benefit from the mentorship, friendship, guidance, patient wisdom, faith, and strength of Valerie A. Smith. It is to her that I owe my deepest gratitude for sharing her extraordinary intellectual support, her spiritual fortitude, grace, and vision. This book is a testament to her faith in this project from its very beginning.

Many years ago, my older sister Renel returned home from college one weekend with James Baldwin, Toni Morrison, and Alice Walker tucked away in her overnight bag. For sharing her love of African American literature and culture with me and for supporting me in multiple ways, I extend my love and thanks to her and to her husband Tommie Moon. To my brother Nate, his wife Sally, to my nieces and nephews Nadya, Trae, Megan, Michael, Melissa, and Anthony, and to my entire extended family and to those beautiful loved ones who have passed on, my enduring love and thanks.

Finally, it is to three people that I owe my greatest thanks of all. To my brave, adventurous, and determined aunt Lodell Matthews, I am so very grateful to her for encouraging me to live, work, think, and fight with spirit and conviction. Thank you to my luminous, courageous, and compassionate mother Juanita Kathryn Watson Brooks and to my late father, the brilliant, visionary, and fiercely loving Nathaniel Hawthorne Brooks, Sr. To them I owe every ounce of my courage to write, to teach, and to mentor. They have inspired me to to tell the stories of all those who have gone before me. This book is dedicated to their dreams and to my father's everlasting memory.

# INTRODUCTION

erformance is on the run in William Wells Brown's 1857 play *The Escape, A Leap for Freedom*. A sly revision of Harriet Beecher Stowe's *Uncle Tom's Cabin*, Brown's abolitionist tale of fugitive resistance features characters who utilize a combination of wit and brawn to slip free from the bonds of slavery. The first drama published by an African American, *The Escape* crosses and compresses racial melodrama with satire, the slave narrative form with picaresque adventure in order to imagine how black figures might shrewdly determine ways to emancipate themselves from servitude. Armed with a skillet for a weapon and an insurgent impulse rooted in American patriotism, archetypal hero Glen and a band of his compatriots dash headlong into a grand tableau denouement that literally fulfills the promise of the play's title. Yet well before the fugitives make their climactic "leap" to Canada, Brown's drama mounts its most spectacular escape in the unlikely hands of Cato, an expedient house servant who wages a one-man, slow-burning insurrection of blackface minstrelsy in his solo bid for freedom.[1]

Although he professes to have initially traveled North "wid ole massa" to uphold the Fugitive Slave Act and "to hunt" his fellow slaves, Cato's decision instead to "hunt Canada" comes in the wake of his having taken sartorial liberties with his "owner." North of the Mason-Dixon line and donning the clothing of his slumbering master midway through act 5, Cato delivers one of African American dramatic literature's earliest and most illuminating monologues on the paradoxes of black identity formation. He marvels,

> I wonder if dis is me? By golly, I is free as a frog. But maybe I is mistaken; maybe dis ain't me. Cato, is dis you? Yes, seer. Well, now it is me, an' I em a free man. But, stop! I muss change my name, kase ole massa might foller me, and somebody might tell him dat dey see Cato; so I'll change my name, and den he won't know me ef he sees me. Now, what shall I call myself? I'm

now in a suspectable part of the country, an' I muss have a suspect-able name. Ah! I'll call myself Alexander Washington Napoleon Pompey Caesar. Dar, now, dat's a good long, suspectable name, and everybody will suspect me. Let me see; I wonder ef I can't make up a song on my escape! I'll try.

As he subsequently confesses in song, Cato has literally stolen the clothes off his "ole massa's" back. "I dress myself," he proudly proclaims, "in his bess clothes, an' jump into de street." Piling on an excess of ironically inflated monikers bestowed upon the enslaved, Cato inverts his own crisis in naming himself by turning that dilemma into a multi-vocal, insurrectionist act. In his soliloquy, he transmogrifies his own self-fragmentation into signifying parody. Speaking on dual frequencies as both captor and captive, gentleman and minstrel clown, Cato (re)dresses himself both in the role of the "suspicious" fugitive as well as the "respectable" master, conflating and perverting the boundaries between each role. His drag act simultaneously stages the spectacle of a fugitive asserting his subjectivity through the tools of performance and using those same tools to mock and destablize the subjectivity of the ruling class.

During this moment of self-making at the site of masquerade, Cato thus rejects the unchanging condition of burnt-cork "blackness" and instead har-nesses the pleasures of fugitive emancipation borne out in costume. He has, in effect, traded in the sycophancy and self-abnegation of blackface persona. Whereas, for much of the play, his minstrel antics traffic in slippery and unsavory racial caricature, Cato's unlikely conversion from feckless burnt-cork puppet into ruminative and resistant runaway manifests the socio-political commentary at the heart of *The Escape*. Stringing together an in-ventive combination of ironies, malapropisms, and neologisms, he turns exis-tential crisis into spiritual jubilation, self-estrangement into ecstatic self-realization, and haphazard disguise into philosophical enlightenment. "Free as a frog," Cato encounters self-reckoning at the site of his alien condition and wriggles free of enslavement to perform a counternarrative to that of min-strelsy's master script. In his search for "a place where man is man, ef sich dar can be found," he locates this site in the act of disguise.[2]

Cato's encounter with himself at the very moment he commits to quite literally "putting on ole massa" provides the occasion to contemplate the profound ironies of black identity formation and self-recognition in the cen-tury that marked African Americans' freedom from enslavement. His startling and paradoxical movement toward self-recognition and a kind of alien(ated) awareness of the self—"I wonder if dis is me?"—confronts and transforms slavery's putative "social death," turning that estranged condition into a rhetorical and social device and a means to survival.[3] *The Escape* thus articulates a critical theme in the work of nineteenth- and early-twentieth-century black cultural producers by registering the disorienting condition of social marginalization and the resourceful ways that African Americans rehearsed methods to transform the notion of ontological dislocation into resistant performance so as to become the agents of their own liberation.

By translating alienation into self-actualizing performance, *The Escape* repeats and revises a signal trope in the nineteenth-century black cultural imaginary. In the context of an evolving African American literary tradition questing for existential meaning and an avenue to state with conviction that "I was born," a diverse array of political activists, stage performers, and writers utilized their work to interrogate the ironies of black identity formation. Against the backdrop of a turbulent and changing international theatre culture, these figures invoked multiple performance strategies, performative ideologies, and new popular cultural technologies to counterintuitively articulate and redeploy the discourse of socio-political alienation. Wedding social estrangement with aesthetic experimentalism and political marginalization with cultural innovation, these resourceful cultural workers envisioned a way to transform the uncertainties of (black) self-knowledge directly into literal and figurative acts of self-affirmation. Their work confronted the "strange meaning" of African American identity formation in the ominous historical arc stretching from the period of antebellum slavery into the early twentieth century. Repeatedly, each individual's work asked a variation of the classic question posed by W. E. B. Du Bois at the dawn of the twentieth century: how do we articulate and narrate the experience of "double-consciousness"—this feeling of "two-ness," of being both "an American" and "a Negro"—and how might African Americans use this dissonant condition to forge discursive as well as embodied insurgency?[4]

## Afro-Alienation, Eccentricity, and the
## Opaque World of Transatlantic Performance

*Bodies in Dissent* traces the pioneering acts of nineteenth- and early-twentieth-century performers who drew from the condition of social, political, and cultural alterity to resist, complicate, and undo narrow racial, gender, sexual, and class categories in American and British cultures. This book's list of characters defies simple categorization; yet taken together they exemplify the sheer heterogeneity of black popular performance culture from the decade before the Civil War through the Gilded Age. Colorful and unconventional, transient and resourceful, each of the figures included in this book developed risky, innovative paths of resistance in performance. For Henry Box Brown, a fugitive who escaped from slavery by mailing himself in a crate from Virginia to Philadelphia, the culture of spectacle and illusion would eventually inform his efforts to create a large-scale visual exhibition to protest the peculiar institution. His contemporary, Adah Isaacs Menken, would, conversely, turn those very same resources back onto her own racial ambiguity in order to gain international fame while performing equestrian acts in a flesh-colored body suit. Combining Box Brown's visual spectacle techniques with Menken's corporeal masquerades, the turn-of-the-century Bert Williams and George Walker theatre company announced the mainstream emergence of postbellum black musical theatre that contested the cultural legibility of racial representations and the black musical form itself. Out of this moment, two women would each respectively imagine the epic potential of performance to challenge the spatial, historical, and political limitations placed on African Americans. Vocalist-turned-novelist Pauline Hopkins used fiction to consider the utility of spiritualism and singing as intertwining keys to diasporic liberation, while her contemporary Aida Overton Walker, a world-renowned cakewalk dancer, dared to yoke her modern dance choreography with New Negro revisionist racial and gender ideologies.

These characters shared much more than it appears at first glance, for their complex and at times confounding work and that of many others evolved out of a dynamic transatlantic cultural matrix. Each channeled varying forms of alienation and dissonant identity politics into his or her performances and, in doing so, stylized alternative forms of cultural expression that cut against the grain of conventional social and political ideologies. Like Wells Brown's Cato, they seized on the potential of unruly performance to articulate heterogeneous identities. These cultural innovators managed their alienation by turning the disorienting condition of marginality and subjection into dense performances that ranged from formal and highly orchestrated concert hall events to literary endeavors and spontaneous, quotidian encounters.

A loaded term in both theatre criticism and diaspora studies, "alienation" emerges in *Bodies in Dissent* as a specific strategy of black Atlantic performance. In what I call "Afro-alienation acts," the condition of alterity converts into cultural expressiveness and a specific strategy of cultural performance. Afro-alienation recurs as a trope that reflects and characterizes marginal cultural positions as well as a tactic that the marginalized seized on and reordered in the self-making process. Akin to both Bertolt Brecht's pioneering theories in drama as well as to black feminist and diaspora scholars' theories of the black experience in the Middle Passage, Afro-alienation acts draw from what Hortense Spillers describes as the "dehumanizing, ungendering, and defacing" conditions that African peoples encountered in the New World. Having little access to the culture of property, to the culture of naming, or to patriarchal wealth, the mythically rendered black body—and the black female body in particular—was scripted by dominant paradigms to have "no movement in a field of signification." Born out of diasporic plight and subject to pornotroping, this body has countenanced a "powerful stillness."[5]

Erupting, then, out of this putative "stillness," Afro-alienation is thus encoded with the traumas of self-fragmentation resulting from centuries of captivity and subjugation. Yet it also manifests the counter-normative tactics used by the marginalized to turn the horrific historical memory of moving through oceanic space while "suspended in time" not only into a kind of "second sight," as Du Bois would have termed it, but also into a critical form of dissonantly enlightened performance. In Afro-alienation, the "strange" situation of "looking at one's self through the eyes of others" evolves into what Brechtian feminist Elin Diamond describes as the enlivened position of "'looking at being looked at ness.'" Calling attention to the hypervisibility and cultural constructions of blackness in transatlantic culture, the historical agents in this book rehearsed ways to render racial and gender categories "strange" and to thus "disturb" cultural perceptions of identity formation. Just as Brecht calls for actors to adapt "socially critical" techniques in their performances so as to generate "alienation effects" and to "awaken" audiences to history, so too can we consider these historical figures as critically defamiliarizing their own bodies by way of performance in order to yield alternative racial and gender epistemologies. By using performance tactics to signify on the social, cultural, and ideological machinery that circumscribes African Americans, they intervene in the spectacular and systemic representational abjection of black peoples.[6]

Afro-alienation acts invoke largely anti-realist forms of cultural expression in order to call attention to the hegemony of identity categories. This strategy also provides a fruitful terrain for marginalized figures to experiment with culturally innovative ways to critique and to disassemble the condition of oppression. Generically diverse and dissident, Afro-alienation acts draw from the tactics of heterogeneous performance strategies—in visual media, Victorian magic, religious, classical, and secular song, breeches and drag performances, transnationalist musicals, spiritualism, and modern dance—in order to defamiliarize the spectacle of "blackness" in transatlantic culture. In particular, these acts rewrite the ubiquitous master narrative of minstrelsy, with its colonizing and constrictive figurations of grotesque and immobile "blackness." These "strange" and disorienting "cultural moves" challenge the tragic spectacle of suffering endemic, as Saidiya Hartman has shown, in nineteenth-century racial melodrama. Rather than depending on conventional realist methods to convey the humanity and value of black subjectivity, Afro-alienation opens up a field where black cultural producers might perform narratives of black culture that resist the narrow constraints of realist representation. In short, these singular figures questioned (or perhaps eschewed) the high (and unrealistic) bar of credibility set for them by dominant culture in representing and (un)doing themselves, favoring instead dissenting methods of narration and aesthetic articulation. These figures combined a diverse array of cultural tools to voice the rich and resonant contours of black identity formation with all of its contradictions and conceits. Through their efforts, they waged a battle to reverse the crisis of representational timelessness projected onto blackness.[7]

Spectacularly "eccentric," the characters in this book imagined and stylized ways to make their subjugated bodies move more freely by embracing what Carla Peterson calls an "empowering oddness." In Peterson's provocative reinterpretation of the eccentric, the term connotes a "double meaning: the first evokes a circle not concentric with another, an axis not centrally placed (according to the dominant system), whereas the second extends the notion of off-centeredness to suggest *freedom of movement* stemming from the lack of central control and hence new possibilities of difference." Working outside constrictive racial and gender paradigms, the figures discussed in *Bodies in Dissent* rehearsed "off-center" identity formations to disrupt the ways in which they were perceived by audiences and to enact their own "freedom dreams." Each figure developed a means to move more freely and to be culturally "odd," to turn the tables on normativity and to employ their own bodies as canvases of dissent in popular performance culture.[8] Restoring movement and history to individuals in the cultural margins, their unpredictable performances cut through the tyranny of stillness evolving out of the Atlantic world's dominant racial and gender narratives. Suturing together hybrid and sometimes profane cultural materials to rewrite categories of self-representation, these path-breaking individuals experimented with ways to express their dissonant relationship to dominant culture and plotted ways to subvert that dissonance.

*Bodies in Dissent*'s motley crew of characters emerges in the context of an unfolding transatlantic popular cultural landscape. In this volatile universe, they performed their own unique versions of revisionist cultural politics.

Working within a "transatlantic imaginary," these performers drew inspiration and innovation from a lively cultural space owing less to geographical cartography and more to the landscape of popular culture. From the mid-1800s to the early 1900s, this dense cultural terrain traded, recycled, and reinvented various theatre tropes, forms, and entertainers themselves.[9] In the transatlantic imaginary, the performing body shifts, converts, and evolves across the imbricated genres of phantasmagoria shows, spiritualism, Victorian pantomime, extravaganzas, magic, and minstrelsy. This fanciful sphere, familiar to audiences on either side of the Atlantic, was a fertile zone for ingenious figures to experiment with alternative ways to critique presumably fixed notions of cultural identity. Many of these characters crafted a means to "doing" themselves in ways that would signal their movement in and through "overlapping diasporas." Aware of their agency as "multipositional historical actors," they produced work that engaged with multiple and imbricated cultural sites of knowledge and, particularly in the late nineteenth and early twentieth centuries, some experimented with ways to interrogate the politics of "diasporic consciousness" through performance.[10]

Just as these figures utilized multiple and alternative strategies of cultural expression to disturb "New World configurations of value" assigned to blackness, I draw on multiple scholarly disciplines and critical methodologies to examine the diverse content and dimensions of their work.[11] My aim is to make visible what was a broad and ambiguous transatlantic cultural network of racial and gender typologies and signs. I therefore employ interdisciplinary critical methods including literary criticism, performance studies, social and political history, cultural studies, music history and musicology, theatre and dance history, and visual theory to explore the socio-political and aesthetic complexity of Atlantic world racial and gender performance. At its core, this study is inspired by the advances of black feminist theorists who have opened up new ways of considering the representational politics of the black body in the cultural imaginary.

As the recent anthologies *Recovering the Black Female Body* and *Skin Deep, Spirit Strong* and Deborah Willis's and Carla Williams's photographic collection *The Black Female Body* have shown, black women's bodies continue to bear the gross insult and burden of spectacular (representational) exploitation in transatlantic culture. Systemically overdetermined and mythically configured, the iconography of the black female body remains the central urtext of alienation in transatlantic culture. Hegemonic hermeneutics consistently render black women's bodies as "infinitely deconstructable 'othered' matter." Yet there are ways to read for the viability of black women making use of their own materiality within narratives in which they are the subjects. Such women might put their own figures to work for their own aesthetic and political uses and "image their own bodies" in such a way to "set up a constructive dialogue between poststructuralist and humanist views of identity." Rather than "either reducing the black woman's body to sheer ground or matter or, to the contrary, using that body to validate disembodiment," such figures invent ways to maintain the integrity of black female bodies as sites of intellectual knowledge, philosophical vision, and aesthetic worth.[12]

Shaped foundationally by black feminist ideology, *Bodies in Dissent* concerns itself with mapping out moments in which black cultural producers and black women in particular negotiated ways of manipulating the borders of the material and the epistemological in transatlantic performance culture. The figures in this book experiment with ways of "doing" their bodies differently in public spaces. We can think of their acts as opaque, as dark points of possibility that create figurative sites for the reconfiguration of black and female bodies on display. A kind of shrouding, this trope of darkness paradoxically allows for corporeal unveiling to yoke with the (re)covering and re-historicizing of the flesh. Dense and spectacular, the opaque performances of marginalized cultural figures call attention to the skill of the performer who, through gestures and speech as well as material props and visual technologies, is able to confound and disrupt conventional constructions of the racialized and gendered body. In what we may refer to as a "spectacular opacity," this cultural phenomenon emerges at varying times as a product of the performer's will, at other times as a visual obstacle erupting as a result of the hostile spectator's epistemological resistance to reading alternative racial and gender representations. From either standpoint, spectacular opacities contest the "dominative imposition of transparency" systemically willed on to black figures. Unlike the colonial invention of exotic "darkness" which has historically been made to envelop bodies and geographical territories in the shadows of global and hegemonic domination, this form of black performative opacity, as Saidiya Hartman suggests of black song, has the potential to "enabl[e] something in excess of the orchestrated amusements of the enslaved" or, I would argue, to instill movement in "free" yet socially, politically, and culturally circumscribed bodies.[13] As the characters in this study clearly traffic in cultural excesses, layering aliases and costumes, devices and genres atop one another, they demonstrate the insurgent power of imaging cultural identity in grand and polyvalent terms which might outsize the narrow representational frames bestowed on them. Reading these particular negotiations of black performance provides, then, a means to recuperating a narrative strategy that, for the nineteenth-century socially, culturally, and politically marginalized circumvents the dichotomy between being visible and abject and being "pure" and disembodied.

## The Spectator in the Archive

The archives of nineteenth-century black performance are characterized by their own dark gaps and elisions, and they present multiple challenges in tracing this cultural history of eccentric movement and Afro-alienation. One of my greatest concerns in mapping this transatlantic network of unruly black cultural performance has been whether I would be able to translate effectively and bring to light the complex layers of this work as it remains documented and recorded in libraries and historical archives today. "Where is the text in nineteenth-century performance?" a good friend once asked me. To manage and mark the distinctions between the agenda of the (mostly) white male recorders who experienced these marvelously unpredictable cultural events and the socially off-center performers who supplied the entertainment, I would have to negotiate an alternative path of historical and critical reading. My greatest anxiety while working on *Bodies in Dissent* has been that it would turn into a study of the most hostile and confused white spectators who witnessed the work of Brown, Menken, and the Williams and Walker Company in particular. While dominant audiences and critics are central to this study, the chapters ahead document a more complicated and dynamic cultural space than either an exclusive narrative about performers or a discussion of spectators could possibly reveal. Rather, I piece together periodical reviews, epistolary exchanges, actor's articles, playbills, and personal documents with fiction and biographies aiming to present a more vibrantly textured cultural landscape of black performance. This approach highlights an electrifying dialectic between, for instance, the scabrous review of an unconventional play and the dissonant gestures of performers embedded in that same review which sometimes tell a different story of the event in question. Searching for and mapping such tensions became a major effort in my work.

*Bodies in Dissent* seeks to make the work of various marginalized cultural performers more audible and, to borrow Robert Allen's language, "legible" in our studies of nineteenth-century African American culture and theatre history.[14] Yet I recognize my own role as a spectator in the archive. As a black feminist critic who is most concerned with bringing to the surface the narratives buried at the bottom of the historical troves, I recognize the critical exigencies of my own agenda. I hope, however, that by unearthing a more nuanced cultural landscape in these performances and by paying close attention to who performed, who documented these diverse acts and productions, why they did so, and in what context, I may to draw attention to the mechanisms of power in the transatlantic imaginary and at the site of the archive. My goal is not to suggest a totalizing narrative of nineteenth-century black performance, but rather to continuously ask "what do we know about these performances?" and "how do we know what we know?" In the case of historical figures such as the slippery Adah Isaacs Menken, this book aims to create an epistemological intervention in how we approach studying the work and cultural identity formations of subjects who remain the source of archival controversy. Following the lead of Hartman and others, my aim then is to "to write a different account of the past, while realizing the limits imposed by employing these sources, the impossibility of fully recovering the experiences of the enslaved and the emancipated at the risk of reinforcing the authority of these documents even as I try to use them for contrary purposes."[15] In sum, this book aims to read the tensions between what the archives record of the performers at hand and the ruptures and blind spots where these same performers defy the expectations and desires of the audience member/recorder. *Bodies in Dissent*, then, emerges out of that fraught and volatile dynamic and oscillates between attending to the observer's (sometimes hidden, sometimes naked) desires and the performer's equally complex agenda. In the performance of dissent, everything is in play.[16]

### Fugitive Bodies

This book begins by contextualizing the politics of African American performance and by examining the evolution of spectacularly racialized bodies in nineteenth-century theatre culture. Chapter 1 interrogates the nexus between transatlantic cultural and performance genres ranging from spirit-rapping to minstrelsy, and it reads Dion Boucicault's *The Octoroon* (1861) and Mansfield and Sullivan's American adaptation of *Dr. Jekyll and Mr. Hyde* (1887) as texts that sensationally exhibit racially liminal bodies in transatlantic theatre culture. Each production transforms the scopophilic display of racially indeterminate bodies in transatlantic theatre culture into an expression of (white) ontological anxiety and theatrical control over corporeal representation. This chapter contests the mythical boundaries between Victorian and American theatre cultures in order to expose an imbricated genealogy of Atlantic world performances that hinged on racially phantasmagoric spectacles. Likewise, the chapter examines a range of theatrical technologies that nineteenth- and twentieth-century black performers appropriated and redeployed for their own ends.

The remaining chapters of *Bodies in Dissent* examine the ways that various historical and cultural figures engineered and experimented with diverse cultural innovations and, in doing so, crafted new forms of narrative agency and corporeal representation in theatricalized spaces. Chapter 2 considers the ways that the work of black abolitionist Henry Box Brown potentially disassembles and renegotiates narratives of the black body and the spectacle of slavery through the lenses of theatre, performance culture, and visual technology. The chapter explores the two vastly different Box Brown slave narratives and places them each in dialogue with his ambitiously staged moving panorama exhibitions, presented in both North America and England. Box Brown, I argue, manipulates the corporeal to produce a renegade form of "escape artistry" in his distinct fugitive autobiographies, his use of visual technologies and popular song and in his public re-enactments of his flight from slavery.

Chapter 3 explores the theatrical work as well as the cultural legend(s) of the racially ambiguous actress Adah Isaacs Menken. The chapter considers the ways that Menken's 1860s performances open up critical questions regarding the metaphorical politics of race and racial performance in the nineteenth century, and it demonstrates how her work calls attention to the fluid ways that racialization attached itself to unconventional cultural (and often female) figures in performance culture. "Blackened" at the root by her profession and her professional choices, Menken's iconicity exposes the fallacies of racial and gender politics in the theatre of the transatlantic imaginary. Chapter 3 thus re-situates Menken in a black feminist cultural context in order to reread her performances in *Mazeppa* (1861), her "protean" drag acts, and her controversial blackface revues. This study of Menken also traces a dialectic between her performative strategies and that of the pioneering innovations of Sojourner Truth, a figure who produced critical interventions in (black) women's corporeal performances.

The final two chapters consider the place of performance in post–Reconstruction-era liberation movements. Chapter 4 examines the experimental theatrical innovations of Bert Williams's and George Walker's traveling musical *In Dahomey* (1902–4), a production which, I contend, poses a radical intervention in turn-of-the-century black nationalist and Pan-Africanist discourses. The chapter demonstrates the ways in which the musical intervenes in black corporeal and cultural representation. Rather than eschewing the cultural and political significance of the so-called back-to-Africa musicals, Chapter 4 explores how *In Dahomey* critically rewrites dominant constructions of black theatrical corporeality. Drawing from a range of spectacular performance technologies, *In Dahomey* defamiliarizes the minstrel show tradition to instead mount a series of complex inversions of cultural representation and to challenge oversimplistic racial, gender, and national categories.

*Bodies in Dissent* concludes with an examination of the intersections between postbellum black performance culture and turn-of-the-century black liberation ideologies. Chapter 5 traces the intertextual dialectic between the fiction of black feminist playwright and novelist Pauline Hopkins and the postbellum stage work of cakewalk dancer and choreographer Aida Overton Walker to explore the relationship between gender politics, performance, and New Negro activism. Through a study of Hopkins's fiction and Walker's dance productions, this chapter re-places the artists and their characters within a fertile matrix of rich and resourceful black women's performances. It also seeks to demonstrate the ways in which black feminist activists invoked performance strategies in the context of racial uplift movements. Chapter 5 charts the intersecting worlds of black women's literature, song, and dance in the postbellum era and the ways in which these artists used multiple aesthetic forms to articulate individual as well as communal desire. While Hopkins's *Of One Blood* weaves together performance tropes and transmigration politics as a means to rewrite black women's narrative and political agency, Walker's *Salome, the Dance of the Seven Veils* choreographs new directions for black female cultural representation in the twentieth century. Taken together, Walker and Hopkins, Williams and Walker, Menken and Brown negotiate ambiguous and unlikely forms of cultural movement that speak back to dominant culture. By imagining ways to perform their heavily contested bodies in different registers, they scripted alien(ated) racial and gender narratives for a new era.

## Crossing the River in Black Performance

*Bodies in Dissent* draws inspiration from both the path-breaking antebellum acts of Cato in *The Escape* as well as the postbellum resistant strategies of valiant characters in Pauline Hopkins's *Peculiar Sam* (1879), the first full-length musical written by an African American. Deft at juggling disguise as resistance, the characters in *Peculiar Sam* map out methods of escape that, like Cato's "act," illuminate the dizzying experience of performing alienation as a means to liberation. Hopkins's musical emphasizes the critical transformations open to African Americans as they gradually cross the divide from bondage to freedom. Akin to Cato's odyssey, *Peculiar Sam*'s characters embark on a journey to inhabit and utilize shifting forms of disguise in their quest to be free. Marked as "peculiar" because of his rebellious vision, the title character Sam masterfully draws from his performance skills to create a path to freedom. In the closing scene of the first act, he appears in costume as the overseer Lucas and sets into play his plot to deceive the black overseer Jim and throw him off of the trail to track his comrades' escape route. In a standoff that serves as the centerpiece to act 2, Sam and Jim confront and wrangle with one another in a spectacular showdown of wit and artifice. While Jim at first holds the upper hand in their battle, decoding Sam in his disguise as Caesar, he nonetheless fails at his own hand in tricksterism. Unable to put on a convincing mask of his own in his plot to apprehend the band of escaped slaves, Jim falls prey to Sam as well as to Caesar's superior ability to see beneath the garments of his costume. The play presents Sam as the superior trickster, the more seasoned masquerader of the two men. Sam thus emerges as the master of insurgent performance in the text who leads his fellow characters into the hopeful era of Reconstruction.[17]

In spite of its optimistic ending, *Peculiar Sam* is a text that articulates, as did *The Escape* before it and the performances of Williams and the Walkers, Brown, and Menken, the profound anxieties and questions attending strategies of performing black identity. Inasmuch as Sam and his cohorts benefit from phantasmagorically donning their arsenal of aliases, these characters also struggle with a nagging anxiety of identification for much of the play. The elder Mammy frets over her ability to recognize her own son in performance, confessing, after encountering him in disguise, "boy I hardly knowed you!" Again and again, Sam is made to confront a cast of characters who wrestle with their own ability to read the codes of his character's drag. In this way, they recycle Cato's fundamental questions of self-recognition for Sam himself. That is, in chorus *Peculiar Sam's* characters repeat in a different register the question that Cato posed in his antebellum performance, "how do we know ourselves" both as a people and individually in the wake of slavery's traumas? Who are we as we make this leap from slavery to freedom? In writing *Peculiar Sam*, Hopkins composed a narrative that sang the ballad of black alienation, once again converting existential crisis into its own liberatory waltz. Literally singing their way to freedom in act 3, crossing the banks of a river while laughing, shouting, and shaking hands, *Peculiar Sam's* cast of characters ultimately emancipate themselves by using their myriad gifts of performance to build a bridge out of abjection. Following the lead of *Peculiar Sam's* brave and resourceful characters, *Bodies in Dissent* aims to cross that bridge as well.

# 1. OUR BODIES, OUR/SELVES

*Racial Phantasmagoria and Cultural Struggle*

Something was amiss on the dance floor in 1853 America. This according to the Reverend Hiram Mattison who that year published *Spirit Rapping Unveiled!*, a slim and somewhat obscure manifesto in which Mattison sought to expose what he read as the treachery and fraudulence of spiritualism, the grassroots cultural movement that claimed to promote communication with the dead. In his pamphlet on the subject, Mattison mocks and debunks this "grand climax" of "all other superstitions, delusions, and isms" which had, nonetheless, by 1850, a reported two million followers. Waxing incredulous throughout his little book, Mattison is perhaps most mystified and offended by the "spirit-dancers" in his midst, spiritualist practitioners who claimed to summon multiple spirits in rapid succession through their bodies while in the throes of dance. In what Mattison viewed as a bogus and blasphemous hoax for the ages, these dancers would proceed, enraptured by movement, parading a string of " 'national characters' " from a "shaker" and "a negro" to an " 'old maid,' [and] an Indian chief," meeting in the veil, and "descend[ing] upon a circle of media, enter[ing] their bodies, and set[ing] them to dancing." The alleged performance reaches a climax when the spirit-dancers end their "physical demonstration" by "act[ing] out the . . . characters that had entered them."[1] A spectacle of miscegenous encounter, spiritualism creates, for Mattison in this scene and others, a horrifying taxonomic crisis as women, Indians, and Negroes collide and coalesce on the dance floor. Coupling and conjoining at the site of the spiritualist medium's body, these ethnic phantoms find voice in the figure of the most often white and female spiritualist who captures and reanimates marginal "characters" across the great racial, cultural, and spiritual divide, "acting out" and performing their residue long after they have withdrawn from their host. Like the "racially equivocal" figures of Victorian fiction that operate as "feminized penetrated figures" who are "vehicles of impurity," the spirit-dancing body "contaminates," "confounds and confuses" putatively impermeable racial and cultural borders.[2] Accordingly, Mattison's attempt to "unveil" these rappers manifests a deep-rooted anxiety of loss, the loss of social and cultural categories, the loss of a simplistic ontological certainty born out of naïve and solipsistic Eurocentric patriarchy, and perhaps most prominently the loss of epistemological clarity in reading, categorizing, and circumscribing bodies through discursive, political, and juridical means.[3]

But while Mattison may have aimed, through his fire-and-brimstone text, to halt the onset of spiritualist mania, he had clearly overlooked the fact that this alternative religious zeal was hardly anything new. With its spectacular display of possessed mediums and commanding trance speakers, spiritualism owed much to a hybrid jumble of popular nineteenth-century show culture rituals and diasporic religious practices. Erupting out of a broad transatlantic network of social and cultural performances that depended on corporeal conversion and fluidity, spirit-rapping, like other early-nineteenth-century theatrical genres, rehearsed the convertibility of the body. Spectacles of transfiguration were manifest in the spectral technology of early 1800s English show culture. Phantasmagoria shows, as they were known, served as the centerpiece of "illusionistic exhibitions" in which "magic lanterns" cranked out "specters" for spellbound crowds.[4] For many, the fundamental attraction of the phantasmagoria show resided in its ability to stage the illusion of ephemeral bodies—"phantoms"—parading before audiences while altering size, advancing toward and retreating away from spectator, and passing into and through one another.[5] Appearing to be both riddled with ontological breaks and ruptures and yet fluid and concatenate, these metamorphic and "discontinuous" bodies floated through an evolving English popular cultural imaginary.

American spiritualism absorbed the corporeal fundamentals of phantasmagoria and resituated these tropes in a volatile pre–Civil War landscape. A radical act of "desegregating the dead," the spirit-rapping sensation of mid-century North America further disrupted a country wrangling with borders between north and south, black and white, master and slave. Practiced principally by whites, spirit-rapping flourished largely within racially circumscribed confines. Historian Jon Butler in fact maintains that the movement "never transcended the lines of class and race as it spread across the country."[6] Yet one could argue that, despite its putative social divisions, spiritualism's philosophical emphasis on metamorphosis posed an ideological resistance to the cultural politics of segregation. In its spectacular dance contests alone, spiritualism continuously flirted with the disruption of presumably arbitrary racial, gender, and class boundaries.[7] In this regard, perhaps no cultural performance ritual figuratively and corporeally encompassed the turbulence of 1850s American culture and reflected the dissonant landscape of nineteenth-century transatlantic popular culture more so than spirit-rapping.

## Bodies (Un)Bound

A kind of "gothic romance," spiritualist practices were not unlike the narratives that Toni Morrison has famously found to be so densely suggestive and evocative of early-nineteenth-century America. Like Melville's oceanic frontier narratives and Poe's haunted excavations of the psychic wilderness, spiritualism too served to articulate Americans' "fear of boundarylessness, of Nature unbridled and crouched for attack. . . . their fear of loneliness, of aggression both external and internal. In short, the terror of human freedom—the thing they coveted most of all." In the same way that Morrison identifies a "dark, abiding, signing" Africanist presence which haunts early Anglo-American literature, so too might we think of Anglo spiritualism as "haunted" by African religious practices. It, in effect, unveiled a repressed and "African way of remembering" (black) bodies and the "socially dead." Toiling at the intersections of the spirit and the flesh, roaming the unmined borders of the afterlife, the spiritualist imagination mirrored that of its literary counterpart. By attempting to elasticize the framework of mortality, spiritualism aimed to "conquer fear imaginatively" by pursuing questions of liberty and self-possession, loss and recuperation.[8] The rituals challenged the limits of freedom in both the spirit and the flesh. To the many social and political reformers who were quick to embrace this movement, spiritualism represented a renewal in faith and offered both the opportunity for "self-purification" and a broader spiritual reawakening of the nation.[9]

Geared toward fostering a "co-mingling of souls," spirit-rapping negotiated the provocative conflict between the ambiguous affirmation of self-possession and corporeal agency and the abdication of that very autonomy. Opening up the body to serve as a conduit of transpersonal contact, communal desire, and knowledge, the movement promoted the spectacle of cultural encounter and likewise manifested the conflicting agendas of abolitionism. With its struggle to simultaneously endorse the individualism and sovereignty of the enslaved, abolitionism similarly promoted an empathic process of identifying with and thereby perhaps eclipsing the subjectivity of the enslaved altogether. Not surprisingly, Anglo-American abolitionists as many and varied as Amy and Isaac Post, Harriet Beecher Stowe, and William Lloyd Garrison championed spiritualism at various stages of their careers. Other reformists seized on spiritualism as providing an additional sounding board for the millennial movement's ominous jeremiad of the 1850s, a wishful foretelling of America's (re)unification with the spirit world.[10]

But whereas some high-profile antislavery figures evolved into even "more ardent champions of spiritualism," others such as Lydia Maria Child and Thomas Wentworth Higginson "constantly tried to distinguish their own beliefs from those of the mass of Spiritualists who flocked to witness sensational demonstrations."[11] Hiram Mattison rose out of this latter pack to underscore his role as a reformist and a fervent antispiritualist. In his written work, Mattison strove to reveal the "fraud" of the ephemeral "frontier" which the Posts and others attempted to traverse. But unlike Child, Mattison waged a fight against spiritualism that rested less on exposing the movement's threat to conventional religious practices and the "authority of the Bible" (Braude, *Radical Spirits*, 28) and more so on literally exposing the body of the medium. His *Spirit Rapping Unveiled* goes to great lengths to detect and destroy the work of a colorful array of alleged crooks, charlatans, and bohemian interlopers. Likewise, his text takes aim at spiritualism's Swedenborgian-influenced "theory of 'progress.'" Nothing could be more absurd, *Unveiled!* suggests, than the notion that spirits have the ability to advance through evolutionary spheres (*SRU*, 20–21).[12] Roaming this haphazard universe of "porous bodies" and reckless soul swapping, Mattison works assiduously to separate and re-stabilize the "magnetized" figures (*SRU*, 54) from opposing electrical states who couple, collide, and collude in a turbulent intercourse of the spirits.

Yet in this raucous world of transgressed spheres and dissolving barriers where bodies remain vulnerable to violation and penetration, Mattison confronts a troubling ontological dilemma. "But suppose," he queries, "one of the 'lower spirits' . . . having got possession of the medium's body, and crowded his soul out into the disembodied state, should refuse to go out of the body . . . what would the poor medium do?" Sensing the chaos that might erupt on the medium's corporeal frontier, Mattison appears to recognize how spirit-rapping dangerously fostered a culture with no borders at all. Only a bit of sardonic wit might provide a salve to this otherworldly anarchy on the horizon: "In the case cited by Mr. Ballou, the spirit of a deceased *gentleman* enters the body of a young *lady*! Adin's soul in Alice's body!! Well, then, which is it, Alice or Adin? a lady or a gentleman?" (*SRU*, 68–69). Perplexed by the distressed boundaries at hand, Mattison waxes anxious about spiritualism's potential to render bodies completely unreadable. Under the aegis of the "Sacred Scriptures," he sets out in his text to discredit and to still the mobility of spiritualist practitioners.

Mattison would direct much of his ire toward the female spiritualist in particular, and his *Unveiled* would serve as a critical platform on which to disparage "the medium [who] must give herself entirely up to the control of the spirits; that is, abandon herself to her imagination" (*SRU*, 55).[13] The very question of female agency and the use of the female body as an instrument of some "other" (aesthetic, spiritual) power runs as a seething subtext to Mattison's presumably high-minded social and sacred concerns. Still more, his quest to unveil the "truth" about the spiritualist female figure affords him a Coverdale-esque "veil" of his own. Beneath the aegis of his altruistic agenda lies a prurient spectator who imparts a patriarchal gaze of detection onto the bodies of liminal mediums. For as he speculates, this damned mob of rapping women might, in fact, harbor some essential "electrical affinity" which makes them more susceptible to communications with the dead. Mattison conflates his naked suspicion of spiritualism with his more subtle paranoia of women, and he speculates that the female domination of the field perhaps owes to the fact that "ladies would . . . be less liable to detection and exposure?" Hence, he assures that "[w]hether the 'spirits' think of it or not, we mortals know that their *sex* and *costume* is a fine security against detection" (*SRU*, 58).[14] The crux of his discursive manhunt remains exposure. Abject and "unveiled," the medium remains under attack here as Mattison aims to restrict the ephemeral and ideological mobility of spiritualist practitioners. The text insists that women's "natural" sex covers over the flesh and essentially veils them. In Mattison's charged and unstable universe, women are naturally fraudulent and thus always threatening with a hidden agenda, and to be sure, always in need of a vigorous "unveiling." The tactical aim of his book, then, remains to strip these eccentric bodies of their polyvalent power, to make the spiritualist's figure speak a singular and innocuous "truth." Forced into a cyclical maze of logic, Mattison's work depends on unseating the spirit-rapper's potential for intellectual and aesthetic polymorphousness and ambiguity. Yet simultaneously the text imbues these same women with social and cultural abstraction by reacting to their putative power to mask and convert their bodies into instruments of deception.[15]

With his palpably anxious regard for border crossing apparent, it comes as little surprise that Mattison would carry his obsession with ambiguous (female) corporeality forward and directly into the culture of slavery. Turning to yet another sort of corporeal medium, he focused his attention on the "300,000 mulattos" rearing their disconcerting faces in America's racial quagmire.[16] Still fascinated with liminal bodies when he turned toward the plight of "the Octoroon," Mattison translated his interests and anxieties into racial terms. In 1860, Mattison took up the cause of Louisa Picquet, a freed Louisiana slave who was touring the midwest and the northeast struggling to raise funds to free her mother in bonds. Mattison's subsequent participation in the production of the 1861 text *Louisa Picquet, the Octoroon: or Inside Views of Southern Domestic Life* is such that he alternates between interviewing the former bondswoman and intervening as narrator in Picquet's abolitionist text and her quest for freedom. Displaying a relentless interest in the (un)readability of the light-skinned Picquet, Mattison assures that no one "would suspect" that she "had a drop of African blood in her veins."[17] Peculiarly drawn to "white slaves" and physical affliction, Mattison repeatedly returns in his interrogation of his subject to the petrified flesh of Picquet and others who "looked like her," who faced the whip and who were "stripped and examined" under the evil eye of slavery.

The strategic abolitionist rhetoric of this questioning is, no doubt, evident here.[18] The racial liminality of "mulattas" such as Picquet exposes the inevitable fallacies of a system that relies on the mythical quantification of blood to define racial categories. Although slavery was fueled by the "power" to "make all slaves black regardless of their seeming whiteness,"[19] "white" slaves served as the ultimate appeal to abolitionist audiences since they called into question the logic of enslaving people according to "blackness." Conversely, the white mulatta's bondage threatens to destabilize the security and authority of the white reader/spectator whose subjectivity is fundamentally challenged by this spectacle of confluence. For, as many have noted, it is at the point where difference is indiscernible that problems occur. Unlike "the ideal spectator" who, Kristina Straub claims, "is not only detached from the spectacle [but] almost, indeed, invisible himself in his relation to the visible . . . benignly distant from the objects of his gaze," Mattison's interrogator/detective is, himself, *unveiled* through the body of Picquet. The white mulatta's body of evidence, her figure (encom)passing the uncanny traces of the familiar and the foreign, makes the violence of his white supremacy spectacularly visible and yet disturbingly contiguous with blackness. By discursively excavating and exhibiting the body of the octoroon, Mattison uncovers the body of white power itself and paradoxically leaves traces of its impurities.[20]

No surprise that Mattison's work hinges on exposing and spectacularizing the white mulatta's figure as a means to demarcate the boundaries of racial difference. In a lengthy exchange between Mattison and Picquet, he asks of her whether she was whipped "hard, so as to raise your marks?" and whether she was "cut through [her] skin?"[21] By framing his interrogation repeatedly in terms that force Picquet to deliver and demonstrate the economy of her physical torture, Mattison defuses the "octoroon's" body of its perplexing, multivalent resonance by reducing her flesh to pure and naked petrified matter. Although he repeatedly draws attention to her visible "whiteness" throughout the narrative, he maintains a steady aim and desire to ritualistically "strip" Picquet of her complex social and historical lineaments in order to clarify and calcify racial boundaries—even at the cost of "whitening" slavery. He assures his readers that "notwithstanding the fair complexion and lady-like bearing of Mrs. Picquet, she is of African descent . . . an octoroon or eighth blood," and he marches righteously toward his fiercely segregatory conclusions.

Fixated as much on the confusing ocular politics of race as he is on the confounding porousness of the female medium, Mattison holds a penchant for "scrutinizing the body for signs of buried black life" and this obsession steers his literary collaboration with Louisa Picquet.[22] As he had before in his anti-rapping treatise, Mattison steams ahead here toward properly resituating Picquet's haphazard, racially phantasmagoric body in mythically stable blackness. For Mattison, Louisa Picquet's narrative pivots on the reader's acceptance of his insistence that she is "black" despite her phenotypical "whiteness." His race for Picquet thus manifests "a factitious public discourse concerning the 'blood' and 'breeding,' the dominant mode [which] succeeds in transposing the real into the mythical/magical."[23] Like the spiritualist medium, Picquet's white mulatta body "functions as a floating signifier . . . [s]he is perpetually being erased or effaced in an effort to stabilize (reify) the tenuous, permeable boundaries between white and black, high and low, male and female, England and America, pure and impure" (Brody, *Impossible Purities*, 18). In response to this "category crisis," Mattison anoints himself as a discursive street-cleaner of sorts, wiping away these "polluted" bodies from the interstices of social and cultural dislocation. His work as author/editor "projects white desire onto 'mulatta' bodies by emphasizing the paternal and the patriarchal, the phallic and juridical Law of the (white) Father."[24]

In this universe of transient white mulattas, shape-shifting mediums, vanishing whiteness, and hard-to-read blackness, Mattison's nightmares reverberated across a vast horizon of sectional controversy and turbulence. Between the publication of Hiram Mattison's anti–spirit-rapping text and his project with Picquet, U.S. culture was itself a kind of phantasmagoria show. The spectacle of "white" bodies made "black (and vice versa) in Mattison's Picquet interrogation thus sensationalized what was an already present loosening of the perceived "ordinary boundaries between inside and outside, mind and world, illusion and reality." Though the Compromise of 1850 was putatively designed to demarcate north and south more clearly, its Fugitive Slave Act blurred those divisions, causing southern law to bleed north and the northern imagination of writers such as Harriet Beecher Stowe to drift south. The desire for order manifested itself in antebellum America through increased attempts to mete out clarity in equivocal bodies. Mattison's own fastidious form of ethnic cleansing revolved around maintaining a surveillance and circumscription of "those tell-tale mulatto, and quadroon, and octoroon faces" who "stand out unimpeached, and still augmenting as God's testimony to the deep moral pollution of the Slave States."[25] His obsessive fascination with both spirit-rappers and white mulatta figures reveals his impulse to institute systems of racial and ontological order and meaning onto bodies that show dangerous signs of erupting out of conventional categories.

Bodies of polymorphousness, the spirit-rapper and the racially liminal octoroon challenge facile readings of racial, gender, and corporeal identity politics, and each serves as an example of a transatlantic body of social and cultural conflict and turbulence. In this chapter, I explore the terrain of these phantasmatic figures and the production of a "transatlantic body" of performance in nineteenth-century culture. By considering the spiritualist medium alongside these other liminal bodies of transatlantic popular culture, I mean to suggest that spiritualism bore a relationship to this peculiar and vibrant universe of phantasmagoric entertainment. Key icons in this period of social and cultural unrest and transition, the dissonant bodies of the spiritualist medium and the racially liminal figure emerged in concert with the raucously disruptive figures of the English pantomime, the American minstrel show, and transatlantic sensation melodramas. In an effort to make the dialectic between these cultural forms more visible, the first half of this chapter traces the genealogy of that body. By considering a heterogeneous array of phantasmagoric bodies ranging from pantomime figures and minstrel performers to sideshow freaks, I trace the intertextuality inherent in the invention and spectacularization of this sort of iconography. This chapter also marks the progression of what I am calling racial phantasmagoria on the stage from the antebellum to the post-Reconstruction era. I contend that these technologies of the transatlantic body spectacularize the process of cultural alienation in ways that would yield reactionary as well as resistant cultural performance strategies in nineteenth-century culture.

The second half of the chapter considers the ways in which this transatlantic body operated at the center of conflicting social and political agendas in two radically divergent nineteenth-century theatre productions. I juxtapose Dion Boucicault's *The Octoroon* (1861) and the American stage adaptation of *Dr. Jekyll and Mr. Hyde* (1886) in order to demonstrate the shift from the sensational exhibition and exploitation of racially phantasmagoric female figures to the equally disturbing performance of white patriarchal "bodies in distress." *The Octoroon* and *Jekyll and Hyde* emerge from a broad cultural genealogy that transforms the spectacular display of racially indeterminate bodies in transatlantic theatre culture into an expression of (white) ontological anxiety and theatrical control over the representation of the body. Each of these productions operates as a manifestation of a culture obsessed with the porosity and excesses of the corporeal and intrigued by the spectacle of encounter and contact in and across the fictions of the body. But beyond serving as an icon of sociopolitical alienation and anxiety in the pre–Civil War era, the transatlantic body in performance clears a space for ante- and postbellum black cultural producers to re-narrate discourses of "blackness" and the body in Atlantic theatre culture.

## Genealogies of the Transatlantic Body in Performance

The theatrical body emerging in the years leading up to the Civil War was no doubt a corporeal manifestation of a turbulent era. If, as it turns out, 1848 was the year in which the pre-adolescent Fox sisters triggered the spiritualist phenomenon in their Rochester, New York, bedroom, it was also a year that emblematized the many conflicts and battles typifying the pre–Civil War era in the United States. During this period of what the critic Michael Rogin calls the "revolution on American soil," a range of "bitter political controversies" erupted—from sectional battles over the spread of slavery to labor tensions and suffragist activism.[26] This was the era of Seneca Falls, the emerging Compromise of 1850, the Astor Place theatre riot, and an omnibus of social, cultural, and political debates that dominated headlines in the northeast, the south, the Midwest, and the west. Following suit, minstrel productions and theatrical melodramas showed signs of absorbing and converting these brewing tensions, creating something of "a kind of civil war on the stage."

In the topsy-turvy world of Hiram Mattison, this "civil war" repeatedly showed signs of erupting in and out of the very bodies that populated the cultural imaginary of the antebellum era. "A playful ontological instability," which was, as Robert Allen reminds us, "reproduced all too threateningly on a social level this side of the footlights" took shape in an era in which social ideologies of the body remained sharply in flux. Shaped by the "professionalization of authority, wage labor, the logic of slavery and abolition, as well as the women's rights movement," the "new bodies" of modernity that Rosemarie Garland Thomson argues "felt alien to the ordinary citizen" were figures responding to the challenges placed on "the common citizen's sense of autonomy and mastery over his own" corporeality, as well as that of others.[27] The culture of performance responded to the uncertainty of corporeal autonomy by producing a range of liminal and embattled types and icons. These figures prowled the colorful world of nineteenth-century transatlantic theatre and performance, a universe that trafficked in a panoply of phantasmagoric bodies. Just as in America, where the liminal bodies of mediums and mulattas alike were met with an anxious gaze, so too were a myriad array of theatrical amalgams treated with differing degrees of fascination and horror in English culture. Indeed, the parallels between Victorian spectacles of transfiguration and American conversion rituals are numerous and stunning.

As Nina Auerbach has shown, " '[t]heatricality' " was a "rich and fearful word in Victorian culture." Having gradually developed forms of melodrama and comedy that exhibited a heightened and often hyperbolic "mixture of fantasy, low comedy, trick effects, and spectacle" from the eighteenth century forward, English theatre absorbed and transposed onto the performing body the turbulence of its own fast-changing nineteenth-century social landscape, marked by industrialization, scientific advances, and theological queries.[28] Dubbed pantomimes, the Victorian versions of these productions showcased narratives and performances of metamorphosis and transfiguration. In particular, the "metamorphic energy" of popular Victorian fairy tale pantomimes such as *Cinderella*, *Mother Goose*, *Aladdin*, and *Peter Pan* gives evidence of how the genre was "directed to the ends of fantasy, to delight not only in the reproduction of a fairy and transcendental world . . . but also in theatrical effects of light, colour, costume, and pictorial beauty." Scenery, plot development, and characters—not to mention scripts themselves—were engineered to shift shape, form, and direction markedly within and in between performances.[29] The transformation scene rested at the center of the genre's amorphous mayhem with its fixation on characters and landscapes that were relentlessly subject to distortion. This "metamorphic abundance of pantomime," with its wild elixir of "paradise and terror," is "the seductive essence of Victorian theatricality."[30]

With ever-increasing technological advances, Victorian performance culture produced narratives of bodily transfiguration and instability. Pantomimes provided the terrain on which to wrangle with philosophical questions of self and to marvel at physical and environmental transmutation. In turn, the genre's metamorphoses came to symbolize "the dangerous potential of . . . invad[ing] the authenticity of the best self." Like the phantasmagoria shows from earlier in the century which "made it possible to put into words perceptions and effects new in human experience," pantomimes and the extravaganza shows which grew out of them aimed to visualize the previously "unrepresentable" by bringing to the stage vividly fantastic imagery and morphological amalgams.[31] By the 1880s and 1890s, British audiences began to anticipate and demand the representation of "a chaos of species" in stage characters, the "jumble of creatures whose mad metamorphoses subvert not only the primacy of humanity, but its existence."[32]

As the pantomime peaked in popularity in England, the theatre of sensation and spectacle crossed to American shores and into a variety of generic forms. *The Black Crook*, for instance, in 1866, became the most successful American stage extravaganza of the nineteenth century. Capitalizing on technological spectacle, *The Black Crook* exploited the visual wonder of semi-nude female performers, fanciful gnomes, amphibea, and Faustian villains, as well as sensational plot twists with "displays of fire, water, transformations of all sorts, phantasmagorias of horror, caverns, grottos, necromancy and conjury" for a run of nearly five hundred shows at Niblo's Gardens in New York City. Critics argued that the show was "merely an excuse for presenting a continual succession of spectacles, ballets, transformations, [and] enchantments."[33] But the show most powerfully exemplifies the extensive cross-pollination of transfiguration strategies in nineteenth-century transatlantic culture. Perhaps the grandest example of the extent to which English pantomime tropes permeated American theatre and performance, the successful extravaganza production carried on the pantomime tradition in which "the activities of the players—transformed by the good spirit or fairy from the characters of the opening—themselves constituted a grotesque, physical, and topically satiric social and urban fantasy."[34]

As was the case with a number of popular mid-century theatre ventures, *The Black Crook* was ripe for blackface parody and was, in fact, turned into a successful burlesque by Christy's minstrels for three months. This kind of parodic minstrelsy absorbed the surplus representation of Victorian pantomime and contemporaneous American extravaganza productions. Like the "problematic femininity" coursing through Lydia Thompson's midcentury burlesque with its "monstrously incongruous" spectacle of female performers behaving outside the bounds of conventional gender codes, minstrelsy pushed the spectacle of the transformed and transfigured body in racial drag and promoted a frenetic concoction of phantasmagoric theatrical forms. Gary Engle contends that because *The Black Crook* "was the epitome of theatrical excess, it was particularly well suited as an object of minstrel burlesque." This "excess," rooted in the mythical black body, provides the crucial link between minstrelsy and pantomime-influenced theatre. With its notorious dependency on the spectacle of duality and contradictions mapped across unruly bodies, the minstrel show lends itself to curious and provocative comparisons with other phantasmagoric performances. Resituating minstrelsy in a broader critical and contextual framework of theatrical corporeal spectacles underscores the shifting currencies of the transatlantic body, especially how and why that body remains a vestige of sociopolitical conflict *in* performance. By complicating minstrelsy's position in genealogies of the transatlantic body, my aim is to emphasize the tension erupting in the transatlantic theatre world, the cross-pollination of midcentury social and cultural anxieties that were cyclically imported and deployed onto bodies in performance.[35]

Reaching its greatest popularity between 1846 and 1854, the minstrel tradition is often cited as a centripetal force in the making of American popular cultural and national identity formations.[36] Less attention has been paid, however, to the significance of minstrelsy's particular role in the making of a spectacularly incongruous body *as* a performance strategy unto itself. Perhaps more than any other critic, Saidiya Hartman has worked to demonstrate the "Manichaeanism at the heart of minstrelsy," which, she argues, "was the division between the races. The seeming transgression of the color line and the identification forged with the blackface mask through aversion and/or desire ultimately served only to reinforce relations of mastery and servitude." Hartman illuminates the ways that minstrelsy posited multiple and yet mythically separate and competing bodies in the blackface figure. This duality was frequently reproduced and reinforced through the distillation of minstrel images in print and media culture. The popular circulation of minstrel sheet music heightened and spectacularized the contradictions in blackface performance. Sheet music, Robert Toll contends, often "emphasized that minstrelsy was a white man's charade by featuring portraits of groups in formal wear without makeup, sometimes accompanied by contrasting illustrations of them in costume and blackface." If anything, these images serve to further commodify the spectacle of duality inherent in minstrelsy. Moreover, minstrelsy's promotion of "white self exploration" through what Hartman identifies as the "elasticity of blackness and its capacious affects" led to an inevitable method of performance that depended on containing difference and dissonance in one (acting) body. Minstrelsy thus anticipates a malevolent strain of what Elin Diamond might call "alienated acting." "Keeping differences in view instead of conforming to stable representations of identity, and linking those differences" to a politics of white supremacy and white working-class desire, minstrelsy produced and displayed the "differences within" blackface as a means to the possession and domination of blackness which, Hartman rightly contends, lies at the tactical root of the minstrel show genre.[37]

In this way, minstrelsy extended and transformed the iconography of the transatlantic body, simultaneously racializing and policing that body for the purposes of mass consumption and collective desire. Both the American minstrel show and Victorian spectacular pantomimes rode waves of curiously similar cultural obsessions with physical metamorphoses; the exhibition of (in)authentically transfigured and socially "deviant" bodies—white men masquerading as black caricatures—radically recalls the pantomime narratives' emphasis on a surplus corporeality and superabundant representation as central thematic and visual attractions of the productions. Yet, unlike pantomime, minstrelsy made systemic and repeated attempts to circumscribe the very surfeiting body that it produced. As Hartman observes, if "grotesque bodily acts like rolling eyes, lolling tongues, obscene gestures, shuffling, and the like animated the body . . . [b]eatings, blows, and brawls reestablished the identity of those who defied the boundaries of race and status." In sum, minstrelsy's "performances of blackness regulated the excess they conjured up with the threat of punishment and humiliating discovery."[38]

Minstrelsy valorized a grotesquely humorous and often erotic exhibition of racial transformation, structuring entertainment elaborately around the titillating display of bodies in distortion and the corporeally transfigured white male figure. Early American minstrel show productions focused—like extravaganzas—heavily on "spectacle" as opposed to narrative. Lott argues that these minstrels

> relied first and foremost on the objectification of black characters. . . . If the primary purpose of early blackface performance had been to display the "black" male body as a place where racial boundaries might be both constructed and transgressed, the shows that developed in the mid-1840s were ingenious in coming up with ways to fetishize the body in a spectacle that worked *against* the forward motion of the show, interrupting the flow of action with uproarious spectacles for erotic consumption. (Lott, *Love and Theft*, 140; emphasis added)

The "vulgar spectacle" of the disfigured or the strangely transfigured minstrel performer in burnt cork, wig, and dress, with protruding mouth and flashy and "dandified" costumes, literally shaped and steered the direction and format of the genre. This performance of the mutated and blackened body, ever shifting positions from song to song, structured and provided the central focus of the minstrel show. Rather than displacing plot, in these shows the "blackened-up" white body became the narrative focal point. The very evolution of American minstrelsy from "narrative dramas to chopped pastiche" by the 1840s exposes the primacy of the body *as* plot in the genre. Although W. T. Lhamon contends that minstrelsy's "formal slipperiness was a way of tempering and deflecting the clanging political pressures imposed" on the theatre, the evolving scarcity of plot in the genre signals the theatre's propensity for fetishizing surplus and surfeiting blackness as a narrative unto itself in performance. The minstrel show stylized, racialized, and redeployed a transatlantic body of embattlement in nineteenth-century culture.[39]

Minstrelsy racialized the English pantomime tradition by appropriating the nursery-rhyme language and imagery of pantos, inverting that genre into a heavily sexualized and sensationalized enactment of power over and through the iconography of the black body. While Engle speculates that minstrel troupes had little interest in pantomime since it "was a distinctly non-American art" and because pantomime "could not easily be burlesqued," he overlooks the primacy of the spectacular body in both theatrical genres. Whereas the pantomime employed the "Benevolent Agent" or "fairy godmother" character of the conventional nursery rhyme and fairy tale genre as a means of inserting play and possibility into the production of identity,[40] the minstrel show relied on a repertoire of "nonsense" songs, puns, and physical humor which fixated on "the relentless transformation of black people into things" (Lott, *Love and Theft*, 143). Blackface jokes and songs revolved around the transmutation of black bodies into animals, furniture, and—quite obsessively—food. This "schoolyard culture," as Lott calls it, focused on malleable constructions of black corporeality which, in turn, were used to demarcate the rapidly transmogrifying racial, social, and political borders of mid-nineteenth-century culture. With its "struggle over the seating of chaotic energy," minstrels seemingly adapted the tropes of masquerade and fairy tale transfiguration into an inverted abolitionist rhetoric; in the world of burnt-cork, black bodies systematically converted into "things" and thereby rectified sociojuridical barriers between black and white, free and enslaved.[41] In other words, "blackface developed distinct responses to 'amalgamation'—not by attacking but by enacting miscegenation." Thus, "the donning of blackface restaged the seizure and possession of the black body for the other's use and enjoyment" (Hartman, *Scenes of Subjection*, 31–32).[42]

Like the bodies of spirit mediums and racially hybrid figures, like theatre itself, the blackface body operates as a point of encounter, as an imaginary site of contact and conflict, a frontier on which to locate both "terror and pleasure." This sort of body comes to the fore and is quite clearly the fulcrum of a number of the most popular subgenric minstrel productions such as *The Quack Doctor* and Shakespeare burlesques such as *Desdemonum*. *The Quack Doctor* emblematized the genre's frequent attempts to attack, deflate, and discount African American class mobilization in the antebellum era by mocking the credibility of black socioeconomic leadership and professionalism. As Engle reveals, like "earlier European forms of popular stage humor," farces such as *The Quack Doctor* "made use of stock comic types such as pompous savants, frustrated lovers, dandies, and dictatorial parents, and placed them in situations where pretention could be deflated and insincerity punished, usually to the accompaniment of graphically violent horseplay. What distinguished the minstrel farce from its European forebears was that each character type was a simplified version of the blackface clown."[43] This major distinction resembles what Hartman might call the "stage of sufferance" and the "suffering black body" in formal theatrical space, a figure which *The Quack Doctor* stylizes and centralizes as a mode of performance spectacle. With its insistence on repeatedly foregrounding blows to the body, scenes of mutilation, amputation, and gouging, *The Quack Doctor* illustrates and ensures that the making of "the corporeal enactment of blackness" would be "a pained one" in minstrelsy (Hartman, *Scenes of Subjection*, 27). Likewise, *Desdemonum* extends minstrelsy's hostility toward nascent black professional culture. By utilizing the grotesque black body as a means to distorting and satirizing the gravity and ambitiousness of black classical theatre productions, midcentury minstrel Shakespeare burlesques inevitably signified on the threatening power and potency of black thespian forebears such as James Hewlitt and Ira Aldrige.[44] As a counterpoint to flourishing black performance culture, minstrelsy sought to naturalize a spectacularly abject and hyperexcessive black body in nineteenth-century theatre.

The white minstrel performer's production and navigation of a violently deformed black corporeality highlights how alienated acting shored up white supremacist ideology. Brecht, for instance, envisioned a gest that would liberate spectatorial perspective and subvert tyranny by way of requiring actors to resist "complete transformation," instead calling on them to "conserve," "contain," and to hold differences in suspension with oneself so as to "discover, specify, imply what [one] is not doing." Conversely, white minstrel show performers exploited the genre's premise of spectacularly racialized difference in order to reaffirm the superior skill of white performers to invade, occupy, and ventriloquize alien "blackness." If minstrelsy's alien (black) acts were frequently deployed as an expression and a performance of white working-class solidarity and desire, as an increasing number of critics have claimed, it goes without saying that the heterogeneous body of the blackface figure performs "blackness" while simultaneously (en)acting and producing "whiteness." Minstrelsy conserves the performance of "whiteness" and "blackness," holding them in tension with one another and grotesquely exposing the mutual constitution of the former with the latter. The blackface minstrel performer defamiliarizes both racial categories, calling them strangely into conversation and proximity with one another and revealing the way that, in Joseph Roach's opinion, genealogies of performance in the circum-Atlantic world "attend not only to 'the body,' . . . but also to bodies—to the reciprocal reflections they make on one another's surfaces as they foreground their capacities for interaction."[45] What I wish to suggest is that we closely consider the strategy of alienating the body and "blackness" in minstrelsy, how the practice of alienation participated in the making of a dissident theatrical figure that traveled the stage in the mid-to-late nineteenth century and found itself at the center of both hegemonic and resistant social and cultural ideologies.

At home everywhere and nowhere in performance culture, the transatlantic body resembles that of the American sideshow freak who, as Rachel Adams has shown, "suggests an intolerable fragmentation and dissolution of meaning." This body which resists categorization therefore requires, in the context of "freak show" culture, "narratives about exotic places, miraculous events, or horrifying accidents that might give coherence to bodies" that resist social and cultural taxonomies.[46] In effect, it is a body that defies a singular context and national culture. It is a body without a nation, and yet like the sideshow freak, the transatlantic body in performance is repeatedly called on to forge some kind of national consciousness, at the very moments in which its figure exposes and affirms the tenuousness of nationalism and its fictions.

Perhaps no theatrical figure summoned up the contradictions of transatlantic performance culture and corporeality more intensely than that of Irish playwright Dion Boucicault's construction of the "octoroon." Developed in the interstices of minstrel shows, pantomime, melodrama, and spectacular theatre, Boucicault's 1859 production of The Octoroon worked with the ideological elements of each genre to produce a theatrical drama that became salient to audiences on both sides of the Atlantic. Far from functioning as a representative work of either nineteenth-century American or British drama, the play situated itself at the center of a highly volatile Atlantic theatre world obsessed with racial as well as gender transfigurations and slippage. With its dual, transatlantic endings, The Octoroon stands both outside and centrally inside American and English culture, ambiguous as the title character Zoe's body itself, protean in its shifting forms and plot machinations. Decidedly anarchic in its inevitable move toward spectacle, social, cultural, and finally environmental dissolution, *The Octoroon* drew from minstrelsy and melodrama, as well as spectacular theater and phantasmagoria shows in the making of a distinctly transatlantic body. Boucicault's traveling melodrama of sensation and dystopian reform restyled the transatlantic body as an icon of sectionalism that served to reconstitute nationalist order as well as imperialist desire. As we will see, it is the genre of melodrama itself that ultimately allows for the exposure of the "truth" of the racialized body—that is, that it is spectacularly inauthentic.

## Law and (Dis)Order: Melodrama, Manichaeanism, and Superabundant Bodies in Dion Boucicault's *The Octoroon*

> He has taken up bodily the great "sectional question."
> —"The Octoroon," *New York Times*, December 15, 1859

A renegade amalgamation of multiple theatrical genres, Dion Boucicault's *The Octoroon* (1859) amplified and reassembled the tradition of racial melodrama set into play by the mammoth success and influence of Harriet Beecher Stowe's *Uncle Tom's Cabin* (1851–52) and its many subsequent theatrical adaptations, parodies, and burlesques. Stowe's novel and its various cultural incarnations did much to promote the nexus between minstrelsy and melodrama. *Uncle Tom's Cabin* combines the deeply entrenched relationship between the "noble" whippings endured by enslaved martyr Tom with the "farcical blows" delivered to the clownish Topsy. Stowe's text exposed and intensified the contiguity of melodrama and minstrelsy, the ways in which each genre borrowed from and informed the other in the culture of midcentury popular theatre; this generic cross-pollination is clearly borne out in the theatrical adaptations of the novel. Lott, Hartman, and Linda Williams have each shown how the novel's adaptations manifested tropes of minstrelsy, even as they revised and redeployed these familiar tropes for ostensibly antislavery purposes. Moreover, all three critics have demonstrated the extent to which melodrama and the contiguous genre of sentimental fiction were mutually constitutive with minstrelsy in their midcentury incarnations. Minstrelsy borrowed as much from melodrama as melodrama borrowed from minstrelsy in the production of a spectacular and "suffering" black body.[47]

The diversity of *Uncle Tom's Cabin* productions makes plain the distinct sociopolitical markings of their period. Whether putatively abolitionist or proslavery, "they all took up in their very formal structures the sectional division, based on competing economic systems, that would soon culminate in civil war. . . . To produce the play was by definition to engage in a divisive cultural struggle" (Lott, *Love and Theft*, 212). In the wake of the *Uncle Tom's Cabin* plays, sectional debate "henceforth became theatrical ritual, part of the experience of *Uncle Tom*" (Lott, *Love and Theft*, 223). If, however, the "Tom plays" translated the controversy of the Compromise into formal theatrical ritual, *The Octoroon* converted the grammar of staged sectionalism into a corporeal allegory. At once a hybrid concoction of spectacular and sensation melodrama, minstrelsy, and phantasmagoria shows, Boucicault's play produced a spectacular transatlantic figure that would, as the *New York Times* aptly observed, take up "bodily the sectional question."[48]

*The Octoroon* built on the success of *Uncle Tom's Cabin* but diverged from it in significant ways. It would have been difficult for the European immigrant playwright Boucicault to escape the experience of "Tom-mania" at its height. In 1853, the same year that Mattison first published his antispiritualist treatise, the eccentric Irish theatrical entrepreneur Boucicault traveled to America, having already spent over a decade writing, producing, and acting in a string of successful romantic comedies, gothic melodramas, and pot-boiler productions for the London as well as the Paris stage. His arrival in New York along with actress-wife Agnes Robertson marked the beginning of what was to be "the most successful and lucrative part of [his] caree[r]."[49] Boucicault spent most of the 1850s—including a brief sojourn in New Orleans—honing and to some extent revolutionizing the genre of spectacular melodrama by basing much of his work on the specificity of his cultural environment.[50] Hailed by English critics for making "one of the most popular forms of English entertainment," Boucicault's technological fantasy productions earned him a reputation as a "master" of Victorian spectacular theatre.[51] Yet to read Boucicault's work exclusively within the rubric of Victorian or American theatrical paradigms would be to overlook the ways in which his production of *The Octoroon* flouted regional categorization and, in turn, disrupted national and generic boundaries.[52] The playwright did much to stylize a transatlantic form of spectacular theatre which specifically served to heighten the iconicity of liminal bodies in performance culture.

Boucicault's brand of spectacular theatre both cleaved to and contrasted greatly with the modes of fantasy and distortion already present in the pantomime and in the extravaganza productions of the era. His distinct style of sensation in theatre shares the pantomime's emphasis on manipulating and underscoring fantastic, visual stage events. Yet Boucicault's spectacle melodrama differed from the pantomime in its invocation of realism and in its effort to theatrically reconstruct all the "grandeur" and wonder of "natural" settings and phenomena. The genre was often defined as a kind of plot-enhanced panorama show with its detailed representations of landscape and its efforts at producing "emotional, physical, and social sensation" through "the painting of a highly selective, highly coloured portrait of modern society and modern urban life in as 'realistic' a way as possible." Spectacular melo-drama paradoxically sought to recreate extraordinary acts of nature, fires and floods for example, as sensational, *super*-natural events onstage. Such scenes were believed to have enlivened melodrama and heightened the dramatic complexity of the numerous moral dilemmas at the center of these narra-tives.[53] Boucicault's innovations and investment in the culture of spectacular melodrama are inextricably linked to his production of the body of the "tragic octoroon" on stage, and indeed this kind of use of the spectacle had far-reaching effects on the ways in which race and the body were subsequently performed in transatlantic culture.

Like minstrelsy, the play's production of a transatlantic body disrupts the primary codes of melodrama, even as it services these very same generic strategies. The racial melodrama of *The Octoroon* clearly situates the trans-atlantic body as a means to reconstituting order; the play presents and exposes this body of excess in order to finally purge it from the community. At the same time, the production manipulates melodrama's mechanistic strategy of exposure in order to reveal epistemological "truths" that undo the very bina-ries that the genre seeks to establish. Like the ritual of spectacle in spectacular theater, *The Octoroon* ultimately exposes "race" itself. Race emerges, in *The Octoroon,* as an elaborate stunt, a construction of gargantuan and highly spectacular proportions. In the end (quite literally), the play's production of a spectacularly "real" transatlantic body predicated on the title character's alienated racial and gender formations opens the text up to (English) na-tionalist as well as imperialist identifications and appropriations.

From its opening at the Winter Garden Theatre in New York City on December 6, 1859, *The Octoroon* articulated complicated and contradictory ideologies about race and the body in antebellum popular consciousness. Boucicault thematically and theatrically transformed Mattison's mid-decade nightmare of porous bodies into a trope of spectacular racial melodrama and freakery that proved complex and disruptive in multiple ways. A "narrative of diaspora and enslavement in the plantation economy," *The Octoroon* show-cases a kind of racial spectacle and phantasmagoria that conceptually, thematically, and generically challenges the arbitrary boundaries between genres, geographical territories, and popular culture itself in the nineteenth century.[54]

Both the title character—the tragic heroine Zoe—and the play's much-talked-about scenery bind the production generically to spectacular theatre and melodrama, and both function dually to create the kind of sensational drama that became the playwright Boucicault's trademark. The plot finds character and setting equally vulnerable. Protagonist George Peyton has returned to his family's Louisiana plantation, Terrebonne, to find it in financial ruin. Peyton's deceased uncle, a profligate judge, has left behind a string of debts and an illegitimate daughter by a former slave, the octoroon servant Zoe. Unaware of Zoe's history, George falls in love with her, and Zoe is forced to reveal her racial origins to him before professing her passionate feelings for him as well. Their bliss is destroyed by the sale of the plantation and the villainous Yankee overseer M'Closky's treacherous plot to purchase Zoe along with the Peytons' land. In a bid to intercept payment of the Peytons' debt, M'Closky resorts to staging a one-man ambush of mulatto slave Paul and his Indian companion Wahnotee. The play reaches a climax as Scudder (the valiant Yankee) and Wahnotee avenge Paul's death and M'Closky, in a fit of fear and rage, sets a nearby steamer on fire before perishing as well.

This final sensational plot turn proved a highpoint in the play, second only to the fate of Zoe, a controversial narrative development that Boucicault was later forced to revise after *The Octoroon*'s debut in London. In the original American version, Zoe opts to commit suicide—a gesture having more to do with her aim to ease her lover's pain than to resist M'Closky's advances.[55] But death by poison also allows Zoe to stave off George's potential emasculation, having lost the "possession" of his lover to a higher bidder at the Peyton slave auction. Zoe's suicidal sacrifice in turn offers George the freedom to marry and seal a financial union with Dora, the wealthy neighboring planter Sunnyside's daughter. The American debut of *The Octoroon* closes with Zoe's final profession of her endless love for George while dying in his arms.

Both the American and English versions of *The Octoroon* highlight the perils of the title character by invoking a number of theatrical forms: Victorian spectacular theatre's emphasis on (super)natural cataclysm, sensation drama's obsession with hidden identity, American melodrama's emphasis on the Manichaean split between characters and the restoration of domestic order, and minstrelsy's fascination with racial masquerade and in particular its fetishization of fair-skinned, "high yaller gals."[56] Zoe's body operates as an allegorical vessel that allows for adulteration and the tumultuous mixing of diverse generic forms. Her iconic figure also corporeally manifests the play's socio-political equivocations, which Boucicault publicly endorsed. In a complaint filed with the Winter Garden Theatre management, the playwright openly argued that the production represents "slavery as a social fact without intending to touch any of its political bearings but only to use its dramatic element."[57] In this instance and many others, Boucicault played fast and loose with politicizing his production, seeking largely to soften and obfuscate the incendiary edges of his play in order to appeal to the widest constituency possible.

Yet avoiding the social and political maelstrom of sectionalism and slavery was impossible for a play like *The Octoroon*. Staged on a frontier where "human difference, like a selvage, forms the seams at which separate worlds meet," and operating as "a narrative of encounter, a dramatization of Anglo-American contact with the creolized interculture of the Latin Caribbean," *The Octoroon* mounted this topography of difference through the body of its title character (Roach, *Cities of the Dead*, 180–81), a "semantic marker, already fully occupied by a content and an expectation." In either version of the play, Zoe exists for others—and a particular male other. A "victim of sacrificial expenditure," her mulatta iconicity stands as "the transgressor before the law" (181–82).[58] A confoundingly "unreal, impossible ideal," Zoe remains the "corrupted and corrupting constitution" in the play, the focus of the drama's ideological energy. For her body bears/bares the history of racial encounter and remains "open" to violation as a result of her racial and gender identity.[59] Zoe's "miscegenous body" stands at the crossroads of juridical debates concerning race, family, and property. She is the manifestation of the crisis that miscegenation law sought to police. As Eva Saks maintains, miscegenation law "upheld the purity of the body politic through its constitution of a symbolic prohibition against the dangerous mixing of 'white blood' and 'black blood.'" Embodying the loss of (white) racial "purity," Zoe corporeally allegorizes the nation's simmering state of disunion as it gradually prepared to go to war with itself over social, economic, and political issues related to slavery and state sovereignty.[60]

Press reaction to *The Octoroon*'s New York City opening translated these tensions into apprehension and confusion toward the title character. The aggressively proslavery New York *Herald* writer James Bennett Copperhead raged against the broader implications of the play as a drama of "the abolition aroma" which "prostituted" the stage "to the work of disunion and treason." Other journalists fixated more specifically on the play's heroine as a source of allure. "[W]hat was an octoroon?" queried the literary journal *Albion*. "While he harbored 'an arithmetical suspicion' that 'it might be something like a

1. "That lady is a genuine white woman!" *The Octoroon* illustration cut-out. Courtesy of the San Francisco Performing Arts Library and Museum.

double quadroon,' he was forced to the shameful admission that curiosity goaded him to find out what the 'strange creature' really was like."[61] The *New York Times* even found good reason to be "disturbed by 'the wildest rumors,' " that *The Octoroon* had "impress[ed] the public mind with a sense of something awful and 'irrepressible.' "[62] More threatening than didactic abolitionist tirades, the taxonimic (in)determinacy of Zoe's body posed an epistemological crisis that challenged the order of things in antebellum culture. Evading the "repression" of the national imaginary, her miscegenous body would yield and sustain a spectacular act of looking in midcentury melodrama.

Zoe emerges in Boucicault's play at the center of an extended racial phantasmagoria act. Played by Boucicault's European wife Agnes Robertson, her character shifts repeatedly throughout the play. Even before Zoe's initial stage entrance, her identity is a tentative, shifting, and contested source of discussion. Initially, Scudder greets George and Mrs. Peyton by commenting on having seen the former with Zoe and looking much like his uncle. "O, aunt!" exclaims George, "what a bright, gay creature she is!" Scudder responds by sharing his own "view" of Zoe:

> What, Zoe! Guess that you didn't leave anything female in Europe that can lift an eyelash beside that gal. When she goes along, she just leaves a streak of love behind her. It's a good drink to see her come into the cotton fields— the niggers get fresh on the sight of her. If she ain't worth her weight in sunshine you may take one of my fingers off, and choose which you like. (139)

Scudder assures that Zoe is physically equal in beauty to any European woman, but he also creates here a triangulated scene in which "niggers get[ting] fresh on the sight of her" is its own titillating spectacle. At the apex of ludicious scopophilia, Zoe is here both whitened by her beauty and blackened by her juxtaposition with other racially abject bodies who are spectacularly erotic in Scudder's aroused universe. Scudder's open articulation of her cross-racial desirability renders her racially suspect as well. For surely no white woman could generate such open lust and looking. Hypervisible and invisible, Zoe, then, remains in danger of disappearing in the text and yet rests at the center of many characters' most vivid desires. While the planter Sunnyside and his daughter Dora literally overlook Zoe in this opening scene, George assumes that they simply "do not notice [her]." Showing early signs of his cultural obtuseness, George is blind to Zoe's "impossible" status as a racially liminal character. Within the confines of plantation law, he innocuously misreads her as a "lady" despite her enslavement. His error fans the flames of Zoe's increasing racially and socially equivocal status as an enslaved heroine whose exquisite "beauty" surely trumps that of any European women that George may have encountered. M'Closky's subsequent advances toward Zoe, however, resituate her as a racially and sexually vulnerable character who exists perilously outside the bounds of true womanhood's social codes. In turn, the overseer reminds Zoe, "I'd marry you if I could, but you know I can't" (146). He offers her, instead, a life in concubinage as "mistress of Terrebone," at once binding the contractual deal of her blackness and her status as sexual property and ensuring that she will embody racialized pain, suffering, and perpetual vulnerability at the hands of a domestic tyrant.[63]

Zoe's shifting identity politics throughout the play pose a particular problem within the context of spectacular melodrama. At its most basic level, conventional nineteenth-century melodrama produces a world which is "subsumed by an underlying manichaeism." Such plays sustain "the excitement of [their] drama by putting us in touch with the conflict of good and evil played out under the surface of things." In short, melodrama operated as an instrument designed to impart order and stability. The genre's consistent moral conflicts aim to "recognize and confront evil, to combat and expel it, to purge the social order" through "spectacular enactments." As a vehicle that intervened in a world "where the traditional imperatives of truth and ethics have been violently thrown into question," melodrama delivers and depends on its "striking revelation" and "evidence" in the form of Manichaean character constructions. "Radically democratic, striving to make its representations clear and legible to everyone," melodrama is, as Peter Brooks concludes, "the principle mode for *uncovering*, demonstrating, and making operative the essential moral universe in a post-sacred era."[64]

Predicated on exposure, nineteenth-century melodrama emphasized and promulgated moral legibility through the development of its characters. Yet this morality was often scripted in racially charged metaphors of the dark and the light, the swarthy and the fair. In this universe of corporeal binaries, then, "white and black signified as morally coded terms in melodrama" which "could be (mis)applied to racially white or black figures" (Brody, *Impossible Purities*, 52).[65] Bound up inextricably with race and the body, the moral ethics of melodrama produced a form of not only moral but "racial legibility" as well.[66] The genre depended on a corporeal language to clarify, materialize, and essentialize this split. That is, as much as melodrama relied on the poetics of dramaturgical gesture and the conventions of nineteenth-century acting methods which were " 'immediately translatable and unified 'ritualized' physical expression of emotion,' " it also required that the actor's body speak and perform a particular notion of "truth" that was, in some cases, deemed more valuable than the character's discursive expression. Melodrama's body conveys a kind of "moral truth in gesture and picture that could not be fully spoken in words" and manifests in "visible bodily signs" the essence of character.[67]

But if the language of melodrama requires the body to speak loudly, the discourse of miscegenation law attempts to silence figures such as Zoe. *The Octoroon* dramatizes "the chief tensions of American miscegenation law" and reveals "the power of legal language to construct, criminalize, and appropriate the human body itself, as Zoe was appropriated by law to her father's estate." An equivocal figure, the "truth" of Zoe's body is, in effect, "unspeakable" in the face of the law and must be juridically muted. As Linda Williams reminds us, typically "the 'unspeakable' truth revealed in the sensation scene is the revelation of who is the true villain, and who is the innocent victim of some plot. The revelation occurs as a spectacular moving sensation." But what happens when that revelatory spectacle derives from the figure of the racially liminal body? For while melodrama was quite good at meting out racial distinctions, yoking blackness with suffering and linking moral and racial legibility to a poetics of pain, it was less certain about what to do with Zoe's body of excess, a transatlantic body in flux.[68]

Boucicault's play and its heroine threaten to disrupt both the Manichaean split as well as the legibility of race and the body in antebellum culture. By producing a figure that was potentially illegible and by presenting blackness that was "ambivalent and contradictory," *The Octoroon* participated in racial melodrama's increasingly ambiguous manipulation of "the disparity between substance and surface." The play "explored the pleasures and dangers of racial travesty in tales of distressed quadroons and octoroons" (Hartman, *Scenes of Subjection*, 28).[69] Zoe's body is all the more spectacular because of this "travesty." A ritual of visual surveillance of her figure permeates the text. In perhaps the most famous scene of the play, Zoe demands that George stand witness to her willfully fluid transformation from fair young maiden to slave bearing/baring "the ineffaceable curse of Cain." (154). She invites him to travel the "gulf between [them] which is as wide as [George's] love, as deep as [her] despair" (153) in order to "take her somewhat obtuse lover on a frank fact-finding tour of her body" (Roach, *Cities of the Dead*, 219). Held in stunned and rapt attention, George assumes the role of the spectator and reads her figure within a certain set of racial codes. Zoe abidingly beckons her lover:

> George, do you see that hand you hold? look at these fingers; do you see the nails are of a bluish tinge? . . . Look in my eyes; is not the same colour in the white? . . . Could you see the roots of my hair you would see the same dark, fatal mark. . . . I'm an unclean thing—forbidden by the laws—I'm an Octoroon! (154)

Revealing her Other half, Zoe makes her blackness visible for the first time to a literally colorblind American expatriate. Her declaration is a stunning admission predicated on the use of her body as a spectacular terrain of liminal and nightmarishly tantalizing possibilities. Here and elsewhere in the play, "it is the purpose of the octoroon to pose (as) the problem of racial discernment."[70] Zoe's exhibition of her racial markings finally re-places the play in melodrama's grand tradition of exposure. Staging an erotic spectacle within a spectacle—that of a white(looking) woman/slave inviting her lover/master to chart what she reads as the trappings of her own body—the scene showcases the text's obsession with voyeurism and visually policing racial liminality. Zoe's meticulous emphasis on the shameful details of her hair and skin operates as the most unimaginative of stripteases, one in which her black body is unveiled for putatively "moral" clarity. Her actions affirm how "race remains eminently visible and undeniable, thus giving license to the fantasies of the white male spectator [and] allowing Boucicault room for a melodrama of sensation."[71]

### Waste Not Want: Excess, Phantasmagoria, and the Spectacle of "Race" in *The Octoroon*

As Zoe strips away the layers of indeterminacy veiling her body, the spectator is made privy to the elements of excess that Boucicault's play gamely attempts to navigate. With a "sense of burdensome superabundance so characteristic of Anglo-American responses to the teeming human and material panoply of the circum-Atlantic cityscape," *The Octoroon* presents "multiplied instances of interracial and intersocietal contact" to such an extent that, Roach concludes, "among Boucicault's dramatis personae somebody must be superabundant." This surfeiting "surplus of difference" shapes and steers the direction of the play. Manifested in scenes of the gest of racial phantasmagoria that finally disrupts and transforms the codes of melodrama, this excess services the same codes. If one considers Elin Diamond's observation that the "Brechtian 'not . . . but' is the theatrical and theoretical analogue to 'differences within,' " and that "the truth-modeling that produces self-identical subjects in coherent plots gives way utterly to the pleasure and significance of contradiction," then racial phantasmagoria, the spectacle of this "surplus of difference" *in play* and the spectacle of the liminality of the body, remain central to *The Octoroon*.[72]

At the heart of this excess lies the "uncanny double" of *The Octoroon*. A phantasmagoric figure of excessive representation, the octoroon e/merges as the "twinned and entwined entities" of white and black Victorian women, "beings whose complex imbricated identities illustrate the categorical contradictions of the culture."[73] This spectacle of superabundance is most evident in act 3's infamous slave auction where Zoe comes to the horrific conclusion that she is "[a] slave! a slave! Is this a dream—for my brain reels with the blow?" (163). As in previous scenes, the "mixed-race heroine undergoes several transformations in which her contradictory body is pushed and pulled between its multiple significations" and according to a higher system of racial laws. The slave auction closes the act and solidifies how the play draws on the history of theatrical spectacle in slavery and the underlying sensation of the auction space.[74] Similar to the New Orleans "fancy-girl auctions" which exploited the sensation of selling white(looking) bodies into slavery, *The Octoroon* offered the metatextual thrill of watching Boucicault's young spouse, Agnes Robertson, portray Zoe's perilous route into enslavement. For the audience, the chiasmic twist of witnessing Robertson feign (white) blackness and Zoe earnestly claiming (black) whiteness served as a climactic spectacle which would go unparalleled in the production.

The *New York Tribune*'s review of the play testifies to the amount of cultural attention lavished on *The Octoroon*'s slave auction. Like other papers, the *Tribune* obsessed over how "a beautiful creature—white except to the eye of an expert—is sold like a dumb beast to gratify brutal lust." Such attention proves that while Zoe's body is the object of illicit desire within the text, Robertson's figure was always equally under scrutiny, a stunningly "beautiful" white thing whose mere masquerade as (black) property remained, for audiences, an alarming development in the play. In the end, the *Tribune* article equates the scene's vividness with the spectacle of the closing steamboat fire in the sense that both are "scenically" thought to be "the most striking and effective" in the whole play.[75] The auction, then, serves as the ultimate point of Zoe's reification in *The Octoroon* as the larger socioeconomic and political circumstances of slavery necessitated her transformation from white to black, from (semi)respected lady into vulnerable sexual property. The scene intensifies the spectacular juxtaposition of whiteness alongside blackness. Using the "liminal status of the Quadroon Girl" as a point of entry and as "a space for erotic play . . . facilitated by the duality of the subject," Boucicault's production disrupts the roles of (white) spectators and voyeurs who had perhaps positioned themselves as remote participants in the drama's spectacle of race. The textual excess rooted in the body and distilled throughout the play manifests itself fully as white bodies are finally put up for sale in the drama (Roach, *Cities of the Dead*, 222–24).

Zoe's "surplus of difference" and the discourse of white slavery and white bodily subjugation remain significant subtexts throughout *The Octoroon*. Identities, enfranchisement, and the sovereignty of the play's (white) characters are "infected" by Zoe's presence, thrown into disarray, and called into question. George is caught between European mores that seemingly "free" him to profess his love for Zoe and the American lineage which forbids it. Scudder laments the breakdown of the boundaries between (white) gentry and (Indian) savages, pleading to the quarreling George and M'Closky that "if we can't behave like Christians, let's try and act like gentlemen" (169). M'Closky is divested of his Christian patriarchal privileges and, in the end, lynched for his expedient transgressions. For, Scudder observes, "it is the white man, whose laws [M'Closky] has offended" (174). Murdering an innocent mulatto slave, M'Closky stages his own transformation from "gentleman" into "savage." Tellingly, Wahnotee, the speechless Indian, moves from falsely accused miscreant to moral judge, meting out punishment to his oppressor and demonstrating the way in which even white men are made vulnerable in the play.

This excess in character borne out in multiple, parallel, converging, and intersecting acts of surrogation is also akin to melodrama's excess which creates " 'a plenitude of meaning' that restores melodramatic subjects to a fullness of expression." As a restorative act, melodrama's "payoff is in the final ability of the mode to speak the unspeakable, to express the inexpressible."[76] But excess

surfaces differently in racial melodrama where the transatlantic body is present. In *The Octoroon*, the transatlantic body, rather than the melodramatic
form, does the work of "speaking the unspeakable"; Zoe's figure serves as the
catalyst for the excess of the melodramatic mode. Within this context, excess
should be understood as an articulation of the heterogeneous complexity of
bodies and identities in nineteenth-century transatlantic culture. These racial
melodramas consistently reconstitute order—presenting and exposing excessive bodies in order to finally purge them from the narrative altogether.

By these means, Boucicault's play aims to rein in the very excess it has
produced in its title character. Just as minstrelsy's "performances of blackness
regulated the excess they conjured up with the threat of punishment and
humiliating discovery," *The Octoroon* worked toward the ultimate reinstate-
ment of social stability and "clarity" (Hartman, *Scenes of Subjection*, 31). Zoe's
decision to choose death over slavery in the American version of the play
succeeds with a final ironic and reactionary twist, executing a parting transformation which undoes her looming black status. As she drinks from a vial
of poison, George remarks in horror that she is "suffering—your lips are
white—your cheeks are flushed" (182). With her "eyes changing color" as well,
Zoe is at once "cleansed" of her blackness and blackened by the act of suffering as a horrified array of onlookers watch her racially transmuting body. The
final spectacular phantasmagoria is all the more bittersweet because of what
the *New York Times* called the "superfluousness" of her sacrifice. In this brutally tragic death scene, "[o]ut of the ruptured chrysalis of the Octoroon's
body floats a miraculous White Goddess" (Roach, *Cities of the Dead*, 224).
"[F]loating" like a phantasmagoria specter, like a spirit hovering above a
medium at a séance, Zoe converts into (ethe)real racial phantom. Her final
ghostification produces "a strange process of rhetorical displacement" that
anticipates how the trope of blackness circulated in the wake of the Civil War
in America—increasingly as an ideological construct of fear and a mystifying
presence requiring expulsion from social and cultural spaces.[77] Beyond merely
becoming "white," she transgmogrifies into the "mythical" like the notion of
the "mulatta" itself.[78] In America, then, Zoe's death aims to reorder the antebellum grammar of racial liminality by "cleansing" the nation as well as the
melodramatic form of its troubling "disunification."[79]

*The Octoroon* thus restores whiteness at precisely the moment when blackness is spectacularly wasted in the play. The metatextual politics of Agnes Robertson, a prominent white actress, playing a figurative black(face) role, makes
this point especially clear. In her memoirs, Robertson describes the American

audience's rabid interest in her performance of a black(ened) woman on the brink of being sold into slavery. She writes, "I was solemnly warned that if I attempted to play this scene I should be shot as I stood on the table to be sold. I confess I did feel rather nervous, for I was clad in a long white gown, and so, of course, a mark for every eye."[80] Her comments here point to two ironies. First, they convey the perplexing contradictions of a patriarchal chivalry that threatens the safety of a white actress in order to "protect" the iconography of (white) womanhood from (representations) of slavery. Second, her statement exposes *The Octoroon*'s spectacular strategies of shoring up "whiteness" and its imperiled value in the context of slavery. On the sensational slave block in a "long white gown," Robertson performed a "white" femininity under siege and reinscribed that racial and gender category as hypervisible. Thus, her comment ironically reverses racial visibility, shifting whiteness and not blackness to the center of sensational and spectacular optic desire. Whiteness in the infamous slave auction scene produces a blinding light, eclipsing the plight of the blackface "slave" characters and negating their representational "worth."[81] Paradoxically, although "Zoe would have had to strip, and she would have been stripped by association in the minds of the viewers as she stepped upon the tabletop," her spectacular exposure works to reinstate white supremacist order by both making the black body of the white actress bare and by baring the white actress of her blackness.

The American *Octoroon* would, then, on the one hand, expose, circumscribe, and reduce the transatlantic body, even as it trafficked in challenging presumably fixed racial categories. At the same time, however, the theatrical genres in which it was situated worked to contest this circumscription. If anything the genre of spectacular theatre exposed the hoax of "race" itself, turning it once and for all into an optical, illusionistic, phantasmagoric stunt. Spectacular theatre's presumption that "realness" can only be expressed through majestic, spectacular, and indeed, highly artificial means would surely then complicate the "truth" of Zoe's body. Through its equation of spectacle with race, *The Octoroon*, therefore, uncovers the social frictions of race and the body in transatlantic culture. By yoking the spectacle of the closing steamboat fire with the auction scene and the death of Zoe, the play situates race and the body as heightened theatrical objects of inquiry in a series of sensational convertibility scenes. Yet, in the coming months and years to follow, as Boucicault and Robertson first left their own New York production over legal squabbles and eventually took the play to London, the English public would, it turns out, have no such ending.

## Another Country: Spectacles of Conjugal Colonialism
## and the Empire's Body in the English *Octoroon*

After returning to Britain in 1860 to present his critically acclaimed Irish epic *The Colleen Bawn*, Boucicault again opened *The Octoroon* in November 1861 at the Adelphi Theatre. Though English audiences were equally obsessed with the figure of Zoe, the slave auction, and the steamboat fire—the so-called sensation scenes of the production—they detested the death of the title character. The *London Times* reported that "such a popular person was the Octoroon in her hands that several of the audience were dissatisfied with her unfortunate end, and refused to understand why George could not marry his devoted 'Yellow Girl.' "[82]

Boucicault tried in vain to counter these attacks with a letter of clarification to the editor which appeared in the paper the day following the opening. He suggested that he intended for his play to complicate the English public's views on slavery in the wake of "Uncle Tom mania." Unlike the novel and stage productions of *Uncle Tom's Cabin*, *The Octoroon* aimed to represent the "happiness" and the American slave's putative complicity in his or her own oppression while also stressing the moral and psychological toll of slavery on those living in its midst. Boucicault proclaimed that "in the death of the Octoroon lies the moral and teaching of the whole work. Had this girl been saved, and the drama brought to a happy end, the horrors of her position, irremediable from the very nature of the institution of slavery, would subside into the condition of a temporary annoyance" (*London Times*, November 20, 1861). The playwright maintained that his work presented an "authentic" representation of Southern life and served as a cautious indictment of a system working outside of the laws of "morality" (November 20, 1861). But the London debut of *The Octoroon* teetered on the brink of financial failure largely because of the British audience's scorn for Zoe's demise. Thus, several weeks later the playwright capitulated to their demands. The ad for the New Theatre Royal, Adelphi pronounced that "in obedience to the universal request that the Slave Girl in *The Octoroon* should be saved, Mr. Boucicault has altered the drama and brought the story to a happy conclusion" (December 7, 1861). This revised production not only closed in the fifth act with George's triumphant rescue of Zoe and their subsequent escape to England but was also "crammed with thrilling episodes which appeared nowhere in the original text."[83] A series of sensational plot twists from a canoe chase to M'Closky's thwarted abduction of Zoe fill out the final scenes of this version before George and Zoe joyously reunite and declare their intent to leave the United

States and legalize their union. This new version was a smashing success in London.

The new and "improved" *Octoroon* pushed the production into yet another generic sphere.[84] In spite of Boucicault's specific intentions, this version functioned less as a "picture" of Southern life and more as a hybrid work of English nationalist and imperialist theatre. As a result of the transgressive romantic relationship between George and Zoe, the play's emphasis on the representation and the construction of the "American" landscape, and the redeployment of the socially and culturally "deviant" (black) body, Boucicault's melodrama reaffirmed English subjectivity, even as it attempted to undo American systems of racial and class power and tyranny.

The need for a production that might participate in enlivening the English midcentury nationalist imaginary would perhaps not have been lost on audiences of the period. Although, for instance, the Great Exhibition of 1851 and the completion of the Crystal Palace were conceptualized as symbols of England's aesthetic, cultural, and political dominance, the subsequent midcentury unrest in British colonial conflicts such as the Indian mutiny of 1857 challenged the empire's perception of its own stability. Cultural entertainment and representations of a placid and victorious England were meant to cover over the widening rips and tears in the thinning imperial fabric. England positioned its high-profile cultural productions of grandeur and opulence as bids to uphold and reassert an imperial powerbase increasingly threatened by indigenous discontent and colonial competition with other countries. "Entertainment and propaganda" thus converged in Victorian England as instruments of suppression and as a means to "embrace the control and exploitation of existing Empire and the communication of the justifications for that to the populace of the imperial state."[85]

In relation to the United States, the issue of slavery served as the means by which British culture attempted to reformulate a discourse of moral superiority in relation to its former colonies. Having abolished slavery in its own colonies beginning in 1833, and serving as a central asylum for high-profile African American abolitionists such as William and Ellen Craft, Frederick Douglass, and Henry Box Brown, England reappropriated America's self-representation as "the land of the free."[86] Arriving in London in 1861 as the British read press reports of the military conflict in America, Boucicault's play was a morality tale ripe for English self-aggrandizement. Sensation novelist Mary Elizabeth Braddon, for example, was one of several authors who recognized this particular element of the narrative's potential. In her serialized novel *The Octoroon*, she characterized the institution of slavery as distinctly

American and un-British, boasting that "to the Briton there is no such word as slavery."[87]

Boucicault's production dramatized England's moral and cultural superiority to the United States. These sorts of power relations are clearly at work in the play's representation of George Peyton, a feckless American expatriate who, upon his return from England, finds himself, in a sense, born again and strangely out of step with the social and political mores of the South. After showing respect for Zoe, George inadvertently disavows his Southern family ties. As Mrs. Peyton warns, "my nephew is not acquainted with our customs in Louisiana, but he will soon understand" (141). The narrative fashions George as a cultural outsider and this move, in turn, reinforces the play's value as a work of Anglocentric and morally imperialist theatre. George's social otherness enables him to sustain cross-racial desire with the black family servant. His ability to transcend merely desiring Zoe—as does Scudder—and his determination to transform that desire into a legal and contractual commitment come to fruition in the English ending and underscore the moral virtue of the English character—even as they keep intact American laws which forbid interracial marriage.

George and Zoe's union exemplifies what Mary Louise Pratt calls a romantic relationship of anticonquest within the survival literature genre. In the eighteenth and nineteenth centuries, and "throughout the history of early Eurocolonialism and the slave trade, survival literature furnished a 'safe' context for staging alternate, relativizing, and taboo configurations of intercultural contact." These narratives, Pratt reminds us, detailed the European penetration of foreign cultures in ostensibly "non-hostile" terms by authorizing such odysseys through an establishment of "new transracial social orders." The putative subversiveness of survival plots that featured transgressive social and cultural relationships were subsequently contained through the conclusive restoration of the European protagonist. In the end "the survivor survived, and sought reintegration into the home society. The tale was always told from the viewpoint of the European who returned."[88] This "survival literature" endorsed the use of foreign and exotic locales to stage narratives of (sexual) encounter and (European) renewal through the body and often at the expense of the female other. In these narratives, precolonized territories offer the European traveler the opportunity to function outside conventional systems of law and to deliver that law, most of the time allegorizing this imperialist desire through sexual relations with the "native" populations.

Little wonder, then, the English public's obsession with "saving the Octoroon." In the "happy English ending" of the play, the London Illustrated

*News* reported that "the fair Octoroon is thus set at liberty; and the piece concludes with a declaration that in another land Zoe and Peyton will solemnize a lawful union, and live for happiness with each other" (December 14, 1861). The *Times* effusively proclaimed on December 12, 1861, that "the Octoroon dies no more! . . . The public . . . did not see why the gallant George Peyton should not bring the beautiful Zoe over to England, where neither laws of the land nor of society would thwart his inclinations. . . . Thus, the curtain drops merrily on a brace of prospective weddings, instead of gloomy veiling over a scene of death and desolation." Even the sardonic dramatic correspondent of *Punch* remarked that "suicide is always an unpleasant and immoral act to contemplate; and I shall go and see the Octoroon with vastly greater willingness, now that a marriage peal is substituted for a cup of poison" (December 21, 1861). Still, however, the conjugal ending of this *Octoroon* asserts the politics of the anticonquest narrative, a "transracial love plo[t]" wherein "European supremacy is guaranteed by affective and social bonding; in which sex replaces slavery as the way others are seen to belong to the white man; in which romantic love rather than filial servitude or force guarantee the willful submission of the colonized."[89] English subjectivity is affirmed through the transatlantic body, a vessel of self-righteousness for the expatriate traveler to acquire and bring back to Europe, his newfound home. In the comfort of this allegedly "free" country, the hero may take liberties to compare his lover to all those fine European girls who, we've been reminded, do not hold a candle to her.[90] Although Zoe's marriage and emigration enable her ostensible freedom, they reinforce the perpetual precariousness of her subjectivity. By burning a steamer and sending the couple to England, Boucicault aimed to follow his own law and render plot obstacles into "minor annoyances" which in the end can be, unlike slavery, smoothly resolved.

While Zoe's fate is briskly settled in each version of *The Octoroon*, the situation of slavery remains deeply fetishized, sensationalized, and unresolved. Faced with the initial threat of losing her estate, the plantation widow Mrs. Peyton laments her potential separation from the "black, ungainly faces" of her home. Perhaps too sanguinely aligned with contemporaneous, transatlantic minstrel culture, *The Octoroon* depended on a healthy supply of grotesque images of black subjects complacent in their enslavement and embedded in the play's pastoral landscape. To English audiences in particular, the play generated simple, seductive, and thrilling "American scenery." Henry Silver, the dramatic correspondent for *Punch*, found the play visually "attractive," and the "sensation scenes" associated particularly with American culture became the central obsessions of some critics. Silver marveled over "the excitement of the Slave Sale, and the rush across the stage when the steamboat is on fire" (*Punch*, January 4, 1862). The spectacle of setting and landscape thus critically intersects with the display of the transatlantic body in this *Octoroon*.

The retention of the play's grand conclusion was surely no surprise to Boucicault's fans, considering his reputation for usually extravagant scenes. As George Rowell has pointed out, "none of his melodramas would be complete without a thrilling sequence on which the resources of the Victorian theatre were fully extended to produce a novel and spectacular effect."[91] Following suit, his English *Octoroon*'s "sensation scenes" were very much bound up in exoticizing as well as eroticizing the American "scene" of slavery. In the production, slavery and the figure of the strangely liminal "slave girl" emerge in a series of tableaux, removed from any sort of meaningful sociopolitical context. If, as Judith Fisher claims, Boucicault "made sensational action manifest a universal moral order," then her further contention that "the predominant characteristic of Boucicault's sensation scenes is that the outsider figure, and not the conventional hero, is pivotal in the action" is a revelation.[92] George Peyton, as American outsider, operates as the interloper in the infamous slave auction sale, bent upon "buying" Zoe out of her troubles and safely rescuing her from the villain and the steamboat fire in the English finale. His actions affirm the neocolonizing impulses of the American-turned-Englishman who is intent on returning order to an uncivilized America on the brink of chaos.

The English audience members are the most crucial organizing agent in relation to these sensation scenes. Viewing this "American scenery" and these "American homes," they transform Boucicault's equivocal antislavery drama into a melodramatic panorama. Panorama shows popularized the exhibition of enormous scenic paintings of landscapes and geographical territories during the height of their popularity in midcentury England. They underscored fantastic scenery and "gained dignity as a quasi-cultural institution . . . meant to illustrate history as it was being made." Their popularity coincided with the height of British imperialism and the movement of the English army into foreign territories.[93] Large-scale picture shows, panoramas cultivated a domestic fascination with imperial supremacy. These exhibitions were the ultimate anticonquest narratives in which travelers/spectators "are chiefly present as a kind of collective moving eye on which the sights/sites register."[94] A kind of visual accompaniment to popular anticonquest travel literature, panorama shows were constituted around "scenes" rather than action, the topographical rather than the topical. Panorama exhibitions underscore the anticonquest narrative's impulse of the imperial gaze as invasion by emptying out foreign territories and those territories' inhabitants of their subjectivity and history while affirming their pleasurable access to the spectator. All the while, the landscape is represented as "uninhabited, unpossessed, unhistoricized, [and] unoccupied."[95]

The panoramic American "scene" coupled with the spectacle of the octoroon's body under siege afforded British audiences the chance to gaze upon American social and cultural instability and to reflexively resolve that instability. Yet this English interception eschews an engagement with the deeper American sociohistorical context in which the play is situated. Rather, in this version, the spectacle of slavery literally gets equated with the body of its title character. This *Octoroon* emerges as America allegorized and sentenced to function as the U.K.'s illicit lover. Zoe remains the "mythical," dehistoricized, and sexually available focal point of the narrative, a product of the white, phallic, and juridical imagination. In England her evisceration is made complete as she transforms into a free-floating cultural symbol, disconnected from the very systems of oppression that bore her. In this way, Boucicault's play works to fortify English nationalist ideology while also promoting the imperialist impulse to reconquer the colonies via the body of the octoroon.[96]

A surrogate, a medium, a pantomime stunt, a dual body of blackface entertainment and Manichaean melodrama, Zoe encompasses the shifts and evolution of the transatlantic body in the cultural imaginary. An impostor, a counterfeit, a body containing too much or too little of something, she floats oddly between continents. Both strangely nationless and an icon of nation building, her imbricated body bears/bares the weight of midcentury transnational and ideological crisis. Curiously, in the years following the Civil War, a new body of excess would manifest the power struggles of the nation and on the stage. This time, however, the (counterfeit) body of surplus would come in the form of a white, Scottish male.

### Hyding in America

If the transatlantic body of antebellum melodrama worked in the service of nation building and domestic housecleaning on both sides of the Atlantic, the English and American cultural imaginaries redeployed that same figure in drastically different terms in the latter half of the century. In the cultural worlds of both postbellum America and late Victorian England, superabundant figures morphed into spectacular and highly specular expressions of sociopolitical terror and horror. Whereas productions such as *The Octoroon* ritualistically and erotically circumscribed and sacrificed racially liminal bodies for the purposes of fortifying the myth of communal homogeneity, late-nineteenth-century performance culture transformed the iconography of polymorphous corporeality into a more resolutely foreboding incubus. Titillating excess and duality increasingly held a threatening place in fin de siècle culture where the presumed dissolution of moral and material boundaries produced, according to Judith Halberstam, a particular strain of Gothic aestheticism fueled by "a vertiginous excess of meaning." Victorian culture's emerging confrontation with "dangerous consumptions and excessive productivity" gave birth to a particular kind of "monstrous" body, a symbol of "interpretative mayhem" in an era marked by the chaos of nascent modernity. Within this context, the "ornamental excess" of people, places, objects, and "rhetorical extravagance" elicited "the experience of horror" which "comes from the realization that meaning itself runs riot." Halberstam concludes, then, that the Gothic "marks a peculiarly modern emphasis upon the horror of particular kinds of bodies." It "condenses various racial and sexual threats to nation, capitalism, and the bourgeoisie" in a singularly "disruptive figure."[97]

In America, that "monstrous" body was none other than the "mulatto/a" herself; a figure previously marked as benignly "tragic," was now, in the post-Reconstruction era, reconfigured as an unmanageable teratology. As Saks observes, the "horror at the conflation of difference was replicated in the mythology of the 'mulatto.' Scientific, legal, and popular mythology deemed" this liminal figure mutant and extreme. The "mulatto monster" was deviant and inferior to whites as well as blacks, "therefore doubly deviant, the other of the other." This modern perception of the mulatto as "monstrous" clearly came as result of the devaluation of "white skin when black skin ceased to signify slave status" in the postwar era. As the miscegenous body threatened the collapse of power derived from the conflation of whiteness and property rights, "miscegenation jurisprudence" responded by promoting a discourse of racial monstrosity linked to both blackness and the convergence of whiteness and blackness in one presumably terrifying figure.[98] Joel Williamson finds that "the simple existence of mulattos after the war militated against the white man's sense of identity. The dichotomy of free versus slave had died, but the dichotomy of white versus black lived on—and grew. Indeed, the white sense of self depended in part upon maintaining that separateness, and white 'being' somehow lay close to the tensions involved in maintaining and refining distinction."[99] Like the Gothic monster who, "as a creature of mixed blood, breaks down the very categories that constitute class, sexual, and racial difference" (Halberstam, *Skin Shows*, 78), the mulatto figure posed a clear and present danger to the preservation of white supremacy.

White supremacist ideology's Gothic reinterpretation of corporeal liminality was perhaps most notoriously vivid in British cultural production. During the 1880s and 1890s, a new trend, "something like the cult of the beast," was epitomized in classic late-Victorian works featuring male characters who are inextricably and, therefore, tragically linked to "the animals [which] they are supposed to have risen above."[100] An iconographic text of this period, Robert Louis Stevenson's *The Strange Case of Dr. Jekyll and Mr. Hyde* (1886) reimagines corporeal excess and metamorphosis in nightmarish terms. Stevenson's narrative, which documents Dr. Jekyll's invention of an alterego to exorcise his "deviant" desires, offers critical commentary on Victorian culture's repressive moral and social constrictions. The text produces a Gothic monster as "a disciplinary sign, a warning of what may happen if the body is imprisoned by desires or if the subject is unable to discipline him- or herself fully and successfully" (Halberstam, *Skin Shows*, 72).

A haunting parable of British subjectivity's tormented internal conflicts, Stevenson's Gothic antihero embodied the tempestuous social landscape from which he had evolved. Derived, in part, from the scandalous legend of William Brodie, an eighteenth-century Scottish deacon who divided his life between the public image of a prominent professional and a nocturnal world of debauchery and dissipation, *Jekyll and Hyde* sustained social currency as a narrative manifesting the simmering conflicts between a repressive bourgeoisie and its violent subcultural underbelly. But the social and political context of post–Reconstruction-era America set the stage for distinct cultural and regional translations of *Dr. Jekyll and Mr. Hyde*. A Gothic narrative which "tracks the transformation of struggles within the body politic to local struggles within individual bodies" (Halberstam, *Skin Shows*, 78), Stevenson's text was ripe for postbellum American adaptations. Like Jekyll's body, the American national corpus wrangled internally as the end of Reconstruction, the beginning of Southern reconciliation, the burgeoning labor and class conflict of events such as the Haymarket Affair, Jim Crow segregation, and racial mob violence each threatened regional as well as national order in late-nineteenth-century America.

Fiction writers made this link between national discordance and the Gothic body of excess explicitly clear. In her 1900 novel *Contending Forces*, black feminist writer and activist Pauline Hopkins invokes the Jekyll and Hyde split as an allegory to address dire socioeconomic conditions in the postbellum African American community. The "Negro," according to the novel's Du Boisian hero, had become the "Hyde" of America, a brutalized figure whose presence ate away at the stability of "the white man's refined civilization!"[101] Hopkin's narrative confronts the numerous obstacles facing African Americans as the modest political and economic gains of Reconstruction were gradually curtailed in the wake of the country's 1873 economic depression. Like a domino effect, the Compromise of 1877 and the Supreme Court's 1883 declaration that the Civil Rights Act of 1875 had been unconstitutional each encouraged the reconciliation between the white North and South. A wave of legislated racial segregation culminating in 1896 with the Supreme Court's *Plessy v. Ferguson* decision, federally accepted such laws. Widespread mob-rule in the form of Southern lynchings became a method of securing these changes and exerting terror and control over black communities.[102]

Within this context, the *Jekyll and Hyde* mythology conjured a corporeal allegory of post-Reconstruction America in flux which Mark Twain envisioned as well in his 1894 novel *Pudd'nhead Wilson*. Twain's tale of twins, one black and the other white, who are switched at birth in the antebellum South and forced to endure tragically entwined lives metaphorically illustrates the (im)possibility of social, cultural, and racial division in America. Twain's narrative engaged fully with the crisis in delineating the fictive borders of racial and class identity in the aftermath of Reconstruction. The cryptic wish of the eccentric title character that he "owned half of that dog. . . . Because I would kill my half" illustrates the obsession with severing and slaying what were presumed to be monstrously excessive appendages to the body politic. Twain's Wilson articulates the impossible effort to bifurcate and purge the (white) body politic of its putative racial excesses and otherness. If one could simply "kill off half" the dog, the body, the country, then somehow the nation might recuperate a romanticized prewar era steeped in mythic racial and cultural purities.[103]

In the midst of Hopkins's and Twain's two Americas, the first major theatre adaptation of *Dr. Jekyll and Mr. Hyde* arrived in the United States in 1887 and played to capacity crowds for close to a year.[104] The play's popularity in the post-Reconstruction era is critically significant in its deployment of a monstrous transatlantic body. American actor Richard Mansfield and playwright Thomas Sullivan's popular stage adaptation of Stevenson's text provides evidence of how the cultural imaginary's fetishistic interest in polymorphous bodies shifted away from *The Octoroon*'s racially liminal female body to a more fantastically hideous and threatening phantasmagoric figure at war with itself. Mansfield and Sullivan's *Dr. Jekyll and Mr. Hyde* makes plain the many ways in which Stevenson's "strange case" of a white, wealthy, patriarchal body in distress vividly engages with turn-of-the-century American social, political, and cultural conditions. Both the original text and the American adaptation of the play embody and allegorize the United States' shifting anxieties and attitudes toward race and spectacular corporeality in the 1880s and 1890s. This transatlantic body which Mansfield performed with terrifying acumen on the stage diverged from Agnes Robertson's portrayal of a "tragic octoroon" in critical ways. Although both Boucicault's play and *Jekyll and Hyde* centralized the performance of the disturbingly interstitial figure, the latter marked dominant culture's evolving resistance to corporeal "differences within." Beyond functioning as an expression of the dissolution of social and cultural boundaries, Mansfield and Sullivan's production performed the crucial task of enacting (super)abundant bodily expenditure presumed necessary to the preservation of such boundaries.[105]

A play that eerily evokes and anticipates the era of Jim Crow segregation, *Jekyll and Hyde* stylized a mode of spectacular theatricality in which the white body metaphorically cleansed itself of the blackness it had trafficked in during the peak years of the minstrel show era. The production makes explicit the task of purging the (unclean) white male body and the community of its difference.[106] This "cleansing" effect tells much about the place of white and black theatrical bodies in the postbellum era, a period when African Americans took to the stage in larger numbers as professional, wage-earning entertainers, composers, and producers and when popular mainstream theatre responded to such changes with an anxiety that surfaces at the very site of theatrical performance rituals. Black performers, in effect, began to transgress the limits of performative mastery which white entertainers had so prided themselves in articulating through the minstrel show form, creating a critical climate for the arrival of Richard Mansfield as a Gothically monstrous transatlantic body.[107] *Jekyll and Hyde* thus served as a theatrical manifestation of resistance to black class mobilization off the stage as well as on it. The production ushered in a theatrical era in which the performance of the control and manipulation of the white male body served as a symbol of dramaturgical power and skill while also communicating a nation's efforts to exorcise and contain the figure of the other in the theatrical sphere.

A metanarrative, then, about white performance agency in an era marked by the threat of emerging black professional theatrical culture, *Jekyll and Hyde* emerges on stage as a production about racial purity, the enactment of (white) representational control via performance and the spectacular disciplining of deviant racial embodiment. As we shall see, in the postbellum era theatrical phantasmagoria would shift to an investment in the reconstruction of white, autonomous subjectivity. In *Dr. Jekyll and Mr. Hyde*, the pre–Civil War minstrel figure and the deviant, racialized body were elaborately expelled in an

attempt to communicate a resilient form of Anglo patriarchy, socially, culturally, and politically renewed, restored, and, above all else, in control of the
stage.

### Racing Mr. Hyde

Many critics have noted *Jekyll and Hyde*'s narrative currency as an expression of racial hostility and xenophobic ideology. Much of this work has focused on Rouben Mamoulian's 1932 cinematic adaptation of the novel. In the
film, Frederic March's beastly Hyde references a set of familiar codes associated with contemporaneous racist caricatures and efficiently signifies on racial, gender, and class tensions in the Depression era.[108] Most notably, however, critics such as Patrick Brantlinger, Richard Boyle, and Judith Halberstam
have convincingly revealed the way in which the novel constructs Hyde's
deformity as dependent "at least partly upon racist conceptions of the degen-
eration of the species" (Halberstam, *Skin Shows*, 77). While Brantlinger and
Boyle point out the similarities in the text's "ape-like" representation of Hyde
and that of British culture's stereotypical image of the Irish, Halberstam
cogently demonstrates how "Hyde combines within his repulsive aspect the
traces of nineteenth-century stereotypes of both Semitic and black physiog-
nomies" (80). Indeed, the novel's construction of Hyde references a familiar
set of minstrel codes signifying blackness as "wild," "dwarfish," "monkey-
like," exuding a "savage laugh" and "a dusky pallor."

But Hyde is further "blackened" by his highly theatrical (un)covering
which lies at the center of the narrative. In other words, the text most consistently racializes Hyde through the characters' impulses to unveil Hyde's body.
Recalling the antebellum gesture to strip and expose phantasmagoric corporeality, Stevenson's text repeatedly reenacts the impulse to expose the racially
trangressive body. Hyde's figure, like that of a tragic octoroon, remains an
unreadable or a misread text to those who encounter him in the narrative.
This crisis reinforces Hyde's racial marking and, moreover, it repeats the ritual of policing and controlling racially deviant bodies through spectatorial
tactics.

Over and over again, the process of seeing Hyde surfaces as an elaborate,
theatrical scene which makes plain the myriad ways that deviance is created
and maintained through public and spectacular acts of looking and being
looked at. Viewing Hyde remains a heavily contested transaction in each of his
startling encounters in the text, and the voyeuristic gaze remains central to the
narrative. Numerous characters recount sightings of Hyde. The scene in which
lawyer-turned-detective Mr. Utterson hears of Mr. Hyde for the first time from

his confidant, Mr. Enfield, shapes the direction and flow of the plot, and yet it is a decidedly vague and repressed recollection. Having attested to the stranger's merciless trampling of a young girl in the thick of a foggy downtown street, Enfield struggles to find words to characterize Hyde's countenance:

> He is not easy to describe. There is something wrong with his appearance; something displeasing, something downright detestable. I never saw a man I so disliked, and yet I scarce know why. He must be deformed somewhere; *he gives a strong feeling of deformity*, although I couldn't specify the point. He's an extraordinary-looking man, and yet I can name nothing out of the way. . . . I can't describe him. And it's not want of memory; for I declare *I can see him this moment*.[109]

Upon encountering Hyde himself, Utterson finds that "he gave an *impression* of deformity without any namable malformation" (40; emphasis added). The "feeling" and the "impression" of deformity convey a vague yet nagging recollection, something Enfield and Utterson already know but cannot name. Each man's failure to describe Hyde in terms other than the way he *seemed* to each of them suggests that Hyde's repugnant appearance emerges, in part, from the dark repressed interiority of those who encounter him.

Utterson's obsession with Hyde, in particular, illustrates the level at which he encounters Hyde's Gothic monstrosity as a kind of racial stereotype. Forebodingly, he harbors phantasmagoric visions of Hyde which run through "his mind in a scroll of lighted pictures" (37), stirring in him an undying curiosity to see the stranger for himself. In these nightmares, however,

> the figure had no face by which he might know it; even in his dreams it had no face, or one that baffled him and melted before his eyes; and thus it was that there sprang up and grew apace in the lawyer's mind a singularity strong, almost an inordinate, curiosity to behold the features of the real Mr. Hyde. (38)

Utterson's desire to "but once set eyes on [Hyde]" (38) seizes hold of him intensely, for he feels that Hyde's countenance "would be a face worth seeing . . . a face which had but to show itself to raise up, in the mind of the unimpressionable Enfield, a spirit of enduring hatred" (38). Although Hyde's facial characteristics might be "unnamable" to many, gazing upon his appearance remains the goal of their quest. For "in 'seeing' (constructing a representational system for) the Other, [they] search for anatomical signs of difference such as physiognomy and skin color"[110] so as to begin to build a material discourse based on Hyde's (the racial other's) deviation from and, therefore, inferiority to the self. The act of uncovering Hyde operates as a step toward expelling him from their world.[111] Manifesting the submerged fears and desires of the spectator, he is the monstrous invention of those who look upon him and those who are determined to (un)cover him. Like the racial stereotype which is "at best a nominal construct and a phantasmatic space,"[112] the protean figure of Hyde "fixes sexual and racial difference within a body which combines horrific effect with Semitic and Negroid features" (Halberstam, *Skin Shows*, 82). For this reason, the novel's characters are both alarmingly aware of and yet refuse to see Hyde for what he is—a reflection of themselves. A body that materially necessitates the community's fear and desire for order and purity in the narrative, Hyde exists so as to be spotted, exposed, and sacrificially executed in order to reinforce communal boundaries. This kind of detection and expulsion is necessary in order to clarify racial and class differences which were less certain in both Victorian and postbellum American culture.[113]

Yet inasmuch as the text's preoccupation with uncovering and covering Hyde works to racially mark him, I wish to suggest that we might also read *Jekyll and Hyde* as a Gothic blackface narrative gone haywire. If *Jekyll and Hyde* is a tale of the "amplitude of costume" which exposes the ways that the Gothic is, in essence, a genre of cross-dressing, "perverse costume," and "grotesque transvestism" (Halberstam, *Skin Shows*, 60–61), then I would argue that it is possible to also read the narrative as a cautionary tale about racialized drag, the potential for the parasitic costume to bind and finally suffocate its host, the potential for blackness to, in effect, kill off and cover/hyde whiteness permanently. For this reason, the text performs the repeated ritual of attempting to (un)cover Hyde, to both shroud him and to sweep back the curtains that veil him so as to separate black from white and divide "queer" from "normative" bodies. In Stevenson's universe, this extravagant body born of theatrical disguise is a site of gross anxiety in the text, just as it is in the world of late-Victorian theatre.

Although many turn-of-the-century drama critics were skeptical of the novel's adaptability to the stage, the text exhibits a remarkable preoccupation with the theatre.[114] *Jekyll and Hyde* repeatedly calls attention to, for instance, the doctor's "surgical theatre," the space where he concocts and consumes the elixir that transforms him into Mr. Hyde. Utterson, as well, harbors a vexed and perhaps telling relationship with the stage. The narrative's opening paragraph relates how, for instance, "though [Utterson] enjoyed the theatre," he "had not crossed the doors of one for twenty years" (29), and his nightmares about Hyde are also steeped in dramaturgical imagery "as he lay and tossed in

the gross darkness of the night and the curtained room" (37). Hyde's mysterious figure lurks, in Utterson's imagination, behind a stagelike veil, until "the
curtains of the bed plucked apart, the sleeper recalled, and lo! there would
stand by his side a figure" (37).

Utterson's irrepressible aversion to theatrical space offers a provocative link
to the novel's racing of Hyde and fundamentally bespeaks the social and
cultural anxieties at the core of the text. The coupling of Mr. Hyde's image with
that of theatrical space is a telling one, for it suggests the nexus between the
process of transformation and the theatre as perceived threat in the late-
Victorian period. Cultural critics of the theatre warned that the stage allowed
actors to engage in insidious forms of transformation and self-invention. Thus
in 1895 George Moore openly lamented the fact that "the actor is applauded not
for what he does, but for what he is—that of late years the actor has been lifted
out of his place, and that, in common with all things when out of their places,
he is ridiculous and blocks the way."[115] If actors and actresses were given a
terrain on which to play (others), then, Moore's text seems to query, what
would stop them from crossing class or racial, gender or sexual borders? Moore
counters and declares emphatically that he, for one, has "no belief in the
amalgamation of classes, and still hold[s] by the old distinctions."[116] In this
tense cultural climate, the faithful servant Poole's cautious decision to "loc[k]
the door of the theatre behind" him (73) after discovering Hyde's deceased and
disfigured body reads as a potent gesture. Lying at the threshold of a new era of
corporeal convertibility, Hyde's body provided evidence of liminality's deadly
effects. It was a scene that was ripe for American shores.

### The Beast in the Jungle: Performance as
### Property in Post-Reconstruction America

In postbellum America, Dr. Jekyll's prescient realization "that man is not
truly one, but truly two" typified burgeoning segregationist ideology, and his
subsequent conclusion that if man "could but be housed in separate identities,
life would be relieved of all that was unbearable" (82) succinctly crystallized
evolving Jim Crow culture. Within this climate of heightened segregation, a
revised discourse on race emerged which equated African Americans with
dangerous disorder. And so it was that "[b]etween 1865 and 1890 the fact of
slaveholding miscegenation by white masters and the fear of black slave rebellion were together transformed into the specter of black crime and con-
tamination—the Negro as mongrel or 'beast.' "[117] Subsequently, the "New
South" and its Northern, Republican supporters led the political as well as the
social movement to socially expel the Hyde-like, "evil" specter of blackness in

(white) America from within its borders. The "mongrelization" of the white race could presumably only be halted and contained through these sorts of absolute divisions. As Philip Bruce would contend in 1889, "the South cannot remain permanently half black and half white."[118]

"Whiteness" required additional juridical preservation during this postwar moment when the end of slavery and Reconstruction threatened to obfuscate racial and class taxonomies. As legal theorist Cheryl Harris has argued persuasively, the concept of "whiteness" has evolved out of "centuries of custom" and has been "codified by law." As a result, "whiteness may be understood as a property interest."[119] Instilled with the power to differentiate "the legal status of a person as slave or free," white identity "conferred tangible and economically valuable benefits, and it was jealously guarded as a valued possession, allowed only to those who met a strict standard of proof." From this standpoint, Harris concludes that whiteness, that is, "the right to white identity as embraced by the law—is property if by 'property' one means all of a person's legal rights."[120] In the postbellum era, the emergence of both a black propertied class intent on claiming ownership of land and self, as well as the persistent presence of "miscegenous" bodies who confounded familial genealogies and inheritance rights, challenged the logic of conflating whiteness and class power. Thus whiteness as property was, with vigilance and tenacity, protected from the threat of a "blackness" that was redefined as monstrous and deadly in the latter half of the nineteenth century.

As journalist Ida B. Wells first made clear in her postbellum investigative reports, the myth of the monstrous "black rapist" was the key to white supremacist propaganda invested in sustaining racial and class hierarchies. The mob violence and terror inflicted onto black bodies in ritualistic lynching ceremonies were aimed at reinforcing the notion of black malevolence and preserving white citizenship. Sandra Gunning observes that, "for many white supremacists" of the period, "the stereotype of the black male as sexual beast functioned as an externalized symbol of social chaos against which all whites, regardless of class, could begin to unite for the purpose of national renewal." This act of lynching black bodies, Robyn Wiegman argues, paradoxically affirms the disembodied and thus superior citizenship of white men. By "impos[ing] . . . an extreme corporeality that defines his or her distance from the privileged ranks of (potential or actual) citizenry . . . lynching emerges to reclaim and reassert the centrality of black corporeality." Conversely, the production of black monstrosity and its ceremonious execution rejuvenates the power and preservation of the white body (politic).[121]

What *The Strange Case of Dr. Jekyll and Mr. Hyde* offered an American culture grasping for the protection of white (ontological) property was, on the surfaces of the dominant body, a parable regarding the necessity for segregation. Capitalizing on the theme of the "mongrel" other lurking literally within, the 1887 American stage adaptation of the *Strange Case* performs the "ritual expulsion" of the (blackened) beast out of the play's Anglo hero. The production effectively shifts the performance of the liminal body, in the wake of the Civil War, to a conscious attendance to the white patriarchal figure. The phantasmagoric genres of minstrelsy and racial melodrama invert so as to symbolically purge the white body politic of its black sins. Through the spectacle of the white male body, the production employs the figure of the racially marked beast as a mere vehicle to self-knowledge and sovereignty. In turn, this spectacle serves as a terrain on which to allegorically reassert (white) social, cultural, and political stability. Beyond its currency as Jim Crow allegory, the production and particularly actor Richard Mansfield's portrayal of the title character(s) work to revalue white performance as a guarded asset and interest. In an era marked by the rise of black theatricality, the stage production of *Dr. Jekyll and Mr. Hyde* enacts the spectacular attempt to recover both white mastery of the performing body and performance itself as property.

Transatlantic performer Richard Mansfield was said to have read *Dr. Jekyll and Mr. Hyde* in the spring of 1887 and immediately expressed an interest in bringing the text to the stage. Portraying the role of the title character was a challenge that the actor felt might showcase his versatility as a performer; thus he enlisted his playwright colleague and friend Thomas R. Sullivan to draft a script based on Stevenson's text. After an ill-fated early version of the play was vetoed by Mansfield, the final draft of *Dr. Jekyll and Mr. Hyde* debuted at the Boston Museum on May 9, 1887. Audiences responded with enthusiasm and the production proved so popular that it spawned a number of copycat dramatic renderings.[122] Mansfield's portrayal of the tragic doctor was the most successful, and eventually he took the show on the road to New York City that fall. At the urging of British stage actor Henry Irving, Mansfield finally performed the dual roles of his Jekyll and Hyde at London's Lyceum Theatre in the summer of 1888 and later toured the United Kingdom. Although Mansfield would reprise the role numerous times throughout his career, the original Boston performance lasted just one week. The actor ceased to perform the role because it "was far too emotional, tragic, and absorbing either for himself or for his audiences during the summer" of 1888.[123]

The stress of performing *Jekyll and Hyde* could have arisen from the extreme characterizations that Mansfield was required to enact on a nightly basis. In one of several critical deviations from Stevenson's original text, the

Sullivan and Mansfield script reimagined Jekyll in less morally ambiguous terms. C. Alex Pinkston argues that "Sullivan faced the necessity of creating a principled, sympathetic Henry Jekyll, establishing meaningful relationships between Jekyll and other characters."[124] Remarking on this revision, the *London Times* observed that "Mansfield has made the 'Jekyll and Hyde' story in America, as he will in England, by humanizing Jekyll, making him hate Hyde, and suffer mentally from his knowledge of Hyde's villainies."[125] Unlike the novel's representation of Jekyll as a closeted bohemian questing for the release of his libidinous desires and initially in collusion with his alterego, the American dramatic version of the narrative subscribes to popular melodramatic conventions and hyperbolically dichotomizes the characterizations of Jekyll and Hyde.

This split led to a clearer construction of Jekyll as a heteronormative and "civilized" hero who is engaged to be married to the daughter of Danvers Carew, Hyde's lone murder victim in the novel. With a conventional damsel-in-distress figure introduced into the plot, the production allowed for Hyde in America to morph into a more traditionally menacing villain. Sullivan's play spectacularly highlighted Hyde's criminality, for instance, by placing the murder scene in the opening act. Hyde's attack on Danvers follows Jekyll's chivalric attempts to break his engagement with Danver's daughter Agnes so as to protect her from the beast within himself.[126] Here, as Pinkston observes, "Agnes Carew provide[s] the love element essential to the stage success, and her betrothal to Jekyll [gives] Hyde's murder of Sir Danvers an important significance it did not have in the book" ("Stage Premiere," 37). Unlike the novel, which is notoriously lacking in female figures, the play's invention of a prominent female character and Jekyll's romantic relationship with her transforms the narrative into a more generically identifiable plot. By forcing Jekyll to choose between self-pleasure or protecting his fair damsel, the play returns Stevenson's distinctly homoerotic text to the realm of heteronormative chivalry.[127] It also translates the threat of Hyde into more specifically racial and gender terms as well.

Sullivan and Mansfield's production takes a notably more emphatic stance in representing Hyde's violence against women. In the novel Hyde "tramples over" a small girl, but in the play he plots to murder Rebecca Moore, the housekeeper of his lavishly hedonistic abode. Theatre critics such as William Winter endorsed the play's extreme construction of Hyde's subcultural pathologies. Winter argued that "Mansfield wisely and widely deviated from the novel, by surrounding the miscreant" in a separate lodging "with profuse but disorderly luxury,—not that of taste, but that of exuberant sensuality."[128] This sort of scenery and set direction only intensified the production's engagement with racial and class coding. Hyde's violent deeds coupled with his material extravagance recall the racist mythology of black dandy discourse in the nineteenth century. Antebellum culture's construction of the Northern black dandy whose awkwardly epicurean habits and whose "miscegenating proclivities" were meant to counter black class mobilization is here, in the figure of Hyde, conjoined with postbellum lynch law's invention of beastly (black) masculinity which preys on innocent and "pure" white womanhood.[129] Although numerous critics trace Hyde's misogynistic violence in subsequent versions of *Jekyll and Hyde* to the influence of the contemporaneous Jack the Ripper murders, one can mark the evolution of the narrative's brutalization of women to the original Mansfield-Sullivan debut in America.[130]

This production surpassed its literary predecessor perhaps most significantly in its extreme visual construction of Hyde's body, a feat carried out in part by the play's notable lighting technology. Sullivan used "atmospheric" calcium lights to cast a decidedly "green gloom across the room" during Hyde's appearances (Pinkston, "Stage Premiere," 27). These unsettling rays heightened the imminence of terror and horror in the production and contributed to the "transformation of personality" necessary to the play ("Stage Premiere," 28). Lighting intensified the audience's gaze toward the alien and intrusive body of Hyde. Wilstach maintains that "one of Mansfield's purely theatric devices for horror was to convey the suggestion that Hyde was coming." For the audience, the "gray, green-shot gloom" which coincided with Hyde's appearances "whetted every nerve. . . . At such a stage as this (the audience having seen Hyde before) the anticipation . . . the searching of the black corners for the first evidence of the demon all begot an hypnotic effect on the hushed, breathless spectators that held them in the fetters of invincible interest." Crouching in the darkness of the stage, waiting to reveal himself, Mansfield's Hyde depended on the sensational effect of the eerie light to emerge in all his hideousness. Repeatedly the audience's attention drifted toward this visually amplified Hyde. The power of the lighting was so intense in steering the audience's focus that several reviews of the play even critiqued the special effect for overwhelming the other aspects of the production.[131]

Mansfield's corporeal technology and his performance of Jekyll and Hyde was, however, reportedly even more potent than the "green gloom." His persuasive interpretation radically translated and spectacularized the trope of bodily transformation in Stevenson's narrative for theatre audiences. The actor was said to have "foreseen an extraordinary triumph if his powers could visualize to an audience . . . the contrast between Dr. Jekyll and Mr. Hyde, the weird transformations of the man into the fiend and back again." In particular, Mansfield anticipated and relished the challenge of "controlling the reversion from Hyde to Jekyll."[132] Pointing to the play's emphasis on pantomime-like conversions of character and its fetishistic engagement with "the horrors of the body," Mansfield's phantasmagoric skills did not go unnoticed by the theatre press. The *New York Herald* maintained that the actor's character changes "made in view of the audience were really wonderful and the whole impersonation was on the whole . . . powerful and consistent." Similarly, the *Boston Evening Transcript* noted Mansfield's Hyde with his "sharp eyes . . . rasping voice, and above all the mouth with its leering bestiality."[133] So fixated was the press on Mansfield's physical depiction of Jekyll's transformation to Hyde that a mild controversy ensued among critics as to the source of Mansfield's ability to make such a character change.[134] The actor's performance of a hideously deviant body on stage coupled with the way in which this body had the ability to eclipse and transcend plot concerns illustrates how the production extended and transformed minstrelsy's fetishization of the sensationally corporeal. With its focus on bodily disfigurement and disruption, Mansfield's performance translated the generic body into a Gothic form of excess that typified postbellum social and political hysteria.

If minstrelsy emphasized "Negro peculiarities," Mansfield recontextualized such signs of corporeal deviance in his performance of Hyde. In early minstrelsy "the body was always grotesquely contorted, even when sitting; stiffness and extension of arms and legs announced themselves as unsuccessful sublimations of sexual desire."[135] Mansfield's Hyde invoked these features, emphasizing the villain's "protruding lower lip" (Pinkston, "Stage Premiere," 34). But the less obvious and more encoded manipulation of the body in Mansfield's performance of Hyde—how he "poised in a crouching position on his toes, swaying and bounding with an agility which gave a weird, spectral quality"—grounded the construction of his character even more firmly in blackface imagery.[136] Hyde's stoop, his gait, his gruesomely "distorted fingers," and his rapid stage movements are strikingly similar to the antebellum minstrel dancer who Hans Nathan recalls as having moved with great speed and acumen and whose body "was always bent and twisted," with legs "wide apart."[137] At the same time, however, Mansfield's deft redeployment of minstrelsy also represents something of a mutation of the form. He ironically appropriated the gestures and imagery from that "counterfeit" genre, stealing back eerily familiar images of visceral disfigurement and distilling them into late-nineteenth-century Gothic melodrama in order to deploy a revised, encoded image of danger and deviance combined. The propagandistic philoso-

2. Richard Mansfield in
*Dr. Jekyll and Mr. Hyde.*
Courtesy of the Billy Rose
Theatre Collection, New York
Public Library for the Per-
forming Arts, Astor, Lenox
and Tilden Foundations.

phies of "the happy darky" which early minstrels promoted and celebrated are radically reversed in *Dr. Jekyll and Mr. Hyde.* Whereas minstrelsy presented what James Weldon Johnson called a "fixed tradition of the Negro as only an irresponsible, happy-go-lucky, wide-grinning, loud-laughing, shuffling, banjo-playing, singing, dancing sort of being," *Jekyll and Hyde* unleashed the (blackened) fiend.[138]

Mansfield's Hyde thus manifests a "major effort of corporeal containment" which serves as a restorative act of power in and through the white perform-ing body. Like blackface caricature, Mansfield's dual anti-hero becomes the site of communal and cultural exchange and exorcism. In both the novel and the play, Jekyll's urge to "like a schoolboy, strip off these lendings and spring headlong into liberty" (86) parallels the minstrel performer's aim to make " 'blackness' flicker on and off so as simultaneously to produce and disinte-grate the body."[139] The *Jekyll and Hyde* narrative participated in this tradition of manufacturing desire and performing the annihilation of it. The phantas-magoric split of the body in the Mansfield-Sullivan production represents the efforts of a nation to both divide itself and to revel in the transgressive spectacle of that division. In this way, *Jekyll and Hyde* embodies the post-Reconstruction climate in which Anglo-American popular culture shifted its representation of African Americans so as to thwart the post–Civil War political and economic advancements made by the formerly enslaved. Gone was the image of the feckless and benign clown begging for guidance, and in its place was that of the beast urgently in need of expunging from the American body politic. The conclusion of the play reads, then, as a cautionary tale on multiple levels. In what Pinkston describes as the "most challenging" point in the production, Mansfield's Dr. Jekyll assumes a noble and heroic stance by trying to ward off an "involuntary transformation" into Hyde ("Stage Premiere," 35). Found alone and disfigured on the laboratory floor as the curtain drops, Mansfield's Jekyll symbolizes the miscegenated body of the nation which, was itself, in this "strange case," at "the nadir of the new segregationism . . . now the freak, separated and rejoined over the black body." Mansfield performs a spectacular act of wasting away this tainted, dual body (politic) as Jekyll perishes along with Hyde, unable to reconcile the difference within himself. The final act thus stages a grand tableau of sorts in which the figure of the "freak," or the "dark, deviant body" has been sacrificed so as not to infect and destroy the national body.[140]

This conflation of racially marked otherness and horror offers a response of sorts to the sociopolitical shifts in the American landscape and in the theatrical world as well. Mansfield and Sullivan's construction of Hyde erupted onto the American theatrical scene during a period of heightened awareness of literal black bodies on the stage. With the rise in prominence of the African American minstrel performer in the post–Civil War era, the presence of black figures in the public sphere posed a problem to dominant cultural audiences even as it intrigued them. As the pre–Civil War argument that the "skill" and "precision" of the white minstrel entertainer transcended that of the black performer gave way to an interest in African American minstrelsy, the rhetoric of performative mastery shifted to an emphasis on the white performer divorced almost altogether from blackface. Nathan's contention that in the early 1840s white minstrel showmen were "expected to excel in precision, speed, near-acrobatic flexibility, and endurance" had, by the 1880s and 1890s, shifted to an assumption that black minstrels were uniquely capable of incorporating a discourse of authenticity into their performances. Responding to the demands of the market, African American minstrel troupes often promoted this rhetoric themselves in the years immediately following the Civil War, "claiming to be ex-slaves" and "minstrel experts at portraying plantation material." Anglo performers reacted by gradually steering away from portraying overtly "Negro" subjects in the stage productions of the latter nineteenth century.[141] The growing perception that black minstrel troupes delivered "something fresh and original" to the genre was thus coupled with the presumption that these performers excelled solely as a result of their putatively essential "spontaneity."[142] Debuting in the era immediately preceding the explosion of black musical performance, the Mansfield-Sullivan production of *Dr. Jekyll and Mr. Hyde* mounted a Gothic allegory of the spectacle as well as the circumscription of these potentially threatening black bodies on the stage.

It is imperative, then, to read the work of white performers such as Richard Mansfield within the context of nascent postbellum black theatre activity. For I would suggest that this metanarrative of Mansfield's performance overrides and occludes the bleak suicidal ending of the play. Unlike the subsequent film adaptations of the *Jekyll and Hyde* narrative in which "science" functions as a potential form of "weaponry" against social deviance, the American theatrical production presents the act of performance itself as metatextual tool which eclipses and quells dominant cultural anxieties of social disorder. The "deaths" of Dr. Jekyll and Mr. Hyde were, in effect, the "birth" of a new era of white performance power. Even as it kills off its lead character, the play reaffirms the skill and mastery of the white, patriarchal figure in theatre. The way to finally control the racialized body on and off the stage, the American phenomenon of *Dr. Jekyll and Mr. Hyde* suggests, is through a reassertion of superior Anglo-American performative skills.[143] That is, since Hyde as black deviance and blackened spectacular performance in postbellum culture threatens to literally and figuratively cover/hide whiteness, Mansfield/Jekyll's final act is to undress this "Gothic transvestism." If Hyde can be understood to be "the disappearance of Jekyll" (Halberstam, *Skin Shows*, 67), then in the stage adaptation of the novel, Hyde also embodies what was perceived to be the frightening disappearance of the white and normative performer on the stage. "Dressed up" in Gothic drag and under the "cover" of both Jekyll and Hyde, Mansfield *re*covers white mastery of the performing body, even as his act recalls and embodies the deviant codes of post-Reconstruction blackness.[144]

The attempt to preserve the notion of a superior, white patriarchal performative craft as black minstrel and theatrical troupes began to form and tour the country may explain why critics and audiences fixated on Mansfield's "skill" as an actor. Many critics were reportedly "less interested in the mystery and complexity of the double character of Jekyll and Hyde than they were in the technical manner in which Mansfield acted the two parts" (Pinkston, "Stage Premiere," 39). Praise for Mansfield's performance focused on his technique and elocution as an actor in ways that recall the accolades heaped on early white minstrelsy performers. Wilstach argues, for example, that Mansfield "thrilled" audiences "with simple, lofty, and invincible art." Likewise, his contemporary Winter gushed about Mansfield's portrayal of the dual role, marveling over the way "the actor possessed great volume of voice and great impetuosity of nervous force, and his acting of Hyde, viewed simply as execution, furnished conclusive evidence of his exceptional resources."[145]

The controversy over whether or not Mansfield relied on his thespian skills, stage tricks, or make-up to perform the transformation from Jekyll into Hyde and vice versa only intensified popular interest in Mansfield's acumen as an actor. He was said to have "told the simple facts" regarding his performative acumen and "caused them to be repeatedly published, that his only change was in the muscles of his face, the tones of his yielding voice, and the posture of his body." Mansfield consistently claimed that his shift into Hyde was entirely brought about through his own physical labor as an actor; he even went so far as to publish a letter in the *New York Sun* which elaborated on his characterizations of Jekyll and Hyde.[146] Mansfield's affirmation of his own theatrical deftness, then, bespeaks an attempt on the postbellum actor's part to claim a bodily authenticity in performance. The actor's self-promotion articulates an effort to compete with the "naturalness" of the new black performer of the day: these efforts remind the public of how his "beast in the jungle" emanated from some Jamesian, "natural thing" within.[147] Mansfield and Sullivan's production of *Jekyll and Hyde* was, then, as much about "white showmanship and skill" as it was about controlling the (encoded) image of the black body and enacting an overriding assertion of narrative authority in performance. Although Mansfield performed a potentially alienating form of Gothic racial drag, the result was yoked in the reactionary rather than the resistant, the comforting as opposed to the countercultural. His performances were some of the surest signs that white male entertainers were determined to maintain control of corporeal technologies on the postbellum stage.

This effort did not to go unnoticed across the Atlantic where an inversion of roles in minstrelsy led Anglo performers to replace African Americans in blackface putatively as a result of the suggestion that black performers lacked skill, maturity, and responsibility to work the minstrel show circuit. In his memoir, Harry Reynolds, the former British burnt-cork performer, argues that in England "the white man gradually replaced all the coloured men, as the public seemed to prefer the imitation nigger."[148] But audiences of the Atlantic world would indeed gradually turn their attention to black performers who redirected conventional performance practices in the nineteenth century, who mastered the art of spectacle, (representational) excess, and duality, and who signified on the politics of racial "imitation" in order to reinvent the transatlantic cultural playing field from abolition forward.

# 2. THE ESCAPE ARTIST

*Henry Box Brown, Black Abolitionist Performance,*
*and Moving Panoramas of Slavery*

N early as unimaginable as the thought of the bondsman Henry Brown crouching in a crate and mailing himself to freedom is the idea of a fugitive Brown rehearsing this act in the years following his heralded flight from slavery. But in the 1850s, the "age of anxious escape," the enslaved Brown's repetition of his boxing act evoked an imaginative commentary on the ambiguities of liberty and bondage for African Americans in the decade preceding the Civil War. Although he had succeeded in fleeing a Richmond, Virginia, plantation in 1849 via the U.S. postal service, the pro-slaveholder concessions of the Compromise of 1850 made even the most high-profile fugitives such as Brown spectacularly vulnerable. With the advent of the Fugitive Slave Act and a subsequent brush with slave catchers in August 1850, Brown's second escape—this time to England—set the stage for an encore demonstration of his wondrous feat. Packed in a replica of his original box and accompanied by his co-conspirator, J. C. A. Smith, a free black Virginian, Brown agreed to ship himself "from Bradford to Leeds" where "he was taken out in the presence of spectators."[1]

## Through the Looking Glass

Part shrewd publicity stunt and part abolitionist propaganda, Brown's living reproduction of his claustrophobic escape route illuminates the complex and cyclical patterns of performative resistance which fugitive slaves mounted as a response to the reactionary federal legislation of the 1850s. Traveling throughout New England and later transgressing the geographical borders of other countries, a number of black abolitionist activists such as Brown, William and Ellen Craft, and William Wells Brown agreed to revisit their often unique and spectacular methods of liberation for curious audiences who paid to see and hear the "horrors" of that peculiar institution.[2] By returning with vividness and a putative authenticity to the "scene of the crime" in their pulpit addresses and exhibitions, these activists contributed to the movement to "erec[t] a moral cordon around America that would isolate her from the international community." They at once removed themselves from U.S. soil and used the abolitionist lecture circuit abroad to mount a critical and argumentative path back into the American social and political landscape.[3]

Brown's return to the box that paradoxically freed him thus came in the midst of a wave of black transatlantic mobility and aesthetically innovative political dissent in the years between 1848 and 1854. If, in the wake of Frederick Douglass's *Narrative of the Life of an American Slave* (1845), the 1840s construction of the fugitive slave revolved around his transformation into the "American hero" and into an agent of his own destiny, that agent became an 1850s peripatetic icon whose migrant travels were put forth precisely to expose the ironies of U.S. domestic enslavement.[4] Responding to Thomas Carlyle's condemnation of abolitionism and widespread theories of racial hierarchies, black Atlantic abolitionists repositioned themselves as international figures called on to exemplify the essential humanity of African Americans and to body forth the atrocities of the slave trade on a global stage.[5]

Motion, migration, and flight worked as operative tropes in the black abolitionist cultural production of the slave's narrative from this tumultuous period. The geographical sojourns and manipulation of borders in works such as Henry Bibb's *Narrative of the Life and Adventures of Henry Bibb* (1849) and Solomon Northrup's *Twelve Years a Slave* (1853) literally and figuratively suggested that there was no (safe) place for black bodies in America. Stripped of his freedom as was Northrup, or perpetually nomadic as was Bibb, fugitive authors produced a number of narratives from this period that foreground the transient positions of protagonists who are repeatedly and often willfully displaced and set to roaming.[6] Box Brown would make this kind of generic black (male) experience painfully clear with his restaged, mobile imprisonment. Affirming the trope of the "outsider manque" and bringing such a status literally and figuratively to life, his use of the legendary box symbolically communicated a decision to re-move himself from the visible world while *still moving through it*. In doing so, his traveling entrapment offered a signifying metaphor of physical resistance to the antebellum period's rigorous literal and figurative colonization of black bodies.[7]

Brown exemplifies the role of the alienated and dislocated black fugitive subject, and the repetition of his escape "act" before audiences abroad provided a heightened and alternate expression of conditional and fleeting liberty "on the run" in the 1850s. Perhaps emboldened by a sharp increase in northeastern black militancy, particularly in Boston, where hostile federal legislation generated passionate public protests, Brown and his traveling comrades sought increasingly spectacular and creative means to attack slavery.[8] The (r)evolutions of various antislavery exhibitions which incorporated lectures, slave spirituals, and aesthetic displays established aggressive and performative responses to the juridical surveillance and circumscription of captive bodies. These public events often built on the initial content of the written slave narrative testimonials by attempting to visually translate representations of slavery for Northern and transatlantic audiences. In this context, Henry Brown's grand re-emergence from the box was part of a continuum of public events designed to sustain an elaborate and serialized critique of the Southern slave labor system. Having published a U.S. version of his memoirs in 1849 with the significant aid of amanuensis and Anglo abolitionist Charles Stearns, Brown decided to erect a "moving panorama" of slavery in 1850. On the eve of his intensified status as a fugitive, his decision suggests that the resourceful activist was seeking alternative forms of intertextual expression in the battle to end slavery which might, in turn, continue to (aesthetically) free him in multiple ways as well.

In an elaborate appropriation of the popular panoramic form for antislavery purposes, Brown employed the visual and theatrical innovations of that genre to imagine reentering the American landscape on his own terms, in turn developing a fugitive form of political expression that was collaborative and multigeneric in its execution and vision. This reinvention of the representation of geographical, social, and cultural space allowed for a formalistically challenging abolitionist project which extended the bounds of Brown's radical passage out of slavery and disrupted the politics of the discursive slave narrative genre as well. A kind of escape from his previous textual "autobiography," in a sense, this panorama offered another way of "signify[ing] and interpret[ing] the borders of other-consciousness" by creating a resistant and yet oft-overlooked bridge into the later edition of Brown's written text.[9] Relying on Gothic metaphor, revisionist landscape art, and corporeal dissent, this panoramic exhibition event would yield a crucial intervention in the cultural construction of black body, narrative voice, and nation building in the transatlantic antislavery movement.

This chapter traces Henry Brown's insurgent movements from his "boxing" journey to his use of the moving panorama and his own body in reenactments of his famed escape. Boldly experimental and iconoclastic, Brown effectively transcended the discursive restrictions of the slave narrative and redirected the uses of the transatlantic body toward politically insurgent ends.

In this regard, Brown engineered multiple ruptures in the cultural arm of midcentury transatlantic abolitionism. His 1849 U.S. slave narrative manufactures a number of conventional editorial constrictions placed on the slave narrative genre. The discussion below traces the critical tensions between this text and Brown's subsequent cultural work. The core of the chapter explores the far-reaching impact of Brown's ambitious decision in 1850 to erect a moving panorama exhibition, the *Mirror of Slavery*, on both sides of the Atlantic. Significant continuities of strategy and tactic exist between Brown's discursive and visual slave narratives. Brown's aesthetic innovations helped forge and perfect new methods of "escape artistry" among fugitive slave activists. Like that of his contemporary William Wells Brown, Box Brown's performative activism dynamically illuminates how, as Paul Jefferson contends, "the act of fleeing is an existential act of self-creation."[10]

The latter half of this chapter interrogates the poetics of Brown's "self-creation" outside the panorama and in the later edition of his slave narrative. Reading Brown's "boxing" reenactments as a kind of politically subversive "escapology," at once referencing Victorian magic and spiritualist culture and prefiguring the work of turn-of-the-century escape artists such as Harry Houdini, this chapter limns the sociopolitical and aesthetic complexity of Henry Box Brown and his renegade cultural work. In sum, it seeks to make plain Brown's significant contributions to nineteenth-century transatlantic culture. Through the looking glass of new technologies available to him in both the northeastern United States and the United Kingdom, and through an invocation of nineteenth-century spectacular theatre and spiritualism in his intertextual cultural productions, Brown negotiated alternative forms of self-representation and, in turn, expanded the terms of black abolitionist activism. His (auto)biographies, panorama, and public exhibitions must be considered, then, as concatenate parts that create a sprawling, epic text, one which Brown the author, artist, and performer might leap through, escaping from one art form into the next in his quest for emancipation.

### Boxing the Text

Like the "3 feet long, by 2 feet wide, and two feet deep" wooden crate in which the future abolitionist smuggled himself to freedom, *The Narrative of Henry Box Brown* is noticeably slim in size. This version of Brown's life story positions him as a self-proclaimed survivor of "that dreadful system of un-hallowed bondage" (11) who, on his birth into slavery in 1816, holds the unusual opportunity to spend most of his youth in the immediate care of his parents and his younger brother.[11] The first portion of the text eschews the

graphic descriptions of torture, abjection, and dislocation present in the canonical slave narratives of the 1840s and 1850s such as William Wells Brown's
and Solomon Northrup's popular autobiographies. Rather, Box Brown's narrative illustrates how the most putatively benign forms of bondage remain
unbearable.[12] His text is not a tale of "horrid inflictions of the lash upon [his]
naked body" but it claims to be "the very best representation of slavery which
can be given" (12).

This sardonically "humane" experience in bondage eventually gives way to
a confrontation with the fateful machinery of the slave system. Although
Brown develops a limited degree of financial and social autonomy while
working in a "tobacco manufactory," he is forced to confront his status as a
pawn of the Southern plantation market economy. No degree of financial
freedom on Brown's part can protect his wife Nancy and their newborn infant
from the whims of the slave trade. The systemic abuse of Brown's wife and
child by various masters announces a critical crisis that culminates in Brown's
inability to purchase his family's freedom and results in their subsequent sale
to a North Carolina Methodist minister. Professing rage and devastation,
Brown acknowledges that for him, "slavery now had no mitigating circumstances, to lessen the bitterness of its cup of woe" (56). In 1848, this severance
from family, the text suggests, provides him with the final impetus to begin
plotting his escape. In hatching his plan, Brown enlists the assistance of Samuel Smith, a white Massachusetts native, and James Caesar Smith, a free black
dentist and merchant.[13]

From the explicit proclamations of its title page, *The Narrative of Henry
Box Brown, Who Escaped from Slavery Enclosed in a Box 3 Feet Long and
2 Wide. Written from a Statement of Facts Made by Himself. With Remarks
Upon the Remedy for Slavery. By Charles Stearns.* moves rapidly toward the
moment of escape. Mired in numerous enclosures, it is a text that has, in
effect, already ended even before its introduction. The length of its title alone
binds the narrative to the spectacular point of liberation and casts its own
form of textual entrapment onto the subsequent body of the narrative. Even
as the *Narrative* reveals the physical ordeals and vicissitudes of enslavement,
Brown's "autobiography" consistently assures its readers that the point of
escape is imminent.[14] Repeatedly the text acknowledges its audience's "eager[ness] to learn the particulars of [Brown's] journey from freedom to liberty" (56), and it reminds the reader that "the heart-rending scenes which give
the principal interest" (40) are close at hand. The work pivots on the reader's
(as well as the editor's) presumption that the slave's body will ultimately and
literally disappear from view. Looming large in this tightly wound vanishing

act is none other than Brown's amanuensis, the industrious Charles Stearns. Passionate in his concern for the enslaved, Stearns's editorial body multiplies in size while Brown's figure gradually dwarfs and collapses into the very box of his escape. Little surprise that Brown's infamous crate resurfaces imagistically at the climax of the narrative. The "boxing" episode (coined by Brown and Smith during their initial lecture tour) shapes and manifests the *Narrative*'s discursively claustrophobic tone and form.

The image of entombment reverberates throughout the "autobiography" in multiple instances, of which the escape plan is the most well known. The tightly oppressive contours of the box, for instance, impress upon the language of Brown's *Narrative*, an account of slavery which Bernard F. Reilly argues is "filled with images of death and burial."[15] Crouched in a fetal position for twenty-seven hours, armed with a beef bladder "filled with water," and provided with "three small gimlet holes" drilled for "fresh air," a boxed Brown operates as the major shifting ideological and representational trope in the text. Similar to the "linguistic narrow spaces" which Harriet Jacobs must negotiate in her own narrative of bondage, the suffocating restrictions of "this dreadful position" in a "narrow prison" (60) permeate the structural patterns of Brown's text as well.[16] Beginning with a series of negations, the narrator waxes repressive with the opening proclamation that "I am not about to harrow the feelings of my readers by a terrific representation of the untold horrors of that fearful system of oppression. . . . It is not my purpose to descend deeply into the dark and noisome caverns of the hell of slavery" (11). The text affirms a representational lack, a thematic absence in the context of the male slave narrative genre which depends on exposure and graphic detail. With its professed resistance to the articulation of violence, Brown's narrative erects a cordon of its own around slavery's explicit abjection, purposefully muting the horrors of captivity in order to reaffirm for readers the ironies of this the more palatable side of the system (11–12). Echoing the denial of white abolitionist Charles Stearns's preface, which assures that Brown's *Narrative* exists "not for the purpose of administering to a prurient desire to 'hear and see some new thing'" (v), the *Narrative*'s opening paragraph assures that it will restrict the audience's vision to the presentation of a "simple and touching narrative" (v). The remnants of the "hell of slavery" are assuredly extinguished from this narrative of Brown's life.

This sort of structural elision and elusion comes to bear on the 1849 edition of the *Narrative of Henry Box Brown* in numerous ways. The text oscillates between narrative imprecision—the narrator's confession that he "cannot correctly describe" the anticipation of liberty (32) and a repeated visual occlusion in which Brown as narrator is removed from the position of witnessing the violence inflicted on fellow slaves. In an early passage from the text, Brown and his brother encounter captives from a neighboring plantation who are subjected to chronic whippings. Yet he and his sibling only hear the "screams of these creatures, suffering under the blows of the hard-headed overseer" (24). These cries of agony which "sounded in [their] ears for some time" (24) are emblematic of the text's emphasis on visually distancing the physical abuses of slavery.[17] Only the residual *sound* of torture is representationally available for the narrative's readers at this stage. These moments of syntactical negation, descriptive imprecision, and ocular impairment have much to do with the heavy-handed influence of Charles Stearns, Brown's ubiquitous ghostwriter and author of both the preface and a document entitled "Cure for the Evil of Slavery" which immediately follows the body of the *Narrative*.

Stearns's somewhat controversial and well-analyzed role as amanuensis and his two editorial documents work perhaps most critically to confine Brown's account of slavery, entrapping Henry Box Brown's "autobiographical" experience in the hyperbolic prose of (white) abolitionist propaganda. James Olney argues persuasively, in fact, that Stearns "dress[es] up" Brown's story in "exotic rhetorical garments" so that "for every fact there are pages of self-conscious, self-gratifying, self-congratulatory philosophizing" by the editor. "[I]f there is any life here at all," Olney concludes, "it is the life of" Stearns who "expresse[s] in his very own overheated and foolish prose."[18] Stearns's appended documents extend and amplify this discourse of entrapment. A kind of barricade to the central text, the preface lavishly appropriates images of enclosure for its own purposes. Here Stearns prepares his readers for Brown's journey in "a portable prison," while simultaneously reimagining his audience as victims of a kind of (emotional) suffocation as well. Through a deft rhetorical transposition on the part of Stearns, Brown's ordeal serves as the catalyst for the resuscitation of his audience. Stearns coaxes his readers into heightened sentience, exhorting them to "let the deep fountains of human feeling, which God has implanted in the breast of every son and daughter of Adam, burst forth from their enclosure" (v). The text is put forth to release "human feeling" in the audience, to free them from their own emotional entombment. Metaphorically manipulating the growing nineteenth-century anxiety of live burial and confinement, Stearns's preface efficiently shifts the fear of entrapment and the quest for liberation to the (white) reader.[19]

This act of displacement recurs in Stearns's attempts to compare the risks of William and Ellen Crafts' famous masquerade and flight out of slavery to that of Brown's. Stearns enacts a clear and reckless slippage between audience and narrative subject, making this sort of conflation vigorously apparent. Initially referring to the Crafts, Stearns asserts that "they were not entirely helpless; enclosed in a moving tomb, and as utterly destitute of power to control *your* movements as if death had fastened its icy arm upon *you* . . . as was the case with our friend" (vii, emphasis added).[20] Stearns's oscillation from the third person to the second and back to the third person positions Brown at the center of a confounding disappearing act. Momentarily, the reader, rather than Brown, is tucked in this cramped and hazardous place of hiding and faces mortality as the fugitive slave is forced out of the text's frame. Stearns's insistence on evoking the brutal specifics of this harrowing escape depends on the habitual and often strategic gestures made by white abolitionists to transform the "horrors of slavery" into an experience which the Northern reader might ultimately own and inhabit at the expense of the ex-slave.[21] With a lengthy closing essay in which Stearns lobbies for "a new government at the North" to uphold antislavery ideologies in the free states, the *Narrative of Henry Box Brown* thus seems subject to its own rather familiar discursive incarceration. These "testimonial," corroborating voices are meant to legitimize the experiences of the author and to assist in building a putatively empathic bridge between the reader and the fugitive slave. However, the tradition of framing that Stearns exploits threatens to box Brown's (narrative) body from beginning to end.[22]

The eclipsing language and structural whims of Stearns's editorial vision follow the trajectory of form which Robert Stepto outlines in his influential work on the slave narrative tradition. Identifying the varying degrees of authorial control and representation in the genre, he asserts that at the most basic of levels, the slave narrative assumes an "eclectic" form which is characterized by a multiplicity of "authenticating documents and strategies" designed to corroborate the voice of the author. Prefaces, letters of support, and epilogues are appended to the texts to confirm the "authenticity" of the author's accounts; yet "there is no exchange, no verbal bond," indeed no dialogue established between the documents which frame the narrative. Rather, the myriad textual appendices operate in discursive isolation, separated by a gulf of social and cultural difference as well as the organizational vision of the "publisher or editor" who ultimately "assembles and manipulates the authenticating machinery" of the text as a whole.[23] Indeed, critics often allude to Brown's 1849 narrative as a casebook study of the erasure of black subjectivity in the fugitive slave narrative genre. It is a text in which the slave's body is, in effect, buried and displaced by the voice of a white editor. By appending his own lengthy "authenticating machinery," Stearns sustains a dialogue "with white America across the text and figurative body of a silent former slave."[24] The general understanding of the 1849 text, then, is one in which, as Olney emphatically concludes, "there is precious little of Box Brown (other than the representation of the box itself)" that remains in the narrative.

Nevertheless, I would argue that we might consider rethinking the significance of this image of the legendary box, if we are to understand the anti-slavery activism of Henry Box Brown more fully. Although Stearns's excessive appendices threaten to eclipse the central Brown text, the 1849 *Narrative's* concluding page with its illustrated "representation of the box," an image of a lone crate, strapped with five hoops and marked for Philadelphia transit, offers the most critical point of reversal in the *Narrative of Henry Box Brown*. Far from eroding the body and subjectivity of the fugitive, this image operates suggestively as an act of narrative combat, as a means toward defensively "boxing," the editors and readers enacting control over his (textual) body. From this standpoint, Brown's spectacularly present absence inside of this "portable prison" executes its own dueling authority with Charles Stearns's narrative control. The image of Brown's self-engineered captivity provides a paradoxical and open-ended critique of the white abolitionist impulse to "remov[e] the slave from view as pain is brought close" through a displacement of black flesh for white (Hartman, *Scenes of Subjection*, 20).

A parting, ambivalent riddle of sorts, a symbolic and corporeal refusal, the spectacle of Brown's self-engineered captivity signifies on the implicit suggestion inherent in the slave narrative genre that the text will operate as a transparent looking glass, free of artifice and exposing the ordeal of bondage. Such a notion gets turned on its head here as the deployment of the box enacts a final gesture of spectacular opacity to (en)close the text. Disrupting the "prevailing metaphor" of "invisibility and translucence" in Afro-American letters, Brown's crate announces a staged resistance to the gaze and presumed spectatorial authority of his readership.[25] An enigmatic representation of enclosure perched at the end of the narrative, the illustration of the box starkly contrasts with the opening portrait of Brown that sits opposite Stearns's preface. While this sketch of Brown in formal dress contributes to the system of putative "truthfulness" and self-exposure manufactured by the slave narrative genre in order to lend veracity to the ex-slave's existence, the "representation of the box" potentially unseats this initial "existential claim" of absolute material presence.[26] The "boxing" image poses a philosophical query regarding the tenuous position of the fugitive slave in both his own narrative and more broadly in American culture. Brown is present and yet discursively entombed, forced underground into a manhole of his own making once again

3. Portrait of Henry Box Brown. From *Narrative of Henry Box Brown* (1849). Courtesy of Manuscripts, Archives, and Rare Books Division, Schomburg Center for Research in Black Culture, New York Public Library, Astor, Lenox and Tilden Foundations.

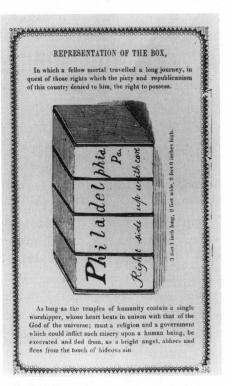

REPRESENTATION OF THE BOX,

In which a fellow mortal travelled a long journey, in quest of those rights which the piety and republicanism of this country denied to him, the right to possess.

*Philadelphia. Pa.*

*Right side up with care*

3 feet 1 inch long, 2 feet wide, 2 feet 6 inches high.

As long as the temples of humanity contain a single worshipper, whose heart beats in unison with that of the God of the universe; must a religion and a government which could inflict such misery upon a human being, be execrated and fled from, as a bright angel, abhors and flees from the touch of hideous sin.

4. 1849 illustration of the box in which Henry Box Brown escaped to freedom. Taken from the last page of the *Narrative of Henry Box Brown*. Courtesy of General Research and Reference Division, Schomburg Center for Research in Black Culture, New York Public Library, Astor, Lenox and Tilden Foundations.

as Stearns's overbearing and "ghostly" editorial hand threatens to place a stranglehold on the text. The box resurfaces at the conclusion as an abolitionist rhetorical device meant to reinforce the "piety and republicanism of this country denied" Box Brown, and it also doubles as a figurative break on Brown's part from Stearns's narrative surveillance.[27]

The placement of this image of the box forces us to consider its economy more rigorously in relation to both the *Narrative of Henry Box Brown* and, more broadly, to the cultural work of Henry Box Brown. An object which potentially conjures what Stephen Greenblatt might read as both "resonance" and "wonder," this illustrated box is both arresting and restlessly in conversation with a dense network of social, cultural, and political signs. According to Greenblatt, resonance and wonder operate as two distinct strategies of exhibiting and viewing art objects; the power of the object on display either promises to evoke "wonder" by steering the viewer's imagination toward the magnetic pull of the object and that object alone, or to encourage a "resonance" that forces the viewer to shift contemplation outward and into the thick field of historicity engulfing the display. Wonder generates an "enchanted" form of looking at an object which "draws a circle around itself from which everything but the object is excluded." Conversely, a "resonant exhibition often pulls the viewer away from the celebration of isolated objects and toward a series of only half-visible relationships and questions"; this resonance draws attention to the "permeability" of the object and its volatile circulation in and across multiple contexts.[28] An object that resists the silencing ahistorical powers of the wondrous, the image of Brown's crate potentially mutes Stearns's loud histrionics. Pulling the reader away from the voice of the editor, the "representation of the box" redirects the viewer's gaze toward Brown's flight and redelivers the loaded trope of hidden human cargo and treacherous (middle) passages which serve to fundamentally haunt the text. A box of metonymic resonance, Brown's crate creates a conclusion which forces the reader into a suspended state of historical meditation and contemplation.[29]

This narrative ends, then, with a representation of (en)closure that, in turn, yields a fundamental lack of closure. The return of the box here establishes a shift in narrative authority from Stearns to Brown and opens up an extended escape route for the fugitive slave. Its image generates what Hortense Spillers might read as an "*intervening, intruding* tale . . . as a *metaphor* of social and cultural management" for the enslaved in flight.[30] With its appended documents which at once contradict and articulate Brown's captivity and liberation, Box Brown's 1849 *Narrative* manifests *in form* the discourse of escape which propels the slave narrative genre. A discordant image of both circumscription and liberation, the box offers a critical climax of resistance and emancipation. If, as Andrews asserts, in the slave narrative "freedom becomes the crucial property and quality *of* a text—not just *what* it refers to, but *how* it signifies" it, then Box Brown's narrative must be read as a living document *in struggle* and one which is (willfully) trapped in a repeating negotiation of confinement and bold flight. It is a text that foreshadows Brown's volatile re-enactments of his escape artistry in the years following the *Narrative*'s publication.[31]

In this sense, Brown's work literally and figuratively heightens Raymond Hedin's claim that "the narratives which are so emphatic in closing off the narrator's escape story are equally emphatic in emphasizing that the real story, slavery continues."[32] The central aim of the slave narrative is in fact not to close but to urge for a transformation of circumstances which comes about through the reader's indignation over a *lack* of closure in the national narrative of slavery. By "refusing to assimilate to his literary landscape," a (re)boxed Henry Brown at text's end overturns the critical notion that "once the protagonist achieves his freedom, the nineteenth-century slave narrative terminates."[33] Although the discursive text concludes, this box of wondrous resonance creates a fitting bridge to a "third" narrative space between abolitionist pulpit and the literary slave narrative. Brown's moving panorama exhibition provides an intervention in white abolitionist editorial constrictions on black authorship and strategies of fugitive slave cultural and political expression. The popular cultural form of the panorama delivers an alternative method for reading and reinterpreting the slave narrative genre. By mounting a moving panorama of slavery, Henry Box Brown embraced a freedom of representational form which, in turn, allowed him to reenter the text of his own narrative and, in so doing, make new the landscape of fugitive slave autobiography.[34]

### Peristrephic Revolutions

[E]very people should be the originators of their own designs, the projector of their own schemes, and creators of the events that lead to their destiny.

—Martin Delany, *Condition, Elevation, Emigration, and Destiny of the Colored People of the United States*

Some time between 1849 and 1850 and within a year of both Henry Box Brown's and William Wells Brown's respective traveling exhibitions, the latter Brown visited a newly refurbished building in London which was believed to have epitomized the grand aesthetic and technological "progress" of English spectacular entertainment. Like many fellow London spectators and theatre-goers, Brown was mesmerized by his trip to the heralded reopening of the Colosseum, an imposing cylindrical structure that featured a lushly over-sized landscape panorama. Originally completed in 1832, the Colosseum had housed the most ambitiously mounted, cyclical, painted canvas in the U.K. With a change in ownership and a series of renovations, the Colosseum of the late 1840s regained its prominence, first by complicating its original pano-rama of London by day with a display of London by night, and second by presenting *Paris by Night* to packed audiences who were fascinated by the brewing French Revolution of 1848.[35]

Like the many spectators who would attend the *Paris by Night* exhibition at the Colosseum, abolitionist, fugitive slave, and elected International Peace Congress delegate William Wells Brown gushed over how he and his party "found [themselves] ... upon the summit of some high building in the centre of the French metropolis, and there, all brilliant with gas-lights, and favored by the shining moon, Paris lay spread far out beneath [them], though the canvas on which the scene was painted was but half a dozen feet from where [they] gazed in wonder." Brown's total immersion in this scene which "seemed natural, from the twinkling of the stars above" him perhaps provided him with an opportunity to experience the grandeur of social and political up-heaval within the "wide topographical sweep" of the panoramic form (Altick, *Shows of London*, 129).[36] Roughly one year later and possibly riding the mo-mentum from his Colosseum experience, Wells Brown and his transatlantic black abolitionist colleagues would exhibit their own "panoramic views" of U.S. slavery, a kind of moving revolution in space, time, form, and content.[37]

Internal schisms within the transatlantic abolitionist movement made the concept of mounting an antislavery panorama especially appealing to African American antislavery activists. While Anglo abolitionists had weathered a number of conflicting ideals and "crippling division(s)" resulting in the lack of any "unified abolitionist movement" after 1840, black antislavery activists harbored their own discontent with white reform power structures through-out the decade and chafed at being forced to operate on the peripheries of the antislavery movement in relation to their white colleagues.[38] Frederick Doug-lass's decision to break with the mentorship and political ideologies of Wil-liam Lloyd Garrison in 1847 represents just one of the more famous examples of those black activists who began working autonomously in a bid to develop alternative abolitionist agendas. These conflicts which manifested the dissen-sion between pacifist Garrisonian followers and radical abolitionists more willing to consider violent tactics helped usher in a new era of urgency, direction, and "endorsed violence" in the wake of the Fugitive Slave Act.[39] After 1840 and well into the 1850s, African American antislavery activists sought to strengthen their agency and collective voice by organizing and participating heavily in national conventions and social projects designed to redirect and rigorously articulate the terms of black reform in the antebellum era.[40]

A provocative space to mine the politics of freedom, travel, and representational agency, the genre of the moving panorama experienced a resurgence in popularity at precisely the moment when larger numbers of black abolitionists began to fan outward and into transatlantic culture in their battles to end slavery. Created in 1790s England and consisting of a large, still, painted canvas which was mounted inside specially designed, circular buildings, stationary panoramas were, for the most part, hybrids of landscape art and evolving theatre culture. Often featuring grandiose representations of geographical space and historical battle scenes, these full-scale displays evoked a sense of visual impressiveness by virtue of their size and their ability to "convey the illusion of reality" (Altick, *Shows of London*, 188). Still panoramas could span up to 360 degrees, filling the walls of buildings where they were exhibited from a distance by spectators who paid an admission to view the scene from platforms within the central "rotunda" area and on staircases where they were perched.[41]

Although there was "no 'performance'—no spatial or temporal beginning or end" to these epic scenes, viewers were "held in the panorama's frozen moment, a fold in time."[42] The forceful grandeur of these early panoramas—a term derived from Greek and meaning "all-embracing view" (Altick, *Shows of London*, 132)—led to the popular perception in the early nineteenth century that they were educational and entertaining, a kind of large-scale "pictorial journalism" capable of recording and registering "history" as it would unfold in grandly "oversized" terms.[43] Although panoramas were marketed as "a respectable alternative to the theatre," theatre culture quickly adapted the form as versatile stage background and scenery.[44]

Moving panoramas took this concept of spectacularly rendered representation a step further. Dubbed "peristrephic" in 1819, an invented term meant to suggest "turning round, revolving, or rotatory" (Altick, *Shows of London*, 201), these "motion pictures" literally altered the landscape of English and later U.S. show culture and negotiated a radical reconceptualization of time and space in the context of theatre.[45] Developing primarily in the late 1840s and early 1850s, moving panoramas were devices comprising "a lengthy series of related scenes painted on a single cloth" (Altick, *Shows of London*, 199) which was harnessed at each end of the stage by two large cylinders where stage hands were called on to roll the cloth across the stage from one end to the other in order to evoke the sense of large-scale spatial movement. These "changing panoramas," which in their earliest form had kindled an interest in "arm chair" travel with the opening of the imperialist spectacle *Aegyptania* in 1802 London, achieved the pinnacle of their popularity in mid-nineteenth-century England and America (A. Miller, "Panorama," 41). Flourishing in the midst of increasingly visible black abolitionist agitation, the moving panorama phenomenon would ironically popularize a reactionary rendering of the Mississippi River journey as an idyllic and peaceful trope of national uniformity and expansionism.[46]

New York painter John Banvard's enormously successful 1848 exhibition of the Mississippi River, which boasted "no fewer than 36 scenes" of that body of water "from the mouth of the Missouri River to New Orleans" (Altick, *Shows of London*, 204), announced the marketable transformation of the moving panorama from primarily novel show culture scenery into a folksy regionalist excursion and revived the popularity of the form in both England and America. The English and American publics, however, harbored divergent reasons for their fascination with the spectacle of local color. Altick speculates that in the United Kingdom, "apart from the novelty of so gigantic a panorama, Banvard's success owed something to the fact that American subjects were more or less unhackneyed as far as panoramas were concerned" (205). As was the case with Dion Boucicault's *The Octoroon* a decade later, the virgin "newness" of the American landscape offered a nonthreatening space where the English spectator might mine his imagination and satisfy his pastoral nostalgia in the midst of industrialization. In contrast, midcentury American culture's overwhelming fascination with the river panoramas had everything to do with a national interest in expansion and a kind of conquering of domestic territory. As Angela Miller points out, "the development of the round into the moving panorama satisfied the optical (and geographical) hunger of American audiences by artificially compressing space in a manner anticipating mechanized travel, unrolling the American landscape before the eyes of audiences" ("Panorama," 38). These river panoramas "represented an unfolding temporal process, showing the regional part in relation to the national whole" and heralded "an unfolding vista of national progress and western settlement" (46). In these exhibitions of the 1840s and 1850s, then, "America" as a nation presumably followed the "natural" currents of its most imposing body of water, moving forward, outward and into an industrial future of progress and efficiency.

Absent from the moving panorama's "trips" down the river were any signs that it was a route of terror in the culture of slavery where it perpetually operated as an iconographic symbol of rupture and disintegration for slave families forced to watch their relatives "sold down" its treacherous watery path. A mammoth geographical minefield, the Mississippi River remained a literal as well as a figurative obstacle which the Southern fugitive was forced to confront and traverse on the road to freedom.[47]

In their search for alternative spaces in which to express themselves and to assert their agency, several key abolitionists such as William Wells Brown and Henry Box Brown embraced the moving panorama despite its conspicuous erasure of national conflict and what was apparently the blind spot of slavery in some corners of popular consciousness. Indeed, Wells Brown proclaims in the pamphlet description of his own exhibition that part of the impetus behind his decision to create his own visual display was to counter the "very mild manner in which the 'Peculiar Institution' of the Southern States was represented" in the 1847 "Panorama of the River Mississippi" which he attended in Boston.[48] Black abolitionists such as Wells Brown fixated on the moving panorama as a site whose narratives of the nation and narratives of slavery needed urgent revision. The rejuvenated and reorganized black activist resistance to slavery in the mid-nineteenth century propelled African American abolitionists to seize on this form of narration dependent on movement and visual convertibility. By reinserting the brutal histories of slavery into these popular exhibitions, the panoramas became a communicative medium and a terrain on which to interrogate what critic Cynthia Wolff reads as "the multiple 'passages' and 'transformations' that constituted the escaped slave's unique version of an American heritage." Black abolitionists became invested in the panorama as well for the formal and representational opportunities it provided. A rolling, potentially radical unframing of the genre of the (circumscribed) slave narrative, the landscape panorama offered a critical point of possibility for fugitive slave narration.

Reworking the content of these river panoramas and extending many of the formal peculiarities latent in this new cultural technology, black abolitionists saw heretofore unrecognized representational and narrative possibilities in this pop cultural genre. The renewed activist resistance to slavery in the late 1840s and early 1850s perhaps propelled black abolitionists to adopt and adapt a public forum fundamentally built with the passion of (r)evolution and representational revolt. A terrain that literally moves and (r)evolves, the moving or "peristrephic" panorama provides a representational space which perpetually enacts a kind of escape in its visual translation of the slave narrative.

Each scene functions as a passage, a collapsing into contiguous parts so that the exhibition manifests in its very form a continuous possibility of exiting, a way out. Its sheer spectacular size alone suggests an excessiveness, a mechanistic unframing which potentially spills the representational scene over and out of its original containment. Richard Altick argues, for instance, that by "its very nature, the circular panorama enjoyed . . . a great advantage over conventional art as well as theatrical scene painting" because "*it had no frame.*" (Altick, *Shows of London*, 188; emphasis added). The form of the panorama alone, then, manifests an unbridled spirit that provides for the possibility of transgressing fixed and constrictive representational boundaries. Whereas the "testimonials" of others in discursive slave narratives threaten to "enclose" the black abolitionist text "by the very act of providing a formal framework" (Hedin, "Strategies of Form," 25), the panorama contests narrative borders.

Yet simultaneously, in spite of its extravagant, superabundant structure, the panorama posits a kind of spectacular veracity onto a scene, offering the fugitive slave a most unorthodox and paradoxical way in which to affirm the "truthfulness" of what s/he has seen/scene in slavery. This majestic "realness" which the panorama captured, its insistent effort to "convey the illusion of reality," proved useful to black abolitionists who attempted to disseminate their own voices through cultural forms that didn't rely on white "authenticators" to enforce the legitimacy of their narrative. The moving panorama's treatment of historical process "as a spectacle whose truthfulness was authorized by its striking illusionism" (A. Miller, "Panorama," 46) could, in turn, pose its own alternative space for crafting a renegade narrative agency.[49] Thus, while much scholarship reveals how the panorama has served imperialist impulses on both sides of the Atlantic with its renderings of "the newly colonized regions of the world," the black abolitionist appropriation of the panoramic genre has yet to be fully considered as its own unique "escape" route and as a generic form of narrative authority for African Americans in the international antislavery movement.[50]

No doubt, black abolitionist panoramas were clearly subject to co-optation for nationalist and global imperialist agendas, as Audrey Fisch reveals in her study of the complexities facing black antislavery activists in the United Kingdom. In regard to Henry Box Brown's exhibitions in England, Fisch contends that "the spectacle of 'Box' Brown himself, displaying his personal life experiences and commodifying his suffering for display in front of British strangers" strategically functions on a continuum of public "spectacles of America and of American inferiority" which affirm and secure the strength of British national identity and dominance.[51] Others have rightly insisted that Box Brown squarely places the American South "on trial" in his 1850 moving panorama the "*Mirror of Slavery*," making plain the "transformation of Americans into savages by the horrors of slavery."[52]

Yet the *Mirror of Slavery*'s power resides in its ability to unseat and transcend competing English and Anglo-American political agendas. African American abolitionist moving panoramas such as Brown's, in fact, often operated as evidence of oppositional and autonomous black political expression that established conversations with American slavery and English imperialism. Like the discursive slave narratives, these panoramas were "constructed as a transatlantic product" and refocused attention on the narrative powers of the black abolitionists who mounted them.[53] Brown's *Mirror* creates and commodifies a self-consciously disruptive space, a chaotic zone that foregrounds the creative agency of the African American activist-turned-artist. The exhibition's emphasis on social dystopia, fugitive escape, and Gothic apocalypse enacts a visual and performative insurrection which Brown deployed as an abolitionist activist and cultural producer. Brown's moving panorama interrupted the solipsism of other visual displays by placing black performative and representational revolt at the center of his exhibition. His project was perhaps just as committed to renegotiating the heroic fugitive's agency through performative and multimedia means as it was insistent on directing self-reflexive images back at British and Anglo-American audiences. What his exhibition finally makes plain, then, is that the national American body politic is itself subject to dissolution in the fugitive slave's pursuit of freedom. And in this sense, the *Mirror of Slavery* contributes to the growing abolitionist move to claim a kind of "Americanness" which comes precisely as a result of its rebellious ideology. "American" nationhood is here ultimately and purposefully at odds with itself and in a perpetual state of (r)evolution.[54]

Black abolitionists such as Henry Box Brown, then, put the moving panorama's "subversive possibilities" (A. Miller, "Panorama," 59) to politically revisionist ends. By relating visual technology directly to a fundamental quest for narrative agency, early African American panoramas aimed to circumvent British and Anglo-American nationalist impulses and the largely colonialist and industrialist manipulations of mid-nineteenth-century visual entertainment in transatlantic culture.[55] With its espousal of "illusive realism," the panorama provided a launching point for channeling black nationalist Martin Delany's vision of African American autonomous, self-designed emancipation, an event of their own creation which might, in real time, help to actively foresee "their own destiny." At the forefront of this artistic and political movement, Henry Box Brown's panorama led the way toward aesthetic and representational emancipation by producing a mobile "revolution" within the revolving panorama, wherein the black body is cloistered, (re)captured, and finally reinserted into an epic topography of dissemblance. Mounted in music halls and concert stages, first in Boston and later throughout Britain in cities such as London, Leeds, and Manchester, Brown's unique exhibition ambitiously sought to controvert systems of U.S. geographical expansionism and presumptions of historical progress.

### The Escape Artist

In the immediate aftermath of his grand escape, Henry Box Brown reportedly made use of a "considerable theatrical flair" which would serve him well as he embarked on the antislavery lecture circuit towing his famous box.[56] Having arrived by mail on March 24, 1849, in Philadelphia, Brown quickly made his way to New York and on to the "fugitive 'depot'" of New Bedford, Massachusetts, where he resided for much of the month of April in the home of staunch white abolitionist Joseph Ricketson Jr.[57] By the early 1850s, Box Brown gathered together a circle of free African American comrades in struggle, including his co-conspirator J. C. A. Smith, and Benjamin F. Roberts, the black Boston printer responsible for "print[ing] speeches, reports, pamphlets, and other items for antislavery and black organizations." From public appearances at conventions where Brown and Smith "entertained the assemblage with a song they had written about Henry Brown's 'boxing'" to more elaborate presentations of Brown's autobiographical anecdotes, the act flourished into a sophisticated performance where Brown became "a living exhibit, telling stories of his slavery days and singing spirituals." With Roberts's initial managerial efforts, this traveling event evolved into the *Mirror of Slavery*, an exhibition first presented at Boston's Washingtonian Hall in April 1850.[58]

Where Box Brown gained inspiration for his exhibition remains the subject of scholarly conjecture. Jeffrey Ruggles has, for instance, uncovered the striking similarities between Brown's panorama script and the artist and author Charles C. Green's illustrated poem *The Nubian Slave*, published in Boston in 1845. Ruggles's brilliant research outlines the numerous overlapping themes in Brown's script and Green's text, and he has retrieved corresponding images from the original volume, which, he speculates, may have been used as a template for the *Mirror of Slavery*.[59] In addition, we might consider the cultural and political influences shaping Brown's aesthetic vision in this project. Certainly his subsequent association with Wells Brown, who had completed a panorama script in 1847, would have proved a formative professional experience for him. Likewise, the increasing visibility of black artist-activists such as James Presley Ball and Robert Duncanson indicates the maturing vision of African American art that may have registered as an influence on Brown's work. The renegade entrepreneur Ball had by 1847 opened his Great Daguerrean Gallery of the West in Cincinnati, Ohio, the largest exhibiting space of its kind in the region.[60] Both Wells Brown's and Ball's activities provide evidence of the black abolitionist aesthetic network in which Box Brown's creative efforts may have fermented. In addition, historians Kathryn Grover and Nancy Osgood have argued that Box Brown's stay in the bustling New England seaport of New Bedford may have informed his work. Artists Benjamin Russell and Caleb Purrington debuted their *Panorama of a Whaling Voyage* in that city in December of 1848 before moving the display to Boston in April of 1849, thus coinciding with a significant period in the activist's decision to create his own panoramic display.[61] From this standpoint, it is clear that Brown cultivated his project in the convergent context of a dynamic and experimental period of popular visual production and black antislavery cultural innovation.

Brown's ambition and resourcefulness enabled him to enlist the painterly skills of reformist Josiah Wolcott. Details of this collaboration are scarce, but an April 1850 advertisement in *The Liberator* provides an account of Wolcott's involvement in the endeavor as well as the extent of pre-production labor and preparation for the exhibition.[62] Wolcott was a "passionate and determined artist, deeply involved in some of the key social movements of his time"; his New England reformist visions met head on with Box Brown's fugitive escape tactics in the vast span of the panorama's eye. An Associationist at heart, Wolcott embraced that movement's promotion of communitarian values and cooperative communities in lieu of capitalist industry. The artist appears to have had a particular hand in shaping the panorama's concluding regional polemics. The initial *Liberator* announcement regarding the *Mirror*'s debut specifically points out that the "last scene . . . is a view of a township, according to a plan of Charles Fourier, and given by the artist to indicate his idea of the fruition of emancipation." The iconography of New England reform looms large in the panorama and remains the parting image in Box Brown's exhibition.[63] Multiple and intersecting aesthetic and political ideologies thus shaped the *Mirror of Slavery*. For the most part during this period in abolitionism, "antislavery orators rose in prominence as the movement grew" and visual artists of the movement "tended to occupy a . . . more tangential position." In contrast, Brown's panorama enacted a critical merging of "art" and political oratory by placing both on equal footing.[64] The basic structure and content of Box Brown's exhibition yokes the politics of Anglo reform, black abolitionism, and new popular and aesthetic technologies. Advancing beyond the confines of contemporary visual art and popular theatre culture, Brown's *Mirror* unites the elegant grandeur of landscape artistry with the dynamic performance theatrics of Brown and his "associates" as rotating impresarios. Brown appears to have co-opted Banvard's performative flourishes from his own panorama exhibition in order to create an alternative form of revisionist abolitionist activism. Banvard had made a fortune from combining the exotic and sprawling views of early stationary panoramas with popular elements of minstrelsy endmen repertoires, which consisted of joking banter, transforming his exhibition into a hybridized form of performance and visual spectacle. Brown's project shows signs of having apparently eviscerated Banvard's popular production of its folksy elements, divorcing the panoramic spectacle from its minstrel and variety show aberrations and, in their place, wedding the form with antislavery performance propaganda. The earliest New England presentations of the *Mirror of Slavery* offered audiences a multimedia experience of a moving diorama painting, an "enterprise" all the "more interesting" according to one observer for "the whole is conducted by colored men." As one of the narrators of the panorama, Box Brown traded off lecturing duties with his colored comrades. The *London Times* describes the synchronicity of this performance, how "[a]s the different views of the panorama presented themselves in succession," Brown "explained them in a kind of lecture, in which he enlarged upon the horrors of slavery, and the cruelties to which the slaves were subjected."[65] Brown's event would then reanimate Banvard's act to highlight the vocal prowess of the fugitive narrativist who stands adjacent to— and quite crucially, not merely inside—the gruesome world of slavery depicted in the panorama. In a spectacular act of recovery, Brown, like a deft spiritualist in his exhibition, presumably crosses over to the other side of the *Mirror*, to witness his own ingenuous escape on canvas and to provide an ending in the flesh for his audiences.

Unlike other black antislavery panorama exhibitions, no accompanying pamphlets, pictorial reproductions, or theatrical documents such as programs or posters remain from Box Brown's exhibition.[66] Hence, the bulk of the information on the *Mirror of Slavery* has been culled from surviving newspaper advertisements, articles, reviews, and descriptions of the exhibition which surface in abolitionist epistolary exchanges. On May 3, 1850, *The Liberator* ran one of the earliest descriptions of the scenes: "NEW AND ORIGINAL PANORAMA! HENRY BOX BROWN'S *MIRROR OF SLAVERY*, designed and painted from the best and most authentic sources of information."

The following are the scenes:

PART I.

The African Slave Trade.
The Nubian Family in Freedom.
The Seizure of Slaves.
Religious Sacrifice.
Beautiful Lake and Mountain Scenery in Africa.
March to the Coast.
View of the Cape of Good Hope.
Slave Felucca.
Interior of a Slave Ship.
Chase of a Slaver by an English Steam Frigate.
Spanish Slaver at Havana.
Landing Slaves.
Interior of a Slave Mart.
Gorgeous Scenery of the West India Islands.
View of Charleston, South Carolina.
The Nubian Family at Auction.
March of Chain Gang.
Modes of Confinement and Punishment.
Brand and Scourge.
Interior View of Charleston Workhouse, with Treadmill in full operation.

PART II.

Sunday among the Slave Population.
Monday Morning, with Sugar Plantation and Mill.
Women at Work.
Cotton Plantation.
View of the Lake of the Dismal Swamp.
Nubians, escaping by Night.
Ellen Crafts, Escaping.
Whipping Post and Gallows at Richmond, Va.
View of Richmond, Va.
Henry Box Brown, Escaping.
View of the Natural Bridge and Jefferson's Rock.
City of Washington, D.C.
Slave Prisons at Washington.
Washington's Tomb, at Mount Vernon.
Fairmount Water Works.

Henry Box Brown Released at Philadelphia.

Distant View of the City of Philadelphia.

Henry Bibb, Escaping.

Nubian Slaves Retaken.

Tarring and feathering in South Carolina.

The Slaveholder's Dream.

Burning Alive.

Promise of Freedom.

West India Emancipation.

Grand Industrial Palace.

Grand Tableau Finale—UNIVERSAL EMANCIPATION.[67]

Box Brown's panorama divides into two major narrative arcs. Part I appears to deploy a loosely structured series of events which represent the initial points in the circum-Atlantic slave trade odyssey, beginning somewhere amid the "beautiful lake and mountain scenery in Africa," passing through the "gorgeous" landscape of the West Indies, and descending into the deep interiors of the U.S. South's multiple "Modes of Confinement and Punishment." The opening image of the "African Slave Trade" and the exiting shot of a Charleston Workhouse "Treadmill in full operation" establish the relentless movement of slavery's persistent commerce, while the internal scenes oscillate between charting the localized ordeal of a "free" "Nubian Family's" fall into captivity and the globalized progressions of a "Spanish Slaver's" seaward journey to the Americas. Part II utilizes the trope of community as its thematic bookends. The introductory "Sunday among the Slave Population" is visually matched with the reported communitarian finale. In turn, Part II's internal structure conveys a grand visual struggle between captive labor and the labor of escape; the panels in this second half appear to mount and mete out the tensions between gross subjugation and heroic flight in the fugitive slave's experience. Various forms of imprisonment and torture are juxtaposed with images of the "heroic" slave in flight. Part I's visions of pastoral elegance are here replaced with the cartography of U.S. liberty; the manifest iconography of "Jefferson's Rock" and "Washington's Tomb" unfurls along the fugitive's path to freedom. Escape is presumably rewarded in the Grand Tableau Finale where the vision of "Universal Emancipation" affirms the revisionist reflection that this *Mirror* attempts to effect and re-flect.

With the iconography of the river conspicuously absent here, Brown's exhibition eschews the dominant conventions of the panoramic genre. The significant chronotopic symbolism of the river panorama alone, its ability to

represent "an unfolding temporal process, showing the regional part in relation to the national whole" (A. Miller, "Panorama," 46), is bypassed in the
*Mirror of Slavery* completely in favor of a repetition of scenes which evokes the
fundamental regressiveness of the nation, its overarching lack of national
progress. Brown's exhibition suggests that, in spite of its industrial aspirations
embodied in the developing city scenes of "Richmond, Va." and the "City of
Washington, D.C.," slavery nonetheless ensnares the nation in whirling stasis,
causing it to repeatedly fall backward into the nightmare of bondage, forcing
it to succumb to the undertow of its gruesome specter. Foreshadowing Walter
Benjamin's extensive criticism of mid-nineteenth-century ornate urban displays and "the myth of automatic historical progress," Box Brown's exhibition
stages an elaborate reversal of the popular panorama's functionality as a tool
of what he identifies as "mythic history."[68] Just as Benjamin's criticism recognizes the ways in which such mythologizing enacts a critical and spectacular
method of "forgetting," Brown's panoramic rebus attempts to "expose 'progress' as the fetishization of modern temporality" and thereby challenges the
spectator to resolve slavery's conundrum.[69]

With the allure of progress embedded in its very structure, the *Mirror*
conspicuously feigns epic movement through space and time. By opening
with an image of the "African Slave Trade" as its constructed etiological core
and by pushing toward a climax with the forecast of a future-perfect utopian
culture, the exhibition imagines a kind of complicated linearity. Epic in theme
as much as in size, the *Mirror of Slavery* represents one of a handful of
attempts in black abolitionist cultural production to articulate a trajectory of
experience from African "freedom" to the point of enslavement and finally to
a futurist view of a land wherein slavery has been effectively eradicated. At the
same time, the panorama's narrative movement repeatedly stalls and disrupts.
That is, rather than allowing his panorama to operate purely in a develop-
mental historical arc, Brown dismantles the progressive temporality of the
form in order to "*de*mythify the present" state of the Union.[70] Time itself is a
property subject to transmogrification in this dystopian scene of slavery. The
viewer is chronotopically entrapped, forced to submit to the rehearsed slippage between (emancipated) space and the tightly fixed walls of captivity.
Shifting rapidly from the prelapsarian imaginary of a "Nubian Family in
Freedom" to the "Seizure of Slaves," from the pastoral scene of West African
landscape to the confinement of the "Slave Felucca," and the lush image of the
West Indian Islands to the "Interior View of the Workhouse," Part I of the
*Mirror* oscillates between a past idealized wide, open, spatial freedom and an
urgently present imprisonment; for instance, it couples the incarceration of

captives with a roving view of Caribbean topography. This particular "rhythm of history," this "pulse of events in which the audience was allowed vicarious participation" (A. Miller, "Panorama," 55), sustains a vertiginous movement in time and space between liberation and enslavement.

By reaching back to the topography of Africa and stretching itself into what Wolff calls a "pastiche that combined actuality and visionary possibility" in the future (36), Box Brown's *Mirror* yokes together images of slaves' experiences with the volatile social and political landscape of slavery, as well as the very make of the land in its "all-embracing view" of the peculiar institution.[71] The capture, removal, and commodification of an entire African family is set in relation to "mountainous" scenery; images of fleeing Nubians are coupled with the ironically noble grandeur of monuments and "water works." As one English critic observed, the tableaux included "representations strikingly illustrative of American institutions and inconsistencies. The noble House of Congress stands at the top of one picture, and in the foreground is to be seen a slave auction; also General Taylor (as president) driving in state into the city of Washington, whilst his four grey steeds are frightened by the cries and groans of a gang of slaves."[72] These visual juxtapositions aspire toward critically rehistoricizing and re-placing the black body in the fabric of nations, indeed in the landscape of African and American scenery altogether.

This strategy is particularly apparent in Part II, where a similarly complex and repetitious narrative pattern resurfaces in the depiction of four fugitive slave escape scenes which play out in five separate junctures of the exhibition. In a section that we might imagine as a kind of escape suite, "Nubians, Escaping by Night" cut a path to freedom for the "Ellen Crafts" (as they are referred to in the script), Henry Bibb, and Henry Box Brown, but in a reversion of movement recalling that found in Part I, the unnamed "Nubians" are eventually "retaken" in a later scene which closes this series of flights in the panorama. Time and again, the spectator watches the replay of escape and return to slavery, as if to witness the plucking of individuals out of the hands of the tyrannical South one by one. Even as Brown's panorama moves toward imminent escape, the belated scenes of slaves "recaptured" and tortured delay spectatorial desires for resolution and stability. The structural dislocation of the conventional slave narrative which, Raymond Hedin argues, is meant to suggest "the disconnectedness of slave life" itself, mutates and intensifies in this black abolitionist panorama.[73] By inserting a conventional narrative arc into the frame of the display and focusing on the perpetual reenactment of fleeing slavery, Brown's *Mirror* revises the panorama's emphasis on "portrayals of scenes rather than of actions" (Altick, *Shows of London*, 178). The action and agency of the fugitive slave assume dominating and contravening features in the panorama's circular narrative fluidity.

Brown's *Mirror* revised the conventional panorama's insistence on providing an "expedited, edited, and misleadingly simple passage through a simulated reality" (A. Miller, "Panorama," 40). The illusion of movement, which is embedded in the genre, comes undone in the exhibition.[74] The *Mirror* punctures the quietude of the spectator's gaze by insisting on a return to the problem of slavery. If the general "panorama experience rested on the conviction that whatever else happened, the scene would change, by the very necessity of the device itself" (A. Miller, "Panorama," 49), Brown's work paradoxically inverted this concept by delivering a treacherous replay of the same event in its varying forms. Whether it surveyed the cramped "Interior of a Slave Ship" or of a "Slave Mart," or whether it traveled with "the Ellen Crafts" in their beguiling cross-dressing plot, or whether it made the perilous journey in the box with Brown to his "release" in Philadelphia, the panorama's investment in deploying the scene of escape interrupts the comforting stability in the traditional genre. Unlike its mainstream predecessors, the exhibition's refusal to easily "furnis[h] . . . a steady, constant flow of images" reveals the ways in which the black abolitionist panorama revised the form, employing its "vicarious visual experience of the real" (A. Miller, "Panorama," 49) for disruptive ends.[75]

Through a manipulation of the panoramic form, the *Mirror of Slavery* works both to make the slave's odyssey a historical subject worthy of heroic representation and to use that form as a tool for enacting historical change. If, as Marcus Wood maintains, midcentury aesthetic representations of fugitive slaves inevitably scripted these men and women as passive and unheroic, as suffering and powerless, then Box Brown's exhibition rewrites that iconography in grandly overt terms.[76] Situating African American subjugation and resistance in a charged historical context, the panorama aimed to re-represent slavery. The span of the *Mirror*, with its move between continents and its telescoping of scenery and mass social struggle, catapults the fugitive experience into the historical imaginary and presses for a present and forward-reaching "realization" of historical transformation.[77] The exhibition reversed the popular French and English panorama's steam roll of "spatial extension" meant to signify "the passage of time and the grand sweep" of an imperialist and eclipsing history (A. Miller, "Panorama," 36). Rather, it reflected its potent rays of hope and horror in a rapidly unfolding series of events leading up to emancipation, and its "Promise of Freedom" assured by the splash of a fiery "Grand Tableau Finale."

This intervention in history, this radical looking glass, a prism of resistant and restorative agency in the movement(s) of the fugitive slave, cuts an opaque ray of light across the landscape panoramas of the 1850s circum-Atlantic imaginary. Brown's display reversed the roll of Banvard's Mississippi panoramas which had effectively erased the black figure from the American landscape. Having notoriously vacated American landscape of African Americans, Banvard's *Panorama of the Mississippi and Missouri Rivers* had left behind only traces of (violent) African American experience in slavery. His exhibition's script charts, for instance, a sterilized river journey, at one point targeting "an old dead tree scathed by the fire, where three negroes were burnt alive."[78] The *Mirror* used black bodies of evidence to point out the myopic elisions of the dominant panorama and contemporary landscape art of the period. The tranquil roll of the Mississippi in Banvard's panorama is replaced in Box Brown's *Mirror* by a turbulent path out of the unbearably "peculiar" situation of slavery. As if to signify on the erasure of black corporeal waste, Box Brown's visual project fills in the gaps of Banvard's artificially pastoral odyssey. It is a road paved to hell and back, one in which the success of the spectator's journey depends on submitting to the apocalyptic visions of a nation coming undone. Punctuating the American landscape with "burning" bodies, the "tarring," "feathering," and "whipping" of black flesh in the wide open fields and cityscapes of Richmond, Virginia, Charleston, South Carolina, and Washington, D.C., this *Mirror* replaces the phantom menace of blackness in the popular panorama. In effect, Box Brown's display transformed the lay of the American panoramic land so as to include, according to *The London Times*, "pictures" of "the flogging of female as well as male slaves, and also the burning of slaves alive." In doing so, his project responded to the contemporaneous efforts of those white artists who constricted and at times altogether extinguished black figures from nineteenth-century American landscape art.[79]

Like the popular 1850s panoramas, this genre of painting was deeply associated with expansionist rhetoric and nationalist identifications.[80] An art form that yoked the realist and the sublime as a means to locating and evoking a putative "American" character inextricably linked to "Nature," nineteenth-century landscape art sought to align the social and political evolution of the nation within a naturalized cycle of meaning. Geography and national identity merge in popular American landscape art to create what Angela Miller calls a "Romantic nationalism" of dehistoricized visual imagery intended to forge a national body politic.[81] A "quasi-utopian endeavor" (*Empire of the Eye*, 13), the landscape painting of this period enacted a visual order and stability onto an unwieldy American topography and spoke back to the threatening sociopolitical tensions bound up in sectionalist debates and fiscal instability.

Box Brown's moving panorama, then, reappropriated the conventions of landscape art, reversing and revising this nationalist rhetoric for black abolitionist ends. The *Mirror of Slavery* rehearsed and redeployed the painterly techniques of African American artist Robert Duncanson, called by some the "greatest landscape painter in the west."[82] Just as Duncanson used literary subject matter in his paintings which "helped to organize the meaning(s) of landscape imagery" around identifiable narrative and thematic structure, Box Brown imported the content of his own autobiographical text into Part II of the panorama.[83] Like Duncanson, Brown revised "the old formulaic comprehension of the 'magisterial gaze' (as an evolutionary movement from wilderness to civilization) to one about slavery and emancipation." But whereas art historian Sharon Patton has argued that Duncanson's work invoked the "escapism embodied in landscape painting" so as to level "a critique at the abusive social order that produced the need for such escape," Box Brown tapped into the genre so as to (re)frame the utility of landscape painting altogether.[84] Brown's use of landscape painting recycled the generic tactics of this visual form for counterrepresentational purposes. His *Mirror* posed the ability to interrupt the conventional "magisterial gaze" of the viewer, carrying him/her back into the "wilderness" of plantocracy America in order to realize social and political revolution. Unfurling itself out of a transnational ordeal of captivity and punishment, his panorama barreled into a reformist future by affirming the necessity of millennial upheaval and a fundamentally violent rupture with the antebellum present. If "millennial thinking" turned on the "unanswered question central to national identity: where was the country headed, and where was it situated in the millennial timetable?" (A. Miller, *Empire of the Eye*, 109), Brown essentially responded to this mode of inquiry by creating a panorama which posits the "future" as unapologetically Fourierist in the final frames of his exhibition.[85]

Black abolitionist panoramas such as Henry Box Brown's complicated the fundamental "aim of nearly" all art of the antislavery movement, which Reilly contends was produced "to create an ennobling image of the African, arouse the compassion of white Americans for the plight of the slave, or generate outrage among northerners toward the South." Instead, the *Mirror of Slavery* posed a way for the fugitive slave to literally and figuratively work his way out of the social, political, and editorial mazes erected by white abolitionists and white supremacists in the antebellum era. This "fleeing," exhibitory space transformed the spectacle of escape into revolutionary fugitive art. It offered a way of responding to the "suffocation" of the circumscribed slave narrative by mounting a wide open space in which to map a representational frontier. It enacted a kind of peristrephic insurrection, a revolt in perpetual, moving process which grates against the political restrictions and the representational constrictions placed on fugitive slaves and black abolitionist cultural and political production. Redirecting the rebellious spirit of Nat Turner, whose legend reverberates as a distant echo in the 1849 edition of the *Narrative of Henry Box Brown*, Brown's panorama imagines a land of simultaneous Gothic abjection and emancipation, a nightmare of disunionism and apocalyptic redemption. Rather than merely representing the scene of the crime—America itself—this *Mirror* converts the nation into a rough and uncanny outback frontier, a monstrous "other" place for both U.S. and U.K. audiences alike.[86]

Box Brown's *Mirror* reflected back a multiplicity of "revolutions" in space and time, a kind of dystopian visual translation of the captive's experience aimed at freeing the nation of its bondage and imminent destruction as a slaveocracy. Anticipating the biblical and bloody anarchy actuated by abolitionist John Brown some nine years later, Brown's exhibition merged this philosophy with the pacificist Garrisonian ideology of "root and branch abolitionism" and millenarian landscape art. His fugitive panorama took the gruesome visions of (corporeal) ravishment and waste in slavery and suggested the painful yet paradoxical ways in which this "slash and burn" representation of the nation, this display of the ruination of flesh and land might bring about the eventual overturning of political power structures.[87] Deploying a miasma of black torture and desolation to operate alongside the heroic escape, the *Mirror* purposefully convolutes landscape imagery so as to unmake and rehistoricize mythical "America." Like a mobile representational storm, Brown's panorama produces scenes of harrowing and unrecognizable nationhood. This teeming swampland, in effect, on display for transatlantic audiences announced a kind of representational unruliness and operated as a radical form of black abolitionist cultural production and narrative authority for the fugitive slave.

### Geography without Boundaries

According to newspapers, advertisements, and printed testimonials, the *Mirror of Slavery* opened its doors to a largely sympathetic audience of clergymen, educators and schoolchildren, journalists and antislavery activists.[88] Lauded by fellow abolitionists as a major contribution to the movement, Box Brown's display successfully circulated in the United States in northeastern antislavery hubs of dissident activism for some four and a half months before its subsequent reappearance in the U.K. Yet despite seeking asylum in Great Britain and encountering British audiences who were largely swayed by black abolitionist sentiment, Brown would face his most notoriously resistant spectator while in England. After the editor of the tiny *Wolverhampton & Staffordshire Herald* printed slanderous remarks on the panorama, Brown sued his detractor, and an English jury ruled in Brown's favor. The episode remains a significant example of how the exhibition and Box Brown's complex network of performance strategies posed a representational crisis to viewers who were seemingly tethered to narrow and troubling racial authenticity politics.[89]

The *Herald* ran its scathing review of the *Mirror* in two separate segments in March of 1852, while the exhibition was on display in Staffordshire, a northwestern part of the industrial Black Country in England. The initial review disparages the exhibition for "its very partial, unfair, and decidedly false view of American slavery." Condemned for its "gross and palpable exaggeration," the *Mirror*'s seeming representational transgressiveness and hyperbole presents a quagmire of visual potholes and pitfalls for the *Herald* journalist. Placing Brown's panorama into direct dialogue with the sterilized ahistoricism of contemporaneous American panorama shows, this particular critic's heated review bristles with unchecked racial hostility:

> If the best and most authentic descriptions of American slavery are to be credited; if the pictorial illustrations of the Southern States, given us by Banvard, Ripley, Smith, Russell, and other artists; if the evidence of travellers in the slave States is to be relied upon; and lastly, if the statements of even former slaves themselves are to be accepted and credited—then is Mr. Box Brown's panorama without a feature of resemblance, and his so-called 'eloquent and poetical address' a jumbled mass of contradictions and absurdities, assertions without proof, geography without boundary, and horrors without parallel. The representation, to our thinking, instead of benefitting the cause of abolition, is likely, from its want of vraisemblance and decency, to generate disgust at the foppery, conceit, vanity, and egotistical stupidity of the Box Brown school. To paint the devil blacker than he is is, certes, [*sic*] a work of supererogation, and to make the slave States a series of inquisitorial chambers of horrors—a sort of Blue Beard or Giant Despair den, for the destruction, burning, branding, laceration, starving, and working of negroes; and the owners of slaves a class of demi-fiends, made of double-distilled brimstone is about as reasonable as giving his Satanic Majesty a coat of black paint to increase his hideousness. How clergymen and other respectable individuals could lend themselves to such a juggle,

we do not know; but testimonials from such men (who doubtless received Box Brown's descriptions as unmingled gospel), are read before the audience, and they are full of fullsome compliment to the bejewelled "darky" whose portly figure and overdressed appearance bespeak the gullibility of our most credulous age and nation.[90]

This visual site which defies "resemblance" to any recognizable place proves an outrage to the critic invested in the simple and picturesque images of the American South commodified and exported by panorama entrepreneurs, travel writers, and even a dubiously perceived array of "former slaves themselves." Lying at the root of the critic's embittered response is a resistance to the *Mirror*'s engagement with spectacle as a means unto itself, as a device conveying extravagant representation which lacks "vraisemblance." An errant and "indecent" endeavor, this panorama defies and transcends the genre's paradoxical goal of validating the "truth" of history via spectacular theatrical illusion. It also deviates from the slave narrative's attempts to deploy a discourse evoking authorial transparency and veracity. Rather, according to the observations of this nonplused critic, the exhibition manifests "a jumbled mass of contradictions and absurdities, assertions without proof." The strategic scrambling of "historical" progress, the trace of black figures made captive and yet again making themselves free, are images scripted as "absurd" in the eye of this spectator.

While New England's *Liberator* praised Brown's exhibition for "advancing the anti-slavery cause" and for producing "a faithful delineation to the eye of the principal features of the traffic in human flesh" and while the English *National Anti-Slavery Standard* marveled at the *Mirror*'s putative accuracy, its "vivid and genuine description of each passing scene," the *Herald*'s editor remained stymied by the panorama's failure to execute narrative veracity. Such a critique however, perhaps veils the publication's deeper concerns regarding black labor, black capital, and black aesthetic innovation in the antebellum era. The conflict with the *Herald* demonstrates how Brown's moving panorama show perhaps offered *too much* of something for the average spectator. As one audience member reportedly "called out when the performance was half done, 'Mr. Brown, we have seen sufficient; not that we are tired, but you show too much for so little charge.' "[91] What was it that the *Mirror* had reflected back too extensively, too fully, too relentlessly? What line had Box Brown's display transgressed? For the *Herald* editor, the superfluity of the panorama alone elicited a response that was at once oblique and yet dogged in its attempts to police black narrative agency and innovation.

In the March 17 review of the display, the critic calls the panorama's excess of representation into question; its "geography without boundaries," its "horrors without parallel" provide evidence of the crime of "supererogation." The subtext of this discontent bears the question, how can this place of ritualistic imprisonment and torture, how could this be "America"? Or perhaps these remarks simply demand, how could this elaborately rendered "American" scene in all its "foppery, conceit" and "vanity," how could this rousing machinery of "artifice" from the "Box Brown school" come forth from the mind and mouth of a fugitive slave? For these images appear to follow no previous script; they deviate, according to this incredulous and discriminating viewer, from even the texts of "former slaves," those essentially truth-bearing icons of experiential wisdom. The *Mirror of Slavery*'s scene titles and the scathing critique suggest that this moving panorama was willing to disrupt the codes of a "[n]ineteenth-century high theatrical realism." By rendering "the slave States" as "a series of inquisitorial chambers of horrors—a sort of Blue Beard or Giant Despair den, for the destruction, burning, branding, laceration, starving, and working of negroes," Brown's panorama exacerbated the restrictive aesthetic conviction that "the [panoramic] picture" remain "utterly faithful to external reality" (Altick, 189) and that African Americans remain deeply entrenched within putatively anti-extravagant expressive forms.[92]

It comes as little surprise, then, that the *Herald* critic's review would so clearly conflate the presumed excesses of the panoramic exhibition with Brown's own body (of work). What begins as a diatribe over the inauthenticity of the display's representations of slavery devolves into a condemnation of sartorial and corporeal transgressions emanating from Brown's own "bejewelled," "portly," and "overdressed" figure. To the *Herald* critic, the chaos of graphic images of slavery parallels the disorder elicited by a "dandyfied" black fugitive redressing the body in accoutrements of leisure and wealth. For this flummoxed viewer, the panorama's spectacular visual politics are, by extension, reanimated in the body of Box Brown himself. In a provocative leap of logic, the putative extravagance of the black abolitionist figure runs counter to the credibility of the panorama's political goals; the sartorial markings of this performing body threaten to yield what can only be read by this cynical spectator as a meretricious narrative about "blackness" itself. The *Herald* journalist makes this point even clearer one week later in his second article on the *Mirror*. Revisiting the spectacle of a "bejewelled and oily negro," the critic counterposes Brown's body to that of the exhibition's political intent in even more blatant terms. Accordingly, Brown's "obese and comfortable figure and easy nonchalance" is said to "remin[d] one of various good things and sumptuous living at the expense of those whose marvel-longing developments have been called into 'lively exercise,' by the terrible wonders" of the panorama.[93] With its own bit of florid and equally excessive prose, the article places Brown's free and "easy" corporeality at odds with the liberationist platform of the exhibition. Brown's vestibularity here contravenes the purpose of elevating the cause of the enslaved.

Wedding Brown's figure to the "supererogation" of the panorama, however, exposes the complex social and cultural anxieties running amuck in the *Herald*'s reports. The critic's insistence on utilizing the trope of "blackness" lays bare the true "offense" of this black abolitionist project. If Brown's *Mirror* adds "coats of black paint" to an already "hideous" endeavor, his project presumably resembles an elaborate minstrel act. Like blacking up with burnt cork, laying the "black paint" on thick calls attention to both the object of inquiry and the subject wielding the paintbrush. Thus, to rephrase the above observation: "to paint the [fugitive slave] blacker than he is" places the expected transparency and artlessness of the black abolitionist narrator in doubt. It is Brown's narrative skills which are on display and which, like those of late-nineteenth-century African American minstrel performers, raise all sorts of questions regarding racial performance and property. Akin to "the elements of derision" involved in blackface culture which were, according to Eric Lott, "an attempt to 'master' the power and interest of black cultural practices it continually generated," the *Herald* review works to divest black artistry of its social and cultural power and meaning.[94] Writ large in both the panorama's broad strokes of spectacular imagery and in Brown's questionable self-stylizing practices are the "painterly" skills of the artist in question. In turn, the newspaper offers a counternarrative aimed at resituating this disorderly black body of work in its "proper" place.

By remanufacturing and reframing the *Mirror* production as a figurative blackface act, the *Herald* journalist shifts the referent of Box Brown's performance so as to return it to the realm of white authorial control. Both the May 17 and the May 24 articles redeploy Box Brown's speech patterns in thick dialect. Brown's accounts of torture and subjugation in slavery amount to "de burnin of slaves to death for stealing, and de beating dem wid hard wood bored troo wid holes." Such descriptions reinforce this critic's effort to render the black body static in minstrel caricature, frozen in popular blackface racial typologies which discount and disrupt African American vernacular systems of expression.[95] The use of approximated dialect insidiously conjoins Box Brown's aesthetic work to that of white supremacist artistry. In other words, if antebellum culture heavily policed blackface minstrelsy in such a way that "the standard was set by whites," then the redeployment of minstrel dialect here safely reconfigures Box Brown's appearance so that it remains dependent on white expressive forms derived from African American culture.[96] The introduction of dialect holds Brown's otherwise superabundant project in abeyance, potentially disrupting the scope, range, and political efficacy of black performance. As if to emphasize the *Herald*'s histrionics, the *London Times* offers a sobering counterpoint to this description of Henry Box Brown's public appearances. Noting the curious spectacle of the activist's sartorial guise, the *Times* reports that "his dress was rather fine, and he displayed some jewellery [*sic*] about his person." The *Times* article likewise observes that Brown's "manner of giving his evidence was quiet and creditable; and his pronunciation altogether correct" while in court.[97] If, for the *Herald*, Brown's visual grandeur precludes narrative credibility, it remains only a passing incongruity for the *Times* reporter.

The fixation on Brown's dialect-ridden speech highlights a struggle over black performance strategies and discounts the politics of black labor in a transatlantic context. Labor is in fact the central topic in the *Herald*'s second review of the *Mirror*. Setting out to sardonically "judge" Brown's lecture on the merits of its "eloquence, poetry, and truth," the article attempts to reveal his "ludicious and semi-baboonish agility" as a speaker by offering yet another dialect-laden narrative of bondsman's labor and exploitation in the slaveholding states. Here Brown's speech imports the sermonizing of his own master who reportedly proclaimed that

> "My dere brederin—De white man was made by Ger Amity with sish white delekit hands that He saw at once he was not fit nor able to work, and He therefore made de black men to work for dem; but de black man were so idel he no work, and Gor Amity give him a whip to make him work, cos he was such a nasty idel nigger he no work. But he could no work wid his hands, and in answer to de prayers of de white man Gor Amity sent a shovel and a hoe, and I shall sing a song about it gemmen and ladies, dat is ladies and gemmen at de close, a shovel and a hoe in bag, so dat de damn'd idle nigger should hah no 'scuze for not working." Now den dere's a pretty master for you.[98]

The reproduction of the sermon is key as the text reveals Box Brown's effort to expose religious hypocrisy resulting in the exploitation of black slave labor so as to preserve and protect "white delekit hands" from the hardships of plantation life. Buried in this crude transcription, the content of Brown's narrative shrewdly underscores the southern plantocracy's brutal intent to utilize black bodies as instruments of labor and to legitimize this effort via theological doctrine which putatively recognizes both that white men are neither "fit nor able to work" and that black men must conversely work for them as both a punitive and disciplinary measure. More still, Brown's retelling of the sermon demonstrates the extent to which the enslaved are rendered "idel" and inept, incapable of "working wid [their] hands" and are in need of "a shovel and a hoe in bag, so dat" [they] will "hah no 'scuze for not working." Dialect is transposed onto what other critics noted to be his "correct" and "eloquent" pronunciation so as to seemingly divest Brown's words of their cogency. Yet the resulting intertextuality of the master's "song about . . . a shovel and a hoe" offers an alternative agenda to that of which neither Brown's master figure nor the *Herald* critic is perhaps fully aware. Brown's insertion of the "shovel and hoe" minstrel song, a melancholic composition which laments the passing of an "Uncle Ned" who is worked to death in slavery, sets up Brown's reclamation of black labor in his public performances.[99]

Perhaps the troubling situation of U.S. black labor remains the greatest "horror" for this particular English audience member. The labor exploitation of African American captives problematizes nationalistic chauvinism for Englishmen who might take Brown's extensive rendering of black torture and abjection as a competitive slight. The "burnin of slaves to death for stealing," the "whippin wid de lash till de blood bathes de ground and dey swim in it," these "scenes of subjection" yield a call to arms for the English critic invested in affirming the superior hardships of his own nation's artisan underclass.[100] As this journalist sees it, the "fact is that bad as slavery is, the condition of the American slave generally is infinitely superior to many of our agricultural and even our be-tommied slaves, and all reliable testimony corroborates it." Brown's panorama competes for philanthropic and political attention; his images threaten, from this critic's viewpoint, to obfuscate the problem of English poverty and industrial exploitation. In this context then, the overriding obsession with excess only intensifies the construction of Box Brown as a spurious and representationally feckless black dandy figure. For just as such a figure embodied the class conflict and racialized labor competition in the U.S. northeast of the 1830s and 1840s, so too did this figure, perhaps, pose a similar threat to English laborers struggling simultaneously to assert their unchallenged role as victims of a tyrannical class system and their (social) superiority to black transatlantic figures.

Lost in an abyss of blackness, the panorama's audiences are, to the *Herald* editor, in danger of losing sight of their most pressing domestic class privileges and problems. It would seem as well that, from this critic's standpoint, they are in danger of losing sight of themselves altogether. With its shades "dark and gloomy" and with its dense visual imagery, the panorama's surfeiting "blackness," its surplus representation, poses an obstruction to the mystified Englishman who cannot visually identify, locate, and police his own subjectivity in the scene before him.[101] Further still, the *Mirror*'s "black excess" threatens to resonate as a kind of contagion; its opaque spectacles run the risk of swallowing the spectator's gaze altogether. The *Herald* journalist's condemnations of excessiveness and his analogous pairing of the panorama's representation of slavery with a blackening effect convey a deeply rooted fear and hostility toward the putative disease-laden stain of "blackness." Though the extra "coat of . . . paint" presumably "increase[s]" the "hideousness" of representation, its very opacity proves an uncontainable threat to the reviewer. This relentless resistance to excess points to the spectator's fear of his own implication and abjection in the scene of slavery, of becoming caught up in the sweep of the panorama's "bottomless pit." Warning the spectators to "be chary in giving credence to the astounding and horrified details," the *Herald* articles anxiously attempt to protect Brown's "wide-mouthed and wonder-gasping audiences" from swallowing the poisonous blackened narratives leaping from the frame.[102]

The *Herald* editor's palpable repulsion toward the *Mirror* makes visible the panorama's darkest mysteries. The critic's seeming obsessions with the darkness of the exhibition begs the questions: what is the form and content of this "blackness" running through Brown's fugitive art and why do these spectatorial opacities prove so troubling to some? From where does this opacity figuratively emanate and toward what end? To answer such questions, Brown's *Mirror* demands that its audiences step into a "third representational space" where the complex subjectivities of the fugitive escape artist are made manifest. In a sustained performance of resistance, Brown's realism-eluding "vision" of a dark and submerged fugitive frontier poses a critical reversal of Charles Stearns's ghostwritten proclamation that the purpose of Box Brown's 1849 narrative is not to "descend into the dark and noisome caverns of the hell of slavery" (11). Instead, the *Mirror* boldly attempts to forge precisely this kind of a journey while underscoring Brown's agency as a narrator and impresario of the panoramic form by making plain his manipulation of hyperbole and "artifice" to construct the "Truth" of slavery's many levels of "hell."[103] Brown's exhibition affirms and occupies a generic "wildzone" outside of the conventional slave narrative. In the process, it speaks back to the elisions of the fugitive slave autobiographies with, according to Raymond Hedin, "no gap, no ambiguous period of floating free—not to mention roaming wild—in the interim" period between slavery and freedom.[104] It is a visual narrative wherein the spectator is made to hover—like the slave in flight, like William Wells Brown above the Parisian Tuileres—between bondage and liberation as the panels progress and collapse into poetically elliptical strategies of narrative upheaval and revision.

### Dark Adventures: Trapped in the I/Eye of the Opaque Swamp

> It is the only thing which gives you an idea of what Milton meant when he talked of darkness visible. There is a kind of light to be sure; but it only serves as a medium for a series of optical illusions; and for all useful purposes of vision, the deepest darkness that ever fell from heavens is infinitely preferable.
>
> —William Wells Brown, "A Description of William Wells Brown's Panoramic Views"

One of the most chilling images in Henry Box Brown's panorama, the "Dismal Swamp" scene was perhaps foreshadowed by its absence from the "Song, Sung by Mr. Brown on being removed from the box." Brown reportedly broke into a spirited version of the fortieth Psalm once Still, McKim, and company cut loose the hoops strapped to the crate of his confinement.

A Psalm of lament, the scripture's first four verses detail the trials and tribulations of a biblical sufferer who proclaims that s/he is waiting patiently for the Lord:

> he inclined to me and heard my
> cry.
> He drew me up from the desolate
> pit,
> out of the miry bog,
> and set my feet upon a rock,
> making my steps secure.
> He put a new song in my mouth,
> a song of praise to our God.
> Many will see and fear,
> and put their trust in the Lord.
>
> Blessed is the man who makes
> the Lord his trust,
> who does not turn to the proud,
> to those who go astray after false
> gods![105]

In contrast, Brown's celebratory "Hymn of Thanksgiving" extracts key verses of Psalm 40 in order to create a new narrative of survival and resurrection. His verse announces:

> I waited patiently, I waited patiently for the Lord, for the Lord,
> And he inclined unto me, and heard my calling;
> I waited patiently, I waited patiently for the Lord,
> And he inclined unto me, and heard my calling;
> And he hath put a new song in my mouth,
> Ev'n a thanksgiving, Ev'n a thanksgiving, Ev'n a thanksgiving unto
>     our God.
>
> Blessed, Blessed, Blessed, Blessed is the man, Blessed is the man,
> Blessed is the man that hath set his hope, his hope in the Lord;
> . . . The Lord be praised.[106]

Marcus Wood has argued that Brown's hymn operates as a resistant vernacular mode of performance that Brown preserved and crafted in the wake of Charles Stearns's "sanitized account of his experience" ("All Right!," 81). "[I]ts enthusiastic repetitions and energetic anti-intellectualism" offered a refreshing alternative to "the sobriety of the lecture hall or biblical scholarship" (83). Yet the elision of verse 2 of the Psalm, a conspicuously haunting passage which alludes to the biblical speaker's past ordeals trapped in the well of a "horrible pit" and ensnared in "miry clay," points toward a more complicated and intertextual reading of Brown's song. The curious excision of Gothic imprisonment and trauma from the popular "Hymn of Thanksgiving" remains a significant conundrum in the abolitionist's multifaceted work. All the raging torment and suffering from which the fugitive slave flees is subsequently displaced in the joyousness of Brown's hymn, which celebrates the "new song" that has been put in his mouth. The hymn eschews horror in favor of joy, entrapment in favor of redeemed liberation. It creates a discursive gap between the effusive ebullience at work in Brown's song and Psalm 40's wary and tempered oscillation between past despair and present reinvigoration.[107]

The key verse which Brown's performance eradicates is all the more provocative in that it resurfaces as an indelible image in his abolitionist panorama. Positioned as the fifth installment in Part II of the *Mirror of Slavery*, the "View of the Lake of the Dismal Swamp" scene disrupts and redirects the process of viewing, at once obstructing and resituating the spectator's wide and roving gaze, which Part I of the exhibition has cultivated to inspect the scene of slavery. Figuratively ineluctable, the image of the Dismal Swamp looms like a deep and aphotic representational cavity at the center of Box Brown's panoramic storm. The site of the swamp marks the most crucial turning point in the panorama. Deeply entrenched in antebellum historical memory, the Dismal Swamp scene synechdochically references a legacy of past slave rebellion as well as future revolts. In the *Mirror*, it provides the narrative bridge out of captivity and into fugitive escape and apocalyptic reform. Operating as the liminal space between entrapment and freedom, between the excruciating labor and relentless sunlit fields of the "Cotton Plantation" and the stealthy nocturnal routes of "Nubians, escaping by Night," the "Dismal Swamp" scene triggers the exhibition's critical transmogrification from a trajectory of abject turmoil into one of intensified fugitive resistance. The panorama's "Dismal Swamp" iconography serves as a dense form of black abolitionist narrative subversion and as a device that registers the return of the "pit of tumult" from its mysterious submergence in the "Hymn of Thanksgiving."

The swamp was linked in the antebellum period to upheaval and historical liberation, a site familiar, if only by its mythology, to Box Brown. As a fugitive of Virginia, Box Brown perhaps utilized the *Mirror* to excavate metonymically the infamous topography of his state of enslavement. Located on the borders of Virginia and North Carolina, the Great Dismal Swamp was a territory linked by legend to the Nat Turner rebellion. Immortalized by historian Samuel Warner in his account of the Southampton Revolt, Virginia's Dismal Swamp garnered cultural infamy as a haunting and treacherous territory. Warner imagines a suffocating ecological universe at the heart of the South:

> [T]he ground of the swamp is a mere quagmire, impression is instantly filled with water. The skirts of the swamp, towards the east, are overgrown with reeds, 10 or 12 feet high, interspersed every where with strong bamboo briers. . . . Near the middle of the Dismal the trees grow much thicker. . . . Neither beast, bird insect or reptile, approach the heart of this horrible desert; perhaps deterred by the everlasting shade, occasioned by the thick shrubs and bushes, which the sun can never penetrate, to warm the earth.

A place of eerily "everlasting shade," this "vast body of filth and nastiness" swirls in "noxious vapors" which "infect the air round about, giving agues and other distempers to the neighboring inhabitants."[108] Written while Turner was still a fugitive, Warner's text announces to readers the viability of the swamp as a space where fugitives might spirit themselves away, and where, within "the deep recesses of this gloomy Swamp" and "beyond the power of human conception," the runaway Slaves of the South" might "secret themselves for weeks, months and years, subsisting on frogs, tarrapins, and even snakes!"[109]

Warner's description canonized antebellum perceptions of the Great Dismal as an ominous environmental obstacle course, and Turner's vigilant band of insurrectionists perhaps gained additional notoriety for their steely demeanor as they sought refuge from capture in the swamp. As redeployed through Warner's text, the legend of Turner's fleeting maroonage made explicit the link between swamp territory and black rebellion. Swampland imagery became particularly synonymous with radical black subterfuge and resistance efforts in the antebellum era.[110]

This crucial territory of social significance for the runaway was thus an identifiable marker of black liberation efforts; the lore of the swamp as a site where revolt might gestate informed its lingering status as a charged and tumultuous symbol in slavery's cultural imaginary. Thus the Dismal Swamp imagery in the panorama potentially signifies on the collective consciousness of that dark and foreboding territory. The script's positioning of the swamp as a site that prefigures Brown's personal maroonage in the box establishes a vital link between that tropical location and fugitive escape. We might, then, examine the potential for swamp iconography to signify on the politics of representing black resistance efforts in antebellum popular culture. The *Mirror*'s ability to tap into the historical memory of black revolutionary machinations underscores the critical and creative utility of the swamp panel in the panorama.[111]

Although plantation authorities sought to quell the practical threat of swamp-residing black maroon warriors, the image of the bellicose and bloodthirsty guerilla fighter with weapon in hand and plot afoot while lurking in the everglades had a lasting impact on antebellum perceptions of swamp territories. Long utilized as an allegory for self-immolating, psychic distress and cultural anxiety in American letters, nineteenth-century cultural images of the swamp often focused on its foreboding psychological suggestiveness, how it symbolized a region that "lives off its own decay and produces so much vegetation that it can actually be seen to strangle itself."[112] Nevertheless the aestheticization of the swamp in mid-Victorian literature underwent a dramatic shift in perspective and intent. "[T]he distinctive 'imagistic' features of the landscape: the arabesque of its vines and tendrils, the shifting patterns of light that played about its fastness, the surprising prospects offered at almost every step" all transformed from serving as the thematic locus of infection and entrapment into "more positive" emblems of self-renewal, discovery, and imaginative agency in the 1850s (D. Miller, *Dark Eden*, 3).

In the literature of slavery and abolition, however, cultural images of the swamp remained vexed through the onset of the Civil War. In the immediate aftermath of the Turner revolt, perhaps no other Southern writer articulated dominant cultural anxiety toward the swamp as a domain for black resistance more than Edgar Allan Poe. Beyond importing the visual specificity of Warner's text, the imaging of "ghastly landscape" in Poe's fiction communicated Anglo fears of "insurgent slaves hiding in the shadows of the Dismal Swamp." By repeatedly returning to the metaphorical entanglement of whiteness and blackness in the swamp, as well as the abyss of the sea, and in the thick and blackened centers of the forest, Poe's work continuously envisioned the nightmarish scenario in which "white becomes utterly imbricated in and absorbed by blackness." Poe's Gothic tales set in motion a particular cultural discourse of Southern anxieties regarding black seditiousness buried in the mire of the swamp. Whether dreading the threat of being consumed by this darkness, as did Poe, or fearing the risk of being hunted down in the tendrils of the Dismal's everglades by murderous figures in black, as did Robert Frost, American writers persisted well into the twentieth century in imagining swamp terrain as a nightmarish site where black rebellion was on the loose.[113]

Abolitionist literature sought varying ways of appropriating the construction of the swamp from the point of view of the tremulous white voyager and conversely worked to manipulate, rewrite, and redeploy the power of this image in the fight to eradicate slavery. Particularly in the genre of the fugitive slave narrative and as early as Henry Bibb's 1850 text, African American authors made reference to the swamp as a site of protection and subterfuge. Dense and often foul and repellent regions that were primarily scattered throughout parts of the South, swamp lands posed both a threat to and an opportunity for the resourceful fugitive. An unseemly home for amphibious creatures, thick, unwieldy, harsh weather, disease and pestilence, swamp territories represented the thorny geographical minefields awaiting runaways in the flight for freedom. In his 1853 narrative, Solomon Northrup, for instance, describes a number of wetlands which he is forced to traverse during his torturous odyssey into captivity. These "haunted place[s]," were the site of the "paths of wild beasts," "alligators," and "serpents," "a dreary picture of desolation," and they represented the hazardous terrain which the fugitive must learn to conquer and command in a bid for survival.[114] Yet as these authors demonstrate, it is the threateningly perilous opacity of the swamp itself that simultaneously offers an avenue for fugitive liberation. Although Longfellow weeps, in his famously romantic racialist vision of the tragically abject "Slave in the Dismal Swamp," for the "hunted Negro" who lays passive, static, debased, and "mangled," crouching like "a wild beast in his lair," other antislavery sympathizers saw fit to champion the powers of black agency accruing power at the site of the swamp.[115]

Most notoriously regarded for having popularized the image of the docile slave in *Uncle Tom's Cabin* (1852), Harriet Beecher Stowe utilizes the trope of the swamp as a means to revising representations of black resistance in her 1856 novel *Dred.* In a radical departure from her construction of a Christ-like and passive martyr Uncle Tom, *Dred*'s title character recalls the subversive legacies of Turner and Denmark Vesey, as well as the aggressively resistant rhetoric of Frederick Douglass and Harriet Jacobs. As Robert Levine contends, Stowe drew from the activism of the aforementioned figures as well as William Cooper Nell's historical text, for which she provided the introduction, in order to create a novel that might participate "in the political terror inspired by the prophetic tradition of the black heroic deliverer." Levine argues that Stowe "presents violent rebellion as a logical, perhaps even sacred, response to slavery," and she situates this rebellion as emanating from a swamp terrain that neither Warner, Poe, nor Longfellow could imagine.[116] Although written six years after Henry Brown introduced his swamp in the *Mirror* to U.S. and British audiences, Stowe's construction of that physical site as a trope of black sedition illuminates the narrative suggestiveness of the swamp in the panorama. If *Dred* "ultimately asks its readers to consider slavery from the point of view of black revolutionaries lurking in the recesses of the Dismal Swamp," then the *Mirror* demands that audiences, at a critical juncture in the exhibition, submit to a narrative and epistemological shift in the display's series of images.[117] In this context, the swamp serves as an allegory for a distinct readerly opacity, in the same vein as Stowe and before her Herman Melville in his *Benito Cereno* equally played with exposing the blindness of the spectator who is unable to properly identify and translate the emergence of black revolutionary activity before his very eyes. If, as Levine has argued, Stowe builds on Melville's strategy of exposing "the limits of whites' perspectives on slavery and race," then I would suggest that it is the metaphorical darkness of swamp iconography itself which transforms the *Mirror*'s narrative trajectory and offers a critical commentary on the seen/scene and the unseen/unscene of slave culture.[118]

The swamp forces the *Mirror*'s travelers to make a radical shift in vision, to accept the wild, dark, and unknowable frontier of the narrative landscape. Like the readers of *Dred* who must succumb to the novel's transition into the swamps and its focus on black revolutionaries, the panorama shifts its lens out of the scene of abjection to follow the path of the runaway; it therefore demands that the viewer resituate his/her gaze to follow a new narrative, one that tracks a fugitive movement toward agency and freedom. Passing through this dismal location with the slave in flight, the spectator's perspective must presumably shift to look a different way at the conditions of the captive who has broken free of his bonds.

In the darkness of the swamp, in this place known for its lack of light, a kind of clarity presents itself. The figurative opacity presents multiple forms of liberation as the panorama moves swiftly toward its spectacular emancipatory images. The rich and symbolic darkness of the swamp is itself a form of black aesthetic resistance. It signifies on the potential for imaginative possibility and creativity agency. Just as Stowe drew on images of "[u]ncontrolled growth, allow[ing] no expanse" as "the source of the dense and convoluted nature of the swamp . . . as a metaphor" (D. Miller, *Dark Eden*, 97) for her black rebel Dred's imagination, the swamp's "superabundance of life" (120) yields a kind of (representational) excess linked to black fugitive imagination. As the site of ecological excess, overflow, and unmitigated foliage, the swamp allegorically extends the surplus form and content of the panorama. It is the place where the unbridled strategies for historical black insurrection could literally take root, and figuratively its iconography represented yet another moment when the exhibition exceeds the putative limits of black representation and white spectatorial control.[119] Moreover, this imagery marks a significant philosophical turning point in black fugitive narration. The opacity of the swamp arms the black escape artist with perhaps his most potent weapon.[120] For it is this scene that resituates the centrality of the opaque as a mode of narrative agency for the fugitive slave activist who might manipulate darkness as a trope of narrative insurgency, discursive survival, and epistemological resistance. Resonating as a visual signifier that calls into question the very politics of representing slavery, it is this black hole of the swamp which affords Brown a rich method of apocalyptic narrative revolution in the panorama.

The *Mirror*'s darkness enables a different kind of spectatorial sight, and it makes spectatorial blind spots visible. At the same time, darkness in all its myriad shades instills the fugitive with multiple forms of power. In this era of, what David Reynolds calls, the "Dark Adventure" narrative, the *Mirror* utilizes the trope of darkness to conjure intersecting literary, theological, and social meanings. A genre which flourished from the mid-1830s to the Civil War, the mode of dark adventure "featured pirates, monsters, orgies, the macabre, and other sensational topics with apocalyptic endings." Consonant with the broader millenarian-inspired, apocalyptic melodramas of the period which envisioned catastrophe as a necessary and inevitable bridge to social reform and communal redemption, this subgenre of popular narrative manipulated the trope of harrowing, metaphorical darkness embedded in cultural anxiety of the apocalypse in order to level social and political critique.[121] Darkness in this context alludes to bleak and decadent environmental conditions; it serves as an allegorical trope for a cataclysmic and amoral universe. With its sequential images of violence strewn across the road to freedom, the *Mirror* effectively resituates the dark adventure within an abolitionist context. Both the fugitives of the panorama and the spectator alike must traverse the darkest images of slavery before reaching earthly emancipation.

The "darkness" of the panorama appears to extend beyond the stark and generic trappings of apocalyptic effect to illuminate the complexities of fugitive narration, as well as epistemological, ontological, and theological turmoil and transformation located at the philosophical center of Box Brown's exhibition. As religious studies scholar Vincent Wimbush suggests, darkness is "a particular orientation, a sensibility, a way of being in and *seeing* the world. It is *viewing* and experiencing the world in emergency mode, as through the individual and collective experience of trauma."[122] Darkness is an interpretative strategy, a structure of reading the world through a dark lens and from a particular and dark position. The introduction of the Dismal Swamp image can be read, then, as both a reinsertion of the "dark script" of the Bible into Box Brown's fugitive narrative and as the announcement of an epistemological juncture in the panoramic exhibition. For as Wimbush himself queries, "darkness is not necessarily the end" but perhaps "one can survive it and can see things differently in and through it."[123] In this light, the "Dismal Swamp" scene serves as a kind of plateau in the panorama that presumably redirects the spectator's strategy of looking (at the scene of slavery). No longer enmeshed in the "Sugar Plantation and Mill" or toiling alongside the "Women at Work," the panoramic traveler's perspective must shift at the point of the swamp. The figurative darkness rooted in swamp imagery elevates fugitive slave narration at this very moment of transition in the display.

This movement into the "unknowable" is of unique value to the black abolitionist narrator, and it is a move that places the *Mirror* firmly within the literary and cultural tradition of the Gothic. For the scene of the swamp, a "dark and grotesque" netherworld in the abolitionist literary canon, makes plain the complexities of fugitive slave narration.[124] Slightly akin to the theological darkness described by Wimbush, this Gothic opacity invokes the discursive mode of terror in order to expose and emphasize the powers of black abolitionist public expression, the potential blindness of the spectator, and the unseen/unscene horrors of slavery. By playing on the portent of black rebellion in-the-making, Gothic opacity shifts the balance of authority to the putatively transparent slave on the run.

Gothic narration depends on the negotiation of two critical and yet arguably oppositional modes: terror and horror. Each subgeneric style, as Robert Hume contends, mediates the boundaries of discursive opacity and disclosure. Terror operates as a narrative device of deflection and deferral, while horror pivots on sharp and disturbing exposure. Terror manipulates the use of "suspense or dread," while horror exploits that which is most fearful to the reader. Terror-Gothic "works on the supposition that a reader who is repelled will close his mind . . . to the sublime feelings which may be roused by the mixture of pleasure and pain induced by fear. Horror-Gothic assumes that if events have psychological consistency, even within repulsive situations, the reader will find himself involved beyond recall." Through concealment, terror holds the audience in the realm of anxious and apprehensive waiting, while horror assumes that through the act of revealing, readers become irreversibly immersed in narrative development.[125] Thus Gothic opacity exploits the narrative intent of terror. Shrouding its secret of horror, the Gothic opaque has the ability to conjure anxiety at the site of the unknown. As the Gothic narrator who possesses the knowledge of what lies beneath, of what swims in the terrifying murkiness of the swamp, the fugitive slave narrator utilizes Gothic opacity as a way to signify on the limits of what can be retrieved, restored, and re-membered in slavery. The fugitive may know, but may choose not to tell. Through its use of opaque symbolism, the panorama illustrates how "darkness emblematizes the gothic's disruptive potential."[126] By calling attention to the dark spaces in representing slavery, Brown's politically oppositional *Mirror* plays with narration and epistemological stability at the site of the swamp. The *Mirror* utilizes the politics of horror-Gothic by unveiling the most gruesome narratives of the nation and by converting "America" into a treacherous frontier populated by marauders and torture victims. Yet the "Dismal Swamp" scene's topography of terror also provides the pivotal point of liberation in black abolitionist discourse. The hidden escape route of the fugitive slave is paradoxically exposed as a dark and impenetrable zone of illumination and elusion for the escape artist.[127] This very "foul blot on the star-spangled banner" operates as a transitory medium for the panorama's runaways as they engage in their "nocturnal antics."[128]

The opacity of the swamp creates a trick mirror of its own as it provides the hunted with a source of refuge and release. This darkness visible serves in the panorama as a historical affirmation of the role of opaque landscape as a resource for fugitives and as a site of figurative representational refuge for black abolitionist cultural producers searching for methods to protect their own narrative agency. In short, the swamp scene's resonant darkness serves to powerfully underscore the trappings of visibility. Similar to the panopticon devices which, Foucault asserts, "arrang[e] spatial unities that make it possible to see constantly and to recognize immediately," the view offered by the panorama promotes the inflated sense of far-reaching vision, a way of seeing which enacts an enclosure over all objects on display. This "panoptic mechanism" ultimately "reverses the principle of the dungeon; or rather of its three functions—to enclose, to deprive of light and to hide—it preserves only the first and eliminates the other two. Full lighting and the eye of a supervisor capture better than darkness, which ultimately protected. *Visibility is a trap.*"[129] Brown's mammoth exhibition perhaps poses an affront to the panoramic viewer's encroaching spectatorial eye/I, an eye which has the power to free him from the residual bonds of slavery and yet also threatens to visually fetishize his fugitive body on display through the "new physics of power represented by panopticism." Panopticism's focus on policing "irregular bodies, with their details, their multiple movements, their heterogeneous forces, their spatial relations,"[130] hovers as an obstacle which Brown must confront as the author of this panorama if he is to finally claim the exhibition as a truly "fugitive" art form, if he is to finally subvert the "trap" of visibility which pursues ocular possession of a "bejewelled and oily negro" in the frame of the canvas and on the stage.

Brown's exhibition scrambles and undoes the systemically punitive dynamics of the panorama. If panopticism depends on the invisibility of the viewer and the hypervisibility of the viewed, then the spectacular opacity of the swamp reorders these spectatorial dynamics. Just as the panorama offered a "way of seeing" (A. Miller, "Panorama," 47), it also opened up a possibility for transforming the viewer into "an instrument, a tool for producing vision, not one who passively reproduces reality. As such, the spectator is himself open to manipulation" (A. Miller, "Panorama," 51).[131] Brown's *Mirror* plays with the optical agency of the viewer, thereby allowing for the visual technologies of nineteenth-century spectacular culture to take an unlikely twist. Perhaps in this panorama show, there is no escape for the spectator.[132] Tellingly, it is the *Wolverhampton & Staffordshire Herald*'s own reportage that exposes the very ways in which the panoptic viewer's disappearance remains impossible in Box Brown's panorama. Wary of the pestilence of the panorama and the seductiveness of its "calumny in colors," the critic attempts to police the spectator's empathic entanglement in the *Mirror*'s narrative. Fixating on the "blackness" of the exhibit at hand, the *Herald* editor's language renders the panorama analogous to that of the infectious atmosphere of a swamp. His passionate bid to the audience to look away from Brown's display makes plain his fears that it is the viewer who runs the risk of becoming trapped "beyond recall," affected and thus "infected" by the dark epistemological cavities at the center of the exhibition. In Box Brown's panoramic narrative, the panoptic viewer's disappearance is thus denied, in part by executing the very thing the *Herald* journalist fears so much—by capturing the (white) audience in the eye of its storm.[133]

The *Mirror* resuscitates "the pit" of tumult from the Psalter, then, as a way to make darkly vivid the existence of a "completely wild and untamed state" of black historical change in-the-making for the panoramic spectator. Like the "black hole at the center of every slave narrative," the "Dismal Swamp" scene operates as the emphatically opaque center of the *Mirror of Slavery*, yet it turns this mortal coil and excruciating struggle into a renewal and resistance.[136] With a "new song" and an old box, Henry Brown would triumphantly emerge out of the pit of his exhibition with a few more tricks up his sleeve and on his journey toward liberation.

### Performing Deliverance: A New Song, an Old Box, and a (Black) Magic Trick

Was Henry Box Brown singing his "Hymn of Thanksgiving" during the English exhibitions of the *Mirror*? The *London Times* fails to specify but reports that he performed various "sacred songs" during his U.K. exhibitions in the summer of 1852.[135] If the songs were indeed "sacred," then, in all likelihood, Brown would have found a place to insert at least one version of the hymn made legendary at the time of his "resurrection" from the box. Both the 1849 and 1851 versions of his narrative describe how Brown emerged from his entombment to perform a spiritual melody. A song of deliverance, the "Hymn of Thanksgiving" fulfills what Richard Newman reads as the "prophecy" of Psalm 40 by responding to the scripture's call for a "new song." The presence of song in both the unboxing episode and in the panoramic exhibit makes plain the ways in which singing serves as another method of spectacular escape for Brown. If the panorama restores the excised "pit" of lament, then perhaps a sacred song of deliverance allows for Brown to once again stage his own rescue from within this apocalyptic visual exhibition. From this standpoint, Brown's translation of Psalm 40 from lament into exaltation creates a path out of despair and into an even broader performative cultural universe. A kind of escape vehicle in its own right, Brown's "new song" emerges along a continuum of spectacular exits in his transatlantic activist career. Vividly bringing to life Joanna Brooks's cogent claim that "near death experiences yield more movement" for the marginalized, Box Brown would surface in the years following his initial mounting of the *Mirror* in order to reproduce the act of his own flight and deliverance in a variety of ways.[136]

Brown ambitiously enacted a crucial kind of discursive liberation from one form of sacred text into another. An able revisionist, he appears to have independently composed the transformation of Psalm 40 into his "Hymn of Thanksgiving." Indeed, he was said to have carefully envisioned building the Old Testament scripture into the very poetics of his flight. William Still describes how Brown reportedly "remarked that, before leaving Richmond he had selected for his arrival-hymn (if he lived) the Psalm beginning with these words: 'I waited patiently for the Lord, and He heard my prayer.'" Brown's 1851 retelling of the incident, however, casts the moment as highly spontaneous. "I had arisen," the narrative states, "from the dead; I felt much more than I could readily express; but as the kindness of Almighty God had been so conspicuously shown in my deliverance, I burst forth into the following him [*sic*] of thanksgiving."[137] In either version of the event, the choice of Psalm 40 remains significant as it represents Brown's engagement with the Psalter's mediation of visceral extremes. Brown's greatest challenge in utilizing Psalm 40 as his oral entrance back into the world of the living was that he had to figure out a way to turn that closed and impervious scripture of suffering, stasis, and "patiently waiting" for divine salvation into a vehicle and a verse that literally and figuratively *moves* him (and presumably his audience) to a new state of being.

Psalm 40 is a particularly distinct "song of lament" that stands apart from others in the genre precisely because of its relative uniformity. Unlike other psalms of its kind that "begin with lament and end with praise" and thus are texts of transformation and "significant change," this psalm, for the most part, remains the same, in a holding pattern of longing and supplication. Although Psalm 40's content resembles other canonical scriptural passages that function as affirmations of faith in times of trial, its structural quirks call attention to the elliptical nature of human suffering and redemption. If other psalms of lament are characterized by transitioning out of abjection, if these other texts end with blessed reversals of fortune, Psalm 40 asserts an emphatic cyclicality by ending with a plea. While verse 9 proclaims to have "told the glad news of deliverance in the great congregation," verse 17 returns the speaker to the place of waiting, enduring, and identifying the Lord as the speaker's "help and . . . deliverer; do not tarry, O my God!"[138] The passage simultaneously calls attention to a deferred liberation since it delays the point of deliverance. Ending

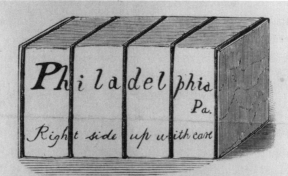

**Engraving of the Box in which HENRY BOX
BROWN escaped from slavery in Richmond, Va.**

## SONG,

*Sung by Mr. Brown on being removed from the box.*

I waited patiently for the Lord ;—
And he, in kindness to me, heard my calling—
And he hath put a new song into my mouth—
Even thanksgiving—even thanksgiving—
    Unto our God !

Blessed—blessed is the man
That has set his hope, his hope in the Lord !
O Lord ! my God ! great, great is the wondrous work
    Which thou hast done !

If I should declare them—and speak of them—
They would be more than I am able to express.
I have not kept back thy love, and kindness, and truth,
    From the great congregation !

Withdraw not thou thy mercies from me,
Let thy love, and kindness, and thy truth, alway preserve me—
Let all those that seek thee be joyful and glad !
    Be joyful and glad !

And let such as love thy salvation—
Say always—say always—
The Lord be praised !
    The Lord be praised !

Laing's Steam Press, 1 1-3 Water Street, Boston.

5. Song, Sung by Mr. Brown on being removed from the box. Courtesy of the American Antiquarian Society.

with a biblical "cliffhanger" of sorts, Psalm 40 does not progress like other texts of its kind, and thus, in its original state, it is perhaps an inappropriate accompaniment for Brown's emergence from the box. Brown must, for his own pressing purposes, figure out a way to make the passage move differently.[139]

Just as Stearns's constricting editorial maneuvers erected high walls for the fugitive narrator to scale, so too does Psalm 40 appear to offer no exit outside the sphere of lamentation. Yet in spite of these hurdles and using the raw material of the original scripture, Brown successfully creates "a new song" to resolve the turmoil that plagues the primary text. While others in the antislavery movement had tackled revising and transforming this verse, Brown's version manifests the most complex and interlocking musical traditions shaping fugitive culture.[140] Brown not only performs the deliverance of the desired passage but also, with religious faith as his steerage, he delivers himself. He imports the specific structure and content of African American divinity forms to improvise and open up the language of this particular Psalter scripture as a means to create a safe passage to freedom via his hymn. In this way, song operates as yet another form of wily escape for a fugitive known for his resourceful innovations.

Turning biblical verse into celebratory lyric, Brown's hymn buoyantly leaps over its dark valleys and into the repeated expression of exuberance and praise for the speaker's Lord:

> Even a thanksgiving, even a thanksgiving, even a thanksgiving unto
> Our God
> Blessed, Blessed, Blessed, Blessed is the man,
> Blessed is the man that has set his hope, his hope in the Lord;
> Oh Lord my God, Great, Great, Great, Great,
> Great are the wondrous works which thou hast done.
> Great are the wondrous works which thou hast done,
> Which thou has done . . .
> Let thy loving kindness and thy truth always preserve me,
> Let all those that seek thee be joyful and glad,
> Let all those that seek thee be joyful and glad, be joyful,
> And glad, be joyful, be joyful, be joyful, be joyful, be joyful
> And glad—be glad in thee. . . .
> The Lord be praised,
> The Lord be praised.
> Let all those that seek thee be joyful and glad,

And let such as love thy salvation, say always,
The Lord be praised,
The Lord be praised,
The Lord be praised.[141]

The jubilation in Brown's "Hymn" marks it as a distinct and separate entity from that of the psalm, and its ecstatics are more than an oversimplified black folk cultural gesture. The hymn operates as an additional contribution to the abolitionist's burgeoning aesthetics of escapology, a kind of performance that Brown would continue to cultivate during his public sojourns in the U.K.[142]

Although Brown's "Hymn of Thanksgiving" does not appear to resonate as black vernacular expression, it did run parallel to and at times stylistically overlap with key elements of the Negro spiritual repertoire. The complex and storied tradition of the Negro spiritual reflects a dedication to rigorous aesthetic innovation and an almost ritualistic investment in revision and improvisation. Religious music scholar Mellonee Burnim contends, for instance, that the "craftsmanship of the song leader was broadly recognized and highly applauded in the slave community. The desire and ability to re-create, rather than merely imitate, was nurtured and reflected a value which lies at the heart of African American cultural expression."[143] Like the evolving Negro spiritual form of the period, Brown's sacred song depended on the simultaneous repetition and transformation of scripture. Spirituals relied on creative borrowing, revising, and suturing, building new texts by quilting the old together. But as Eileen Southern maintains, it "must be remembered that in every instance, the spiritual is a refashioning of verses and motives from the parent hymn or hymns and *not* simply a different version of the hymn."[144] We might then read Brown's composition as a sacred song indebted to multiple nineteenth-century black religious musical forms of expression and as having evolved out of various folk practices that demonstrate African American efforts not merely to express but to *transform* the condition of textuality and the textuality of one's condition.

As a sacred song which proclaims deliverance, "Hymn of Thanksgiving" reflects and fulfills what John Lovell, in his influential work on spirituals, contends is the "fundamental theme of the genre," the "need for a change in the existing order." As a translation of Psalm 40, Brown's song then stands as evidence of the phantasmagoric promise of black religious musical performance. Brown's "sacred ballad" extends the hallowed tradition of deliverance hymns such as "Steal Away to Jesus," "Children, We Shall Be Free," and "Go Down, Moses," by creating an entirely new musical structure built almost exclusively around expressing the ecstasy of deliverance itself.[145] A dual expression and an enactment of transformation, Brown's song midwifes the humanity of its performer as it articulates and constitutes the movement from putative "thingdom" to personhood. In this regard, Brown followed the tradition of captives who made functional use of sacred song and who sought to create, as Lawrence Levine asserts, "a new world by transcending the narrow confines of the one in which they were forced to live. They extended the boundaries of their restrictive universe backward until it fused with the world of the Old Testament, and upward until it became one with the world beyond . . . they creat[ed] an expanded universe, by literally willing themselves reborn."[146]

Performance in this context becomes constitutive of Brown's deliverance from enslavement and his subsequent "rebirth." Not only does Brown's lyrical revision fulfill the original scripture's "prophecy" but also the act of song occurs at a critical moment in Brown's odyssey. Arising from the crate and "bursting" into his hymn, Brown further signifies on the condition of enslavement by willfully and publicly embracing the embodied act of performance. To perform, to add movement to his previously still and cargoed flesh, the song completes Brown's journey into subjectivity and marks a necessary rupture from his putative abject state. His insurgent musical performance demonstrates the ways that, as Lindon Barrett has shown, the black singing voice "provides a means by which African Americans may exchange an expended, valueless self in the New World for a productive, recognized self." If, then, as theologian Thomas Briendenthal has eloquently observed, divine "faith" has the power to "return one to oneself," then Brown's hymn, a musical proclamation of faith, was a way in which the fugitive might return (value) *to* himself, by using song to cut through the bonds of captivity.[147]

Brown arrived singing in an antislavery world very much accustomed to yoking sacred song with political resistance. The 1840s and 1850s saw the explosion of popularity in publishing antislavery songbooks as well as the composition of abolition hymns performed in Northern churches for individuals who had withdrawn from proslavery congregations. However, only a small group of African American activists composed and performed these songs for public antislavery audiences.[148] During the compressed period between his 1849 entrance into abolitionist circles and his rushed exit to England in 1850, Box Brown seems to have capitalized on his singing abilities, appearing at antislavery organized gatherings such as the 1850 Syracuse, New York, abolitionist convention and extending his use of his song into the secular and satirical realm to rewrite minstrel melodies from a radical black abolitionist perspective. An "old tune" set to "new words," Brown's and James "Boxer" Smith's revamped rendition of "Uncle Ned" calls further attention to the bold compositional and performative abilities of the former and makes plain the extent to which song played a central role in Box Brown's abolitionist career.[149]

A deft and signifying rumination on labor, the "Uncle Ned" of Brown's performances revised the original 1848 Stephen Foster text, a standard feature of many minstrel show revues of the period, in order to once again deliver Brown, and more broadly the black laboring figure, from the condition of enslavement. While Foster's chorus laments the passing of "Old Ned," who "lay down de shubble and de hoe" to die, having weathered the severe punishment of unchecked labor with fingers "long like de cane in de brake" and "no teeth for to eat de corn cake," Brown would recast himself in his version of the song as having "laid down the shovel and the hoe / Down in the box he did go / No more Slave work for Henry Box Brown / In the box by express he did go." Brown's composition labored, so to speak, so as to displace the grotesquely corroded corpus of the slave in Foster's racial romanticist vision (not unlike Longfellow's slave in the swamp) in order to insert his own willfully vanishing body into the text. As would be the case in his subsequent panorama exhibitions and in his 1851 *Narrative*, Brown would repeatedly return to the question of black labor, and aesthetically he would seek to resituate his own body to labor in resistance to the peculiar institution through the poetics of spectacular performance. An old box would prove his greatest prop in this endeavor.[150]

The box that had initially set Brown free would in fact play a central role in his continuing efforts to publicize his own metamorphosis from "slave into man." Like black song, Brown's crate of liberation would serve as a portal to the sphere of subjectivity, transforming the Middle Passage narrative "into its opposite by converting the very stringencies of an African slave ship into a blueprint for freedom." But in a complicated twist, Brown's post-boxing efforts would move him far beyond the symbolic gesture of "translating" black captive cargo into humanity. Rather, Brown's spectacular re-boxing act recognized the benefits of converting his own commodity as a slave into that of cultural commodification.[151] An inverted magic act of sorts, Brown's recycled boxing altered what would eventually become the "classic" magic trick of metamorphosis which hinged on dramatic substitutions of one person or thing for another. He instead used the spectacle of his own entrapment to stage publicly Frederick Douglass's legendary and demonstrative proclamation in his own autobiography: "you have seen how a man was made a slave,

6. The Resurrection of Henry Box Brown at Philadelphia. Courtesy of the American Antiquarian Society.

now you shall see how a slave was made a man."[152] In the United Kingdom, where fascination with fugitive slave celebrity remained high throughout the 1850s, Brown marketed the sight of his own conversion, once again imagining new ways of dually utilizing his body as a source of his own capital and political propaganda.

In the midst of Box Brown's high-profile tour of English townships, the *Leeds Mercury* gave the most detailed description of Brown's May 1851 "boxing" appearance. The report describes how, with the assistance of J. C. A. Smith, he had mailed himself from Bradford to Leeds, "packed in the identical box" in which "he first made his escape from slavery." The article announces that Brown's exhibition at the local Music Hall

offers for inspection a representation of the horrors of slavery in America. He was packed up in the box at Bradford about half-past five o'clock, and forwarded to Leeds by the six o'clock train. On arriving at the Wellington station, the box was placed in a coach and, preceded by a band of music and banners, representing the stars and stripes of America, paraded through the principal streets of the town. The procession was attended by an immense concourse of spectators. Mr. C.A. Smith [*sic*], a coloured friend of Mr. Brown's rode in the coach with the box, and afterwards opened it at the Music Hall. The box is 3 feet 1 inch long, 2 feet 6 inches high, and 2 feet wide. Mr. Brown's last "resurrection" (as he calls it) from the box took place at a quarter past eight o'clock, so that he had been confined in the space above indicated for two hours and three-quarters. He was very well received by the small audience who attended, and after a short but interesting account of his adventures, he proceeded to exhibit his panorama.[153]

In a clear and dauntless gesture that signifies on the American abolitionist Henry Wright's call for the public to see Brown's box, "look into it, and there behold American Republicanism and American religion," Brown's Leeds appearance unveils a grossly sardonic contrast in images. The pomp and circumstance of "stars and stripes" and the music of the band are offset by the dissonant sight of a fugitive of the States made to seek safe harbor in a box.[154] Brown and Smith's act redeploys the nationalist pageantry of coach-drawn processions and street parades toward abolitionist ends, skillfully segueing this scene into Brown's self-engineered "resurrection" before an audience. The structure of this program again makes plain the ways that Brown perhaps envisioned his diverse cultural work as concatenate parts of a whole. Boxing spills into lecturing which creates a bridge into the *Mirror*.[155] The boxing event serves as a critical introduction to the evening as it underscores Brown's control over both his body and his narrative, which he makes available for public consumption.

For nearly three hours on a spring evening in Leeds, Brown's box trick announced to a "small audience" of onlookers that excruciating confinement could be recycled into a symbol of corporeal subversion. Brown's resourceful performative labor appropriates still more Gothic tropes—entrapment and abjection—converting them into spectacular and cyclical methods of escape. If the iconography of the slave in St. John de Crèvecoeur's *Letters from an American Farmer* (1782) typifies the image of the trapped and decrepit, "[h]alf dead and half-alive . . . rotting corpse" hanging in a cage, Brown's display of endurance crouching in his crate converts the slave's body into an elastic tool capable of transgressing and transcending extreme corporeal limitations.[156] Theatrically prescient and forward-looking, Brown's work is both directly and figuratively tied to the imbricated fields of Victorian magic culture and transatlantic spiritualism, both of which were practices gradually beginning to flourish in the England he encountered in the early 1850s.

Known for its imperialist and misogynist ideological underpinnings, mid-nineteenth-century magic culture nonetheless might have inspired Box Brown as he cultivated his boxing routine. Karen Beckman astutely reminds us that magic "transforms the emerging political voices of women and other 'others' into bodies that move with apparent ease from the realm of the corporeal to the realm of fantasy. In short, magic tries to convince us that 'surplus' bodies can be evaporated harmlessly and without trace."[157] Conversely, however, Brown appears to have reanimated magic's illusory play of the body in order to harness its functionality for African American liberation tactics. Working at the borders of spectacular and "nineteenth-century high theatrical realism [which] prided itself on challenging the viewer . . . by seeming to have nothing to hide, by seeming to show it all . . . 'right before your very eyes,' in the magician's traditional phrase," Brown's reconstructions of escape used the black body as a tool of defiance, as a site of illusion, theatrical mastery, and reinvention.[158] Less a vanishing act and more an antecedent to early-twentieth-century magic show "escapology," Brown's boxing spectacle reaffirmed an African American appropriation of the black body, making that body "vanish" in the midst of the panoptic culture of slavery and under the peculiar institution's diligent and watchful eye.[159]

Brown's reenactments of boxing would seemingly anticipate Victorian magic's increasing use of cabinets, crates, and trunks as critical stage devices. Although box escapes which featured a performer's self-liberation from sealed receptacles and nailed packing cases did not gain popularity until the early twentieth century and in the wake of Harry Houdini's dominating success as a magician, confinement imagery nonetheless played a central role in the burgeoning magic culture of the mid-Victorian era.[160] The famous cabinet act of teams such as the American Davenport brothers in the 1850s and 1860s and the infamous "box Trick" of Englishman J. N. Maskelyne in the 1860s and 1870s contributed to a lively show culture intrigued with the mysteries of entombment. Bound and tied in a cabinet with instruments which were made to seem as though they were played by mesmeric forces, the Davenports engaged in "profitable seances" in the States and England, where the two men were "invited to prove the wonders that invisible spirits could perform when mediums were enclosed in a dark cabinet."[161] Unlike the brothers' act, Brown's was no hoax, and his use of confinement as performance made corporeal agency as opposed to passivity the central focus of his appearance. Brown's boxing reenactments stressed the powers of his body to withstand the torture of slavery.

The art of escapology served as a way for Brown to comment on his relationship to the corporeal, to reassert his triumphant defeat of subjugation. Like Houdini, who would perfect a version of boxing for his own theatrical purposes, Brown perhaps realized that "the knowledge that he could always rely on his body was essential to the control of his mind," and he used boxing as a way in which to assert the ultimate power and sovereignty which he heroically claimed over his own flesh.[162] Settling into the box "for two hours and three-quarters," Brown willed his body to endure the suffocating restrictions of the crate as defiant spectacle and as a potential affirmation of his ultimate autonomy. This sort of appearance aided Brown in overturning the terrible abjection of his imprisonment, which he relates at length in both versions of his narrative, how the confinement caused him to break into a "cold sweat," how his eyes began to "swel[l] as if they would burst from their sockets," and how "the veins on [his] temples were dreadfully distended with pressure of blood upon [his] head."[163] The emphasis on the pain he endured during this form of prolonged and self-willed torture in order to obtain freedom sheds strategic light on Brown's skillful abilities and his depth of endurance in claiming control and ownership over his body.

Brown's greatest feat as an escape artist, however, may have been his uncanny ability to cheat (social) death in slavery. Repeatedly compared to a "Lazarus" figure with the power to "rise again" from his entrapping box, Box Brown reinvented the traditional role of the resurrected biblical figure, "the surrogat[e] detailed to investigate, experience and if possible exorcise, on behalf of the rest of us, the great mystery" of death.[164] Faced with ubiquitous images of live burial in slavery and Victorian popular culture alike, Brown's boxing followed abolitionist discourse in a bid to reappropriate the harrowing iconography of Crèvecoeur's "slave in the cage" imagery for resistant purposes.[165] As "the essential Gothick situation," the theatrical box escape subsequently provided Brown with the opportunity to revisit the question of mortality and to signify on the symbolic uses of the box as a metaphysical "threshold, that point of elision between life and death."[166] Perhaps Brown recognized, like Houdini, that "his life was tolerable only if he could assure himself, time after time, that he could defeat [death]," that he could defeat the peculiar institution at its own game of transforming people into things.[167]

Transcending the limits of the body which slavery sought to place on him, Brown's boxing act gave the activist a public forum to performatively interrogate the politics of death and resurrection and thus seems closely aligned as well to the evolving spiritualist movements of the period on both sides of the Atlantic. Not surprisingly, spiritualism seems to have contributed to the graduated theatricality of Brown's work late in his public U.K. career when the magic of his boxing seems to have transmogrified into full-blown spiritualist demonstration. The road from nineteenth-century magic to that of spiritualism was not a long one. Midcentury spiritualism mediums "became the first 'escape artists'" as they increasingly relied on cages and contraptions to heighten their putative connection to the netherworld.[168] Brown's work tapped into the evolving art of escapology, but the very presence of his cabinet-like crate may have imbued his act with a timely spiritualist currency as well.

Functioning as the messenger of "survival" for his audience, the figure who had traveled to the dark "underworld" of slavery and lived to tell about it, Brown eventually imagined a way to engage with the spiritualist elements of his escape, transforming that interrelated symbolism into a gesture that would combine multiple theatrical strategies to create yet another new and multifaceted spectacle. In 1859, eight years after his initial U.K. tour, the activist resurfaced with a second wife to mount a revised version of his initial panorama production which reportedly brought the spiritualist politics of his cultural production to the fore. Spiritualism, it seemed, was literally the final frontier for Brown to traverse as an abolitionist reformer.[169] The return of the *Mirror* to England in 1859 was hailed, according to the *West London Observer*, "with breathless interest and loudly applauded" at Town Hall in Brentford.[170] Yet Brown had noticeably altered his "grand original panorama of African and American Slavery" in significant ways. The article marvels over the exhibition's alterations, noting that Brown

> has since added to his entertainment some dioramic views from the Holy Land, which are excellently painted, and ably described by Mrs. Henry Box Brown. Since the sad revolt in our Eastern Empire has occurred, Mr. Brown has had a panorama of the great Indian Mutiny painted, which he now exhibits alternately with his great American panorama, either of which affords a most excellent evening's entertainment. . . . To conclude the evening's entertainment on Wednesday, Mr. Brown, together with Professor Chadwick . . . introduced several experiments on mesmerism, human magnetism, and electrobiology, which proved most successful, and afforded the crowded audience much pleasure and amusement.[171]

A maddening elixir of panoramic grandeur, abolitionist visual display, neo-imperialist propaganda, spiritualist and magic spectacle show, Brown's last recorded *Mirror* appears to present more questions than answers about the political and cultural direction his work was taking a decade after his fabled flight. The geohistorical scope of Brown's exhibition has here stretched to include "dioramic views from the Holy Land." Even more puzzling still, the mysterious Mrs. Brown strikes a startling role. A lone female voice on the stage who reportedly "introduced the panorama of the great Indian Mutiny" on some nights as well, this Mrs. Brown accompanies the panoramic tourist on a journey that shifts from night to night between holy location and colonial conflict.[172] Joined by Chadwick on the stage, Brown adds mesmeric stunts to a variety-show repertoire in what were reported to be "his first experiments in public."[173]

The sheer excess and overload of these lesser known Box Brown–helmed programs has led some scholars to question the extent to which these later exhibitions were more opportunistic events than politically minded affairs. In particular, Audrey Fisch speculates that Brown's representations of the mutiny and his experiments with "popular science" may have been driven by economic pressures to appeal to an English public whose interest in American abolition had "wan[ed] by 1859." Fisch points to the favorable notices of Brown's exhibition, despite its introduction of material on the Indian Mutiny, as evidence in part of the fugitive's complicity with English imperialist propaganda. In the midst of post-mutiny English hysteria and xenophobic paranoia, no oppositional discourse on the British army's defeat at the hands of Indian rebels would have been tolerated by a public still licking its wounds from defeat. Thus Fisch concludes that the Box Brown of 1859 London was, in all likelihood, pandering to imperialist sentiment with his inclusion of this additional panorama in his act. She reflects on whether " 'Box' Brown's 'entertainment' " is "very different from the thousands of exhibitions of exotic spectacle which crowded Victorian popular culture?"[174]

Fisch's observations raise a string of concerns about the credibility of this Box Brown of late 1850s London, concerns that have haunted his body of work in the years since he climbed out of the box.[175] At best, the Brown of this exhibit was a busy entrepreneur capable of yoking multiple forms of entertainment into a challenging and conflicting cultural exhibit; at worst he was, as Fisch suggests, a venal pawn of British popular culture and "a supporting actor in a larger drama about the state of the English nation."[176] To counter this latter claim with any certainty at all by suggesting that, for instance, Brown was in fact staging a "mutiny" of his own on the English stage by placing his *Mirror* in a dialectic with dissonant images of a crippled English empire would be a difficult endeavor. I would, however, like to offer an alternate reading of this exhibit based, in part, on its sheer heterogeneity. For despite the fact that British spectators may have found "pleasure" and "amusement" by looking in the *Mirror* once again, I would urge us to consider the historical and political blind spots that these viewers may have encountered in the display, opaque connections that leave open ways of reading for the signifying elements of the exhibition. In short, I would argue that the incorporation of historical mutiny and mesmerism at this late juncture in the public display of his panorama suggests that Box Brown may have exploited these juxtapositions so as to yoke his visions of millennial reform with the spiritualist elements of his boxing.[177]

At the very least, the connections which Brown made in his 1859 *Mirror* between spiritualism and abolitionism were most likely not as incidental as one might initially presume. As R. Laurence Moore reveals, the links between mesmerism and reform developed over the course of the 1840s and 1850s, attracting the likes of influential abolitionists such as Garrison and Gerrit Smith and others, who found "something in spiritualist teachings to bolster their own particular ideal of free association."[178] While Garrison appeared with Brown on several occasions during the early weeks of his New England lecture tour in 1849 and early 1850, it is Gerrit Smith who perhaps was a critical figure to Brown in formulating his public career as an abolitionist and in forging his interests in spiritualism. Smith, who distinguished himself as a radical abolitionist in his career, attempting at one point to "establish a black agricultural settlement" and later "conspir[ing] with John Brown to incite a slave insurrection at Harper's Ferry," was in fact believed to have been one of the key financiers of the original *Mirror of Slavery*.[179]

With the abolitionist connections to spiritualism politically and professionally close to him, Box Brown manifested in this new version of his panorama what were already the suggestively latent elements of his act. The chaotic images of mutiny combined with the sensational spectacles of "human magnetism" and "electrobiology" to create a disparate landscape of black abolitionist escape art. Following the fascination of "many of America's millenialist reformers [who] saw the raps as signs of a prophecy heralding the beginnings of an age of perfect human brotherhood," Brown perhaps deployed mesmerism as the natural evolution of his millennial visions which he had hatched in his original exhibition.[180] Spiritualism's foregrounding of the turn of the body from the material to the nether world lent to the popular perception that mesmeric acts were ultimately a precursor to millennial change; hence, the "seance manifestations" were believed to have had "portentous significance for modern times."[181]

The Fourierist township image, which provided an ominous closing frame to the early 1850s *Mirror*, works, then, as something of an ultimate precursor of its own in Brown's political and performative career. His production's emphasis on Fourierism again reflects the extent to which Box Brown's work asserted itself at the crossroads of reformist ideologies. In a sense, his panorama built on the "poetic and vigorous vision, apocalyptic themes, indignation at the unjust state of the world and desire for its betterment" which spiritualist leaders such as Andrew Jackson Davis fostered and embraced in the late 1840s and early 1850s.[182] Brown would seemingly build on these kinds of conflations of political reform and spiritualism, transforming them into black abolitionist cultural expression. His moving panorama withstood the test of time in reflecting the imminent and turbulent change that the United States' national body was itself on the threshold of confronting in 1859. Read in this context, this *Mirror* reflected the turbulent events ahead and affirmed a spiritualist vision that would serve as a bridge for the fugitive slave to revolve himself out of social death and into a future unknown.

### Coda: The Trap Door Narrative and the Return of the Mack

Henry Box Brown was well into his first U.K. lecture and panorama tour when the "first English edition" of his *Narrative* was released in August 1851.[183] This "new" narrative differentiated itself from the 1849 text with its very title, *Narrative of the Life of Henry Box Brown, Written by Himself.* Gone were the suffocating details of the dimensions of Brown's box, as well as any mention of Charles Stearns. Yet this alternate text poses (and perhaps exacerbates) its own set of complicated questions regarding the authenticity and existence of an "original" Henry Box Brown narrative. James Olney observes that the differences in the 1851 edition suggest that Stearns had worked from a version of the manuscript for this English publication, "or from some ur-text lying behind both." He suggests that Stearns's editorial work is "very much in play in this text"—whether the fugitive literally authored the work or not. Olney concludes that if it was "really written by Brown," then the text reveals the ways in which "the abolitionist style insinuates itself into the text and takes over the style of the writing even when that is actually done by an ex-slave."[184] But the 1851 version of Brown's *Narrative*, whether literally authored by the activist or not, distinguishes itself as an intertextual cultural production, a narrative which finally and emphatically affirms Brown's use of performative strategies to transcend the corporeal as well as the discursive restrictions laid upon him as a fugitive slave.

The prefatory material and documents appended to the 1851 narrative alone set up a direct relationship with the previous edition of Brown's autobiography, while also immediately suggesting a representational transcendence of that text. As a significant juxtaposition to the title's descriptive reductions, the Manchester-issued edition includes on its first page the popular 1850 lithograph of Brown's "unboxing" from slavery, entitled the "Resurrection of Henry Box Brown, at Philadelphia."[185] The positioning of the lithograph on the initial page serves as a concatenate image to that of the final representation of the box from 1849. With head and shoulders carefully emerging from the crate, Brown is placed at the center of this illustration, fully dressed and staring forward with even aplomb while three white and one black abolitionist onlookers ponder the scene. The image foreshadows the ways in which this *Narrative* might expose rather than cloister Brown's body (of work), how it might extend the cultural productions which he has thus far staged within his career as an activist.

This attendance to intertextuality permeates the structure of the 1851 edition of the *Narrative*. Although it lacks the sophisticated literary style of William Wells Brown's subsequent travel writings, which were often laced with panoramic imagery and a roving, vigorously descriptive narrative eye, the English edition of Henry Box Brown's *Narrative* creates a direct and fundamental dialogue with the *Mirror of Slavery*.[186] A new preface displaces Stearns's "self-conscious, self-gratifying, self-congratulatory philosophizing" in favor of opening remarks which present a generic problem that Brown's cultural work will consistently address: how to negotiate the void between the experience of slavery and its representation.[187] Presumably the narrator of this new preface, Box Brown speculates that the ordeals which he has endured at the "lash of the whip" will "never be related, because, language is inadequate to express" such events (Brown, *Narrative of the Life*, 1851, ii). This comment establishes an initial crisis in mounting visual proof of the fugitive slave's experiences which the subsequent introduction to the *Narrative* will attempt to resolve through an intertextual engagement with Brown's celebrated boxing (re)appearance and his panorama.

This introduction includes multiple letters from those who serve as "witnesses" to either the initial scene of unboxing or to the touring English exhibition of the panorama, and speaks back in multiple ways to the problem of linguistic "inadequacy" in the representation of slavery. The remarks of the famed abolitionist James Miller McKim, one of the primary Philadelphia activists canonized in the scene of Brown's "resurrection," extend the narrator's initial points concerning visual corroboration. In one of the opening letters, McKim "confess[es]" that "if I had not myself been present at the opening of the box on its arrival, and had [I] not witnessed with my own eyes, your resurrection from your living tomb, I should have been strongly disposed to question the truth of the story" (iv).[188] The latter "testimonials," as they are introduced, provide a kind of response to this problem of visual representation by foregrounding the claims of those who witnessed the panorama. British Reverend Justin Spaulding's effusive letter describes the panorama as "almost, if not quite, a perfect fac simile of the workings of that horrible and fiendish system. The real life-like scenes presented in this Panorama, are admirably calculated to make an unfading impression upon the heart and memory" (iv).[189]

The introduction's sustained referencing of the panorama production, in particular, complicates the conventional structure of the slave narrative genre. Although the narrative's compilation of appending documents appears to follow the rudimentary structure of Stepto's "eclectic" narrative format with its letters of authentication, the intertextuality of these documents suggests that each of Box Brown's cultural productions act as "authenticating narratives" for the other.[190] The 1851 *Narrative* is meant to corroborate and further contextualize his panorama exhibitions, his boxing reenactments, and vice-versa.

This imbricated interplay of cultural work which the 1851 version of Box Brown's *Narrative* brings to fruition diverges from the content of the 1849 text most critically in its revised incorporation of performance as a strategy of renewal, transformation, and liberation for the fugitive. Performance figures early as a sign of both passive and aggressive objectification in enslavement. In this new version of the narrative, Brown describes the instance in which one of his "kinder" overseers, Henry Bedman, "was very fond of sacred music and used to ask me and some of the other slaves . . . to sing for him something 'smart' . . . which we were generally as well pleased to do" (21). In contrast to this coerced singing to which Brown confesses, he later renarrates "the revolting case of a coloured man, who was frequently in the habit of singing" and who is later tortured for this transgression which reportedly "consumed too much time" according to the especially tyrannical overseer John F. Allen (24). The text problematizes the limits of performance in slavery, how it threatens to operate as a whim of the master's will and as a catalyst for enacting power over the enslaved.

Yet the *Narrative* also allows for a significant shift and a strategic reappropriation of performance from the bonds of the slaveholder. Situated as the eighth chapter in the 1851 text, a new portion of material presents a detailed account of Brown's involvement as "a member of the choir in the Affeviar church" in Richmond, Virginia (47). His experiences in the choir foster several transformations in Brown's life; as a result of this activity, he develops an increasing resistance to white supremacist Christianity and an awareness of the hypocrisy of "slave-dealing christians" (48). He also gradually comes to recognize the ways in which the performance of sacred music might also enact altruistic awakenings within individuals. The chapter's description of a choir performance in which Brown participates emerges as a crucial turning point in the text which ultimately alters the spiritual condition of choir partner J. C. A. Smith. Moreover, Brown himself professedly resolves after the Christmas choir concert of 1848 to "no longer [be] guilty of assisting those bloody dealers in the bodies of souls of men" by "singing" or "taking part in the services of a pro-slavery church" (49). The performance of sacred song here paradoxically perpetuates the regime of slavery and potentially aids in its dismantling by psychologically and emotionally freeing Brown from complicity with the system. From this incident of sacred performance, the narrative segues into Brown's resolution to conspire with the aforementioned Smith to box himself to the free states, finally redeploying performance toward overtly liberatory ends.[191]

In yet another twist of narrative fluidity in the many "acts" of Henry Box Brown, the fugitive slave in the climax of this text is allowed full rein to emerge from the box of his escape singing, thus exiting the crate in similar fashion to the way in which he entered it. The English edition of the *Narrative* returns Box Brown's "him [*sic*] of thanksgiving" to its originating context, on his emergence from the box in Philadelphia. Having previously been situated in the bowels of Stearns's 1849 preface, the hymn is positioned, as Wood points out, "in its proper context" in the 1851 text, where Brown is able to "replac[e] the earlier linguistically sanitized account of his experience with his own language and cultural form" (Wood, "All Right!" 81). Stretching itself from the exuberance of Brown's final, repetitious exclamations in hymn that "The Lord be praised," the *Narrative* rides this legendary performative spectacle as a bridge into the politicization of Brown's performances on the lecture circuit. This act elasticizes even further in the final pages of the text, where it evolves into the original "Uncle Ned" composition which manifests the confluence of autobiography, performance, and political critique which Brown would embrace throughout his career as an abolitionist activist.

The final shift in this transmogrifying, "authenticating narrative" turns out to be his introduction of "Uncle Ned." Transforming literary labor into the labor of performance in song, Brown's second *Narrative* offers yet another surprisingly "dark" and parting gesture as this chapter of his adventures comes to a close. Even in this most joyful moment of liberation, the spectators of Box Brown's many varied acts may never fully come to terms with either the terror or the horror of slavery and the box of both entrapment and freedom. This final song functions, like so many that came before and after it, as "a veiled articulation of the extreme and paradoxical conditions of slavery."[192] Brown reminds us of the visible darkness of captivity which he has both remanufactured and simultaneously obscured and eluded. The song, in this way, operates as yet another sensational trap door for Box Brown to both construct and pass through on the road to freedom.

He was called, according to Jeffrey Ruggles, the "African Prince," the "King of All Mesmerisers." The Henry Box Brown who made his way across Great Britain in the mid-1850s was apparently every bit the showman he had intimated himself to be when he first unveiled his *Mirror of Slavery* in America. From "march[ing] through the streets in front of a brass band, clad in a highly-colored and fantastic garb"[193] to pursuing a full-fledged career in mesmerism and magic, the phantasmagoric Box Brown reappeared on the transatlantic scene with several more acts up his sleeve in the latter half of the century. Ruggles is the first historian to recover the late adventures of the fugitive artist, and he has provocatively suggested the ways in which these particularly eccentric career moves on Brown's part may have pushed him to the margins of abolitionist circles which often privileged conventional methods of agitation and dissent. Simply put, in the end, Brown's brash and spectacular public acts may have indeed proved too excessive, too performative, too "glam" to register as legible acts of social and political resistance to slavery.[194]

We may speculate as to whether Brown was, by the time he resurfaced in 1864 Wales as "the character of an African King, richly dressed, and accompanied by a footman,"[195] performing for his own mischievous pleasure and profit or whether he was actively producing political protest, boldly dancing in the streets and signifying on the imminent reconstruction of black selfhood and sovereignty on the eve of the Civil War's demise. Whatever his agenda, as Ruggles contends, "he was who he made himself to be,"[196] and by the time he re-materialized with his wife and daughter Annie in 1875 New England, he had become the ultimate conjurer: Prof. H. Box Brown, professional magician, a master "blindfolded 'seer,'" a "sleight of hand performer," a drawing-room entertainment spiritualist of the postbellum era. Like the wily, late-twentieth-century underworld heroes of picaresque black urban narratives, like the title character of the underground blaxploitation classic *The Mack* (1973), Box Brown harnessed the "dark arts" of illusion, manipulation, and the spectacularly expedient ruse to "crossover" into his own singular realm of freedom.[197]

# 3. "THE DEEDS DONE IN MY BODY"

*Performance, Black(ened) Women, and Adah Isaacs Menken*

*in the Racial Imaginary*

I was always a wonderful and eccentric child. Never very fond of doing things
because other people did them.
—Adah Isaacs Menken, "Some Notes of Her Life in Her Own Hand"

N umerous stories of fraudulence lurk on the lower frequencies of
nineteenth-century culture. While history has told us much about
the "confidence men and painted women," the thriving industry of
"humbug," and the tantalizingly corrupt culture of imposture brewing in
antebellum and postbellum America, far less attention has been paid to
the curious cases of social, cultural, and political chicanery engineered by
"strangers" emerging from the racial margins of transatlantic culture. More
commonly familiar are the many incidents of intrepid black activists such as
Sojourner Truth who weathered false accusations of social imposture only to
rise up victorious by proving her detractors wrong. But buried in the foot-
notes, epilogues, and postscripts of spectacular tales involving, for instance,
African American conjoined twins in North Carolina, there exist ambiguous
black characters whose actions ranged from the questionably opportunistic to
the brazenly duplicitous. Trapped at the center of various public and litigious
battles in the United States and England, the McKoy twins, Millie-Christine,
reportedly endured exploitation at the hands of white and black charlatans
who sought to make a profit off of the sensational enslaved celebrities.[1] The
crisis of black imposture proved in fact pressing enough to England's *Anti-
Slavery Reporter* that, in 1854, the publication warned of "certain coloured
men," such as Reuben Nixon, who preyed on tractable abolitionist audiences
"already pre-disposed to listen to a skilfully-invented and well-told tale of
woe, and suffering, and hair-breadth escapes. "Such impostors," the *Reporter*
warned ominously, "damage the cause, and bring discredit upon the race."
Even Henry Box Brown, who fended off slanderous barbs from British re-

porters, sustained a protracted struggle with fellow black activist J. C. A. Smith, who publicly argued that Brown had grown fiscally manipulative and opportunistic and was, therefore, "not worthy to be numbered" within the rank of the Anti-Slavery Society.[2]

## Smoke and Mirrors

Despite the relative obscurity of these secondary anecdotes and forgotten tales, the morally ambiguous mavericks at the center of them are fascinating in part because they appear to have either everything or nothing to lose. Risking both the punitive actions of a white supremacist legal system intent on policing black agency as well as the excoriating wrath of black progressive communities who were focused on building a unified front against racism, these anomalous characters nonetheless rejected the altruistic ideals of "race men and women" to advance their own fiscally and socially self-serving plans. Glorifying the art and pleasure of success, profit, and survival, their stories are rarely told in either Anglo-American or even black studies for that matter, and yet their very existence complicates our understanding of nineteenth-century resistance politics, social performance, and definitions of "blackness." The purpose of this chapter is to explore where, how, and if at all the charismatic and adventurous antebellum actress Adah Isaacs Menken fits into this history of identity formation and social equivocation.

In 1859, the year in which Henry Box Brown reemerged in Great Britain with an English wife, a mesmerist act, and a revamped panoramic exhibition, Adah Isaacs Menken, then a young Southern ingenue, broke rank from her husband in Cincinnati and set out for New York City. She had no "magic" box and no original songs to her name, but like Brown, she possessed a knack for (self) invention and a keen eye for the spectacular. With distinctively re-sourceful social skills and a fair amount of hubris, she resettled in a bustling metropolis awash with theatrical and literary possibility. Although she had already made a name for herself while performing in New Orleans and Texas and while later writing impassioned poetry and essays for Cincinnati's bur-geoning Reform Jewish communities, it was in New York where she moved rapidly from margin to center. In that city, she spun her grandest feats of cultural reinvention both on and off of the stage, and she cultivated a place that would eventually serve as a springboard for her final vault into interna-tional fame. Within a year, she had married and separated from a champion pugilist, weathered a public scandal involving bigamy, and worked her way into New York's bohemian intellectual circles, all the while negotiating her reemergence in the world of theatre.[3]

7. Adah Isaacs
Menken, Sarony,
circa 1866. Harvard
Theatre Collection,
Houghton Library,
Harvard University.

Much can be said about Adah Isaacs Menken's uniquely transient and remarkably metamorphic life before she reached New York—as well as the electrifying and tumultuous road that lay ahead of her in the years leading up to her death in Paris in 1868. Menken invoked spectacular technologies to defamiliarize racial narratives in the antebellum era. A pioneer of midcentury theatrical and cultural spectacle, she played with the mythologies of racial and gender categories in order to generate fame and unmatched wealth for actresses in the 1860s. And though her stardom, her fleeting fortune, and her notoriously ambiguous personal history set her apart from other performers, Menken nevertheless evolved, like Box Brown, into an opaquely excessive persona. Like her fugitive abolitionist counterpart, she transformed and transported key elements of midcentury theatrical spectacle and corporeal subterfuge both in and to her work on stage as one of America's first international celebrities. Traveling incessantly from the South to the Midwest, from the East to the West, and from England to Paris, she dazzled her public by embracing the role of a daring, athletic, and controversial breeches actress who played with the boundaries of identity politics. Creating her own performative frontier to traverse, she moved effortlessly from playing man-child heroes who discovered brave and cunning ways to foil their oppressors to sporting gentleman's attire during gambling outings in rough and tumble western cities out on the range.

Assuming a series of heroic leads in English melodramas and working-class crime adventures, Menken dominated the spectacle-driven transatlantic theatre circuit for much of the 1860s. She was best known for performing the eponymous lead in the 1861 preburlesque, equestrian-driven production of *Mazeppa*, a play based on Lord Byron's poem of the same name. Strapped to a black stallion and cutting a treacherous path across the stage in "flesh-colored" tights and a tunic before full-house audiences in the United States and Europe, Menken's voluptuous and yet ambiguously costumed figure created a groundswell of pop cultural fascination. The spectacle of her "disrobing" in the cross-dressed role of a heroic rebel warrior evolved into the central attraction during this nightly extravaganza.

Yet with so much attention paid to what she "laid bare" on the stage, the facts of Menken's personal life have largely remained a source of occlusion and contention. At various moments in time, over a century's worth of biographers imagined Menken to be Jewish, Irish, Spanish, French, and even African American "passing" for white. From the earliest biographical sketch in an 1860 *New York Illustrated News* article through her posthumously published "Notes of Her Life in Her Own Hand," her self-authored alter-egos have surfaced along multiple ethnic, cultural, and class spectrums—a white American working-class survivor, a New Orleans child performer, a hard-knock Memphis heroine, a coddled Franco-Spanish heiress, a Jewish daughter in exile, or an "octoroon."[4] By the time that Menken had passed (on), her conflicting aliases assumed lives of their own in numerous biographies, journal articles, and theatre histories about the actress. She became, as critics have suggested, whoever a biographer, a culture, a movement, an epoch needed and wanted her to be. A tragic female performer punished for her personal and professional choices. An actress who doubted her morals and ethics. A Victorian rebel who actively chose a bohemian life and subsequently served as an icon for future countercultural revolutions. A struggling poet dedicated to her underrated belles lettres. In her own lifetime and in the years immediately following her death, she has been remembered and dismembered according to the whims of paternalist cultural pundits and legendary feminist icons alike.[5] Her circuitous path to "becoming Menken" has left a tangled web of scholarly intrigue to untangle. Moreover, her cultural identity performances have generated the most heated debates for over a century now among biographers, theatre historians, and more recently among feminist and ethnic studies scholars.

While her early public allegiances to the Midwestern Jewish community laid the groundwork for the legend of Menken's Jewish cultural identity,[6] in recent years and most persistently, Menken has emerged in American cultural history and criticism as a woman of African descent, perhaps raised somewhere in or near New Orleans during the antebellum period. Cultural historian Renee Sentilles's recent rereading of Menken's life and career places a new focus on the subject of the actress's thorny cultural identifications. Cautiously wary of the ways in which Adah Isaacs Menken's identity remains overdetermined in popular and critical discussions, Sentilles insists that there exists no empirical "evidence" to link Menken to specifically "African ancestry" (133). Yet she also reminds readers of the ways in which this dependency on textual proof hardly forecloses discussions regarding race and Menken. Sentilles argues that the "fact that no one actually wrote of Menken as being black until after her death does not refute the notion that Americans may have speculated about her racial identity during her lifetime" (135). What makes this latter observation so crucial and provocative is the way in which it complicates her former claims regarding "evidence." For the very concept of racial "evidence" is perhaps called into question when one begins to consider the relationship between collective speculation, public imagination, and the concept of "blackness" itself. Lingering controversies surrounding Menken's cultural iconography force us to scrutinize critical methods for defining race and the tools that we use to measure and evaluate its social and political worth and cultural authenticity.[7] What, in fact, does it mean to rely on "evidence" when discussing "blackness" and how might the concept of Menken's extended social and cultural performances ultimately undo a quantitative definition of her "authentic" identity? As Sentilles questions, "what do we make of an identity based almost entirely on rumor, hearsay, and wishes?" (274).

It is at the site of rumor, hearsay, and wishes that this study of Adah Isaacs Menken in the racial imaginary begins, and it is, as I will argue, the place where "blackness" resides in nineteenth-century culture, the place where a "black(ened)" Menken—to take a page from Jennifer Brody—and more broadly black women reside in the transatlantic imaginary of the antebellum period. We may never know who, what, when, and from where the person who became Adah Isaacs Menken initially sprang.[8] But the distended cultural lore that persists about her iconicity should tell us a great deal about the function of race, gender, class, and sexuality as intersecting metaphors in nineteenth-century culture. If we consider the ways that race itself operates as a fiction made substantial by institutional and discursive hearsay, rumor, and active mythology, then studies examining the ways that Menken matters racially might begin by questioning social and cultural epistemologies that prop up specific kinds of identity "truths."[9]

Reading Menken as without "proof" of blackness risks recycling the very racial and gender epistemologies that her work at times challenged and at other times reinforced. We would be foolish then to not consider the specific ways that a figure like Menken exposes the permeability of identity categories and the critical way that these categories inform each other. As Harryette Mullen has proven, there are ways that certain kinds of silences produce and perpetuate the myth of stable "white" identities. Mullen assures us that such myths reify "whiteness to the extent that it is known or presumed to be unmixed with blackness. 'Pure' whiteness is imagined as something that is both external and internal." Rather than imagining Menken to be "pure" anything at this point (she seems to have run from such a label for much of her lifetime), I am proposing that we read the intersections of her racial and gender identifications.[10]

This chapter demonstrates how race—and specifically "blackness"—continues to resonate in relation to Menken and her cultural work. Specifically, the chapter examines how and why the actress should figure prominently in discussions of race, gender, and corporeal ideologies, and it seeks to demonstrate how these categories evolved in concert with one another in Menken's transatlantic world of theatre. As we will see, Menken may have tricked up an endless array of smoke and mirrors in relation to her personal history during her meteoric rise to fame in the antebellum era, but the tricks themselves open up new ways of understanding the intersectionality of race, gender, class, and sexuality in nineteenth-century theatre culture and likewise the ways in which these categories might mutually constitute one another at the site of performance. An actress who intervened in the representation of her own body politics both on and off stage, Menken remains a confounding site of contradictions and intersections in Atlantic world performance. Her work has rarely been considered in the context of critical black feminist analysis, despite the fact that her iconography is now curiously linked to nineteenth-century black women's cultural history.[11] Likewise, few scholars have attempted to map a connection between dominant racial and gender categories and the nature of her work as a versatile theatre actress. Menken is therefore the center of analysis in this chapter, but she matters, as I will argue, in relation to other women like Sojourner Truth who were spectacularly circumscribed by race and gender, and who, in spite of this, were able to make their bodies move and function differently in the years leading up to the Civil War.

The chapter considers how racial and gender codings get mapped onto Adah Isaacs Menken in transatlantic culture. I examine the spectacle of Menken's body in conversation with public and mobile African American women as a means to understanding how the actress's body politic cannot be separated from that of black women, the ur-text, if you will, of public female mythologies in the nineteenth century. I read against popular and long-standing representations of Menken which fix, reduce, and racially pathologize her stage corporeality, and I resituate the actress in a black feminist theoretical context that allows us to read her as radically using her body as a performative instrument of subjectivity rather than existing merely as an object of spectatorial ravishment and domination. In short, this chapter proposes a way to interrogate Menken's controversial work as a spectacle-driven actress alongside the efforts of other "stripped" women, and it offers a method for examining how the labyrinths of Menken's identity performances complicate the terms of her corporeal "exposure" as a female entertainer. Only by critically recontextualizing biographical as well as theatrical "scenes" in multiple Menken narratives do we come closer to a consideration of the important interplay between her ruptured identity constructions and her equally volatile body politics. What most concerns me in this discussion of Menken is the possibility of locating a performing body that problematizes the ways in which we perceive racial, gender, and corporeal spectacle in nineteenth-century culture. Reading across the gaze of the normative spectator, I am most interested in mining what we might call a politics of opacity that illuminates a way to consider the performances of "black(ened)" women like Menken who traveled through the transatlantic imaginary.

Guiding this study is an overarching question that I seek to answer in the chapter's final section, where I explore Menken's varied theatre work, her breeches roles, as well as her controversial protean dramas which incorporate blackface performances. How and why does race matter in relation to Adah Isaacs Menken and how did her work in theatre simultaneously exacerbate, convolute, and deepen such matters? In an effort to answer this question, I consider the relationship between corporeal subjectivity and cultural agency as it specifically comes to bear/bare on stage Menken. More than any other cultural figure of her time, Menken invoked the opaque as an aesthetic device, as a method of contestation and self-invention, and as a form of social mobility. A phantasmagoric body of (un)truthfulness, Adah Isaacs Menken made prolific use of performance's fecundity, its regenerative power, and its endlessly beckoning riches as a site of (re)covering for public and ambiguously situated women. Strewn out at the intersections of racial, gender, sexual, and class confusion, her corporal technologies signaled a new era in midcentury Atlantic world theatre.

## Black(ened) Adah: Menken in the Racial Imaginary

> Say of me the *Truth* . . . I have many faults. No actress is perfect, not even the "daughter of her father."
>
> —Adah Isaacs Menken, "Some Notes of Her Life in Her Own Hand"

George Barclay may have been one of the first biographers who began the task of fleshing out a history for a "black" Menken in transatlantic culture. Renee Sentilles contends, for instance, that his 1868 biography is the first text to make this claim in print, thus making him the official author of one of the most persistently conflicted and controversial genealogical tales in theatre history. Sentilles claims that mention of Menken's African American identity politics first surfaces in Barclay's short biography about the actress published in Philadelphia in 1868, within months of her death. In that text, Barclay is said to have "stated that Menken had claimed to be the daughter of a free man of color named August Theodore" (Sentilles, *Performing Menken*, 274). She suggests that Barclay's biography includes a potential bombshell. According to Sentilles, Barclay claims that Menken's third corroborated husband, Robert Newell, "was the one who gave him the information on Menken's true parentage. He begins, 'On April 11, 1835, Marie Theodore, the wife of August Theodore gave birth to a daughter in the living quarters of the family tiny general store in Milneburg, Louisiana. . . . The baby was christened Adah Bertha.' He asserts that in 1863, Adah 'in one of her more expansive moods, told a group of abolitionists' that her father had been a 'free man of color.' [Barclay?] goes on, 'There may be some substance to the claim, for she told Newell, while married to him that 'I cannot, as the daughter of an octoroon, sympathize with the cause of the Confederacy' " (Barclay as quoted in Sentilles, *Performing Menken*, 275).

On the surface, the story is an alluring one. Menken's most oddly matched and tragically complex companion, a "gentlemanly" journalist and political satirist who was said to have been initially abandoned by his wife on their honeymoon, on her death confides to another in the waning years of Reconstruction that she was in fact "blackened" at the root. Although Sentilles relies heavily on this portion of the Barclay narrative, it remains something of an archival mystery. The twenty-two copies of this volume housed in contemporary libraries and archives do not seem to have been printed with pages 25 and 26, the pages which Sentilles cites for this anecdote. Whether or not these passages exist, however, an analysis of Barclay's supposed racialization of Menken opens the door to several profound questions and insights.[12]

Sentilles makes plain the questionable nature of Barclay's contention by citing Newell's own memorial scrapbook on the actress in which he describes how Menken in a letter pronounced, "I am an ultra Southerner; I cannot fraternize with the negro—I cannot feel with Abolitionism."[13] As with all vestiges of Menken biography left to be pieced together, the square pegs seemingly refuse to fit into the round holes. Yet these dueling claims regarding Menken's political affiliations perhaps do little to fully refute Menken's material links to an African American past. As Sentilles herself makes clear, although Menken's "many statements supporting the Confederacy" perhaps "undermine contemporary concepts of black identity, which rest precariously on racial solidarity . . . they actually put her on par with many free people of color" in class and color-conscious antebellum Louisiana (276). Certainly, as numerous scholars have demonstrated, antebellum New Orleans culture was in particular the site of fractious and divisive debates concerning racial identification and communal solidarity. While some Louisiana residents who were designated "Free Persons of Color under the Code noir" fought the accretion of laws promoting racial segregation, others became "slave owners themselves, enlisted to fight for the Confederacy" or "disappeared entirely into whiteness."[14] Such important observations complicate facile assumptions about the parallelisms between racial and political identifications in nineteenth-century culture and do more to shed light on Menken's political equivocations than to close the door on questions regarding the putative authenticity of Menken's racial identity.

While the question of whether or not Barclay manufactured an elaborate anecdote purporting to shed light on Menken's racial opacities is itself subject to inquiry, his generic leanings as a journalist and dime-fiction novelist would certainly render him capable of writing a sensational Menken narrative. Immersed in producing mid-to-late-nineteenth-century sensation literature, Barclay was thus closely aligned with a literary tradition preoccupied with identity fraud. Moreover, his professed familiarity with figures close to Menken leaves open additional and tantalizing questions about the veracity of his narrative versus the extent to which he grafted blackness onto Menken's persona before her corpse had even grown cold. Elsewhere I have suggested that the genre of sensation itself obsessively revolves around controlling the (secret) identities of heroines bold enough to imagine self-reinvention and that Menken's elusiveness (and allusiveness) in divulging facts about her own past created a space for others to invent a sensational past for her.[15] Introducing Menken's narrative into the realm of his dime-novel pamphlet market, Barclay perhaps wrote a Menken who insisted that she was "the daughter of an octoroon." And while scholars have yet to vigorously explore Barclay's authority in this matter, the possibility that he published such a charged anecdote about her identity might tell us quite a bit about the race for Menken in the 1860s. Indeed, from the standpoint of cultural memory, the veracity of Barclay's claims is, in the end, perhaps altogether irrelevant when it comes to considering the complex relationship between race and Menken iconography. For just as intriguing as the idea that Barclay held some rosetta stone in regard to the actress's racial DNA is the possibility that he fictionalized it in the first place. If Barclay did design a new past for Menken, the critical question to ask would be from where did he derive his inspiration? Put another way, what does the road look like on this fictionalized route to black identity? And to what extent does Barclay's potential imagining of this past expose how blackness operates in the transatlantic imaginary as a site of the "cultural vestibularity" of black womanhood in particular?[16]

Such questions seem critical to pose in light of Menken's increasing canonization in African American literary and cultural studies archives. In the wake of John Kendall's 1938 purported revelation concerning her racial background, a "blacker" Menken has surfaced in multiple scholarly endeavors. She appears, for instance, in Arna Bontemps's and Jack Conroy's 1945 examination of African American historical migration, *They Seek a City*, as one of "the 10,000 free people of color who disappeared from the New Orleans census prior to the war between the states." Likewise, a 1965 *Negro Digest* dubbed her "the Negro beauty who bewitched two continents." Even more recently in the 1980s, her *Infelicia* volume of poetry has passed into the *Schomburg Library of Nineteenth-Century Black Women Writers*, and I have myself written about Menken in the context of cultural studies endeavors which examine representations of African American women. Clearly, if Menken was not explicitly written as African American in her lifetime, she has been scripted as such in the century following her death.[17]

But concerns remain as to how and why one of her own contemporaries, George Barclay, would allegedly surface as the only figure to present this racial bombshell within months of her death, with apparently little to no fanfare and even less consequence. Unlike Kendall, who held his flagrant racial biases clearly in view and who argued that only the shameful secret of blackness would necessitate such cloaking on Menken's part, Barclay offered no authoritative spin for his assertion other than the intimate and privileged knowledge of a former (and an occasionally acrimonious) husband. One could perhaps speculate, like several contemporary scholars, that the city of Menken's past had much to do with the evolution of this theory from Barclay's period forward. Bontemps and Conroy have, for instance, argued that Menken's links to antebellum New Orleans, coupled with the timing at which she left that city, suggest a great deal. They contend that "the pattern of her life [was] certainly a classic imitation of a colored Creole passing for white in the United States and England in the middle of the nineteenth century."[18] In this regard, we might consider whether Barclay may have transposed a romantic interest in "runaway girls" onto a narrative that fancied Menken as a plucky New Orleans transient youth. An author who staked a claim in imagining diverse and unique settings in his literature, Barclay roved in his textual explorations from Cuba to the Arctic, from New England to Africa, from Chicago to New York. It is therefore not too much of a stretch to consider how a writer of his lot may have gravitated toward embellishing the transcontinental adventures of a Creole heroine whom he imagined as having transcended her racially oppressed beginnings.

At the very least, as a writer who was in every way preoccupied with contemporary cultural events and controversy, Barclay was probably well aware of the brewing racial imbroglios in antebellum New Orleans, a dynamic cultural space where definitions of ethnic, racial, and cultural identity fluctuated. Originating in part out of colonial encounters, racial intermingling, and border crossings, the Creole identity that Menken indisputably claimed more consistently than any of her other labels typified this diversity of cultures. A liminal racial and ethnic category, "Creole" identity in nineteenth-century definitions "had always been used in Louisiana to signify local birth and foreign parentage." Traditionally the term could also apply to "children of black or racially mixed parents and children of Anglo-American" as well.[19] Social perceptions of "Creole" identity remained, then, broad and amorphous for much of the first half of the nineteenth century in New Orleans.

Gradually, however, shifting social and economic structures in that city produced more arbitrary racial categories. Particularly in the 1850s and 1860s as class structures shifted, so too did "the 'racial' identity of the Creoles." Subsequently, the struggle to redefine Creole identity as specifically "white" or "black" in New Orleans began in earnest.[20] The increasing dependence on clearly defined racial taxonomies, combined with an accretion of legal restrictions toward African Americans in New Orleans during the years leading up to the Civil War, worked to fan the flames of conflict and controversy in the city where a young Menken at least briefly lived.[21] The fomenting of race relations at midcentury underscores the exigencies that may have influenced one Creole ingenue to remake herself by using a number of flamboyant aliases. As the social climate of the adult Menken's New Orleans shifted, so too did dominant definitions of Creole identity, which attenuated and became less heterogeneous in the years leading up to her initial known departure from the region. Having wed Alexander Menken in Galveston, Texas, in 1856, Adah Menken and her husband settled briefly in New Orleans late that year, where she gained early experience performing in the J. S. Charles Theatre Company. By March 1857 they had relocated to Shreveport, moving, incidentally, the same year in which Louisiana had seen the near passage of a major bill restricting interracial marriage between whites and those individuals with even "a taint of African blood." Although the legislation failed, the very fact that the proposal received serious consideration in the Louisiana state legislature "was evidence of increasing white concerns with the growth of a sector of the population of color that was physically Caucasian enough to pass for white."[22]

Whether Menken was actually a fugitive from this newfound New Orleans segregation or whether her biographers simply envisioned her as on the run, this particularly heated sociopolitical context may have served as an impetus for Barclay and others to create for Menken a past that matched the turbulent lore of the city. What is certain, however, is that her anomalous cultural swagger and her increasing tenacity in moving along a continuum of ethnic and national marginalities went against the grain of the heightened panoptic surveillance of the Creole community. If she was merely "imitating" a Creole passer, her actions perfectly mirrored that of the midcentury Creole resolve to "exercise choice over who and what" one was in the face of "epistemological and institutional systems that seem[ed] to stand in [one's] way."[23] Perhaps even more importantly, Menken "emerged from . . . a society shaped as much by West African and West Indian legacies as by French and Spanish colonization" (Sentilles, *Performing Menken*, 282). Exposed, then, at some level to New Orleans' singular brand of circum-Atlantic culture and its fleeting opportunities for self-defining agency, Menken came barreling out of the region with the bravado of an individual who recognized the polyvalence of cultural categories, as well as the innate power rooted in that polyvalence. Thus it is New Orleans itself that contributes to a critical way of understanding Menken's cultural identity politics, regardless of whether her genealogy conventionally affirmed African ties.[24]

The complex history of race relations in New Orleans and the ubiquity of sensation fiction are, however, merely two critical components in what is certainly a much broader grid of cultural throughways that inform the making of a "black" Menken. In many ways, the biographical research and scholarly inquiries that would sensationalize and thereby racialize her past and likewise focus on her regional ties remain posterior readings of her identifications. They tell us little about Menken's racial scripting during the height of her career. Below, I suggest a way of understanding Adah Isaacs Menken as always already racialized in the context of popular and performance culture during her lifetime, and I propose a way of reading Menken's inextricably linked racial and gender identifications in the context of the transatlantic imaginary. Such an analysis acknowledges the ways in which the conjoined paradigms of race and gender served as vessels of fictive ideologies concerning "blackness" and "womanhood." Rereading her across these charged and imbricated spheres affirms the particularly unique "utility of 'black' women (mulattas, octoroons, prostitutes) for the (re)production of certain forms" of racial and gender paradigms that fuel dominant culture.[25] Moving away from hegemonic definitions of race that attach blackness exclusively to phenotypic black bodies, I suggest ways in which we might read race as it surfaces on "other" frequencies in the phantasmagoric world of 1860s performance culture. In short, I propose that we look beyond traces of conventional ethnographical and ethnological evidence in locating Menken's racial identities. Rather, it is the racial codes, the submerged metaphors indicating difference and emerging in a decade fraught with concern over maintaining racial and corporeal borders—it is these codes which tell us the most about how nineteenth-century racial taxonomies circulate in performance culture.[26]

We cannot, then, consider the life, lore, and cultural work of Adah Isaacs Menken without taking into consideration how she operated in relation to racial and gender ideologies in nineteenth-century culture. Below I offer a series of examples of how blackness operates as a traveling trope in Menken studies, how race and performance function in Menken's cultural spheres, and how blackness lingers as an (in)visible metaphor in the theatrical world that she dominated at midcentury. Menken herself produced and circulated several narratives during her lifetime in which she perpetually imagined herself in racially coded terms—even as she maintained conflicting and deeply problematic public positions on race throughout her career. Equally apparent is the way in which the press repeatedly "blackened" Menken by relying on racial tropes and cultural presumptions as opposed to explicit language about her racial identity. Even in her putatively public "whiteness," Menken was ultimately made "black" in such a way that clarifies how Barclay and others may have ended up scripting her as such by the time she died.

One of the most notorious and oft-repeated personal narratives involving the race for Menken was one that she herself circulated and perpetuated in the early years of her fame. The tale of Menken's captivity at the hands of "Indians" on the Texas frontier first surfaced in print in March and April 1860 in the *New York Illustrated News* as an article entitled "Ada Isaacs Menken, the Wife of John C. Heenan." The tale, which reappeared in an extended form in Barclay's text, put into play an ambiguous racial representation of Menken that she herself sustained. In the captivity narrative, which is told in first person (and which Barclay claims had been passed on to him from his friend William Wallis, who may have known Menken in Paris), Menken focuses on a life on the frontier in Livingston, Texas, as "Bertha Theodore." This Menken/ Theodore incarnation is taken into captivity by local Indians who are intent on making her the concubine of Chief Eagle Eye.[27] Theodore is subsequently rescued by an Indian maiden, Laulerack, who guides her to safety before falling victim to a gunshot wound inflicted by a group of traveling white men. Menken's solidarity with the Indian maiden Laulerack and her contempt for the feckless traveling companion Gus Varney reads, on the one hand, as a celebration of "female unity" in keeping with several of Menken's personal narratives (Sentilles, *Performing Menken*, 129). She begins the narrative "a sophisticated lady, the member of a hunting party," but she nonetheless emerges at the end "as a grieving 'sister' who sounds more like a lover" (Sentilles, *Performing Menken*, 130).

Yet the captivity narrative is also critical to reading Menken's racial politics in that it contains one of the few specific moments in print where Menken self-referentially engages with racial categorization, describing herself as "white" at key points in the narrative. Through the lens of performance, we might read these eruptions of whiteness as critical signifying moments in the text which do much to expose Menken's own recognition of the ways that race and power are deeply entwined with one another. Keenly aware of the literary conventions in which she has immersed herself, Menken calls attention to the structures of representation that she is negotiating. Early in the narrative, she declares that "[a]ll the heroines that I had ever read about, upon awakening from unconsciousness, repeated the well-known 'where am I,'" and "consequently I said the same thing" (21). Admittedly "conscious" of her role as "the heroine" in this tale, Menken calls attention to her willingness to utilize (racial) performance as a tool of mobilization. Thus, inasmuch as we know this story to be a spurious one, we may still read for the ways that Menken performs under the aegis of whiteness *and* masculinity in order to generate power, safety, and movement for herself within the narrative.[28]

The Laulerack frontier narrative registers a curious preoccupation with whiteness throughout its compressed plot arc. Crudely caricatured Indians speak broken English and demand the capture of "the white man" in the wilderness, and Chief Eagle Eye licks his chops while basely contemplating a plan to hold Bertha and Laulerack captive so as to have a "white beauty in summer" and a "red . . . in winter."[29] Laulerack repeatedly addresses Bertha as her "pale" or "white" sister, and Bertha fashions herself to be "a white maiden" in distress. What is striking about this string of monikers, though, is how often Menken's Theodore rejects a first-person possession of whiteness here; instead, whiteness often emerges at the site of the third person in the text. When Laulerack addresses Bertha, asking of her, " 'What does my pale sister want?' " the narrator offers an oblique reply: " 'Thy sister is named Bertha Theodore,' said I in Spanish, 'and although I have seen you but once I already love you' " (Barclay, *Life and Career*, 23). Evading a direct response to the question, the narrator's address here shifts from third to first person and is spiked with multiple divisions and layers. Her slightly askew answer proclaims desire (what the "pale sister" wants) without affirming the title bequeathed her. Perhaps equally provocative in its suggestiveness, our speaker makes it known that this exchange is rendered in Spanish rather than English, pointing to an impossible language lapse, something which may (or may not) be lost in translation here.

Even at the moments when race emerges in the narrative as the fulcrum of authority for Menken's Bertha, her character successfully recycles it into disposable and transient utility. In the midst of an intrepid escape from Eagle Eye's camp with Laulerack in tow, for instance, the narrator invokes "whiteness" as a blanket of protection and survival. Scrupulously, our female protagonist trades on race and gender in a bid to save herself as well as her newfound companion, Laulerack, with whom she promises to share a home upon breaking free from Eagle Eye's concubinage plan (Barclay, *Life and Career*, 24). Encountering a band of rangers on the plain, Bertha is resolute in her intent to use white patriarchy as a means to freedom. "I knew these were white men," she confesses, "and I shouted, 'A white maiden seeks protection' " (27). Again resisting the first person, Bertha/Menken employs the "white maiden" moniker in question here as a buy for herself and Laulerack, who have forged a homoerotic relationship counter to that of both white and Indian heternormative bonding rituals. In this scene which is fraught with tropes of western chivalry, the putatively vulnerable "pale sister" renegotiates the conventions of racial power on the frontier in order to escape them entirely. Under the cover and currency of whiteness, Bertha/Menken and Laulerack allow for a way to break free of the ties that bind them in captivity.[30]

Most importantly, the Laulerack tale would, in 1860, introduce the public to a Menken who was provocatively engaged with the ethnic margins of American culture. Menken's narrative of white women and women of color on the frontier together extended a tradition in nineteenth-century letters that focused on colonial encounters in the wilderness of America. Certainly as Sentilles observes, "the idea of a spiritual sisterhood between Native American and Euro-American women and the exoticism of Laulerack colored Menken." But whereas she concludes that Menken ultimately "used the tale to play up her own whiteness," I would urge us to reconsider the meaning of these racial contiguities in the context of transatlantic fiction and culture.[31] There is, I am suggesting another equally complex and provocative trend in nineteenth-century literary representations of "light" and "dark" women that we should keep in mind when discussing Menken's Texas tale. If anything, the juxtaposition of Menken and Laulerack opens up rather than forecloses questions of Menken's racial identity—even as she performs a particular kind of putative white(ned) womanhood in the narrative. Socially and culturally ambiguous "white" women, like Menken, and "morally erect" women of color, like Laulerack, often evolve in tandem with one another in Victorian fiction. If, for instance, Menken skimmed the borders of mainstream and bohemian culture by circulating tales of life on the frontier, she certainly walked a tenuous line similar to that of *Vanity Fair*'s notoriously equivocal parvenu Becky Sharp. That is, she walked a line between her visual "whiteness" and an adventurous and very public personal history that radically diverged from dominant definitions of white womanhood. "Genetically fair but morally or metaphysically black," women like Becky and Menken, who are marked as socially and therefore "sexually deviant are blackened," and their proximity to "virtuous" women of color only calls further attention to their own categorical liminality. As Jennifer Brody has shown, the "proximity of these different types of 'black women' in Victorian narratives emphasizes the fact that each type emerges beside the other. They should be understood as twinned and entwined entities—as beings whose complex imbricated identities illustrate the categorical contradictions of the culture."[32]

Pairing herself with a woman of color, then, became for Menken a way of undoing her own "whiteness" while also producing it. The tale moved her closer to the "blackened" category reserved for those women who disrupted gender and sexual codes while at the same time it sought to rescue her from this position by ultimately extinguishing that person of color from the narrative entirely. This was a pattern of representation to which Menken would return in the second and even more provocative personal narrative that she dispensed about her life for publication. In the highly fanciful "Some Notes of Her Life in Her Own Hand," Menken produced a short and flamboyant memoir of which, in 1862, she began mailing segments to her friend the playwright Gus Daly. In turn, Daly published an edited version of the piece in the New York Times, less than one month after her death, in 1868. Critics have largely overlooked the text as Menken scholars increasingly discounted large portions of the "factual" information which the actress includes: she imagined herself the heir to a monarchical line of French and Spanish nobility, Marie Rachel Adelaide de Vere Spenser, a "wonderful and eccentric child" who never knew her father and who was, in part, raised in New Orleans, educated in Europe and Latin America, an acclaimed performer in Cuba by her teens.[33] Several critics have read the gentrified European politics of this work as an example of Menken's "growing determination to emphasize her whiteness" and to "destabilize the exotic identity that she had cultivated" (Sentilles, Performing Menken, 131). Yet the complicated and circuitous color tropes of the "Notes," entangled with genealogical themes, again point toward a more ambiguous construction of racial categories. Menken's epic "Notes" suggest that the actress was, once again, examining and questioning the mutually constitutive relationship between blackness and whiteness, particularly in her representation of the mother figure in this narrative.

Beginning her tale in France, Menken spins a rather elaborate maternal biographical sketch.[34] Born one of two twins, her mother, in this story, shares the same name as her sister: Marie Josephine Rachel de Vere de Laliette. Blessed with "the same form, the same features, voice, gesture, expression," Menken's mother and aunt seem one, yet they are "so unlike"; the two bear one stark physical difference. One is "a delicate blond, the other a Spanish-looking brunette." In an extravagant plot twist, the brunette Marie is made to drown in a boating accident while the blond sister lives on to become the surrogate mother of Menken. Sentilles has argued that "the story of Menken's remarkably blond mother having a dark *twin* sister disposed of the notion of a quadroon mother at the same time that it suggested a white paternal heritage" (134).

Or did it? There are several significant nineteenth-century literary conventions that Menken's familial anecdote calls into play here. Like her sometimes adversarial acquaintance Mark Twain, who would return repeatedly to the "critical language of twinning, doubling, and impersonation," Menken crafted a narrative of maternal duality that produced (rather than reduced) multiple familial genealogies.[35] Moreover, her complicated twin tale bears the indelible stamp of gothic literary conventions and, specifically, the stylized imagery of a distinct Menken literary influence, that of Edgar Allan Poe. A passionate and outspoken supporter of unconventional literary aesthetics, Menken publicly championed the controversial work of figures such as Poe and her acquaintance Walt Whitman as she sought to cultivate an offstage persona as a serious poet and essayist. In one of her more notable literary articles published in an 1860 edition of the *New York Sunday Mercury*, she readily endorsed Whitman as an "American philosopher" whom she boldly likened to Poe and to herself as having "been drowned in the current of life, because they swam against the stream."[36] The drowning imagery itself recalls that of her darker maternal line, if only in fiction. Further still, her interest in Poe's work is significant here since I would suggest that there is a way to read his influence as having stretched its thorny thematic tendrils into Menken's account of her family history.

An early purveyor of uncanny gothic dualities and tenuous borders between self and other, Poe, as Toni Morrison reminds, gave haunting language, form, and image to "Americans' fear of being outcast, of failing, of powerlessness" and distressed human boundaries.[37] His anxious preoccupation with corporeal as well as psychological hemorrhages and the horrifyingly porous lines between individuals would anticipate nineteenth-century transatlantic culture's fascination with racial phantasmagoria in later decades. In particular, Poe's 1838 short story "Ligeia" plays suggestively with antebellum cultural perceptions of life, death, lightness, and darkness as each of these themes is bound up symbolically in the figure of the racially ambiguous female body. Keeping these thematic obsessions in sight here, we might read for the similarities between Menken's wrenchingly maudlin tale of light and dark girls as it resembles a key plot development in Poe's famous short story. With her inherent "strangeness," her "curly tresses," and "large and expressive" eyes, "far larger than the ordinary eyes," Poe's "Ligeia" "signals the same physiognomic traits as did taxonomists of color in the Caribbean and the South: hair, eyes, and skin" to create a doomed heroine who physically recalls the South's mythically "tragic octoroons" and who is thus mysteriously embedded in the shadowy legacies of slavery and colonialism. Racial tropes swirl just beneath the surface in "Ligeia," and given Menken's fascination with Poe, the similarities between one of his most famous tales of racial duality and Menken's maternal narrative from "the Notes" suggest yet another way that she may have invoked racial metaphors in her self-stylings.[38] Although not biologically twinned, like the mother figure of Menken's "Notes," Poe's "wild" and mysterious dark-haired beauty is nonetheless provocatively attached to a light double who temporarily displaces her upon her death. But whereas Menken's Marie sinks with her darkness to the bottom of "the most beautiful lake in the world," in Poe's nightmarish, Southern gothic dreamscape, his Ligeia resurfaces like indelible drops of ruby red blood in the blond and emaciated body of yet another wife for the narrator.[39] Ligeia's spectacular convertibility in this text functions as an ever-present reminder of what cannot be repressed in antebellum culture: the nearness of "blackness" and "whiteness," the terrifying recognition that intermingling between the races and the collapsing of racial differences might in fact be inevitable. With "Ligeia's" uncanny twinning of light and dark women—the dark one killed off, only to reincarnate into the body of the blond proxy—its familiar racial gothic dyad imagistically reemerges in Menken's mother of the "Notes."[40]

The actress's father figure is, however, another story entirely. In both Poe's uxorious ghost tale and in Menken's subsequent familial "Notes," the legacies of paternity and the present absence of the elusive patriarch remain murky and yet profoundly meaningful points of concern. Whereas Poe is noticeably vague about Ligeia's paternal genealogy inasmuch as his narrator has "never known the paternal name of her who was my friend and my betrothed," Menken, in her "Notes" and elsewhere, offered more confounding details rather than fewer about her paternity.[41] Producing an obfuscating series of conflicting descriptions of her father, Menken frequently altered his name, his occupation, and his whereabouts. The patriarch of Menken's "Notes" is, for instance, a "strong, healthy, and handsome" soldier's son who dies of consumption and leaves behind a two-year-old daughter who claims to have "never known" him. Other Menken narratives of the father created a spectacularly opaque portrait of him as well. The patriarch of Newell's Menken memoir is an ambiguous figure who calls his daughter "Delores," only to watch her reject that name. This refusal of her father's affection seemingly comes about as a result of her allegiance to her mother and the curious estrangement from her father's family that she succinctly describes. "Because," Menken is said to proclaim, "I had spirit and soul enough to work for my mother, the proud relatives of my father refused to own me. I would no longer be called Dolores. Adah is indeed my name."[42] Implicit in Menken's comments here is the suggestion that her father is somehow without "spirit and soul" and that likewise her father's family is perhaps haughty and heartless, a clan determined to reject her as a result of her loyalty to her mother. Clearly, we cannot ever know the extent of Menken's relationship with either of her parents, but we can infer from the accumulation of anecdotes that she maintained a running ambivalence toward them and particularly her father.

Of Menken's father, Sentilles concludes that, whether "she called [him] McCord, Theodore, or Los Fuertes, Menken's focus on her paternity implies that when Americans asked who she was, she saw the answer as laying principally in the identity of her father" (*Performing Menken*, 126). I would go a step further in order to argue that the "answer" that she conjured up for herself as well as the public has less to do with her actual paternal genealogy and more to do with the peculiar entitlement bound up in antebellum white patriarchy. If she was, as she professes to be here, her "father's favorite child," possessing "all his dreamy, thriftless, unreliable nature," Menken was also, it seems, clearly intent on seizing the freedom, movement, and choice emanating from nineteenth-century white patriarchy. Indeed, some of her most provocative comments on record about her father suggest the extent to which Menken sought, through her ambivalent identifications with his absent figure, to regain a unique form of inheritance rights to her paternal line. In Newell's Menken biographical sketch, the actress both maintains a bitter stance toward her "thoughtless father" and equally acknowledges that he "gave [her] strange books to read [and] made [her] the companion of his restless pursuits. Can it be wondered that my nature assumed a marked individuality and self-reliance, and lost the gentler graces which gain a pure love for my sex?"[43]

Menken's masterful identification with the father figure works to position her as the groomed and rightful intellectual heir to "his restless pursuits" and to a legacy of New England masculinist desire and transcendental self-reliance. In this regard, perhaps more than any other way, her father was indeed the "answer" for Menken as she sought out resourceful ways to perform her social and cultural identities. Menken's allusions to her father reaffirm the wealth of the daughter and further re-situate her within the rubric of grand old patriarchal inheritance. Staking a claim to this line of inheritance would potentially instill her with the passion and inspiration to rewrite her social and cultural position via the legacies of the absent father figure. Particularly if we follow a reading of Menken that considers the racial metaphors looming large within her public performances, the careful attention she paid to obscuring her father's identity is telling. Whether black or white (or both or something else altogether), Menken's father operates in her personal narratives as a shifting point of identification for the actress that ultimately steers her clear of slavery's decree that would have her "follow the condition of the mother." A black Menken in 1850s New Orleans would have existed outside of time and the law, solely the property of (rather than the heir to) the father.[44] If, then, in the world of the enslaved, the child is tethered to the mother's social and juridical abjection, Menken seemingly mocked that law by morphing identities as many times as did her phantasmatic father in her personal stories. It was a position that would, in turn, set a black(ened) Menken free. Having staked a claim in owning the property that is performance, this "other" Menken resituates herself within the paternal line that maintains possession of movement and that remains entitled to perform. She, in effect, invents and endows herself with the paternal inheritance rites to which she would otherwise have had no claim as a "tragic octoroon."

Menken's wildly circuitous autobiographical yarns about her past sit alongside and in conversation with equally ambiguous and sometimes scabrous newspaper coverage about the actress, her social reputation, and her character between 1860 and 1868 and during her high-profile years as an international celebrity. Like Menken's own duplicitous accounts of her past, the press would, during these same years, circumvent blunt interrogations of the actress's identity politics, choosing instead to accept and frequently embellish her entertainingly tall tales. Occasionally though, newspaper representations of Menken would work in interesting and significant ways to blacken Menken. These press accounts are critical to take into consideration as they demonstrate the ways that blackness operated as a distilled, free-floating trope that could easily get mapped across unconventional bodies like Menken's. By examining these instances in which the press racially coded Menken, my point here is to emphasize the way that we might dislodge reading her "blackness" as tied strictly to the corporeal. For in transatlantic popular culture, racial tropes were often diffuse and layered signifiers. The metaphorical utility of blackness, for instance, erupts in early visual imaging of the actress. The 1860 *New York Illustrated News* article includes an engraving of Menken which was "notably unflattering, the artist having tossed her wildly curling hair and widened her nose so that she appeared disheveled and coarse." The "heaviness of her features" signifies on "Menken's identity as a notorious woman, picking up on fictional portrayals of fallen women as large and swarthy" (Sentilles, *Performing Menken*, 118).

Menken's "swarthiness" in this portrait, her dark eyes, hair, and broadened nose, calls to mind the triadic relationship between the role of the actress, the "fallen woman," and women of color in nineteenth-century culture. By no means exclusively interchangeable, each category nevertheless depends on conflated perceptions of race, gender, and class that were tightly woven together by popular notions of sexual deviance. That is, both the actress and the woman of color were united by their perceived congruence with sexual availability and promiscuity. A "swarthy" Menken in this portrait provides an early example of how the press straddled her iconography across multiple ambiguous categories of salaciousness and marginality. Even as the accompanying *Illustrated News* story produced what would become a familiar narrative of Menken's presumably working-class white background, her class deviance provided a gateway for visually imagining her darkened roots.[45]

Having first entered into broader public notoriety as a result of a bigamy scandal with pugilist John C. Heenan in early 1860, Menken, from this point on, diligently responded to press images of her which lampooned and questioned her stage work on the grounds of gender propriety and morality. Critics, for instance, greeted her early work on the New York stage by trumpeting her "talent" for "captivation, marriage, and divorce."[46] In the final years of her life, Menken had experienced the kind of publicity that placed her iconic character explicitly in conversation with overt racial and gender caricature. Particularly during the magnificent denouement to her career in Paris in 1867, Menken brushed up against racial scandal and notoriety in the city of light. Following one of her performances, the actress became acquainted with Alexandre Dumas pere, an inspiration for Menken's literary aspirations. Although never officially confirmed, the two were believed to have had a brief intimate relationship, a rumor fueled largely by the circulation of cartes-de-visite photographs of the pair straddled and strewn across one another. One of the more famous of these images features a content-looking Menken nestled on the lap of a relaxed Dumas, leisurely resting her head on his chest. The international outrage and repulsion stemming from Menken's putative relationship with a man both "mulatto" and several decades her senior was palpable as Parisian papers mocked the union and stateside critics registered public dismay and disgust.[47] The Dumas affair catapulted Menken into uncharted territory with regard to racial politics. By placing her squarely at the center of racial miscegenation controversies, it forced the press to reckon with her duplicitous status as a white-looking woman who repeatedly returned to "dark" corners of the transatlantic social and cultural universe. In addition, the scandal created a space in Paris where Menken's iconography might ferment in the racial imaginary. This is especially evident in a notorious incident in Paris during one of Menken's final runs in *Mazeppa* in 1867.

Briefly bed-ridden with a stage injury, the actress sat out a series of stage performances that would prompt an odd yet telling publicity stunt. Seemingly seizing on the opportunity to capitalize on Menken's lighting-rod European

8. Adah Isaacs Menken and Alexandre Dumas. Harvard Theatre Collection, Houghton Library, Harvard University.

fame that year, the managers of rival Paris theatres sought to generate public interest and excitement around the *Mazeppa* production by threatening to replace Menken with "Sarah l'Africaine, the dusky Hippodrome ecuyere." With press descriptions stylized to conjure up images of Sarah Bartmann, the "Venus Hottentot" of southern Africa who had, some thirty years previously, been put on display in Paris as a result of her "deviant" genitalia, Menken's imaginary "rival" was meant to shadow her in the most grotesquely racialized terms. Bernard Falk recounts that "Paris enjoyed the fictitious exchange of correspondence" between the two theatre managers and "the idea of comparing the lovely American with a primitive negress from tropical South Africa [which] appealed to their sense of comedy." As would become the case in the biographies written about her, Parisian newspapers would utilize the body of Menken as an instrument of white, patriarchal power and order. For, presumably, setting up the public distinction between the African "savage" female and even the most bohemian of white(ned) women was tantamount to midcentury colonialist impulses of Europe and the Americas.[48] At the same time, the incident works once again to illuminate the ways that Menken and "l'Africaine" were forever conjoined in transatlantic fantasies of race and gender and critically reveals the ways in which, "when the display of the black woman became indecorous, the decorative, less overtly sexual, white-appearing woman stepped in to fill the former's place. Where the sheer 'fact of blackness' . . . produced an aura of *extra*ordinary licentiousness, the face of whiteness became a purely ordinary occurrence. In short, a white-appearing body was inherently and mystically less vulgar than a black-appearing body" (Brody, *Impossible Purities*, 44). Menken's "mystic" whiteness here is fueled by "the most primitive negress" and fills the void created by the erasure of "Sarah" from cultural memory. Conversely, her blackness was itself phantasmagoric, materializing and vanishing as called for by the press and by herself as she played with the boundaries of social and cultural identifications.

Increasingly in the last year of her life, Menken's iconography emerged at the site of charged cultural imagery bound up with race and particularly entangled with mythical representations of women of color. These juxtapositions highlight the moments at which the contemporary public of her time considered Menken as a sort of racial metonym positioned conveniently and contiguously in relation to othered bodies.[49] Dualities remain, in fact, constant in the iconic images of Menken which the press and the actress equally took part in creating. Perpetually her image evolved as a conjoined subject, attached at the hip, as it were, to the marginalia—the Indian maidens, twinned mothers, vanishing patriarchs, "mulatto" old men, and Hottentot Venuses—

the "circus freaks" haunting the public in the midcentury Atlantic world. "Blackened" by these dark and duplicitous associations just enough to tantalize the public rather than to set a racially divided world against her, Menken nevertheless continues to be read as a woman without a history, a figure without an identifiable cultural past.

If Menken was indeed "blackened" equally by her own machinations and those of the press, then surely her representational complexity demands a critical methodology that considers the politics of her racialization, how her body was scripted and how she allowed for her body to rewrite that script in certain contexts. In this regard, it is, I argue, imperative to consider how Menken's metaphorical racialization compares to that of antebellum black women who were violently constructed in relation to their bodies of work. Paired differently and with other kinds of women, Menken and her performances might perhaps yield alternative ways of perceiving of her body. With this in mind, I wish to offer an alternative examination of Menken. Juxtaposed with the extraordinary activist and visionary Sojourner Truth, a "black(ened)" Menken may in fact have complicated narrow, one-dimensional representations of the female body. Reading Menken in concert with Truth's overtly black feminist performance thus allows for a way to understand the broad and heterogeneous continuum of insurgent social and cultural performances bravely deployed by very different women in the antebellum era. More still, exposing Menken and Truth's overlapping methods of corporeal performance forces us to acknowledge the intersections of theatrical performance and what were perhaps spontaneous and boldly improvised scenes of performance in the culture of abolition. Thus, below and in an effort to rehistoricize Menken, I consider how both Menken and Truth offer ways of "doing their bodies" that open up fields of knowledge about race, gender, and identity in nineteenth-century culture.

### Stripped and (Re)Covered: The Truth about Menken

I feel that if I have to answer for the deeds done in my body just as much as a man, I have a right to have just as much as a man.
—Sojourner Truth

An equivocal, shape-shifting opportunist, Adah Isaacs Menken seems anything but "Truthful" in the life that she led. Her ambiguities force us to consider the social and political strategies of nineteenth-century individuals who are figuratively awash with racial codes and imaging but putatively estranged from the conventional terms of political resistance. Once arrested on the suspicion that she was a Confederate spy, Menken professed a fondness for her portraits of "Jeff Davis, Gen. Van Dorn, and Gen. Bragg," and at various times claimed to have had a "faithful" black slave and a domestic servant to whom she was deeply attached. Although, as her career evolved, Menken's iconography gradually and subtly blackened in popular culture, she performed a brand of social and cultural "whiteness" that was both brash and capricious as her celebrity grew. For every uncorroborated anecdote that would have her claiming to be "an ultra Southerner" who "cannot fraterniz[e] with the negro," there is an alternate image of Menken pledging allegiance to the Union, or, in one case, even privately confessing to Dumas that she was "a quadroon."[50] Race was a site of extreme equivocation for the actress, but in the public imaginary of the 1860s, Menken's social and political formations pushed her far away from political and ideological "blackness." She expressed no public identifications with "sisters in bondage," nor was she ever subject to the Northern juridical backlash that black antebellum New Yorkers had faced in the decades leading up to the war. She was anything but an antebellum black feminist icon, and thus coupling her with a figure like Sojourner Truth would, on the surface, only seem to perpetuate the myths and political fantasies imposed onto her legend in the contemporary era.

Yet in spite of her ambivalent relationship to race, Menken is in fact a critical figure to read alongside a woman like Truth. An alternative context for examining Menken's self-representational practices enables us, for instance, to draw parallels between the cultural work of (white) women in theatre and the urgent and innovative performance strategies of black women living within slavery's specter. In this regard, we can read Menken's range of corporeal performances as sharing the kinds of aesthetic complexities rooted in black female performance work under duress in the antebellum era. Juxtaposing Menken with Truth thus demonstrates the applicability of black feminist performance practices in multiple antebellum cultural contexts. Menken's onstage acts translate and transform midcentury theatrical genres, mixing and matching them in order to create new and unpredictable ways of representing race, gender, and the body in public cultural space. Although often unrecognized, her identity performances are, however, also indebted to a tradition of African American double-vocality and particularly black feminist multi-vocality produced as a means to (re)covering one's own flesh. Just as Menken seemingly depended on the abilities of her athletic and racially indeterminate body to belie the detection of audiences and acquaintances alike, so too did African American female cultural producers come to embrace complex ways to perform the body at critical moments when they were seemingly stripped of their rights to claim it as their own. Tracing the ways that Menken's public acts were *akin* to that of the activist Truth's thus opens up an understanding of black women's use of theatrical and performative models as methods of antebellum social and political disruption.

When the landmark abolitionist and feminist activist Sojourner Truth claimed equality by virtue of the "deeds done" in her body, she articulated a means to rescuing that very body from nineteenth-century proscriptions of racial and gender abjection by locating agency precisely within her flesh. Like Menken, Truth's image has weathered a mangling for over a century in some of her most prominent biographical narratives. She too has served as the fodder for mythical legends of corporeal spectacle in cultural history and has been canonized as a kind of primitivist vision of feminist piety. History has immortalized Truth as an illiterate, "Amazon" lecturer whose "witnessing" of slavery before all-white audiences depended on a deployment of the "violated" slave woman's body, reconfigured as a site of "physical endurance."[51] As is the case with Menken, history perceives of Truth's body as speaking just as loud—if not louder—than her words. Yet the efforts of contemporary feminist theorists to reappropriate Truth's body from these sorts of fetishistic agendas clears a space for considering the transformative power of "bodily deeds."

Truth's lifelong illiteracy and a scarcity of self-authored documents leaves a void in critical work on her life and activism. As historian Nell Painter speculates, Truth's "biographical problem becomes a larger question of how to deal with people who are in History but who have not left the kinds of sources to which historians and biographers ordinarily turn."[52] Like the majority of Menken biographies, which simultaneously document and reinvent the legend of the "free-loving" actress, the myths and false reports regarding Truth are clearly "all the more valuable as a reflection of Truth's mid-nineteenth-century persona."[53] The representation of the socially "deviant" woman's constructed persona in both these cases reinforces the ways in which racially marked female bodies occupy a vexed and contested terrain in scholarly (and not so scholarly) discourse. In turn, the conspicuous voids in discursive material on Truth and Menken have contributed to this intense privileging of their bodies as "authentic" texts of identity. The question becomes, then, what kinds of critical methodologies might we use to interrogate the subjectivity of historical figures such as Truth and Menken, figures who have been largely denied the right to fully claim discursive property as well as the patriarchal fantasy of "writing themselves into being." Does the scene of performance offer itself as an avenue for these women of the flesh to instead *act* themselves into being, to act themselves into history?[54]

These questions continue to circulate in current critical debates which perpetuate the reduction of Sojourner Truth into "authentic," corporeal knowledge, a source of labor for some other agenda. As black feminist critic Deborah McDowell cogently observes, Truth is too often employed as a sign to "rematerialize" poststructuralist, epistemological theory, particularly in the work of contemporary white feminist scholars where she is frequently "summoned from the seemingly safe and comfortable distance of a historical past" and transformed into a material and iconographic bridge to "experiential" politics. McDowell's points here extend the work of, among others, Valerie Smith, Margaret Homans, and Patricia Williams. Rather than "either reducing the black woman's body to sheer ground or matter or, to the contrary, using that body to validate disembodiment," these critics maintain the integrity of the black female body as a site of intellectual knowledge, philosophical vision, and aesthetic worth.[55]

Within this critical framework, I suggest that we read Truth and Menken as pioneers of eccentric black(ened) women's performance in the nineteenth century. With their distinct methods of "off-centeredness," each woman harnessed what Carla Peterson marvelously refers to as black women's eccentricity, a "freedom of movement stemming from the lack of central control." Indeed, each woman used different forms of "oddness" to protect, empower, and mobilize herself at unlikely moments.[56] Each created parallel and profane methods to convolute the categories to which each was relegated. And in this way, it is possible to locate the Truth about Menken. Truth restrategized the public spectacle of her body through performance politics, transforming her corporeality into a contested terrain of social and cultural knowledge. As Peterson demonstrates, "Truth was alternatively and overdeterminedly constructed as either invisible or visible, constituting either lack or surplus." But, as I will argue, a reconsideration of Truth's "surplus" body in performance might allow us to (re)cover revisionist female subjectivities that we might finally apply to reexamining Menken.[57]

Faced without the protection of a sturdy box in which to hide or the wide and diverting artifice of a moving picture show in which to roam, Truth found herself situated perilously in the public eye in the fall of 1858. In one of the more indelible and oft-recounted scenes in antislavery social memory, Truth stood before a "promiscuous" assembly, that is, an assembly of men and women who were putatively flummoxed and fearful spectators in rural Indiana. Having completed her antislavery remarks, she was greeted with an insolent proposition. As reported by William Hayward in *The Liberator*, a man identified as Dr. Strain "demanded that Sojourner submit her breast to the inspection of some of the ladies present" so that the question of "her sex" might be "removed by their testimony." Several distinct agendas were hanging in the balance of this brutal and awkward scene. In an openly abolitionist stance, Hayward had pegged Strain a "mouthpiece of the slave Democracy" who was intent on framing Truth as "a mercenary hireling of the Republican party." Under this auspice, Strain had proclaimed that it was in the speaker's best interest to bare her breast and clear the air of the suspicion that she was a man. And thus, while the doctor openly attempted to shame Truth of her credibility, dubbing her "an impostor," *The Liberator* aimed to expose the specific adversarial politics swirling about the room.[58]

In spite of the implicit scuffle between the antislavery journalist and the proslavery doctor, it is Truth who rises victorious above the fray in one of the most extraordinary public acts of black women's corporeal dissent and resistant performance recorded in antebellum history. As Hayward recounts, after Strain made his demand,

> Confusion and uproar ensued, which was soon suppressed by Sojourner, who immediately rising, asked them why they suspected her to be a man. The Democracy answered, "Your voice is not the voice of a woman, it is the voice of a man, and we believe you are a man.". . . Sojourner told them that her breasts had suckled many a white babe, to the exclusion of her own offspring and she quietly asked them, as she disrobed her bosom, if they, too, wished to suck! She told them that she would show her breast to the whole congregation; that it was not her shame that she uncovered her breast before them, but their shame.[59]

Perceived "as unruly and excessive" Truth confronts an audience intent on stripping her of her surplus worth. Yet this very "excess of body and speech" creates subterfuge at the site of subjection. In this passage, wherein Truth remains potentially buried in the discourse of dueling spectators, her use of the corporeal as a narrative strategy amounts to performative mutiny. Interpolating another Truth into this scene, she revalues her exploited flesh and instills it with an alternate textual meaning. Coerced into disrobing, Truth enables her breasts to articulate the history of a submerged slave past. These "deeds done in [her] body" mark her violation as a slave woman and potentially (re)cover her flesh as excessive and perhaps unreadable to a "shamed" congregation forced to acknowledge their spectatorial and social complicity in her abjection. For the Northern audience to read Truth's figure as she deploys it requires that they affirm the unseen/unscene atrocities of slavery that her body harbors and that they face their own implicit role in that scene.

Truth's demand to have her audience "see" her body according to her own narrative framing establishes a way to read for the opacity, or for what Elin Diamond might call the "non-truth," of the scene.[60]

With this unveiling of Truth before her audience, there appears to be more than one black female figure meeting the gaze of Dr. Strain here. The moment of initial supposed transparency which enables Truth's male spectators to seemingly view the dominant script of the mammy figure whose breasts are made available for "suckl[ing]" transforms into a point of visual excess and occlusion, a suggestion of the extraneous corporeal (sub)texts which the spectator cannot, in fact, see at all. By reminding her audience of her own absent offspring whom she is denied the right to nurse, Truth splinters the security of the viewer's intimacy with her body. The hidden narrative of black "motherhood" rather than "mammyhood" operates as a looming disruption that Truth invokes, a specter of contradistinction to the (un)veiled black body of deception who speaks not like a woman. This voice alone calls attention to Diamond's extended refiguration of feminist mimesis-mimicry as a destabilizing "alienation-effect," a point "in which the production of objects, shadows, and voices is excessive to the truth/illusion structure of mimesis, spilling into mimicry, multiple 'fake off-spring.' "[61] A kind of "excessive" representation which overturns the subjectivity of the viewer, Truth's appearance recycles the role of the exploited, stripping slave and then rejects that role by offering "shamed" spectators a body which is a text of multiple social and historical inscriptions which double and cover over each other. From the darkness of the void which she creates, surplus Truths are put into play.

It would seem that a moment encapsulating Adah Isaacs Menken disrobing could have little in common with the complex distillation of power at work in the moment of Sojourner Truth's exposure. Obviously separated from Truth by her class and by a public construction of whiteness which kept the overt hardships of American racism at bay, Menken engaged with corporeal representation from the standpoint of relative privilege. Yet, like Truth, and in the context of nineteenth-century racial and gender politics, she discovered a way to redress her body eccentrically. With gumption and material resources at her disposal, she put her restive body to use as a central tool in self-making and as a canvas of narrative authority which, similar to Truth's efforts, went against the grain of self-abnegation. Such is the case in an illuminating anecdote reproduced by Menken biographer Allen Lesser. Shrewdly wrapping her body in the mosaic of mythography, the Menken of this tale stages a critical striptease that brings to fore the strategic elements of her performative acts. Upon meeting with her acquaintance, the French journalist

Adrien Marx, Menken was said to have "revealed" herself to him during an interview which followed one of her sold-out performances. As Lesser describes:

> The Menken nonchalantly stripped to her form-fitting tights and then put on her costume for the next act in full sight of her visitor . . . he was certain that she had stood completely nude before him. "She changed costume," he recalled, "and let me see, without modesty and without embarrassment, the marvelous beauty of her body." . . . In answer to a question about her childhood and youth, about which everyone was curious, she launched into a fantastic narrative compounded of every adventure story she had ever read. Indians had captured her in her youth, she said, bending down so that he could feel "the depth of the scar left on her head" by a tomahawk flung at her when she escaped. She had also fought for the south disguised as a soldier, she added, pulling her skirt up above her thigh to show him "the trace of the balls she had received in war."[62]

Stripping of her own accord, Menken encounters Marx in a universe entirely removed from the coerced moment of uncovering Truth in Indiana. Exultant in her fame and wealth, comfortably in conversation with the fabulist historicity of her body, Menken exploits the legendary elements of her iconic persona. Branded "naked" by the press and the public, she puts on an exhibitionist show for her one-man audience that would be neither appealing nor accessible to a black female evangelical abolitionist and suffragist like Truth. Yet what resonates as similar in both scenes is the resolute opacity of the ostensibly exposed female body, putatively exposed to meet the lubricious demands of the male spectator and yet confoundingly and performatively surplus at the very moment of exposure.

The Menken of Marx's passage is a dauntless creature who showcases the spectacle of her "completely nude" body standing "nonchalantly" before Marx's ogling gaze. Marx marvels over Menken's unchecked boldness and apparent candor at allowing him to sneak a peak, "without modesty, and without embarrassment." In this presumed moment of intimacy and bonding, Marx presses onward with his interview, querying the actress in regard to her childhood. The disingenuous responses that Menken offers, the largely discounted captivity narrative as well as the equally fictitious cross-dressing war tale, are corroborated through the marks and scars inscribed as text onto her body. The initial scene of disrobing transforms into a moment of (re)covering. At this very moment in the anecdote we are made to bear witness to the way in which Menken uses her body, not as evidence of some

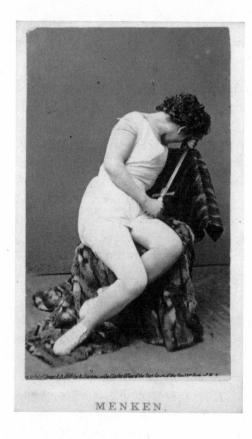

MENKEN.

9. Menken (un)covered.
Harvard Theatre
Collection,
Houghton Library,
Harvard University.

"incontrovertible truth" but as an instrument of ontological deception, and central to the performance of Menken's passing her body before a rapt and naive spectator. Like Truth, she ruptures and re-covers her body from the gaze of a rabid spectator. Yet unlike Truth she shrouds that body in the historical fictions of her making.

Both Menken and Truth transformed their naked bodies, the former into an opaque terrain of mythmaking, the latter into the site of historical density and value. Menken's bodily deeds are privileged transmutations of Truth's efforts to survive in a terror-filled, white supremacist and patriarchal world. Taken together the acts of these two women offer glimpses of the disparate scope and range of female corporeal performances in antebellum culture, and they each remind us of the renegade ways that racially marked women used their bodies in dissent of the social, political, and juridical categories assigned to them. Menken imported Truth's performance of the surplus body in order to remain mobile and elusive. Mastering the art of "the pass," she made her identity the source of elaborate and ever-changing social transactions, repeatedly dislodging it from the clutches of the ontological. Her cultural moves, as Herman Gray might call them, underscore the way that passing "is not so much a willful deception or duplicity as it is an attempt to move from the margin to the center of American identity."[63]

Menken "passed" her body, as it were, from margin to center and through multiple identity categories. Like a seasoned pro, she sat at the helm of what Amy Robinson has referred to as "the apparatus of the pass," a kind of "triangular theatre." Comprising competing figures—a passer, a (hegemonic) dupe, and a "literate member" of the passer's "in-group" community—the triangular theatre of the pass charts the transmigration of a floating subject from one group to another. The pass, Robinson insists, can only be successful when it is witnessed by the literate in-group member. Although Robinson has publicly complicated her own points on this subject, I want to hold on to the fundamental principles of her theories here—not to impose an essentialist reading onto Menken but to call attention to Menken's multivocality as a subject and the complexity of her identity transactions in flux.[64] As readers of Menken's as well as Truth's biographical and performative narratives, we can assume the role of the "in-group" member with a particular kind of literacy. We can imagine ourselves entering into the intimate dressing room scene with Menken and Marx (and Lesser for that matter). But acquiescing to a different kind of "truth," we might recognize that we can only see the magnificent "pass" and the constructedness of Menken's body and multiple, mythical identity performances *in play*. Such analysis might be especially useful in rereading Menken. If we assume that Menken operates in her biographical canon as what Jennifer Brody would call a "mulattaroon" figure, an "unreal, impossible ideal whose corrupted and corrupting constitution inevitably causes conflicts in narratives that attempt to promote purity," then the exigencies for this sort of critical methodology are all the more apparent.[65] Interrogating the negotiation and the site of the pass in the context of this mulattaroon actress's many varied performances forces us to read through and across not one but potentially two hegemonic dupes—that is, those in the narratives of nineteenth-century public, racialized women and the biographers who manufacture their narratives. Entering into the theatre of Menken, we might pay close attention to the ways that she reanimates the innovations of Truth's performances. Through her highly stylized, "semi-nude" acts, Menken stages a veiled redeployment of her own controversial corpus. In this sense, then, her work manifests the currency as well as the legacies and transmogrifications of black(ened) women's performances, and, most importantly, it creates (dis)order at the site of performing her own bodily deeds.

## Shape and Substance: Performing "Nude" Menken

A flummoxed Mark Twain wrote one of the more famous reviews of a Menken performance. Heaping on his signature wit, Twain gave an account of a night at the theatre in which he waxed utterly mystified at the sight before him. A showy piece every bit as turgid and hyperbolic as the theatre production it describes, Twain's review fixates on what was allegedly a ball of confusion before him. He wrote of how Menken "works her arms, and her legs, and her whole body like a dancing-jack: her every movement is as quick as thought; in a word, without any apparent reason for it, she carries on like a lunatic from the beginning of the act to the end of it." She is, he would later conclude, a "shape actress" who apparently "didn't have any histrionic ability or deserve any more consideration than a good circus rider!"[66] Throughout her career Menken generated the impassioned reactions of fellow actors, critics, and theatre audiences across two continents who wrestled with the conundrum that Twain voiced: was she an actress or merely a sensation act? An earnest and inspired artist or a hack talent and charlatan? Did she show innovation in her craft or merely bend the rules of a rapidly shifting antebellum theatre world so as to accommodate her paltry gifts as a performer?

In the years following her death, the debates regarding her aesthetic merits in theatre lingered, along with the popular lore that she was, in short, a dreadful actress. Despite early reviews that hail the then "Mrs. Heenan" as "an actress of versatility," many of her earliest biographers cleave to patronizing, if sometimes inadvertent, disdain for her work as a thespian. Several in fact appear to relish retelling an infamous anecdote involving Menken and the Shakespearean actor James Murdoch. After allegedly weathering a haphazard production of *Macbeth* with the actress, a supercilious Murdoch reportedly offered Menken some prescient and parting advice. "Search out," he suggested, "some 'sensational spectacle' in which your fine figure and pretty face will show."[67] Slithering into her "pink fleshlings" each night, the Menken of sensational New York theatre culture, the rough-and-tumble Comstock Lode out west, and high-flying bohemian Europe would seem to have taken the veteran actor's edict to heart. A performer of reputed little substance, Menken the abject body spectacle shapes up to be, at first glance, the godmother of those nineteenth-century burlesque performers "who reveled in the display of the female body" and who would seize the spotlight on the heels of Menken's swift ascent and early demise.[68]

Always lauded for her ability to strike a pose, Menken, to some critics, was most adept at revealing, uncovering, and exhibiting her remarkably athletic and voluptuous body in grand equestrian productions such as *Mazeppa*, shows that were believed to have been especially designed to call attention to her frame. As a result, that famously curvaceous and, for a time, healthy body threatened to dwarf any potentially shrewd, cerebral, or lyrical choices that Menken may have made as a performer. If she was not roundly condemned in parts of New York and London for what appeared to be a lubricious road show, many critics maintained that her performances lacked serious dramatic depth. Her acting, one English critic scoffs, "consists principally of attitudes. She poses better than she speaks." To some, she was "the very essence of carnality; her whole life was rooted and grown in fleshliness." Others lamented of her posthumously that, had she been "less weighed upon by the flesh, [she] might have been what female obituary notices call 'an ornament to her sex.'"[69] But to these critics and others, she was too much of the body onstage; she was, to them, no actor, "she merely showed herself . . . she revealed herself to be what she was: a woman" (Allen, *Horrible Prettiness*, 125–26). No journalist espoused this viewpoint with more vituperation than onetime Menken acquaintance William Winter. In a tendentious review called by some "the worst" that Menken ever received, Winter stridently attacked Menken's *Mazeppa* as it made its long-awaited debut on Broadway. Writing of her 1866 performance in that production, he proclaimed, "[She] has not the faintest idea of what acting is. She moves about the stage with no motive, and therefore, in a kind of accidental manner; assumes attitudes that are sometimes fine, and sometimes ridiculous; speaks in a thin, weak voice and with bad elocution. . . . in short invites critical attention, not to her emotional capabilities, her intellectual gifts, or her culture as an artist, but solely to her physical proportions."[70] Divested of her vocal power, the actress in this review is made to flail in her own flesh. Lacking dramaturgical vision, control, and intent, Menken's command of her craft eludes her in Winter's review; her meager skills as a thespian presumably force her to depend on nothing more than the weight of her body.[71]

Her body was, however, quite an asset to Menken in her career-long engagement with performing opacity. Particularly in her performances of *Mazeppa*, she made great use of it as a critical device that called attention to mid-nineteenth-century spectacular theatre's representational inversions and complexities. First adapted for the stage in 1830 by English playwright Henry Milner, the two-act play dramatizes Byron's epic poem involving the servant-turned-royal-Tartar-heir Cassimer, who finds forbidden, interclass and interethnic love with the Polish Castellan's daughter Olinska. Disguised in Polish armor, Cassimer infiltrates the royal court to do battle with Count Premislas for Olinska's love and subsequently faces the Castellan's punishment for wooing his daughter and for assailing his rival in a deadly duel. At the hands of his captors, the Poles, he endures humiliating subservience that culminates in an elongated act of public torture. Demanding that his servants "[t]ear the garb of our royal house from off" Cassimer's "miscreant limbs," the Castellan Laurinski strips Cassimer of his class insurgency and seeks to set him on a different course. Defrocked and bound, Cassimer is strapped to the back of a "wild" and fiery steed trained to carry him to his death in a brutal ride across the plains and "precipitous mountains" of Tartary. Rife with New Testament imagery, the turning point in *Mazeppa* occurs in the scene of Cassimer's lustrous transformation from stripped and bound boy into the swashbuckling prince Mazeppa who performs several miraculous feats in a swift blaze of glory. Cassimer's moribund suffering in the wilderness, a torture evocative of "the passion," only ceases once he makes the prodigal return to his homeland. Basking in his own mettle and fortitude, he survives the violent ride, is crowned King of Tartary, reunites with his father Abder Khan, executes a scheme to win back Olinska, and leads the Tartar combatants to victory over the Poles in a "grand and imposing tableau."[72]

With its majestic display of ethnic warfare, heroic rebellion, and chivalric redemption, *Mazeppa* would seem like an easy sell to critics and theatre-goers alike who were confronting the bloody chaos and social dislocation of civil war. Resurrected from its earlier 1830s run, the production ostensibly resembled a string of other theatrical diversions during "the turbulent war years," when "theater managers discovered that audiences would put aside news of war's horror for an evening if offered something novel and sensational to witness onstage" (Allen, *Horrible Prettiness*, 94). This production, however, was anything but a sobering panacea for the nation's ills. Both unusual and nearly scabrous in its strategy of putting a sparsely dressed female performer on a live horse made to ride up steep scaffolding, Menken's distaff version of the equestrian play appealed to a public clearly working through social and political desires and fears. Those fears and desires were given space to roam in the play's redeployment of Byron's "Romantic representations of the Orient as exotic locale." No doubt, the Eurocentric ideologies of the original *Mazeppa* epic are retained and deeply embedded in the structure of Menken's production, a melodrama which clearly depended on the "reduction and flattening" of Tartary into the kind of spectacle that predictably "re-structured" the mythical Orient into a topos for Western consciousness. Menken's *Mazeppa* would find success by annexing the mythical Orient for 1860s American culture and by speaking to its exigent cultural and political needs and desires.

Her version of the epic predictably emptied the Orient of its meaning for the solipsistic pleasures of its Western audiences, but it simultaneously raised conflicting questions concerning race, gender, and the body in transatlantic performance culture. A pastiche of extravaganza theatre, equestrian performance, spectacular melodrama, and panoramic exhibition, the play offered an oblique and unpredictable rumination on heterogeneous identity formation and social upheaval as the war haltingly drew a curtain on the antebellum era.[73]

Mocked and upbraided for its blend of bawdy sensationalism and highbrow-aspiring drama, Menken's production triumphed in its busy use of her figure as a theatrical centerpiece. Although she was not the first woman to assume the role of the Tartar prince, she was most certainly the first performer to pulsate, at the very heart of the production, as a transatlantic body of spectacularly real deception.[74] Menken's extratextual notoriety and ambiguity as a cultural celebrity functioned as a feature which conjoined *Mazeppa* in various ways to the evolving, midcentury extravaganza show and, more specifically, to playwright Dion Boucicault's influential innovations in "realist" spectacle. With its sprawling scenery and elaborate visual mechanics, Menken's and theatre entrepreneur E. T. Smith's *Mazeppa* aspired to Boucicault's paradoxical method of representing "realism" through a distinct reliance on the spectacle of artifice.[75] In *Mazeppa* this effort was enacted through and across the site of Menken's spectacularly "real" and curvaceous female body. If Menken increasingly used the press to market a certain kind of self-exposure, folding her tall and mendacious tales of youth into publicity for her stage work, then the show itself effectively mimicked and extended this opaque act of (un)covering. With Menken decked out in "flesh-colored" tights and strewn across a horse each night in the show, *Mazeppa* invited audience members to gaze on "a formidable array of theatrical illusions. But the two most sensational illusions of all were the voluptuous figure of Adah Isaacs Menken as Ivan Mazeppa, a sexual transformation requiring an extremely willing suspension of disbelief; and more sensational still, the nakedness of the star" (Mankowitz, *Mazeppa*, 18–19). *Mazeppa* passed the spectacle of Menken's "nakedness" off as "authentic" despite the fact that the actress wore stockings to maintain the "illusion" of nudity. Like the burning steamboat set against a broad scrim in Boucicault's English *Octoroon*, like the scenes of subjugation wrestling within the frame of Box Brown's moving panorama of slavery, the spectacular image of Menken costumed as nude telescoped the mechanics of nineteenth-century spectacular theatre into one formidably ambiguous corporeal form. Paradoxically, spectacle resided in the (in)authenticity of Menken's disrobed figure on the stage. Shamelessly pandering to the contemporary public's desire to be deliciously and spectacularly deceived and left to wondering whether Menken "was or wasn't" nude, the show earned its proper place alongside other epic productions that valued the ability to lure the audience into a state of inviting (dis)belief.[76]

Menken's legendary bodysuit hedged the production ever closer to the realm of Victorian pornography. With its "loose folds of white linen" and "flesh-coloured tights" that traced her "lovely female form," her *Mazeppa* costume easily conjoined the spectacular theatre genre with contemporaneous pornographic codes of (un)dress, the latter of which transgressed and circumvented the modestly clothed female form of the period by "flaunting the ankles, calves, knees, thighs, crotch and upper torso."[77] These sorts of vestiary devices, according to Tracy Davis, encouraged a way of "seeing nudity" ("Spectacle," 323). In everything from ballet to burlesque, the Victorian simulacra for female nudity made elaborate use of clothing which kept "the referential body to the fore" (326). Pink tights and tightly bound white gauze and wrappings served their purpose by generating the notion of nakedness; as misleadingly elegant props, such garment devices led spectators to believe that they were, in fact, witnessing a nude—and importantly, a resplendently nude "white" female body like the kind marketed in pornographic postcards and publications.

Victorian pornography's use of white veils, however, only serves to highlight the slippery contiguity of prostitutes, actresses, and "blackened women," especially as the latter two figures were perpetually scripted in terms of their sexual availability in midcentury transatlantic culture.[78] The sheer stark whiteness invoked in this kind of coding points to the odd contradiction of nineteenth-century popular culture wherein nudity was collectively idealized and "whitened" for public cultural consumption; yet black(ened) female flesh lurked in the penumbra of the gauze, made vulnerable to sudden and aggressive exploitation and violation. The point here is not to suggest that the political and socioeconomic position of white women who supported themselves through the theatre is at all equivalent to that of free black women who, beginning with Maria Stewart in the 1830s, risked ridicule and sometimes bodily harm in order to publicly speak in support of abolitionism, temperance, and suffrage, among other causes. Rather, that both groups were perceived as inhabiting and revealing bodies that were vulnerable and open to varying degrees of public possession provides a significant and challenging context when reconsidering Menken's performances of Mazeppa. For just as the white actress was expected to display "what is cloaked (anatomically and experientially), supposedly revealing truths about womanhood . . . promulgating a mystery as deep and as artificial as the colonial photographer's penetration in the Oriental harem" (T. C. Davis, "The Actress," 121), so, too, was the black woman's body, according to Peterson, "always envisioned as public and exposed."[79] Menken's body sat at the crossroads of these cultural significations.

Despite its lurid codings, the public outcry over Menken's perceived nudity in *Mazeppa* was decidedly chaste and circumspect. While theatre critic H. B. Farnie's bilious review in *The Orchestra* bemoaned "this corruption from America" during the month of *Mazeppa*'s London debut, the campaign to repudiate such criticism and to legitimize Menken's performance in tights frequently relied on drawing analogies between the production and the world of sculpture. Menken led the charge on this front herself. In a widely published letter rebutting Farnie's heavy-handed criticism, the actress defended herself on the grounds that, having "long been a student of sculpture," her attitudes were "selected from the works of Canova" and "present a classicality which has been invariably recognized by the foremost of American critics."[80] Even Mark Twain observed that in her "thin tight white linen" garments, she "dressed like the Greek Slave." But unlike Hiram Powers's iconic symbol of naked morality, Menken and her postures, Twain asserts, were not quite "so modest." At the time of her performances, much attention was paid to debating the links between Powers's work and Menken's state of undress in *Mazeppa*. However, given the complicated ways in which her act depended on the cultural surrogacy of whitened female bodies substituted for black ones, Menken's stripped Mazeppa shares perhaps much more in common with the sensational imagery of John Bell's 1868 sculpture *The Octoroon*, a work completed (in perhaps a fantastic act of surrogation) in the year of Menken's death. If, in that work the "octoroon repines unresistingly in the almost ornamental chains of her bondage" and recalls the positioning of *The Greek Slave*, Bell's *Octoroon* also, like Menken's Mazeppa, panders to public fascination with white-looking female bodies which, when stripped and chained, are excessively eroticized for the public's pleasure, pathos, and pain.[81]

Like the Bell sculpture with its rendering of an unveiled body, Menken's *Mazeppa* hero/heroine rides a formidable continuum of double drag which ultimately complicates notions of racial and gender-marked, corporeal exposure. Her work insists on a form of counterintuitive viewership that paradoxically sensationalizes the way that the female figure is obscured. Just as the Bell statue and a subculture of antebellum slave auctions promoted public fascination with the eroticized subjugation of "white-looking" black bodies, Menken's Mazeppa enticed and seduced audiences through a demand to gaze on the spectacle of corporeal contradiction—a body costumed in "masculinity" and yet retaining some putatively inherent womanhood and a body which conveys "whiteness" but simultaneously professes the constructedness of "whiteness" itself. In spite of the nuances of this astounding scene, most Menken critics have focused their energies on reading the sexist regime of scopic vulnerability and victimization at the sight of her "shape show," overlooking the complexities of what she (un)veiled on the stage altogether. True, to crowds of heterosexual men who made up the overwhelming majority of her audiences in places like Virginia City, Nevada, Menken's stage wardrobe surely "excited masculine imagination," since her "'classic Dress' concealed none of the exotic delights to which they had looked forward" (Lesser, *Enchanting Rebel*, 135).[82] But focusing solely, as do some, on Menken's abjection and her "attenuation of self" as a result of her corporeal exposure in *Mazeppa* risks transforming her into a figure as lapidary and motionless as the stone statues with whom she found ideological company.[83]

For feminist theatre historians who have done much to point to Menken's career as an example of "the problem of the body," the state of undress in nineteenth-century theatre leaves few options for female performers. Faye Dudden observes, for instance, that "the actress has been equated with the whore so persistently that no amount of clean living and rectitude among actual performers has ever served to cancel the equation. Acting is linked to sexuality because it is an embodied art—in contrast to the relatively disembodied business of writing. . . . To act you must be present in the body, available to be seen." In short, Dudden reads the "crisis" of the (white) actress as a "problem" which forces the female performer to be "present in the body" and "taken as a sexual object against one's will." This corporeal crisis, she insists, unfolds into a "hall of mirrors" which "rob[s] women of any authentic sense of self." For all the historical complexity that Dudden's important study brings to our understanding of women and theatre, her points also provoke specific concerns which, to me, are threefold. Among the many troubling elements of this argument lies the implicit suggestion that "embodiment" and aesthetic expression are somehow diametrically opposed to, rather than deeply entangled with, one another.[84] Such claims also overlook the brutal sociopolitical and material challenges of women who, regardless of whether they wrote or acted, were afforded no choice in being "present" or absent in the body. For these women, the utility of performing and potentially transforming what may have been, in various cases, the only canvas they had—their own bodies—to create "art" cannot be underscored enough. For these women, performance exacerbates the moment of exposure and opens a

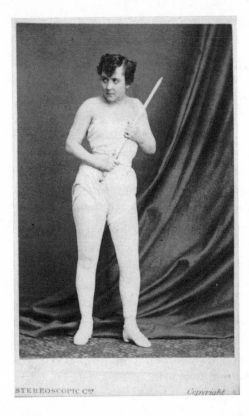

10. Menken "on guard."
Harvard Theatre
Collection,
Houghton Library,
Harvard University.

path to finding the "Truth," to disrupt and obfuscate scopic desire precisely through a calculated use of "embodied art."

"Black"(ened) already by the infamy of rumors and scandals, Menken "lifted up her skirt" to speak as a public woman in a different way in nineteenth-century theatre culture. Strapping on the tights and playing with the notion of nudity onstage, she wrestled with a means to making her body move a different way so that she might become its own agent. What for one critic might resonate as a corporeal quagmire may have, from a different perspective, provided Menken with a delicious strategy of theatrical illusion, an extension of the discursive "humbuggery" that she crafted with great care.[85] Dancing directly into the dreaded "hall of mirrors," she transformed her corpus into the crux of spectacular theatre and its attendant devices. Keenly aware of the mechanics of her act, one English critic dismissed the controversy of Menken's performances and sought to recenter her work where it rightfully belonged, in "the office of drama" where "concave mirrors are not only made but sold" and where "*nature*" is regularly "distorted."[86] Menken provided the distortion sought out by a public already ravenous for deception and made her body the source of fraud. Trafficking in inauthenticity and publicly exploiting it with a kind of light-hearted recalcitrance, she presented the altogether novel idea of turning a nude act into just another method of coverup. In the process, she mounted a robust and an elegant method of performing a heterogeneously coded female body in transatlantic theatre culture.

Reviews and epistolary accounts of Menken's *Mazeppa* performances suggest that during the peak of her career performing in cities like San Francisco and London, the actress was able to rely on a visible physical vigor and energy rooted in her body. She was apparently able to place that physical strength and athleticism in concert with a sharp, nimble, and an intelligent gift for expressing palpable emotion. Perhaps the most naked thing about Menken was her ability to create great drama on the stage, drama that had the power to transcend and transform the flesh. Leave it to a female journalist to offer one of the most trenchant and detailed accounts of Menken's formidable use of her body in performance. Writing in the spring of 1864, several months into Menken's phenomenally successful run on the west coast, Tessa Ardenne sought to convey the shock and awe that Menken's performance had conjured in her. Ardenne writes about her experience of watching Menken perform as a moment of redemption for both Menken and herself. In a witty travel-narrative epistolary article detailing her tour of San Francisco, she resolves to her readers that she is "about to make a confession. . . . I went—[awful pause]—to see THE MENKEN, And, another awful pause—I am *not* sorry for it." Presumably the salacious denouement to her narrative, the actress's act ends up restoring and conserving Menken's own as well as Ardenne's respectability via her austere and controlled performance.

> I came away with a sorrowful sort of respect, for which I know she would not thank me;—for she asks no one's sympathy. Physically she is a glorious creature, proud and defiant as a goddess. Her forte is in the almost superhuman power she has over her body. It obeys her. It is the servant of her will. It assumes every possible attitude at her bidding while her face, with its luminous eyes, tells the story of joy and sorrow, hope and fear, more plainly than the tongue of another can speak it. But visible to one who studies her face at all, are marks of a hard battle fought single-handed with the world, fought and won—much of it perhaps for that "daily bread" for which we pay.[87]

Ardenne frames her comments in the lace and frills of sensational pathos. Menken is the paradigmatic literary heroine of sentiment and sensation, valiantly struggling with the hard fought battle of this mortal coil and striving for her "daily bread."[88] But at its core, the article creates a kind of inverted bathos wherein the cliché-ridden elements of female tragedy are turned on their head at the site of Menken's sublime work as an actress exhibiting prodigious strength of the body. Ardenne's description conjures up the histrionic superlatives of "superhumanity," but Menken's "goddess"-like powers work in the service of her own body. Indeed, Ardenne's language waxes mildly sadomasochistic in its description of Menken's "power . . . over her body." This body which "obeys" and is "the servant of her will" is a seductively pliant creature which bends into "attitudes" with seeming fluid and elegant precision. Manifesting superior control over her countenance, Ardenne's Menken executes a valiant balancing act between the body and its emotive and cerebral center. And this kind of punctilious performance allowed Menken to narrate her flesh with great pulchritude and opacity in her *Mazeppa* performances.

### Prodigal Menken: Drag/Racing *Mazeppa*

Perhaps no one talked a better game about the iconoclastic blaze of glory that Menken's Mazeppa was destined to burn across the theatrical horizon than Menken herself. "I will create a new sensation. Depend on it. And thus my claim to the 'most versatile artiste' in the world," she declared in a shrewd, self-promoting letter to friend and playwright Augustin (Gus) Daly. It was a supreme act of braggadocio and hubris, even in an epistolary exchange between two friends. But for Menken in 1862, these words may have only confirmed what audiences and, to a lesser degree, critics had been expressing for over a year. Following her successful and highly publicized debut in the role of the valiant Tartar hero at Albany, New York's Green Street Theatre on June 6, 1861, Menken gradually transformed what could have been a hackneyed horse-act into a physically arduous tour de force. The *Mazeppa* performance cemented her reputation as a daring and skillful equestrian performer, and it aided her in garnering respect and accolades in some—if not all—corners of the fickle transatlantic theatre world. In particular, one of the premiere New York theatre publications, the *Spirit of the Times*, hailed Menken as "one of the few great actresses of the age." Thriving on this kind of a buzz, Menken toured the east coast, Midwest, and finally the South from June of 1861 until early July of 1863 and built a solid reputation as a breeches actress who could execute multiple roles of which Mazeppa was but one. By the time she and husband Robert Newell packed their bags and headed for San Francisco, she had tackled a full range of rugged (and often male) adventurer roles. Yet as the Byronic hero, she found her niche performance and her entrance to unprecedented heights of celebrity.[89]

The "new sensation" that Menken cultivated in *Mazeppa* fermented at the site of her hyperactive body. Stripped and flung atop an enormous and fast-moving animal and re-dressed in the sumptuous and brightly colored lineaments of *soi disant* exotic royalty, Menken as Cassimer led a mass entourage in insurgent warfare while romancing a fellow actress on the stage. Because of its frenetic mix of horseback daredevil tricks and the suggestion of female skin, her performance most often surfaces in critical discussions of equestrian spectacles, breeches roles, and early burlesque culture. On horseback, Menken created a Mazeppa that informed female equestrians for years and which was, even in costuming, intended to operate as a classic revival of the famous horseback scene as it had been established in the 1830s. Yet according to Mullenix, this *Mazeppa* was most influential in the way that it affected "the image of the breeches actress," shifting her iconography "from an innocuous boy, a feminine hero, or even a directly transgressive masculine woman to a silent sexualized object."[90] Cited as a forerunner to the fast-approaching late 1860s burlesque craze led by Lydia Thompson and others, Menken's *Mazeppa* revival generated a recognizable obstacle for the actress whose body bore "the burden of signification" (Allen, *Horrible Prettiness*, 81).[91]

In this role, Menken's body of signification erupted with meaning in such a way that it surpassed the limitations of what Robert Allen calls the "feminine spectacle" of her day. Her *Mazeppa* drew from multiple theatrical genres and on a spectacular scale grappled thematically with war, bondage, ethnic autonomy, and rebellion. That it most often gets folded into the genealogy of burlesque risks obscuring the play's generic heterogeneity. Moreover, to read Menken's *Mazeppa* solely within the framework of theatre history limits our understanding of a production whose imagery, themes, and characters were all entangled with Civil War social and cultural ideologies, and, more specifically, popular antebellum racial and gender representation.[92] In reconfiguring the "supposedly nude woman" of Victorian pornography as a metatextually transgender, transethnic, and transracial hero at the center of the adventure, this *Mazeppa* production both anticipated and exceeded burlesque's "monstrous" incongruities in unpredictable ways (Allen, *Horrible Prettiness*, 26). If burlesque would make "no attempt to bring all its parts together into a unified and ideologically monovocal whole" (Allen, *Horrible Prettiness*, 28), so too did *Mazeppa* and particularly Menken in the title role manifest the threat of chaotic racial "amalgamation" and class fragmentation bleeding at the root of the nation's internecine conflict.

In many ways, a bellwether play that forecast the carnage and upheaval that typified the 1860s, *Mazeppa*, as one San Francisco playbill advertised, sent its

"Messenger of Death" riding into a 'Splendid Tableau.' "[93] That it concluded with the prodigal return of a figure so marvelously diverse sent perhaps a different kind of ideological message to its audiences, however. With Menken's liminal performance of the title character at its helm, *Mazeppa* confronted and negotiated questions of race, gender, and nationhood through both its spectacular form and content. Yoking together the phantasmagoria of *The Black Crook* with the melodrama of *The Octoroon*, employing panoramic devices to add a historical sweep to its narrative, the production retained and recuperated multiple and familiar tropes and themes but also scrambled them to create something altogether new. With its many excesses coursing through Menken's performance, it was a production that was in fact deeply entangled with war and political rebellion and just as deeply and surprisingly at odds with the conventional theatre landscape of its time. Indeed, its reportedly panoramic set design is itself a synecdoche for the larger historical and political implications of the play. Riding through the scene of revolutionary return with "a blur of equine movement," Menken reportedly held tight to her steed "against a moving landscape drop . . . lighted by bursts of stage lightning" (Allen, *Horrible Prettiness*, 99). A vestige of imperialist spectacle, the play's panoramic scenery recalled the large-scale moving panorama exhibitions of the 1850s that underscored the perception of temporal and visual progress and fueled the myth of ever-expanding empire.[94] But figuratively Menken converted the raw energy and brutal power of that panoramic movement into the spectacle of her mobile body. Read in this way, panoramic movement provides Menken as well as *Mazeppa* with a Box Brown–like escape route out of the confines of melodrama as well as imperialist spectacle and into the grand and limitless possibilities commensurate with spectacular and extravaganza theatre. Set against the progressivist ideology of the panorama, Menken rode into a future where women slipped into and out of the parts of (Tartar) men to save other women and the world.

While many critics have suggested that Menken's *Mazeppa* did little to challenge the values and attitudes of its audience, her production utilized the tropes and machinations of conventional theatre in concert with the phantasmagoric body in a way that articulates and speaks back to the critical fears, questions, and concerns engulfing antebellum American culture. Audiences may have flocked to theatre during the war as a form of respite, but the popularity and success of *Mazeppa* across multiple regions of the country just as easily suggests that the public was willing to use the theatre as a space to engage with the tumultuous uncertainty and ambiguity of the war (Allen, *Horrible Prettiness*, 94–95).[95] Bringing together the tensions of slavery, bondage, and ethnic conflict into one production, *Mazeppa* signified on sectional-ist warfare politics and the culture that it spawned. Yet just as well, *Mazeppa* resonated with images of the immanence of the bound, the wounded, and the enslaved potential for uprising. What audiences encountered was perhaps more than politically timely "delicious danger" (Sentilles, *Performing Menken*, 114). Through Menken's eccentric performance, the play offered a radical response to theatre culture's attempts to police the transatlantic body.

Particularly on her 1863 arrival in California, a land of miners, migrants, and new industry, Menken's *Mazeppa* outsized the expectations of west coast audiences who had been primed for the actress's debut.[96] The sharp business acumen of theatre manager Tom Maguire, who struck an unprecedented deal to bring the "ascendant" Menken exclusively to perform at his plush new San Francisco Opera House venue, provided the impetus for her debut in the late summer and fall of 1863. The local press greeted the actress with intense anticipation and curiosity. But if early promotional pieces generated excite-ment for Menken by hyperbolically ticking off her list of alleged accomplish-ments as "a graceful dancer, excellent vocalist, rare linguist, and remarkably original poetess," the reviews following her west coast debut paid even more dutiful attention to the specifics of Menken's work as a thespian. Hailed within a month of her premiere by one *Golden Era* critic as the "bright particular star of . . . the New American School of Acting" and lauded by the *Daily Alta* as "quite an actress—calm, considerate, careful and judicious," Menken garnered overwhelming praise from local critics who celebrated her control of gesture and movement on stage.[97]

Surprisingly serious and attuned to character, Menken performed a kind of sincerity that was, on the one hand, consistent with melodramatic heroism of the period. Played straight, so to speak, and not for laughs, her Cassimer-turned-Mazeppa character was meant to convey a measured degree of forti-tude, earnestness, and righteousness. But as the rebellious moral center of the drama, she turned on its head the assumption that women on the stage should retain the conventional markers of "true womanhood" while "providing so-cial and moral stability in a rapidly changing world." Instead of performing "purity" and moral transparency in the female body, Menken delivered an adulterated body that was cloaked in the lineaments of artifice. Dressed as a man-servant, stripped into a simulacra of "nude" womanhood, and reclothed as a valiant, prodigal heir to the Tartar throne, she wrapped the "truth" of her lead character in a dizzying maelstrom of multiple identities (Allen, *Horrible Prettiness*, 84). Performed in the midst of an era in which sociopolitical and geographic boundaries were mutating, her *Mazeppa* blurred sociocultural

11. Menken as Mazeppa. Harvard Theatre Collection, Houghton Library, Harvard University.

divisions and dared audiences to consider the "pure" and heroic authenticity of an "impure" lead figure in the play. If burlesque later "delight[ed] in incongruity and miscegenation" (Allen, *Horrible Prettiness,* 147), then Menken anticipated that cultural craze by making incongruity and (theatrical) miscegenation manifest in *Mazeppa.* Although many have argued that the actress "blunted the force of her potential transgressiveness" by depending on "familiar and comforting melodramatic ideology" (Allen, *Horrible Prettiness,* 101), Menken, in fact, entered the sphere of melodramatic theatre only to mix and pollute its form and content. As Mazeppa, she was thus " 'resistant and excessive to the very discourses' " from which she emerged. Rising up out of the confines of melodrama, she offered a body of equivocation that utilized spectacular mechanisms in order to overturn and convert the structure of racial melodrama and that genre's dependence on Manichaean identity split.[98]

What has gone nearly unnoticed by critics of Menken's work is the crucial significance of her contiguity to that popular genre of theatre, as well as the ways that her own vertiginous performance choices created a powerful dissonance in 1860s dramatic representations of race and gender. From the Pacific coast to the hallowed halls of English theatre, *Mazeppa* played in a theatre climate heavily affected by racial paradigms, some of which Menken herself promoted. Even in London, midcentury audiences' perceptions of racial typologies were distinct and deeply entrenched. In handwritten and scrawled comments on one 1864 playbill of the London *Mazeppa* performance, for instance, a theatregoer describes a *Mazeppa* cast member as "niggerish."[99] Produced in the midst of minstrelsy and racial melodrama's popularity on both sides of the Atlantic, *Mazeppa* cannot and should not be separated from the ideological impact of those genres. Moreover, the very contiguity of Menken's *Mazeppa* with theatre entrepreneur Dion Boucicault's brash innovations in melodrama and spectacle remains a little discussed and yet a particularly significant point that helps to underscore the disruptive racial and gender dimensions of Menken's performances, as well as the counterintuitive elements of her stage work.

Having come close to working with one another to produce the London 1864 premiere of *Mazeppa*, Menken and the equally idiosyncratic and risk-taking Boucicault had shadowed one another in theatrical fame and notoriety for several years prior to that missed collaboration.[100] Boucicault's controversial New York City production of *The Octoroon* opened in December 1859, one month before the actress left Alexander Menken to resettle in New York. The plantation tear-jerker was even more closely associated with Menken's San Francisco stage appearances where, in the final weeks of her stint in that city, *The Octoroon* played to enthusiastic audiences with a cast of leads who had performed concurrently with Menken throughout her stay there. While overlapping work for actors and actresses in multiple productions was hardly uncommon, the fact that San Francisco celebrity players both worked with Menken and performed in *The Octoroon* suggests the extent to which audiences may have experienced Menken's productions in concert with Boucicault's brand of spectacular melodrama. The performer who made this connection perhaps most apparent was none other than Menken's costar in multiple San Francisco plays, favorite local actress Sophie Edwin. Edwin had balanced her principal roles alongside Menken in productions of *Mazeppa* (as Olinska) and in *Black Ey'd Susan* (as Susan) with that of a lead performance as Zoe in the spring 1864 production of *The Octoroon*. Her performance of the title character of the latter play came just weeks before her turn as the beleaguered sailor's wife in *Black Ey'd Susan*, again suggesting the lively, Boucicaultian context for Menken's *Mazeppa*.[101]

"Zoe-mania" may not have been as rampantly prevalent in San Francisco as in places like London, but *The Octoroon* still managed to spawn sharp and passionate cultural responses that reflect the degree to which west coast theatre culture was engaged with questions of race, gender, and slavery during Menken's appearances in San Francisco. *The Octoroon* of Menken's western sojourns seems to have particularly fueled the flames of racial romanticism and simultaneously called attention to the imminent fire in the hole as the war was, in 1864, reaching its bloody climax. As was the case in New York and later London, the San Francisco *Octoroon* piqued the public's interest in the subjugation of the enslaved. And like the pathos generated by the English production, the angst of slavery was articulated in a poem published in an 1864 issue of the *Golden Era*. Entitled "Zoe, The Octoroon" and dedicated, ironically, to Sophie Edwin, the poem echoes the sentiment of the original stateside version of the drama in its rendering of the enslaved as legible only in suffering. Where it diverges, however, is in its jeremiad-like forecast of an apocalypse on the horizon and its climactic vision of "a time of reckoning come/A dark and fearful hour/When like your minions ye shall quail/Before a higher power." This Zoe poem uses the occasion of racial melodrama to envision millennial upheaval and the kind of apocalyptic conflagration which punctuates the end of the revised English production. Appearing in the *Golden Era* alongside a lengthy rave review of Menken's turn as the sailor William in the nautical drama *Black Ey'd Susan*, "Zoe, The Octoroon" provides evidence of the ways in which San Francisco writers, literary readers, and critics were engaging specifically with questions of slavery and its aftermath.[102]

San Francisco's 1864 *Octoroon* run and the mixed media surrounding that production provides a fuller and a more complicated context for reading Menken, particularly in her performances of the Tartar Prince. Placed alongside one another, Boucicault's *Octoroon* and Menken's *Mazeppa* create an unlikely yet stirring tableau of racial and gender identity formations in flux at midcentury. If *The Octoroon*'s patiently suffering Zoe was made to die in the American production of the play, her tragically cleaved body hardening into blackened flesh while a blanched "white" soul ascends to heaven before sorrowful audiences, then one might also read Menken's high-powered *Mazeppa* performances as a surfeiting response to *The Octoroon*'s arbitrary and exacting economy of race, gender, and tragic mulattaroons. Having rejected the death of the racially phantasmagoric body in both her personal life and in her public work, Menken introduced a prodigal hero/heroine into the overlapping worlds of spectacular theatre and melodrama. Lavish and extravagant in corporeality, her Mazeppa ultimately restylized the transatlantic body by restoring and redeploying the superabundance of racial melodrama's pathos-producing figures who have been repeatedly sacrificed and e/raced. Out of the wreckage of racial melodrama, Menken's *Mazeppa* emerges.

Rather than producing clear and stable melodramatic characterizations in *Mazeppa*, Menken delivered a performance that was built on an endless series of contradictions and falsities. With care, she cultivated an extratextual persona that was swathed in misinformation and served up a production that depended on similar paradoxical dimensions of concealing at the very point of revealing. Despite her reputation for masquerade and mischief making offstage, her performance of the drama is often read as conserving and reinforcing the restrictive cross-dressing habits of Victorian theatre and scopophilic representations of actresses. Certainly, dressed in drag as the Tartar heir, Menken performed *Mazeppa* in a way that seemed, on the surface, to reinforce gender demarcations and the circumscription of the breeches actress performer. She may have been praised by the press for having convincingly assumed the role of "a warrior" who "dealt blows with more muscular strength," thereby challenging fixed gender categories on the stage, but as several feminist critics have noted, this kind of identity obfuscation was potentially undercut by the actress's varying states of dress and undress in the role. Forced to endure the humiliating turpitude of stripping before his foes, her warrior-like Cassimer was believed by many in attendance of the play to have nonetheless revealed a decidedly "naked" female form. In this way, critics have argued that her *Mazeppa* "tested the waters for a new kind of stage androgyny: a woman revealing her female sexuality through a male role." In nineteenth-century transatlantic theatre culture, gender cross-dressing for actresses often "highlight[ed] rather than disguis[ed] sexual difference" (T. C. Davis, "The Actress," 106–7). Within this world of paradoxical striptease wherein the female body is made bare through the spectacle of covering it, Menken biographer Kendall claimed with confidence that Menken "had the kind of figure which never looked so alluringly feminine as when clad in male attire."[103]

Yet this approach to reading Menken's *Mazeppa* performances as purely hampered by the limiting representations of female sexuality in Victorian theatre risks overlooking the ways that Menken's extratextual racial formations may have complicated her stage "exposure" and created mayhem at the site of melodrama. As Marjorie Garber points out in her study of transvestism, we reduce and delimit the complexity of the cross-dresser when we attempt to read only one dimension of that performer's identity politics. Readings of Menken in drag must attend to the intersectionality of her culturally and racially transitive persona.[104] Having promoted an ambiguous, transracial body in the press, Menken drags herself across the stage, as it were, through multiple layers of masquerade that should make us wary of reading what was exposed and what remained cloaked in her *Mazeppa* performances. As she embraced identity transgression and transmogrification throughout her career, it seems only fitting that she repeatedly inhabited a role that allowed her to perform ethnic marginalization. Sentilles has pointed out that her Tartar Prince capitalized on the increasing colonialist fascination with the Orient and its oppressed inhabitants. As became the case in multiple corners of her life's work, Menken used tropes of whiteness to temper her ethnic drag. Yet importantly, her use of "pink tights" to connote nudity suggests the inverted cultural vestibularity of "whiteness" as well. Her famous "flesh" which is made "nude" through costume covering might convey the fakery of "whiteness." We might read the display of the bodysuit as yet another form of racial drag at the very moment in which masculine drag appears to come undone. From this standpoint, Menken as the mulattaroon appropriates Victorian pornography's fetishization of "white" female corporeality, "unmask[s] the performative nature of whiteness," and "expos[es] the construction" of racial and not just gender (im)purities.[105]

Menken's racial drag is, however, only one in a series of moves that invigorates and intensifies the complexity of her spectacularly liminal performance in *Mazeppa*. Just as the delicate pink gauze of her nude costume signifies on representations of "whiteness," so too does the actress's colorful and splendiferous Tartar warrior costume work in surprising ways to reappropriate the uses of (male) drag. Draped in the bright and colorful silks of mythic Asiatic royalty, her rebel prince cuts a startling figure on the stage, resplendent in the threads of wealth and monarchical power restored. Matching her famously androgynous "Byronic curls" with a curvaceous frame decked in pantaloons and a head scarf, Menken's (clothed) Mazeppa recycles the vestiary tropes found in imperialist spectacle dramas such as William Dimond's *The Aethiop*. More still, her sumptuous garb reinforced the intersecting codes of gender and colonial identity by exposing the mechanics of (white) patriarchy on the antebellum stage. As a vanquished prince of "the Orient," Menken fulfilled the romantic racialism of the period that longed for spectacles of exotic adventure and ethnic insurgency that could be safely contained or distanced from immediate American contexts. At the same time, her performance destabilized the patriarchal hegemony of such roles by effectively mimicking, negotiating, and "experience[ing] 'male authority and territory and entitlement' " in ways that for her would eventually spill off the stage as well.[106] She both trafficked in imperial theatre tropes and, at the same time, intervened in the mythical normativity of these tropes by interpolating her alien(ating) and eccentric moves into the form.

Her Tartar prince drag thus reminds us that the tradition of male cross-dressing performance has "turned on the artifactuality of women's bodies" as well as the bodies of people of color. This is especially apparent in highly spectacular forms of nineteenth-century entertainment such as the circus where "feminine disguise was used to enhance the skill of the acrobat or the equestrian." In such spaces, the mythically normative white male body remains intact beneath the disposable female skin. Conversely, we might think of Menken as having inhabited the acrobatic role of Mazeppa and having disrupted the use of women's bodies as mere spectacular props.[107] She inverted the use of feminine disguise to enter and utilize the masculine form as a means to performative agency. Her princely costuming provides multiple sources of movement and opportunity for Menken as she transitions across the great racial and gender divides of nineteenth-century performance culture and overturns the patriarchal fantasies literally and figuratively embedded in the costume. From this standpoint, both racial and gender cross-dressing, manifested in the transgressive female's invocation of the phallus and ethnic insurgency, present a crucial critique of identity construction in nineteenth-century popular culture; for the artifice of both "manhood" and "white" supremacy are put into play and stripped of their arbitrary power.

A conduit of vigorous movement and strength, Menken's *Mazeppa* retools and reimagines the utility of masculinity to intervene in the Victorian sexual reification of the female body in theatre. This was most acutely apparent in the climactic scene of the horseback ride, a scene which was a significant extension of her drag act—even as it depended in the plot on the spectacle of her "nudity." In a stunt which she performed so frequently in the 1860s that many have speculated that the brutally demanding act may have led to her early demise, Menken rode horseback in the shadow of incessant publicity that marketed her as a vulnerable damsel in distress aboard a reckless beast. Each night, she manipulated and reinvigorated the horseback scene as the ultimate display of risk and vulnerability. A playbill from *Mazeppa*'s London run zealously promotes "the terrific scene of cataracts of water and tearful precipices, when the feelings of the audience are sympathising with Mazeppa, who is condemned to a dreadful death and hurrying on to destruction." Like similar advertisements in other cities, this poster tags on a rambling lyric derived from Byron and presumably adapted to exploit the spectacle of a female performer in the role of the tortured male servant Cassimer. "Wild was her look," the poem declares, "wild was her air/Back from her shoulders streamed from her hair." The "wildness" of Menken was, thus, somewhat legendary by the time she reached England. Save for the scopic titillation of the play's impending "nudity," no scene generated more rabid fascination and collective fear than that "dangerous horseback ride" as it was performed by a woman.[108]

What was to some nothing more than crazed and jejune spectacle with a sexual lexicon embedded in its very form was to others an opportunity to witness a (female) body holding the reins of a scene and questing for control.[109] In the highly anticipated ride, Menken weathered an obstacle course of scenery meant to evoke the deathtrap of the Tartar landscape. Particularly in San Francisco, where Maguire had reportedly rigged up an impressive mountain trail "winding up between jagged rocks, across a perilous bridge" and "above a roaring stream to vanish on heights unguessed," she faced down scenery nearly as rough and prodigious as the horse itself.[110] As one review described the scene, "when the animal starts off and gallops up the mountain, affrighted by the glare of fires and goaded . . . the interest is painful in its intensity, overpowering in the wild whirl of excitement it evokes." As the production for *Mazeppa* grew and flourished, Menken was reported to have played an increasingly central role in purchasing and training her horses for the ride.

Studied and strategic in her horseback effort, Menken transformed what could have been a scene of violent abjection and prurient delight for spectators into the pinnacle of her performance. West coast audiences were particularly keen on her fabulously daring spirit and stamina, and San Francisco critics were quick to produce encomiums celebrating her feats. "She vaults," the *Daily Alta* gushed, "on the back of the 'fiery and untamed steed' (represented by a full blooded California mustang) with all the daring and aplomb of a Sebastien or a Franconi." Menken, in this reviewer's eyes, carries "the horse by storm, and both the horse and rider made the aerial flight with due precision and effect."[111] Before reaching California, Menken took it on herself to circulate word of her remarkable ride, reiterating in a letter the words of one critic who claimed that "[n]othing daunts the intrepid and fearless girl." But once out West, she encountered a public who appreciated her equestrian skills and who were perhaps "more fascinated by Adah's horsemanship than by her nakedness."[112]

The stunning horseback demonstration marks the site of *Mazeppa*'s most powerful intervention in conventional theatre. It was where Menken set her transgender spectacle to revisionist ends and where her body was finally allowed to carry the production out of the shadow of Victorian pornographic spectacle and into the definitive realm of transformative performance. Mastering the ride allowed Menken to tap into a "masculine body aesthetics." The scene gave her the opportunity to vanquish her own "nude" body and to ride off into the sunset each night as a "masculine heterosexual woman" who "reject[ed] . . . the strictures of femininity." Her athleticism rescued the static and statuesque heroine from melodrama and imported and converted the sublime ecstasy of the horseback ride in Byron's poem into a site of specifically rugged transformation for the breeches actress.[113] More than the sum of a circus acrobat, pre-burlesque actress, or the tragic heroine in a melodrama, Menken's Mazeppa sutured together a body strong enough to endure occasional spills from the horse, yet appealingly soft and fleshy enough to kindle the desires and fascination of both sexes. This "duality of sex," as one critic of her time referred to it, profanely elasticized femininity and masculinity to create a new category of performance.[114]

Confusing the terms of desire, Menken consistently forced her audiences into states of categorical disarray and fluid and unpredictable points of identification. Profoundly bewildered by and sometimes pleasurably stupefied into their own states of realigned sexual and gender desire, some of her most passionate critics and fans wrangled with the turbidity of her sexual politics, as well as their own. San Francisco journalist Florence Fane, for instance, publicly berated "Perfidious Cassimer" for having duped her into capitulating to "his" spectacle of manhood. But while Fane lamented that her "brave . . . beautiful and suffering hero [was] *only* a woman," she recognized that some of her female companions "had the hardihood to declare that they admire—nay dote on Cassimer, knowing he was a woman!"[115] Menken herself brashly attested to the effect she had on women (who, by her accounts, were made to swoon in the aisles at the sight of her on horseback), but there is evidence that she was equally successful at disordering the terms of the hegemonic male gaze as well. While doting admirer Charles Warren Stoddard easily folded into fan-like submission and genuflected to Menken's shifting gender economy, confessing that in her he "saw . . . a boy," others confessed to an even more intense internalization of her act. One admirer recalled having seen Menken in a production of the breeches melodrama *Jack Sheppard* rather than *Mazeppa*. Yet the erotically charged and seemingly satisfying gender confusion erupting from this experience seems to recall that of Fane's and Stoddard's reactions to her Tartar prince performance in a remarkable instance of Menken's ability to both manifest and simultaneously incite liminal identity formations. Writing many years in retrospect of his Menken theatrical encounter, one fan delighted in describing how "in my childish dreams of romance, my flightiest nightmares of adventure, I was Jack Adah Sheppard Isaacs, a dare devil boy and siren girl combined in one ideal hero." More than simply disturbing the ground of heterosexual male desire and "confusing the distinctions on which desire depended" (Allen, *Horrible Prettiness*, 148), as did burlesque, the unique effect of Menken's work was that she was able to encourage in her audience intense pleasure at the site of identity confusion.[116]

The sociopolitical climate of Menken's Civil War world created fertile ground for her to derive an "epitome of both masculinity and femininity" in her *Mazeppa* character and for audiences to respond gradually to her coun- terintuitive performances with sometimes prurient and other times passion- ate interest and engagement. The war itself created a space where the concept of "duality" and all its attending allegorical abstractions might demand an iconic body in which to be housed. Uncertain of the Union's future, American audiences in particular gravitated to *Mazeppa*, a shadow of itself in the waning years of war, ravaged and resilient, undone and ambiguous, aged and yet inchoate. In her turn in the title role, Menken returned to the stage the political, class, and identity "duality" of racial melodrama but discovered a way to conserve rather than kill off that genre's iconically indeterminate body. Audiences hungered for a solution, for a way to resolve the terror and chaos of national and cultural transmutation. By providing a Civil War nation with a means to reinventing and redressing itself at the site of her phantasmagoria, Menken successfully performed an effigy of melodrama's "tragic octoroon" while simultaneously rewriting the body of that effigy. Pregnant with mean- ing, the body of Menken's *Mazeppa* paraded through the cities of New York and Milwaukee, Baltimore and Virginia City, London, and Paris, forecasting the news that the terms of the racialized and gendered body in transatlantic theatre had been born anew.[117]

## Crimes and Misdemeanors: Blackface Menken and Other Outlaw Acts

> You know I am a vagabond of fancy; no home—no plans—no ideas. I was born a
> dweller in tents—a reveler in the 'tented habitation of war'—consequently my ideas of
> life and all it involves are rather disreputable in the eyes of the just.
> —Adah Isaacs Menken, "Some Notes of Her Life in Her Own Hand"

Among the many excuses that *Golden Era* journalist Tessa Ardenne gave as to why she attended a Menken performance in 1864 was that she was "curious to see the being who could cause such a flutter; to see if she really was 'black as she is painted.'" Ardenne's sly and perhaps Shakespearean allusion would seem to transform Lady Macbeth's contemptuous disregard for "a painted devil" into an oddly ironic barometer of Menken's acting capabilities.[118] Could Menken really, Ardenne seems to ask, fulfill the legend of hearsay? Could she perform a role with the kind of genuine authenticity that would live up to the grand accounts of her work in the local press? With the turn of a key phrase, Ardenne's description of her night on the town attending a Menken show opens up a field of racial and theatrical innuendo. What may have amounted to no more than a witty proverbial aside about "black paint" is ironic given

Menken's contested identity politics and given the fact that Menken literally painted herself black with burnt cork in some of her most successful non-*Mazeppa* productions. As risky and as ambiguous a move as the Byronic equestrian act may have been, Menken's supplementary performances in these minstrel shows, as well as multiple-role "protean" productions, nautical and military melodramas, picaresque frontier tales, and outlaw adventures would in fact stretch her image far beyond her valiant *Mazeppa* persona.

At the same time, however, the diverse performances that Menken cultivated particularly between 1862 and 1866 must be read as linked with her signature role. If *Mazeppa*'s "nudity" blackened Menken in the cultural imaginary, then playing the "rebel" character and, particularly donning blackface in some of these key other performances became a way to at once inhabit the trappings of white patriarchy and to divest it of its power. No longer the ethnic hero in these varied productions, Menken played the role of the sometimes overtly white, sometimes overtly working-class, and always recalcitrant outsider, the blackface trickster, the jailbird on the loose, the falsely accused sailor. The actress made it clear through the sheer diversity and eccentricity of her work that she would remain a "vagabond" until the end. Restive and enigmatic, Menken remained thrillingly elusive as a stage performer through the many productions she staged in concert with *Mazeppa*. She utilized inventive, unpredictable, as well as socially and culturally unseemly ways to distort and redirect the "black paint" in which she swam. In each production, she fashioned herself an escape via the mechanics of racial phantasmagoria and put to use the future tools of Dr. Jekyll in order to create a new way to Hyde.

The protean and multiple-role performances that Menken staged concurrently with *Mazeppa* in various U.S. cities provide evidence of her long-standing interest in maintaining a grand spectacle of movement in her stage work. While some of the shows in which she performed such as *Rookwood* and *Eagle Eye* incorporate *Mazeppa*-like equestrian stunts designed to carry her through the theater at top speed, the most potent movement that Menken harnessed in all her productions evolved out of and in between characters.[119] Some have observed that Menken "seemed to have been obsessed with protean changes" and indeed, the actress was said to have had a hand in writing, producing, and reviving a number of multiple-role theatre pieces such as *Three Fast Women*, *The Unprotected Female*, and *The French Spy*. Particularly in her San Francisco production of *Three Fast Women*, Menken drew critical attention for taking on multiple roles in what was considered by some to be one of her most challenging productions. Assuming a series of characters ranging from "an organ girl" to a sea-sailor, a "sporting duck" to "a minstrel"

12. Outlaw Menken? Perhaps in costume as Jack Sheppard. Harvard Theatre Collection, Houghton Library, Harvard University.

figure, Menken tapped into her performative "versatility" in a phantasma-goric series of transformations; she "pass[ed] from character to character with almost lightning-like rapidity." Once again, in San Francisco Menken garnered her greatest praise for these performances which, to some crit-ics, strayed away from *Mazeppa* and showcased a dominant and "vigorous originality."[120]

A survey of the many characters Menken performed reads like a who's who of lone rebels, rabble-rousers, and charming miscreants. Some of the roles during her Bowery run in the early 1860s were standard fare and a few were perhaps expected choices in the wake of the mushrooming *Mazeppa* fame and legend attached to her. Her turn as Joan of Arc, for instance, gave Menken the opportunity to further develop and cultivate her reputation as a tortured soul and martyred icon, and her performance as the title character of *The Whistler*, "a savage Highland youth," enabled her to continue playing figures who were resistant to authority. Likewise, her short-term and uneven attempts to per-form in alternate extravaganza pieces, such as the popular and panoramic standard *Tom and Jerry* and the poorly executed *The Child of the Sun*, none-theless provide evidence of her dependence on racial and class spectacle, albeit in productions that returned her from "the Orient" and placed her in urban and agrarian settings closer to home.

Immersed in contemporary urban argot, the American adaptation of William Moncrieff's *Tom and Jerry* created a space for Menken to play multiple roles in a production that was known for ambitiously staging epic views of modern city life. *Tom and Jerry* also gave her the opportunity to appear in a play that influenced popular perceptions of a nascent, urban young white male culture in the early nineteenth century. Rollicking and roving through the streets of London, dapper Tom and his provincial cousin Jerry make, according to Moncreiff's finale, "[l]ife in London one holiday" where "[b]idding frolic and merriment reign." The burletta of this production only elevated the joviality of the original and featured a scene in a "Chaffing Crib" in the house of Corinthian Tom, a role that Menken would perform in her own versions of *Tom and Jerry*. In particular, the "Chaffing Crib" scene enabled Menken to continue to cultivate a pleasure-seeking, masculinist persona as her character took his "pals" on a tour of his room where he "unbends" and where he coaches Jerry as they prepare for an evening in the "gay and bustling" city. As the two men prowl the night, they encounter a host of urban characters, including African Sal, a "Negro" prostitute, and Dusty Bob, a "Negro" coal worker.[121] Such minstrel subplots were not uncommon in various Menken productions. *The Child of the Sun*, for example, placed Menken at the center of what resembled the maelstrom of a plantation spectacle. Written by the American actor and prolific dramatist John Brougham, *The Child of the Sun* called for a large cast of actors playing "peon slaves, brigands, Negro attendants, field hands, [and] Mexican peasants." It also called on Menken to play what was listed on its playbill as "a Creole" character. Little is known about the details of Menken's *Child of the Sun* performances, other than that the play was a critical and financial fiasco. But both *Tom and Jerry*, which she performed during her peak months at the Bowery, and *The Child of the Sun*, which she briefly mounted while in England during the latter years of her career, reveal the extent to which Menken continually returned to large-scale sensation productions as a terrain on which to showcase her abilities as a performer.[122]

The gild of some of these showier endeavors may have led some critics to disregard Menken's serious creativity as an actress and to label her a one-note acrobat who was addicted to fame. While the latter may be true, a close examination of Menken's other frequent and alternative roles demonstrates the ways in which she gradually refined and stabilized a diverse, traveling repertoire. Throughout the 1860s, Menken selected and inhabited a cluster of roles that deepened and complicated the image that she was concurrently developing in *Mazeppa*. Her long-term experimentation with impersonations of famous players such as Charlotte Cushman, M'me Fabbri, Ed Forrest, Ed Booth, and especially Lola Montez suggests her running attachment to spectacles of transformation and convertibility of which *Mazeppa* had only hinted.[123] Above all else the roles that Menken inhabited on her nights when she was not playing the Tartar Prince suggest a provocative thematic consistency. They centered on the tensions between captivity and escape, oppression and insurgency, stasis and mobility. In these roles, she found the space to forcefully transgress many of the rigid social and cultural limitations of white patriarchal order. Particularly in the dizzying protean productions, she executed her character transformations with a kind of ease and alacrity that made her as elusive to pigeonhole as the many outlaw characters she enlivened on the stage.

Not surprisingly, however, Menken ended up clinging to white patriarchal supremacy's protective aegis in these supplementary productions and shows. I would argue in fact that the work Menken conducted outside of *Mazeppa* provides even more powerfully confounding evidence of the actress's long-term cultural and political equivocations as an entertainer. In her less legendary productions of *Jack Sheppard*, *The French Spy*, and particularly *Black Ey'd Susan*, Menken continued her carefully orchestrated dance of ideological conflict which would carry her far beyond the saddle of Milner's play. Nowhere were those contradictions more strikingly on display than in the actress's protean shows, and it is to those performances which incorporated blackface to which I will finally turn in order to confront the ethical politics of Menken's (un)conventional deeds as a performer.

With astonishing frequency, Menken returned to scenes of bondage and extreme subjugation in her performances. While *Mazeppa* certainly displayed her adept skill at playing the vulnerable captive who stages a grand and splashy revolt, many of Menken's other roles would also call uon her to confront or withstand torture, imprisonment, and the threat of public execution. In *The Whistler*, she breaks free from the captivity of mysterious soldiers by committing patricide, only to face a gruesome death at the bottom of a boiling cataract.[124] Even more successful were her frequent stagings of J. B. Buckstone's *Jack Sheppard*, a popular English melodrama based on the legendary life of the eighteenth-century criminal who robbed from the rich, gave to the poor, and staged innumerable jailbreaks from Newgate prison during his short but colorful life as a thief. A tale of "love, vengeance, and injustice at the hands of vicious authority," the melodrama *Jack Sheppard* was believed to have fostered a "working-class contempt for authority" from its debut in England in 1839. With a woman most often assuming the title role of a "sprightly young dare devil" who makes off with the ladies as well as the riches of the aristocracy, *Jack Sheppard* enabled Menken to once again showcase her unique abilities to effect escape resistance, as well as a masculinist breeches swagger.[125]

Escape is one of the overarching themes of *Jack Sheppard*, and Menken's repeated gravitation toward this role reveals her penchant for working spectacular elusion into the center of her repertoire. Buckstone's play worked perfectly for Menken as it celebrates the brilliant charm and tenacious resourcefulness of an "erstwhile bandit king, highwayman and general all-around thief" who foils his captors and seeks shelter among the "poor of the countryside."[126] Climaxing with an intricate, Houdini-esque scene set to music in which the hero picks a padlock and sets himself free from jail, *Jack Sheppard* provided Menken with the opportunity to articulate, enact, and perform the art of individual resistance and liberation. In the title role, she found ample room to create a romantically insolent hero. Buckstone's Jack brashly declares in act 4, "I battered the strong wall of the red room, the thick doors of the chapel, the stone and the iron barriers that met me on my way; bolts, nails— all becomes my humble servants with *your* help and *my* strength and patience!" Savvier than Cassimer and more cunning and debonair in fashioning his escape, the *Jack Sheppard* role nonetheless reinforced Menken's gravitation toward characters that invoked stamina and corporeal power to surmount treacherous circumstances. The play fleshed out more fully the outlaw persona that Menken continued to craft from role to role and as she traveled the war-torn country in the 1860s.[127]

While *Jack Sheppard* showcased Menken in the role of the bandit, her turn in the "sensation-drama" *The French Spy*, in a triad of roles, returned her again to the realm of the imperial and militaristic epic. As Mathilde De Meric, Henri St. Alme, and Hamet Carmaully, Menken slipped into a palimpsest of characters in J. T. Haines's melodrama of the "siege of Constantina." Set against the French colonization of Algiers in 1830, Haines's play restages France's insistence that the "tri-color must wave" in North Africa by collapsing imperialist desire into the erotics of an intrepid breeches heroine who navigates Franco-Arab conflict in drag.[128] *The French Spy* created the opportunity for Menken to play a bellicose transgender protagonist whose intricate subterfuge and escape tactics surpassed those of Mazeppa. As the French nobleman's daughter Mathilde, Menken inhabited a mute female character so devoted to her colonel lover that she follows him into the deserts of Algiers,

13. Menken as the
French Spy. Harvard
Theatre Collection,
Houghton Library,
Harvard University.

masquerading in drag as the faithful servant Henri St. Alme and keeping a
watchful eye over her betrothed as military conflict ensues.

In the context of Menken's rotating repertoire, her role in *The French Spy*
distinguished itself as one of her few staple female characters and one in which
she could turn the metatextual spectacle of her breeches performances and the
acuity of her physical stage presence into a central plot development. Particularly in the opening act, Mathilde's mute lancer Henri dominates the
energy and activities between characters, expressing an obsequious devotion
toward Colonel Bernelle, who is too illiterate to read his lover's pass. Most
provocatively, Haines's script gives free reign to the character of Mathilde/
Henri to flout sexual and gender codes by playing a "saucy swaggering dumby
[*sic*]" who flirts incessantly and explicitly with the General's daughter Marie
and who equally competes with and mocks her feminized suitor Tony. When
Henri climaxes his antics in act 1 by "snatch[ing] a kiss from Marie" with "the
sound of their lips" loud enough to "make Tony suddenly turn round" (10),

14. Menken perhaps in costume as Mathilde/Henri. Harvard Theatre Collection, Houghton Library, Harvard University.

the play reinforces the outer limits of Mathilde's transgressions—passing as a man in order to invert the dynamics of chivalry and dabbling in explicit homoerotic flirtation afforded her by the movement of transvestism.

*The French Spy* demanded of Menken a different kind of physicality in its insistence on a female lead who could make her body speak with cerebral and emotive complexity in the part of the mute. Playing Mathilde enabled Menken to distinguish herself to many critics who had remained skeptical of her acting abilities. *The French Spy* is, as one critic gushed, "an illustration of this wonderful actress' power," in part because it "is not dependent for success upon beauty of person alone." Instead, the play called on Menken to use "her expressive face" to reflect "every emotion of the mind, whether of hate, love, or fear, so that her pantomime can be as well understood as the spoken words of another." *The French Spy* provided a gateway for Menken to prove to critics that she "stands peerless in every play where such physical and mental conditions are the elements of success." In this triple role, she manipulated "the play of her countenance" and used her much-described "personal attractions" in pursuit of the "intellectual illustration" and "perfect outward vraisemblance of the assumed characters."[129]

In spite of this critical triumph, Menken's repeated performances of this play underscore her explicit association with the business of empire and racial hegemony in her theatre work and through the spectacle of female corporeality. The rhetoric of Orientalism, a virulent contempt for the Arab underclass, and the Frenchmen's rallying cry to "storm Constantina" and "plant the tricolor on their walls" (12) simmers to a boil in the play. To be sure, the basic plot arc of *The French Spy* fundamentally reinforces the rudiments of imperial theatre by annexing Mathilde's drag act and placing it in the service of French espionage and military conquest. If the "Arab spy" Mohammed is initially captured in act 1 spewing venomous death threats toward France (11), Haines's drama counteracts and quells colonial insurgency by requiring that Henri suit up in the service of France as the ideal spy, a "deranged" "Arab of the Desert," Hamet Carmaully. Essentially killing two birds with one stone, the drama retrieves Mathilde from the margins of gender and sexual normativity, replacing her in the recognizable confines of the European heroine in peril, while simultaneously extinguishing Arab insurgency. Moreover, it reestablishes the mechanics of racial and gender hegemony by returning Mathilde to the context of her original trauma. Muteness afflicts her, we are told in act 1, as the result of "those cursed Moors'" massacre of her family (6). By penetrating the walls of the Arab encampment, Mathilde/Henri sets in play French military advancement and the symbolic vanquishing of her family. Mathilde's costume, disguising her in the familiar and fetishistic garb of the Orient, resembles Mazeppa's baroque threads. Yet in her subsequent unmasking, Menken's heroine transforms into the symbolic and necessary female pawn of empire. In the hands of the sexually rapacious Achmet, Mathilde is "instantly clothed in the habillments of her sex" and threatened with rape by a lecherous Arab (2.3.21–22).

Inasmuch as Haines's script depends on the ascending vulnerability of female sexuality and the commensurate threat of a French imperial and militarist power on the verge of defeat, the closing tableau reaffirms the virility of patriarchal empire by interrupting the scene of Mathilde's violation and rendering the Arab army prostrate. Even the emasculated Tony, who has proven less attractive than Henri to the general's daughter, stands "cross-legged over a dead Arab soldier shouting" while "the whole country" is "awfully illuminated" (3.2.24). *The French Spy* thus inverts the romanticized rebellion of *Mazeppa* and places Menken squarely in a propagandistic drama that celebrates the conquests of the imperialist phallus. Paradoxically, it enabled Menken to break new ground in performance, but its narrative logic proved to be one of her most reactionary roles.[130]

Like *The French Spy*, the nautical drama *Black Ey'd Susan* created a province for Menken to experiment with playing characters who manipulated the tensions between outlaw transience and nationalist identity formations. Each drama enabled Menken to play both sides of a sociopolitical coin, dipping into anti-establishment vagrancy and yet ultimately resurfacing in the service of nation building. In the case of *Black Ey'd Susan*, she tapped into the adventures of the transnational English sailor. Her highly lauded turn as the hero William remained a staple performance that she kept in her repertoire during many of her extended engagements in various American cities. In *Black Ey'd Susan*, critics recognized her sharp ability "to take advantage of the pathos of the character and really to show herself an actress in the assumption." Another added that Menken in the role of William transcended the limitations of her previous "spectacular plays," where "beauty of form and graceful attitudes were all that was required." Conversely, in *Black Ey'd Susan*, this critic argued, she flexed her muscles "as a great melodramatic actress."[131] Yet rather than thinking of that play and *Mazeppa* as polar opposites—the former a "classic" melodrama and the latter a standard spectacle and sensation— we might instead consider the ways in which her William was a role that enabled Menken to amplify the performative innovations that she was concurrently cultivating in *Mazeppa*.

Working more explicitly with the intersecting thematics of gender and nationalism which had remained implicit in *Mazeppa*, Menken performed William as both a boisterous nomad and a stalwart leader. She was, in effect, assuming the character of a dashing sailor who had become synonymous with the familiar English archetype "Jack Tar," a figure that J. S. Bratton calls, "the most powerful instrument of imperialist ideology on the nineteenth-century stage." Within the codes of British nautical melodrama, the "tar" embodies a wealth of contradictions. He is "powerful and compassionate, superhuman and common, heroic and comic, able to utter the loftiest nationalist rhetoric" as well as "puns and malapropisms." The "mature Jack," comes as a result of "the genius of [actor] T. P. Cooke and of Douglas Jerrold coming together to create William" in 1829. In short, Cooke's and Jerrold's collaboration in creating *Susan* worked to elevate the "tar" figure to a new level of "maturity," transforming that figure into "an emissary of virtue against villainy."[132] This version of the "tar" part was seemingly made for Menken to inhabit and redeploy in the service of both American patriotism and the insurgent working-class rhetoric of midcentury theatre. As the sailor figure who returns home from abroad, she tapped into the original production's romance of the outsider who is forced to figure out his relationship to family and to nation.

The Jack Tar hero in *Black Ey'd Susan* enabled Menken to exploit her meta-textually marginal persona and recontextualize that image within a drama invested in shoring up nationalist masculinity. Like the "tar" figure who emerges "from nowhere, or from outside, beyond the known world" and who must "make himself understood by the locals," so too did Menken assume roles that reinforced the rhetoric of loyalty to home and statehood. In her turn as William, she received high marks for her interpretation of a fiercely uxorious sailor threatened with death in the wake of protecting the honor and chastity of his wife, the very "Black Ey'd Susan." Having protected Susan from the disreputable advances of fellow sailor Quid, William is locked away and forced to confront the wrath of his superiors and an unyielding court authority. Whereas *Mazeppa*'s spectacle of violation turned on a wordless Menken's intrepid calisthenics and steely reserve, her William depended on the eloquence of his own visceral exhortations and the grave and passionate honor of character to rescue him from death by hanging. It was a part that required of Menken a different kind of transformative energy than that which she had displayed in *Mazeppa*.

Inverting the thematics of that part, the role of William called for Menken to play the noble and courageous rebel leader who rallies his people into resistance through a conversion in demeanor rather than atop a horse. Shifting from a jovial and yet mildly reckless gallant into a persecuted and quietly steadfast patriot, William at one point kneels and leads his fellow sailors in prayer while embracing the Union Jack. Menken's character acts here as "a human sacrifice" for both the strength and principles of the nation in a scene that efficiently rehearses imperialist melodrama's reliance on "talismanic patriotism in the form" of the flag.[133] Once again playing the persecuted resistor to strict and unyielding authority, Menken found in William a way to bring together her unique aesthetics of voice and body on the stage. By enlivening the transgender poetics of her body with a voice equally as multivalent and unpredictable, Menken created a William that disrupted the logic of patriarchal iconography and displayed her reserve as an androgynous performer who fluidly rewrote the utility of her own body in performance.

Her success in the role was especially evident in reviews of her 1864 San Francisco encore performances that marveled at her seemingly effortless ability to mix and match gender codes with a distinct and convincing physical grace and ease. In one of the most comprehensive local reviews of her work from that season, the *Golden Era* paid an extensive farewell tribute to Menken and the anomalous figure that she had crafted in several of her most popular roles. In her William, the publication argued, Menken created a virtuous masculinity, a sailor with "dash" but "without a touch of his actual vices." Clad in a "neat and natty costume" that "sets off her charming figure to the best advantage," Menken's feminine form paradoxically imbues her sailor with a masculine aplomb and a suave form of dignity and charisma:

> Her beautiful little feet fairly twinkle in their shining shoes, her white and delicate hands peep out from under their blue cuffs without a shade or suspicion of tar upon them, a jolly little hat is perched on the top of her curls. . . . She throws herself into the part with the most perfect carelessness and *abandon*, hitching up her trowsers, and flinging her feet in an out-and-out hornpipe as naturally and unaffectedly as though she had sailed all her life from the Downs. Her voice is as cheery as a fair breeze. . . . And then when the sentimentality of the piece comes in—ah, there is a sweet William for you! How he dashes on the villain officer who has insulted and would outrage his wife, cutting him down, to use his own words, "as though he were a piece of old junk." Bravely and defiantly in the cabin he stands up when the sentence of death is passed upon him by the cruel looking old chaps in cocked hats, flinging out his soul in vindication of his honor as freely and bravely as though it were a commodore's broad pennant, only melting when he bids farewell to "Susan."[134]

A "cheery voice," small feet, and milky "white" hands free of sailor's "tar" racially feminize Menken's soft, jovial, and sartorially smart sailor here. But the core of her performance seemingly resides in the zeal and zest of her physical execution, her "careless abandon" for hiking up her breeches and dancing a hornpipe jig. The sentimentality of *Black Ey'd Susan* rests on the shoulders of William, who transforms (much like a child prince) into a man of force, vigor, and principles as the drama progresses. In Menken's portrayal of the character, the power of William's English manhood plays out in her movements which, in this particular case, appear to push her hero from the trappings of feckless youth and into the expansive and imperious stance of a virulent naval officer who "dashes on the villain officer who has insulted and would outrage his wife." In a whirl of character transmogrification, Menken's William storms and cuts at his adversary and turns the energy of airy insouciance into the bravery to withstand oppression. In this final scene, "the finest exhibition of power" as one critic observed, the apparent eloquence of language serves her William well as he invokes words to "flin[g] out his soul in vindication of his honor."[135] Menken's performance turns on the weight and magnitude of her voice and its ability to extricate her character from incarceration and impending death. By infusing her protagonist with her trademark "duality of sex," her performance both shores up the romantic valor of patriarchy and undoes it.

Rescripting (white) "manhood" in a richly realized breeches performance, Menken created a William "handsome enough to turn the heads of all the girls in any port her ship may enter." The intimacy that she crafted with San Francisco costar Sophie Edwin depended on her ability to match a face "alive with joy and happiness" with hands that have "a language of their own," warning and commanding, threatening and "fall[ing] lifeless toward the earth in sorrow." According to one reviewer, Menken's arms are the vessels of her sensuality and they bond her with Edwin on the stage:

> Every touch, every time they smoothed Susan's hair, softly stroked her cheeks, gently touched her shoulder or drew her to her arms, was the very embodiment of tenderness; an expression of Love in its highest form . . . loving the object for her own sake; tender, watchful, gentle toward her; but flashing like a sword from its scabbard if she is assailed. It is a conception of *man's love* in its highest form such as makes a woman's heart beat with joy and pride to have inspired.[136]

Performing "man's love" with the skill of a woman, Menken once again disrupted gender epistemologies on the stage. Although conventional Jack Tar roles called for an emotionally demonstrative hero who readily bursts into tears at the drop of a hat, Menken's breeches interpretation posited a queer intervention in the Tar image's conflation of national and domestic desire. Whereas Jack Tar was often made to weep over "his own eloquence on the subject of his ship/girl or girl/ship or even his devotion to his superior officer," Menken and Edwin worked a physical intimacy into the interpretation of their characters that complicated and overshadowed the nationalist dimensions of William's verbal rhetoric. While loyal Menken fan Charles Stoddard argued that her "sweet William" was the "embodiment of all that was deliciously melancholy, melodious, and unmasculine," the sum of her stage gestures amounted to an insurgent revision of normative gender roles.[137] The language of arms, hands, fingers, sensual strokes, and soft embraces is likened to "an expression of Love in its highest form" and stages a metatextual scene of homoerotic passion within the framework of the production. Just as Menken's "conception of man's love in its highest form" makes "a woman's heart beat with joy and pride to have inspired," her William also makes masculinity subject to vulnerability, open to the conveyance of sexual passion, an unpredictable cross between tenderness and bellicose watchfulness of the "object" of his affection. In the formidable role of William, then, Menken scrambled gender identifications by constructing an idealized masculinity that was molded out of the detritus of "true womanhood" iconography.

What is most provocative and least discussed about Menken's *Black Ey'd Susan* role though is the way in which William's heroics are couched in the steadfast inflation and preservation of a very particular kind of racialized masculinity. Indeed, race figures prominently in versions of Jerrold's *Black Ey'd Susan* as it comes to bear on the protagonist's attempts to lay claim to his wife and his sovereignty in a rapidly changing colonial environment. Published in 1829, the original script for *Black Ey'd Susan* provides telling documentation of the ways in which England and its culture of empire grappled with redefining itself as the system of slavery began to gradually dissolve in its colonies. As the grip of English slavery continued to loosen in the late eighteenth and early nineteenth centuries, culminating in the 1833 Act of Parliament which freed slaves throughout the British empire, *Black Ey'd Susan* offered a way to recuperate the subjectivity of its transnational agents of the sea. Jerrold notes of his play that it aims to "present a picture of manners" and to rectify what he perceives as the lingering specious folklore about the English sailor. Claiming to have had an early stint of his own in the British navy, Jerrold declares as much in his preface, arguing that the "English sailor,—so far from being a blusterer, is a creature of reserve: his bravery and endurance are accompanied by that taciturn doggedness which foreigners ascribe to us as one of our principle characteristics."[138] Yet in revising the iconography of the English sailor, Jerrold's original text depends on drawing attention to the perils of white masculinity while baldly and randomly translating that vulnerability onto black figures in the narrative's background. White masculinity is, in *Black Ey'd Susan*, restored to power through the impending disposability of invisible yet very present black corporeality.

We must, then, imagine Menken delivering lines that required of her to play the part of a sailor who negotiated the social and cultural chaos of colonial regions in flux. Having returned from a long sojourn at sea, William describes his travels in St. Domingo where, "when the fleet was lying off . . . in the West Indies—the crew liked new rum and dancing with the *niggers.*" The pleasure and danger of revelry across racial boundaries and its attending confusion is, however, immediately pulled into check by the bizarre and gruesome sea tale that William delivers to a crowd of listeners held in rapt attention.

"One morning" he offers, "there was a black bumboat—woman aboard, with a little picanninny . . . afore you could say, 'about ship,' the little black baby jumped out of its mother's grappling, and fell into [a shark's] jaws;— the black woman gave a shriek that would have split the boatswain's whistle! . . . Tom Gunnell saw how the wind was. . . . Overboard he jumps. . . . And when Tom came up, all over blood, with the corpse of the baby, and the shark turned upon its side . . . such a cheer.[139]

With a nod to minstrelsy's most violent spectacles of black torture and mayhem played for laughs, Jerrold's "melodrama" commences by addressing a nagging social incubus: how to restore the honor of a prodigal seaman who fraternizes with "the natives" in tropical climates. The transgression of the "bumboat" woman who penetrates the sanctity of William's vessel makes plain the exigencies of this problem and reinforces the need for returning power and control into the hands of the English sailor. Enter shipmate Tom Gunnell who, in William's retelling of the incident, restores the heroic order of English manhood. As a result of Gunnell's "valorous" act, the English sailor reasserts his willingness "to brave every call of duty" at the expense of blackness which is here infantalized and subject to carnivorous ravishment.[140]

From its egregiously grotesque beginnings to its melodramatic ending in which William evades death and transforms into an iconic symbol of courage and moral rectitude, *Black Ey'd Susan* works to recuperate the patriarchal leadership and agency of the English sailor. As William, Menken slipped into a role that magnified and reaffirmed the enduring centrality of white masculinity. She both called attention to ways of undoing the arbitrary power of race and gender by performing "man's love" with clear and convincing detail and managed to keep the symbolic machinery of white masculinity and empire in place through this role by capitulating to the earnestness and sententiousness of its melodramatic arc. Surprisingly, it is in Menken's scabrous and controversial work as a protean blackface performer that we find the residue of resistance and disorderly conduct teeming within the familiar and malignant semiotics of burnt-cork impersonations and musical variety shows.

The so-called protean shows that Menken performed both on the east coast and even more successfully in San Francisco remain, for critics, the most enduringly divisive and enigmatic in Menken's repertoire. Although they were, during her lifetime, hailed as deliciously hypnotic trifles of entertainment, her performances of the burlesque productions *The Unprotected Female* and particularly *Three Fast Women* raise even greater questions about the extent of Menken's counterhegemonic vision as an artist and entertainer. In

15. Menken as William
in *Black-Ey'd Susan*.
Harvard Theatre
Collection, Houghton
Library, Harvard
University.

the former production, the actress's subversive strengths are fully on display
in her diverse performances that prefigured the fast-approaching burlesque
phenomenon and its most potent early signature, that of the "threatening
electric charge" of female speech. What was additionally refreshing and original about Menken in *The Unprotected Female* was her keen ability to playfully
and irreverently mix up the forms of a night at the theatre and offer "extem-
porized soliloquy and singing and dancing interlude, lasting half an hour" or
longer. Amplifying the singing abilities that she had employed in *Jack Sheppard* and *Black Ey'd Susan*, Menken's "rollicking Polly Crisp . . . revealed a
voice that had amazing variety." She balanced masterful impersonations of
"serious actors of the time" with French and Italian songs, and numbers made
popular by fellow sensation actresses such as Menken acolyte Lotta Crabtree.
In short, *The Unprotected Female* provided Menken with an outlet to combine
her cogent use of a voice that was said by some to "transcend every other
impression" with her dancing and a keen intuitive ability to slip impersona-

tions of Cushman and Booth "into her lighter plays as if these dignified thespians had assumed frivolous roles."[141] Everything was turned on its head in *The Unprotected Female* in a way that seemed to exhibit the scope, range, and depth of Menken's cultural disobedience and in a way that appeared to demonstrate her potential as a pioneering actress unafraid of playing with theatrical conventions.

And while her professedly original production *Three Fast Women* seemed to build in fast and furious ways on *The Unprotected Female*'s seeds of early burlesque by showcasing Menken's scrappy and unpredictable use of voice along with "mocking male impersonations" and "streetwise language" (Allen, *Horrible Prettiness*, 28), *Three Fast Women* was Menken's most troubling and ideologically conflicted work. A brassy and exhaustingly elaborate extravaganza performance for one actress, *Three Fast Women* is compelling, seductive, and stunning. It reaffirms Menken's blatant creativity and versatility as a theatrical entrepreneur as well as a performer. The show was billed as a new and original production in San Francisco, but there is evidence that she had performed it as early as December 1861 at the Louisville Theatre. There the production was advertised as a showcase for Menken's "great protean characters in this the greatest drama of the day, being a famous extravaganza written by Miss Adah Isaacs Menken entitled *Three Fast Women*. New Features, New Characters, new Songs, new conundrums, new jokes, new dances." *Three Fast Women* proved a particularly durable and portable piece that Menken adapted and sold to local audiences in different cities, but most successfully in San Francisco where, as a "burletta," it reportedly "abounded in local allusions and settings, including a scene at Squarza's famous gathering place" from an earlier era in the city's history.[142]

Assuming up to nine roles and "including five men's parts," Menken put to use her "broad comic talents" in a show that enabled her to flex her imaginative insolence in a broad cross-section of character impersonations. The voice that could slip in an instant from rendering a number with "vehemence" and "gusto" to "harp-like" tenor and soprano came into full bloom in *Three Fast Women*.[143] Her voice served as the backbone of her performance and carried her across a panoply of American caricatures with flamboyantly provincial names and pedestrian titles. In her act, she wove between belting out the "Bully Lager Beer" song in the part of Lovely Nancy, the organ girl, to playing the fop, Montague Fitzherbert. She could prance through the role of Yankee girl Jerusha Sparks singing "My Johnny is a Soldier" and just as quickly inhabit the parts of Tom Bowling, a horn-piped sailor, and the dashing sporting duck Harry Scarlet. As young Mose, a fireman, she slipped into the iconography of the "Bowery b'hoy," a creature of popular culture who gradually yoked working-class subcultural desire with the "racial modality of blackface."

Her Mose fireman is, in fact, a critical figure to recognize in *Three Fast Women*. It is a role that adumbrates and reinforces the significant ideological utility of black cultural forms in this production. For just as Mose's symbolic class dissent eventually merged with blackface minstrelsy in an expression of dissonance and insurgent "class travesty," so too did Menken incorporate burnt-cork performance into her "burletta" as a grotesquely conventional and yet subtly parodic expression of difference and dissent. In Menken's hands, minstrelsy showed the potential to operate as a vehicle turned back on itself; it exposed the ruse of the very patriarchal forms that she inhabited.[144]

As "Rosebud" and "Bones," Menken refined stock blackface caricatures to anchor the third act of *Three Fast Women*.[145] In a sequence that was advertised on playbills as "the Great Champion Female Minstrels" performing with the "best band in the States," "Miss Adah" made her entrance "as Bones in 7 Songs, 3 Dances, and a Bone solo." By all accounts, this segment of *Three Fast Women* was a run-of-the-mill "Olla Podrida of Ethiopian minstrelsy, consisting of songs, dances . . . jokes, and conundrums." The scene likely showcased the impertinent ethnic and political jokes, regional banter, dialect, and musical elements of minstrelsy's recognizable opening sequence featuring "the two unruly end men, Mr. Bones and Mr. Tambo" and additionally incorporated olio skits that "burlesqued [San Francisco's] Barbary Coast with its whores, criminals and gallants." With a cast that drew both from the more stately entertainment of Maguire's as well as the ruffian world of local minstrel houses, *Three Fast Women* brought together the two opposing theatrical spheres that Menken had long straddled in her career. As Frank Sweet notes, one can only "imagine the sedate thespians attempting to maintain their dignity in the midst of the rollicking minstrel band. The incongruity is suggested by the heterogeneous cast" with names like "Joe Highbrow and Joe Lowbrow."[146]

Menken distinguished herself in this motley crowd as the star of what was an extremely successful and well-received production. Although as a female performer she was not alone in her work in blackface entertainment—friend and associate Lotta Crabtree famously dabbled in the form as well—her turn as the familiar minstrel figure Bones figure ensured her reputation as an actress who was forever willing to cross racial and gender lines in popular theatre. As Bones, the keeper of the minstrel flame and one half of the two-pronged anchor endmen of the minstrel set, she assumed the role of the court jester. Greased up in black paint, suited up in oversized vestments, "gaudy swallowtail coats, striped trousers, cumberbunds, top hats, [and] cravats," cracking "naughty jokes," and smoking a stogie, Menken inhabited a familiar vision of black masculinity emasculated and deformed for popular consumption. In *Three Fast Women*, the offstage Menken who had caroused with male companions along the Barbary Coast in casinos and braved the saloons of Virginia City took yet another flamboyant, socially and politically turbid step toward "gain[ing] access to patriarchal privileges" on the stage.[147] As many have rightly observed, her work in minstrelsy spectacles such as *Eagle Eye* clearly exposes the ways that "[n]o expedient was too rash for Menken; the public must be dazzled, startled, awed—at whatever cost to her life and limb." Performing in a medium renowned for its racist misogyny appears to reinforce a short and controversial lifetime's worth of ethically bankrupt and self-serving choices that Menken made to protect herself and to further her career. Her minstrel work thus undermines a reading of Menken as a performer invested in rigorously and consistently subverting racial and gender categories in midcentury transatlantic culture.[148]

Still, Menken may have utilized her blackface acts to call attention to the hegemony of mid-nineteenth-century theatre. For particularly in her steadfast attempts to purchase the (performance) rights of white men, she remains a critical figure to examine in relation to the resistant cultural acts of the marginalized. Considering Menken's hubris in appropriating patriarchal cultural paradigms should not diminish our recognition of minstrelsy's violent and relentless assault on black (and particularly black female) bodies in nineteenth-century culture and beyond.[149] Rather. the contradictions and surfeiting ironies involved in Menken's entrance into this realm of theatre do much to expose the machinery as well the fallibility of white cultural patriarchy. We might, then, read her minstrel characters as similar to her breeches melodramas and sensation pieces in that they transgressed white patriarchal circumscription from within its very borders rather than simplistically succumbing to its seductive burnt-cork rhythms.

In a theatrical tradition largely dependent on the absence or present vacuity of (black) female figures and a (white) male homoerotic gaze intent on controlling and emasculating black male bodies, Menken inserted her own ambiguous body, shrouded in drag and adorned with greasepaint. If minstrelsy had grotesquely pornotroped the sexual availability of "light-skinned" women and "mulatta coquettes" by burdening them with operating as the objects of erotic pursuit, then Menken's breeches (counter)act in *Three Fast Women* must be considered as another paradoxical parody on her part.

Double-crossed, as it were, in her dressing, she inverted the deployment of masculinity "in a dress" that was, as many critics have pointed out, a paradoxical staple of minstrelsy's fundamentally masculinist rhetoric. In this way, her blackface acts disrupted the stasis of the "wench" archetype character from within the genre. Her presence as a woman in this chaotic theatrical minefield calls attention to the ways that minstrelsy "reified the white male's position as enabler of his own gender and cultural politics on the popular stage." Menken thus appropriated the tools of the trade in a way that once made legible the artifactuality of white masculinity.[150] She laid claim to the property of performance and called attention to the mythical perceptions of who is entitled to perform and in what way in antebellum culture. At the same time, it is crucial to point out that minstrelsy most certainly shored up an implicit and yet convincing cultural perception of her own identity politics. More than any other role, the Bones act enabled Menken to publicly and spectacularly perform whiteness, even as she called attention to the cultural invention and preservation of that category through the act. No doubt, Menken's act underscored *her entitlement* to perform blackness in a space dominated and preserved especially for white men at midcentury. It is therefore her most provocative social and political revolt as an entertainer, and it is also her most vehemently reactionary legacy as a performer.

Under the aegis of whiteness, then, Menken continuously put forward her own expedient plan. In doing so, she joins a long and unheralded list of figures in the margins of culture who have been difficult to pigeonhole in cultural histories, and particularly the histories of nineteenth-century people of color. Romantically capitulating to a familiar rhetoric of resistance, we may in fact choose to ignore the complex dynamics involved in Reuben Nixon's masquerade as "Hill" the fugitive "house servant" from Baltimore or those in Henry Box Brown's allegedly willful "abandonment" of his family, but overlooking the quotidian and the conflicted, the (extra)ordinary and the equivocal social and political acts of these individuals risks airbrushing them of their remarkably unique, sometimes heroic, at other times politically repugnant, and always strikingly complicated humanity.[151] As Robert Allen pointedly observes, it is "tempting to view resistant forms of cultural production as unproblematically and unambiguously progressive—as if there were a solidarity among the discourses of subordination" (*Horrible Prettiness*, 32–33). Instead of oversimplifying the workings of dominance and resistance, we would do well to recognize in Menken's case the frequent "slide" that Allen describes as moving "from one register of social power to another—from class to gender, from

16. Menken of Mystery.
Harvard Theatre Collection,
Houghton Library,
Harvard University.

class to race." It is a slide that Menken perfected from the moment that she became visible on the mid-nineteenth-century cultural radar.

Was it a crime that Menken, a mysterious outsider, used white patriarchal tactics of performance from which to profit and protect herself? Did the sybaritic choices that she made throughout her life amount to a form of sociopolitical malfeasance? If so, how do we reconcile her maddening expedience and equivocations with her clear interest in upsetting certain dominant paradigms in nineteenth-century culture? In the end, what kind of a critical lexicon might we use to discuss and contemplate these figures who live in the gray areas of cultural, political, and racial memory? We might consider what sort of a precedent they perhaps create for the kind of late-twentieth-century contradictions that Hortense Spillers identifies and re-imagines in a figure like Toni Morrison's Sula. A character who, as she observes, "reverses the customary trend of 'moral growth' and embodies, contrarily, a figure of genuine moral ambiguity about whom few comforting conclusions may be drawn," Sula's "unalterable 'badness,' black and female are now made to appear as *single* subject in its own right, fully aware of a plenitude of predicative possibilities, for good and ill."[152]

A woman who was as much a product as an architect of midcentury entertainment, Menken trafficked in a particular kind of "good and ill" predicative possibility. She slid into the burnt-cork tradition with all its attendant prevaudeville strategies and thrived as a performer who continuously changed the representational terms of her body. What is then most compelling about her legacy in transatlantic culture is that, far from playing the familiar role of the black(ened) heroine left to die like Zoe by her own hand, she proved herself capable of mixing up, reassembling, and in some cases burning down the boundaries of white supremacist patriarchal forms in her work. In doing so, Menken forecast a new era of contrapuntal performances choreographed and led by equally eccentric, bold, and brave African American artists in the decades to come.

# 4. ALIEN/NATION

*Re-Imagining the Black Body (Politic) in*
*Williams and Walker's* In Dahomey

**W**ere it not for the consternation of British theatregoers, the Bert Williams and George Walker breakthrough black musical *In Dahomey* would not have been forced to begin where it previously had ended. But following its debut at London's Shaftesbury Theatre in the spring of 1903, the splashy Pan-Africanist extravaganza was given a quick face-lift to appease its audiences. Having conquered a skeptical Broadway public in the fall of 1902, the Williams and Walker Company decided to launch its tour of Britain in the heart of London's theatre world. Billed as a historic production staged completely by "real coons" from America, *In Dahomey* had already generated a fine amount of publicity which had focused primarily on the anomalous spectacle of its all-black cast. The press trumpeted the arrival of African American performers in a musical of their own making and encouraged the public to attend the production, if only to observe the odd miracle of African American theatre. Curious and remarkable in form and content, *In Dahomey* greeted its audiences with a flurry of sound and movement on its opening night. Flaunting a vast array of colorful contradictions, the musical sparked a rather startling cultural contradiction. A renegade production both stunningly seductive and yet mystifying and untranslatable to audiences, *In Dahomey* was forced to end with an ad-hoc version of "God Save the King" in order to assuage the "confusion" of its British audiences.[1]

### A Rumble in the Jungle

Much of that confusion erupted in response to *In Dahomey*'s original ending, a lavish scene which featured a pantomime-transformation act, Victorian theatre's popular ritual involving elaborate costuming and spectacular technology designed to transform the stage into a site of fanciful upheaval and carnivalesque disruption. The crux of Victorian pantomime was its celebration of metamorphosis, and the form consistently provided an "occasion for masquerade, disguise and processions," as well as "role-reversal [and] gender-switching." Delightfully familiar to British theatregoers, pantomimes were a staple of Victorian culture and its persistent obsession with transmutability and "patterns of conversion."[2] But Williams and Walker's use of the form as a punctuation mark for their three-hour musical confounded many Britons. Situated, according to one incredulous British critic, in an "exotic" locale amid verdant scenery with "mud swamps" and "grinning skulls," the concluding scene clearly re-animated popular theatre's spectacles of grand transformation for audiences who were invited to gaze upon a darkened stage filled with chorus members adorned in camouflage costumes. Covered with leaves "to look like foliage of the swamp," the cast of In Dahomey used the site of a surreal "jungle" terrain to convert the lay of the land in pantomime. Transmogrifying from scenery into a song and dance revue, the chorus performed a splendiferous transformation of "Dahomey" for nonplused audiences who watched as the song "My Lady Frog" was sung "by two idealized lovers in frog costumes who float down the stream in a canoe."[3] Bodies out of swamps, swamps into bodies, this grand tableau created a brassy and colorful link between its characters and the African kingdom of elusive promise in the musical. In short, the cast of In Dahomey became Dahomey onstage.[4]

Wondrously vibrant and flamboyant, In Dahomey's original ending would seem appealing to Edwardian audiences well seasoned in the ways of spectacular theatre, thus making the English confusion with regard to the show's finale all the more puzzling. For surely the musical's extravagant, panoramic staging would have been familiar to British spectators who were ever seduced by the imperialistic rhetoric of late-nineteenth- and early-twentieth-century popular culture. After all, theatre was, in a way, just one more outlet to affirm and negotiate systems of what Mary Louise Pratt describes as "territorial surveillance, appropriation of resources, and administrative control" over exoticized, colonial landscapes and their inhabitants. Dramatic productions in the second half of the nineteenth century particularly sustained what Michael Hays reads as the perpetual re-inscription of "fictions of English superiority." Such plays repeatedly offered images of distant territories that could be imaginatively annexed in the service of expanding the mere notion of an "imperial domain." Like the European explorer traipsing across a foreign territory, British patrons could enter the theatre with an "improving eye," encountering habitats as well as inhabitants who "must be produced as empty and unimproved"; for "the Eurocolonial future" is one predicated, as Pratt points out, "on absences and lacks of African life in the present."[5]

Emerging out of this era, In Dahomey seemed on the surface to reproduce the Dahomey of the imperial imaginary, a land of unmarked and unmoving territories that encourage the spectator's putative pleasure to conquer through the languid gaze of his or her roving eye/I. With marching Caboceers and magnificent Cannibal Kings in its cast of characters, the original third act transformation scene seemed theatrically to re-animate the prodigious work of early-nineteenth-century English explorers who did much to shape European perceptions of the African continent.[6] Yet despite its clear dependence on recycling the "Africa" of the white supremacist imagination, there were those English critics who ultimately recoiled from In Dahomey's representation of a fanciful, sub-Saharan locale dominated by dancing frogs and transmogrifying swamp lands. Indeed, while several journalists argued that the pantomime scene was nothing short of anticlimactic and unimpressive, others waxed altogether mystified over what seemed to be the finale's baffling, absurdist imagery. One critic remarked that "the action of the piece is not In Dahomey until the last act, and when it gets there it goes all to pieces in a manner which is little short of bewildering." Added another, "when the scene changes to Africa, what thread of story there was is entirely lost sight of; and a succession of apparently irrelevant pictures of native life are given."[7]

Missing from the closing sequence was the nostalgically rendered Africa of a bygone era, a prelapsarian province of Edenic native culture which the European spectator might weep over, even as he recognizes his complicity with the imperialist and systemic acts involved in conquering such territories. Rather, this Dahomian scene could only be posited by onlookers as supremely "strange," as a machination sustained in order solely to "show us the African unenslaved, the African in his native majesty, by way of contrast to the Americanized African" who travels the transatlantic divide toward the play's end.[8] The pantomime scene would prove troublesome to some because the crux of the spectacle confirmed that this musical was anything but "nostalgic" in its rendering of African landscape. For the notion of the "putatively static savage societies" which serves as "a stable reference point for defining (the felicitous progress of) civilized identity" metaphorically comes undone as a result of an oddly fanciful "rumble in the jungle." In the dense, green moving foliage of "Dahomey," the stasis of the "native" is set to unravel as "nature" and the racial paradigms attached to such a construct are transfigured and re-imagined through the mechanics of transatlantic theatre. In Dahomey's pantomime act, then, ensured that this production would conclude with a distinctly flamboyant lack of closure.[9]

Yet In Dahomey's infamous transformation scene, on the one hand, threatened to reinforce European fantasies of African atemporalism. Certainly the pantomime's most startling images flirt with collapsing into what Anne Mc-Clintock reads as the "anachronistic space" so central to classic Eurocentric explorer narratives.[10] Williams and Walker were no doubt juggling dangerous representational forms as black entertainers at the turn of a new century. At the same time, I would argue that the racial dynamics of *In Dahomey* were distinct from the recognizable racial caricatures of nineteenth-century traveler tracts and blackface minstrel shows. *In Dahomey*'s "African scene" is different because of its fullness, rather than its emptiness, its "busy-ness" rather than its pedestrian structure, its sardonic subterfuge rather than its rudimentary barbarism. At its core, Williams and Walker's musical set a precedent for yoking broad strokes of romantic whimsy with black political intent and activist vision. Indeed, the musical's seeming "incoherence" to some is in fact a cue for us to pay close attention to the ways that this black theatrical production broke new ground and challenged the terms of representational coherency in relation to race.[11] From its phantasmagoric ending to its large-scale, frenetically paced choruses, *In Dahomey* was a production that dared to couch new images of African American culture within the old. The musical imagined spectacles of black transformation and black plenitude and embedded those concepts in its libretto as well as in its song and dance. Even as the producers and performers ostensibly pandered to the demands of its audiences by resituating the last scene as a prologue, the musical held fast to the play of transformation and forecast its centrality as a theme that would course through the very heart of the production.

The pantomime sequence in Williams and Walker's *In Dahomey* was, then, just the beginning of a series of disruptions along racial, gender, and national lines within the musical. It was a production founded on an abundance of figurative and literal instabilities. Little wonder, then, that a range of transatlantic critics nonetheless voiced their disappointment with the musical's "thoroughly American and up-to-date quality," proclaiming that this was their "chief grievance against *In Dahomey*. . . . We thought it was to be 'negro' from beginning to end. . . . What we really get is negro-America. We do not get the negro in the rough . . . [but] Yankee veneer" (Green, "*In Dahomey*," 29). Indeed, a fair share of English and American critics took the production to task for not pandering to a more recognizable set of racial codes. Particularly in America, as theatre historian Henry T. Sampson reminds, numerous touring black musicals were "severely criticized by white critics for being insufficiently 'Negroid.'" The critical responses to *In Dahomey* illuminate the extent to which racial typology was already scripted in transatlantic theatre culture and the extent to which *In Dahomey* dissented from that typology.[12]

17. A Song and Dance "Broadway in Dahomey." Courtesy of the Victoria and Albert Picture Library, Victoria and Albert Museum.

The "mourning" evident in these critiques reveals the complexity of a musical often dismissed for its inability to engage with sophisticated character constructions and resistant performative strategies. As David Krasner has demonstrated in his study of turn-of-the-century black theatre, some of the earliest black musicals played with both re-inscribing and undoing racist tropes while also bearing the burden of their contiguity with a bygone (white) minstrelsy era. This chapter extends this sort of query by examining the bold and iconoclastic black musical theatre of the Williams and Walker Company at the turn of the century. Their complex and experimental musical *In Dahomey* (1902–4) serves as a critical example of African American cultural identity formation and performance politics in flux. Within this colorful landscape of change and transformation, I explore the textual and cultural volatility of this production in order to demonstrate the ways that *In Dahomey* operates as a musical that posed a series of complex representational inversions of race, gender, and nation.

Despite its textual sophistication, *In Dahomey* remains a play that is often dehistoricized and demetaphorized by contemporary critics who fail to read the daring and transgressive images running rampant in the production. Although Eric Sundquist suggests that "back-to-Africa musicals were mostly vaudeville routines transferred to a cardboard Africa, with virtually nothing African about them," below I suggest the ways that *In Dahomey* is not so much about literally being present "in Dahomey."[13] Instead, it is what happens in the brief yet startling transmutative sequences when one is "there" that serves as a catalyst and a recurring, figurative trope that repeatedly critiques and rewrites racial categories and conventional notions of identity formation. *In Dahomey* thrives less on affirming and reinforcing dominant racial caricatures and more on unmaking and challenging those very representations through contending with boundaries of self and black "nationhood." Given the wildly controversial spectacle at play's end, the abrupt rendition of the British national anthem at curtain call suggests finally that the state had been (symbolically) summoned to restore order and coherency to the musical. It was left up to a spirited round of "God Save the King" to delimit the carnivalesque, supremely ambiguous, and radically unsettling elements of the first all-black musical to be produced in a major Broadway theatre and to be staged triumphantly in London's theatre district.[14]

### "This Heterogeneous Yet Indivisible People":
### Rupture and (Re)Vision in Turn-of-the-Century Black Theatre

To Sylvester Russell, *In Dahomey*'s pure and unadulterated international success was hardly in the air on September 8, 1902, the night of the musical's stateside opening in Stamford, Connecticut. The leading voice of Gilded Age African American theatre criticism, Russell insisted that the musical had sparks of verve and promise, energy and originality, but he was also quick to identify the production's uneven edges, its "draggy" first act, and its occasionally confusing visual scenarios. Russell adumbrated the comments of English critics when he wrote that the third act of *In Dahomey* was "a dramatic fiasco," a melange of incomprehensible plot developments and implausible twists. Writing for a black readership, he proclaimed that there is "not a literary merit to be found in a band of American Negroes taking a trip to Dahomey merely to bluff the people around them after they get there. We must remember that we belong to an oppressed race ourselves and Jesse Shipp must scratch his head and write the third act over again."[15] However infamous this closing act would later become, Russell's early and explicit critique of *In Dahomey*'s denouement illustrates the extent to which Williams and Walker's musical faced the dual demands and desires of black as well as white audiences. Russell's admonition that African Americans must remember the conditions of their oppression in making and enjoying art bespeaks the rallying cry of racial uplift ideology. In an era of heightened black awareness of the mechanics of racial representation and during a period in which the originating seeds of the "New Negro" era were planted, Williams and Walker's show debuted alongside multiple breakthrough innovations in black literature, poetry, visual art, photography, and essays. At the same time, however, key elements of the play remained disconcertingly archaic, owing as much to the more insipid forms of blackface minstrelsy as they did to late-nineteenth-century progressive art, music, dance, and fiction. As a result, the musical played fast and loose with conventional racial and gender images, walking a fine line between disrupting the master narratives of theatrical "race" performance and simultaneously capitulating to familiar and debilitating caricature.[16]

*In Dahomey*'s disquieting double-vocality manifests a broader conflict in turn-of-the-century African American culture caught between ascribing to the ambitiously sweeping aesthetics of black nationalist writers such as Pauline Hopkins and Sutton Griggs and struggling to get up from under the shadow of old minstrel forms that Sam Lucas and others had worked in as a way to gain entrance to the stage. Even as "politically minded" novelists such as William Wells Brown and Charles Chesnutt slipped at times into notoriously ambiguous strategies of black characterization, it was black theatre that perhaps waged the most ambivalent uphill battle to rewrite white supremacist constructions of blackness.[17] Though the gutsy and original African Company had, in the 1820s, offered a critical paradigm for autonomous black theatre production and management, only in the late nineteenth century did the performance circuit fully blossom into a viable social, economic, and political terrain for black entertainers.[18] With the genealogical roots of minstrelsy as well as the coon song phenomenon spectacularly visible, post-Reconstruction black theatre weathered a taxing gestation period as it struggled to garner the support of African American critics and patrons and as it aimed to earn the respect of mainstream culture. Historically, the black press had given very little attention to black minstrel troupes surfacing at midcentury. Conversely, white minstrel performers responded ambivalently to the presence of professional competition.[19] On either side of the Jim Crow divide, however, minstrelsy remained the elephant in the room. White entertainers struggled with new ways to maintain a foothold in the business, while black performers confronted the harsh reality that this racially crude and malevolent form might serve as a gateway to new professional ventures. Inevitably, blackface minstrelsy evolved into a critical site for black musical theatre's gradual innovative development and popularity by providing a necessary entrance for African Americans to cultivate employment as show business entertainers, playwrights, composers, and eventually producers.

The roots of these opportunities can be traced to the 1850s, a period of broad social, cultural, and political dissonance in transatlantic culture, and one in which the landscape of black performance underwent radical up-heaval. While African American abolitionists crafted and reworked fugitive forms of cultural and political expression, this period also gave birth to orga-nized African American minstrel troupes, the earliest of these northeastern "colored minstrels" dating back to 1855.[20] Following the Civil War, minstrelsy afforded black performers the room to move, socially, economically, and geographically. Put another way, blackface minstrelsy bequeathed African American cultural workers the critical tools to transport themselves literally across the country, to new economic heights, and imagistically out of the desert of blackface abjection. Wealth, mobility, and respect might eventually provide them with the "rare opportunity" to experiment with tidying up the detritus of stereotypes born out of blackface popular culture.[21] Yet the lin-gering irony in the postbellum period's black minstrelsy phenomenon was that even in this profession black labor was largely managed, marketed, and (mis)handled by white entrepreneurs who disproportionately profited from their efforts, particularly by the time of the early 1870s, as Reconstruction began to wane in earnest.[22] As white minstrel entrepreneurs such as Callendar and Haverly continued to promote primitivist notions of black culture, Afri-can American minstrel productions were caught in a vortex of retrograde slavery images. These plantation productions eerily mirrored the erasure of Reconstruction's black enfranchisement efforts even as they made visible a new kind of black (theatrical) labor class asserting its freedom and creating its own aesthetic and economic property.[23]

In many ways, one could read the explosion of the "coon song" phenome-non in the late nineteenth century as an aesthetic instantiation of black social mobility even within the context of the "colored" minstrel show. At the height of their popularity in the 1890s and subsequent decades, coon songs were a distinctly crass and inglorious celebration of grotesque minstrel caricature compressed into syncopated black American folk music melodies. While the most popular numbers re-attached pornographic sloth, social recklessness, and gluttonous excess to blackface blackness, these songs were marked by their postbellum white-supremacist paranoia of Civil War amendments and black socioeconomic autonomy. Songs like "Coons on Parade" and "When a Nigger Makes a Hundred" greeted the aspirations of newly migrant African Americans in the North with a sour wink and a smile.[24] Yet the great irony of the coon song rage was that it too, like minstrel revues before it, became a source of bread and butter for the very individuals it mocked and scorned. As many black entertainers, songwriters, and burgeoning producers began to profit from creating and marketing xenophobic pop songs for a new age, they paradoxically went about the business of nurturing and funding a newly moneyed class of artists intent on developing a black musical theatre of an entirely different order.[25]

Out of this class came the creators of *In Dahomey*. Well-traveled, well-schooled, and well-skilled, their specific aim was to push African American performance in a new direction for a new century. Whether they could advance past the weight of burnt-cork end men and chicken and watermelon serenades was a question that some black critics publicly posed as the curtain went up on Williams and Walker's grand and ambitious endeavors. It is a question that contemporary scholars continue to ask as they revisit the rocky terrain of *Dahomey* and other back-to-Africa musicals from the Gilded Age. Importantly, as critics continue to search for the "cracks in the public mask of the black man" that Sandra Richards locates in her pioneering work on Williams and Walker, we might also continue to refine our method of sussing out the provocative "cracks" in postbellum black performance. Were dissonant expressive strategies discernible to audiences and critics searching for signs of uplift then as well as now? If so, how do we recuperate and mark these moments when, to borrow a phrase from Malcolm X, (coon) singing turned into swinging?[26]

The itinerancy of early black musical theatre's entrepreneurs and performers had much to do with the form's latent insurgency. As an increasing number of African Americans became immersed in the sweeping culture of migration at the turn of the century, the structure and content of black performance manifested and responded to the conditions of movement, resettlement, and dislocation. Foreshadowing the wily tricksters in George Schuyler's 1930s satiric novel *Black No More* who benefit from "observation and contact" with the master (white) class, the pioneers of the Gilded Age's black theatre circuit would gradually reformulate, stylize, and create a rupture in minstrel and coon song forms by way of a similar strategy.[27] Perhaps no turn-of-the-century black performer articulated an interest in observation and contact and thought and theorized more provocatively on the process of white performance and African American theatre craft than George Walker. In two high-profile articles published during the height of his company's fame, Walker wrote at length about nascent black theatre strategies and detailed his dual commitment to black entertainment culture and racial uplift politics. In a brilliant and oft-cited 1906 *Theatre Magazine* article published three years after *In Dahomey*'s ambitious debut and five years before his untimely death, Walker outlined the bursts of inspiration and youthful creativity that led to the Williams and Walker partnership and the company's risk-taking theatrical endeavors. Part autobiographical sketch, part editorial polemic, the article reads as much like an American migration narrative as it does a rumination on African American performance tactics and political intent. The detail that Walker assigns to his roots in Lawrence, Kansas, as a "lad" who latched onto colored minstrelsy and medicine shows proves helpful in tracing some of the cultural experiences that would no doubt influence his later work with Bert Williams. Walker incorporates rich detail in his description of "roughing it" all the way to California, encountering picaresque show business characters who mentored him in the art of observing white minstrel performers and who assisted him in stylizing his own craft. His comments create a lively record of black spectatorship and the evolution of African American turn-of-the-century theatre aesthetics.[28]

Walker's account of meeting "quack doctors doing business in the West" and his forthright assessment of racial politics in entertainment culture shape the structure of his narrative. Implicit in the article is the suggestion that moving around the country enabled him to engage in methods of observation and contact which ultimately informed the development of Williams and Walker's successful craftsmanship. If, as Walker observes, "in those early days of the black man on the American stage," it remained hard to believe that African American men "would ever rise above being a mere minstrel man," the actor's *Theatre Magazine* piece illuminates his fierce dedication and strategic commitment to reversing that trend through his work as a performer. Anticipating the shrewd, racialized business acumen of Schuyler's protagonist Max Disher some thirty-three years later, Walker declares that his "experience with the quack doctors taught me two good lessons: that white people are always interested in what they call 'darky' singing and dancing; and the fact that I could entertain in that way as no white man could, made me valuable to the quack doctors." Walker suggests that this revelation led to his and Williams's subsequent forays into the world of white performance culture. Amplifying the detective roles that they would inhabit in their *Dahomey* musical, the Williams and Walker of the 1906 *Theatre Magazine* piece troll the world of west coast theatre in a bid to document and evaluate the mechanics of white minstrelsy.[29] "When we were not working," Walker reports,

> we frequented the playhouses just the same. In those days black-faced white comedians were numerous and very popular. They billed themselves "coons." Bert and I watched the white "coons," and were often much amused at seeing white men with black cork on their faces trying to imitate black folk. Nothing about these white men's actions was natural and there-

fore nothing was as interesting as if black performers had been dancing and singing their own songs in their own way.[30]

Walker's statement is a remarkable cultural document for several reasons. First, it makes visible the daily craftsmanship of the black actor and gives a strong and public voice to the figure of the black theatre spectator. Black performance emerges as craft and labor in this piece, and it demands an investment in time and preparation as the two actors commit themselves to visiting other venues and processing the skills of fellow actors. The most stunning detail of Walker's narrative is his description of how he and Bert would "watc[h] the white 'coons'" with a mixture of amusement and seeming disregard as these performers floundered in what he reads as a hopeless effort to embody the "natural." It is a rich moment, and it is one that recalls the many undervalued instances of African Americans registering and evaluating what historian Mia Bay refers to as the "white image in the black mind."[31] Second, Walker's anecdote of black performers encountering whites in blackface slyly reverses a key primal scene in minstrel history. If the lore of white entertainer T. D. Rice spying a disabled black man "jumping Jim Crow" and transforming that dance into the earliest of minstrel shows was legendary nineteenth-century knowledge, Walker's tale of encountering bland and ineffectual white racial mimicry repeats the moment of observation and appropriation in order to reject the "counterfeit" act and to clear a space for bold, colorful, and, what he here calls, "natural" black performance.[32]

Walker was a notorious stickler when it came to proclaiming and embracing the authenticity of African American performance practices, even as his comments, as well as the form and content of his subsequent theatrical work, suggest a more complicated approach to articulating racial identity formation. As Williams and Walker gained global notoriety, Walker seldom shied away from discussing and comparing white and black performance practices. He was indeed the savvy business partner half of the duo and exploited controversial topics as both an expression of forthright conviction and as a means to publicity, often playing with images of the black gaze, racial authenticity politics, and what he openly perceived as the fallacies of white mimicry. The aesthetic differentiation in segregated theatre culture particularly drew his ire. Again documenting his and Williams's research of white and black performances in the black periodical *The New York Age*, Walker pointed out a disparity that "began to agitate [their] gray matter. . . . We noticed that colored men had to be . . . athletic comedians." Conversely, he observes that "the white man gets the desired results without perspiring." What made Walker perhaps most ingenious is that he was able to channel his palpable discontent regarding the inequities of Jim Crow theatre practices into performances and publicity stunts that directly addressed questions of racial competition and appropriation. Challenging a white business tycoon to a well-orchestrated cakewalk duel in 1898 called attention to racial discordance in performance culture by way of a satiric cultural spectacle. For Walker, the quest to level the playing field between white and black performers remained an urgent concern, and he dedicated himself tirelessly to stretching the boundaries of what "colored" performers could and could not do on the stage. He seemed to care most about providing opportunities for black actors and rectifying the problem of white minstrels who "stood in the way of black actors, and thus he pledged "to do all [he] could to get what [he] felt belonged to us by the laws of nature."[33]

George Walker was joined in his professional crusade by a cluster of key players who challenged the boundaries of the color barrier through resourcefully imaginative means. Called by some the "strongest theatrical combination" of the early twentieth century, the Williams and Walker Company served as a base for black performers and theatre workers to imagine and execute forms of expression which flagrantly transgressed the color line.[34] Through diligent and diverse methods of encountering and turning the gaze back onto white supremacist performance culture and by melding rigorous imitation with surreptitious bastardization, and bold parody into new forms, a group of impassioned young black performers in their twenties and thirties, from places like Kansas, California, and Washington, D.C., came together in New York City to collaborate and to create a fast-moving and unpredictable musical of enormous proportion. A mobile class of artists, their work seemed to mirror and manifest the politics of movement and dislocation. The son of a Bahamian immigrant family, Bert Williams moved, for instance, from the Caribbean to Florida and on to Riverside, California, before making the trek to northern California, where he had intended to enroll at Stanford University. His subsequent meeting with Walker in San Francisco led to the inception of their sixteen-year partnership. Celebrated for being a "master of gesture," Williams honed a dissonant method of performance that went, as Camille Forbes suggests, "against the discourse of minstrelsy" in order "to ascribe new meanings to his black body."[35]

Likewise, in his intricate and wildly influential compositions for the most prominent and successful black theatre productions of the era, heavyweight composer Will Marion Cook created musical material that manifested his own unique Du Boisian "two-ness." As the heir to a prominent, "talented tenth" family who found his initial success in coon songs and colored musical revues,

Cook waged a tortuous and complicated struggle to negotiate between an elite classical music training and the limited employment opportunities available to African American entertainers at the turn of the century. Cook's remarkable pedigree which took him from Oberlin Conservatory to Berlin and on to New York City's National Conservatory where he studied with Joseph Joachim and Antonin Dvorak resulted in his ability to draw from a potent elixir of European and African American forms in his "genius" compositional aesthetic. A composer who once advised a young Duke Ellington to find "logical ways" of making art and then avoid them and "let your inner self break through," Cook is often recognized for having executed a way to "mov[e] fluidly between black and white styles, drawing on the breadth of his training as a musician."[36] As the principal composer for In Dahomey, he brought a sharp, cosmopolitan musical aesthetic to the production which he daringly matched with unpredictable experimental flourishes in musical form.

A professional mentor figure to many of the players in the Williams and Walker Company, Cook presided over a group of inspired artists such as Jesse Shipp, who enjoyed a reputation for being an enormously successful stage manager in New York. Shipp was one of the key figures in the production team. A veteran of colored minstrel shows, he is credited with having written the bulk of the In Dahomey libretto and for helping to manage the production demands of the company's domestic and U.K. tours. The grace and grand vision of these elegant and imaginative theatre men—from Williams and Walker to Cook, Shipp, and composer-lyricist Alex Rogers—were matched by the contributions of several trailblazing women who worked in and traveled with the In Dahomey company.[37] Singers Abbie Mitchell, Lottie Williams, and Hattie McIntosh drew critical attention for their roles in the musical, and the activist actress and choreographer Aida Overton Walker garnered praise from journalists and audiences that often rivaled that of the stars of the show. These women's participation in the company reinforced the belief that theatre could serve as a particularly viable field of opportunity for African American women of the new century. Moreover, that three out of four of these women were married to principal members of the production team illuminates the extent to which the world of postbellum black musical theatre was populated by a unique class of African American heterosexual couples with similar professional, political, and social aspirations. In its vibrant professional couplings, the Williams and Walker Company to some extent mirrored the visions of postbellum black women's club visionaries such as Pauline Hopkins and Frances Harper who, in their turn-of-the-century fiction, imagined and theorized the exigencies of lively and creative cross-gender partnership as central to racial uplift. Together these performers created and moved through colorful cultural spaces.[38]

Although musical theatre "became one of the few avenues of black mobility in a white world," this socioeconomic movement coupled with the experience of social encounter afforded by black theatre's appeal to black as well as white audiences established a strikingly dissonant situation. The great irony in performing a musical like *In Dahomey* which focused on black emigration, entrepreneurial pursuits, and class aspirations was that it presented these themes in the midst of a space where, as one critic remarked in 1903, "the color line ha[d] been drawn." And thus, for all its lavish images of high-stepping, globe-trotting, and social-climbing African Americans, *In Dahomey*'s Broadway debut at the opulent New York Theatre was nonetheless subject to the constrictive tyrannies of segregated seating plans. More than one thousand black patrons reportedly turned out for opening night on February 18, 1903, dressed to the nines, despite the fact that they were shuttled away to "the bleak and inhospitable gallery."[39] In spite of the sting of this insult, the musical event itself created a space where black patrons were able to *imagine* themselves moving through time and space, across land and nation, from costume to costume. At the very least, these black Manhattanites took the occasion of a night out at a Broadway theatre to adorn themselves in the kinds of elegant sartorial items—"evening gowns, tuxedos, and swallow tails, just the same as the 'white 400'" in the house. For these black patrons the event became another way to contest the boundaries of the color barrier, "crossing over" into the fabulous world of New York social life. In short, during an era in which the color line fortified itself in law and social spaces, black theatre performers took advantage of stretching their own as well as their audience's movement and opportunities for social encounter. Through the musical form they claimed "a space for creative, joyous, and powerful body movement unencumbered" by blackface caricature.[40]

For the African American women and men who worked in black musical theatre, the long-term goal was simple and clear: create black art by, for, and about black people. As pioneering songwriter and composer Bob Cole (one half of the period's other dominant black theatre team Cole and Johnson) put it in his 1898 "Colored Actor's Declaration of Independence," the aim of the colored musical companies was to write, manage, and produce their own shows. But to this manifesto Cole would add the important pledge to wage a war against the color barrier by insisting that there must be "[n]o divided houses—our races must be seated from the boxes back." Writing from the vantage point of the flourishing Harlem Renaissance, James Weldon Johnson documented the bustling activities of this distinct and lively group of black theatre actors and entrepreneurs who worked to fulfill the vision of Cole, Johnson, and others. The "new phase of life among coloured New Yorkers" and the swelling numbers of black migrants fresh from places like Georgia, Florida, and Tennessee delivered vital energy to the city. Midtown Manhattan's Tenderloin area took root as the space where black actors, musicians, and managers began to congregate and create aesthetic as well as political coalitions. George Walker was a major organizer in this regard. In addition to his keen managerial skills, the actor was quick to establish a space, known as "the Williams and Walker flat," where black theatre artists congregated. He also played a key role in spearheading the creation of The Frogs, a landmark professional organization designed to promote and legitimize black theatre so that productions were not "lumped" by white audiences into "circus attractions."[41]

This vibrant community of spirited collaborations and buoyant social gatherings yielded increasing triumph for New York's black actors, musicians, and composers. The rousing rooftop success of 1898's *Clorindy, or the Origin of the Cakewalk* served as a precursor to *In Dahomey*'s and evolved out of the connections made in the core group from "the Williams and Walker flat." A late-night summer entertainment atop the Casino Roof Garden, *Clorindy* took shape as a result of Cook's compositions, arrangements, and his prescient collaboration with celebrity poet and Midwest transplant Paul Laurence Dunbar. While the two had initially met in Chicago, it was in the Tenderloin area that Cook and Dunbar wrote the music and lyrics for what became *Clorindy*.[42] The partnership was an infamously fraught one, despite the fact that Dunbar was, in every way, Cook's lyrical counterpart. Like Cook, Dunbar famously wrestled with tensions between classical forms and vernacular expressiveness in his highly successful post-Reconstruction poetry; he too notoriously straddled an aesthetic divide as expansively complex as Cook's music. Born in Dayton, Ohio, Dunbar moved around the Midwest, Northeast, and the United Kingdom and had made a name for himself as a poet capable of writing both crisp and elegant "odes" to Africa as well as salty, dialect-driven verses born out of the mythical mouths of "the folk." Eventually finding his way into the Williams and Walker circle of lively and prolific black Manhattan, Dunbar's work with Cook would serve as an all-important precursor to *In Dahomey*.

That the two were able to make some sort of peace to work on *In Dahomey* seems miraculous considering Cook's proclamation that he could not work again with Dunbar. Likewise Dunbar had registered a palpable horror on

*Clorindy*'s opening night when black people were "laughing at themselves" and "offering themselves as objects for the laughter of others." At the time, he vowed that "*Clorindy* would be his last coon show." But in spite of (or perhaps directly as a result of) this conflict, a second fuller and remarkably ambitious production emerged. Perhaps this professional friction resulted in a "collaborative dissonance" (to borrow a phrase from Brent Edwards) which informs the quirky, off-center nature of Cook and Dunbar's work in black musical theatre. At the very least, the conflicts that they weathered only added to each artist's tortured efforts to reconcile mainstream success with aesthetic integrity. Cook waged a struggle to balance blackface composition with classical experimentation. Similarly, Dunbar was attempting to mediate his interest in eighteenth-century English comedies of manners and the financial necessity to write for minstrel shows.[43] At the heart of both Cook's and Dunbar's work was a quest to produce art that might speak to "the difficult question of progress after emancipation, the adjustments of reconstruction, the perils and the promise of migration to Northern cities, and the paradoxes of portraying 'Negro' life authentically while a residue of stereotype remained strong in society on the whole." In the midst of these myriad struggles and conflicts, these two brilliant men came together to make art that seemingly registered their difficulty with each other as well as the alienating experience of black life in postbellum America.[44]

Although undoubtedly heterogeneous in their multiple and diverse professional aspirations, the core creators of *In Dahomey* were united by a single passion to experiment with form and a dedication to advancing the field of black theatrical performance to new levels of innovation and imagination. Desiring to break new ground for black performers, George Walker envisioned a musical that might make what he called a dramatic "leap" forward in theatre. Critically, this goal meant working on a two-pronged front to both disrupt the minstrel form and to offer what Walker purportedly believed to be more "earnest" representations of black people. As he ominously recounted in *Theatre Magazine*, in the duo's early years, "we saw that the colored performer would have to get away from the ragtime limitations of the 'darky,' and we decided to make the break, so as to save ourselves and others." Williams and Walker were intent on creating a rupture in the minstrel form and "making a radical departure from the old 'darky' style of singing and dancing" in order to think "along new lines."[45] They did so with a new musical that veered left of dominant racial authenticity politics at the turn of the century and that diverged in critical ways from previous African American expressive forms as well.

Within this climate in which people like Williams, Walker, Dunbar, and Cook were actively experimenting with ways to break free of form and create new ones, *In Dahomey* took shape. In particular, Williams and Walker gained specific inspiration for creating the musical as a result of what Forbes might call the duo's unique "bilateral racial" interaction in the late 1890s and early 1900s. These extraordinary encounters served as evidence of their own profound (and perhaps aesthetically fortuitous) sites of social and cultural dislocation, and they shaped and informed the duo's sense of theatrical experimentation. To Walker, the experience of watching white men imitating black people presented a profound crisis for black performers who were rendered absent and unnecessary by the acts of "white coons." A double-negative of sorts, black performers like Walker and Williams stood in the shadows while the grotesque, mythical antiheroes of white minstrelsy created and assumed the roles of black figures in the cultural imaginary. For those black men and women who eventually entered the profession, Walker famously remarked that nothing "seemed more absurd than to see a colored man making himself ridiculous in order to portray himself."[46] For Walker, the sheer alienation in watching white men "blacking up" and black men doing the same served, in part, as a catalyst for him to create a space for what he called the "natural" black performer. But a chance encounter in San Francisco ultimately redirected the way that he and Williams articulated and grappled with "the natural" in black performance in significant ways.

Hired as last-minute "sham native Dahomians" at San Francisco's Midwinter Fair in 1893, the duo were, as Walker describes, "brought into close touch with native Africans" who were incorporated into the large-scale imperial exhibition. The idea of two postbellum black performers being paid to perform the "part" of Africans who had yet to arrive from their native land was extraordinary enough as it is. But what made the incident all the more remarkable was George Walker's enterprising resolve to create something entirely new out of the encounter. Indicative of the ideological struggle apparent in his *Theatre Magazine* article which oscillates between a capitulation to "the real" ("real coons" and the "laws of nature" in black performance) and a commitment to the aesthetically imagined, Walker came out of the Dahomian encounter with an interest in somehow attempting to straddle the boundaries between an "authentic" and a fanciful "blackness" in theatrical performance. "We were not long in deciding that," he claimed in hindsight, "if we ever reached the point of having a show of our own, *we would delineate and feature native African characters as far as we could, and still remain American,* and make our acting interesting and entertaining to American audiences."[47]

Walker's comments make plain the pair's interest in producing multivocal black cultural expressiveness. But his comments also reflected something richly anticipatory of what Bertolt Brecht later envisioned as a kind of theatrical alienation. Inasmuch as Walker's actor attempts to remain the actor while "showing" the (African) character for the audience in question, he engages in a method that prefigured Brecht's twentieth-century efforts to create a theatre in which the "performer's self-observation, artful and artistic act of self-alienation" prevents "the spectator from losing himself in the character completely."[48] From this standpoint, we might call Walker's ambitious efforts to perform the hyphenated self a kind of Afro-diasporic alienation effect. While the ethnographic impulse in Walker's statement is undeniable, and his aim to display "the native" plainly borrows the language of exhibition culture of the period, his comments also reveal an impulse to imagine a space where black performers might straddle the dually elusive (illusive as well as allusive) spheres of "African" and "American" identity. Walker and Williams were thus deeply immersed in questioning how and in what ways to articulate the dissonant multivocality of black identity in performance space.

Not surprisingly, Walker would claim with certainty and pride that "we were the first to introduce the Americanized African songs," numbers such as "My Zulu Babe," "My Castle on the Nile," and "My Dahomian Queen" in *In Dahomey*. The actor was intrigued with ways of performing the condition of (re)imagining "Africa" through African American eyes. Born in the interstices of Walker and Williams's detective-like observations about white coons and Dahomians in the city by the bay and placed in an imperial pop cultural universe clambering for exhibitions of "the real" and "the native," *In Dahomey* arrived on the transatlantic musical scene. Williams and Walker's production conjured up a new paradigm for black performance that mixed, scrambled, and churned back out disruptive images of burnt-cork bodies and displaced "natives" in order to express the distinct experience of African American alienation at the turn of the century. The duo and their company created a rupture in the inherited forms of black representation in order to re-envision social and cultural survival, and they sought to reclaim "blackness" as a kind of property invested with wealth and induced with real social and cultural power for African Americans.

*In Dahomey* first opened in Stamford, Connecticut, on September 8, 1902, against a backdrop of increasing U.S. imperialism and in the midst of an evolving transatlantic popular culture invested in the display of indigenous peoples. It was a period in which U.S. expansionist efforts were in fact commensurate with the disfranchisement of U.S. people of color.[49] Imperial exhibits like "Darkest Africa" in the United States and the "Dahomeyan Village" displays in both the States and the U.K. additionally marketed black primitivist paradigms for public consumption and sustained an oddly tense juxtaposition with turn-of-the-century black theatre.[50] Strangely and disquietingly heterogeneous, *In Dahomey* inserted itself in this volatile cultural fabric of ethnological spectacles and scientific exhibits by offering a vertiginous combination of forms and images. While it featured much of the structure that became standard in early black musicals—an overture, chorus, some improvisation, featured singers, specialty entertainers, company song and dance numbers, humor scenarios, and magnificent displays—the musical nevertheless represented a break, not only from plantation minstrel shows featuring black performers but also from earlier African American show business productions. Mixing multiple forms, the show borrowed liberally from the spectacular unpredictability and visual impressiveness of the extravaganza form in its utilization of a large cast, lavish costumes, and a fast-moving plot like that of the 1890s colored minstrel variety productions like *The Creole Burlesque Show*. The show also bore some resemblance to midcentury burlesque productions like 1869's *Robinson Crusoe*. At the same time, however, critics have argued that it is *In Dahomey*'s Will Cook–engineered musical composition which "consistently transcends the expressive straitjacket that the prevailing coon song style imposed on black artistry in the realm of popular music and theatre." With an impressive array of solos, chorus compositions, and instrumental dance numbers woven into the production, *In Dahomey* manifested a trailblazing cultural and generic diversity.[51]

What made the production such a formidable endeavor was its amorphousness, its ability to stretch and change forms as it progressed and evolved over 1,100 performances from 1902 to 1905. At the core of this fluctuating program was the fluid and frequent use of interpolations. Musical theatre historian Thomas Riis has done much to demonstrate the extent to which *In Dahomey* was the product of many different voices and visions, in part because it featured a multiplicity of songs that were mixed, matched, and interchanged across multiple and distinct productions mounted in New York, London, and Boston. Although the element of change is certainly nothing new to the culture of turn-of-the-century dramaturgy, this kind of moving workshop of tooling and retooling the show was critically important to black performers. *In Dahomey* was a place where African American cultural producers improvised themselves into consciousness. Just as the production "was simultaneously one thing and many things, a story told in dialogue, song, and action, yet never quite the same on successive nights," so too did it reflect the "changing same" of black identity formation. Indeed, the shifting form of the show became the fulcrum of the black identity paradigms that *In Dahomey* brought to life onstage every night.[52]

The remainder of this chapter, then, reads *In Dahomey* as a site of shifting textual possibility for black performers in this new era of possibility. The chapter focuses most fully on the initial version of the script published in the United States in 1902 in order to explore the provocative disjointedness and the fecund ruptures embedded in that very text and in subsequent performances of the script. Taking the prevalent theme of terrible transmutation in coon songs as a point of departure, *In Dahomey* appropriated the concept of transformation in its very form.[53] By aggressively mixing and matching genres and material, it created something indeed new and, at times, baffling to even the likes of Sylvester Russell. But it would also, as black journalist R. C. Murray observed in hindsight of the musical's globetrotting success, come to encapsulate a "history of the progress of this heterogeneous, yet indivisible people" at the dawn of a new century.

### Nappy Edges

Can the Ethiopian change his skin? the leopard change his spots?
—George Moore, *Impressions and Opinions*

An "irresistibly protean" work in progress, *In Dahomey*'s plot underwent frequent revisions as the production traveled from the Northwest and on to the U.K. before returning to the States in 1904.[54] Yet across two continents and over a thousand performances, the musical's skeletal narrative remained essentially the same: finding themselves embroiled in an odd quest to return a family heirloom to its proper owner, the transient dandy Rareback Pinkerton (Walker) and his socially inept sidekick Shylock Homestead (Williams) embark on a journey which takes them from Boston to Florida and the home of Cicero Lightfoot, the "President of a Colonization Society," and finally to the West African region of Caboceer in Dahomey, where the two protagonists, accompanied by a large and motley entourage, choose to relocate in order to build a "broadway in the jungle."[55] During their travels, Rareback and Shylock encounter a diverse assortment of characters who are, like them, obsessed with social climbing. They run the gamut from Lightfoot's glamorous bourgeois daughter (Aida Overton Walker) who longs for the pleasures of the social aristocracy to a smooth-talking urban hustler intent on reaping the benefits of black colonization in Africa.

Concerned with the politics of place, (re)settlement, and African American (dis)placement, *In Dahomey*'s first act slyly pronounces these themes by commencing its action in front of an "Intelligence Office" located in downtown Boston, circa 1902. With the theme of espionage hovering provocatively in the backdrop, the curious setting invites audiences to enter into a world of subterfuge and duplicity. Most critics of *In Dahomey* have overlooked this seemingly small detail of place in the musical's opening scene in favor of focusing on the larger implications of transnationalism embedded in the plot. Yet the presence of this mysterious "office" would prove thematically resonant in the context of the production. From the minor role of George Reeder (reader), the figure who runs the Intelligence Office, to the more pronounced activities of the would-be detectives Pinkerton and Shylock, *In Dahomey* is fundamentally a work that articulates the ways that postbellum African Americans were constantly sleuthing for answers to their own condition. As private eyes hired to retrieve Cicero Lightfoot's prized silver casket, Williams and Walker's turns as "Rare and Shy" might, on the one hand, seem to merely provide a convenient vehicle for the two entertainers to engage in what the script directions often richly refer to as "business," carefully inspired physical and verbal improvisation (1D1, 69). But the detective figure may serve as another indicator of just how oppositionally situated the musical imagined itself to be. After all, as the Sherlockian Shylock remarks toward the end of act 1, "What's the use of being a detective if you can't ask questions"? (1D1, 72).[56]

The questions and concerns the musical repeatedly asked were often housed in the figures of its seemingly innocuous detectives. In George Walker's lengthy monologue from act 2, scene 2, for instance, Rareback recounts and reanimates the adventures of the dime-novel detective hero Nick Carter for his partner. His tour-de-force performance allowed for the comedian to turn on his "electric smile" and to make use of "wild gestures" and "long words" in the middle of the production in what is often read as a scene which merely enabled the performing veteran to showcase his abilities (1D1, 76–78). But the riddle of Rare's spirited narration of "Old Sleuths" and robbers on the run perhaps has a resounding answer in the figure of Bert Williams's "Jonah Man," his signature song that he often inserted at the end of the Nick Carter narrative. While "Jonah Man" would become a Bert Williams classic upon its interpolation into *In Dahomey*, its particular placement within the musical complicates the stock figure of the detective in the narrative. As Forbes contends, Williams's Jonah Man figure "deepened the usually simplistic 'darky' character. . . . Not merely miserable, or unlucky, the unfortunate Jonah Man. . . . Communicated the experience of the wretched."[57] A kind of call-and-response sequence rendered in comedy and song, Walker's Rareback comes to life in the form of a "first-class detective" figure who, in his entertaining tale, apprehends thieves and saves the day, while Williams's Jonah Man emerges as an existential response of sorts. Ever seeking a place to "homestead," Shylock can only sing the blues about his "hard luck" and his "old, old tale" of falling down a "coal hole" (1D1, 85). Together this oblique juxtaposition of lively detective work and lost men gives greater metaphorical meaning to the role of the detectives in *In Dahomey*. In short, Shylock's shiftlessness is a contrast and a problem that Rareback will try to rectify by encouraging him to seize on fulfilling employment as a detective—or at least to get rich and climb the social ladder as he intends to do. As a team, Rareback and Shylock sleuth toward the promise of African American identity remade and resurrected somewhere along the journey to Dahomey.

That journey toward revision and reinvention begins, however, long before Rare and Shy make their comic entrance in act 1. Outside Boston's Office of Intelligence, the musical commences its adventure with a gaggle of nameless characters seduced by the promise of corporeal convertibility. Gathering together in the street, they listen to the noisy pitch of the boisterous "Dr. Straight," a figure who, the program's cast of characters relates, is "straight" in "name only" but is, in fact, a "street fakir" trafficking in fraudulence. Above the orchestrated din of Tambo and Bones, two joke-cracking end men (1D1, 66), relics of the minstrel tradition which this all-black company will, through the course of this production, attempt to disassemble, the (dis)honorable Dr. Straight makes his opening appeal to a curious throng of onlookers and attempts to peddle an oddly concocted product with shockingly potent powers. To his entranced audience, Straight unveils a mysterious potion "made from roots, herbs, barks, leaf grasses, cereals, vegetables, fruits and chemicals warranted by myself, to do all that I claim, even more" (1D1, 66).

With his penchant for malapropisms and mangled monologue, Straight would seem to serve no greater purpose in the production than to provide additional continuity with the minstrel show tradition. But Straight's ideological and symbolic agency exceeds the limitations of minstrelsy in critical ways. A flamboyant charlatan, Straight is visibly linked to a genealogy of blackface performance culture. A popular figure from the medicine show circuit, he embodies the theatrical traditions on which cast members like George Walker initially cut their show business teeth. He also operates as the transitional bridge for cast and characters alike between postbellum black cultural performance and theatre proper. Most importantly, Straight opens the musical with a radical proposition that speaks to the fundamental hopes and desires of each of *In Dahomey*'s curious combination of desiring, oddball characters. He claims that his potion can transform "any dark skin son or daughter of the genius Africanus" into "an Apollo or Cleopatra with a hirsute appendage worthy of a Greek goddess" (ID1, 66). With an arsenal of "natural ingredients" by his side, Straight here plays with the boundaries of racial categories. Right before the audience's very eyes, Straight shrewdly flaunts the possibility that this organic product might ultimately "denaturalize" racial physiognomy for all who dare to use it. More than the sum of the fraud which his name belies, Straight's project is one which pivots on a process (pun intended) of literally transforming and transfiguring corporeal blackness into a sign of canonical, European-fetishized "beauty" marks.[58]

But this potion changes more than skin tone. As Straight proclaims, "this compound known as Straightaline is the greatest hair tonic on earth." It has the power to "make hair grow on bald-headed babies. It makes curly hair as straight as a stick in from one to ten days. Straightaline straightens kinky hair in from ten to thirty days and most wonderful of all, Straightaline straightens knappy or knotty hair" (ID1, 67). Straight peddles a potion which cuts to the heart of black representational politics by addressing the racial signification of hair itself. As Kobena Mercer has argued, "black people's hair" has "been historically devalued as the most visible stigmata of blackness, second only to skin." For this reason, he adds, "where race is a constitutive element of social structure and social division, hair remains powerfully charged with symbolic currency."[59] In this remarkable opening scene *In Dahomey* confronts the loaded semiotics of race and hair with sharply coded language and disorienting imagery. Disassembling and restructuring (racial) body parts on the medicine show market, the scene confronts and renders chaotic Jim Crow systems of logic which sought to discipline black "dress, walk [and] comport[ment]" in the postbellum era. In a moment which forecasts the fundamental social and political insurgency of the musical, all hell breaks loose in Dr. Straight's funhouse of racial cosmetology where the conventions of the "white coon" minstrel shows are shown to the door.[60]

Gradually and methodically, the "stigmata" of hair as well as skin in this scene are turned topsy-turvy, for Straight's product turns out to be an elaborate linguistic and metaphorical pun. As the crowd slowly works itself into a frenzy over the Straightaline sale, the doctor presents yet another product to bolster his claims which he refers to simply as "Oblicuticus." The " 'Obli,' " he explains, "in this case, being an abbreviation of the word 'obliterate.' 'Cuti'— taken from the word 'cuticle,' the outer skin, and 'cuss' is what everybody does when the desired results are not obtained, but there is no such thing as 'fail' " (ID1, 67). A disturbing concept indeed, this attempt to "obliterate" blackness rests on a teasingly disruptive premise, however, since it suggests that even the biologically fixed topography of skin can be converted into a terrain of artifice, a point of trickery. Straight describes how "this wonderful face bleach removes the outer skin and leaves in its place a peachlike complexion that can't be duplicated—even by peaches. Changing black to white and vice versa." What is striking about Straight's pitch is the way that his language insists upon the oddly "un-real" quality of this skin-lightening transfiguration. Rather than endorsing an oversimplified mimesis of whiteness, Straight promises his customers that Oblicuticus will yield a "peachlike" complexion which remains weirdly incomparable—even in relation to the thing which it ostensibly mimics. Rather perversely at this moment, instead of becoming "white," the Oblicuticus consumer becomes something beyond or strangely outside of—perhaps even signifying on—whiteness. He or she embraces an "ambivalence of meaning" in his or her representational politics, challenging rather than delimiting the parameters of identity.[61] The power of Straight's product, then, lies in its ability to disturb and undo ontological categories presumably linked to "race."

Straight's appeal comes to a close with a spectacular physical manifestation of racial ambivalence. Pulling forth an attendant who the stage directions describe as "made up to be half white and half black" (1D1, 67), the doctor assures, "Straightaline and Oblicuticus are the most wonderful discovery of modern times. This young man is a martyr to science. Here you have the work of nature. Here the work of art. Here is the kinky hair, here the bronze of nature, here the peachlike complexion" (1D1, 67). Plucked from the crowd to model the wonders of science, this patchwork racial Frankenstein registers a mockery of contemporaneous scientific theories bent on erecting biological borders around racial identities. The exhibition of this racial amalgam blatantly foils the "ambitious schemes" which proliferated in the post-Darwinian era and which focused on "the futile search for criteria to define and describe race differences." For clearly his bronze and peach body of wonder attests to the complexities in asserting the politics of racial difference.[62] Straight's comments playfully scramble racial paradigms, matching "kinky" black hair with "nature" and white skin pigmentation with "art." In this regard, his speech generates a trenchant critique of whiteness and its conflation with social and cultural normativity. Although Straight's monologue, on the one hand, panders to popular stereotypes asserting the primitive "nature" of blackness, his words also level a subtle critique of the "white" side of this perambulatory scientific experiment. Classifying the body in question not as "art" but as "artifice," oddly outside the "real," "peachier" than a peach in its complexion, the scene jarringly places whiteness under construction for a captive set of onlookers. In a surprising break from late-nineteenth-century black class mobility politics, which often trafficked in concepts of physical as well as cultural assimilation, the Dr. Straight scene delivers the first of In Dahomey's many iconoclastic scenarios.[63]

For a production, then, that is so often catalogued as being, at best, the innocuous entertainment vehicle of a fledgling black actors troupe, and at worst the manifestation and promulgation of unbridled self-hatred in the black community, In Dahomey's bold and clever transformation scenes are particularly offbeat and surprising. This version reinforces the extent to which the musical engaged in adapting and transforming racial paradigms to spectacular ends. Dr. Straight's extended appeal not only celebrates the power of artifice and corporeal reinvention but his staged medicine show-turned-meta-performance translates and transfigures the Victorian pantomime scene. Straight's act effectively turns the Benevolent Agent character of the classic phantasmagoric sequence, the central figure who activates a set of imaginative transformations, into a trickster character invested in marketing hair and skin products that heighten racial aesthetic masquerade. If, in fact, as historian Immanuel Geiss suggests, emigrationist movements directed toward resettling in Africa were fundamentally fueled by a racist American society which "at every turn reminded" black Americans of their "non-normative" physical features, then these scenes from In Dahomey turned that psychological terrorism on its head. The production revised the classic site of phenotypical colonization and abjection—that of skin color and hair texture—into a source of fluid and parodic play.[64] Thus, moving the closing pantomime scene to its eventual anterior positioning only seemed to strengthen and reinforce the spectacularly coded representational power of the opening act proper. This series of visually stunning scenes virtually lays the production's politics of trickery bare before its audience.

The metaphorical and illusory play of In Dahomey's prologue and opening act should not be overlooked, especially given the ethnological expectations and desires placed on black performers in nineteenth-century theatre culture. Despite the fact that one American critic claimed that, "ethnology on the stage is not of itself very exhilarating" (HTC), nineteenth-century polygenetic discourse would prove itself to be a thick and myopic lens through which many (white) critics read the production and its African American cast members. Ethnology's classic definition, that it is "the science which treats of races and peoples, and of their relations to one another, their distinctive physical and other characteristics," paradoxically fixates on racial difference through a comparative analysis and anxiety of sameness, of what's "in relation" to what, how the geography of one's own bodily cartography gets mapped out differently across the face of (an)other. Although as a number of social historians and cultural critics have noted, the "science of racial difference" was well beyond its peak by the early twentieth century, the desire to perfect some scholarly, physiological system of marking, categorizing, and ultimately "knowing" race deviation only seemed to intensify in a new, post-Darwinian era. Importantly, as David Krasner asserts, theatre served as a central cultural venue to deploy an ethnological discourse grounded in the politics of racial "authenticity" at the turn of the century. He reminds us that "the newly derived modernism promoted the idea of 'authentic' African Americans on stage as opposed to white minstrel imitations in blackface. Unfortunately, the image was based on racist presumptions that utilized newly formed 'scientific' data in manufacturing distortions" (Krasner, *Resistance*, 35).[65]

Critic after critic in both England and North America gravitated toward a fascination and a simultaneous frustration with cataloguing physical and racial typology in the musical, all the while gleefully pursuing the show's spectacle of difference for their readers. While there were many, especially in the United Kingdom, who were overwhelmingly receptive to the production, several critics could not surmount the racial anomaly that was *In Dahomey*. One New York writer presented an exhaustive catalogue of variations of skin pigmentation in cast members, wryly remarking that "local color abounded" on the Broadway stage. Others expressed a resistance to comprehending anything beyond the physical spectacle of racial difference in the theatre, insisting that there was a certain "difficulty of understanding the speech . . . the eye [had] grown accustomed to the sable coloring of their faces."[66] The *London Times* theatre critic revealed himself to be nothing short of nonplused in his review of *In Dahomey*'s U.K. debut, for the production seemingly posed a linguistic obstacle in terms of how to articulate difference. The British journalist is inevitably reduced to expressing his bewilderment at the "so curiously disquieting" elements of the production which left the "resultant impression of . . . strangeness, the strangeness of the 'coloured' race [which] blended with the strangeness of certain American things." Although this particular critic assures his readers that this trope of deviance is an exotic and beloved quality to be treasured in art, the article sustains an excess of concern with the disruptively alien elements of the musical—referring to its "strangeness" no less than fifteen times throughout the course of the review (HTC). Repetition here exposes a crisis in language regarding this "new aesthetic 'thrill'" of difference on the stage. To its befuddled audiences, something had run amuck in *In Dahomey*, and this critic, like several others, struggled to find the words to explain the crisis at hand.

Confronting the alien and the brave new world of black musicals, critics of the production often returned to safe and familiar racial tropes in their reviews. Like the imperial scientist who employs systems of collection and taxonomy as a means to establishing notions of order and stability onto previously "chaotic" and "unknowable" foreign subjects, journalists who reviewed *In Dahomey* projected totalizing scripts of racial deviancy onto its performers.[67] For the *London Times* critic, the solution was to dehistoricize and empty out these black figures on the stage, transforming them into comforting ciphers of blackface deviance. In this way, the *Times* critic can cling to a reading of *In Dahomey*'s black performers as functioning exclusively in the realm of the physically aberrant, of the "merely ugly . . . and strange." He assures that the "difference of colour will tell. We may be wrong, but these people seem to us, in their timid, half-averted gaze, to be mutely pleading for toleration; 'mislike us not for our complexion,' they seem to say. The spectacle is just a little painful—painful and strange" (HTC). His proclamation that color itself "will tell," indeed narrate, the course of the production suggests the extent to which white audiences and critics would look to race as the guiding trope of *In Dahomey*, transcending plot and obfuscating the performative execution of cast members.

Forward leaning in content and form, *In Dahomey* created its own "alienating" effects, making "the incidents represented" on the stage each night appear indeed quite "strange to the public." Increasingly, the musical created an obstacle for those who diligently struggled to locate and categorize black figures who refused and fled from the pathologizing systems of minstrel theatre. Aching to recuperate what has apparently been lost, these writers left *Dahomey* longing to relocate the recognizable and "*signified* black" from bygone theatrical and musical fantasies. As the Williams and Walker Company steadily and persistently bucked tradition in its directorial choices to, for instance, cast black performers of varying shapes, hues, and sizes, critics publicly reacted to the startling heterogeneity of non-blackface blackness unfolding. Such was the case in a review of the 1907 Williams and Walker production *Bandanna Land* as one critic wondered, "What is the management's object in permitting most of the men and nearly all of the women to wear straight hair is, however, difficult to understand. The types would be very close to natural if it were not for this hair. But it really does not matter, and the singing of the straight haired chorus is just as vigorous as it would be with kinks" (BRT).[68] Lurking beneath the surface of this statement is a concern that this physical difference might aggravate the prescribed behaviorial role associated with race. At the base of his comments is the potent desire to naturalize blackness, to will these figures to at least perform a certain notion of race even if their physical "kinks" have all but disappeared. One British critic complained in his review of *In Dahomey* that "the fact that Bert Williams blacked-up confused matters" because it "made his darkness visible." This comment reflects the widespread difficulty white spectators had when confronting race and racial artifice on the stage. Like Henry Box Brown and Adah Isaacs Menken before him, Bert Williams disoriented and disturbed the expectations of audiences who were surprised to find that he was "not so black as he is painted."[69]

No wonder, then, that so many critics went to such extraordinary lengths to champion the putative "essence" of blackness in theatre. For these opening sequences of *In Dahomey* enacted the mutability of phenotypical characteristics which were so necessary to sustaining dominant ideologies of racial inferiority. In their perceptions of black musical theatre, white critics and audiences alike often clung to an agenda that willfully assigned regressive, caricatured meanings to black performers. Even in Great Britain, a one-time shelter for black expatriates where, by the turn of the century, a black presence had dwindled and where racial tension began to rear its own uniquely British head, audiences came to expect and depend on narrow racial performances.[70] The legendary lore of the cakewalk, for instance, became a necessary addition to *In Dahomey* since British audiences expected black Americans to perform the dance (Green, "*In Dahomey*," 23). This "dancing," some observed, "seems the natural expression of a racial instinct, not the laboriously acquired art of the schools" (HTC). To be sure, the effort in these comments is twofold: to reduce the performative labor of *In Dahomey*'s cast down to essentialized luck (as it were), and to render the production artless and free of performative complexity. If anything, white critics repeatedly voiced a hunger for authenticity, for "real negro music," unadulterated and uncomplicated in scope and range (Green, "*In Dahomey*," 27). To stray from such an expectation resulted in the scathing or even the utterly bewildered review. Several British journalists expressed a deep disappointment with the *In Dahomey* production, declaring that "it is a pity, because it gives us the negro who has assimilated what is worst in European civilization instead of the negro at his best, in close and sympathetic touch with nature" (HTC). The lament is a predictable one, in that it oscillates between a familiar "sense of disorientation and loss" and "an obsessive urge to discover an 'authentic'" black body in the wilderness of theatre culture.[71]

Despite this adoration of "the negro" in touch with his "natural" side, critical praise was often lavished on Bert Williams and George Walker for their ability to engage in an adept kind of bodily technology which ultimately deployed and reified popular notions of "blackness." This sort of paradoxical gesture is most evident in an elaborate pictorial spread on the performing duo that appeared in the pages of *Vanity Fair* during the second-leg of their American *In Dahomey* tour. The headline of the spread reveals the contradictions undergirding turn-of-the-century black minstrelsy and (white) racial fetishization: "Williams and Walker, nature's black-face comedians in a series of specially posed facial stunts." A total of sixteen photographs arranged in a rectangular sequence and featuring a series of close-ups, profiles, and poses of each actor in a range of costumes border the two-page article. The concatenate structure of the layout creates a panoramic spread; its photographs fall into a sequential, almost phantasmagoric pattern of development wherein each performer's facial contortions run the gamut of emotions from vaudevillian clownishness to tragic pathos. George Walker shifts from the extremity of a twisted scowl in one shot to a euphoric, wide-eyed, joyous smile with mouth agape in the next (BRT).

The text that accompanies this montage affirms that "colored actors have frequently failed because they aimed higher than the white theatregoing public wanted to look, or because they set too low a mark for their efforts." Implicit in the article's praise of the performing duo is a positive reception to their ability to revel in "nature" in such a way which might "gras[p] the secret way to attract white patronage." Yet the same article expresses a fascination and admiration for the "peculiar style of dramatic humor"—indeed, seemingly the graceful skill—of the "specially posed facial stunts." Although Williams and Walker engage in the "natural," the article celebrates the "novel" quality of their "posed" "stunts," their staged acts. Even the two middle photos of Bert Williams applying his burnt-cork make-up in his dressing room reinforce the striking juxtaposition between the white press's fascination with essentialist racial categories and the constructedness of such roles. At the heart of this spread is a deep-seated interest in spectacularizing the corporeality of these performers. Nestled between two close-up shots of George Walker in his famous "dandy" top-hat attire, for instance, rests a shot of the entertainer standing shirtless with his back to the camera, arms slightly bent and suspenders loosely falling around his hips. It is the only photograph in the article which features a full standing shot of either performer's torso; stripped and nearly faceless, save for the hint of Walker's profile, his body intervenes in the portraits of facial masquerades as if to suggest that the faceless spectacle of the

Colored actors have frequently failed because they aimed higher than the white theatre-going public wanted to look, or because they set too low a mark for their efforts. Bert A. Williams and George W. Walker, a few years ago, grasped the secret of the way to attract white patronage on a big scale, and began laying plans to succeed in a field where they as well as others had met disaster. "In Dahomey," a vaudeville farce, acted, written and stage-directed by colored people from start to finish, witnessed a hit and generous support by the white

18. Williams and Walker pictorial feature, page 1 (in *Vanity Fair*). Courtesy of the Billy Rose Theatre Collection, New York Public Library for the Performing Arts, Astor, Lenox and Tilden Foundations.

element. These prototypes in color of the white Rogers Brothers drew crowded houses to the New York theatres, won plaudits in England, and came back to renew their American success at the Grand Opera House. New York critics generally agreed that not only Williams and Walker but the entire "In Dahomey" company set a pace for white comedians and comediennes to follow in an entire absence of slap-stick comedy and in a strict regard for only niceties in fun-making. "In Dahomey" is under the direction of Hurtig & Seamon.

y Fair, is believed to be the only series of the two colored artists to be posed for and peculiar style of dramatic humor make this page of exceptional value, and of what—to say the least—is a most novel and valuable set of faces.

PICTURES OF THE SEASON AND WORTH THREE TIMES THE REGULAR ADMISSION PRICE!!

19. Williams and Walker pictorial feature, page 2 (in *Vanity Fair*). Courtesy of the Billy Rose Theatre Collection, New York Public Library for the Performing Arts, Astor, Lenox and Tilden Foundations.

passive corporeal will inevitably compete with the bodily agency of the black entertainer for the white public's interest.

More troubling still is the assumption that the (black) body will always persevere as the fundamental plot for the white spectator. Given this type of preconceived scripting, it's little wonder that a disproportionate number of critics in England and North America were steadfast in their insistence on the plotlessness of *In Dahomey*, for the production consistently deviated from reductive, oversimplistic representations of the black body. One British critic assured readers that, in regard to the plot, "what it is about we are unable, even with the assistance of a printed 'argument,' to fully understand" (Green, "*In Dahomey*," 24). The *London Times* critic contended even more aggressively that the production was an "example of plotless drama . . . perhaps without a rival" (HTC). Most forcefully, however, one English critic proclaimed that "here was the coon in music, naked and unashamed, merry, pathetic, eager, and alive with emotion," urging the spectator finally to "forget purpose, plot, reason, and coherence, simply look and listen" (Green, "*In Dahomey*," 33).[72] The frustration with plot was, in actuality, frustration with *In Dahomey*'s departure from conventional minstrelsy plot machination, resulting in an insistence on the critic's part to dehistoricize and simplify the narrative by rendering it as "plotless," and by asserting that the production "was written without any other object than to amuse." For, in the end (quite literally), despite chiasmic scene revisions and negations, *In Dahomey* continuously refuted prescribed racial roles and what Marianna Torgovnick calls "the secret" of the "primitive" in the twentieth century, that "the primitive can be—has been, will be . . . whatever Euro-Americans want it to be." The musical proved time and again to be a production invested in transgressing the borders of the color line as it affirmed the inauthenticity of "color" categorization itself. Repeatedly, *In Dahomey* whispered its own secret—that the Ethiopian could, indeed, change his own skin.[73]

### Alien Nation

We are not so sure a second visit to it
is to be recommended to anybody with nerves.
—*In Dahomey* review, London, 1903

On April 28, 1903, five hundred people "from white and colored society" turned out in the grand salon of a New York City ocean liner to fete the Williams and Walker Company as it made its glamorous exit from the North American theatre world. On that night, America's most successful black theatre company threw a swank party and prepared to set sail for England. Initially booked for a six-week run at London's Shaftesbury Theatre, the troupe was already strategizing ways to adapt their act to the fickle tastes and demands of British audiences weaned on their own beloved forms of black-face minstrelsy. The constraints of English audience expectations were not unforeseen by Bert Williams, who described in great detail the troupe's preparations for their performance: "We did all our work without dialect. Once or twice I turned loose . . . little broad 'coon' talk on them, but they couldn't understand." He adds that the troupe decided not to "depend too much on our 'acting' and none on our dialect."[74] Williams and his cohorts knew full well that in the shadow of minstrelsy's long arm their bodies meant more on the stage than their words to English audiences who privileged the racially spectacular corporeal. The cast gambled that an emphasis on mute black figures would offer an attractive accessibility to the musical which performative verbosity somehow curtailed.

Yet as it turned out, the eccentricities of *In Dahomey*'s racial body politic did little to placate critics who debated the show's ability to "attract," "amaze," "distract," and "disturb." Called by one journalist confoundingly "untranslatable," *In Dahomey*'s spectacle of "garrulous" colored performers embroiled in intricate plots and intrigue proved too much for some (BRT). Even the show's staunchest U.K. supporters overlooked or disregarded the play's narrative possibilities, choosing instead to pay homage to the frivolity of black entertainment in novel settings. This problem was not lost on Sylvester Russell who, in keeping with his outspoken style of journalism, chastised the "white critics, likes James Montague, who like to give a colored show a 'jolly' instead of good advice in criticism."[75] Russell's indictment exposes the level at which, in past and present critical circles, the black musical's plot and textual complexity languished as an undertheorized work of drama. A closer examination of *In Dahomey* reveals, however, that the musical's narrative manifests some of the text's most potent and coded subversions. Rather than re-asserting the domination of (white) spectatorial desire, the musical's unique plot devices combined with its spectacular construction of the black body waged a unique battle against the circumscription of black corporeality as well as narrativity. The key to the musical's revisionist plot rested on its unpredictable engagement with contemporaneous black nationalist ideological concerns, and the production's emphasis on the politics of capitalistic land ownership, (e)migration, and the creation of nationhood yoke together in unconventional ways to masterfully reformulate visions of Pan-Africanist cultural and political ideology.

Despite the lingering and often pejorative characterization of their careers as "blacks-in-blackface" entertainers, Bert Williams and George Walker developed a number of early-twentieth-century theatrical projects that were informed by contemporaneous black nationalist political platforms. In a famous post-performance interview following a production of *Bandanna Land*, for instance, George Walker articulated a decidedly militant viewpoint regarding the role of black theatre and further asserted a theory of race pride which added additional meaning to *In Dahomey*'s appearance-obsessed opening scene. Walker boldly claimed that "you can't get the best out of a boy by telling him that his hair should be straight instead of kinky, that his nose should be classic instead of flat. Nor can you expect a colored girl to realize the best there is in her if you make her believe that a black skin cannot be beautiful" (BRT). Walker followed up this hearty embrace of "black beauty" with a fervent endorsement of black theatre as a means to communal rejuvenation and economic autonomy, gushing that his "greatest ambition . . . is to get money enough together to build a theatre—if possible to build one in New York, one in Philadelphia" (BRT).[76] Walker was a visionary in his belief that African American entertainers should have access to owning their performances. He and his cohorts used *In Dahomey* as a platform to enact and interrogate the possibility of black economic autonomy in a transnationalist context.

Theories of fiscal empowerment and capitalist aspirations abound, albeit in odd shapes and forms, in *In Dahomey*. Faithful servant and manumitted slave Cicero Lightfoot has, for instance, fortuitously inherited his former master's Florida plantation at the musical's opening, and his vicissitudes have subsequently thrown the Lightfoot family into an extended state of reveling in their new bourgeois roles. Daughter Rosetta pledges herself to becoming the "leader of the colored aristocracy," singing that "all I need is lots of dough, for that regulates the social scale, you know" (ID1, 80). The majority of *In Dahomey*'s characters, in fact, commence a fevered quest for economic transformation. Upon meeting Pinkerton and Homestead, the mysterious "Hustling Charlie" explains that he is "goin' to join this Colonization Society, blow over to Africa with them and get the money" which the continent has to offer (ID1, 71). Even the newfound landowner Cicero desires additional prosperity and social mobility for his youngest daughter, Pansy, whom he instructs in the song "Society" not to "cultivate sobriety but rather ostentation." Cicero asserts that "a royal prince my little girl shall wed, for since the days of lords and dukes have sped, it takes a prince to put you at the head of the best society!" (ID1, 76). Dr. Straight demonstrates his own dogged entrepreneurial spirit with his hair and skin products and speculates as to whether he might convert Cicero into a wealthy customer whose hair he "might straighten" as well (ID1, 75). Each character weaves into the fabric of a post-Reconstruction era landscape of black economic desire littered with the promise of social transformation and financial opportunity. In this way, the show embraces key black nationalist ideals which champion the importance of capitalist autonomy as a central step toward social and political empowerment.

Even so, the kind of black nationhood that *In Dahomey* imagined for its audiences was remarkably dystopian. The musical presents not so much the articulation of a nation as the expression of postbellum black consciousness rooted in *alien*ation which ultimately guides and unites its characters. A musical about "chicanery and heritage," *In Dahomey* expresses black national identity and nation-building sentiment in vastly different ways from early-nineteenth-century black nationalism which, as Eddie Glaude points out, is rooted in negotiating "the common insult of slavery, the persistence and entrenchment of white supremacist beliefs in the social and political fabric of early nineteenth-century America." Evolving out of a turn into a new century and faced with the strange and bitter fruits of postbellum disfranchisement and mob rule, the architects of *In Dahomey* created a musical that parodied and critiqued the politics of racial solidarity in the midst of changing times.[77] Instead of coalition building, this was a production that repeatedly obsessed over the individual pursuit of property and the loss of precious family valuables.

If, then, early-nineteenth-century black nationalism was characterized in part by a sense of moral obligation, "we-intentions—a sense of being one of us," *In Dahomey* marked a break from this kind of thinking. From one brutal twist to the next, its characters cheat and manipulate each other. A minor character like the New England "widow" "clothes dealer in forsaken patterns" Mrs. Stringer imagines swindling black Southerners ("stringing them along" perhaps) into purchasing old goods (68–69), while the Syndicate's Straight, Reeder, and Hustler, the "high society . . . gentlemen from the North wid great reputations" (76), befriend the newly minted Lightfoot family with less than noble intentions. Just as shady are Shy's dreams of landing a job with no work involved (70) and Rare's scheme to get a slice of Cicero's treasure (71). Bitter ironies are piled atop one another in a script that eviscerates its own "back-to-Africa" ideals midway through the second act of the American script. In that version, Cicero declares his aim to put his trust in a "gentleman down in Cheaterville dat can find the Royal ancestors for anybody dat got fifty dollars" (81). With yet another thief potentially lurking just around the corner, Cicero's transnational nostalgia for "a time when every darkey was a king" rings particularly hollow. Rather than promoting the notion of a mythically unified black nation-state, the script articulates the kind of existential fragmentation in black consciousness that presumably threatened to disrupt and disturb conventional postbellum racial solidarity politics. *In Dahomey* grapples with the (in)authenticity of racial identity formations, as well as the viability of racial unions in the wake of migration patterns, class mobility, and the increasing heterogeneity of African American experiences in the wake of seismic social and cultural change. In this regard, the musical's capitulation toward chicanery and the characters' rampant distrust and disloyalty toward one another operate as a broad rumination on the profound experience of postbellum black Americans' social, political, and cultural estrangement from one another and from the larger systems that held them captive.[78]

The oft-overlooked prop that articulates the condition of Afro-alienation most profoundly appears in the first scene of the musical. Inexplicably positioned behind Dr. Straight as he lassoes his crowd into his pitch, the ambiguously titled "Intelligence Office" (1D1, 66) opens up a full range of questions regarding citizenship and patriotic allegiance for *In Dahomey*'s characters. Audience members are left to wonder who runs the "Intelligence" at the office and to what ends. Certainly the presence of the Syndicate, a heady cabal featuring Reeder, Dr. Straight, and Hustling Charlie, alluringly signifies on the possibility that one or all of the musical's characters are spying for or on something for some mysterious cause. The potential for double-agency hangs ominously in the air of this office of intelligence where subterfuge, cloistered surveillance, and covertly alien identity lurk beneath the surface of the scene. Its presence points to something "foreign" and something infiltrating beneath the layers of *In Dahomey*'s back-to-Africa plot.[79] Politically provocative, the tropes of "intelligence," "spying," and "treason" imaginatively reanimate black nationalist agendas which asserted, as Sterling Stuckey reminds, a "disaffection with American life" and a "distrust" of U.S. government sociopolitical structures. Certainly this sentiment was shared by the likes of W. E. B. Du Bois, who, in the same year of *In Dahomey*'s debut, famously documented in *The Souls of Black Folk* the myriad ways in which African Americans were forever foreigners in their own country. Pioneering nineteenth-century black nationalists such as Martin Delany thus "emphasize[d] the importance of a territorial base away from white America," which, in turn, created the seeds of Pan-Africanism that find a home in *In Dahomey*. At the same time, however, the production is remarkably unique in its ambitious twists and turns away from familiar black nationalist conventions. And although the musical's various plot developments gradually move its characters out of "white America" and toward the promise of a far-off and forgotten continent, the text largely eschews classic Pan-Africanism. In a clear ideological break from the norm, rather than locating the return to Africa as a necessary endpoint in black liberation politics, the script favors a more daring and open-ended notion of diasporic emancipation and identity production altogether.[80]

Whether audiences are greeted into the "jungles of Caboceer" as a prologue to the musical or whether they make it to shore with the cast in the original final act, the "Dahomey" scenes remain the most complicated and contested in the entire show. Yet these "African" scenes remain the most critically disregarded plot machination in the whole production—despite the musical's title. If anything, when the trope of emigration is broached by critics, its analysis has historically resulted in frequent attempts to discount the musical as anything beyond a replication of white minstrelsy productions. Allen Woll contends that, in most cases, the back-to-Africa plot was written off by white as well as black critics who failed to conceive of its political and cultural relevance. Woll reminds us that, "despite the lofty expectations of George Walker, In Dahomey did little to enlighten audiences about African culture. Indeed, some critics believed that Williams and Walker had gratuitously put their old vaudeville routine into an African setting without the slightest thought." Black businessman Albert Ross, in a well-known epistolary exchange with the performing duo published in Variety, warned Williams and Walker that if "your ideals are degenerative you are succeeding and prospering personally and financially at the expense and to the injury of your own race and people."[81] Many read Williams and Walker's theatrical efforts and particularly the back-to-Africa musicals as extraneous at best and politically and representationally harmful to black Americans at worst. This gesture perhaps stemmed in part from the long-standing, controversial position which the topic of emigration and territorial separation sustained within the black community and broader American politics at the turn of the century.

For many pundits, the desire to emigrate suggested an implicit critique not only of white America but of African American communities as well. In Dahomey's Mose Lightfoot, the prevailing voice of emigration in the narrative, announces early on, "I'se just naturally disgusted with the frivolities of the colored population of dis country" (1D1, 67). His sentiments speak to an undercurrent of despondency in certain black nationalist circles which seemingly depended on an aggressive critique of African American communal politics in order to endorse a subsequent literal movement out of what was conceived of as a fundamentally oppressive and debilitating environment.[82]

Mose carries on a spirited debate regarding the risks and merits of territorial separatism with Henry Stampfield, a letter carrier who is ambiguously positioned at the door of the "Intelligence Office," and who is specifically characterized as harboring "an argument against immigration" in the stage directions (1D1, 66). Stampfield admits that "your exalted opinion of the ideal life to be found in a barbarous country is beyond my comprehension" (1D1, 67). Around and around it goes as Mose laments the state of black America embodied in Straight's antics while Stampfield critiques Mose for his romantic attempts to mythologize Africa. With layered and savvy badinage, the scene mounts a lengthy exchange between the two characters which articulates prevailing black anxieties regarding racial identity politics and emigration.

Which view the production ultimately favors is, however, a bit more difficult to ascertain. Stampfield's prediction that the Colonization Society is destined to find *In Dahomey* a "barbarous country" whose "natives" will "look upon you as intruders" matches many of the popular black postbellum ideas about Africa and the question of emigration. While Mose chastises Stampfield for his seeming overexposure to "white folks here in the United States," his own comments reveal a contempt for African Americans and Dahomians alike. No doubt, Mose's disdain for "the frivolities of the colored population of dis country"—coupled with his equally regressive images of an Africa with a climate so "fine" that it is "just the right thing for raisin' chickens and watermelons. It never snows so you don't need no clothes" (1D1, 67–68)— makes a mockery of his own political convictions. As the official mandarin of the colonization movement in the play, Mose, with his questionable politics, is just as equivocal as the Straight man before him. Described in the script as "a calcium artist," a performer who whitens his skin, Mose and his minstrelizing visions of Africans and African Americans seem to do much to critique conventional emigration proponents who knew or cared little for black communities on either side of the Atlantic.[83]

Tellingly, the debate between these two characters in the first scene prefigures the extent to which *In Dahomey* strays from black nationalist and nation-building rhetoric from the previous century. Unlike early-nineteenth-century black activists and theorists who embraced a mode of racial solidarity that stressed unity and "moral obligation," Mose and Stamp fail to articulate a language of common struggle. Mose's vexed position on diasporic relations mirrors the ambivalence of postbellum black historians toward the continent of Africa and its connections to black Americans. As Dickson Bruce points out, black scholars of the period "saw little to be proud of in contemporary African life" and thus this sort of sentiment fueled a "civilizationist" view of the continent which even the most radical black nationalists endorsed. Such sentiments rise to the surface as recurring tropes throughout *In Dahomey*. Mose, in fact, conceives of "get[ting] a few franchises from the king to start street cars, 'lectric lights and saloons to running" on his arrival in the Dahomian state (ID1, 68). Mose's civilizationist rhetoric and his wholesale disregard for pre-existing Dahomian culture collapses into a familiar kind of nineteenth-century black nationalism whose goal was "the establishment of black 'civilizations,' which would give evidence of the black man's capacity for self-government."[84]

Rare and Shy reiterate this sentiment with zest in the show tune that closes act 1, "Broadway in the Jungle." In an absurdist song which catalogues each man's screwball plans to appoint animals to high offices once in Dahomey, Rare and Shy elaborately detail a black psuedo-imperialist fantasy focused on building department stores and railways in the pure and untouched wilderness of Africa (ID1, 72–73). The return to "Africa" in *In Dahomey*, then, is in part a movement engineered by African American characters to retain social, political, and economic freedom but which can only be realized through mimetic rehearsals of American and European imperialism and colonization. During a period of rollicking U.S. prosperity when the gross national product soared, "wages were rising," and "American factories were running full tilt," the Williams and Walker musical reflected the Gilded Age boom by envisioning its African American characters as eager participants in American imperialist experiments. Dahomey's promise of "plentiful" "gold and silver" (ID1, 68), as Mose imagines it, hovers before the play's characters as an enticing incentive. Africa symbolizes for these characters a tempting territory open for exploitation, an "original Klondike" beckoning the likes of Hustling Charlie to penetrate and pillage the country (ID1, 71). Mose and Hustling Charlie each express a desire not just to return to the land of their putative ancestors but to repossess it in a way which, not surprisingly, mirrors the kinds of socio-economic systems of oppression from which they initially aim to flee.[85]

This sort of neo-imperialist ideology is driven home in the musical's hackneyed racist caricature of Me Sing, the "Chinese cook" played by the African American actor George Catlin. Perhaps more than any other character in the musical, Me Sing endures the most overt forms of racial discrimination as he is made to weather the racial epithets hurled at him by Mrs. Stringer and the random passersby (71). As the local cook, he thus genuflects to the orders and demands of the loud and brash dressmaker. On the one hand, the double-vocality of the musical leaves open the possibility for Me Sing to operate as a cutting, satiric figure who exposes the rise of black racism toward Asian immigrants in late-nineteenth- and early-twentieth-century American culture. However, any satire in the play is undercut by the script's dependence on unchallenged racist allusions to "pigtail" Me Sing and the "rats in [his] kitchen" (71). If anything, Me Sing's role as the much-maligned cook seems to play into a popular strain of racial hostility toward Chinese laborers in the mid-to-late nineteenth century. As historian Gisele Fong points out, the black popular press of the 1850s and 1860s provides evidence of a complicated midcentury relationship between African Americans and Asian immigrants. For its part, the black press occasionally reinforced the public perception that African Americans were in danger of losing their domestic and custodial positions to "coolie labor."[86] In this light, *In Dahomey*'s brazen contempt for Me Sing reads as a knee-jerk expression of black socioeconomic anxiety channeled into xenophobic racial humor. What's more, the musical's subtle capitulation to the kinds of white supremacist, anti-Chinese propaganda which had already informed the passage of the Chinese Exclusion Act paradoxically "Americanized" a musical which seemed intent on questioning the viability of life in America for people of color. By disparaging Chinese immigrants, the musical implicitly sought to make its black characters more "American" by calling attention to the grotesque physicality and uncleanliness of Me Sing. Unable to equally share in the scheming plans of Stringer and the others, Me Sing silently follows the rest of the cast all the way to Dahomey. His presence, however, reminds us that *In Dahomey* appears to present romantic notions of emigration only to deflate them by exposing the ugly underbelly of black greed, xenophobia, and expediency that threaten to undermine such movements.[87]

All these elements of *In Dahomey*'s plot taken together suggest some of the valid reasons for the musical's critical dismissal in contemporary debates. Theatre historians and cultural critics have rightfully taken to task the reactionary elements of the production which reinforced a broad range of racial and cultural stereotypes concerning Africa as well as African Americans at the turn of the century. Without overlooking its abundant and disturbing political ambiguities, I do however wish to re-engage discussions of black nationalism in the musical in order to consider unconventional representational systems and thematic developments embedded in the script. Following the lead of Herbert Martin and Ronald Primeau, who observe that Dunbar's work has often been "misread in ways that overlooked his ironic humor and effective parody," I want to suggest that we re-interrogate *In Dahomey* from within a contemporaneous social framework that exposes its cutting and sometimes confounding ironic humor. Who can say, for instance, that the very name of the Syndicate, whose members scheme ways to lie, cheat, and steal from their black brethren, is not in itself a signifying reference to the white entrepreneurs who dominated theatre of that era?[88] In short, certain contextual twists, I argue, do much to challenge the more problematic ideological points in the production.

The very terms of *In Dahomey*'s political ambiguity work in the service of establishing a terrain of struggle regarding (black) identity politics and push forward the terms of black cultural agency and political expression in the postbellum era. *In Dahomey* manifests the ways that Cook, Dunbar, as well as Williams, the Walkers, and others were wrestling with racial, cultural, and national identity formations, and it staged its own tumultuous and highly ambivalent process of (re)conceptualizing (black) nationhood and nationalist desire. The musical contested simplistic notions of "positive" versus "negative" racial images in ways which anticipate contemporary theories of "new ethnicities" posed by Stuart Hall, among other cultural studies theorists. Hall writes that "there is another position, one which locates itself *inside* a continuous struggle and politics around black representation, but which then is able to open up a continuous critical discourse about themes, about the forms of representation, the subjects of representation, above all, the regimes of representation." Within this context, *In Dahomey* provocatively distanced itself from an oversimplistic identification with the evolving "New Negro" rhetoric of the period which rested on the production of what Henry Louis Gates Jr. calls "fictitious black archetypes" of class assimilation. It also differentiated itself in unlikely ways from developing Pan-Africanist discourses of the post-Reconstruction era so as to stage a "continuous struggle" of diasporic black identity "becoming."[89] This process is staged dually through the musical's recurring tropes of (e)migration and a fundamental (re)invention of "Africa" in the text. Both themes do much to undo and rewrite black identity in ways that transform how we might choose to read early black musical theatre's relationship to nationalist discourses.

Even if *In Dahomey*'s cast of characters were to never reach their final destination of West Africa, their migratory movement serves as a culturally thematic disruption set against the African American migration narrative unfolding contemporaneously in the United States. The economic promise of the North lured "an average of 6,700 southern blacks" to uproot in Northern cities annually between the years 1870 and 1910. By the close of the first decade of the twentieth century, approximately 200,000 African Americans had moved north in search of sociopolitical and economic empowerment as well as relief from the mob violence spreading across the South.[90] Indeed, this massive uprooting was, in part, fueled by the economic prosperity which *In Dahomey's* characters so desire. Significantly, however, not only do these characters choose to follow the path of emigration over migration, a choice endorsed by few African Americans at any moment in American history, but, importantly, their route is decidedly nonlinear, making pointed stops along the continuum of diverse and shifting black cultural communities.[91]

*In Dahomey* inverts the direction of the African American migration narrative, anticipating the thematic re-visioning of late-twentieth-century literary works. Through the course of its travels, the production underscores an implicit critique of Northern as well as Southern social and cultural obstacles facing black Americans. In the North, for instance, we are introduced to Mose Lightfoot and an entourage of disgruntled black Bostonians willing to reject the hollow promise of Northern opportunity and move in search of social stability and the fulfillment of economic desire. Homestead's inventory of his Northern experience in act 1, scene 1, adumbrates the critical (re)visions of the musical:

> Shy: No, I ain't mad. I've been laughing every since we got off that boat we come up on from down south. Ha, ha, ha. (sarcastically) I'm laughing 'cause I worked all the winter and then got worked for every cent I made while I was on the boat coming up here. I'm laughing 'cause three days after I git in town after workin' all the winter, I've got to blow the bass drum in the Salvation Army to keep from starving to death. (1D1, 69)

That the script calls for "sarcasm" further exposes the musical's acerbic method of signifying as it pointedly critiques a Northern culture laden with black economic hardships. Homestead's bitter words underscore the extent to which the North might be a place worthy of fleeing in 1902. Like the "Jonah Man" that he will prove to be, Shylock laughs from the belly of the whale, turning the occasion of his tragic luck into a rumination on the false promises of black migration to the North, labor exploitation, and a cycle of poverty he cannot escape. As Shylock, Williams's lines here not only foreshadow the musical's reverse geographical movement for its black characters—from north to south—to someplace else entirely—but his insistence on calling attention to laughter itself creates a richly dissonant moment in the production. This succinct and "sarcastic" narrative about laughter refuses blackface normative codes of humor by rejecting the scorn of white supremacist spectators and by making plain Shylock's language of double-vocality.[92]

Rather than departing the United States from the shores of Boston, however, *In Dahomey* insists that its characters re-enter the South, presumably in order to (spiritually? culturally?) recuperate that historically vexed territory before moving on to Africa. Thus, on reaching the lush gardens of Cicero Lightfoot's Florida home, brother Mose, his "Intelligence Office" cohort George Reeder, and the rag-tag Pinkerton and Homestead are met by a chorus of singers performing the celebratory regional tune, "For Florida." This Florida, the chorus proclaims, is one of "verdant vale to arid stand . . . 'ere a summer land." Passionately, they declare their "loyal hearts are dear . . . Tho' rude and black our faces be / Our hearts are brave, our hands are free / And as we sing, so shall we strive" (ID1, 73). The song's odd championing of region and (free) labor is placed in opposition to the mournful remnants of slavery retained in Cicero's plantation, the very land which its singers celebrate. But the lyrics also convey a black tenacity in joyously reclaiming this (Southern) territory as one's own and disrupting regional alienation born out of a share-cropping economy; the song revels in the fruits born out of now "free hands" and one's own body of labor. Like the Emancipation Day parades of the 1890s in South Carolina and Georgia "in which African Americans successfully asserted their right to occupy" the "most prominent streets" in the South, "For Florida" signifies on acknowledging rightful ownership of a land over which black folk forever toiled. The arrival in Florida, then, resembles Harlem Renaissance black migration narratives such as *Cane* in which, according to Farah Griffin, the South "is not a place of racial horror and shame" but "a site of history and redemption."[93] Here and elsewhere in the production, *In Dahomey*'s penchant for "romancing" the land and its plenitude is evident. As with other epic numbers, "For Florida" makes use of its large cast to colorfully and energetically occupy space, to fill up the stage with "moving, dancing, singing all at the same time" to create what Riis has called its indelible "kinetic quality" unlike any other spectacle of its time.[94]

The spectacular apotheosis of Florida is, however, sharply curtailed and ultimately deromanticized in one of the play's many screwball episodes. All the characters, including the local Cicero, finally rejoice at the promise of leaving for Dahomey as a result of a financial windfall in the form of a hidden treasure discovered by Cicero (ID1, 81). Hurriedly, the production pushes forward a movement which spurs the characters in search of a nation where "evah darkey is a king."[95] This constant deferral in reaching Africa, the desired endpoint of emigration that arrives so conspicuously late in the production, is quite significant in reconsidering *In Dahomey*'s political discourses. For the "return" is seemingly less important than the negotiation of mobility. One might conceive of this movement as akin to James Clifford's work on the dialectic between dwelling and mobility and his reconceptualization of "culture as travel."[96] Yet just as Clifford is cautious to *not* advocate or romanticize a kind of "nomadology," I am also wary of suggesting that black identity is by definition dislocated or that "travel" is free of the markers (paradoxically so) of class privilege in one sense and economic stability in another. Instead, we might consider the ways that *In Dahomey* posits a poetics of identity that comes as a result of the willed process of cultural and geographical transition and transaction. The musical's performance of travel actualizes Anna Deavere Smith's postmodern claim that "American character lives not in one place or the other, but in the gaps between the places." Smith suggests that performance itself operates as a kind of crossing of spaces in the formulation of identity.[97] Such an oppositional practice dislodges the reductive and essentialized readings of *In Dahomey*'s racial politics. The "return" in the Williams and Walker production is constantly stalled in the service of producing a revised form of Pan-Africanist discourse and diasporic identity improvised in mobile intervals.

Despite the claims of Wilson Moses that Pan-Africanism "is essentially a transatlantic phenomenon," little critical attention has been paid to the symbolic relationship between travel in *In Dahomey* and its revisionary stance in relation to black nationalism. This may owe, in part, to the Pan-Africanist conception of emigration championed by mainstream nineteenth-century black activists which involved reaching a territorial space where "political enclosure and national edifice can be reared, established, walled, and proudly defended on this great elementary principle of original identity."[98] Coupled with the extravaganza finale which commences on the characters' African arrival, *In Dahomey*'s deferred "return" in the production critiques and questions this notion of Pan-Africanist etiological desire. What gets recuperated in the place of some notion of "original identity" by the production's concluding act is the total foreclosure of a desired "black" etiological core. Instead, *In Dahomey* hinges on a series of spirited falsities of identity and nation(hood) which comes further undone with the production's final staging of "Africa."

### Dragging It Back to "Africa"

When the characters of *In Dahomey* finally reach the "Gardens of the King of Dahomey," it seems at first glance that they have stepped into a land of the lost—or at least a world that resembles the caricature-laden "Africa" of colonial expeditions and European travel journals. With a superabundance of pageantry, the musical's finale/prologue celebrates the "local custom" of Dahomey by piling on a series of ornate images which, as Riis points out, seem as though they could be ripped from the pages of Richard Burton's infamous *Mission to Gelele.*[99] Marching bands and extras spill onto the stage and a women's drill team "costumed as Amazons" makes way for the Caboceer army, who execute their own "precision marching drill." One flamboyant entourage celebrates the arrival of another until, as the script demands, the stage fills with a chorus dressed as "African chiefs, soldiers, natives, [and] dancing girls" (1D1, 83). Together this motley crew must

> com[e] to the front of the stage, knee[l] and sin[g] choral descriptive of glories of Cannibal King and Caboceers. At the middle of the choral, they rise at the words "Mighty ruler of our nation: and sway to and fro with swinging palm leaves. At the end, the chorus falls prostrate to the floor on their faces to greet Shylock Homestead and Rareback Pinkerton dressed as Caboceers. (1D1, 83)

Certainly, the scene recalls the most familiar Western travel guide images of exoticized grandeur where customs of foreign and frivolous "cannibal kings" and their tractable subjects abound. Resplendent in this world of swaying foliage, the Dahomian royalty and attending Caboceers retain the "pompous ceremonial activity" that typifies Burton's popular text from 1864. So popular were the "Amazon warrior" figures, in fact, that they had become already a staple of the ubiquitous "Dahomeyan village" exhibitions from the previous century. Translating American minstrelsy into imperialist popular caricature, Walker in this scene, as one critic would put it, "blossoms forth in gorgeous raiment and becomes a leader of black face society."[100]

Perhaps this scene marked the birth of a new tribe of burnt-cork figures, but if it did recycle and re-order such images, few critics responded favorably to the twist. Although the pantomime had shifted into a prologue, reviewers again dismissed the abridged finale of *In Dahomey* as incomprehensible fluff. As one journalist scoffed in mystification, "the performance on Saturday night closed rather abruptly with a scene in an African swamp, in which the two principal comedians appeared as a savage king and queen—though with what artistic intention was not quite clear, unless to indicate a return to primitive barbarism as the ideal of the negro race" (BRT). To such critics, the "Dahomian" scene affirmed the primal and essentially "savage" brute embedded in black performers who were artistically aimless, save for their ability to execute the "barbaric" roles of "jungle" royalty. What critics failed—or refused—to see, however, was the extraordinarily multivalent forms of spectacle and masquerade involved in a scene which required the musical's lead performers to don exotic costumes while preserving their principal roles. Once they are dressed in "Caboceer" wardrobe, however, what Williams and

Walker literally and figuratively "become" in this performance of the "Daho-mian" scene remains open for debate.

On the one hand, their re-emergence as "leaders of the colored aristoc-racy" reinforces the neo-imperialist leanings of the production. Hailed, in the British version of the script, as "the Czar of Dixie" even before reaching Dahomey, Walker's Rareback Pinkerton has apparently seized the kind of leadership and status that all the characters have been seeking in the musical. This "czar" title foreshadows the ways that he and his Syndicate cohorts briefly "rule" in *In Dahomey* with an iron fist, spouting brutal language, and threatening to "discipline" the "chocolate drops" who may "get gay" and dissident (lxx).[101] Re-dressed in the role of "African" leaders, they run the risk of ruling "jes lak white folks," as Dunbar sardonically suggests in his 1899 "one act operetto" which anticipated the shape and content of *In Dahomey*. That Pinkerton is even referred to as "the Czar of Dixie" provocatively aligns him with the Deep South plantocracy of Cicero's former master John, the original "czar" in an earlier version of the script (1D1, 81).

Whether one reads this transition from white czar into African neodictator as a sly commentary on black leadership run amuck or as a dig at the fall of white rule in the post–Civil War era depends on a consideration of the musi-cal number "The Czar," a composition with lyrics by Alex Rogers and music by Will Cook and his brother John. In that number, "one of the longest" in the production, "black folks" celebrate this "modern man" with a "modern plan," the "President, the Mayor, and the Governor," a "guiding light" and a "leade[r] of his race" who "is the brightest star" (33–43). The exuberance of the number comes physically to life in the Walkers' spotlight dance routine during "The Czar," the critics' favorite and a moment noted for its "de-lightfully free and graceful character." In musical and choreographed lan-guage, then, "The Czar" operates as a synecdoche for postbellum communal harmony. An icon of black leadership realized, "The Czar" brings to life black cosmopolitanism and serves as a New Negro beacon of light for a people in transition.[102] In both versions of the script, "The Czar" number appears toward the close of the second act and serves as bridge into the third. Exuber-ant in its proclamation of rejuvenated black social and political vision shep-herded in by a "gentleman," "a scholar," and "a diplomat," the song paves the way for the musical's most curious scene of convertibility, staged in the wil-derness of a far-off country. In the gardens of Caboceer, *In Dahomey* emerges fully as iconoclastic in its approach to re-imagining and re-articulating Afri-can American identity formation in the postbellum era. Employing the spec-tacle of drag as a centerpiece for this "African scene," the musical poses its most powerful representational intervention. Far from "barbaric," Pinkerton's and Homestead's new threads create the occasion for reveling in a disruptively urbane form of postbellum pageantry that might guide this cast of characters, in "czar-like" fashion, into a new era of black performance entirely.

Although photographs of the costumes worn by Bert Williams and George Walker during this concluding version of *In Dahomey* are scarce, two images of Walker in pseudo-"African" regalia illuminate the complexity of this sartorial sequence. In the first, which was presumably taken out of the context of the show, the photograph features the actor in his *In Dahomey* costume. A full, curly wig softly frames and feminizes Walker's face and several sets of beads and shell necklaces loop around and across his neck and chest like chokers and chains. Baubles and shells swath the shoulders of Walker's sleeveless, low-cut garment, which reveals a hint of his thick muscular frame, sinewy arms, and sculpted chest. Without archival annotation, it remains impossible to know the full context for this image. If in character, Walker, who looks tremulously into the camera, could be conjuring Rareback's terror in the revised climax to the musical. Perhaps he is bringing to life his character's recognition that all has gone terribly wrong in Dahomey. At the very least, the image of a timorous Walker staring into the camera accentuates the tense line that *In Dahomey*'s cast walked between creating fluid, insurgent and alien images that resisted the gaze of its desiring audience and falling privy to being "captured," so to speak, on film and in the act of negotiating multiple layers of popular caricature.[103]

Making fuller sense of Walker and Williams "going native" requires, however, paying attention to the broader context of the duo's—and particularly Walker's—sartorial politics, both on and off the stage. We might look, for instance, to other images of the actor in "back-to-Africa" productions. In a well-circulated photo of Walker in character as "the Cannibal King" in the 1906 version of *Abyssinia*, the costume attests to the extravagant representational politics of these musicals which paradoxically eschewed the sartorial simplicity of the "native" in favor of redolently majestic costumes.[104] A towering headdress shaped by two tusk-like horns and a cluster of feathers sits atop the actor's crown. Walker also wears an abundance of jewelry, from loose chains and angular earrings which frame the performer's forehead to thick, wide bracelets on either wrist which fall just above his clenched fists; heavy facial makeup sharply highlights his eyes and lips. Several layers of feathers, beads, and fur drape the actor's bare torso and a midlength animal skin covers his lower body from waist to knee. If Walker's *In Dahomey* costume resembled

20. George Walker in *In Dahomey*. Bert and Lottie Williams Album. Courtesy of the Yale Collection of American Literature, Beinecke Rare Book and Manuscript Library, Yale University.

that of this lavish *Abyssinia* outfit, then his portrayal of Rareback Pinkerton in the former production would have undergone a final spectacular transformation. Pinkerton's and his partner Homestead's quest for wealth is realized and manifested in the ornate, richly detailed costumes which they adorn in a sequence where both characters metamorphorsized into "royalty."

Just as African Americans like Henry Box Brown faced the attacks of the English public for his sartorial excess and particularly his offensive display of jewelry in the 1850s, Williams and Walker's postbellum hypercostuming generated strong reactions as well.[105] Donning their splendiferous garments at the height of post-Reconstruction hostility toward African American social mobility, the duo played with the limits of black material extravagance, turning inside out the spectacle of native primitivism. The appearance of Walker and Williams dressed in costumes which referenced West African tribal costuming circumvents an easy engagement with Western fantasies of the "savage." Rather, their "African" outfits deploy a kind of drag which works as a triple transgression of sorts—disrupting racial and class as well as gendered categories. The duo's appearance in full regalia yet still in the guise of their Pinkerton and Homestead roles plays with the boundaries of racial masquerade, producing what Amy Robinson might call a form of "Brechtian drag" wherein the

21. George Walker in *Abyssinia*. Courtesy of Photographs and Prints Division, Schomburg Center for Research in Black Culture, New York Public Library, Astor, Lenox and Tilden Foundations.

"drag calls attention to the act of impersonation and foregrounds its status as imitation." Williams and Walker, it seems, cannot simply be read as "African" because the production demands that one sustain seeing them in elaborate tribal costuming *and* as the bumbling characters who have journeyed toward Africa from the production's commencement as well. Thus one critic's observation, that the conclusion offers "irrelevant pictures of native life" but that "Messrs. Williams and Walker execute a kind of 'coon duet,' 'Dahomian Queen,' in which the histrionic talents of both find excellent opportunities," inadvertently reveals the paradox of the duo's performance (HTC). Their skill at rendering "native life" underscores their talent as thespians and their ability to thus deploy racial paradigms which require "histrionic," that is, hyperbolically constructed, execution.[106]

One can easily push a reading of this scene's representational mayhem by examining *In Dahomey*'s relationship with the discourse of camp. Much has been written about the politics of camp in recent years, mostly in response to Susan Sontag's controversial 1964 essay "Notes on 'Camp'." In his introduction to *The Politics and Poetics of Camp*, Moe Meyer attempts to revise and reappropriate the dominant definition of camp popularized by Sontag. "Pop Camp," he argues, depoliticizes and denies camp its relevance, indeed, its centrality as a queer sociocultural negotiation. Sontag's camp, Meyer contends, effectively "kill[s] off the binding referent of Camp—the Homosexual" in favor of conflating a number of "rhetorical and performative strategies such as irony, satire, burlesque, and travesty."[107] Choosing instead to reread camp specifically as "postmodern parody" which "is an intertextual manipulation of multiple conventions" (Meyer, introduction, 9), Meyer further asserts that "there are not different kinds of Camp. There is only one. And it is queer" (introduction, 5). Here and elsewhere Meyer aims to redeploy camp on the grounds of queer political agency and social intervention.

Meyer's concerns regarding the politics of resistance might help us to consider the layered elements of parody at work in *In Dahomey*. Yet by locating *In Dahomey* within the parameters of camp which Meyer has boldly redrawn, my aim here is not to extinguish the queer politics of Meyer's agenda. Indeed, the military penetration of "the dark continent" seemingly necessitated a kind of "queering" of colonial relations in that the phallus of imperialist projects encourages an often homoerotic objectification of male indigenous subjects as well as women. Instead, I would argue for the repositioning of camp as a politically disruptive tool in the process of marginalized identity production, that it is an equally significant element in the negotiation of African American identity construction. In this regard, I find it useful to trace

Chuck Kleinhans's provocative elaboration on "low Camp," as well as Sontag's reflections on "dandy" camp, in relation to *In Dahomey*'s spectacle of drag and artifice before returning to an extended consideration of Meyer's argument as it relates to the conclusive spectacle of the cakewalk in act 3.

Dissonantly excessive, the Dahomian drag sequence of the Williams and Walker musical is a vivid example of low camp spectacle in black musical performance. Marking a distinction between various forms of parodic camp, Chuck Kleinhans contends that low camp distinguishes itself from the high in that it gaudily calls attention to the underpinnings of masquerade. While high camp is "seamless" in its "illusion of female impersonation . . . low Camp accepts the deconstructed gender presence of drag queens . . . celebrat[ing] bad taste and often intentionally offend[ing] aesthetic and social sensibilities in order to make a statement." As the "king and queen" of *In Dahomey*, Williams and Walker sustain roles which pose multiple low camp ruptures in representation; the actors mediate dual masking mechanisms as black performers in figurative "blackface" and as characters in "tribal" as well as queer costuming. The competing identity representations in this scene suggest a kind of parodic drag which does not simply hyperbolize "the primary intelligibility of the anatomical" and racial "body of the performer," but which renders the construction of that body as pivoting on multiple falsities, doubling and palimpsested, one after and on top of the "other." Adorned in his perennial "blackface" makeup and the "African" costuming of a "queen," Bert Williams dallies in a triple drag of sorts which magnifies the racial (in)authenticity at the core of this "Dahomian" world. The musical duo's performance demonstrates Stuart Hall's critical observation that the black body in popular culture was often "the only cultural capital we had." Hall speculates that, "[w]e have worked on ourselves as the canvases of representation." From this standpoint, Williams and Walker's final act in the production operates as corporeal stylization and as an execution of multivocal narrative agency.[108]

Yet to some, as the lead characters "go native," the musical problematically returns to its dual roots in both imperial popular culture and minstrelsy since it ostensibly freezes its social climbing black characters in a state of perpetual "barbarism." Sylvester Russell even suggested that if "Mr. Walker would dress up as an American gentleman in citizen's clothes it would be more in keeping with the situations and the character."[109] Yet there is a way, I suggest, to read George Walker's jewelry, feathers, and facial paint as the "cannibal king" as swerving free of emasculating postbellum black masculinity in order to articulate what Marjorie Garber calls a disquieting "narcissistic macho." In this context, black male drag converts systems of social power by exacerbating the narrow categories of identity construction open to African American performers. Walker's drag as the Cannibal King "turn(s) inside-out the valuation of cross-dressing, male-to-female and female-to-male, producing it not as an imposed and enslaving act of castration or ungendering, but rather as a language of reassignment, empowerment, and critique." More still, I would argue that the sartorial markers of Walker's double role as "king" Pinkerton are in many ways congruent with the smart "gentleman's" clothes that the actor donned with verve and elegance offstage. Both clothing choices illustrate the ways that Walker and his cohorts worked to reconfigure the (black) body as a text of artistic manipulation and as a form of cultural critique. In short, *In Dahomey* complicates the trope of black cross-dressing by linking Williams and Walker's (over)abundance of costuming in this finale to George Walker's spectacular offstage dress.[110]

Costumes were a trademark for Williams and Walker productions. By midcareer, Walker had earned an impressive reputation for donning what one critic described during the 1907 run of *Abyssinia* in New York City as "exceedingly 'proud clothes' which he wears [to] illustrat[e] the love of his race for things sartorial" (BRT). "Dressed," as Russell admiringly put it, "in the richest teutonic style and with his large cluster of real diamonds, George Walker" distinguished himself as the " 'colored fashion plate' of his race" while performing on Broadway in 1903. Walker's lush formal street attire and his love for top hats, white gloves, and elegant suits offstage provoked puzzled and obsessive disdain from the white press. A shrewd businessman, Walker used "his own clever manipulation of the press to create an aura of stardom about himself." Within the panoptic fish bowl of postbellum black celebrity culture, journalists grappled with the performer's "extravagant and costly stage costumes and good expensive street clothes" and even at times demanded that Walker provide an explanation for his dress (BRT). The public's fixation on Walker's wardrobe is hardly surprising given the way that Walker's lavish wardrobe both in and out of character easily aligned him with popular nineteenth-century dandy iconography. However, if the traditional dandy that nineteenth-century French culture bore was a "highly stylized, painstakingly constructed self, a solipsistic social icon," the black dandy figure who adopted similar traits was the most threatening of creatures in antebellum and particularly post-Reconstruction America. For, resituated in the context of free(d) urban black migrants, the hedonism, decadent narcissism, ostentation, and artifice associated with the European dandy potentially violates class boundaries. The black dandy's refined clothing communicated a pleasure in bourgeoisie lineaments and threatened the delicate balance of racial and class

22. George Walker and Bert Wiliams in *In Dahomey*. Courtesy of Photographs and Prints Division, Schomburg Center for Research in Black Culture, New York Public Library, Astor, Lenox and Tilden Foundations.

relations in the wake of slavery's abolition. The seemingly small event of dressing was, then, looked on by whites and blacks as a way to symbolically bridge the gap between the upwardly mobile dresser and the leisure class.[111]

For Walker, the dandy aesthetic seemed to operate as its own phenomenal will to power, a nightly transgression of social boundaries that had often appeared impermeable. By re-dressing the black male body within the material codes of sybaritic pleasure offstage, Walker flaunted the visual poetics of class fluidity. Yet the isolativity of this kind of image alone was enough to incur a legacy of white supremacist scorn, ridicule, and sometimes violence. As early as the 1830s and 1840s in the Northeast, the notion of the black dandy existed primarily in the fearful imagination of a white urban, working class who grew increasingly threatened by the presence of an evolving black middle class. Black dandies manifested the white supremacist nightmare of African American class aspiration realized. Transformed into the postbellum caricature of the "Zip Coon," the "slick, urbane," amoral, and mythically dangerous figure of 1880s coon songs, the black dandy icon and his grotesque Zip Coon counterpart symbolize the extent to which black male socioeconomic mobility remained terrifying and troublesome in the post-Reconstruction American imagination. Critics directly perceived Walker's wardrobe in this light, observing that "clothes help to advertise his and his partner's theatrical business" (BRT). This "high visibility–notoriety and stylish dress" of black performers such as Williams and Walker appeared, "at least to the predominantly white, working-class mob, to embody the black bourgeoisie" on the whole.[112]

Within this context, the drag of dandyism was both a threat and a catalyst toward the public adulation of the black body. Walker seemed conscious of the ways his wardrobe both sustained a form of persona commodification and offered access to self-authoring as well. During a 1907 press interview, the actor related an incident in which two white men approached the performer in order to ask why he wore "such flashy clothes and that large diamond ring." Walker contended that "white people would not believe I was George Walker if I did not wear them" (BRT). His statement attests to the level at which Walker was aware of the fundamental artifice, in a sense the drag, involved in deploying a public persona as a black theatre performer. The actor consciously and successfully constructed "George Walker" through a metonymic relationship between his musical characters and the figure who left the theatre in the evenings. As Russell speculates, his "English dress suit and white pointed cut vest," his "English silk hat and overcoat were something a little too smart for" America. No doubt, the spectacle of George Walker's costuming further managed to disturb and disrupt the essential racial "nature" which white audiences expected *In Dahomey* to evoke.

What black dandyism best exposed was black socioeconomic and cultural desire in a new era of class transmogrification and redefinition. Onstage *In Dahomey* hyperbolically articulated the hopes and aspirations of African Americans who aimed to master the art of social climbing. Ironically, no character embodied and articulated these dandyish desires more vociferously than the figure of a young woman, the ingenue Rosetta Lightfoot, played by an actress James Weldon Johnson once called "the brightest star among women on the Negro stage," Aida Overton Walker.[113] In three of *In Dahomey*'s best-known numbers, Rosetta's character leads or enables the charge to climb. In her famous solo performance of "I Wants to be an Actor Lady," she showcases her character's desire for professional success and mobility. Written by the white composer-publisher Harry von Tizler and lyricist Vincent Bryan, "Actor Lady" was "a jaunty ragtime number" interpolated into the musical. In her rendition of the song, Walker revealed her ability to inhabit material not expressly written for "colored performers," reanimating the song to fit and reflect the oft-invisible desires of black and particularly black female performers who longed to "star in the show . . . no back row shady." For a few dazzling minutes in act 2, then, Walker would take center stage with "nothing but a wheelbarrow," presumably the prop of a soon-to-be-discarded rural existence, "and a looking glass" through which Rosetta might see herself and her dreams of a new life as a performer, "the real thing" who matches the talents of Ellen Terry and Carrie Brown. Rosetta's blazing ambition echoes later in act 2, scene 3, when she robustly declares her goal to become "the leader of the color'd aristocracy." This show-stopping performance, "all full of female whimsicalities," affirmed her status as "the greatest coming female comedy star of her race" and, "with a grand star reception from the audience," she actualized the ambitions of her alter-ego Rosetta in one fell swoop each night onstage.[114]

Aida Walker's Rosetta Lightfoot operates as the archetypal voice of black social climbing in the musical. Moreover, she figures as the crucial distaff side of her husband George's offstage dandy persona within the context of the production. While other characters scheme and plot crooked plans to seize wealth and success, Rosetta articulates through song her embrace of the "show" involved in obtaining and maintaining success across and in spite of the color line. If she is a "troublesome young thing," as the script suggests (ID1, 66), and an "enfant terrible," as the British press pegged her character, the "trouble" she creates stems from her "ambition" for "recognition" which "Leader of the Colored Aristocracy" jubilantly details for the audience.[115] Structured as a call-and-response number, Cook's and James Weldon Johnson's song finds Rosetta imagining her own triumphs "mov[ing] on a social plane, so very high" while the chorus reaffirms that "she has a yearning" and "has been learning" to, as Rosetta puts it, "make the proper show" (ID1, 80). Again and again the musical returns to these themes of cultural performance, the need to cultivate "ostentation" rather than "sobriety," as Cicero puts it in the number "Society," in order to break into new social circles. In short, Rosetta's showy materialism was its own kind of "drag" show aimed clearly and almost ritualistically toward transforming her conditions and her social position, which were always in the forefront of her mind.[116]

Like Walker and Williams offstage in top hat and tails, Overton Walker's Rosetta onstage wrapped herself in the lineaments of fine things to move herself up and through the world. And it is Rosetta who repeatedly makes these aims explicit throughout the musical. In yet another interpolated von Tizler number, "Vassar Girl," Walker was believed to have sung about the wily chronicles of the "first dark belle" who "startl[ed] the nation" by passing for white and entering Vassar. This remarkably subversive tune, which recounts the way its heroine feigns a Madagascar identity and plays her "part so well" so that all the boys thought her "swell," amplifies the musical's preoccupation with transgressing the color line and positions Rosetta's character as the icon of social mobility (ID1, 74). More still, "Vassar Girl" stages its own particular reversal of popular coon song passing themes which often scripted the social aspirations of upwardly mobile African Americans as the mere desire to become white. For the heroine of "Vassar Girl," education rather than whiteness is the welcome fruit of passing. Rosetta's number here reverses popular coon song iconography which stressed the "pretensions, vanities," and "greed" of black women who longed "to change from black to white in order to gain status." Instead, the desires expressed in songs like "Actor Lady" and "Vassar Girl" gave voice to a modern—indeed perhaps a "New Negro" womanhood—committed to bettering herself professionally as well as intellectually. Walker's Rosetta thus rewrote coon song female social climbing as postbellum uplift and rescripted the "mercenary vixen" of such songs as the would-be leader of the new "colored" elite.[117]

The tricky line that *In Dahomey* walked, then, was in its emphasis on both endorsing and critiquing the passionate and sometimes selfish social aspirations of Rosetta and others. Repeatedly the musical played with the boundaries of envisioning the mobility of some of its characters while mocking and parodying the avarice of others and warning audiences of the pernicious effects that social climbing could have on black solidarity. Audiences were continuously forced to travel through a labyrinth of artifice and modes of social and cultural performance when attending the Williams and Walker musical. In this context, drag then is not so much an abrupt, non-sequitur stunt staged in the jungles of In Dahomey's Caboceer as it is a stylized method of performance that signifies on the complex and ambiguous politics of social mobility within and all the way to the outer limits of In Dahomey. In turn, the metatheatricality of the two principal characters' masquerade as "king and queen" operates on a continuum with the lavish offstage clothing of its stars and disrupts and decentralizes the base of Williams and Walker's performances. The competing sites of drag at the heart of the show work to unseat the tyranny of racial authenticity politics imposed on black performers by undoing ostensibly arbitrary categories of representation. That this form of masquerade surfaces most overtly in the final act of In Dahomey is particularly significant since the drag spectacle consistently disarmed critics' attempts to naturalize not only In Dahomey's performers but the "African" landscape as well. The production's finale suggests that although even Joseph Conrad in his literary visions of a raped and pillaged dark frontier "could not grant the natives their freedom, despite his severe critique of the imperialism that enslaved them," the turn-of-the-century black musical, with its spectacular, hyperbolic visual excess, potentially transformed the politics of liberation through an unconventional intervention in representing the "African scene."[118]

### The (Re)Invention of "Africa"

Nature with itself be a-vieing / A-singin' while my babe and I parade.
—"My Dahomian Queen"

Behind the curtain of "drag" in In Dahomey there lies a stunning critique of the romantically essentialized notion of the "dark continent" which perpetuated and enabled imperialist ideology in the late nineteenth and early twentieth centuries. The musical's perplexing "African" imagery not only competed with conventional representations of an "uncivilized" frontier but it also threatened to revise how Africa might be narrated and ultimately who would narrate that mysterious land in Western cultural consciousness. Founded in the early seventeenth century, the kingdom of Dahomey (which is now a portion of present-day Benin) figured prominently in the transatlantic slave trade. Bartering and brokering extensively with European slave traders, eighteenth-century Dahomian King Agaja (1716–40) played a key role in establishing a port where captives were transported into the Atlantic world. In the late nineteenth century, the country struggled violently with civil unrest, political tyranny, and French colonization, particularly in the 1890s and as African American intellectual discussions and scholarship increasingly focused on African history and culture. *In Dahomey* auspiciously debuted in the wake of what West African historian Boniface Obichere describes as France and Great Britain's " 'dishonorable scramble' for territory" in the Dahomey-Niger hinterland. This battle for land resulted in the dissolution of two more African kingdoms, subsequently jeopardizing the notion of West African autonomous territories which seemed in danger of extinction by the early twentieth century.

The kingdom of Dahomey was, in the 1890s and early 1900s, another African territory annexed by adjacent European colonies in what seemed like an unstoppable steamroll of sub-Saharan expansionism peaking with the Boer War of 1902. Only Abyssinia avoided imperialist rule and, in a dramatic inversion of military strength, warded off and defeated the advances of Italian colonizers in an 1896 battle that created an international sensation. This event, perhaps more than any other, galvanized the rhetoric of global Ethiopianism and rejuvenated a vision of a liberated African continent which critics read as the underlying theme in the eponymous 1906 Walker and Williams production.[119] Compared to the Abyssinia show and the legendary circumstances which it loosely referenced, *In Dahomey* seems to lack a sophisticated engagement with contemporaneous African politics. Nonetheless, it uniquely subverts systems of nationalist and imperialist spectacle by working *outside* conventional notions of what constitutes Pan-Africanism and diasporic cultural politics. In doing so, the musical renegotiates viable forms of postbellum Pan-Africanist representation.

We might in fact think of the "Africa" in *In Dahomey* as dressed up in its own kind of marvelous drag. Re-appropriating the pomp and circumstance of an imperial ceremony, this Dahomey is all glamorous parade and jubilee. Two of the extended musical numbers in act 3 mount elaborate images of monarchical pageantry. "My Dahomian Queen" celebrates the unification of a nation through the conjugal coupling of a "royal" king with his betrothed. In that song, a smitten monarch imagines that love " 'twill be the grandest thing, just to hear the natives sing, as loyally they fall before my throne. Caboceers will be our sentry, 'Rabian knights will be our gentry, / The wonder of the twentieth century, / A-makin' even sunlight fade" (ID1, 83). Drenched in gauzy, romantic yearning, the song provides the occasion for its singer to woo a "Moorish maiden . . . so sweet and serene / fresh from the jungle green." On the threshold of a blissful future, "My Dahomian Queen" imagines a world where the sun has finally set over colonial empires, "fading" into a new era of black self-rule. Taken together, songs like "My Dahomian Queen," "Evah Darkey Is a King," and George Walker's signature tune "My Castle on the Nile" play with notions of romance, wealth, inheritance, and genealogical reclamation. In its assertion that all "dahkeys" are linked to a royal line and, likewise, in its aim to "live extravagant[ly] in my ancestral castle on de Nile," each song translates the conjugal romance of "Dahomian Queen" into a love song directed toward the sybarite's vision of "Africa." Each tune celebrates an extravagant fantastical landscape of promise and renewal.[120]

Ushering in this new era of independence, the Caboceer drill teams mark this transition in power and the exuberant reclamation of space. Cook's "Caboceers Entrance" amplifies the triumph of sovereignty. Subsequently in the song, Dahomey prepares to rise up. Ominously, its subjects warn that "before his Majesty all nations prostrate fall . . . / Their power all victorious, / Like gods of light before us, / They come, the world to sway." The Caboceers celebrate the army's fortitude and dedication to battle. Their "armor brightly flashing, with bayonets a clashing," they pledge to "hunt the fray" at any cost. The image, like so many moments in *In Dahomey*, is a politically ambiguous one. The figure of the war-mad, hunting native is a powerful icon entrenched in the Western imaginary and employed as a legitimizing agent in suppressing the indigenous masses, and it was not uncommon for sensational extravaganza shows and circus entertainment to feature this kind of regimented drilling in their repertoires as a form of exoticized entertainment.[121]

Yet we might reread the use of drills in this scene as a sharp signifying sequence that visually references concurrent black uplift cultural rituals. The musical's Caboceer drills, for instance, should be understood in the context of the "spectacle of black militia units, proud in their military uniforms and . . . regularly drilling on . . . city streets or marching in major parades" in the latter half of the nineteenth century. As "disconcerting" to whites and to some blacks as these sometimes "garish" acts of exhibitionism were, such marching spectacles were frequent reminders of the many ways that postbellum African Americans celebrated and defiantly flaunted their contested access to public space and affirmed "the collective use of the black body for parodic play."[122] The scene of the Caboceers' entrance avoids, then, the re-articulation of mere "coon song" pomp and parade, most remarkably in the complex musical composition which accompanies this sequence. In short, Will Cook's sprightly and inventive number encompasses and articulates the heterogeneity of black cultural identity formation. *In Dahomey* thus took the grace, precision, and swagger of the drill rituals and resituated these events in a transnational context for African American characters seeking ways to claim "Dahomey" as a new cultural site of resistant expression.[123]

All the romance of In Dahomey's grand spectacles, though, cannot dispel the often troubling images of bellicose "natives" that erupt at various stages in the production. To be sure, such characterizations fall in danger of merely reproducing grotesque stereotypes of African peoples for a transatlantic audience rabid for blackface. In particular, the Syndicate characters assume minstrelized aliases as they embark on their journey to the African continent; Pinkerton's "Cannibal King" / "King Eat-Em-All," Shylock's "Emperor of Blasasus," Reeder's "Lord of Jungletta," Straight's "Discount of de Apis," and Charlie's "Duke Monkey Faceteen." Whether these titles expose the Syndicate's inherent fraudulence or whether they take a signifying dig at Anglo-Americans who travel abroad in search of inflated gentrification (as Dunbar would attempt to do in his own variation on this theme), the Syndicate's new names recall the ways that minstrelsy mockingly eviscerated the potency of black leadership through primitivist caricature. Likewise, the conflict that these characters weather with their African peers suggests that the show was none too optimistic about the viability of African and African American social and political relations.[124]

Keeping these ambiguities directly in sight, we might nonetheless consider how the discourse of the spectacle might have worked in the service of African American entertainers and toward potentially revisionary ends. For if, as Guy Debord reveals, "the spectacle is the existing order's uninterrupted discourse about itself, its laudatory monologue," then it is possible to read In Dahomey's conclusive succession of spectacles, its invocation of wide-scale ceremony and jubilant musical numbers which spiritedly bled one into the other, as a suggestion that this mythically rendered West African region rests on the brink of renarrating itself in extravagant terms. In Dahomey transforms the function of the spectacle, the means through which nations are made and preserved, by recasting the terms by which African Americans might participate in such a process.[125]

Beyond transforming the site of the body into a terrain of dissonant dis/play, the production uproots the imperialist dream of a statically "savage" territory open for violation by re-appropriating the sensational exhibition of the "dark continent" and redeploying such imagery as a model of ontological intervention. In Dahomey responds to the always-expanding, generic empire's need to naturalize the boundaries of nations and essentialize historical memory by hyperbolically calling attention to the fictions of "Africa" promulgated by a Western imaginary.[126] The musical's "barbaric" "Africa" underscores its own artifice and its superficiality. Its superfluous pageantry and performative ritual lays bare the juncture between the dis/play of the nation and the territory which such spectacles aim to represent. This construction of an "other" Dahomey illustrates the provocative ways that the musical generates an imaginative ideological discourse of nationhood which potentially eludes the circumscription of Western spectatorial desire. No scene in the musical played with the limits of the imperial imagination more than the notorious finale/prologue. Billed in the script as a "scenario," a form that anticipated the African American pageants of the coming decade, the original act 3 dissolves plot almost entirely in favor of emphasizing musical numbers, colorful costumes, and populously decorous tableaux. In its early form with the scenario tacked on to the end of the show, the script moves its characters out of the States and into "Africa." Simultaneously however, the narrative grows weaker, seemingly incapable—or, perhaps refusing—its own representational cogency. This "other" place where its African American characters end up cannot, the musical suggests, finally be conventionally represented. In turn, Africa is reinvented as "Africa" in the Williams and Walker musicals, in much the same way that black bodies masquerade in the production, as an unstable point of play which transforms and re-appropriates mythically disfigured conceptualizations of race and place.

The point of *In Dahomey*, then, is not to represent Africa at all but to conjure an unrecognizable "African" territory that countered the nineteenth- and early-twentieth-century desire for scientific "accuracy" and a tyranny of authenticity which denied black narrative authority.[127] The imperialist mission that depended on the notion of Africa as an "underdeveloped wilderness" is turned on its head in *In Dahomey*, where the spectator is challenged to look on a fictitiously resilient terrain of artifice. Through layers of drag and a montage of multiple musical numbers in what was a shifting repertoire, *In Dahomey* affirmed its ability to remain "unmarked." In many ways, *In Dahomey* resembles that which critic Robert Eric Livingston defines as Negritude's twentieth-century "drama of decolonization." Livingston's description of the "anti-colonial" work of Negritude poet and playwright Aimé Cesaire runs akin to the Williams and Walker musical. Just as in the drama of Negritude, where "character becomes construction" and "development takes place through the recurrent disintegration and rearticulation of the dramatic scene," *In Dahomey*'s fantastic and phantasmatic rendering of another country suggests that what cannot be identified can no longer be conquered. The musical anticipated Cesaire's "theatre of development" in which mounting the spectacle would itself become "a moment of cultural negotiation."[128]

The production, then, inverts Edward Said's influential notion of an "imagined empire" by calling attention to the cognitive and narrative agency of the performers who act out this odd "other" place. In a powerful reversal, *In Dahomey* demonstrates the possibility of boldly re-appropriating the imperialist strategy of inventing so-called native regions as a means of building a stronger "Europe." The musical, instead, articulates the complexities of African American identity production and the quest to invoke an aesthetic of fantasy as a counterhegemonic response to the concept of an essential territory. Moreover, *In Dahomey* converts Pan-Africanism's accursed "psychological dissociation" of its emigrants, turning the crisis of cultural dislocation into an alternative form of identity articulation. The Williams and Walker musical enacted a struggle to dream intensely, and to employ what could only be read as fantasy sequences which served as responses to a naturalizing discourse which render Africa and African Americans as dreamless subjects. As cultural documentation alone, *In Dahomey* reveals "things Negroes were not supposed to think about, or were considered incapable of thinking about."[129]

The musical also offers sobering critiques of romanticized black transnationalist thought and postbellum popular culture's increasing nostalgia for slavery. Neither the conventional black nationalist emigrationist longing for an idealized homeland nor the sentimental nostalgia for the "simple life" of plantation culture are beyond the musical's skewering. It is little wonder then that the British script firmly squashes Mose's quixotic African dreams of prosperity. His final lines in act 3 find him declaring that "[t]hings have been misrepresented and I for one should go back to from where I came from. And when chickens and watermelons give out in the United States, I'll be satisfied with plain pork chops" (lxxi). And though Rare, Shy, and the other characters may, in this version's end, follow Cicero's plans to head back to the States as well, the production has already roundly condemned Cicero's delusional nostalgia. In both scripts, mother and daughter Lightfoot express little tolerance for Cicero's archaic sycophancy toward the memory of his former master (ID1, 78, 81). The competing desires of multiple Lightfoots in the production underscores how these characters stand precariously between slavery's past and the promise of a new century. No doubt, his yearnings threaten to stymie Cicero's ability to imagine a world of black life beyond the confines of his Florida home. In this regard, *In Dahomey* was perhaps most startlingly incendiary and committed to black uplift ideology by way of its iconoclastic ideology and its refusal to endorse any single political line. By deromanticizing various lines of political and social thought, the production created an unlikely space for political debate and cultural interrogation by including multiple critical perspectives.[130]

The "dream" of *In Dahomey*, as it were, further lends itself to a project of revising black nationalism. If, as Benedict Anderson contends, nationalism "is not the awakening of nations to self-consciousness: it *invents* nations where they do not exist," then the musical (re)invents an "imagined" nation-state which comes as a result of the plot's back-to-Africa movement. However, this "Africa," this fanciful "place of indeterminacy" is nowhere at all; it is a place which resists "realist" representations even as it ostensibly panders to such categories. And while British audiences reveled in the unknowability of this spectacle, "laugh[ing] and scream[ing] with merriment" over their own inability to comprehend the narrative's significance, this act of (mis)reading registers a significant allegorical moment of disjuncture between audience and theatrical spectacle; for finally, this region of "otherness" cannot be identified, it cannot be co-opted entirely into the world of an incredulous spectator. By re-imagining "Africa" and the boundaries of (black) nationalist desire, *In Dahomey* wages an unlikely theatrical "revolt against empire" which came to a head at once during the musical's stunning finale and, in particular, within the context of its legendary encore performance at Buckingham Palace.[131]

### "Swing Along" to the Palace: Cakewalking and the Politics of Emancipation

> There was a cakewalk threatened at one stage.
>
> —Anonymous critic, Billy Rose Theatre Collection

Rather than recentering "Africa" in Dahomey, the London version of the musical made good on fulfilling the "threat" of a cakewalk for its much-contested finale. Although the dance served in the 1900s as "a conduit for African Americans to white show business" culture, the decision among the show's performers to unveil the cakewalk as a centerpiece to the closing act was anything but harmonious. As biographer Mabel Rowland notes, the dance "was introduced into London, only upon the insistent demand of the royal audience. The Williams and Walker Company had not the slightest intention of including this dance in its repertoire, because it was passe . . . in America . . . but in England they had heard much about it and the Mother Queen was anxious to see it." Within a week of the show's premiere, the English *In Dahomey* reached its spectacular finish with a choreographed extravaganza that brought to life in dance American race relations and black identity formation at the turn of the century. Following the "monarchy's" entrance and a second rendition of "Evah Darkey Is a King," *In Dahomey*'s script calls for the narrative to shift into two musical numbers, "On Emancipation Day" and "That's How the Cakewalk's Done," along with a "triumphant" dance of the same name. Theatre historians speculate that this routine lasted a whopping twenty minutes.[132] The transition into a cakewalk song and dance routine was a much anticipated tradition in the early black musical genre which *In Dahomey* ostensibly fulfilled. A dance which had its cultural roots in slave gatherings designed to reference the culture of white masters, cakewalking continues to endure as a lingering source of critical debate concerning racial authenticity politics; fundamentally at issue is the question of who is "imitating" whom in this legendary two-step romp. The dance experienced a resurgence of popularity in the postbellum era of black stage performance at which time the event was featured as a grand and elaborate conclusion to vaudevillian productions such as the traveling *Creole Show* of 1890 and as a spectacular processional event which served as an evening's entertainment unto itself. By the turn of the century "the cakewalk would become the most popular element of the minstrel and early black theatrical stage, usually a grand finale with elaborate choreography and costumes."[133]

To cakewalk at the end of *In Dahomey* was to some a way to conclude and contain the narrative with a return to the familiar terrain of the "happy darkey" plantation motifs often associated with the dance (Sundquist, *To Wake the Nations*, 276). Certainly the popularity of "operettos" and revue sketches such as *Clorindy* encouraged these kinds of expectations. Such productions had found great success in presenting the cakewalk as a jubilant conclusion to their shows. As Aida Overton Walker remarked famously in an interview with the London *Tatler* during *In Dahomey*'s U.K. tour, the dance was meant to convey a seamless and an infectious joy for performers and audiences alike. Arguably the leading dancer of her era and the principal choreographer of many of the Williams and Walker productions, Walker urged her colleagues and pupils who danced the cakewalk to hold "sunshine in [their] hearts. Think of moonlight nights and pine knots and tallow dips, and of lives untouched by the hardness of toil." Subsequently, from Walker's insistence that "the success of cake-walking depends largely on temperament" came British interviewer Constance Beerbohm's assertion that the black dancers' "faces must be interested and joyous, and as the cake-walk is characteristic of a cheerful race to be properly appreciated it must be danced in the proper spirit—it is a gala dance" (GEC).[134]

While the public may have found it easy to associate the dance with wide grins and bubbly galas, critics in more recent years have convincingly contested the easy elision of cakewalking's social and political salience in American culture. Sundquist demonstrates, for instance, how "the cakewalk occupied a liminal territory with a significant potential for resistance, a psychological and cultural space in which the racist appropriation of black life in offensive mannerisms gave way to an African American reversal of the stereotype" (Sundquist, *To Wake the Nations*, 277). The notion of black performers imitating white performers who, in turn, were believed to have been imitating African Americans gives pause not only to consider what Amiri Baraka calls the "remarkable irony" of cakewalking and minstrel show theatricality but also to explore the ways in which the dance engaged with the politics of imitation, satire, and parody as black political and cultural resistance. Sundquist's work affirms the way that cakewalking, under the rubric of black minstrelsy, functioned as a strategic "re-appropriation of significant elements of African American folk life, surviving from slave culture and early blackface minstrelsy alike [which] signified on the racist theory of imitation. African American minstrelsy was imitation with a vengeance" (Sundquist, *To Wake the Nations*, 286).[135]

Similarly, Chuck Kleinhans has argued that cakewalking works as a kind of parody, building his use of the term on Linda Hutcheon's significant contention that parody represents a "repetition with critical difference." Kleinhans specifies that parody is the technique which "involves the articulation of a critique by expressing a meaning different to the stated or ostensible meaning through a repetition or doubling." According to Kleinhans, black entertainers' performance of the cakewalk parodied white aristocratic culture through a performative ritual which simultaneously went against the grain of dominant culture and yet was safely contained in its forms. Sundquist adds that through this notion of parody, black performance culture and, in particular, cakewalking preserved certain syncretic elements which were not merely "parodic attack alone" but which "recall[ed] in performative expression a cultural meaning separate from and prior to enslavement" (Sundquist, *To Wake the Nations*, 280). The insistence on locating the presence of "Africanisms" within the cakewalk is a crucial element in coming to terms with the representational significance of the dance, for such arguments reveal the political currency of the act as an embodiment of cultural identity.

Adding to this critical discussion, David Krasner expands on exploring the cakewalk's negotiation of imitation as subversive parody by foregrounding what he reads as Aida Overton Walker's highly stylized transformation of the dance into oppositional "hybridized aesthetics." Krasner advances the theory of reading the cakewalk as "double-voiced parody: a hybrid of African dance and satiric gestures aimed at whites"; he specifically considers Walker's manipulation of the dance's shifting semiotics and cross-cultural "lexicon of movement" to pose a hybrid form of subaltern expression for the black performer.[136] Borrowing from Homi Bhabha's notion of hybridity as sustaining multiple meanings, he contends that Walker "understood how cakewalking's fluid cultural baseline worked" and used it to her advantage in reshaping the dance aesthetically along the margins of African and Western forms. Walker, Krasner concludes, "devised a choreography that was protean, flexible, and cognizant of the mechanisms of cultural expression."[137]

Each of these critical observations aims toward a recuperative project and works to effectively demonstrate how the cakewalk served as "an example of the principles of subversion and indirection essential to the evolution of African American cultural expression" (Sundquist, *To Wake the Nations*, 279). Moreover, these analyses reveal how cakewalking yielded a dynamic representation of African American identity at the turn of the century. Krasner, for instance, makes a crucial link between Walker's "hybridized choreography" and Du Bois's theory of double-consciousness, which delineates black identity's ongoing "twoness" of self, its "two unreconciled strivings; two warring ideals in one-dark body."[138] Cakewalking transformed the ever-present "push and pull" of the Negro into a perambulatory spectacle which weaved in and out of a seemingly endless vortex of cultural "imitation" to deploy a dynamically fluid representation of African American identity. It was, according to Walker herself, "more of a walk [and] less of a dance" (BRT). In other words, cakewalking served as a performance of travel that literally walked the color line of identity politics.

This latter point calls attention to the limits of defining the dance solely in terms of "cultural expression" and parodic mimesis, indeed as a radically vertiginous "hall of mirrors," as Krasner puts it.[139] For while such claims do much to advance an understanding of black performative agency and representational authority within the context of cakewalking, they do little to reveal the ways in which one might read the dance as not merely an expressive act but one which is, in part, *constitutive* of African American identity in the early twentieth century. From this standpoint, cakewalking operates as a strategy of Butlerian identity enactment, a performative practice which, through the dance itself, establishes and continuously re-assesses Du Bois's legendary formulation of an identity constantly in contestation with itself.[140] Walker's description of the dance foregrounds the processual politics of the cakewalk, how the performance forever comprises shifting and alternating paradigms and meanings which contribute to the strategic *production* of African American identity. She describes how, "in the walk you follow the music, and as you keep time with it in what is best defined as a march you improvise. Gestures, evolutions, poses, will come to you as you go through the dance. The partners may develop steps which they think will impress the judges. Every muscle must be in perfect control" (GEC). Walker's instructions call for the constant (re)birth of character and the performer's own "improvisational" style of "gestures" and "poses" which set up a dialectic with the forever-rigid structure, the dominant paradigm embedded in the dance.

At the close of *In Dahomey*, each of the cakewalking couples danced their way through and across the "problem of the colorline." In hoop gowns and black tie, these performers elegantly enacted what Randy Martin avows is the political intent and process of dance itself. As Martin contends, dance "does not name a fixed expression but a problem, a predicament, that bodies might find themselves in the midst of, whose momentary solutions we call dancing. Unlike most political practice, dance, when it is performed and watched, makes available reflexively, the means through which mobilization is accomplished." Mobilizing themselves into the "twoness" of Du Bois's new-century "blackness," the company's cakewalkers repeatedly disassembled and re-ordered the articulation of black identity formation. No doubt an "extended repetition with critical difference," cakewalking was more than an act of parody. While this kind of reading is clearly accurate, it nonetheless falls short of fully coming to terms with the ways in which the dance operates as political intervention and identity critique.[141] Such a gesture belongs, as we have seen—and rightfully so—to the discourse of camp as Moe Meyer contends. Camp, Meyer argues, is "the total body of performative practices and strategies used to enact a queer identity, with enactment defined as the production of social visibility." It is a definition "based on identity performance and not solely in some kind of unspecified cognitive identification of an ironic moment" (introduction, 5). Similarly, I find it necessary to push the politicization of black musical performance and, in particular, cakewalking as part of a strategy of performative and rigorously oppositional identity production and not merely as an expressive moment wherein identity is conveyed. In short, I propose that we read cakewalking as a form of camp, not to replicate an erasure or colonization of queer identity politics and critical discourse but to broaden Meyer's definition of camp's currency and to make visible camp's black genealogical roots.

Although Meyer aims to extend the definition of parody into a "process whereby the marginalized and disenfranchised advance their own interests by entering alternative signifying codes into discourse by attaching them to existing structures of signification," his analysis rests on the insistence that camp works as a specifically ontological critique and that such a critique is an exclusively "queer signifying practice." Reading camp as only queer, Meyer replicates an erasure of parallel marginalities based on race and class.[142] It goes without saying that camp has a crucial resonance in queer discursive histories and cultural practices; it may, in fact, be the fulcrum of queer identity politics as Meyer and others suggest. Yet I would argue that camp as a strategy is also linked to African American performances such as the cakewalk in that both the cakewalk and a broadly defined process of camp embrace and celebrate an unfixed identity which repeats its own dissonance and lack of closure. With this in mind, rather than displacing queer positionality, I am arguing for a way to consider the relationship between these oppositional performances. Queer camp and the camp of cakewalking are not a conflated form of identity production; rather each works in the service of dismantling a dominant ontological paradigm.

This reformulation of cakewalking as a kind of camp and as a constitutive strategy in renegotiating marginalized identity politics necessitates a more focused consideration of the dance's positioning as an extended, twenty-minute performance at the close of *In Dahomey*. The majority of critics tend to decontextualize the cakewalk as a performative act, suspending it from narrative depth and significance. They choose to read the dance as a complex, yet plot-free, non-sequiturial theatrical moment which either holds the narrative in abeyance or delimits its parameters altogether. In her study of African American dance, for instance, Jacqui Malone suggests that *In Dahomey* served as a "vehicle" which, nonetheless, "lifted the cakewalk to the status of an international dance craze after the show's smashing London run of 1903."[143] A number of critics tend to foreground the production's ability to present the cakewalk as a cross-over success which captured the fascination of white audiences; yet little critical attention is paid to the relationship between cakewalking and plot development, specifically how cakewalking advanced the play's fundamental themes.

Not surprisingly, to contemporary reviewers of the musical, the cakewalk finale additionally accentuated the rapid dissolution of *In Dahomey*'s already "flimsy" plot development. The bewildered London *Times* critic viewed the dance as a predictable conclusion and a manifestation of the production's chaotic structure, observing with a tinge of ennui, "[o]f course, *In Dahomey* concludes with a 'cake-walk,' a real cake-walk with a real cake, which is awarded, by acclamation of the audience, to the most frenzied among the pairs of dancers. In 'epileptic' dancing these coloured people are, as was to be expected, quite unrivaled" (HTC). The musical ended, to these reviewers, as it had begun—in absolute disorder.

Aida Overton Walker's interviews and articles on cakewalk instruction and the fastidious discipline of the cakewalk dancer whose "every muscle must be in perfect control" (HTC) counter this kind of oversimplification of the performance, as do the many analyses of the promenade which link its rhythmic marching style and music to an "explicitly military nostalgia" (Sundquist, *To Wake the Nations*, 289) evolving at the turn of the century. If anything, cakewalking's two-step pattern appropriated the patriotic marching band aesthetic which, Malone argues, "seemed to embody America as it liked to see itself— cocky, stepping to a proud beat, ready for any change."[144] Read from this perspective, the finale of the cakewalk as a transmutated marching band parade with its hubris and extravagance ushered in the change of (black) identity which the dance, itself, continuously (re)enacted through camp. This extended repetition of difference—of African American identity in motion— appropriately capped *In Dahomey*'s conclusion as it reached the alien terrain of "Africa."

More than anywhere else in *In Dahomey*, the characters find the rhythm to "swing along" in the cakewalk finale and, in doing so, they tap into a choreographed "response" of sorts to the dense and equally heterogeneous musical "call" which opened the show. Both the music and lyrics of "Swing Along" forecast the pomp and circumstance of the musical's journey. "Singing in unison and fortissimo, and anchored by forceful orchestral accents on the beat," the cast proclaims the pleasure of parade and the splendor of exhibitionism. In "Swing Along," *In Dahomey*'s characters seize back from the hands of white show business managers and entrepreneurs the right to proudly exhibit themselves. Cook's number thus encourages black subjects to "swing a-long chillun, swing a-long de lane, Lif' yo' head and yo' heels mighty high." The number lyrically rewrites minstrelsy's grotesque lampooning of black soldiers, marching units, and parades. Whereas minstrelsy conceived of African Americans as "harmless strutters," "Swing Along" imagined an insouciant black strut that was all the more disconcerting because of its marchers' carefree joy and direction. With culturally informed political intent, the song metatextually signifies on the exigencies facing black performers in a crossover musical production; "Swing Along" disruptively reminds that "white fo'ks awatchin' an' seein' what you do," and in doing so, makes a sophisticated gesture toward foreshadowing the Brechtian actor's "awareness of being watched." The key to Cook's savvy composition is to turn the constrictions of the gaze into a moment of longing, in effect to expose the deep-rooted cross-racial desire informing white spectatorial politics. "Swing Along" assures that "white fo'ks jealous when you'se walkin' two by two, So swing a-long chillun swing a-long." Originally positioned at the end of the show, "Swing Along" celebrates the emergence of a black subjectivity proudly willing to occupy public space and to revel in the pleasure of grand and impressive communal elegance and camaraderie. If, as Riis compellingly argues, "Swing Along" "stands as no less than a synecdoche for the entire production," then the cakewalk finale represented that composition's translation into corporeal movement.[145]

Two additional musical numbers often performed during or near the finale amplify the engagement of "Swing Along" with white spectatorial desire. Dunbar and Cook's ragtime number "Emancipation Day" and J. Leubrie Hill's "That's How the Cake Walk's Done" envision parodic inversions of identity which clear a space for renegotiating "black" and, more broadly, American identity in the spirit of the cakewalk. The former proclaims that "On Emancipation Day / All you white fo'ks clear de way / Brass ban' playin' sev'ral tunes, / Darkies eyes look jes' lo'k moons." The lyrics juxtapose residual minstrel codes with visions of a presumably post-enslaved black culture built on artifice and disguise. Viciously lampooned in minstrelsy, the Emancipation Day parades of postbellum black culture resurface in *In Dahomey* in the hands of a new world order. In this remarkable universe "coons" are "dress'd up lak masqueraders, Porters arm'd lak rude invaders," and "White fo'ks try to pass fo' coons on Emancipation Day." The vision here is not so much a facile inversion of power dynamics and social positioning, where African Americans displace "white folks" in the system of aristocratic order. Rather, the song celebrates a "pass" of another sort, a mode of exchange in which blacks and whites experiment with the "Straight" practices handed down from act 1. And while white folks may "try to pass" across the color line, the song assures that the darker races will succeed in donning the garb not of whites but of masterful "masqueraders." On "Emancipation Day," the song suggests, the black performer will discard the "coon's" clothing and enter into the cakewalk's continuous space of transformation and renewal.[146]

Elaborating on these themes, "That's How the Cake Walk's Done" describes a world where social and cultural borders are disrupted by the "dance craze" which, as Krasner maintains, "was one of the first culturally expressive forms to be used as a cross-over commodity and to transgress the racial divide." The land which *In Dahomey*'s characters find themselves in by act 3 is one beset, as the lyrics put it, by a "Cake-walking craze, it's a fad nowadays / With black folks and white folks too / And I really declare it's done ev'ry-where." Cakewalk fanaticism in the song's vision spreads across racial as well as national borders so that even "[t]he Parisians, you know, they all walk just so / They call it ze cake walk dance / But with me you'll agree / That the folks from Paree / In this cake walk would have no chance." This global phenomenon opens a field of possibility for a romanticized transnational unity sustained by the enactment of the dance. Likewise, the dance follows Kleinhans's extended characterization of camp as well, in that the song demonstrates how the cakewalk "draws on and transforms mass culture." The cakewalk in *In Dahomey* threatens to intercede in and revise global power relations through the spirit of the dance. Yet the lyrics simultaneously remind audiences that none of its new disciples compare to the (black) dancers who demonstrate the processional in the song. Cakewalking, thus, unifies even as it calls attention to the superior skill and narrative authority of the "Black folks in Tennessee" who, according to the lyrics, "introduced [cakewalking] years ago down in Dixie."[147]

This magisterial promenade at production's end, then, mounts a dual performance wherein the process of "becoming" and of rehearsing African American identity is staged and where a final, imperialist intervention is waged on "Emancipation Day." This sort of extravagant ending was not, however, palatable to some British theatregoers. For despite the fact that London "audiences expected black Americans to dance the cakewalk," this performance of the promenade left audiences adrift. Most critical observations of the period claimed that this confusion was occasioned by a lingering crisis in plot which permeated the production from beginning to end. One reviewer described how "the audience sat helplessly wondering whether the performance was at an end. It was not till the orchestra, a few minutes later, played the national anthem that the house recognized that the entertainment was over and filed mystified out into the rain" (BRT). Only a rousing rendition of "God Save the King" was said to curb the crowd's perplexity.

Although, as Jeffrey Green points out, this rendition of the national anthem was fairly customary in England for much of the twentieth century ("*In Dahomey*," 24), it is, nevertheless, an extraordinary form of social and political symbolism with which to mark *In Dahomey*'s conclusion. The anthem's presence at all in the context of theatre culture suggests the ways in which imperial regimes systemically constricted and bound the borders of nineteenth- and early-twentieth-century cultural spaces. Further, this recurrence of "God Save the King" at the end of the production each night reflects the turn-of-the-century English dramatic production's shifting politics which were forced to accommodate and "to accept the binding closure of the discourse and practice of imperialism instead of producing a cultural rhetoric of its own." *In Dahomey*'s refusal to follow such guidelines, its inability to reproduce the script of British blackface minstrelsy's entrenched celebration of an imperialist "social and cultural pre-eminence" centered in the U.K., warranted an intervention. Thus, to play the national anthem at the close of this extended cakewalk—a simultaneous performance of black identity production and an articulation of transglobal popular culture—at least symbolically illustrates the state's attempts to contain the insurgent politics of both the dance and the production.[148]

Whatever "threat" that the cakewalk posed to the sovereignty of its British audience's social and cultural positionality, the nightly rendition of "God Save the King" potentially restored a kind of cultural order through what Benedict Anderson calls the "experience of simultaneity" in the language of nationalism. Anderson argues that "there is a special kind of contemporaneous community which language alone suggests," and that singing the national anthem provides a notion of "unisonance" in the making of "imagined" national communities. His point underscores the ways that the generic anthem offers for audiences a sense of belonging to a higher national order, of being united within a chorus of familiarity which celebrates the preservation of a romanticized monarchical forebear.[149] One might consider, then, how cakewalking, in many ways a national anthem of its own, went head to head with the putative white imperial audiences in both England and America by attempting to stage a performance of black nationhood and (counter)cultural sovereignty as a spectacle of resistance. While songs like Will Heehan's 1901 number "Every Race has a Flag but the Coon" disparaged the notion of black social and political identity formation, *In Dahomey*'s transatlantic imaginary, its extravaganza of emigration presented a response to the incredulous white spectator who scoffed at the validity of African American national identity.[150] In this way, the production extended and theatricalized the goals of the Pan-African Congress which, two years earlier in London and with a critical mass of black scholars at its helm, had declared that "the world was called upon to respect the integrity and independence of the free negro states." With aims to seize the global spotlight, the Congress called for an international audience to recognize black sovereignty on the rise.[151] *In Dahomey*, however, translated this performance of nationhood before the imperial audience into a final metatheatrical parody of monarchy and international relations. No moment encapsulated the musical's ability to reinterpret freedom and independence more profoundly than the scene at Buckingham Palace on June 23, 1903, when the cast performed before the royal family.

After a month's run in London, the Williams and Walker Company received a royal invitation to perform what was billed as a "command performance" for a palace birthday party in honor of the young Prince of Wales. The Shaftesbury Theatre was, in its entirety, essentially transferred to the palace grounds with full scenery and costume for the purposes of the production. As Ann Charters describes, "the show had been slightly modified and abridged" for the purposes of performing for the Prince; in turn, the production was received enthusiastically by King Edward VII and his family and subsequently the show maintained a lengthy stint for the duration of the year in the U.K. If there was any tension or apprehension surrounding the Buckingham Palace visit, it was perhaps felt most acutely by Bert Williams, who allegedly had "wondered whether it would be acceptable for him to sing " 'Evah Darkey Is a King' " before the royal family.[152] His anxiety was ultimately dispelled, however, for seemingly the audience and the British press alike read the performance as an innocuous, self-reflexive mockery of black political autonomy. Within days of the visit, the English publication *The Era* commented that, for instance, the palace performance "was a very happy and cheerful note that was struck between the bogus king and the people of a bogus country and the real king—the King of England" (Green, "*In Dahomey*," 36). To the press, the Buckingham Palace production of *In Dahomey* reinforced the inefficacy of a fictitious black nation and its subjects' willingness to genuflect before the godhead of the English empire.

George Walker, however, recalled the scene at the palace quite differently. Recounting the visit in detail, he wrote, "We were treated royally. That is the only word for it. We had champagne from the Royal cellar and strawberries and cream from the Royal garden. The Queen was perfectly lovely, and the King was as jolly as he could be and the little princes and princesses were as nice as they could be, just like little faeries."[153] Walker's infantilization of the ruling monarchy is fascinating in the way that his language safely depoliticizes each member of the family, transforming them into "lovely" and "jolly" hosts who treat their black guests as "kings" and "queens" (for a day). His allusion to the family as "little faeries" is equally daring and peculiar in that his words flirt with infantilizing his monarchical hosts in ways similar to minstrelsy's incessant rendering of black folks as children. Within the context of Victorian and Edwardian culture, there is a way to also read Walker's amusement with the royal family's fairy-like traits as another kind of sly and signifying remark. For his comments effectively transform the king, queen, little prince, and their company into the kinds of a-human, "Ur-child" (non)entities that populated storybooks and pantomime shows of the era. In Walker's vision, the monarchy metamorphoses into the Victorian fantasy figure of the "fairy" whose "nature," as Nina Auerbach points out, is akin to that of a child. Fairies are "always sliding into the other orders of being," and, she argues, they sustained their power in nineteenth-century British culture as an incessant reminder of Great Britain's increasing uncertainty with the Self.[154]

Leave it then to Walker to turn the spectacle of transformation back onto the white (royal) spectator. His topsy-turvy comments were, however, colorfully prefigured on the palace lawn during the demonstration and instruction of the cakewalk which followed the *In Dahomey* performance proper. As legend has it, the dance so caught the attention of the royal family that they staged a subsequent cakewalk contest of their own, with the black performers serving as judges.[155] *The Era* reported that, after having corroborated the authenticity of *In Dahomey*'s cakewalk, "it was noted that while the members of the company were tripping the light fantastic on the improvised stage the children of the Royal Household gave very fair imitations on the beautifully-arranged lawn. Both Mr. Williams and Mr. Walker were enthusiastic as to their reception" (Green, "*In Dahomey*," 37). At Buckingham Palace in 1903 the imperial order's dreaded dissolution and imminent transmogrification of power dynamics was well under way in the form of a cakewalk.

# 5. DIVAS AND DIASPORIC CONSCIOUSNESS

*Song, Dance, and New Negro Womanhood in the Veil*

Writing in 1888 from her newspaper desk in Memphis, Tennessee, the journalist, social activist, and political reformer Ida Bell Wells imagined a world in which the "model" Negro woman would one day own and command the public stage. Neither "stiff," "formal," nor "haughty," Wells's "typical Southern girl" would possess the grace of a gazelle, angelic luminosity, and swan-like pulchritude wrapped in a "sweetness of disposition." An ingenue radiating with nobility, this "type of Negro girl" would use her quietly fierce mettle to burn a shining path into the future for her brethren, "reconstructing womanhood" and African American "personhood" out of the rubble of white supremacist defamation and systemic physical brutality. Not yet twenty-six years old when she wrote "The Model Woman" for the *New York Freeman* and several years away from making her radical strides as an antilynching journalist, Wells was nonetheless already the very embodiment of her published sketch.[1]

## Iola and the Stars

Having embraced the nom de plume "Iola" in a strategic act of "inspired self-fashioning," Wells was every bit the effulgent New Woman heroine of African American social and political culture. A longtime "theatre bug," she discovered in print culture a way to cultivate public voice and to launch revised images of New Negro womanhood in ways that paralleled a career in theatre.[2] Fusing the energy of postbellum black theatre culture's nascent opportunities for a new generation with her visions of "model" Negro girls, "Wells the theater fan" would close her treatise on exemplary Southern women with rhapsodic "inspirational verse" that imagined her heroine walking directly into the Bard's spotlight. "Since all the world's a stage/Upon which, we, the actors/Come and go in every age" her closing lines proclaim, "Live nobly, grandly, aim afar! E'er onward, skyward—be a star!"[3] Wells's climactic lines forecast her own brilliantly incandescent notoriety as an agitator and intellectual. Becoming the "star" herself, Wells would see her own pen name in lights some four years later during a historic evening in New York City. Feted by one of the many black women's club organizations that helped to spearhead African American social reform, Wells watched the name "Iola" radiate with the glow of gaslights on a celebratory dais before a room of admiring supporters and comrades in struggle.[4]

Wells was joined in the spotlight by an accomplished array of "New Negro" women from the South, the North, the Midwest, and the California coast who rushed like comets toward the center of Reconstruction and postbellum America's popular culture universe. Many of these women, entertainers like the Hyers Sisters, Matilda Sissieretta Joyner Jones, Pauline Hopkins, and Aida Overton Walker most certainly became the stuff of Iola's dreams. Balancing aesthetic passion with clear and purposeful commitments to racial uplift, Hopkins and Walker each rose to theatrical prominence in the late nineteenth and early twentieth centuries. In particular, Hopkins's and Walker's respective innovations and their diverse and inspired work sharply contradicted competing images of debauched and demoralized black women in theatre. While Paul Laurence Dunbar could, for instance, only imagine the theatre as a "social cesspool" eating away at the souls of tragic heroine Kitty Hamilton and veteran actress Hattie Sterling in his 1902 novel *Sport of the Gods*, Hopkins and Walker seized on theatre as a viable site of economic prosperity and political intervention for black women.[5] Both Hopkins and Walker burned brightly like "stars" and, while in the limelight, used their celebrity status as a platform from which to speak with bold, Wells-like candor about the exigencies of uplift.

Walker had been performing professionally for more than a decade by the time theatre critic Sylvester Russell anointed her "the greatest coming female comedy star of her race" in 1903. Emerging at the forefront of the musical *In Dahomey*'s large and talented cast, the entertainer made her Broadway debut in the role of Rosetta Lightfoot and was greeted "with a grand star reception from the audience." The part gave Walker the opportunity to work the stage in key solo turns and with little "direct contact" with the show's two stars, husband George Walker and Bert Williams. Going it alone, Walker was hardly a "lonesome little thing," as Russell would playfully describe her in a later review. Rather, by all accounts she filled the stage with energetic performances and solo numbers which prefigured her gutsy solo acts later that decade. From working with wheelbarrow and mirror props to depending simply on her own "novel steps in dancing" which generated "repeated encores," Walker on

Broadway in 1903 was well on her way toward becoming the first international black female dance celebrity.[6]

Rapidly ascending to her heralded status as one of the premier (black) choreographers, dancers, and musical actresses of the Gilded Age, Aida Overton Walker self-consciously imagined her work in theatre as a social, political, and aesthetic intervention in American popular culture. Born Ada Wilmore Overton in New York on Februry 14, 1880, to Moses and Pauline Whitfield Overton, Walker was recognized as a dancer during her grammar school days. Having performed professionally from her mid-teens forward, she eventually danced alongside her actor-husband George Walker and later as a solo artist who dared to experiment with new innovations in musical theatre and who promoted the theatre as a socially and economically viable opportunity for African Americans in the postbellum era.[7] Crossing over into Wells's world, she wrote several prominent articles for the black press in order to firmly endorse the political and regenerative merits of African American performance. "I venture to think," Walker proclaimed, "and dare to state that our profession does more toward the alleviation of colored people" than any other occupation. Emotionally fulfilling stage performance provided, Walker assured, a source of cathartic "pleasure" for African Americans facing the traumas of migration and resettlement, relentless economic hardships, and the Southern horrors of mob terror. In this era of disenfranchisement and thwarted socioeconomic opportunities, Walker recognized the value in aesthetic self-making and representational autonomy. She encouraged her people to embrace the nurturing sustenance of autonomous cultural production and warned readers that "unless we learn the lesson of self appreciation and practice it, we shall spend our lives imitating other people and depreciating ourselves."[8] Walker also championed the stage as a source of employment and self-actualization for young black women. In 1908 she stressed the practical benefits of theatre as a singular field in which "colored women" could have "the advantage of traveling" and in which they could additionally meet "a number of people of different classes."

To Walker, theatre was where "intelligent women," the kind of ingenues that Wells had imagined some twenty years before, would gain the advantage to actualize their unique and wondrous creative apsirations. Walker prioritized cultivating in young African American women the life-affirming desire to create art. Although she had been lucky and shepherded into dancing at a young age by her mother, many black women had yet to discover the replenishing opportunities the arts offered. "We have," Walker concluded, "many dressmakers, many stenographers, many school teachers . . . but how many intelligent women have we whose parents educate them to follow their artistic yearnings?"[9]

Pauline Hopkins was one of those women who had found support at a young age to carry out her expressive intentions. Born in Portland, Maine, in 1859, the only child of migrant Virginian Northrup Hopkins and New Hampshire native Sarah Allen, Hopkins grew up and lived her entire professional life in Boston, Massachusetts. She attended the public Girls High School in Boston and demonstrated an early interest in literary endeavors. Lauded as a popular performer in her own right in the 1870s and 1880s before taking up journalism and fiction writing, Hopkins, like Walker, championed theatre and performance as key political tools necessary for the empowerment of African Americans. Grossly underacknowledged in her distinction as the first known African American woman playwright, Hopkins nonetheless infused theatre work and performance tropes with political intent throughout her career as a highly imaginative and industrious cultural worker and social activist.[10] By the time she published her last and perhaps most ambitious serialized novel, *Of One Blood*, in 1902–3, it was evident that one character's exclamation at a key point in that sprawling epic—"Pleasure! . . . Oh Lord! You've come to the wrong place. This is business, solid business"—could easily apply to Hopkins's views concerning the urgency of black cultural performance and its critical significance as a weapon in the battle for social and political enfranchisement. Hopkins's work aggressively seeks to mix the "business" of African American uplift with the "pleasure" of popular aesthetic production and consumption.[11]

A novelist, journalist, essayist, short-story writer, dramatist, actress, and singer, Hopkins employed multiple generic forms and themes, blending journalism with the sentimental novel, historical narrative with westerns, theatre and performance with sensation fiction, and Pan-Africanist ideology with the culture of spiritualism. Elizabeth Ammons points to the very hybridity of Hopkins's work as evidence of the writer's imaginative "disruliness" as an artist and her distinct "rebellion" against the narrow constrictions of aesthetic genres in the articulation of African American history and culture. Like her more famous contemporaries, W. E. B. Du Bois and Paul Laurence Dunbar among them, Hopkins invoked multiple expressive strategies to contribute to contemporaneous black liberation movements, as well as the burgeoning concepts of a "New Negro" identity, and a postslavery, post-Reconstruction, "modern" African American literature and culture. Hopkins not only participated in this movement in politics and letters but she crafted fiction, prose, journalism, and theatre that collapsed and transgressed generic boundaries and, in turn, helped to create a uniquely popular *and* political form of African American cultural production. From the late 1870s and through what were seemingly her "sleepless" years at the turn of the century, she produced one published dramatic musical, one novel in book form, three serialized magazine novels, a full-length historical survey, and more than thirty periodical articles. She also delivered numerous public lectures during her career as a performer and later as an essayist.

Like Walker, Hopkins achieved her initial stardom by way of her solo efforts on the stage. In late 1870s and 1880s New England, Hopkins's vocal talents garnered the attention of the press, who crowned her "Boston's Favorite Colored Soprano." She reached the pinnacle of her success in theatre, however, as a playwright and musical actress who performed for a brief time in her family's ensemble troupe, the Hopkins Colored Troubadours, a company that included Hopkins, her mother and father, and at least one other male performer. Having published her first musical *Peculiar Sam; or, The Underground Railroad* (1879) at the age of twenty, Hopkins and the Troubadours, along with colored minstrel veteran Sam Lucas, and the already accomplished Hyers Sisters Company collaborated on a version of the production that they successfully performed before large-scale audiences at Boston's Oakland Gardens amusement park in July 1880. The success of this event did not, however, foreshadow Hopkins's rise in the world of theatre. Rather, like Wells, she gradually channeled her fascination with theatre into the discursive, where she considered the viability of cultural performance practices such as spiritualism as forms of black communal and black female uplift.[12]

Like her dancing comrade in struggle as well, Hopkins consistently maintained an interest in investing her performance work with black empowerment politics. The Hopkins Colored Troubadours' repertoire, for instance, consisted of audacious musicals which celebrated and provided narrative scope to a recent black historical past and which tackled weighty concerns such as social reform, emancipation, and Reconstruction's ill-fated promise of economic and social opportunities for African Americans.[13] This fusion of historical events and theatricality clearly left its mark on Hopkins's writing style as she made the successful leap from playwright to popular magazine novelist. With astounding fecundity (Richard Yarborough has referred to her as "the single most productive black woman writer at the turn of the century"), Hopkins spent the early years of the twentieth century spinning marvelously original literary narratives for audiences in the Northeast. Using performance and fledgling Pan-African historical discourse as raw material, she produced her serialized narrative *Of One Blood Or, the Hidden Self* against the backdrop of an increasingly popular contemporary black theatre tradition which Walker and others had dedicated themselves to pioneering. Hopkins's novel marks the end of nearly a century of African American theatrical performance. It is a text which richly, and at times subtly, invokes this tradition, and which, like Aida Overton Walker's comments, seeks to mine the interrelatedness of black female desire, collective resistance, nascent black modernity, and performance culture. Most importantly, it is the earliest novel by an African American woman to figure a black female performer, Fisk Jubilee Singer Dianthe Lusk, as its heroine. Hopkins's last novel thus remains a key cultural narrative that metaphorically queries the hopes, fears, and desires of those women who dared to perform in the service of their community and equally for themselves at the turn of the century.

In their own unique ways, Hopkins and Walker were emblematic of the sort of "New Negro woman" who used performance strategies, both literally and figuratively, to serve themselves as well as their communities. Although Hopkins, a single New England writer, and Walker, a married, itinerant New York performer twenty-one years her junior, led vastly different lives, they shared much in their visions of how black women might utilize performance as a place from which to explore and express the social, political, and sexual politics of black womanhood in America. In the midst of this fruitful era when leading black female activists conjoined the political with the aesthetic in myriad ways and forms, Hopkins and Walker experimented with classic and Pan-Africanist aesthetic practices to imagine how performance culture might serve as a site of revision and self-making for black women and their overdetermined bodies in the cultural imaginary.

This chapter discusses Hopkins's and Walker's unique work and the intersections of two characters they brought to life late in their respective careers in the 1900s. Hopkins's last fictional heroine, *Of One Blood*'s Dianthe Lusk, and Walker's historic reinterpretation of theological "femme fatale" Salome each iconically embodies and renegotiates black women's social, cultural, and political expression in the early twentieth century. Both figures operate as "veiled ladies" who re-animate and revise popular black nationalist discourses as well as dominant scripts of black womanhood in the Gilded Age. Placing both the artists and their characters within a fertile matrix of rich and resourceful black women's performances in the late nineteenth and early twentieth centuries, the middle of the chapter traces the rapidly unfolding world of black women's popular performances. In this regard, the chapter charts the intersecting worlds of black women's literature, song, and dance in the postbellum era and the ways in which these artists used multiple aesthetic forms to articulate individual as well as communal desire. Throughout I seek to pay close attention to the heretofore undertheorized genealogy of postbellum black women's theatrical performances and the ways that this cultural work fused racial uplift with revised black female subjectivity at the dawn of a new century.

## In the *Blood*: Pauline Hopkins's Rebel Women and the "Pecoolar" Dianthe Lusk

When she was twenty years old, Pauline Hopkins imagined three vastly different female characters to anchor her first and only extant musical drama, *Peculiar Sam, or The Underground Railroad*. "Mammy," the mother of the title character, is the first female figure to emerge in Hopkins's script which charts the heroic efforts of plantation slaves who successfully traverse their way across space and time to freedom and the hoped-for romance of Reconstruction. With a lively vernacular wit, Mammy straddles what Hopkins clearly perceives to be the important historical and cultural past of slavery and the promising future for a new generation led by her son Sam and his enslaved peers. Irascibly apprehensive of Sam's efforts to hatch a plan of escape from the plantation, Mammy dubs her dream-into-action son a "pecoolar" fellow and worries that he may in turn bring "disrace onter" her (105).[14]

Rather than propping up Mammy as antiquated plantation caricature, Hopkins utilizes her character and her words as a signifying, double-voiced mouthpiece to fuel the political intent of the narrative. While her lines may articulate a fear of the infamy that Sam's involvement in the Underground Railroad may generate for her family, Mammy's recognition that escape may bring "disrace" (this race) onto her puns and foreshadows the self-actualizing process of liberation and "reconstructed" black identity formation that each character pursues. Just as well, Mammy's dialect-inflected coronation of her son as "pecoolar" supplies the play's title. Seemingly dubbed "pecoolar" (105) because of his Nat Turner–like "spirits a movin' in" him and his vividly fanciful dreams of freedom where "the sun was shinin' bright, in the middle of the night" (101), Sam translates his "peculiarity" and his alterity into a source of material liberation for himself and other characters. Mammy is thus allowed to benefit from her son's philosophical deviance. The senior elder in the script, Mammy makes the journey to a new life with a new husband and her children of Reconstruction, and Hopkins affirms the critical value of African American elders in this new era of change and transformation.

Written originally as "a starring vehicle" for veteran colored minstrel performer Sam Lucas, *Peculiar Sam* was first performed in the spring of 1879. The musical originally consisted of four acts (and was later compressed into three). It called for several different types of solo parts as well as vocal ensembles, including "a women's trio."[15] Hopkins envisioned Mammy as playing "second soprano" to the effulgent "plantation nightingale" Virginia (Jinny) while Sam's stalwart sister Juno would serve as alto. In these two small yet significant parts, Hopkins begins what turned out to be a career-long interest in playing socially insurgent and quest-driven female characters against one another in the pursuit of racial uplift. While Jinny fits the archetypal "young mulatto girl" who is vulnerable to slavery's threat of sexual exploitation and bartering (104), Hopkins gives her a voice infused with the spirit of resistant literary heroines from Harriet Wilson to Harriet Jacobs. Jinny insists that "it is better" to join Sam in his flight than "to remain here, and become what they wish me to be" (567). Ever the songbird, Jinny in her "Home, Sweet Home" solo provides the soundtrack to the characters' departure from their old plantation life in the first act into and through the maroonage of the antislavery underground. As the only female soloist in the musical, Jinny's purposeful vocals anchor one of the key transitions in *Peculiar Sam* and serve as the gateway to freedom in the musical.

Occupying the lower registers of resistant female song in *Peculiar Sam*, Hopkins's rebel character Juno surfaces to sing alto in the script and to perform the role of what is perhaps the most militant (black) female character in nineteenth-century letters. A wily and energetic figure, Juno relishes in guarding the villainous black overseer Jim, brandishing a pistol, "playing" at "shooting" her prisoner and perpetually taunting her charge into an extended state of emotional and psychological submission (116).[16] Sharing her brother's radical resolve to be free, Juno emerges as the black female revolutionary realized. She brings to life the riotous wit and fortitude that Hopkins imagines her black female characters as capable of possessing. Moreover, as the alto, Juno fills out the bright and ethereal vocals of the two sopranos with a singing role meant to operate on the lower ("underground") frequencies of musical as well as thematic performance. Together, Mammy, Jinny, and Juno compose Hopkins's trinity of rebel women—signifying elders, soprano songbirds, and alto combat soldiers.

*Peculiar Sam* enjoyed a brief and yet an impressively high-profile run during its second incarnation in July 1880 when the play was produced at Boston's Oakland Gardens. With a new title, *Slave's Escape, or the Underground Railroad*, and a new cast which included the Hopkins Colored Troubadours, Sam Lucas, and the Hyers Sisters Company (which featured soprano Anna Madah Hyers and contralto Emma Louise Hyers), the musical received glowing reviews and, on one warm summer night, reportedly drew an attendance of 10,000 on the amusement park fairgrounds.[17] In the musical, the "blood" lines were set for strategies of black female characterization that Hopkins extended, developed, and refined much later in her professional career as a writer.

From theatre to stenography work in the 1890s, Hopkins confidently leapt, like so many of her adventurous dramatic and fictional characters, into the worlds of both journalism and fiction writing on a full-time basis. Both fields enabled Hopkins to continue her forays into imagining the lives of radical black women. As the editor and staff writer for the black-owned and organized *Colored American Magazine* (*CAM*), she spent the first four years of the new century contributing dozens of nonfictional black history articles ranging in titles from "Famous Women of the Negro Race" to "Heroes and Heroines in Black." Unsatisfied with merely writing about history's unsung black heroes, Hopkins sought to create fictional African American female characters who might match and magnify the quotidian acts of resistance and survival endemic of black women's lives. From 1900's operatic, political, and sentimental novel *Contending Forces* to the serialized fiction of *Hagar's Daughter* (1901) and *Winona* (1902), Hopkins clearly worked in her fiction to flesh out complex characters whom we might think of as Mammy, Jinny, and Juno's "daughters." More melancholy than their forebears yet even more sophisticated and resolved to achieve success and personal fulfillment, the primary heroines of *Contending Forces*, Dora Smith and Sappho Clarke, debate "race troubles," as well as the pros and cons of marriage, family, and the "woman question." Like Juno and Jinny before them (and with Mammy reincarnated as the Northern postbellum mother Ma Smith), Dora and Sappho once again represent the higher and lower frequencies of New Negro womanhood. To this end, while the former plays the effervescent nightingale-like role of the Northern ingenue who seeks to find her perfect partner in uplift, the mysterious Sappho Clarke negotiates the lower registers, so to speak, of black women's postslavery trauma, with its skein of rape, concubinage, and lynching legacies.

In all these works, Hopkins imagined her black female characters as either central to, adopted by, or recuperated within fractured, rebuilt, or reformulated families and communities. In her post-Reconstruction universe, beleaguered black mothers are lost and found, wounded women are often healed and nurtured, and children are reunited with their lost mothers and fathers. As Carol Allen sees it, Hopkins often transforms her daughter figures into "avenging heroines" who overtly protect and defend family and community.[18] But much of that would change in 1902–3's serialized novel *Of One Blood,* what would turn out to be the last and perhaps the most ambitious of her *CAM* literary projects.

*Of One Blood*'s subtitle, "The Hidden Self," signals that the text is essentially a quest narrative intent on excavating the buried layers of historically thick black identity formation in the Atlantic world. The novel spans three continents while tracing African American protagonist Reuel Briggs's search for cultural, historical, and philosophical meaning and purpose. A successful doctor who, nonetheless, is "passing" for white, Reuel awakens to desire and romantic love for one of his black patients, Dianthe Lusk, a star vocalist member of the Fisk Jubilee Singers. Suffering from presumably fatal injuries following a train wreck, Dianthe is miraculously revived out of a state of only "seeming rigor mortis" by Reuel. The couple, however, faces a crisis of betrayal and conspiracy at the hands of Reuel's friend and confidante Aubrey Livingstone. Out of lust for Dianthe, Aubrey engineers a scheme to dissolve the couple's connubial bliss by procuring for Reuel a job as the doctor on an archaeological expedition to Ethiopia. This turn shifts the remainder of the text into a journey narrative built around Reuel's movement toward the African continent and toward the discovery of multiple "hidden selves" in the narrative. In Africa, Reuel is reunited with what turns out to be his lost tribal community (his buried selves). Through clairvoyance, he learns of Aubrey's duplicity. He also confronts the horror that he, Dianthe, and Aubrey are all "of one blood"; thus, they have been embroiled in an incestuous triangle. In a climactic series of unfolding events, Aubrey resolves to poison Dianthe, Aubrey dies by his own hand, and Reuel ascends to the throne in the fictional kingdom of Telassar where he is united with the bronze Dianthe doppelgänger, Queen Candace.

With its surfeiting plot twists and machinations, *Of One Blood* continues to yield a diversity of critical responses. Several critics have focused on the novel's engagement with postbellum black nationalist discourse and its simultaneous critique of U.S. social and political relations.[19] Within this context, the narrative is often viewed as a kind of fictional manifestation of Pan-Africanist discourse, an elaboration of sorts on the diasporic political queries which Du Bois and others were concurrently developing in prose and journalism. Black feminist critics have made significant strides in pointing out the ways that *Of One Blood* participates in the burgeoning genre of black women's domestic fiction in the postbellum era. Hazel Carby maintains, for instance, that Hopkins transforms the genre's trope of the "search for and discovery of family" into a metaphor of reconnection with a black diasporic community. Still others contend that Hopkins's text demonstrates and compresses a spirited engagement with contemporaneous black nationalist subgenres such as Ethiopianism, which prophesied the return to the "lost" homeland of Ethiopia in millennial scope. Several scholars have convincingly demonstrated the thematic and political connections between the novel and W. E. B. Du Bois's far-reaching theories on mystic historicism and Pan-Africanist discourse.[20]

That Hopkins also shared with Du Bois a fascination for William James's pioneering studies on "new psychology" and the theory of "double-consciousness" remains a source of provocative intrigue. A kindred soul to Du Bois and his critical studies of the existential, the spiritual, and Pan-Africanist desire, Hopkins also used her literary endeavors to "imagine a mystic idea of 'personality' as a means to recovering the hidden self and history of the race." Cynthia Schrager's examination of the politics of race and mysticism at the turn of the century makes plain the striking similarities between Du Bois's invocation of spiritualist rhetoric in his political and social philosophies and Hopkins's own use of mesmeric devices in *Of One Blood* to signal a new era in racial cultural awareness. Schrager and others effectively demonstrate how both authors attempted to yoke a philosophical and historical relationship with "Africa" and the contemporary psychological ideas of their time, which promoted the notion that the "undiscovered country," a second, "conscious" hidden self, lies within individuals. The "hidden self" of *Of One Blood*, then, is both a geographical territory and a spiritually diasporic terrain, much like the one which Du Bois's prototypical black everyman figure in *The Souls of Black Folk* negotiates. Through a kind of discursive dialectic, the two authors taken together weave a complex theoretical tapestry in regard to racial politics at the turn of the century.[21]

Yet other critics have taken the text to task for what they view as its regressive gender politics. Historian Kevin Gaines contends that this notion of a mystically based Pan-Africanist ideology "reflected [Hopkins's] assent to the prevailing view of 'race' as essentially a masculine ideal." Gaines suggests that Hopkins displaces what he sees as the markedly "feminine" terrain of domestic fiction in favor of the " 'male' persona of a scientific expert on the darker races." Still others have pointedly remarked that it is Hopkins's representation of Dianthe Lusk and her tragic death in particular which demonstrate how black women's bodies are ultimately disposable integers in the movement to reclaim an African communal and cultural past. Schrager, Claudia Tate, and Jennie Kassanoff argue that the narrative posits Dianthe as a source of exchange in an incestuous relationship and literally as a body whose agency is suspended and seemingly emptied out at different points in the plot. Most notably, however, Elizabeth Ammons observes that "the American black female artist exists in Hopkins's fable in a state of living death. . . . Dianthe can only be who other people tell her she is; and in racist America, that will not include being an artist."[22]

This chapter, however, revisits this remarkably contested work of post-bellum black fiction in order to bridge the gap in criticism between the thorough consideration of Pauline Hopkins's nationalist, black cultural philosophies and the simultaneous critical dismissal of the text on the grounds that it fails to sustain a meaningful black feminist vision. Below I aim to recenter the discussion of this text in two ways. First, by considering how Hopkins situated her narrative in relation to black women's postbellum historical performances, I seek to demonstrate the ways that *Of One Blood* inherited and translated the field of historical and cultural performance into popular fiction paradigms. Second, I explore the allegorically resonant trope of spiritualism in the text, and I consider how Hopkins redeployed spiritualist "veiling" as black post-Reconstruction era performative articulation and political intent. Rereading the figure of Dianthe Lusk through the dual prisms of postbellum black theatre culture and Pan-Africanist spiritualist practices, I examine the historically, culturally, and politically imbricated position of Hopkins's heroine in the narrative. I interrogate the heroine's role as both diva choir soprano and spiritualist medium in order to reveal how, in *Of One Blood*, black nationalism is reconstituted through the politics of black women's performances. Moreover, the text imagines performance as the insurgent site for dismantling imperialist and patriarchal discourses and centralizes the resilience of black women's bodies.

Lacking the immediate presence of close female confidantes who might join her in a duet or an ensemble singing arrangement, *Of One Blood*'s Dianthe nonetheless emerges unexpectedly and heroically as the fulcrum of Hopkins's Pan-Africanist epic. Indeed, she is perhaps most worthy of inheriting the ambiguous, signifying title that Mammy had bequeathed to Sam in the early Hopkins text. One of the author's most "peculiar" and enigmatic characters, Dianthe negotiates a resistant alterity that ultimately weds song with spiritualist transcendence and, in many ways, speaks, indeed, sings through the multiple questions and concerns to which Hopkins repeatedly returned in her written work. If, in her fiction, Hopkins consistently asked of her readers, What are the tools that African Americans need to survive, to interrogate, and to process trauma in American culture? And how might we define the role of black women in uplift movements?, Dianthe serenades a dense and hypnotic answer to readers.

Hopkins was joined in her visions of veiled ladies and Pan-Africanist desire by the junior artist ingenue Aida Overton Walker. Walker's theatrical performance of Salome, "the dance of the seven veils," and the larger question of black female imaging and black uplift activism during this period expanded a revisionary black female iconography by further engaging the strategy of the African American female performer as a medium and narrative agent of Pan-Africanist desire. Walker's role as the first black woman to perform Salome operates as a dramatic addendum to the spiritualist gender politics that Hopkins explored in her serialized fiction.

## Stealing Away in the Theatre: Hopkins, Histotextuality, and the Fisk Jubilee Singers

Having flirted with stardom as a singer some two decades earlier, Pauline Hopkins returned to the world of song in her final novel. Often eclipsed in critical discussions of the text which favor an emphasis on new psychology, black nationalism, and imperialism, black song and the role of the female singer are nonetheless crucial thematic elements of *Of One Blood*. For all its grand, sweeping, transnational perambulations across three continents and along an electric geographical axis of black political history,[23] the novel imagines one of its most critical journeys as unfolding entirely within the confines of a New England concert hall on one snowy night in November. The trajectory of quest and longing that Hopkins plots out for her "melancholic mulatto/a" characters begins with angst-ridden and suicidal hero Reuel Briggs, who initially surfaces in a state of intellectual torment.[24] A bookish student of occult mysticism and its promise of "the soul's migration," Reuel pours over tracts of new psychology criticism by William James (thinly disguised as the work of "M. Binet") and contemplates a way to enact a flight to the heart of his own deeply troubled universe of alienation. Unable to resolve his own wrought existential queries concerning "good and evil, God and the devil . . . sinner and saint, body or soul" and the overriding question of "which wins in the life struggle?" (448), Reuel turns to the promise of new psychology's burgeoning theories which aim to discover an "unconscious" or "hidden self," a "quiescent" territory (448) somewhere just off the map of his waking recognition. Reuel's studies give him little consolation, however, and it is left up to the impromptu mischief of his putative confidante Aubrey Livingstone to draw Reuel out of his distressed isolation.

Bearing the surname of doomed Scottish explorer and African missionary David Livingstone as well as the hall built to memorialize him at historically black Fisk University, the duplicitous Aubrey visits Reuel in his despair and dangles before his friend what he perceives to be a bit of harmless japery. Aubrey proposes an evening at the theatre since, he adds, "[t]he blacker the night, the greater the need of amusement" (449).[25] Awash in racial overtones, Aubrey's pun is perhaps a product of his own Southern-bred sense of humor, and he soon reveals that, on this "blackest" of nights, his proposed "amusement" is none other than the first professional African American singing ensemble, the Fisk Jubilee Singers. For Aubrey, of course, the night's entertainment is certain to fulfill a seeming cool fascination with ethnographic "oddity" so common in P. T. Barnum's era of exhibition and circus spectacle. Yet Reuel's encounter with the august and elegant sounds of this historic singing ensemble inevitably yields much for him in his journey toward dissecting "the 'mysteries' of the universe." Abruptly and forebodingly, the narrative shifts from Reuel's philosophical interrogations of self and existential positionality and moves swiftly toward the rich, dense respite of postbellum black vocal performance in the round.

The Fisk Jubilee Singers were nearing the end of three decades of touring, fundraising, and educational and religious activism in transatlantic culture when Hopkins conjured up their *Of One Blood* cameo. Formed in the early 1870s at Fisk University at the behest and encouragement of the American Missionary Association, as well as the university's combination of white reformists and benefactors, the Jubilee group evolved out of the exigencies of Reconstruction. Under the tutelage of bleeding-heart Civil War veteran, Freedman's Bureau employee, and Fisk administrative treasurer, teacher, and choir director George White, the original group of young men and women put their vocal gifts to work in the service of generating aid for their fledgling educational home. Composed of former slaves—Greene Evans, Benjamin Holmes, Isaac Dickerson, America Robinson, and Thomas Rutling—as well as free women—Maggie Porter, Jennie Jackson, the youthful Minnie Tate, Eliza Walker, and the gracefully indomitable Ella Sheppard—the first troupe collaborated with White in collecting and rehearsing the "secret hymns" of the enslaved.[26] Working tirelessly at craft and touring for fatigue-inducing months and sometimes years on end, various incarnations of the Jubilees perfected a crisp and sonorous interpretation of the "sorrow songs" of slavery, a combination of "exquisite four-part harmonies and double pianissimi that carried to the back rows of enormous halls" (Ward, *Dark Midnight*, 185, 196, 269) throughout North America and Europe. Raising more than $150,000 for Fisk University on its first three tours (394), the world's first African American celebrity vocal group garnered high-profile endorsements from leading ministers such as Henry Ward Beecher, performed before President Ulysses S. Grant, Queen Victoria, and a wide array of state dignitaries, royalty, and decorated military figures (390–93).

Forty-three years old when she began serializing *Of One Blood* in the *CAM*, Pauline Hopkins had lived most of her professional life with the Fisk Jubilee Singers dominating the Reconstruction and postbellum cultural landscape. Her own experiences performing in the late 1870s and 1880s with her family placed her directly in the Northeastern touring footsteps of the Jubilees, who made their way across the eastern seaboard in the early-to-mid-1870s. The group's influential aesthetic left its mark on her 1879 *Peculiar Sam*, which incorporates at least eight of the songs used regularly in the group's revolving repertoire.[27] Resurfacing in Hopkins's later work, the cultural and political utility of the Jubilees' performances would only amplify in *Of One Blood*. By following Reuel's and Aubrey's sojourn into a luminous concert hall, a "Temple" in "a blaze of light and crowded from pit to dome," Hopkins telescopes "the first appearance of the troupe in New England" (450), fleshing out that "gala night" in masterful detail. She places her characters directly in the run of history and yokes together black postbellum progress with the critical revelation that "the Negro possessed a phenomenal gift of music" (450). Ever attuned to historical context, Hopkins builds up to the concert sequence by alluding to the "passing of slavery" (449), the war which had "passed like a dream of horrors," and the strivings of a people to create a new world of "reconstructed" possibility. Thus, while Du Bois was, in his *Souls of Black Folk*, famously charting his own narrative of the "darker races" out of bondage and the critical role of black musical innovation in America that same year, so too was Hopkins situating the Jubilees at the pivotal center of her own historical epic.[28]

Balancing journalistic reportage with historical narrative, the novel glosses the philanthropic drive which inspired the formation of the singing ensemble, and it vividly details the Jubilees' early tour as the first all-black choir to perform spirituals before white audiences. In particular, the text pays close attention to the phenomenon of racial encounter that remained a source of sensational discussion and debate throughout the group's touring career. Drawing from her resources as a historian, Hopkins reproduces the visceral energy and excitement which the Singers generated and with which their white patrons visibly responded as the Singers made their way up from Nashville, across the Midwestern plains, and into the Northeastern states during the 1871–72 tour. In Hopkins's re-imagined world of the Fisk phenomenon, the "wealthy and exclusive society women everywhere" emerge, vying to shower "benefits and patronage upon the new prodigies who had suddenly become the pets of the musical world" (450).[29]

Yet as accurate as Hopkins's storytelling appears to be, she also pushes beyond the limitations of mere historical reportage in her narrative. Indeed, her spirited engagement with the Jubilees reanimates and extends the terms of what Gabrielle Foreman has defined as the strategy of "histotextuality" at work in postbellum black women's fiction. In her study of Frances Harper's 1892 novel, *Iola Leroy*, Foreman demonstrates how Harper negotiates a "seeming dissonance between her text's sentimental affiliations and its dialogic complexity to articulate" that narrative's "message in various social registers." Harper practices "histotextuality," a method which "marginalized writers use to incorporate historical allusions that both contextualize and radicalize their work by countering the putatively innocuous generic codes they seem to have endorsed."[30] Embedding her popular and particularly sentimental narratives with layers of "socio-ideologically determined language" and historically rich referents, Harper and her activist black female contemporaries created historically dense homonyms and portals of radical discourse in their fiction and for their most politically literate audience members. Such readers, as Foreman asserts, would have been well familiar with issues and debates in the agitating investigative reports of Wells and others.[31]

Like Harper, Hopkins enmeshed layered and intersecting radical referents in the Fisk Jubilee Singers concert scene, one of the most historically allusive, semantically textured passages in *Of One Blood*. Indeed, she utilizes the Fisk Jubilee Singers concert space to effect three intersecting layers of cultural experience. Her novel enters into the Temple hall all abuzz with anticipation and uses that space to map three sets of readerly encounters with the choir's performance: that of white spectators, the troubled black protagonist Reuel, and the black performers themselves. In juggling these distinct and yet provocatively imbricated categories of reception, *Of One Blood* complicates the efficacy of histotextuality and pushes it into the realm of metanarrative. Like other texts of its kind, *Of One Blood* "bastardizes the form" of the "classic historical novel" which "incorporates the past as a prehistory to explain present contending forces." At the same time, however, if the most insurgent "histotextual narrative goes beyond this" by "merging past and present referents to effect change in an as yet not determined future," Hopkins's layering of the form historicizes and articulates the divergent ways that black and white audiences as well as performers processed socially and politically rich musical texts.[32] As the sequence vividly demonstrates, the process of music making and musical reception effects varying and dramatic levels of change in individuals. And thus the scene of Reuel's night in the musical "temple" appeals to *Of One Blood*'s greater discursive readership to recognize the competing historical referents and spectacles of change unfolding in the space of the concert hall.

In the "contact zone" of black postbellum performance where many white audiences witnessed and experienced black cultural workers on the stage for the first time, the Fisk Jubilee Singers concert scene shines a spotlight on the phenomenon of white reformist histotextuality. In this regard, the novel pays much attention to recreating the aura of fascination and fawning which accompanied the Singers throughout their travels. Hopkins effectively compresses and transposes the vaunting status of the choir members at the peak of their success. Well-documented in newspapers and promotional pamphlets by the turn of the century, the Jubilees' popularity as what we might call the first black "cross-over" musical act was a source of postbellum legend in transatlantic popular culture. While they consistently endured the inequities and indignities of Jim Crow America, the Jubilee Singers gradually enjoyed an unprecedented celebrity in popular culture of the Atlantic world, generating a rabid fan base of white admirers. Particularly abroad, where the female singers collected regular marriage proposals (Ward, *Dark Midnight*, 226), frenzied crowds met the group as they entered and exited the theatre (Ward, *Dark Midnight*, 293), and traveling fans presaged the birth of the modern groupie (Ward, *Dark Midnight*, 391), the Jubilees learned to manage the adulation of their large white base of support (Ward, *Dark Midnight*, 351–52). Hopkins dutifully recreates this aura of cultural fetishization enveloping the Singers. The text brings to life the ways in which the group kindles the effusive empathy of an audience who read the Jubilees as literally embodying the epic past of a people and who, deeply affected, melt under the spell of the spirituals. Their experience would mirror that of American Missionary Association officer Gustavas Pike, who best summed up the encounter of many listeners at the ensemble's concerts when he described the impact of "the rich tones of the young men as they mingled their voices in a melody so beautiful and touching I scarcely knew whether I was 'in the body or out of the body' " (Ward, *Dark Midnight*, 153).

In keeping with this sort of testimonial, Hopkins's fictional passage echoes and reiterates the well-documented encounters with the Jubilees' rendition of spirituals in which white listeners, like floating phantoms, were "carried away on a whirlwind of delight" as a result of the performances. In *Of One Blood*, the Jubilee Singers' concert generates so much visceral energy that the house is rendered "spellbound" and speechless, while the "old abolitionist in the vast audience felt the blood leave their faces beneath the stress of emotion" (453). Hopkins thus underscores the expectations placed on the Jubilees to sustain vestibularity, that is, to occupy the role of historical conduit for eager (white) audiences who considered them representative links to slavery and the Civil War. As the text avows, "these were representatives of the people for whom God had sent the terrible scourge of blood upon the land to free from bondage" (452). Presumably so close to the vestiges of bondage, the Jubilee Singers were perceived by many as the physical and aural manifestation of slavery's traumas. They were expected to deliver the "sound" of slavery, all "refined" and "burnished" into classical arrangements, so as to distinguish themselves from minstrelsy's grotesqueries and to better market themselves to elite middle-class audiences and reformers.[33]

In this regard, the Jubilee concert passage reinforces Paul Gilroy's contention that "the Fisk Singers constructed an aura of seriousness around their activities and projected the memory of slavery outwards as the means to make their musical performances intelligible and pleasurable."[34] According to Gilroy, the ensemble's singing was designed to make the memory of slavery palpable, something one could touch and feel, something a listener could grasp and digest for herself. The Singers were thus imagined to be the angels of history for white audiences who, in their intensely empathetic responses, expressed a simultaneous affirmation and disavowal of their own complicity with the narrative of slavery.[35] Accordingly, Hopkins dramatizes this white fascination with the Singers and brings to life their histotextual engagement with songs that were said to both bring them closer to the cultural memory of slavery and push them into renewed service to support the contemporary uplift aims of African Americans. If these "old abolitionists" could find these songs of "suffering" politically intelligible, if they could be called once more into the service of agitation and resistance—both in the narrative and in her broader *Of One Blood* readership—then part of Hopkins's goal to sustain and develop the advances of the New Negro generation would presumably be met.

Prioritizing black uplift in the Fisk agenda proved to be a complicated task in this era which tended to emphasize white audience reactions to the Singers. Many historical narratives on the Jubilee Singers occlude any consideration of the subjectivity of black audiences and, perhaps most importantly, the performers themselves. Rather the spotlight is focused on the audience's reactions to the Singers, which often ranged from the adoring to the befuddled. One critic, for instance, speculated as to why "such simple music, modest and unassuming singing, and unpretentious performances produce so great an effect on the audience." With so much of the public discourse on the Singers generated from the vantage point of the white spectator, the historical memory of the group's indelible performance skills remains firmly lodged in the discourse of audience members as opposed to the black performers themselves. Hence the image of a shy band of Fisk students reticently approaching Professor Adam Knight Spence to sing "old time religious slave songs" that they "did not dream of ever using . . . in public" only fuels the notion of "alien" (W)hite intrusion into these "secret hymns."[36]

This episode and the scene that Hopkins sketches in *Of One Blood* brings to light the peculiar phenomenon of what Jon Cruz calls "ethnosympathy," a kind of fascination and engagement in black cultural forms which evolved out of "the process of discovering black music from a sympathetic perspective" and which "coincided with the notion of salvaging a black cultural authenticity."[37] According to Cruz, what "the Jubilee Singers brought into view was the tremendous positive reception from sectors of the white world for 'authentic slave songs.'" And yet conversely, as the "Negro spiritual emerged as a clearly recognizable cultural form," the cultural, social, and political utility of black sacred song deteriorated. In effect, "a shift in interest emerged" which "severed the spiritual from slavery, the social context in which it was produced." Put another way, the advent of black spirituals into the realm of popular culture seemingly signaled the evisceration of that form's historical and political intent and meaning.[38]

No doubt this phenomenon evolved in tandem with the all too familiar obfuscation of the black artists who created, crafted, and performed the spirituals, the people who opened their mouths "wide" and absorbed, interpreted, mastered, and redeployed the teachings of their fastidious choir director and mentor George White. White initially folded the spirituals into the Jubilees' early classical repertoire of cantatas, hymns, and popular songs and encouraged an "exactitude" in his singers that required a skillful and focused discipline on the part of the performer. He instructed the ensemble "to sing with their mouths open wide enough to fit a finger between their teeth. [They] had to blend with each other, listen to the entire ensemble; no voice except a soloist's was to be heard above another" (Ward, *Dark Midnight*, 115). If their songs "worked to burnish the 'dirty' tonality and improvised arrangements of the folk songs to match the polished, round-toned style cultivated in formal European vocal music," this dulcet and yet forceful material also demanded extraordinary interpretative power, energy, and talent on the part of the singers.[39]

Fisk University's first group of Jubilee Singers was clearly up to the task of what White asked of them in song. In forming the univocal Jubilees sound, the singers brought to the table their own unique musical talents which they had cultivated in slave prayer meetings, churches, work fields, and self-taught instrumental lessons. Yet historically the aforementioned ethnosympathetic gestures of white patrons in particular threatened to eclipse all that hard work and artistry on the part of the singers. Choosing to focus on the black spirituals singer as mythical tabula rasa, the Jubilees' white audiences and critics repeatedly gravitate toward lauding the *effect* of the song rather than the performer who interprets and finesses the material. J. B. T. Marsh makes this point clear in his 1880 *Story of the Jubilee Singers with Their Songs* when he declares that "the power is chiefly in the songs themselves." Playing fast and loose with the myth of the "origins" of the Jubilees' music, Marsh conjures up a Topsy-like etiology of the ensemble's songs which, he argues, "spring into life, ready-made, from the white heat of religious fervor. . . . They came from no musical cultivation whatever, but are the simple, ecstatic utterances of wholly untutored minds." Even Paul Gilroy's contention regarding the Jubilees' ability to transform the positionality of their listeners follows in this vein. He points out that "for their liberal patrons the music and song of the Fisk Jubilee Singers offered an opportunity to feel closer to God and to redemption while the memory of slavery recovered by their performances entrenched the feelings of moral rectitude that flowed from the commitment to political reform for which the imagery of elevation from slavery was emblematic long after emancipation." This sort of an observation, although illuminating, reinforces the assumption that the Jubilees worked exclusively in the service of God and audience, leaving little for the singer, herself, to claim for possession. Instead, it is the spectators who, historically, were made to feel both close and far away from slavery, stricken by the horror of its looming brutality, yet cleansed by the sanctimoniously moral passage to a higher ground which the Singers' labor enables.[40]

In *Of One Blood*, Pauline Hopkins makes a remarkable intervention in this sort of historical erasure of the Fisk Jubilee Singers' subjectivity and artistry as performers. Rather than re-inscribing her narrative with the privileged gloss of white sympathetic fervor, she instead reinvents the playing field of performance in the Jubilee Choir scene. As if to both complement as well as complicate this conventional emphasis on the interiority of white postbellum audiences in flux, Hopkins unveils the emotional and aesthetic transmogrifications of the black performer *in* song. Following the lead of Colin Brown, who was, as Anderson reveals, at the forefront of championing the Singers' "labor of artifice, the aura of folk authenticity, and an 'unpretending' moral sincerity [which] worked together . . . to elevate the performance's power,"

Hopkins works in her narrative to restore an ebullient black subjectivity to the Jubilees' performances.[41]

*Of One Blood*'s concert scene reformulates theatrical space and the dialectic between spectacle and spectator. It transcends a narrow focus on the position of the white spectator in racialized performance culture, so as to explore the complexity of black performative *experience* as well. Indeed, the narrative demonstrates the way in which the two positions are entwined. The narrator recounts how the concert's opening begins in grand ceremony:

> The opening number was "The Lord's Prayer." Stealing, rising, swelling, gathering, as it thrilled the ear, all the delights of harmony in a grand minor cadence that told of deliverance from bondage and homage to God for his wonderful aid, sweeping the awed heart with an ecstasy that was almost pain; breathing, hovering, soaring, they held the vast multitude in speechless wonder. (453)

Heavily ambiguous in terms of who actually reaches "ecstasy" during the rendition of the song, the passage maps a cartography of performance that hovers suggestively between performer and audience, singer and listener, ensemble and individual. For seemingly "the delights of harmony" could potentially "sweep the awed heart" of both the performer as well as the spectator. The "grand minor cadence" of the Singers' notes while "thrilling the ears of listeners" appear to be equally satisfying to the performers who produce such rich, liberatory melodies. With a total lyrical "exuberance," the Singers' voices "stealing, rising, swelling, gathering . . . breathing, hovering, [and] soaring" unleash a rush of movements, ascending and "harmoniously" collaborating, swimming free in an ethereal flourish and hugging a joyful agency in this rendition of "The Lord's Prayer." Though "the vast multitude" is held "in speechless wonder" (mesmerized in a sense), the pleasure which the passage rehearses and recycles in the vocal work of singing remains spectacularly active, transcending the enchanted "multitudes." Rising to the forefront of the scene, the work and craft of the black performer fulfills both the entertainer and the entertained in the concert hall.

The scene also represents "the distinctive patterns of cross-cultural circulation" which the Singers nurtured throughout their career as a choral group.[42] By "sweeping the awed heart" of listeners, the choir establishes a theatre of movement built on a relational model of "contact." The passage recognizes the ways in which the connection between audience and performer is one of improvisation and interaction and one that is fundamentally constitutive of identity. Hopkins revises the power dynamics of the "contact zone" so that, within *Of One Blood*, it comes to signify a terrain of exchange and struggle. This zone is marked not so much by the satiation of white spectators hungering for a re-enactment of slave sorrow but by the tension between the pleasures of the performative agent as well as the wretchedly engaged yet disconcerted spiritual pathos of audiences. Hopkins's theatre serves as a frontier where desire is improvised and renegotiated through and across the waves of spectacle and performance. These oscillations and inversions of agency and authority sustain a textual dynamism throughout the narrative.[43]

There is as well a subtle addendum to Hopkins's poetic rendering of the Jubilees' performance. By tracing the Jubilees' engagement with the song form itself, in this case "The Lord's Prayer," she plays with the Singers' sophisticated interpretative powers. Like the readers of the histotextual narrative in which these characters are immersed, the Jubilees are given the opportunity to translate the historically dense meaning of the text they have been entrusted to sing. To be sure, the spirituals in the Jubilees' repertoire were products of an immediate past for the Singers. The songs were, as ensemble member and long-time assistant director Ella Sheppard reflected, "associated with slavery and the dark past, and represented the things to be forgotten. Then, too, they were sacred to our parents who used them in their religious worship and shouted over them." Having then "softly" learned "from each other the songs of [their] fathers" and mothers, the original Jubilees that Hopkins sought to magically revivify were clearly on their own multivalent journey to learn, retain, and disseminate the music of their elders. Keeping in mind Samuel Floyd's famous contention that "all black-music making is driven by and permeated with the memory of things from the cultural past," we might think of these songs as a (spiritualist) medium, as a site for communion with ancestors. We might also see more clearly the ways that this scene marks the Singers' production of history inasmuch as it also documents their musical travels through history in the pursuit of creating an emancipated future for African Americans.[44]

In this crowded concert hall, Hopkins creates room for yet one more set of spectators enraptured by the sacred sounds of the ensemble. Although historians have paid little attention to the black audiences in attendance at Jubilee concerts, their presence was no doubt significant. Weathering the habitual indignities of Jim Crow segregation, black audience members were greeted in places as hallowed as Princeton University with the instruction to sit "in a distant corner of the church" (Ward, *Dark Midnight*, 196–97, 379). *Of One Blood* disrupts the segregated economy of such spaces and imagines a situation wherein a deeply conflicted African American protagonist who is "passing" for white makes his way into the audience of one of the Jubilees' concerts. The scene creates a sphere for considering the profound impact that the Singers' performances may have had on black subjects who were questing for spiritual and philosophical consolation in the postbellum era. Hence, the passage forwards the movement of the narrative by creating a forum for solving the broad, theoretical questions of self that threaten to consume Reuel Briggs. Reuel introduces the third layer of meta-histotextuality in this scene since, as the ostensible protagonist of the novel, he is drawn into "breaking the codes" of a deeply politicized musical text dense with historical referents during the concert. The solo performance of "Go Down, Moses" by the choir's star singer, in turn, plants the seeds of Reuel's political and cultural evolution. Moreover, it promises to link him to a long-repressed diasporic history by initiating his movement out of emotional stasis and into a providential network of travel that will deliver him to his regal future.

## The Song Remains the Same: Singing Heroines and the Historicity of "Go Down, Moses"

On this marvelous and mystical evening, Reuel enters the concert hall perched restlessly on ambiguous racial borders. He encounters Dianthe Lusk, "a great soprano," for the first time in the flesh (although she has already surfaced in his dreams), and he subsequently undergoes a kind of visceral and emotional ecstasy capable of shaking him out of his psychic torpor. Music, we are told, "soothe[s] [his] restlessness" (452). With "a voice beyond belief," Dianthe and her nuanced performance of the spirituals flirt with carrying Reuel "out of himself." He absorbs her enchanting solo, so wrought with "divine fire" and historical weight that "all the horror, the degradation from which a race had been delivered were in the pleading strains of the singer's voice" (454). On the heels of Dianthe's dramatic rendition of "Go Down, Moses," Reuel must, it seems, reckon with himself in new ways.[45] Faintly echoing and yet also radically diverging from Du Bois's melancholic protagonist John Jones in his *Souls of Black Folk* vignette "Of the Coming of John," Reuel finds himself drawn to the magnetism of Dianthe's mesmeric aria, which yields a startling emotional eruption in him. Anderson demonstrates the ways that Du Bois's drama of John and his fleeting, bittersweet opera house encounter with Wagner's *Lohengrin* traffics in despair and only a brief "transcendence of the veil of racial division." Conversely, we might consider how Hopkins's narrative rewrites the musical romance of emerging racial consciousness by placing a black ensemble and, in particular, a black female choir soprano at the center of her hero's evolving repoliticization and awakening.[46]

The masterful artistry of Dianthe's solo, which "gave tribute to the power of genius" (453), emerges as a key manifestation of the racial mysticism which Reuel must himself learn to master and navigate in his gradual movement toward the African continent and the "lost" kingdom of Telassar. In the concert hall, Dianthe Lusk assumes her crucial place as the bridge in the narrative to Reuel's identity transmogrifications as well as her own. With this character, Hopkins makes a far-reaching statement regarding African American women's roles in performance culture and in the production of turn-of-the-century racial identity formation. "Go Down, Moses" houses critical historical referents that are buried like a secret city in the verses of the legendary spiritual. By singing the song, Dianthe sows the seeds of insurgency in the narrative that Reuel must, in turn, learn to decode and put into practice. Her performance posits a complex diasporic, historicized, and politicized position for Dianthe in the narrative, one which all too often remains "hidden" from the sight of most readers. All too often, critics allude to the scene of Reuel's awakening in the concert hall without considering the historical and political density of the song that anchors the passage. This density, however, cultivates and solidifies the bond between Reuel and Dianthe in the novel. Likewise, the song operates as a clue that Hopkins offers her readers as to the critical position of her heroine in the text.

By the time that Hopkins introduced the classic "Go Down, Moses" into her fiction, it had long been recognized by many as "one of the great freedom declarations of literature and history."[47] Yet few *Of One Blood* critics have considered the rich sociopolitical history of the spiritual, favoring instead readings which re-inscribe the "sorrow" of the song and which equally fold Dianthe's subjectivity into that "sorrow." In a rigorous analysis of the novel, Dana Luciano has, for instance, rightly observed that her "trademark song . . . not only reworks the recent historical experience of slavery but also suggests, in its lyrics, both the physical terrain and the deep historical play of the latter part of the novel." Yet Luciano ultimately capitulates to positing Dianthe and "her vocation" as a singer as the centerpiece of "melancholia" in the narrative, concluding that the "sadness that she transmits clearly emerges from her artistic proximity, as a black Gospel singer, to loss, and not from 'temperament' alone."[48] Luciano's insightful analysis of *Of One Blood* nonetheless eclipses and disregards the radical signifying layers of black performance in the narrative which create ruptures of resistance in Hopkins's putatively mournful epic. By reading Dianthe exclusively through the prism of melancholia, Luciano and others risk privileging the gaze of her white reformist audience at the expense of exploring the insurgent layers of Dianthe's utility as a singer who delivers arguably the most significant political message in the narrative.

In "tones" that, we are told, "awakened ringing harmonies in the heart of every listener," Dianthe performs a resounding version of "Go Down, Moses" for this hall filled with bleeding-heart activists, veterans of the bygone struggle to emancipate their Negro brethren. But whereas Reuel is quick to recognize the dazzling craft of the talent before him ("never save among the great artists of the earth" had he heard "such a voice alive with the divine fire," 453), others in the audience are drawn to their own romantic evaluations of this startling solo performance. Fittingly,

> Some of the women in the audience wept; there was the distinct echo of a sob in the deathly quiet which gave tribute to the power of genius. Spellbound they sat beneath the outpoured anguish of a suffering soul. All the horror, the degradation from which a race had been delivered were in the pleading strains of the singer's voice. It strained the senses almost beyond endurance. It pictured *to that self-possessed, highly-cultured New England assemblage* as nothing else ever had, the awfulness of the hell from which a people had been happily plucked. (453–54; emphasis added)

Sobbing women may pay "tribute" to the "power" of Dianthe's "genius" as a singer, but in the end it seems that this congregation is seduced by the putative spectacle of "suffering" all bound up in "the pleading strains of the singer's voice." What the passage makes clear, however, is that this bird's eye view of Dianthe's solo turn emanates from the vantage point of the "highly-cultured New England assemblage" (453–54). No doubt this audience is hungry to grasp "a distinct, observable, and knowable element of black culture" and the angst-ridden history of slavery's woes.[49] The passage beckons readers to absorb carefully the spectacle of white ethnosympathy for suffering and black art as opposed to merely articulating the transmission of black loss and melancholia in Dianthe's performance. Reading Dianthe's work from the latter standpoint would, in fact, risk confusing white listeners' relationship to black spirituals with the very distinct process of black artistry to which Hopkins is clearly committed. In fact, Hopkins imagines this performance as an intervention in the melancholic narrative introduced by Reuel in the opening chapter.

A song which testified to the "degradation" of bondage as well as the deliverance from the condition of slavery, "Go Down, Moses" was, even by the time of Hopkins's novel, a song with a deep historicity. Often cited as "a masterpiece" in the Fisk Jubilee Singers' concert repertoire (Ward, *Dark Mid-*

*night*, 129), the spiritual was a consistent audience favorite. The ensemble had famously delivered a rendition of the spiritual for Queen Victoria, who reportedly requested it (213), as well as an aging John Greenleaf Whittier at his home in Hampton Falls, New Hampshire (385). In the spring of 1872, the troupe chose to sing the piece at the White House, as Ward sharply observes, "in the wan hope, perhaps, that [President] Grant might see himself as the freedmen's deliverer, though to advocates of the freedmen, Grant sometimes seemed more pharaoh than Moses" (177). Something of an anthem for the group, "Go Down, Moses" was, however, already well established as a popular spiritual by the time that the Jubilees made it their own. The song was in fact the "first publication of the complete text of a Negro spiritual," having had its own unique journey into print. Testifying "unequivocally to the spiritual plight of the contrabands," "Go Down, Moses," as Jon Cruz maintains, "was heard first and foremost as an *antislavery* song, and its reception marked an interpretative desire to connect song and social circumstance."[50]

If, however, and as Cruz suggests, the song had gradually become estranged from its revolutionary roots as a result of (politically) disinterested archivists and scholars who were driven instead by an ahistoricizing racial fetishization, then Pauline Hopkins inserts the song the narrative to disrupt the rapidly evolving cultural amnesia of the postbellum era. She makes use of the song to demand of her characters—in this case, both Reuel and Dianthe—that they exercise their repressed "interpretative desire to connect song and social circumstance." Hopkins imagines a discursive narrative in which singing provides a gateway to philosophical, mystical, and cultural mediation for black women. Dianthe is thus singing in this sequence not in the service of "loss" but in the service of creating both literal, landed property (the historical Jubilee Hall for which the Singers' performances raised funds to build at Fisk University) and artistic property. Through her vocal work, Dianthe generates additional resources for New Negro intellectual life, and African American cultural preservation and promotion as well. Prefiguring the mysterious women in Telassar whose "restored female bodies" become "both a form of art and an historical artifact," Dianthe in song fulfills the role of a "performing effigy" who preserves the past and creates new pathways into the future for sophisticated listeners who can decipher the semantic crosscurrents of her musical text.[51]

Dianthe is thus the feature soloist imbued with the power to carry this great anthem. Like Harriet Tubman, who was known to have used the song "to call up her candidates for transportation to free land," Dianthe uses the spiritual to lead her congregation, like that "female Moses" did to the north, here "heavenward" (453) in song.[52] Her role as soloist is critical to the resistant currents of Hopkins's narrative, and it is a role with which Hopkins would have been, as a former starlet songbird herself, deeply familiar. No doubt, having performed her own set of solos, Hopkins would have been aware of the distinct demands placed on the lead singer. As twentieth-century Fisk folklorist and composer John W. Work maintains, "the leader is a most important factor in the singing of spirituals. It is [she] who sets the pitch and tempo, and it is [she] who sings the verses. The leader sometimes must sing [her] refrain through several times before the group will join [her]. [She] must have at [her] disposal many verses for each song."[53] The leader must push ahead on the song's path to transcendence, clearing a way for her followers and articulating the direction of the spiritual for the rest of the group who will join her in chorus. Specifically, in "Go Down, Moses," the lead singer is called on to assume the booming voice of authority.

In his legendary rendition of the song in 1965 (during the country's "second Reconstruction"), a regal and stalwart Paul Robeson performed a magnetic version which made plain the crucial power of the soloist's vocals. As Robert O'Meally reminds us of this rendition, Robeson's "voice assumes the might and authority of God—remind[ing] listeners of the ongoing struggles against slavery (in varying forms and degrees) around the world: *Let my people go!*"[54] For contemporary listeners Robeson's performance makes audible the singer's ability to transmit agitation, authority, and divine message. In "Go Down, Moses," the lead singer must negotiate the liberation of a people and make "arrangements for the immediate reimbursement to the slave for his unrewarded toil."[55] Most provocatively, perhaps, the lead vocalist must intuitively shift positions within the song to articulate the Lord's divine orders to the group leader's interpretation of God's message. The singer then finally transitions into a choral version that might be sung either alone or in group unison, pulling together a collective voice.

"Go Down, Moses" emerged in the broad collective imaginary following its transcription into print for the first time in 1861 and was available as sheet music by the following year. Linked historically to the moment of emancipation, the song resurfaced at the "stroke of midnight" on New Year's Eve in December 1862 when reportedly it circulated among black assemblages in Washington, who sang the chorus "over and over again" that night. Subsequently, in 1880, J. B. T. Marsh included all twenty-five stanzas of the song in his *Story of the Jubilee Singers*.[56] Although Hopkins only includes specific lyrics to the chorus in the passage ("Go Down, Moses, way down in Egypt's land, Tell ol' Pharaoh, let my people go"), it is likely that her readers would have been familiar with some if not all of the forceful verses of the song.

When Israel was in E-gypt's land: Let my people go, Oppressed so hard
    they could not stand, Let my people go.
Go down, Mo-ses. Way down in E-gypt's land,
Tell ol' Pharaoh. Let my people go.

Thus saith the Lord, bold Moses said,
Let my people go; If not I'll smite your first-born dead,
Let my people go.
Go down, Moses, and
No more shall they in bondage toil,
Let my people go;
Let them come out with Egypt's spoil,
Let my people go.
Go down, Moses, & c.[57]

The structure of "Go Down, Moses" charts a dialectic of communication and
coalition building between the individual lead singer and her choral community. According to John Lovell, the song's arrangement opens up an oscillation
between the lead singer who imparts the first line of each stanza and the choir
who follows her in song. The chorus pronounces the second line, followed
again by "the leader [who] returns with the third line, the chorus with the
fourth and both deliver the refrain."[58] Seizing the multivalent position of
Moses, the Lord's word, and a participant in the collective, Dianthe performs
a lyrical subjectivity which is underwritten by its interconnectedness with
community. Like her antebellum forebear Henry Box Brown, who delivers
himself through sacred song, Dianthe crosses the river of despair in "Go
Down, Moses" to reach an emancipated sphere, and she instructs her listeners
to follow in suit and in song. "Go Down, Moses" is, then, less a "sorrow song,"
the melancholic title bestowed on the spirituals by Du Bois (a Fisk scholar in
his own right), and more a score for the trajectory *out* of sorrow. As one
nineteenth-century critic would note of the song after having heard the Jubilees perform it, this masterful number with "sad, earnest, and pathetic beginnings" reaches a "great swell to rapturous grandeur after the deliverance
of the Israelites."[59] Like a great biblical heroine, or like Tubman traveling
by night up and through the Underground Railroad, Dianthe delivers her
charges to freedom.

Dianthe's movements in song would have been apparent to politically and
historically savvy readers of *Of One Blood* as well as to a gradually awakening Reuel. Her performance makes plain how Hopkins "realized that black
women had to discover alternative ways to participate and receive the benefits

of citizenship" and agency in post-Reconstruction uplift struggles.[60] The act of singing provides an entry point for Dianthe to serve an in-flux community of African Americans working to assert its hopes, desires, and its sense of itself in the wake of emancipation. Likewise, Reuel witnesses her solo effort and the self-making power of African American culture (re)building and renegotiating group expression as Dianthe "performs community" in ways similar to Katherine Bassard's vision of that process in nineteenth-century America. The call that Dianthe sings out through "Go Down, Moses" to Reuel is, in short, a coded invitation to participate in this communal process. Accordingly, his challenge will be to open himself up to what Bassard identifies as the "centripetal pull" of the "spirituals in performance which establishes the bar between outsider and insider, draws the boundaries between participating within the communal performance and those outside the performing collective."[61] Reuel must learn how to perform the role of the "leader" of a transnational black nationhood in *Of One Blood*. He gets his early clues and cues from Dianthe, who is herself the manifestation of a long line of Reconstruction and postbellum songbirds who performed and led a New Negro people forward in the quest for social and cultural freedom.

### The Sopranos: Gender, Singing, and Self-Making in New Negro America

A "great soprano of unimaginable beauty" (453), Dianthe's electrifying success as a concert singer mirrors the explosion of black female musical artistry in the second half of the nineteenth century. During this era, no less than an extraordinary half a dozen African American women performed in concert halls at home and abroad and rose to the ranks of celebrity status. Singing their way through opera, spirituals, and the popular melodies born out of musical theatre, these women paved a way into previously segregated transatlantic cultural spaces, gradually earning the respect and support of incredulous critics and large mainstream audiences alike. By way of Dianthe, Hopkins pays tribute to these trailblazing women who were lauded as triumphant examples of the "colored race's" ability to achieve excellence in the institutional arts. At the same time, however, the tragic set of circumstances which Hopkins imagines for her heroine in the wake of her majestic concert performance suggests that the author was also well aware of the excruciating material, philosophical, and ideological challenges for the archetypal New Negro soprano in the wake of Reconstruction. Witness, for instance, how it is Reuel, as opposed to Dianthe, who surfaces with vibrancy in the wake of the concert to assume his role as the recognizable protagonist of the narrative. For many critics and particularly feminist theorists, the novel's preoccupation with Reuel's rapid ascendance to professional fame, power, and royal authority obscures and ultimately displaces Dianthe's dazzling emergence in song. As some have suggested, only a writer who was vastly pessimistic about postbellum black women's artistry and agency could conjure up a narrative in which a talented heroine survives an accident only to fall into the self-serving hands of ambitious men.

To be sure, even Reuel's successful effort to "reanimate" Dianthe before a room full of incredulous white colleagues seems baldly expedient. Grossly self-aggrandizing, Reuel's aim to marry an amnesia-ridden Dianthe "before she awakens to consciousness of her identity" rings as a kind of inverted fairy tale. Playing prince to her sleeping beauty, he resolves to keep her in a blank state of cultural slumber and, in collusion with Aubrey, denies her access to her own memories. Reuel makes the terms of his agenda explicitly clear, declaring that "[t]here is no sin in taking her out of the sphere where she was born. God and science helping me, I will give her life and love and wifehood and maternity and perfect health" (479). Whisked away by Reuel on chivalry's magic coattails, Dianthe lands in the world of refined New England culture, zombie-like, afflicted with amnesia, and "accept[ing] the luxury of her new surroundings as one to the manner born" (490). Reuel's "miraculous" act appears to work at the expense of Dianthe's autonomy and performative agency, so that, as Jennie Kassanoff concludes, Dianthe "is unable to exert any agency of her own and falls into complete submission to masculine mandates."

Physical tragedy and patriarchal ambition thus thwart the vaunting talents of Dianthe Lusk. Rendered silent and motionless, she ceases to sing. Left with little memory of her successful career as a Jubilee Singer in the wake of her accident, the "fair-skinned" soprano inadvertently "passes" into the New England, white upper class. In what would become the first of many coarse and unyielding plot twists involving Dianthe, the novel flattens out and expels her powerful voice, converting, it would seem, her (vocal) body of strength and propulsion into the "living dead." A distant memory, Dianthe's concert performance appears, on the one hand, to play as a tragic swan song, a final bow before her descent to the depths of patriarchal control and manipulation. It is no wonder, then, that Elizabeth Ammons concludes that Hopkins employs her character to tell "the awful truth about the African American women artist's reality at the beginning of the twentieth-century. In *Of One Blood* the black American woman artist *has* a past. It is ancient, potent, brilliant—full of voice. What she does not have is ownership of that past or a future."[62]

But Hopkins may have conversely imagined both a problem as well as solution to her tragically embroiled heroine's catastrophe. Her precipitous fall from her Fisk Jubilee grace notwithstanding, Dianthe possesses both a "past" history and "a future" purpose. Ultimately reconfigured in the narrative as an allegorical conduit of gendered musical performance, cultural memory, and self-making, Dianthe utilizes song and musical production to open up history and to sing herself across space and time and out of her present material constriction.[63] Song operates as the other frequency on which the black female protagonist is able to articulate voice in the midst of oppressive conditions. Thus Hopkins aligns Dianthe with her historical forebears in song, the "black prima donnas" who stormed the second half of the nineteenth century. For Dianthe, song acts, just as it did for her historic antecedents, as a tool to disrupt cultural and historical amnesia and elision. Moreover, music and song enable her to reunite with her temporarily submerged cultural identity politics. Hopkins thus uses the plight of Dianthe and the very particular spectacles of "re-awakening," first in song and then in the related realm of spiritualist trance, to signify on the cultural, historical, and social role of black women in the late nineteenth and early twentieth century. Song serves as the first historically dense plateau that Dianthe must traverse and remaster in order to regain her social and cultural subjectivity. This reunion with lyrical verse and melody subsequently shapes and influences the racial as well as the gendered political intent of the novel.

By figuring Dianthe's memory loss specifically in relation to song, Hopkins pushes a critical engagement with the politics of black music and cultural memory, as well as the ways in which music and song might specifically operate as the catalyst for black women's social and cultural (re)awakening in the postbellum era. In the wake of her absorption into Reuel's and Aubrey's social circles, Dianthe's amnesia plays out in painstaking terms as it becomes apparent that this loss of identity extends to the beloved realm of her musical "genius." At an "afternoon function" featuring a white women's singing group, for instance, "[t]he grand, majestic voice that had charmed the hearts from thousands of bosoms, was pinioned in the girl's throat like an imprisoned song-bird. Dianthe's voice was completely gone along with her memory. But music affected her strangely" (491). The full-voiced self is apparently at sea here; yet Hopkins uses the occasion of Dianthe's lapsed vocalism to allegorically reference a social and historical mystery illustrative of her own contemporary cultural landscape. Through Dianthe's dilemma in *Of One Blood*, she points up the turn-of-the-century disappearance of postwar black prima donnas and accordingly interrogates the possibility of their resurrection.[64]

More than fifty years before Hopkins gave voice to her singing heroine, Elizabeth Taylor Greenfield initiated what would become a pioneering if fleeting trend of black women's musical artistry in the second half of the nineteenth century. Born into slavery in 1824 in Natchez, Mississippi, Greenfield was later raised by Philadelphia Quakers who supported her interests in the arts. A student of the harp, guitar, and piano, and a mezzo-soprano with uniquely pliable vocal talents, she sang in the private company of benefactors before making her professional debut in 1851 in Buffalo, New York. Often compared to the world-renowned celebrity opera singer Jenny Lind, the "Swedish Nightingale," Greenfield toured the States and Europe in the early 1850s and later taught and organized musical performances in Philadelphia in the 1860s. With "sweetness," "ease and flexibility," and an "unusual compass" of voice, Greenfield unveiled a three-and-a-half octave range for predominantly white audiences who were no doubt drawn to the spectacle of a black woman who "dared" to perform classical material.[65] Anomalous both in terms of race and gender as a public and performing black female artist, Greenfield battled the specter of blackface and the racialized expectations of audiences raised on minstrelsy. She thus negotiated a mixed repertoire of classical standards by Handel and Bellini with the minstrel folk songs of Stephen Foster and weathered an elixir of gushing praise of her "genuine art" with the race-based aspersions of critics who dismissed her act as burnt-cork aberration and "untaught" "imitation."[66]

To several of her supporters, the "solution" to Greenfield's sometimes hostile reception was to encourage her to "de-emphasize the body" in her performances, as Carla Peterson has shown. However much she followed the advice to "conceal" her figure and eschew wearing "colored flowers" and "flowing ribbons" in her hair, Greenfield would maintain a resoundingly transgressive style of singing that set a symbolic and social precedence for future black prima donnas. Greenfield's "phenomenal range, from a low G in the bass clef to an E above high C" generated the perplexed responses of critics who compared her voice to that of a male singer's. This "low register," which was said to have "the full, rich sonority of a baritone," pushed her vocally well beyond the performative sphere of standard sopranos. Figuratively akin to the kind of "excess" in sound that musicologist Susan McClary influentially describes as a "feminine ending," Greenfield's singing refused the hegemonically regulated and gender-circumscribed sphere of the classical soprano by paradoxically venturing onto "masculine" terrain. Greenfield both entered into the realm of classical singing uninvited as an African American woman and bastardized the sphere by vocally traveling outside the boundaries of vocal categories. And while her performances threatened to "masculinize" her already under-siege black female body, Greenfield nonetheless "dared to challenge existing musical proprieties by singing in musical territory dominated by men." Exploring a new field of public expression for black women in song, Greenfield challenged racial, gender, and cultural politics of the mid-nineteenth century. Forever flummoxed by her "sweet" and yet categorically unruly vocals, audiences equally championed Greenfield's talents as a national response to Lind's success and chastised her for choosing a "style of music" which is "evidently not her *role*."[67]

To the women who came after her, what Greenfield perhaps best exemplified was a determined bravery and perseverance to pick and choose her own "roles" in cultural performance. She set the pace for a generation of black female musical artists to move forward into the realm of classical music performance. Many would embrace the genre in a bid to gain the representational propriety denied their foremothers in slavery, to engage in conventional forms of cultivated, "highbrow" cultural expression, and to disrupt the ever-evolving blackface and coon song paradigms of the era. All were clearly intent on rescripting their status as "non-being" through a rigorous engagement with classical forms.[68] Indeed, Greenfield and the classical black female performers who followed her would establish a field of cultural transgression to reanimate their socially circumscribed bodies and make themselves matter in a newly visible cultural context. Greenfield gave birth to a genealogy of black women's cultural play within classical music forms, and she exemplified the ways in which professional singing might operate as a vocation capable of rewriting black female iconography in the cultural imaginary.

Young women like the versatile and industrious Anna Madah and Emma Louise Hyers would take up the torch passed by Greenfield with even greater success. Raised primarily in the late 1850s and early 1860s in Sacramento, California, the Hyers Sisters made a fast ascent in the entertainment world following their concert debut in 1867. Contrasting Anna's "birdlike" soprano with Emma's "dark, rich" contralto, the Hyers carried the mentorship of their parents and the formal training of several accomplished music professors to grand success in touring opera concerts and musical theatre. They became the first significant black musical actresses of the Reconstruction era. Achieving a level of critical acceptance from the press that Greenfield was never fully awarded, the Hyers Sisters were conversely praised for their "refinement, culture, and attractiveness" which they, in turn, used as their own promotional fodder. Performing in the West, Midwest, and Northeast to both black and white audiences, the Hyers Sisters broke new ground in theatre with 1876's

*Out of Bondage*, a production that metatextually signified on the social and political viability of a career in song. Their future collaboration with Hopkins herself in *Peculiar Sam* would have given them the opportunity to extend an investment in musical theatre as a kind of cultural landscape of Reconstruction reform.[69]

Hopkins was perhaps influenced by her serendipitous proximity to this burgeoning and rapidly evolving world of black prima donnas. A young Hopkins would have witnessed these elegant female entertainers who emerged with an enormous burst of creativity and from all walks of life. Based in New England, Hopkins was situated in a regional community which "produced more than its share of African American concert artists undoubtedly because of the opportunity for study at the conservatories in Boston and Providence where blacks were admitted." In her twenties and thirties, then, Hopkins certainly would have heard of and been witness to the meteoric success of women like Flora Batson, the "Double-Voiced Queen of Song," "the Creole Nightingale" Rachel Walker, or Bergen Star Concert Company singer Nellie Brown Mitchell. The cosmopolitan Marie Selika, a Natchez native herself who studied voice in San Francisco, developed a "flair for ornamentation" in her singing, and toured places as far-flung as Europe and the West Indies in the 1880s.[70]

Undoubtedly, Hopkins would have been enraptured by the work of the uncontested superstar prima donna of this era, "New England's Rising Soprano Star," Sissieretta Jones. With a range that spanned the upper registers with a "clear and bell-like" lucidity and swooped, in Greenfield fashion, to "the depth of a contralto," Jones quickly garnered comparisons to the great Italian prima donna Adelina Patti, earning the racialized sobriquet of "the Black Patti." Following her debut in Philadelphia in 1888, she cultivated a career, first as a concert soprano and later, at the behest of her white producers, as the centerpiece of black musical comedy revues. Performing before white as well as black audiences as a solo artist and as the star of her popular vaudeville theatre sketches, she eventually toured Europe, Asia, Africa, and sang at the White House. A pioneer of bold and spectacularly indulgent and unapologetic vocal performance, Jones worked the stage and exemplified the nuances of vocal artistry. She was, as Rosalyn Story contends, "not above showiness; once a journalist reported her 'taking the A above the staff and holding it for fifteen seconds' in an immodest and unmusical display of vocal athletics that delighted her audience." That brassy, luxurious style of singing exemplifies the extent to which Jones indulged in the pleasure, sustenance, and the glorious magnitude of her own extraordinary abilities. As she once proudly declared, "'I love to sing. . . . Singing is to me what sunshine is to the flowers; it is our life.'"[71]

Jones found her own "life" in the song, in the unmatchable high and low notes that she took pleasure in reaching, running toward and alighting from and out into extraordinary points in sound. Like her cohorts, she set an example for negotiating pleasure in ways that prefigured the modern era's blues singers by several decades. Indeed, in the century *before* the emergence of the modern blues singer, Jones and this remarkable group of women found a means to sing themselves into a vibrant presence. They became, "in the moment of performance, the primary subject of [their] own invention." Under the aegis of classical music which struggled to keep the presence of the body in check, these women unveiled the power and cultivation of their marvelous physical strength in vocalization. Unafraid to embrace the "singing voice," which Lindon Barrett convincingly contends "plays upon bodily dimensions of vocal action usually taken for granted," these musical virtuosos used their operatic vocals to rescript their bodies decorously in the raiment of "high culture." By singing, they made visible the power, control, and autonomy of their culturally contested black female bodies and "reclaim[ed] the voice" *for* their bodies. More still, they reveled, as did Jones, in their magnificently complex vocal flourishes. Reaching difficult heights of perfection in their singing, these women enacted strength, endurance, focus, and transgressiveness as performers.[72] The black prima donnas of the postbellum era were no doubt capable of reaching the peak notes in song and traversing the (in)visible ceilings set for them in American culture. These women found "freedom" in the high as well as the low notes.

A fleeting and yet bittersweet magical moment in transatlantic culture performance, this renaissance of black women in song was ultimately swallowed up by history itself. For, as Southern notes, by "the mid-1890s the black prima donna had almost disappeared from the nation's concert halls because of lack of public interest."[73] It was left to Pauline Hopkins to "raise the dead" black female prima donna. In this regard, *Of One Blood* intervenes in the ephemerality of African American history and the evanescence of postbellum black female cultural production. Moreover, Hopkins specifically grooms Dianthe to signify on the specific and very public history of the African American prima donnas in the Fisk Jubilee Singers, the first black women to meld the classical with African American cultural forms.

Although they were never the sort of individual celebrities like their solo concert hall sisters, the women of the Fisk Jubilee Singers—Maggie Porter, Ella Sheppard, Jennie Jackson, Mabel Lewis, and America Robinson among them—were recognized members of the singing ensemble. Importantly, the group members' individual histories were detailed in short biographies and pamphlets by the 1870s and 1880s. On the heels of Gustavas Pike's narratives of the Jubilee Singers' various fund-raising campaigns came J. B. T. Marsh's *The Story of the Jubilee Singers, with Their Songs* (1880), an "abridgement" of Pike's texts which included "personal histories . . . more fully written."[74] With this flurry of publicity, the Jubilee women received a particular amount of scrutiny from critics and audiences who sometimes evaluated their physical traits with the grotesque precision of slave traders (Ward, *Dark Midnight*, 182). Recognizing the "need to be models of rectitude" (186), the Singers practiced the already refined tradition of spectacular (black) comportment as a way to combat mythical narratives of racial immorality. Doubly responsible for performing the "pious nobility" of true womanhood, "the sopranos and altos" of the Jubilees were romantically fetishized abroad. As figureheads of the ensemble, these women "contended with a steady stream of calling cards and forests of bouquets from ardent young admirers" (233).

The publication in various contexts of the Singers' "personal histories" only seemed to encourage this sort of fan frenzy as it reflected the hardships and triumphant survival of their postwar generation. Through these circulated narratives, the regal and imperious star soprano Maggie Porter's painful childhood separation from her sister was recounted and the story of Ella Sheppard's split from her parents and their subsequent vicissitudes in the wake of slavery was packaged into book form. Most ominous perhaps was the story of Mabel Lewis, "an extraordinarily powerful contralto," whose sensational tale of trauma and artistic healing is so distinct that it resonates in more than one Hopkins narrative. Born Marie Bohom to an enslaved New Orleans woman and a Frenchman named Falcoup Bohom, the singer was given shelter at an early age in a New York convent. Renamed Mabel Lewis by her military guardian, the singer was raised in a "strangely detached and insular" New England where she learned French and was forbidden from socializing with African Americans. Educated by nuns and former slaves, Mabel endured a life of physical abuse.[75]

Like their fellow Jubilees, Porter, Sheppard, and Lewis struggled with issues of displacement and familial, and social estrangement recounted in print and absorbed into the cultural imaginary of the late nineteenth century. These three standout performers were also united by their documented dedication to music and the way in which each pursued singing as both a personal passion and a meaningful vocation. Both Porter and Lewis were said to have drawn inspiration to sing from Jenny Lind, and must have found it thrilling to perform before the "Swedish Nightingale" at the height of their own success as Jubilees (Ward, *Dark Midnight*, 221). Porter passed on stories of her habit of listening to music while sitting outside on the steps of churches as a girl in Nashville (90), and Lewis's already extraordinary tale is punctuated by the revelation that she was discovered in her youth by "a Stockholm ballerina" while "singing to a cat." She later strolled the streets of New Bedford, Massachusetts, with an accordion hoping to attract the attention of a benefactor who might fund her with a musical education (193). Devastated by the loss of her "private piano" as a result of poverty, Sheppard negotiated the early mentorship of the black photographer James Presley Ball, who supported her efforts to study music at Glendale Female College (72).

As women who spoke in great detail of their interest in classical song, Porter, Sheppard, and Lewis promoted the aesthetic desires of New Negro black women in musical performance. Moreover, they came into their roles as virtuoso vocalists in spite of and perhaps as a response to the severe traumas of slavery and its lingering legacies. With the ubiquity of these narratives and variations on the themes that each raises apparent, Hopkins used her fiction to engage with the obstacles facing black female singers. Like the Jubilees, Hopkins's heroine weathers social fatigue and the exploitation of others, along with the politics of displacement and dislocation born out of slavery. In *Of One Blood*, Hopkins imagines a way to emancipate her fictional singer from the harsh cruelties of professional life in performance, to instead return her to the realm of performance itself as a sphere of shelter and self-actualization. This is why Dianthe's parlor performance represents such a critical moment in the text and in Hopkins's larger project of recuperating and reanimating black female musical agency.

Repeating the scene of Dianthe's encounter with song with a critical difference, Hopkins returns the narrative to the evening parlor where her heroine is given a second opportunity to stage a reunion with the emancipatory melody of her past vocation. The second time proves the charm. Following an evening of dance and song in her new home, Dianthe is drawn, as if in a trance, toward the parlor piano, where she assumes "a strange rigid appearance" while her "fingers flash over the keys" (501). The electric currents of song itself seemingly pulse through her so that "[s]lowly, tremulously at first, [she] pealed forth the notes" to "Go Down, Moses," which, in turn releases "another voice," a voice other than "Mrs. Briggs." In the wake of this spectacular impromptu performance worthy, according to one stunned onlooker, of a "prima donna for the Grand Opera," memory "return[s] in full save as to her name" (503).

The narrative brings to life the process of singing as the kind of self-making process that Barrett so eloquently describes. The "sly alterity" of Dianthe's musical voice re-emerges, cutting through lapsed personal memory, cultural amnesia, and social dislocation; it pulls her onto another frequency to articulate the invisible and putatively "valueless" life of her former "colored" self. Singing, for Dianthe, re-inscribes her subjective visibility within this world of New England high tea, audacious young scientists, and Southern estate heirs. Singing "insist[s] upon the urgency of [her] presence despite ubiquitous and confining reports of [her] cultural—even human—absence." Singing restores social and cultural meaning to Dianthe's identity formation. Most importantly, singing makes her body—the thing that has been rendered "living dead"—presently *alive in* song. Dianthe's "Moses" melody courses through her as the lifeblood that overrides social invisibility and vetoes the cultural death of nineteenth-century black female prima donnas. As a "counterpresence" in this hushed and astonished elite social gathering, Dianthe redelivers the audibility of slave resistance in a room previously sterilized of such sounds. A medium of memory in song, Dianthe conjures "a weird witchery," not unlike the music of the Hyers Sisters, who, as one critic noted, performed "southern songs, which like the cry of the curlew, tell a story of the soul."[76] In this regard, Hopkins uses the scene to open the door to her heroine performer's value, which exceeds that of merely singing. In this passage Dianthe begins her gradual movement toward assuming the role of mystic performer who bridges time and space in the novel's epic and far-reaching vision of New Negro transnational identity.

Dianthe harbors and masterfully disseminates the exquisite tale of deliverance which "Go Down, Moses" both narrates and lyrically enacts. The deep historical textures of that composition open up the portals to her own personal history as an artist, and they more broadly bridge Dianthe to the historical and cultural legacies of the African American communal past. As Hortense Spillers might observe, Dianthe "[re]turn[s] in fully conscious knowledge of her own resources toward her object" and, as vocalist, seizes back "her particular and vivid thereness" in "an alterable and discrete moment of self-knowledge." She becomes, then, "a good example of 'double consciousness' in action."[77] Displaying the cultural polyvalence of black music, the soprano's performance articulates the plenitude of cultural identity formation. Although it is the music of the spirituals which "returns" Dianthe to her primary, nonwhite subjectivity, the music itself expresses a heterogeneous cultural identity formation indicative of Du Bois's ideal vision of American identity itself. As a virtuoso Fisk Jubilee Singer, Dianthe regains a voice steeped in classical training—indeed, one which would have been historically cultivated, in part, by white choir director George White. White's mentorship of the Jubilees famously led them to interpret the classics through a mediation of European as well as African American aesthetic modes. With this historical tradition of diversity in song, her Fisk Jubilee character would presumably circumvent narrow notions of essentialist expression. Accordingly, Dianthe's performance midwifes a complex construction of interracial identity which advances the theory of cultural heterogeneity.

By way of her singing, Dianthe is free of the tyranny of American culture's racial amnesia which imagines mythically stable, inviolate, and pure racialized subjects. Her vocals "free" her not merely from "white" identity but from the tyranny of white supremacist ideology. That is, she performs along a continuum of cultural positions. She is present in the body, the physical site that generates a dramatic form of vocal mesmerism. Through spiritual singing she further alludes to an identity informed by African, European, and African American cultural forms, and she invokes multiple histories.[78] For Dianthe, black song is, then, the site of excess, the "double-consciousness" that so eludes black women in an American and African American patriarchal culture that fails to see them as complex, multidimensional subjects.

### Divas and Diasporic Consciousness

A pivotal moment indeed, the parlor scene prefigures the crucial role that Dianthe will play as musical and spiritualist medium in the text and as a figure who will bind together musical genius with a female-centered legacy of African American spiritualist practices. At the center of what Earl Lewis might call "overlapping diasporas," Dianthe fulfills her "multipositional" role as a "historical actor" who sings and "sees" her way along the spectrum of a variety of African American experiences in the Atlantic world.[79] Dianthe connects the past of *Of One Blood*'s tortured characters to a future life of resistance in a "mythic diaspora."[80] Her vocal talents ultimately open up transgeographical frontiers and negotiate chronotopical fields to reconnect her character with an individual past as a choir soloist and a collective history of black subjugation and cultural survival embedded in the lyrics of the spirituals. Most importantly, through Dianthe, Hopkins endorses the resistant excesses of black women's cultural identity formation made visible in this performance, and she uses that excess to emancipate herself as well as her fellow characters.[81]

As the singer with "mystic" powers, Dianthe bridges philosophical desire with the transnational in her art. She literally sings herself and the narrative into the African diaspora, and in doing so, she assumes the powerful role of the diva figure, the critical agent of knowledge and change in *Of One Blood*.

Only by reconsidering Dianthe's often misunderstood role of the diva agent do we come to a clearer understanding of the ways that Hopkins signifies on the position of the black female artist at the turn of the century.

A sometimes controversial moniker used to describe (black) women's musical artistry in contemporary popular culture, the term "diva" may have nonetheless been an appealing one to nineteenth-century African American women vocalists who combined their love for song with visions of uplift. As music scholar Rosalyn Story reveals, the etymological roots of the word "diva" trace back to Latin and mean the "goddess, divine one." To be "divine," ethereal, all-seeing, an icon of majestic promise and grace, the black divas of the postwar renaissance were often expected to shoulder the demands that the race put its best face forward. "Divine" as they may seem, these women were often forced to place the material and representational desires of their community before themselves, to perform the hopeful ideals of a people above all else. In this same sentiment, *Of One Blood* seems similarly to position Dianthe as a vocal talent who directs her agency entirely toward shoring up the subjectivity of her partner-turned-brother Reuel.[82]

But the diva figures of the black prima donna era were perhaps drawn, as Hopkins certainly was, to the kinds of theological and mythic signifiers bound up in their high-profile positions. How else to explain the preponderance for biblically regal and royal Pan-Africanist imagery that flourished during the black operatic vocalist boom? From the Hyers Sisters' "operatic bouffe extravaganza" *Urlina, the African Princess* (1879) to the late-nineteenth-century explosion of women who were billed as "Queens of song," black female musical artists embraced diva-like monikers and assumed the role of the regal heroines of their culture. They were presumably performing through song the role of lost royalty to a mythically rendered "African" past.[83] This trend was prefigured when none other than the Fisk Jubilee Singers brought forth their own "queen," the confident, commanding, and stratospherically talented soprano Maggie Porter. In a symbolic directorial decision, Porter was handpicked by George White to perform the lead role in William Bradbury's contemporary cantata *Esther, or the Beautiful Queen* (Ward, *Dark Midnight*, 90).[84] In turn, her vocal inhabitation of the biblical queen who defended her people set a precedent for future prima donnas to yoke regal character with theologically historical narrative; her performance signified in a musical context on the leadership role of queenly figures in delivering a people from subjugation. In the wake of this era of divine queens of song, then, Hopkins recenters Dianthe as a diva in her own right, conjoined to her diasporic doppelgänger, the mysterious Queen Candace, who emerges to greet Reuel in the underground nation. In this twist (of fate), Hopkins plays on these popular images of black vocal queens and works to restore Dianthe's dissident role in the text. She draws not only from black musical history but also from Victorian popular culture and sensation fiction to signify even further on her heroine's fundamental insurgence and cultural resilience.

Drawing from the resonating imagery of mystical queenly energy in Victorian popular culture, Hopkins invokes the shimmering figure of an identical diva (monarch) to imagine her violated heroine "consecrat[ing] herself into a queen with disturbing alacrity." But long before Candace takes her seat alongside Reuel as the female royalty of a new African kingdom, Dianthe has assumed the role as the narrative's diva-"queen." With a name that bespeaks the kind of "malevolent divinity of a lunar, and always feminine, landscape," Dianthe's transmutating character holds the kind of phantasmagoric energy so readily apparent in Victorian regal female iconography. If nothing else, Dianthe is a figure who manifests, brings about, sings of, and ultimately forecasts change in the text. The dyadic Dianthe/Candace combination operates, then, as the unified prima donna heroine in the text. This mystical figure is diasporically phantasmagoric, a dual goddess of transformation and spiritistic energy.[85]

It may be, then, too simple to read Dianthe's "hypnoid" state as a mesmeric medium solely within the framework of abjection and pathology, as do many critics. Her torture-ridden struggle with trance states and physical inertia (475) certainly sets her up to play out the conventional role of the late-nineteenth-century female hysteric. Communicating spiritualistically with both her grandmother Hannah and the spirit of her mother Mira, who reveal to her two generations of black women's sexual, physical, and labor abuse at the hands of white patriarchs, Dianthe initially seems only capable of inheriting the "violence, racism, and misogyny" of previous generations. But Hopkins resolves to repair and vindicate this black female genealogy of abuse and exploitation through Dianthe's spiritualistic powers. As Elin Diamond has noted, "hysteria in feminist discourse has become meaningful precisely as a disruption of traditional epistemological methods of seeing/knowing."[86] Hopkins carefully rescripts the seemingly "hysterical" Dianthe into the key figure who creates a rupture in dominant American amnesia which threatens to render black culture and black people invisible (the hidden selves) in the postbellum era. She enters into the trance realm, in short, to mount and center mystic resistance and spiritualist epistemologies in the text.

Within her final hours, Hopkins's heroine manipulates the perception of her (im)mortality. Evoking the most prolonged of death scenes, such as that of Little Eva's ascension in *Uncle Tom's Cabin*, Dianthe's departure results in a lengthy passage and a final promenade out of her lingering and painful abjection. Unlike Little Eva, however, death carries her not to some blissfully blinding whiteness of heaven replete with angels and harps but presumably back to an "ancient Ethiopia" which greets its "dying daughter of the royal line" by carrying her across space and time fittingly on the strength of a "vast orchestra's . . . low and wailing notes . . . swelling [and] pealing through arch and corridor in mighty diapason" (614). Dianthe as diva makes her final exit in a crescendo of trumpets and "crashing cymbals"; witnessing a symphony which only she can hear (614–15), she transforms death into a site of black and female agency unleashed.[87] Sleep, trances, and indeed death itself are but liminal frontiers of transfiguration and "self-transformation" which enable imminent reunification with her own sovereignty. For Dianthe, the entranced woman of the narrative, her somnambulism "is not passivity but an ominous gathering of power as she transfigures herself from humanity to beatitude" and from sleeping diva into African queen.[88]

Dianthe's dual roles as diva and as spiritualist medium in the narrative equally utilize notions of vocal agency which are interconnected and which turn both acts into aesthetic performance rituals of empowerment and leadership. Hence, despite Claudia Tate's important observation that Hopkins's serial heroines increasingly lack voice and that the author "seems to have silenced the discourse of female agency," we might read for the way that Hopkins subverts and transforms definitions of black feminist activism in *Of One Blood*. In particular, as a spiritualist medium Dianthe engages in a legacy of black women's mystical performances which provide the crucial link between the American and African landscape in the narrative. Hopkins invokes spiritualist performance as an epistemological and politicized strategy in order to intervene in black empowerment discourses that far too often elided the political agency of black women. By reconsidering *Of One Blood*'s construction of the black female medium, I pose a way in which to complicate the parameters of what gets deemed as "political" or "resistant" in black women's postbellum fiction.[89]

Certainly, as several critics have argued, *Of One Blood*'s representation of Dianthe seems to ascribe her to a legacy of female inertia and passive subjectivity.[90] But such readings tend to consider Dianthe within the rubric of a legacy of female exploitation, especially that of spiritualist mediums. Dubbed the "veiled ladies" of mystical exhibitions because of their putative ability to "cross over" the "veil" separating life and death, mediums were no doubt icons of exploitation and abjection. Primarily Anglo-American women, these cultural workers were paradoxically conceived of as exhibitionists with little agency of their own. Although the spiritualist medium who worked as the centripetal force of such sensational gatherings was capable of summoning contact and building a bridge between the material and the nether worlds, the (male) mesmerist doctor remained the fundamental "ringmaster" of these events who controlled and manipulated the body of the (female) medium.[91]

Yet reading Dianthe solely within this framework privileges narrow and Westernized definitions of spiritualism as well as what constitutes political agency itself. For however central spirit-rapping may have been to a white, patriarchal New England culture, many critics have demonstrated the broader circum-Atlantic tradition of cultural rituals akin to and yet perhaps far more politically and culturally expansive than midcentury American spiritualism. Joseph Roach argues, for instance, that the Native American and later African American tradition of the Ghost Dance in 1880s Louisiana functioned both for Indians and for black Louisiana voodoo communities as a means of "resisting the segregation of the dead" by summoning up ancestral spirits from an idealized and re-membered homeland. Given the diasporic roots of spiritualist expression, it is possible to reinterpret spiritualist rituals such as mesmerism, and (most importantly) the role of the mesmerized, from a standpoint which opens up a space for considering Dianthe's social, political, and cultural power and significance in *Of One Blood*.[92]

In *Of One Blood*, spiritualism links and reunites Dianthe to a genealogy of black women's resistant performance in the text. In turn, Hopkins envisions Dianthe's (singing) voice as the tool that reconfigures gender dynamics through her black female diva soprano medium. From this standpoint, scholars who critique Dianthe's lack of narrative authority and action in the text tend to overlook the moments wherein her voice literally serves as a guiding and binding force for other characters. Dianthe's stirring sleep-induced "address" to Reuel and colleagues during one of her early trance states, for instance, holds a room full of curious onlookers in "a solemn silence." Though her initial pleas to her doctor/mesmerist Reuel to "hasten to cure me of my sufferings" seem to articulate a total helplessness on her part, the request that she eventually extends to him suggests her attempt to disrupt the spiritistic balance of power in her relationship with Reuel. She demands of him to "give me the benefit of your powerful will," before ominously proclaiming that she "see[s] much clearly, much dimly, of the powers and influences behind the Veil, and yet I cannot name them. Some time the full power will be mine; and mine shall be thine. In seven months the sick will be restored—she will awake to worldly cares once more" (475).

Far from expressing tractability in this scene, Dianthe holds center stage before an all-male audience and not only lobbies for a more equal distribution of power with her mesmerist but also asserts a startling prophecy which suggests that "the full power" of clairvoyance will eventually be hers for the taking. She forecasts her own liberation from illness, which comes to fruition through yet another moment of vocal articulation. Significantly, it is the characterization of Dianthe's voice during this performance as a "weird contralto, veiled as it were, rising and falling upon every wave of the great soprano, and reaching the ear as from some strange distance" (502), which fully reflects the extent to which Hopkins employs Dianthe's intersecting role as medium and diva singer to disrupt gender hierarchies embedded in spiritualist as well as Pan-Africanist ideologies. Dianthe's voice in both instances undermines the dominant presumption in spiritualism that the "success of spirit communication depended on the ability" of the mediums "to give up their own identity to become the instruments of others." The scene instead demonstrates how the heroine uses her own voice as a tool of "the Veil" which contributes to individual and collective agency.[93]

By situating Dianthe at the center of the spiritualist energy, Hopkins makes an intervention in the field of spiritualist culture to re-imagine how black women specifically might re-inhabit and renegotiate the political and social utility of that movement. The author also signifies on the place of black women in racial uplift agendas. Like Du Bois, Hopkins explores the intersections of spiritualism and the African diasporic liberation movements and applies the existential and philosophical queries embedded in spiritualist culture to questions of racial identity and the politics of the "color line." Spiritualism offered a convenient site for cultural nationalists such as Hopkins and Du Bois to imagine a fluid frontier between North America and West Africa that black Americans might philosophically traverse in their pursuit of racial and ideological revelation. Unlike Du Bois, however, Hopkins employed spiritualism in her work both as a tool for Pan-Africanist sociopolitical movements and as a specific representational tool designed to articulate a black feminist agenda and African American women's quests for narrative agency in the postbellum era.

As the novel suggests of Dianthe and her "celestial" voice, to be "veiled" is to finally see. Like Du Bois's paradigmatic "Negro" who "is a sort of seventh son, born with a veil, and gifted with second-sight in this American world," the singer anticipates her own healing and subsequent rebirth in "seven months," at which time she will reach her full cognitive and intellectual capacity. This trope of the veil in the novel's representation of Dianthe establishes a clear dialectic with Du Bois's landmark theories of that term which yoke spiritualist with Pan-Africanist imagery. Within *The Souls of Black Folk*, Du Bois posits the veil "as a kind of occult tract," which "may show the strange meaning of being black here at the dawn of the Twentieth Century.'" The black "see-er" functions, according to Cynthia Schrager, as an "alternative model of black leadership," one "who mediates between the seen and the unseen, between both sides of the veil" so as to speak for a "disenfranchised" nation in the midst of reinventing itself.[94]

Eclipsing Reuel, the Du Boisian character who is often linked to a potent "second-sight," Dianthe serves as the prevailing "mediating figure" who straddles the boundaries of transglobal and transhistorical cognizance in order to act as an interventionist tool in the revisioning of black nationalist as well as spiritualist ideologies (Schrager, "Pauline Hopkins," 201). As medium, she is the "center of spiritual knowledge and insight," and thus her role as "veiled lady" is one not of "imprisonment," as Brodhead configures this position, but of liminal possibility. Veiling for Dianthe works as a kind of (un)covering of knowledge and representation. Her resistance to the threat of bodily and psychological subjugation in mesmerism comes precisely as a result of her status as the mesmerist's patient, indeed, as the "veiled lady." Resurrecting and reinvigorating the role that her mother Mira once performed under the coercion of slaveholders (487), Dianthe retains the spiritualist power of her black female forebear, transforming that energy into enlightened and resistant alterity. She is the "woman in white" (as the iconography of the spiritualist medium suggests) who, nonetheless, disrupts the violent tyranny of white supremacy. She is the heroine who claims with conviction to have sight "behind the Veil" and thus wrests the position of the "see-er" away from the male spectators who attempt to colonize her female sexuality by penetrating the veil. She is the figure whose "veiled" soprano builds a bridge that reaches to some "strange distance" and which connects the lost souls of folk to a distant, far-off land. While Du Bois may have taken the "feminine" trope of the veil and put it to use in a specifically African American context, Hopkins invented a female protagonist who transformed that "feminine" site into a space where racial as well as gender insurgency could collude and flourish. In the years following *Of One Blood*'s publication, Hopkins's contemporary Aida Overton Walker choreographed a ground-breaking dance which boldly pushed Hopkins's veil(ed) agenda and representations of New Negro womanhood forward and into a new cultural era.[95]

## A Diaspora of the Seven Veils

*The daughter is simply there in order that she may dance.*

—Anonymous critic, *In Dahomey* Review

Ada Overton would have been old enough in 1897 to have observed first-hand the rapid dissolution of black social and political advancement with which Hopkins concerned herself. Yet, at the same time, she grew up in New York City, the center of black theatrical innovation and energy, watching the flourishing artistic experiments and opportunities of a new generation of African American performers, musicians, and composers who seemed undaunted by the ubiquity of racial discrimination. It comes as little surprise that, just one year after the Supreme Court's acceptance of segregation in *Plessy v. Ferguson* (1896), a teenage Overton emerged in the professional labor force as a theatre entertainer. Appearing in the chorus of Black Patti's Fifty Troubadours show, a new vehicle for opera virtuoso Sissieretta Jones, Overton danced her way into the public eye and began what would turn into a rapid ascent toward international show business stardom as a critically acclaimed entertainer and choreographer.[96] In 1898 Overton joined George Walker and Bert Williams's newly formed traveling black musical theatre group. The following year she married the stalwart and ambitious Walker and rose to prominence as the principal choreographer and lead dancer for the Williams and Walker troupe. A "prize" entertainer to critics, she won audiences by exuding a seemingly effortless charm and charisma that she carried through her musical comedy performances. Critics embraced Walker as a paradigmatic example of the "rapid and successful advancement in a race which twenty years ago boasted no such a luxury as a company of popular players."[97]

The year in which *Of One Blood* ran its serialization, Walker was starring as Rosetta Lightfoot, "the troublesome, young" daughter of Southern black patriarch Cicero in Williams and Walker's *In Dahomey* (1902–4). She achieved public notoriety for her singing and her dancing in this musical, performing such numbers as "I Wants to Be an Actor Lady" and the wickedly subversive "Vassar Girl," a song which documented a contemporary incident involving a black student who passed for white in order to enter Vassar College. With lyrics proclaiming her character's desire to "pla[y] you know / Star in the show / Spotlight for me, no back row shady," "Vassar Girl" provided Walker with the opportunity to cultivate a unique public and black female cultural persona. A break from the popular and familiar coon song constructions of expedient black female "gold-diggers" (of which Walker sang her share as well), tunes such as "Vassar Girl" and "I Wants to Be an Actor Lady" were distinct thematic departures for black female comedy performers.[98] These numbers marked new strides in strategies of black female characterization on the stage in that they allowed for ways to articulate black women's often disregarded desires for social and cultural mobility in American culture. Moreover, they imagined passing heroines and clever ingenues, and they underscored Walker's commitment to characters who dared to dabble in the excesses of subversive masquerade. These distinctly disruptive and eccentric performances, then, challenge theatre historian David Krasner's contention that the actress "downplayed the notion of self in order to mollify blacks, particularly males, who felt threatened by her success." On the contrary, from a consideration of her repertoire alone, Walker's work appears deeply attuned to articulating the complexities of "self" and the particularly black female self in the postbellum era. That critics historically have been less invested in reading for the rich layers of characterization in Walker's performances is perhaps best exemplified by the observation of one theatre critic who noted that her Rosetta existed "simply" so that "she may dance."[99]

But she was not there solely to dance. She performed in the service of complicating and confounding early-twentieth-century constructions of race and gender. A New Negro activist committed to utilizing theatre and performance as sites for black representational change, Walker gained public notoriety as a perfectionist performer dedicated to promoting the rich legacies of African Americans and pushing for mainstream acknowledgment of the vital contributions made by black performers in the field of dance. Fiercely outspoken in interviews and in her own articles for the black press, Walker used her time offstage to cultivate a politicized voice deeply invested in exposing and rectifying racial discrimination within the theatre world. In one 1906 interview she railed against the "popular prejudice" toward "love scenes enacted by Negroes"; in another press article she delivered a fiery letter defending her ailing husband from the racist remarks of a former Williams and Walker business manager. Even more frequently in her own writing, she spoke directly to black audiences, encouraging them to work in and support black theatre because "there are characteristics and natural tendencies in our people which make just as beautiful studies for the Stage as any to be found in the make up of any other race, and perhaps far better." Walker's investment in community activism stretched from press editorials into the realm of charity work. Taking a particular interest in the uplift of young black women, she was known for giving benefit performances in and around New York City, performing for audiences such as the students at the White Rose Industrial School for Colored Working Girls in New York City.[100]

At heart a cultural nationalist who found an outlet for expressing her social and political ideologies in theatre, Walker experimented with different forms of articulating and signifying on the increasingly popular (and varied versions of) cultural Pan-Africanism of the period. She starred in each of the Williams and Walker Company's transnational-themed musicals, including *In Dahomey* and *Abyssinia*, and went so far as to change her name from Ada to Aida, reportedly in homage to Verdi's nineteenth-century opera and its imprisoned Ethiopian princess. Whether Walker was attempting to align herself with both classical forms and romanticized "African" iconography, or whether she was slyly rewriting the opera *Aida*'s vision of colonial inhabitants who "seem destined never to escape" and "remain creatures of European will," the name change signaled her consistent commitment to disrupting cultural representations of African Americans. In this regard, she extended her interests in Pan-Africanist imagery into the aesthetics of her choreography when she developed and performed a "ballet" entitled "Ethiopia" in the last Williams and Walker production, *Bandanna Land*.[101]

That 1907–8 production proved to be an especially critical period for Walker both personally and professionally. She seemed to hit her stride as an artist experimenting with new musical numbers, and she was simultaneously forced to bear the weight of her husband George Walker's precipitous decline in health. George Walker's gradual onset of dementia and paralysis led his wife to assume the role of her husband's understudy during his illness. Appearing in drag and assuming the role of Bud Jenkins, "a slightly educated and very extravagant colored youth," Overton Walker performed her husband's signature number "Bon Bon Buddy" and moved from the role of a "farmer's daughter" into the full spotlight of the show. Somewhere in the duress of caring for an ailing husband, Walker harnessed the fortitude to brilliantly drag George Walker's dandy character forward in the production.[102] *Bandanna Land* opened the door to what was perhaps Walker's greatest triumph as an entertainer, that of becoming the first black woman to perform the notorious "Salome, the Dance of the Seven Veils."

Through these professional transitions, Walker held fast to a commitment to promoting the social and political utility of black theatre. She also invested in stretching the representational possibilities for black women and the black female body. Indeed, rather than transcending race or gender, as Richard Newman suggests of Walker, the performer used the realm of dance and her costumed body to foreground blackness and female corporeality. In Walker's elegant and skillful routines, she managed to recenter New Negro womanhood in both corporeal and spiritual terms. Thus she developed new ways of imagining the relationship "between the 'material' body and the body in representation" in ways that would break new ground in early-twentieth-century African American *and* feminist performance.[103]

The politics of "diasporic consciousness" and the black female body provide the intersecting ideological framework for Walker's high-profile performances of "Salome." Initially featuring the dance as an addition to *Bandanna Land* in 1908 and later as an exclusive performance at Hammerstein's Victoria Theatre in New York City in 1912, Walker introduced her "veiled lady" into a busy field of black cultural images preoccupied with this icon of "mystic" consciousness. Made manifest figuratively in the literature of Hopkins and Du Bois, as well as visually in the contemporaneous painting of Henry O. Tanner and the sculpture of Meta Warrick Fuller, the mystical "veiled ladies" of New Negro consciousness romantically beckoned their audiences to see their way through the divinely wrought historical challenges of life along the color line. Well-versed in evolving Pan-Africanist cultural imagery and discourse, Walker may have been familiar with two of the period's most visible images of diasporic veiled ladies—Tanner's 1902 *Salome* portrait and Fuller's *Ethiopia Awakening* sculpture. Although not explicitly politically situated, Tanner's *Salome*, for instance, captures the ambiguity of veiled consciousness that Hopkins and Du Bois imagined. Swathed in shimmering, diaphanous gowns, Tanner's heroine sways demurely in the twilight of racial and visual indeterminacy, enticing audiences to see, question, and look into her luminous garments. Tanner's Salome unabashedly dances to the choreography of Du Bois's *Souls*. Moreover, his painting reflects the era's increasing fascination with women's bodies as conduits of black liberation politics and desire at the turn of the century.[104]

Fuller's *Ethiopia Awakening* positions an "Egyptian noblewoman, aroused and emerging from the cloth and papyrus of the dead" as an emblem of romantic Pan-Africanism during this same era. As art historian Richard Powell observers, "this figure, looming from a cocoon-like sculptural base, gave concrete form and signification to the uprooting and resettlement process experienced by blacks in the early twentieth century." Emblazoned with the mark of Salome-like veils that cling to her tightly like a second skin, Fuller's Ethiopia rises gracefully from the shadows with a somnambulistic and self-contained poise. As an early artistic personification of "Mother Africa," Fuller's work, on the one hand, follows cultural convention by feminizing the figurative iconography of mystic Ethiopia. Yet her work also hints at a crucial gender complexity, even while operating within the confines of allegorical convention. With her head turned, eyes closed, and one hand resting evenly on her chest, Fuller's figure radiates satiation and fulfillment while standing on the precipice of transformation. Beyond merely anthropomorphizing the diasporic nation-state, Fuller's and Tanner's works challenge viewers to ponder the complex and often veiled interiority of womanhood in the New Negro era. Their veils speak, then, not just to the "hidden" self of turn-of-the-century black identity forma-tion but to evolving black womanhood specifically as well.[105]

Within this rich cultural context, Walker choreographed her own inter-pretation of a dance that might contribute to the current conversation. In her performance of "Salome," Walker assumes the role of Pan-Africanist medium and narrative agent of black feminist desire. Walker's performance manifests the innovative complexities in turn-of-the-century constructions of the black female body in popular culture. She both signifies on the veil ideology of diasporic consciousness within the context of black musical theatre and ma-nipulates that loaded trope so that it comes to represent at once a suggestion of both the spiritual and the corporeal in relation to New Negro womanhood. In this way, Walker's pioneering performance conjoins and calls attention to Pan-Africanist as well as black feminist ideologies, so that rather than merely "living in the Veil," she dances in it, making the black female body a source of visceral, visible aesthetic agency and desire.[106]

Walker's decision to add the "Salome" dance to *Bandanna Land* in the summer of 1908 was inspired, at least in part, by an evolving musical theatre market obsessed with "Salomania," as the press pegged it. Just a year before the actress debuted her interpretation of the piece on Broadway, choreogra-pher Mademoiselle Dazie was teaching the dance to her fellow Ziegfeld Follies and numerous other professional entertainers. A rush of female performers flooded the vaudeville circuits with the dance. Walker's performance achieved a particular distinction because she was the first African American woman to play the biblical princess. A number of previews and reviews speculated on the authenticity politics of such casting. One critic defended this version of the drama on the grounds that "the original Salome's skin may have been of a hue resembling that of Miss Walker's" (BRT). Observers publicly wrangled over the "race for" Salome, in spite of the notoriously brazen legend of the heroine and her dance which skirted dangerously close to stereotypes of black female sexuality entrenched in fin de siècle American culture.[107]

There was no way for Walker to avoid the sexually charged legend of the role. For the story of Salome's infamous dance and the spectacle of dan-gerously erotic female desire were inherently inscribed in the original biblical narrative. In the gospels of Mark and Matthew, the Salome legend tells the tale of domestic dissolution in the house of King Herod. Herod imprisons John the Baptist for performing "miraculous" acts and for condemning the monarch's decision to wed his brother's wife. Some time later, the King hosts a banquet and birthday celebration with family and friends. Queen Herodias is present, as is her daughter, who dances before the company. Pleased and presumably aroused by the dance, Herod pledges to the girl her heart's desire. In consultation with her mother, the girl requests the head of John the Baptist on a dish. Herod keeps his word and John loses his head. Helen Grace Zagona argues that over the centuries since the tale first appeared in the scriptures, "the figure of Salome took on more immoral aspects," and that "[i]n their disapproval of dancing, the Church fathers used the Salome story as an example of the evils to which this diversion might lead." Salome evolved over several centuries into "an archetype that reflected male desires, fears, and fantasies about women's eroticism spinning out of control," her dance an example of "hystericalized femininity."[108]

Only in the late nineteenth century was the Salome legend revised from a rebellious perspective. Quite famously, Oscar Wilde transformed Salome into a central protagonist, and his interpretation created a space for the lead performer to explore the depths of the title character's "psychology," shifting the energy of the narrative away from prurient heterosexual male desire and toward a roving, open-ended sexual expressiveness rooted in the female performer's potential agency. Out of this spectacle, the dance ushered in a new era wherein "actresses' bodies were understood to have a new license on the stage." But in true Wilde fashion, the playwright extended his adoration of the heroine into a celebration of murderous eroticism and a revelatory deviance. Sexually and hysterically obsessed with John the Baptist, Wilde's Salome orders his execution as a result of her unrequited love and, with a necrophiliac touch, proceeds to fondle and sashay with the decapitated head of her victim. This *Salome*, critics concluded, was not for opera houses but belonged in vaudeville where the dance's "horrible sensuality" could play out in full fruition. This new version also gave a name to Salome's choreography, dubbing her performance the "Dance of the Seven Veils."[109] Although Wilde's iconoclastic version of the tale enjoyed a celebrated run in Paris in 1896, the U.K. had already shut down the production. The play received an even less welcome greeting during a brief run in New York City in the winter of 1907, one year before Aida Overton Walker assumed the role. But it swiftly found an audience downtown in vaudeville houses where the *Salome* craze became, in turn, full blown.[110]

In keeping with this move, the new turn-of-the-century *Salome* productions found wings in various comedic interpretations which pushed the narrative closer to the racial aesthetics of early-twentieth-century vaudeville.

Iconoclastic bohemian performer Eva Tanguay, for instance, notoriously re-cast the *Salome* narrative with racist referents, in which she delivered the head of a "Negro boy" on "a silver tray" in "a bizarre marriage of minstrelsy and sexual parody." A string of blackface burlesque *Salomes* would follow suit in the era of Walker's debut in the role. These minstrel Salomes, as Susan Glenn contends, anxiously responded to "New women and New Negroes" as "women and blacks threatened to act out new social roles."[111]

Walker entered into this charged cultural context and developed her own version of the dance. Clearly her performance had to negotiate the social and cultural exigencies of an era in which "there arose among black women" what historian Evelyn Brooks Higginbotham defines as "a politics of silence" re-garding black female sexuality. Walker's choice to embrace Salome seems a risky and potentially disastrous move—one that some critics fretted might threaten the New Negro movement's careful project of "reconstructing" black and particularly female images in cultural discourse. The dominant, already scripted notions of "deviant" black female sexuality necessitated that "black women, especially those of the middle class, reconstruct and represent their sexuality through its absence—through silence, secrecy, and invisibility."[112] And many in the popular press read Walker's performance as exoticized spec-tacle. One reviewer observed that her "pantherine movements have all the languorous grace which is traditionally bound up with orient dancing," and another remarked that the performance was "funny," describing the way the actress "commenced to send her hands and arms outward in snakelike jerks, meantime pushing up either shoulder with the regulation 'bear' shrug. It was some 'Salome,' boys, and catch it while it's going" (BRT).

Aida Overton Walker, however, intended her act to be anything but light and vacuous "fun." She was serious about choreographing and performing a dance that would showcase aesthetic innovation and that would ideally prove palatable to concert hall audiences. Walker, Glenn argues, "characterized her black Salome as more artistic than erotic, more spiritual than sensational." Yet with Walker's clear interest in elevating black dance to mainstream recogni-tion, it may seem an unpredictable move for her to have first performed "Salome" under the aegis of the Williams and Walker musical *Bandanna Land* on August 27, 1908. A show which featured the comic star duo engaging in a scheme to swindle a street railway company into paying colored people to move *off* a designated piece of land, *Bandanna Land* presented an even more militant and satiric form of black nationalist rhetoric than its progenitor *In Dahomey*. The musical encoded colorful language and signifying song in its otherwise familiar black musical comedy plot arc.[113]

To be sure, it is precisely *Bandanna Land*'s subversive critique of racial socioeconomic politics in America that made it an ideal platform from which Walker could disrupt several conventions. For in *Bandanna Land*, her Salome connects with the rhetoric of black nationalism to emphasize the serious aesthetic complexity of black dance and extends Walker's effort to revise popular constructions of black womenhood on the stage. By breaking the color line in modern dance and performing her own version of Salome, Walker staged her own coup of dominant cultural forms and recentered them in the context of all-black theatrical narrative. Her interpolation of the dance within Williams and Walker's insurgent musical also affirms her consistent interest in complicating representations of black female characterization in musical theatre culture. That is, her veiled lady created yet another alternative image of black women on the stage, and it enabled her to further unseat the grotesque coon song caricatures of black femininity. In a musical comedy concerned with questions of ownership and property, Walker's "Salome" sig-nified on her own claims to ownership of artistry and representation of her own body in dance.[114]

Walker's pioneering efforts, however, were countered by none other than her costar Bert Williams, who appeared alongside the actress in a bizarre "burlesque version" of the act one week after her "Salome" debut. Wrapping himself in gauze and "remov[ing] his oversize shoes for dancing," Williams sashayed across the stage with a coon song watermelon prop on a platter in lieu of the head of John the Baptist. Such spectacles seem to underscore the tensions that Walker's choice to perform modern choreography must have generated within her own theatre company. As Glenn has suggested, neither white nor black men were fully comfortable with the potent sexual economy of the role and thus sought multiple ways to divest Salome dancers of their power. Yet we might go so far as to read Williams's postscript to Walker's dance in an even broader context of black musical comedy in the late nineteenth and early twentieth centuries. The precedent for Wil-liams's minstrel drag of Walker's "Salome" was set in the previous century by the Black Patti Coloured Troubadours. In that company's acts, conceived by white producers Voelckel and Nolan, the grandly imposing opera singer Sis-sieretta Jones was often placed in the second act of a sketch comedy produc-tion rife with ethnic humor and coon song melodies. While Patti shined in her "operatic kaleidescope" concert sequence, she always shared the stage with banjoists, comedians, and acrobats. The blackface humor of comedian "Jolly" John Larkins sometimes garnered as much attention in reviews as did the work of the star prima donna. Within this context, Williams's ludicrous act

23. Aida Overton Walker as Salome. Courtesy of the Billy Rose Theatre Collection, New York Public Library for the Performing Arts, Astor, Lenox and Tilden Foundations.

conjoins with Walker's "respectable" dance to mimic a larger trend in musical theatre that leaned toward circumscribing the efforts of black female artists who dared to push their work outside the conventions of black comedic forms. The public seemingly accepted Walker in black musical comedy, but her attempts to render a classical piece on its own terms at Hammerstein's Victoria Theatre yielded more critical ambivalence. For these reasons, Glenn concludes that Walker was "unable to transcend the categories to which black performers had been consigned."[115]

Although Glenn rightly points out that white audiences had difficulty "appreciat[ing] black performers outside of certain racially specific entertainment contexts," her reading of Walker's work is perhaps limited by its relation to white audiences. We might do well to reconsider the extent of Walker's "Salome" performances in relation to the specific cultural and political intent that the actress espoused throughout her career. Indeed, as Walker was openly aligned with black uplift and women's era social and political agendas, it is critical to imagine the performer's lifelong dedication to creating art by and for black people, as her husband had similarly proclaimed in a *New York Age* article published in 1908. In this regard, Walker did not, then, just use "Salome" "to try to transcend her identifications with race comedy." Rather, her work was clearly in dialogue with racial uplift, black nationalist, and black women's cultural discourses of the period.

Beyond performing "grace," "propriety," and "classical art," Walker's "Salome," I argue, engages metaphorically and physically with contemporaneous images of black veiled ladies. Like Tanner's liminal heroine, she moves between multiple worlds—from black musicals to uptown concert halls—in order to rehistoricize her flesh. Like Fuller's quiet icon, she emerges poised in self-reflection while spinning in the veil. More still, Walker's interpretation of this dance allows her to absorb and reinterpret Salome's legacy of desire, corporeal expression, and rebellious female vision, thus conjoining her potent legend with that of postbellum New Negro womanhood. Signifying on the politics of black female visibility and the potential for sensual figuration in movement, Walker's "Salome" centralizes the movement of the black female body in dance to choreograph the unspeakable language of black female erotic energy. If she cannot, in this era, make black female sexuality explicitly audible or visible, nonetheless, in similar ways to her nineteenth-century forbear Sojourner Truth, she most surely uses the dance to articulate a complex corporeal presence, abstruse, elegant, and mysterious as opposed to putatively transparent, coarse, and vulnerable. Unlike any other black female dancing body that had come before, Walker dons Salome's veils to chart new territory for black women in performance, and she makes visible the opacities of black women's histories in America. In doing so, her work exposes the "theatrical roots" of black feminist thought and activism at the turn of the century.[116] By reconsidering a methodological approach to reading the dance and Walker's performative strategies, and by further placing the trope of the veil in a black *and* feminist context, we can more fully comprehend the political and cultural significances of Walker's distinctly African American "Salome."

Although the "veiled lady" icon of mid-nineteenth-century culture was a "pallid, fragile-appearing" creature, "unvoluptuous, unrobust," and "unproductive," Walker's "Salome" emerged in 1908 adorned in ornate garments and radiating with physical energy. Swathed in flowing and "bespangled" robes and crowned with a sparkling tiara, her enchanting figure commanded the spectator's gaze. Lavishly costumed, Walker nonetheless faced a nightly unveiling by those critics who insisted on reading the imagined visibility of her (racial and sexual) body beneath the garments. While some critics marveled over Walker's "modest" dancing, they also occasionally took it on themselves to subtly strip the performer in print. One review alluded to "the bronze tights nature placed upon her, covered here and there with shields of brilliants and a dark blue, bejeweled curtain effect in the way of a skirt" (BRT). With her "bronzeness" already visible and presumably available to the leering spectator, Walker danced directly into the spotlight of the spectacular female corporeal in "Salome." As a performance predicated on the act of corporeal revealing, the dance inevitably flirted with the politics of the male gaze and female sexuality made open and available. Thus Walker, an African American woman committed to black women's uplift politics, confronted head-on questions of racial, gender, and sexual representation and autonomy as she assumed this controversial role. As a black female cultural producer clearly aware of the "metalanguage" of postbellum racial and gender categories, Walker would, then, have to confront her own potential hypervisibility in the Salome role, as well as the veil's metaphorical economy of female sexuality, penetration, and the reaffirmation of the potent phallus.[117]

A dance evolving out of the imperialist allure of "the Orient," "Salome" invites the dominance of the colonial gaze that circulates obsessively around disrobing and fetishizing the veiled female figure. In this context of lucrative imperial popular culture, the Salome dance craze of Walker's era evolved out of late-nineteenth-century spectacles such as that of the dancer "Little Egypt" at Chicago's 1893 World Fair. Subsequent Salome cultural mutations kept the dance closely aligned with imperialist and colonialist legacies.[118] As Malek Alloula demonstrates in his study of the colonial harem and the cultural commodification of Algerian women, the veil, the idealized and clichéd colonial garment, is only worn to be removed, to be co-opted as an instrument spectacularizing the act of *un*covering. Alloula contends that the veil, a shroud of "opacity," represents a specular failure. Refusing to be seen/scene, the veiled woman, thus, ostensibly invites her own ravishment at the hands of the male spectator who initially experiences "*disappointment and rejection.* Draped in the veil that cloaks her to her ankles, the Algerian woman discourages the *scopic desire.*"[119] In spite of this thick, violating gaze, there is a way to read Aida Overton Walker's "Salome" as confounding the discourse of this imperialist scenario. Despite the fact that critics attempted to impose or completely drain her performance of its resistant meaning, it is possible to trace the ways that the veiled dancer supplied her own disruptive form of representation to counter colonizing projects.[120] By eschewing the conventions of the imminent striptease spectacle, and by engaging in a crucial form of material (re)covering through her act, Walker's dancing heroine works to reveal a culturally and politically rich body in dance.

Like her pre–Civil War actress forebear Adah Isaacs Menken, Aida Overton Walker manipulated notions of corporeal authenticity in her stage costume.[121] No doubt Walker's work as a choreographer and a dancer extended this project by invoking diverse performative strategies which transformed the politics of the dance as well as her body into lively sites of corporeal reinvention. One Boston review of her "Salome" dance in particular conveys the extent to which Walker challenged conventional representation of the black and female body:

> She gives an original conception of the role, which differs in many respects from that of the other dancers who are appearing in New York. She does not handle the gruesome head, she does not rely solely upon the movements of the body, and her dress is not quite so conspicuous by its absence.
>
> Miss Walker's costume will consist of a full covering for the body and limbs, except bare feet and shoulders. One phase of her art is notable in the fact that she acts the role of "Salome" as well as dances it. Her face is unusually mobile and she expresses through its muscles the emotions which the body is also interpreting, thus making the character of the biblical dancer lifelike.
>
> The poetry of motion is exemplified in this dance by Miss Walker, and she shows as well the passion and emotion which must have consumed "Salome's" body and soul when she realized the awful price she has demanded. (BRT)

The absence of the "gruesome head" works immediately in the service of recentering the spectator's focus on the dancer. Her "bare" feet invite the spectator's gaze but they also shift the visual fulcrum of the dance to its physical and organic foundations, to the core of Walker's performative enactment. The body does not merely move but its execution works in the service of Walker's specific narrative interpretation. The critic observes Walker's efforts to exert her abilities as an actress who is visibly invested in revivifying the Salome figure and steeping her in "passion," "emotion," and psychological depth. Muscles shift and alter exterior surfaces to convey an interiority of character which the dancer, herself, authors. Her movements yield a kind of poetic motion which, to this reviewer, transcend the sensationalism of the narrative to inform the character of Salome with a mediated subjectivity of both body and soul.

Read in this way, Walker's heroine mounts a form of resistance to what dance theorist Susan Leigh Foster observes as the historical evolution in late-eighteenth- and early-nineteenth-century Western dance wherein dancing bodies became "no-bodies." Foster argues that this aesthetic and theoretical movement resulted in a "mastery over bodily display" which "signaled an entirely new relationship between body and self, one that dismissed the body as an intersubjective discursive field." Walker's "Salome," thus, transformed the subjectless, dancing female body into a stylized figure who was narrated by the dancer herself. Her interpretation of the dance deftly negotiated the problem which Foster identifies in the narrative effacement of bodies which threatened to "gestur[e] a vacant physicality and a stereotypic interiority." Her performance referenced discourses outside of the dominant Salome legend to reinvent the narrative itself.[122]

Black critics such as Lester Walton were, however, not easily impressed by Walker's act. Calling her performance "pretentious" and misguided, Walton argued that Walker's interpretation misread the iconography of Salome entirely. By "clean[ing]" up the dance and ridding it of its "suggestiveness," Walker had, according to Walton, failed to fulfill the very essence of the Salome legend. She had fallen short of delivering the original thematic focus of the narrative. From Walton's viewpoint, Walker had also eviscerated the dance of its sinuous body charms, choosing instead to emphasize the character by way of facial expression which, he observes, "gave a more intelligent exhibition of the dance than her body." Finally, and perhaps most critically, Walton chastised Walker for seemingly abandoning black cultural expression and by failing to "originat[e] something peculiar to ourselves." Walton's review registers a disappointment in Walker's decision to experiment with European cultural forms, and he ominously forecasts that "it is doubtful if any colored artist will make a sensation in a dance created by a white performer." For "they will never startle the world." At the root of Walton's hostility toward Walker's "Salome" was his bitter frustration that "one of the most graceful dancers" apparently had aimed to interpret and thereby promote art outside black autonomous circles.[123]

What Walton himself perhaps overlooked was the extent to which Walker was indeed creating a new strategy of African American theatrical performance by way of her "Salome." Combining the ethos of classical dance's emphasis on the spiritual with modern dance's focus on the material body, Walker cleared a space for black women's modern dance that melded the ideals of both forms. With her sublimely elegant and anti-"suggestive" dance, she invoked the "ethereal presence" of classical ballet's iconography replete with "fairies, swans," and "innocent peasant girls." To be sure, Walker's "Salome" may have referenced the "strangely disembodied female" of this particular genre. Yet simultaneously she rooted herself in the modern repertoire's thematic emphasis on strong female characters. If she was said to have emphasized her torso movements less, she nonetheless utilized the Salome role to open up the interiority of her black female heroine through a humanized relationship between facial expression and attending body movements. As Foster reminds us, in the modern dance revolutionized by Walker contemporary Isadora Duncan, the "actual shape of the limbs is less important than the degree of involvement in the dance, evident in the face, the quality of the movement, and the graceful connections among areas of the body." She gives "weight" to her body by instilling it with the character born out of her stylized expressions.[124]

Walker was thus inventing a new representational lexicon for herself as a black female dancer. Yet in reading her dance as mediating intersecting cultural tropes and ideologies, I am also arguing for a way to examine her performance not from the position of the critic who privileges tracing the spectator's desire to see. Rather, I am suggesting that in reading Walker's work, we must focus instead on acknowledging what only the Salome dancer holds and *knows* behind and within the veil. The challenge is to "mak[e] the female body visible in contradistinction to its patriarchal invention," to make the black and female body labor not for the spectator but for the dancer herself and her own social and political desires. In an effort to "comprehend the impact of the dancing body as it performed . . . in its historical time," I draw from Foster's efforts to "situate it alongside other contemporaneous bodies engaged in related cultural endeavors." Rather than dancing the seven veils alone, Walker's Salome performs in conversation with Pan-Africanist as well as black feminist discourses to ultimately re-imagine the cultural territory of the black female body at the turn of the century.[125]

As a dance that depended on the veil as a central metaphorical instrument, "Salome" theatricalized a trope deeply aligned with both sexual as well as racial signifiers in the early 1900s. A phantasmatic space, a "blind spot," the veil would resonate at the turn of the century and in the dominant pop cultural imaginary as a site marking the "sexual and epistemological discovery" of the female body.[126] Yet during this same period, the veil continued to evolve in philosophical and political subculture as a symbol of racial consciousness and transnational alliances. For black nationalist cultural workers such as Hopkins and Du Bois, the mystic trope manifested a diasporic frontier where black identity might assert an insurgent epistemology by embracing the power of black alterity in its own right. By "living in the Veil," the black veiled subject possessed a transglobal "soul" that reconnected her figure across space and time. In this era of conflicted discourses of the veil which asserted its power as a colonial instrument as well as a radical expression of resistant black identity, Walker's "Salome" would have to create an alternative way to dance. She would have to forge a different path from that of Loie Fuller, who famously interpreted the dance at the 1900 World's Fair in Paris and "removed the veil dance from any specific sense of geography" detaching it "from any specific country." Instead, Walker's Salome dances in lyrical conversation with social, historical, and cultural movements, signifying on the symbolic and philosophical iconography of Du Bois- and Hopkins-imagined black nationhood as well as black female corporeal subjectivity. As the first black Salome onstage, Walker, a black entertainer committed to uplift ideology, effectively inhabited and re-historicized this infamous character so that she might dance along the axis of diasporic consciousness with other black veiled icons of the period.[127]

In its symbolic value alone, Walker's dance resoundingly complicates questions of racial and gender presence and absence in turn-of-the-century popular culture. A spectacularly visible opacity, her "Salome" depends on the ideological liminality bound up in veil tropes, richly creating a new path for black women's performative agency. In the veil, where "what is disclosed is what is concealed," Walker's dance clears a space for alternative representations of the black female body. No longer putatively open, available, transparent, nakedly on display, this body dances opaquely on the borders of the visible and the visually indeterminate. Walker's Salome thus conjures a figurative economy of representational freedom for black female cultural workers who might imagine a way both to break free of the bonds of self-imposed corporeal silence and to reject abject forms of sexual expression. Her ambiguous covering in this dance threatens to turn on its head the confession of race as well as sexuality that is, as Foucault reminds us, fundamental to policing the knowledge of the body. Her veil here eludes a mere exposure of the "truth" of sexual, racial, and gendered presence. Instead of calling attention to "the fascination of seeing it and telling it, of captivating and capturing it . . . luring it out in the open" and making that "truth" an object of surveillance, this veil might, in fact, resist representational disclosure. Adorning her body in the lineaments of theatrical experimentation, Walker thus choreographs uncharted territory for black women in performance by evading dominant culture's impulse to "capture" and fix black female bodies in the void of stillness. Her dance of the seven veils becomes the means by which the liminal realm of presence and absence opens up new representational possibilities for African American women in early-twentieth-century culture.[128]

Black female sexuality remained the most complicated subtext in Walker's grand dance. As Krasner sees it, Walker both "hi[d] her sexuality . . . casting off the visibility of her body," and simultaneously "emphasized the sensual and exotic." There is perhaps still more, however, wrapped within the veil of her dance if we dare to consider the sexual metaphors that Walker's performance signified on with choreographic grace. By playing with the visibility and invisibility of the black female body in dance, her work draws an important parallel to the socially and culturally unspeakable: the expression of (black) female sexual desire so closely aligned with Salome. In this era of black women's "silence, secrecy, and a partially self-chosen invisibility," Walker dared to dance a metaphor of female sexual *will*. If, as black feminist critics have clearly demonstrated, black female sexuality has historically been "rendered simultaneously invisible, visible (exposed), hypervisible, and pathologized by dominant discourses," Walker rechoreographed a dance in which she manipulated her own visibility, inherited the language of sexual desire in dance, and confronted, in aesthetic terms, the problem of representing the subjectivity of her body in the cultural imaginary. Rather than repeating a narrative of "silence and secrecy" in relation to her body, she turned the dilemma of present absence and absent presence into a one-woman display of her own masterful control, direction, and vision of her body in motion. What Walker's dance finally celebrates, then, is the kind of "pleasure, exploration, and agency" that, Evelynn Hammonds argues, "have gone underanalyzed" in American culture.[129]

Rejecting the striptease in favor of a "poetic" manipulation of her garments, Walker is both present and absent in her body on stage. The black and female figure in "Salome" is not eradicated. Indeed, Walker's performance necessitates the centrality of the material. Yet her use of the veil also suggests a narrative agency over her body and an insistence on withholding its representation. This negotiation anticipates the discursive strategies of black feminist cultural producers who came after her. Madhu DuBey reveals, for instance, the ways in which contemporary black feminist writers such as Toni Morrison and Gayle Jones "construct character around lack, division, and mutilation" and yet "always retain the notion of a whole and unified self as an unrepresentable, imaginary ideal. The figuration of identity in these novels, then, may best be understood as a contradictory interplay between presence and absence, wholeness and fracture."[130] Somewhere between "wholeness" and allusive (illusive) "fragmentation," Walker's "Salome" refuses to capitulate to a total repressive silencing of the black female body, as was so characteristic a gesture of her contemporaries. Instead, it inserts corporeality into public consciousness through a spectacle of narrative agency and as a space in the margins of representation, mediated by the African American and female cultural producer who is, in this dance, perhaps not alone after all.[131]

When the German composer Richard Strauss first encountered Oscar Wilde's radically reworked biblical daughter, he adopted the play in the libretto for his next opera and "fantasized" that his lead "would display the voice of a Wagnerian heroine and the body of a ballerina. . . . The resolution of these disparate requirements gave birth to the tradition of having a dancer perform the Dance of the Seven Veils." As Toni Bentley concludes, the "subsequent Salome craze owes everything to this two-person solution. *Salome* the dance was born, of necessity," she argues, "from Salome the soprano, and her subsequent life as a visual icon soon competed with her life as aural heroine." Somewhere in the veil, Hopkins's soprano and Walker's dancing princess were meant to meet in song and in dance, creating space for African American female subjects to move, to improvise and become.[132] Two brave heroines emerging from the cultural margins, they might find a way to collaborate rather than to compete. They might in fact discover the room to revel in the choreography of the veil, a symbol which remains dependent on its "insurmountable opacity" and which, to be sure, enables new aesthetic expression and agency for the black female performer. "A dense and full place in space," this "black hole," to borrow Hammonds's eloquent (re)formulation, demands "a different geometry," a new rich logic to theorize its remarkably deep, wondrous, and long-eclipsed dimensions.[133] Together, in the fold of a luminous garment, in the darkness of the veil, they dance and sing their bodies into a new century.

# EPILOGUE

*Theatre, Black Women, and Change*

On a cool and overcast spring evening, some one hundred years after Pauline Elizabeth Hopkins was ousted from her editorial position at the *Colored American Magazine* in 1904, a new wave of black female artists elegantly stormed the barricades of theatre culture.[1] June 6, 2004, marked history in the making as three prizes in major acting categories for women were handed to black actresses at Broadway's Tony Awards. Within the first hour of the program, the youthful Anika Noni Rose had swooped onstage to take the evening's first statuette for her vaunting Broadway debut as the rebellious Emmie Thibodeaux in the musical *Caroline, or Change*. Tearfully, Rose accepted the award and expressed her thanks for her "gift of voice" and the love and support of cast and family. Soon after, luminous theatre darling Audra McDonald received her fourth Tony at the age of thirty-three for her cerebral portrayal of Ruth Younger in the smash-hit revival of Lorraine Hansberry's classic *A Raisin in the Sun*. "Broadway," McDonald rightly acknowledged in her speech, "has been so kind to me." She closed her remarks by emphatically reminding the audience that her award "*belongs* to Lorraine Hansberry," the "brilliant," "prescient," and "legendary" playwright.[2]

Finally Phylicia Rashad broke barriers as the first African American actress to win a Tony for a lead role in a play. As the matriarch Lena Younger in the revival of Hansberry's drama, Rashad brought a renewed and textured wisdom, grace, and wit to the classic role. With a hushed eloquence, the veteran actress confessed:

> I wondered, what does it take for this to happen? And now I know it takes effort and grace . . . tremendous self effort and amazing grace. And in my life that grace has taken numerous forms. The first was the family into which I was born. Parents who loved and wanted me. And a mother who fought fearlessly, courageously, consistently so that her children above

all else could realize their full potential as human beings. Teachers who wanted to be teachers. Art all my life. A brilliant play. A magnificent role. A producer with a vision, heart. And a director who *dares to see me as an artist* capable of many things.[3]

Although some critics chastised Rashad for having delivered a speech with scant overt political content, the contrary could easily be said of her remarks. Indeed, in a stirring description of her network of support and the nurturing that she received as an actress, Rashad delivered one of the most subversive statements of the evening by referencing the historic significance of recognizing her worth *as* a creative force in theatre. Subtly critical of an entertainment industry unwilling to acknowledge and reward black women's artistry, Rashad's speech paid tribute to the director Kenny Leon's skill and vision in recognizing her craft as an actress. That night at Radio City Music Hall, the African American female artist commanded center stage.

In fact, black women were everywhere on Tony night 2004. The three award winners were joined in the audience by fellow nominees Sanaa Lathan (up for her whimsical performance as the ingenue Beneatha Younger in *A Raisin in the Sun*) and Tonya Pinkins, who lost in the night's fiercest competition, that of lead actress in a musical category (despite receiving rapturous reviews for her portrayal of the title character in Tony Kushner's and George C. Wolfe's pathbreaking *Caroline, or Change*). On the stage (and perhaps inexplicably), the R&B pop diva songstress Mary J. Blige delivered a melisma-inflected version of "What I Did for Love," the classic ballad from *A Chorus Line*, reminding the audience of hip-hop music's cultural reign outside the bounds of Broadway. Even the veteran entertainer Carol Channing, having in recent years revealed her own African American familial genealogy, appeared in a confounding yet charmingly improvised song and rap number with recording-artist-turned-actor LL Cool J.[4]

Yet for all of the joy and multicultural conviviality bubbling throughout the program, a subtle yet insidious backlash was in the air that night as well. In what was deemed an upset of enormous proportions, the youthfully driven musical *Avenue Q* captured an astonishing five awards, including 2004's Tony for best musical. Written and produced by a band of heavily hyped, twenty- and thirty-something theatre upstarts, *Avenue Q* was, despite having garnered strong reviews, considered a long shot to win any major awards. That evening, when the show's exuberant, fresh-faced writers and crew dashed to the stage to accept their award, a new take on an old-fashioned trend announced its prominence in theatre. *Avenue Q*'s critical and box-office success reminded the theatre world of the persistently marketable and ever-seductive appeal of minstrel culture at the dawn of the twenty-first century.[5]

Billed as a fast-moving, Gen X "puppet musical," *Avenue Q* transforms blackface costuming into ersatz Muppet characters who swap witty, satirical barbs about race, gender, class, and sexuality on the front stoops of their New York City apartment buildings. Called by some a "mix of *Rent* and *Sesame Street*," the musical nonetheless retains little of the progressive, multicultural politics of either of those landmark shows.[6] Rather, *Avenue Q* showcases an acerbic array of hackneyed racial, gender, and sexual caricatures, from an Asian neighbor wrestling with broken English to a black actress enlisted to play an out-of-work "Gary Coleman," the child television star. Couching its contemptuous rhetoric in putatively sardonic musical numbers such as the egregiously insouciant "Everyone's a Little Bit Racist," *Avenue Q* marks the resurgent popularity of minstrel performance in the form of innocuous puppeteers.

Trading burnt cork for felt marionettes, the musical documents an even broader trend in Generation X popular culture. Raised in the wake of the Civil Rights movement and in the midst of educational integration and popular culture's visible efforts to diversify, a new crop of young artists and producers, fed on *Sesame Street* and *Fat Albert*, *Zoom* and the *Electric Company*, has risen to prominence in the world of theatre, film, television, and music. In this changing cultural universe, a new and subtle sardonic racism, the product of Gen X irony crossed with savvy multicultural education, has reared its ugly head in the works of filmmakers such as Wes Anderson and in pop music's ever-envelope-pushing world of MTV videos. Emerging out of this uniquely ambiguous moment in time, *Avenue Q* presciently announced in its print advertisements the week of the Tonys that "America's Counting on Q!" Counting, indeed. That the musical created such a stir at the awards show reminded anyone and all that racial and gender power struggles were and still are very much underway in contemporary theatre culture.[7]

How subversively serendipitous that the woman who rose up midway through the Tony program to sing a searing protest number appeared in the guise of a character grappling with civil rights, social, political, and personal change. Delivering an intervention, a rallying cry, a glimmer of hope, the brilliant and commanding best actress nominee Tonya Pinkins erupted onto the stage to perform her breathtaking solo performance of "Lot's Wife" from the unconventional Civil Rights musical *Caroline*. Called a "spiritualist" and a "diva" by *Time Out New York*, Pinkins had already enchanted audiences at the downtown Public Theatre before taking the role to Broadway. One of the most complex and challenging black female characters ever brought to the Broadway stage, Pinkins's Caroline was a force with which to be reckoned. In her magnificent and unsentimental portrayal of an African American woman working as a domestic employee in 1963 Louisiana, Pinkins's "soon-to-be-legendary" interpretation of the role gave Broadway its newest, richest, and most densely textured representation of a black female character.[8]

In her Tony Awards show performance, Pinkins compressed and delivered all the smoldering intensity, rage, bitterness, discontent, and tender longing that she had originally instilled in her character. We might think of her performance as palimpsested and metatextual, as one in which she balanced the constrictions and resistant acts of her revisionist "Mammy" role with that of her critically acclaimed power as a resilient musical theatre actress at the peak of her career. With a voice that climbed to emotional highs and swooped to wrenching lows, croaking in despair, soaring in hopefulness, and pulsating with palpable, aching sorrow, Pinkins held the concert hall's attention and delivered Kushner's searing lyrics with vigor and passion:

> I can't hardly read.
> Some folks do all kinds of things and
> black folks someday live like kings
> and someday sunshine shine all day!
> Oh sure it true
> it be that way
> but not for me—
> This also true:
> ya'll can't do what I can do
> ya'll strong but you ain't strong like me:
>
> I'm gonna slam that iron
> down on my heart
> gonna slam that iron
> down on my throat
> gonna slam that iron
> down on my sex
> gonna slam it
> slam it
> slam it down
> until I drown
> the fire out
> till there ain't no air left
> anywhere.

What else
what else
what else
what else God
what else God give me an arm for?

SLAM go the iron
SLAM go the iron
FLAT!
FLAT!
FLAT!
FLAT!

Now how bout that then?
That what Caroline can do!
That how she rearrange herself,
that how she change!

Murder me God down in that basement,
murder my dreams so I stop wantin,
murder my hope of him returnin,
strangle the pride that make me crazy.
Make me forget so I stop grievin.
Scour my skin till I stop feelin.
Take Caroline away cause I can't be her,
take her away I can't afford her.
Tear out my heart
strangle my soul
turn me to salt
a pillar of salt
a broken stone and then . . .

Caroline. Caroline.

From the evil she done, Lord,
set her free
set her free

set me free.

Don't let my sorrow
make evil of me.[9]

Transitioning out of and transforming the economy of her own "sorrow" song, Pinkins's heartbreaking solo punctured the complacency of high Broadway gloss. Ripping through the auditorium like a sonic boom and making audible the palpable fears and desires of a black female protagonist, Pinkins sang a song of liberation *for* and *as* her character Caroline and raged against the machine of a glib, self-congratulatory evening of theatre-world kudos and elite celebration. That night, black women once more brought change to theatre and found a way through performance to set themselves free.

# NOTES

## Introduction

1 William Wells Brown, *The Escape*, 37–60.

2 Ibid., 56–57.

3 Orlando Patterson, *Slavery and Social Death*.

4 Du Bois, *The Souls of Black Folk*.

5 Spillers, "Mama's Baby, Papa's Maybe," 257–79. Spillers argues that the mythically rendered black body operates as a signifier that "has *no movement in a field of signification*" (259, emphasis added).

6 Du Bois, *Souls*, 5. Elin Diamond, *Unmaking Mimesis*, 52. Bertolt Brecht, "Alienation Effects in Chinese Acting," "A Short Organum for the Theatre," in Willett, *Brecht on Theatre*. It should be noted that there are many distinctions I am drawing between Afro-alienation acts and Brechtian alienation-effects. For instance, unlike Brecht, who imagined that audiences might indeed "awaken" to history through gestic performance in theatre, I presume in my work that most audiences were less willing to recognize the ways that black cultural producers negotiated identity polyvalence in performance. Nineteenth-century dominant spectators were less inclined to read the ways that these figures were critically complicating perceptions of race and gender by way of performance.

7 Diamond reminds us that "demystifying representation, showing how and when the object of pleasure is made, releasing the spectator from imaginary and illusory identifications—these are crucial elements in Brecht's theoretical project" (*Unmaking Mimesis*, 44); Herman Gray, *Cultural Moves*; Hartman, *Scenes of Subjection*. See also Paul Gilroy, "To Be Real"; Fred Moten, *In the Break*; Eric Lott, *Love and Theft*.

8 Carla Peterson, "Foreword: Eccentric Bodies," xi–xii; emphasis added. Robin D. G. Kelley, *Freedom Dreams*; Stuart Hall, "What Is This 'Black' in Black Popular Culture?," 32.

9 Gilroy, *The Black Atlantic*; Joseph Roach, *Cities of the Dead*; Hartman, *Scenes of Subjection*; Jennifer Brody, *Impossible Purities*; Lott, *Love and Theft*; David Krasner, *Resistance*; Eric Sundquist, *To Wake the Nations*; Carla Peterson, "*Doers of the Word*."

10 Earl Lewis, "To Turn as on a Pivot," 767, 783. Sundquist, *To Wake the Nations*, 570–72.

11 Lindon Barrett, *Blackness and Value*, 61.

12 Michael Bennett and Vanessa Dickerson, eds., *Recovering the Black Female Body*; Kimberley Wallace-Sauders, ed., *Skin Deep, Spirit Strong*; Willis, *The Black Female Body in American Culture*; Deborah McDowell, "Recycling," 253; Valerie Smith, "Black Feminist Theory," 45. Ann duCille takes to task the problem of black women's persistent role in contemporary academic discourse as "infinitely deconstructable 'othered' matter" in "The Occult of True Blackwomanhood," 70. See also Margaret Homans, " 'Women of Color' Writers and Feminist Theory," 87.

13 Hartman, *Scenes of Subjection*, 36. Hartman declares that her "task is neither to unearth the definitive meaning of song or dance nor to read song as an expression of black character as was common among nineteenth-century ethnographers but to give full weight to the opacity of these texts wrought by toil, terror, and sorrow and composed under the whip and in fleeting moments of reprieve" (36). My use of the term "opacity" here differs somewhat from the Irigarian theory that "women represent the sex that cannot be thought, a linguistic absence and opacity" (Judith Butler, *Gender Trouble*, 9). Rather than arguing for representational absence, I am instead suggesting that "opacity" in this context characterizes a kind of performance rooted in a layering and creating a palimpsest of meanings and representations. From this standpoint, "opacity" is never an absence but is always a present reminder of black feminist agency and the complex body in performance.

14 Robert Allen, *Horrible Prettiness*, 25–42.

15 Hartman, *Scenes of Subjection*, 10–11. Diana Taylor contends that "the archival, from the beginning, sustains power" (*The Archive and the Repertoire*, 18).

16 Following Kristina Straub's lead, I am interested in considering the gaze as a constantly shifting object of struggle, "not the product of a stable position, a clearly defined and unchanging 'place' or subjectivity . . . not the inherent right of some monolithic *Masculinity*" (Straub, *Sexual Suspects*, 15, 18).

17 I borrow the formulation "fugitive bodies" from Bill Lowe. Pauline Hopkins, *Peculiar Sam*.

## 1. Our Bodies, Our/Selves

1 Hiram Mattison, *Spirit Rapping Unveiled!*, 81, 3–4. Future references to this text will be cited parenthetically as *SRU*. The spiritualist medium seems here akin to the "Africanist character" who functions, as Toni Morrison observes, like a "surrogate and enabler" for an "imaginative encounter" between seeming polar opposites (*Playing in the Dark*); Russ Castronovo, *Necro Citizenship*, 125.

2 Jennifer Brody, *Impossible Purities*, 4–12. Future references to Brody's text will be cited parenthetically unless otherwise noted.

3 Nancy A. Hewitt, *Women's Activism and Social Change*, 140. On the rise of the spiritualism movement in America, see Barbara Goldsmith, *Other Powers*; Bar-

bara Weisberg, *Talking to the Dead*; Howard Kerr, *Mediums, and Spirit-Rappers and Roaring Radicals*; Earl Wesley Fornell, *The Unhappy Medium*; R. Laurence Moore, *In Search of White Crows*.

4 Terry Castle, "Phantasmagoria," 27; Richard D. Altick, *Shows of London*, 217–19.

5 Castle, "Phantasmagoria," 27–36. Altick, *Shows of London*, 217.

6 Jon Butler, "The Dark Ages of American Occultism," 74; Brett Carroll, *Spiritualism in Antebellum America*. New work by Gabrielle Foreman and Reginald Pitts suggests otherwise. While unearthing the past of Harriet Wilson, Foreman and Pitts discovered Wilson's involvement in spiritualism as a popular, midcentury "colored medium" who lectured and traveled in concert with several other successful African American spiritualists. See P. Gabrielle Foreman and Reginald Pitts, introduction to *Our Nig* by Harriet Wilson.

7 Joseph Roach, *Cities of the Dead*, 208–9.

8 Morrison, "Romancing the Shadow," *Playing in the Dark*, 37; Castle, "Phantasmagoria," 50; Diana Paulin, "Representing Forbidden Desire," 417. My thanks to the Duke University Press readers for suggesting the formulation of "African ways of remembering" to me.

9 Ann Braude, *Radical Spirits*, 60–76, 57. See also Goldsmith, *Other Powers*.

10 Braude, *Radical Spirits*, 73; Moore, *In Search of White Crows*, 70–101; Goldsmith, *Other Powers*, 29–83; Kerr, *Mediums, and Spirit-Rappers*, 10–11; Hartman, *Scenes of Subjection*, 3–14.

11 Braude, *Radical Spirits*, 28. Hewitt, *Women's Activism*, 142, 169; Goldsmith, *Other Powers*, 31–32.

12 Bret Carroll, *Spiritualism in Antebellum America*.

13 Judith Walkowitz, *City of Dreadful Delight*; Alex Owen, *The Darkened Room*; Goldsmith, *Other Powers*.

14 Moore, *In Search of White Crows*, 115; Mattison, *SRU*, 58. Nathaniel Hawthorne's notoriously duplicitous narrator Coverdale engages in a protracted struggle with suffragists and veiled ladies in the author's Brook Farm parody *The Blithedale Romance* (1851).

15 Braude, *Radical Spirits*, 29; Castronovo, *Necro Citizenship*, 159–68.

16 The estimate is Mattison's own, although Williamson (*New People*, 63) points out that the 1860 census suggests that this total may have been at least 100,000 greater.

17 Hiram Mattison, *Louisa Picquet, the Octoroon*, 5.

18 P. Gabrielle Foreman, " 'Who's Your Mama?' " 505–39; Castronovo, *Necro Citizenship*, 176–83.

19 Williamson, *New People*, 75.

20 Straub, *Sexual Suspects*, 5–6, 8; William Craft, *Running a Thousand Miles for Freedom*, 271–72; Barbara McKaskill, introduction to *Running a Thousand Miles for Freedom*. See also Barbara Christian, *Black Women Novelists*; and Hazel Carby, *Reconstructing Womanhood*.

21 Mattison, *Louisa Picquet*, 12, 15.

22 Mattison, *Louisa Picquet*, 6; Brody, *Impossible Purities*, 49.

23 Hortense Spillers, "Notes on an Alternative Model," 178; Roach, *Cities of the Dead*, 193.

24 Foreman, " 'Who's Your Mama?' " 3, 10.

25 Mattison, *Louisa Picquet*, 51.

26 Rogin as quoted in Eric Lott, *Love and Theft*, 9. Future references to Lott's text will be cited parenthetically unless otherwise noted.

27 Robert C. Allen, *Horrible Prettiness*, 58; Rosemarie Garland Thomson, *Freakery*, 11. See also Mark Seltzer, *Bodies and Machines*.

28 Auerbach, *Private Theatricals*, 4; Booth, *Victorian Spectacular Theatre*, 74.

29 Booth, *Victorian Spectacular Theatre*, 74; Gerald Frow, *Oh, Yes It Is!*

30 Edwin M. Eigner, *Dickens Pantomime*, 42; Auerbach, *Private Theatricals*, 14.

31 Auerbach, *Private Theatricals*, 8, 3–18; Altick, *Shows of London*, 219.

32 Auerbach, *Private Theatricals*, 77.

33 Allen, *Horrible Prettiness*, 29; Myron Matlaw, "Preface to *The Black Crook*," 320. See Allen, *Horrible Prettiness*, 108–17; David Ewen, *Complete Book of the American Musical Theater*, 348, 347.

34 Booth, *Victorian Spectacular Theatre*, 74. This was a style confined largely to the early pantomimes, known as Harlequins. See also Frow, *Oh, Yes It Is!* 38–47.

35 Matlaw, "Preface to *The Black Crook*," 321; Gary Engle, *This Grotesque Essence*, 123; Allen, *Horrible Prettiness*, 121–78. Robert Toll argues (*Blacking Up*, 135) that following the success of *The Black Crook*, minstrel productions evolved into "lavishly produced musical comedies featuring partially undraped women" and employing "spectacular staging" techniques; also see Engle, *This Grotesque Essence*, 41.

36 Toll, *Blacking Up*; Lott, *Love and Theft*; W. T. Lhamon Jr., *Raising Cain*.

37 Toll, *Blacking Up*, 40 (Toll also reveals how minstrel performers occasionally mounted productions which featured onstage progressions from white to blackface, 67; see also 38–40); Hartman, *Scenes of Subjection*, 30–32; Diamond, *Unmaking Mimesis*, 48–49.

38 Hartman, *Scenes of Subjection*, 30–31. Future references to Hartman's text will be cited parenthetically unless otherwise noted.

39 Toll, *Blacking Up*; Lhamon, *Raising Cain*, 32.

40 Eigner, *Dickens Pantomime*, 47.

41 Lhamon, *Raising Cain*, 45; Gillian Brown, *Domestic Individualism*, 42–43; William J. Mahar, "Ethiopian Skits and Sketches," 193.

42 Lhamon, *Raising Cain*, 42; Toll, *Blacking Up*; Lott, *Love and Theft*; Michael Rogin, *Blackface, White Noise*; Hartman, *Scenes of Subjection*, 32; Roach, *Cities of the Dead*, 17–25.

43 Engle, *This Grotesque Essence*, 28. On "terror and pleasure" in minstrelsy, see Hartman, *Scenes of Subjection*.

44 Hartman, *Scenes of Subjection*, especially 25–50; Lott, *Love and Theft*, especially 131–35. The production of this aberrantly transfigured body of pain ensured that black actors would be forced into persistent conversation, contest, and competi-

tion with burnt-cork figures in the popular imaginary. It is possible that *The Quack Doctor* operated as both a socio-political farce directed at the rise of the northern black professional as well as a metatheatrical farce directed at the rise of black performers such as Ira Aldrige, who performed in an 1847 production entitled *The Black Doctor*, a clear reversal of minstrel buffoonery with its romantic tale of a black physician who falls in love with and secretly marries the daughter of a French aristocrat. See *The Black Doctor* in Hatch and Shine, eds., *Black Theatre USA*, 4–24. For more on William Brown's African Theatre and early-nineteenth-century black Shakespeare productions, see Shane White, *Stories of Freedom in Black New York*; Marvin McAllister, *White People Do Not Know How to Behave at Entertainments Designed for Ladies and Gentlemen of Colour.*

45  Bertolt Brecht, *Brecht on Theatre*, ed. John Willett, 137; Lott, *Love and Theft*; Roach, *Cities of the Dead*, 25; Michel Foucault, "Nietzsche, Genealogy, History."

46  Rachel Adams, *Sideshow USA*, 5.

47  Thomas Gossett, *Uncle Tom's Cabin and American Culture*. See also Eric Lott, *Love and Theft*; Linda Williams, *Playing the Race Card*; Audrey Fisch, *American Slaves in Victorian England*. On the connections between Stowe's melodrama and minstrelsy, see Lott and Williams. See also Richard Yarborough, "Strategies of Black Characterization in *Uncle Tom's Cabin*"; Hartman, *Scenes of Subjection*.

48  "The Octoroon," *New York Times*, December 15, 1859.

49  Andrew Parkin, introduction to *Selected Plays of Dion Boucicault*, 11.

50  Parkin, introduction, 12.

51  Michael R. Booth, *Victorian Spectacular Theatre*, 79.

52  Roach, *Cities of the Dead*, 183; Brody, *Impossible Purities*, 46–58. See also Heinz Kosok, "Dion Boucicault's 'American' Plays," 95.

53  Booth, *Victorian Spectacular Theatre*, 74.

54  Roach, *Cities of the Dead*, 183.

55  Dion Boucicault, *The Octoroon*, 177. Future references will be cited parenthetically.

56  Toll, *Blacking Up*, 75–76.

57  Boucicault quoted in Sidney Kaplan, "Drama of Miscegenation," 555.

58  Spillers, "Notes on an Alternative Model," 167.

59  Jennifer Brody, *Impossible Purities*, 4–16.

60  Eva Saks, "Representing Miscegenation Law," 40, 42.

61  Sheldon Faulkner, "The Octoroon War," 35. Copperhead concludes that *The Octoroon* contributed to the wave of literature that "helped to feed the flame of disunion": "Abolition On and Off the Stage," *New York Herald*, December 5, 1859. (The author of the article is cited as Copperhead in Kaplan, "*The Octoroon*," 548–49.)

62  Kaplan, "*The Octoroon*," 548.

63  See Hartman, *Scenes of Subjection*, 210, n.24.

64  Peter Brooks, *Melodramatic Imagination*, 4–5, 13, 15; emphasis added. David Grimsted, *Melodrama Unveiled*, 221–22.

65  See P. Brooks, *Melodramatic Imagination*, 17; Williams, *Playing the Race Card*, 44.

66  Hartman, *Scenes of Subjection*, 28; Misa Oyama as cited in Williams, *Playing the Race Card*, 311, n.1.

67  Alan Downer as quoted in Bruce McConachie, *Melodramatic Formations*, 112–13, Williams, *Playing the Race Card*, 18, 42; P. Gabrielle Foreman, "This Promiscuous Housekeeping," 51–72; P. Brooks, *Melodramatic Imagination*, 11.

68  McConachie, *Melodramatic Formations*, 221–23; Hartman, *Scenes of Subjection*, 26–27; Williams, *Playing the Race Card*, 7, 29.

69  See Saks, "Representing Miscegenation Law," 39; Williams, *Playing the Race Card*, 18.

70  Brody, *Impossible Purities*, 50; Roach, *Cities of the Dead*, 220.

71  Harley Erdman, "Caught in the 'Eye of the Eternal,'" 336; Foucault, *Discipline and Punish*, 195–228.

72  Roach, *Cities of the Dead*, 185–86, 199; Diamond, *Unmaking Mimesis*, 48–49.

73  Roach, *Cities of the Dead*, 216; Brody, *Impossible Purities*, 43–44.

74  Brody, *Impossible Purities*, 49; Roach, *Cities of the Dead*, 220–24.

75  "The Five-Act Drama—The Octoroon," *New York Tribune*, December 7, 1859, 5. The *New York Herald* also called the scene "the most important in the play" and quotes the scene in full in its review of the production. "Winter Garden—First Night of 'The Octoroon,'" *New York Herald*, December 7, 1859.

76  P. Brooks as quoted in Williams, *Playing the Race Card*, 18. See Roach, *Cities of the Dead*; Paulin, *Representing Forbidden Desire*.

77  Castle, "Phantasmagoria," 30; George L. Aiken, *Uncle Tom's Cabin*.

78  Spillers, "Notes on an Alternative Model," 178.

79  Sánchez-Eppler, "Bodily Bonds," 250.

80  Robertson as quoted in Kaplan, "*The Octoroon*," 550.

81  This blinding light recalls that which engulfs the title character of Edgar Allan Poe's *The Narrative of A. Gordon Pym* (1837) as the European seaman confronts "the blackness of darkness" in "savage" territories. Pym's "whiteness," Morrison suggests, erupts in response to this foreign blackness (*Playing in the Dark*).

82  See *London Times*, November 19, 1861. Future periodical references will be cited parenthetically by title, month, day, and year.

83  Degen, "How to End *The Octoroon*," 176. The four-act text, known as "The Happy English Ending," is, in fact, not the originally revised version that Boucicault brought to the stage in 1861. See ibid., 175–78.

84  Ibid., 175.

85  John M. Mackenzie, *Imperialism and Popular Culture*, 5. See Altick, *Shows of London*, 456.

86  Audrey Fisch, *American Slaves in Victorian England*; Clare Taylor, *British and American Abolitionists*; Douglas A. Lorimer, *Colour, Class, and the Victorians*.

87  Mary Elizabeth Braddon, *The Octoroon*, 57. Robert L. Wolff, *Sensational Victorian*, 80. See also Brody, *Impossible Purities*. Several spin-off plays were also devel-

oped during this period which seemed to borrow heavily from both the original Boucicault text as well as Braddon's work. See, for instance, W. B. Donne, *Cora, or The Octoroon Slave of Louisiana Drama*. See also Brody, 46–58.

88  Mary Louise Pratt, *Imperial Eyes*, 87.

89  Ibid., 97.

90  Roach, *Cities of the Dead*, 220; Altick, *Shows of London*, 268–72. See also Anne Fausto-Sterling, "The Comparative Anatomy of 'Hottentot' Women in Europe, 1815–1817"; Sander Gilman, "Black Bodies, White Bodies."

91  George Rowell, *The Victorian Theatre*, 57.

92  Judith Fisher, "The 'Sensation Scene' in Charles Dickens and Dion Boucicault," 164, 162.

93  See Altick, *Shows of London*, 174; Booth, *Victorian Spectacular Theatre*, 3.

94  Altick, *Shows of London*, 180. See Pratt, *Imperial Eyes*, 59; Booth, *Victorian Spectacular Theatre*, 7. On black abolitionist panoramas, see chapter 2.

95  Pratt, *Imperial Eyes*, 51.

96  Booth, "Soldiers of the Queen," 6–7.

97  Judith Halberstam, *Skin Shows*, 2–3, 23. Future references to this text will be cited parenthetically unless otherwise noted.

98  Saks, "Representing Miscegenation Law," 63, 47.

99  Williamson, *New People*, 95; Woodward, *Strange Career of Jim Crow*, 32.

100  Auerbach, *Private Theatricals*, 76. See also Brody, *Impossible Purities*, 130–69.

101  Pauline Hopkins, *Contending Forces*, 273.

102  Theodore Rosengarten, *All God's Dangers*; Eric Foner, *Reconstruction*; Woodward, *Strange Career of Jim Crow*; Robyn Wiegman, *American Anatomies*; Jacqueline Goldsby, "The High and Low Tech of It."

103  Mark Twain, *Pudd'nhead Wilson*, 59; Eric Sundquist, *To Wake the Nations*, 269.

104  The appendix to *The Definitive Dr. Jekyll and Mr. Hyde Companion* lists a much lesser-known and an apparent parody of sorts entitled *The Strange Case of a Hyde and Seekyll*, which was produced at L. C. Toole's Theatre in London on May 18, 1886. Harold Geduld cites the American version as the first dramatic adaptation of the novel; see *The Definitive Dr. Jekyll and Mr. Hyde Companion*, appendices, 215. This version is available in Lord Chamberlain's Play Collection in the British Museum Library's Manuscript Room.

105  Roach, *Cities of the Dead*, 25.

106  Lott, *Love and Theft*, 148.

107  Toll, *Blacking Up*, 160–61, 202.

108  Virginia Wright Wexman, "Horrors of the Body," 288–89.

109  Robert Louis Stevenson, *The Strange Case of Dr. Jekyll and Mr. Hyde*, 34; emphasis mine. Future references to Stevenson's text will be cited parenthetically.

110  Sander Gilman, *Difference and Pathology*, 25.

111  Terry and Urla, *Deviant Bodies*, 6.

112  Ibid., 3.

113 See Halberstam, *Skin Shows*, 53–85. See also Homi K. Bhabha, *The Location of Culture*; Brody, *Impossible Purities*.

114 "Reviews of the First Production," in Geduld, *The Definitive Companion*, 166.

115 George Moore, *Impressions and Opinions*, 128.

116 Ibid., 137.

117 Sundquist, *To Wake the Nations*, 265.

118 Bruce as quoted in ibid., 255; see also 259.

119 Cheryl Harris, "Whiteness as Property," 280.

120 Ibid.

121 See Ida B. Wells, *On Lynchings*; Sandra Gunning, *Race, Rape, and Lynching*, 6; Wiegman, "The Anatomy of Lynching," 455.

122 Paul Wilstach, *Richard Mansfield*, 155–56.

123 Ibid., 145.

124 C. Alex Pinkston Jr., "Stage Premiere," 23. Pinkston discovered the only existing script of Sullivan's play as well as the promptbook and other materials from the original production in the Smithsonian Museum's Costume Collection. However, the public's access to these materials is now restricted. In addition, the play and promptbook have suffered severe damage in storage; only three of the four acts remain intact. My thanks to librarian Shelly Foote and the entire Smithsonian Costume Collection staff for making available to me the partial promptbook and script of Sullivan and Mansfield's text. Given this material's condition and the limited access to the collection, my analysis of the textual elements of the play relies somewhat on a combination of documents. I have utilized the partial script in conjunction with Pinkston's informative article. The latter provides a comprehensive synopsis of the plot. In addition, I make use of contemporary reviews of the play and turn-of-the-century theatre critic William Winter's description of the plot in his biography of Mansfield. See Winter, *Life and Art*, 2:36–47. Future references to Pinkston's piece will be cited parenthetically as "Stage Premiere," unless otherwise noted. See also *Jekyll and Hyde Dramatized*, edited by Martin A. Danahay and Alex Chisholm, which was released too late for inclusion in this study.

125 *Sunday London Times*, July 29, 1888.

126 Thomas R. Sullivan, *Dr. Jekyll and Mr. Hyde*, 10–16; Pinkston, "Stage," 27.

127 See Halberstam, *Skin Shows*, 53–85; Stephen Heath, "Psychopathia Sexualis," 93–108; Eve Kosofsky Sedgwick, *Between Men*.

128 Winter, *Life and Art*, 40.

129 Lott, *Love and Theft*, 131–15; Jacquelyn Dowd Hall, " 'The Mind That Burns in Each Body.' " One could also read the production of the play as an "assault" of sorts on white womanhood. Women were said to have been swooning in the aisles during Mansfield's portrayals of Hyde. The actor subsequently published an article in the *New York Sun* in which he explained the necessity of the play's violence and Hyde's gruesome nature. Here he also articulates his regret that "so

many women hav[e] fainted" during "an evening at the theatre" (Wilstach, *Richard Mansfield*, 161).

130  Geduld, *The Definitive Companion*, appendices, 3–6.

131  Wilstach, *Richard Mansfield*, 146.

132  Ibid., 143.

133  *New York Herald*, 5; *Boston Evening Transcript*, May 10, 1887: 1.

134  Wilstach, *Richard Mansfield*, 147–48. See also Pinkston, "Stage Premiere," 34–35.

135  Toll, *Blacking Up*, 34. See also Lott, *Love and Theft*, 117.

136  Wilstach, *Richard Mansfield*, 148.

137  Hans Nathan, *Dan Emmett and the Rise of Early Negro Minstrelsy*, 75. Charles Dickens, in his *American Notes* travel narrative, confesses to being mesmerized by the African dancer Juba (one of the few black men to gain prominence in theatre during the early minstrel era) and his extraordinary speed and leg-work skill as a performer. The extension of legs and arms was, thus, central to minstrelsy. See Lott, *Love and Theft*, 115–16. See also Nathan's description of this incident, *Dan Emmett*, 73–75.

138  James Weldon Johnson, *Black Manhattan*, 93; Wilstach, *Richard Mansfield*, 57–74; Harry Reynolds, *Minstrel Memories*.

139  Guy DeBord, *The Society of the Spectacle*, 4; Lott, *Love and Theft*, 117–18.

140  Sundquist, *To Wake the Nations*, 249.

141  Nathan, *Dan Emmett*, 71.

142  Weldon Johnson, *Black Manhattan*, 89; Toll, *Blacking Up*, 201; Martin Favor, *Authentic Blackness*; David Krasner, *Resistance, Parody, and Double Consciousness*; Hatch and Ted Shine, eds., *Black Theatre USA*; James Haskins, *Black Theatre in America*.

143  Wexman, "Horrors of the Body," 293.

144  Halberstam, *Skin Shows*, 60.

145  Wilstach, *Richard Mansfield*, 147. See also Winter, *Life and Art*, 2:43; Wilstach, ibid., 154–55.

146  Wilstach, *Richard Mansfield*, 147–48.

147  Halberstam, *Skin Shows*, 59–61; Henry James, "The Beast in the Jungle."

148  Reynolds, *Minstrel Memories*, 165. See Toll, *Blacking Up*, 152; Reynolds, ibid., 163–70.

## 2. The Escape Artist

1  Cynthia Griffin Wolff, "Passing beyond the Middle Passage," 30; *National Anti-Slavery Standard*, September 19, 1850; *The Liberator*, July 11, 1851; *Leeds Mercury*, May 24, 1851; C. Peter Ripley, ed., *The Black Abolitionist Papers*, 1:174–75; Richard Newman, introduction, *Narrative of the Life of Henry Box Brown*, xv–xvi.

2  R. J. M. Blackett, *Building an Antislavery Wall*, 147. Future references to Blackett's text will be cited parenthetically unless otherwise noted.

3  Blackett, *Building an Antislavery Wall*, 6; *National Anti-Slavery Standard*, June 7,

1849; Benjamin Quarles, *Black Abolitionists*, 137; Blackett, ibid. See also Ripley, *The Black Abolitionist Papers*, introduction; Audrey Fisch, *American Slaves in Victorian England*; Blackett, *Building an Antislavery Wall*, 169; William E. Gienapp, "Abolitionism and the Nature of Antebellum Reform," 37–39.

4   William L. Andrews, *To Tell a Free Story*, 98–99; Sundquist, *To Wake the Nations*, 36.

5   Blackett, *Building an Antislavery Wall*, 145; Carlyle, "Occasional Discourse on the Nigger Question," 11–12; Blackett, ibid., 155–57; William Wells Brown, *Three Years in Europe*, 217–18.

6   Solomon Northrup, *Twelve Years a Slave*, Henry Bibb, *Narrative of the Life and Adventures of Henry Bibb*, 51–171; August Meier and Elliot Rudwick, "The Role of Blacks in the Abolitionist Movement," 111; Wilson Moses, *The Golden Age of Black Nationalism, 1850–1920*.

7   Valerie Smith, "'Loopholes of Retreat,'" 216–17; Andrews, *To Tell a Free Story*, 177. Clearly, as well, this construction of allegorical isolation anticipates significant tropes in twentieth-century African American literature, such as Ralph Ellison's representation of his *Invisible Man* protagonist who lives underground in a manhole.

8   Gienapp, "Abolitionism and the Nature of Antebellum Reform,"39; William Still, *Underground Railroad*, 71. The Boston antislavery community's high-profile and not always successful efforts to protect fugitive slaves such as Frederick "Shadrach" Wilkins, Thomas Sims, and Anthony Burns from recapture suggest that Brown was immediately initiated into a radical reformist community led, in part, by white abolitionist William Lloyd Garrison and the Boston Vigilance Committee. Gienapp, ibid., 39–41; Jane H. Pease and William H. Pease, *They Who Would Be Free*, 12.

9   Andrews, *To Tell a Free Story*, 169. Contemporary African American visual artist Kara Walker has commented on the provocative possibilities of the nineteenth-century cycloramas, a derivation of the panoramic form. Walker observes that the "cyclorama carries itself as if it were the highest form of art, because it creates an entire experience for the viewer. It's handcrafted, made by a team, and it's all about making historical moments more real and more present. . . . Their craft forms that are striving real hard to be something that they're not" (interview with Lawrence Rinder).

10  Paul Jefferson, introduction to *The Travels of William Wells Brown*; Marcus Wood, "'All Right!'" 72. See also Wood, *Blind Memory*.

11  Henry Box Brown, *Narrative of Henry Box Brown* (1849), 11. Future references to the American edition of this text will be cited parenthetically as *Narrative* (1849) and future references to the English edition as *Narrative of the Life* (1851), unless otherwise noted. While the *Narrative of Henry Box Brown* states that Brown was born in 1816, subsequent historical studies estimate that Brown was born about 1815. For a detailed biographical account of Brown's life, see Jeffrey Ruggles's excellent book *The Unboxing of Henry Brown*, which makes significant research

advances in the study of Box Brown. Although Ruggles's work dovetails with my own in various ways, my aim in this chapter is to resituate the activist in a broad cultural network of resistant transatlantic black performances in the nineteenth century.

12 William Wells Brown, *Narrative of William Wells Brown*, 21–70; Solomon Northrup, *Twelve Years a Slave*; Leonard Cassuto, *The Inhuman Race*, 112; Frederick Douglass, *Narrative of the Life of Frederick Douglass*, 52; Saidiya Hartman, *Scenes of Subjection*, 3. For more on the representation of torture in slavery, see Hartman, *Sense and Subjection*, 17–48. Michael Newbury, "Eaten Alive."

13 Ripley speculates that Box Brown was most likely married to Nancy in the early 1830s. Within a year of their marriage, she was "sold to Richmond saddler Samuel Cottrell." In the English edition of his narrative, Brown describes his meeting with a free black man, and he relates J. C. A. Smith's assistance in protecting his family and aiding him later in his escape. He also alludes to the assistance of white store owner Samuel A. Smith in his flight from slavery. Ripley, *Black Abolitionist Papers*, 301 n. 11; Brown, *Narrative of the Life* (1851), 38, 51–53; Newman, introduction, *Narrative of the Life of Henry Box Brown*, xv–xvi. See Ruggles, *The Unboxing of Henry Brown*, 3–25.

14 Cassuto, *Inhuman Race*, 86.

15 Bernard F. Reilly Jr., "The Art of the Antislavery Movement," 63.

16 Still, *Underground Railroad*, 67–68; *Narrative* (1849), 91; Smith, "Loopholes," 213.

17 This scene re-emerges in the 1851 version of Brown's text; see Brown, *Narrative of the Life* (1851), 10–11. However, the English edition of this passage leads into a series of increasingly graphic passages in which the narrator witnesses the torture of fellow slaves; these scenes are missing from the 1849 text. In this latter edition, the narrator's insistence on visual authority, that he "saw [his master] do many other things which were equally cruel," signals a divergence in the narrative style of these two texts (ibid., 21).

18 James Olney, " 'I Was Born'," 161; John Blassingame, *Slave Testimony*, xxxiii, xxvii; Olney, 159. See Andrews, *To Tell a Free Story*, 307, note 6. For more on rhetorical "cross-dressing" and discursive drag, see Judith Halberstam, *Skin Shows*.

19 Ruth Braddon, *The Life and Many Deaths of Harry Houdini*, 151; Wood, "All Right!" 88.

20 Wood, "All Right!" 8.

21 Andrews, *To Tell a Free Story*, 99; George Frederickson, *Black Image in the White Mind*, 33; Hartman, *Scenes of Subjection*, 17–23.

22 Raymond Hedin, "Strategies of Form in the American Slave Narrative," 25. Hedin contends that the "black American written narrative tradition" essentially "began 'enclosed' in some ways by literary forms bequeathed to it by whites" (25). See Smith, "Loopholes"; Jean Fagan Yellin, introduction to *Incidents in the Life of a Slave Girl*, xvi.

23 Robert Stepto, "I Rose and Found My Voice," 228–29. On occasion, Stearns acknowledges Brown's presence, affirming in the first line from his "Cure for the

Evil of Slavery," for instance, that the reader has "listened with eager ears and with tearful eyes, to the recital of Mr. Brown" (66).

24 Stepto, "I Rose," 229; Olney, " 'I Was Born,' " 161.

25 Stepto, "I Rose," 229; Hartman, *Scenes of Subjection*, 20, 35; Olney, " 'I Was Born,' " 150.

26 Olney, " 'I Was Born,' " 151–55; Sharon F. Patton, *The Oxford History of African-American Art*, 78. The image of Brown appears on page iv, following an ad for *The Christian Reformer* periodical and on the page preceding Stearns's preface. Questions remain as to whether the portrait is that of Brown since the same image appears on the cover of Anthony Burns's 1854 narrative. See Charles Stevens, *Anthony Burns, A History*; Newman, introduction, *Narrative of the Life of Henry Box Brown*, xxxix. Burns and Brown both circulated in Boston fugitive circles in the late 1840s, and the former prepared his own panorama of slavery in 1858, thus perhaps contributing to the confusion of these images. *The Liberator* announces the exhibition of Burns's "Moving *Mirror of Slavery*"; see *The Liberator*, September 3, 1858. See also Letter from Anthony Burns to the Editor of The Liberator, in MS.A1.2.v.25, 122 in the Boston Public Library, Rare Books and Manuscripts Reading Room. For the purposes of my argument here, the fact that any portrait purporting to be Brown appears at the beginning of the text is significant since this document participates in a critical dialectic with the "mixed media" of the *Narrative*.

27 Reilly, "Art of the Antislavery Movement," 63; Brown, *Narrative of Henry Box Brown*.

28 Stephen Greenblatt, "Resonance and Wonder," 49, 45.

29 Wolff, "Passing beyond the Middle Passage," 27.

30 Spillers, "Mama's Baby, Papa's Maybe," 478.

31 Andrews, *To Tell a Free Story*, 104; Cassuto, *Inhuman Race*, 106.

32 Hedin, "Strategies of Form," 30.

33 Frances Smith Foster, *Witnessing Slavery*, 124; Hedin, "Strategies of Form," 27.

34 Blackett, *Building an Antislavery Wall*, x; John Ernest, "Fugitive Performances."

35 Richard Altick, *Shows of London*, 150. Future references to Altick's text will be cited parenthetically unless otherwise noted. The date of Brown's visit is imprecise; however, one can deduce from his description of having seen the panorama of Paris at the Colosseum building "in the middle of May" that Brown would have to have visited the exhibition between 1849 and 1850 since his European travels commenced in July of 1849 after he was selected by Boston abolitionists to attend the International Peace Congress convention in Paris. Altick notes that the Colosseum displayed its *Paris by Night* panorama from May of 1848 until Christmas of 1850 when "the Paris Panorama gave way to one of the Lake of Thun" (157, 161). William Wells Brown, *American Fugitive in Europe*, 255–56.

36 W. W. Brown, *American Fugitive in Europe*, 255–56.

37 William Wells Brown unveiled his twenty-four-scene panorama in Newcastle-upon-Tyne during late October of 1850, several months after Henry Box Brown's

public boxing "re-enactments" and touring exhibition; Ripley, *Black Abolitionist Papers*, 191; William Wells Brown, *A Description of William Wells Brown's Original Panoramic Views of the Scenes in the Life of an American Slave*; Ripley, ibid., 191–224. In November 1850, abolitionist R. D. Webb speculated that Wells Brown would "not be at all pleased by the competition" Box Brown's subsequent panorama might create. "R.D. Webb Letter to Mrs. Chapman," MS.A.9.2.25, 42 in Boston Public Library, Rare Books and Manuscript Reading Room.

38 Meier and Rudwick, "The Role of Blacks," 117–18; Gienapp, "Abolitionism," 36–37. See also Meier and Rudwick, "The Role of Blacks," 111–15; Quarles, *Black Abolitionists*, 3–14; Blackett, *Building an Antislavery Wall*, 79–117.

39 James Brewer Stewart, *Holy Warriors*, 153; 155–60.

40 See Jane H. Pease and William H. Pease, *They Who Would Be Free*; Gienapp, "Abolitionism," 36; William S. McFeely, *Frederick Douglass*; Henry Mayer, *All on Fire*; Eddie Glaude, *Exodus!*, 105–59; Howard H. Bell, "National Negro Conventions."

41 Russel Nye, *The Unembarrassed Muse*, 186–87.

42 Christopher Kent, "Spectacular History," 7.

43 Martin Meisel, *Realizations*, 33.

44 Altick, *Shows of London*, 136, 176; Meisel, *Realizations*, 33, 51, 174, 184.

45 Altick, *Shows of London*, 198–99. The early moving panoramas were initially mounted as theatrical backdrops to English pantomimes in the first two decades of the nineteenth century. Angela Miller, "The Panorama, the Cinema and the Emergence of the Spectacular," 39; future references to this text will be cited parenthetically as "Panorama." See also Nye, *Unembarrassed Muse*, 186.

46 Altick, *Shows of London*, 199; A. Miller, "Panorama," 47.

47 Harriet Beecher Stowe, *Uncle Tom's Cabin*.

48 Brown declares that while viewing the Boston exhibition, "it occurred to [him] that a painting, with as fair a representation of American Slavery as could be given upon canvass, would do much to disseminate truth upon this subject, and hasten the downfall of the greatest evil that now stains the character of the American people"; *A Description of William Wells Brown's Original Panoramic Views*, in Ripley, *Black Abolitionist Papers*, 191. Ripley reveals that a "number of black antislavery panoramas appeared during the 1850s," *Black Abolitionist Papers*, 217. In particular, the daguerrean photographer and freeman James Presley Ball's 1850 panorama with its accompanying pamphlet remains one of the most ambitious black abolitionist efforts of its kind and featured the work of both the black landscape painter Robert Duncanson and the lectures of Charles Lennox Remond. Deborah Willis, *J. P. Ball Daguerrean*, 237–99; Joseph D. Ketner, *The Emergence of the African-American Artist*, 101–4. Pease and Pease note that "Anthony Burns joined the promoter H. C. Garcelon and toured the country in the late 1850s. In the evenings they showed a panorama called 'The Moving *Mirror of Slavery*' and in the daytime peddled copies of the *Life of Anthony Burns*," 36. While Box Brown was not alone in his decision to mount a black abolitionist

panorama, his work is significant both in the ways that it signifies on his discursive narrative and in that he was apparently the first to have his project visually mounted and produced for an audience. See Allan D. Austin, "More Black Panoramas," 636.

49  Kara Walker observes that "cycloramas create a kind of hyperreality. History painting is all a fictional space"; interview with Lawrence Rinder.

50  Fisch, " 'Repetitious Accounts,' " 24, 28.

51  Fisch, " 'Negrophilism' and British Nationalism," 30–31; Wolff, "Passing Beyond," 24.

52  Wolff, "Passing Beyond," 24; Fisch, " 'Repetitious Accounts,' " 24, 28.

53  Fisch, " 'Repetitious Accounts,' " 28.

54  Stewart, *Holy Warriors*, 162; Sundquist, *To Wake the Nations*, 27–134; David Brion Davis, *The Problem of Slavery*; Sidney Kaplan, *The Black Presence*; Frederick Douglass, "What to the Slave is the Fourth of July?"; Walter Benjamin, *Reflections*, 150.

55  William Andrews, *To Tell A Free Story*, 2.

56  Pease and Pease, *They Who Would Be Free*, 36. By the summer of 1849, "Boxer," as he was spiritedly anointed by his touring colleague and co-fugitive, William Wells Brown, appeared at a number of abolitionist gatherings where it was reported that he related the specifics of his escape. On occasion, senior activists such as Garrison or Samuel May would describe his flight from slavery while Brown stood before a rapt assembly with the box as prop. See the *National Anti-Slavery Standard*, Jan. 31, 1850, and February 7, 1850. See also *The Liberator*, May 31, 1850; *National Anti-Slavery Standard*, June 7 and 14, 1849. *The Liberator*, June 8, 1849, features a speech by Samuel May on Henry Box Brown's escape. See also the *North Star*, June 15, 22, 1849; *National Anti-Slavery Standard*, Oct. 25, 1849; Wood, "All Right!" 75.

57  Kathryn Grover, *The Fugitive's Gibraltar*, 202–3.

58  Ripley, introduction, *Black Abolitionist Papers*, 85; "Panorama Exhibition of the Slave System," which reports that on "Thursday and Friday evenings, last week, a considerable number of ladies and gentlemen assembled at the Washingtonian Hall, in Bromfield street, by special invitation, to witness a Panorama of Slavery and the Slave Trade"; *The Liberator*, April 19, 1850. The *National Anti-Slavery Standard* reports on February 7 that Brown and Smith opened the fourth evening session of the Syracuse Anti-Slavery Convention with songs. It also announces that Brown was, at the time, in the process of "getting up a MIRROR OF SLAVERY." By early 1850, Box Brown's public appearances were diverse, interrelated forms of promotion and publicity; *National Anti-Slavery Standard*, February 7, 1850. In a private correspondence, Ricketson puns his receipt of the fugitive slave, referring to him as a "very valuable consignment of 200 pounds of Humanity," Grover, *Fugitive's Gibraltar*, 202.

59  See Ruggles, *The Unboxing of Henry Brown*, 77–80 and 93–105.

60  Patton, *Oxford History*, 73. The celebrated transatlantic landscape painter Dun-

canson collaborated with Ball on his *Splendid Mammoth Pictorial Tour of the United States* (1855) panorama along with other African American artists. Duncanson's success as a landscape painter of great notoriety in the States and abroad by the late 1850s and early 1860s should not be underestimated as a potential influence on Box Brown's work. Although originally based in the Midwest with Ball, Duncanson traveled to Canada and the United Kingdom, and his work was the subject of great praise and discussion in both the art and abolitionist worlds during this period as well; Patton, ibid., 79–85.

61  Grover, *Fugitive's Gibraltar*, 204. Nancy Osgood, "Josiah Wolcott," 16.

62  The article describes how the panorama had "been for several months past in process of completion by the artist, Mr. Josiah Wolcott, who has been employed for that purpose by the celebrated Henry Box Brown." The article also pointedly observes how, "[c]onsidering the difficulties to be overcome, the time spent upon and the sum paid for it, it is very creditable to the industry, zeal and talent of the artist"; *The Liberator*, April 19, 1850. See also *The Liberator*, April 26, 1850; *Leeds Mercury*, May 24, 1851. An ad for the panorama in the English periodical the *Preston Guardian & Advertiser* lists the three panorama artists as "Wolcott, Rouse, and Johnson, artists of Boston, United States"; *Preston Guardian & Advertiser*, Jan. 18, 1851. Both *The Guardian* and *Leeds Mercury* describe the display as being "50,000 feet" in length with "upwards of 100 views." However, the published list of scenes suggests that the panorama spanned roughly around 46 scenes. See also *The Liberator*, May 3, 1850. Many art historians note that most contemporaneous estimations of moving panoramas were often exaggerated for the purposes of publicity.

63  Osgood, "Josiah Wolcott," 9. A follower of the philosopher Charles Fourier and his views on utopian reform, as well as a one-time member of the Fourierist-inspired Brook Farm commune, Wolcott presumably contributed a utopian and communitarian ethos to Box Brown's panorama project. As Nancy Osgood has demonstrated, Wolcott's work, particularly in the 1840s, was closely aligned with his political views, culminating in his well-known sketches of Brook Farm. Associationism's political philosophies had a far-reaching impact on Wolcott's mid-century work and his involvement in the movement would have created a convenient bridge into developing antislavery visual art on a massive scale like that which he conjured in the *Mirror*.

64  Reilly, "Art of the Antislavery Movement," 49; Guy C. McElroy, *Facing History*, 55; Marcus Wood, *Blind Memory*.

65  *The Liberator*, May 31, 1850; *National Anti-Slavery Standard*, May 3, 1855; *London Times*, July 30, 1852.

66  J. P. Ball, *Balls Splendid Mammoth Pictorial Tour*, 237–301. For a convincing analysis of the similarities between Brown's panorama script and Charles C. Green's illustrated poem *The Nubian Slave*, see Ruggles, *The Unboxing of Henry Brown*, 93–104. Ruggles's work is the first to retrieve illustrated material that may visually correspond with Brown's exhibition.

67 *The Liberator*, May 3, 1850; "Great Attraction at Mechanics Hall," *Providence Daily Journal*, Aug. 5, 1850, 3.

68 Susan Buck-Morss, *The Dialectics of Seeing*, 79. Walter Benjamin, *Reflections*, 149–50; Buck-Morss, ibid., 67.

69 Buck-Morss, *Dialectics of Seeing*, 56, 90, 95.

70 Ibid., 36; emphasis added.

71 Wood, *Blind Memory*, 38. Several other black abolitionists made overtures in their work to situate the experiences of the African American slave within a historical and geographical African diasporic legacy. See, for instance, Olaudah Equiano, *The Interesting Narrative of the Life of Olaudah Equiano*. See also Ball's *Mammoth Pictorial*. Martin Delany's novel *Blake* (1862) represents yet another example of a black antebellum activist attempting to "wrest the American story from white control and to present it from Africa to America"; Martin Delany, *Blake*.

72 *Leeds Mercury*, May 24, 1851.

73 Hedin, "Strategies of Form," 29.

74 Buck-Morss, *Dialectics of Seeing*, 82–83.

75 A. Miller, "Panorama," 49. From this standpoint, Box Brown's panorama overturned the shift from the innovations of Daguerre's diorama of the 1820s which involved literally moving the audience "in the passive mood, from one picture to another" to the scenographic panoramas from later that decade which "achieved also an illusion of relative motion in which the spectator, though not shifted bodily . . . functioned as a moving eye"; Meisel, *Realizations*, 62.

76 Wood, *Blind Memory*, 19, 97.

77 Altick, *Shows of London*, 176; Kent, "Spectacular History," 17.

78 Banvard, *Description of Banvard's Panorama*, 34. Banvard's panoramic journey abruptly shifts into a Poe-like movement toward a purifying whiteness, the "very beautiful cliffs called the WHITE CLIFFS" (34). See also Toni Morrison, *Playing in the Dark*.

79 *London Times*, July 30, 1852; McElroy, *Facing History*, xiii. This kind of erasure has an ironic autobiographical mirroring of its own in the case of the Henry Box Brown Papers, housed at Berkeley's Bancroft Library. In the early 1850s, Harrison Brown (1831–1915), the marine painter from Portland, Maine, was hired by Commissioner John Bartlett to research and sketch landscapes of Northern California scenery and "Indian ethnology." Seemingly, at some point during his sojourns between 1851 and 1853, Harrison Brown took the name "Henry Box Brown," perhaps to capitalize on the latter's notoriety. Whether Harrison Brown ever saw or met the fugitive abolitionist is unknown. Ironically, however, in a number of contemporary art history reference volumes, the Anglo landscape painter is still attributed with having "exhibited panoramas of Africa," thus effacing Box Brown's authorship from historical art records. See *Bartlett's West*, 55; The Henry Box Brown Papers, University of California Berkeley, Bancroft Library, MSS 80/54c.

80 Patton, *Oxford History*, 79.

81 Angela Miller, *Empire of the Eye*, 6–8.

82 Patton, *Oxford History*, 79.

83 Ibid., 83.

84 Ibid., 85.

85 A Frenchman whose views on social reform were fundamentally influential in propelling the broad-based communitarian movement of the 1830s and 1840s in North America, Fourier embraced a notion of peaceful yet fundamental social change through the eradication of western free trade economic systems. Fourier's "critical-utopian" socialism encouraged the "notion of a complete reconstruction of society," and in its most radical, unadulterated form, Fourierist philosophies "offered a comprehensive revolutionary vision" of what America might look like free of capitalism and, to a much lesser degree, chattel slavery. See J. F. C. Harrison, *The Second Coming*, xvi; A. Miller, *Empire of the Eye*, 5; Guarneri, *Utopian Alternative*, 2.

86 Reilly, "Art of the Antislavery Movement," 51; Brown, *Narrative* (1849), 38; Brown, *Narrative of the Life* (1851), 19.

87 Stewart, *Holy Warriors*, 151; Gienapp, "Abolitionism," 36.

88 Newman, introduction, *Narrative of the Life of Henry Box Brown*, xxvii; Brown, *Narrative of the Life* (1851), 9–13.

89 "Summer Assizes. Midland Circuit. Warwick July 28," *London Times*, July 30, 1852. See also Blackett, *Building an Antislavery Wall*, 158–59. The *Times* reported that the jury "found observations made upon personal character" must be weighed "with more rigour, because no man ought to attack the character of another without taking the utmost care to ascertain that he was right"; *London Times*, July 30, 1852. According to the *Times*, the author of the review was the editor of the newspaper. Ruggles cites "T. H. Brindley" as the editor of the *Wolverhampton & Staffordshire Herald*. Ruggles, *The Unboxing of Henry Brown*, 143.

90 "Panorama of Slavery," *Wolverhampton & Staffordshire Herald*, March 17, 1852.

91 *The Liberator*, April 19, 1850; *National Anti-Slavery Standard*, August 3, 1855; *Leeds Mercury*, May 3, 1851.

92 Other press reports attacked Brown's panorama on the grounds that it indulged in hyperbole. Another English critic, in a review of *Uncle Tom's Cabin*, declares that Stowe's "illustrations are not the exaggerations of Box Brown panoramas. She selects no hideous exceptional crimes of individual slave-holders, insisting then upon a general inference. She suppresses, evidently, much authentic evidence available for such a book, and rejects everything that could disgust needlessly or offend unjustly. She paints the bad, but she also paints the good": *Daily News*, August 4, 1852.

93 "The 'Nigger' Panorama," *Wolverhampton & Staffordshire Herald*, March 24, 1852.

94 Lott, *Love and Theft*, 113. The proverbial statement "the devil is not so black as he

is painted" repeatedly surfaces in reviews of transatlantic black and "blackened" performers in the nineteenth century. The reference here could specifically be to *Macbeth* 2.2.50–53: "The sleeping and the dead / Are but as pictures; 'tis the eye of childhood / That fears a painted devil." See also chapters 3 and 4. My thanks to Sarah Meer and Richard Yarborough for assisting me with this reference.

95  Lott, *Love and Theft*, 122; Geneva Smitherman, *Talkin and Testifyin.*

96  Lott, *Love and Theft*, 113. Although Lott's arguments are rooted in a discussion of northeast American blackface performance culture, the *Herald*'s invocation of American cultural practices and minstrel forms here and elsewhere suggests that these sorts of struggles with racial performance politics are very much at work in Britain as well.

97  *London Times*, July 30, 1852.

98  "The 'Nigger' Panorama," *Wolverhampton & Staffordshire Herald*, March 24, 1852. The 1851 *Narrative* includes a version of this material in its appendix, 67–73.

99  Brown, *Narrative of the Life* (1851), 65; Wood, "All Right!" 83–84; Newman, introduction, *Narrative of the Life of Henry Box Brown*, xxiii–xvii. Already accustomed to incorporating music into his public appearances, Brown would have perhaps sung "Uncle Ned" in the context of his *Mirror* lecture as well. One can only speculate, but the potential elision of Brown's self-authored response to the sermon's labor imagery elicits the question as to whether the article is ultimately working to defuse the threat of autonomous black labor by offering the minstrel "Uncle Ned" without his emancipated abolitionist counterpart.

100  Fisch, " 'Exhibiting Uncle Tom,' " 151.

101  Bruce Greenfield, *Narrating Discovery*, 167.

102  Cassuto, *Inhuman Race*, 124.

103  Wood, "All Right!" 79.

104  Elaine Showalter, "Feminist Criticism in the Wilderness"; Hedin, "Strategies of Form," 29.

105  Psalm 40:1–4, Revised Standard Version. See appendix for full text.

106  *Narrative* (1849), ix–x; Brown, *Narrative of the Life* (1851), 57–58.

107  Stearns, preface, ix–x. Brown, *Narrative of the Life* (1851), 57–58; Wood, "All Right!" 80–83; Still, *Underground Railroad*, 70. Wood argues that Brown had chosen this text because "in its original version the theme of resurrection from the pit had a precise relevance" (80). Yet the absence of allusions to the "miry pit" here suggests to me a generic restraint toward articulating the Gothic elements of slavery in a way which is later unbridled in the panorama's narrative. The "gloomy underworld" surging at the center of Psalm 40's "pit of tumult," then, operates merely as a subtext in Brown's "Hymn" which technically leaps from verses 1 to 4 to 5 to 11 to 16, climactically resolving to "be joyful and glad—be glad in" the Lord. For more on the historical readings of Psalm 40, see *The Interpreter's Bible*, volume 4. See also Patrick Miller, *Interpreting the Psalms.*

108 Samuel Warner, "Authentic and Impartial Narrative," 297; David Miller, *Dark Eden*, 92.

109 Warner, "Authentic and Impartial Narrative," 298.

110 William Cooper Nell, *Colored Patriots of the American Revolution*, 227–28; Herbert Aptheker, "Maroons Within the Present Limits," 152; Richard Price, "Introduction: Maroons and Their Communities"; Suzette Spencer, "Stealing A Way."

111 Eugene Genovese, *From Rebellion to Revolution*, 69. As Warner makes clear, there is a significant difference between the Great Dismal Swamp and the Dismal Swamp since the former is sometimes called "Great" to distinguish it from the latter, which was located "in Currituc county," "Authentic and Impartial Narrative," 297. The distinction between these two territories would surface as something of a controversy in Brown's exhibition of the *Mirror*. In the *Wolverhampton & Staffordshire Herald*'s reportage of Brown's appearance, the newspaper recounts a query from the audience about the swamp scene. The *Herald* editor describes how "a gentleman present asked Mr. Box Brown what part of Virginia 'The Dismal Swamp' was in. 'Well, he daint sactly know; taint somewhere in de middle of de state.' 'But,' continued the interrogator, 'is it not on the borders of North and South Carolina?' 'Well, he daint know' you might put it in Carolina, but he taut it was Virginny.' Much laughter followed this confab, but after that section of the exhibition was over, the proprietor said 'There was a swamp in Virginia, but not *the dismal* swamp,' a fact, we presume, which may be predicated of every state in the union." "Panorama of Slavery," March 17, 1852. The editor thus concludes that the *Mirror* is "a very partial, unfair, and decidedly false view of American slavery."

112 As David Miller points out, by the 1850s the "more radical implications of the swamp" began to surface in relation to sectional debates (*Dark Eden*, 10). Future references to this text will be cited parenthetically.

113 Joan Dayan, "Amorous Bondage," 256. Miller adds that Poe's landscapes of swamps are always about "danger and disintegration"; *Dark Eden*, 41, 37, 286–88, note 49.

114 Henry Bibb, *Narrative of the Life*, 119–30; Northrup, *Twelve Years*, 101–5, 187. Northrup's narrative is a complicated example, however, since Olney speculates that his text operates in similar ways to Box Brown's 1849 narrative, as an "instance of the white amanuensis/sentimental novelist laying his mannered style over the faithful history as received from Northrup's lips"; Olney, " 'I Was Born,' " 162. See also Northrup, *Twelve Years*, 114; Charles Ball, *Charles Ball*.

115 Henry Wadsworth Longfellow, *Poems on Slavery*; Dayan, "Amorous Bondage," 255; Vincent Wimbush, "Introduction: Reading Darkness, Reading Scriptures," 17.

116 Robert Levine, introduction, Harriet Beecher Stowe, *Dred*, xxx; William Cooper Nell, *Colored Patriots*, 227–28. For a theatre version of the swamp narrative, see John Brougham, *Dred*, found in the Princeton University Rare Book Play Collection.

117 Levine, introduction, xvii.

118 Ibid., xxiii–xxiv; Sundquist, *To Wake the Nations*, 155–63; Maggie Sale, *The Slumbering Volcano*, 156–72.

119 As evidence of this, look no further once again than to the seething hyperbole of the *Herald*'s journalist's reportage. Alluding to the contested accuracy of Box Brown's swamp, that doubting writer warns that "the bondage of slavery is bad enough, without evoking from the bottomless pit shades dark and gloomy, and auxillary horrors to dress up and horrify with," March 17, 1852. It is no wonder that viewers such as the editor would read the *Mirror* as a hyperbolically unrecognizable and an inauthentic frontier. Even American audience members were apparently put in the service of delegitimizing the panorama's authenticity and, in turn, Box Brown's narrative power. During the exhibition, the *Herald* journalist claims to have brought forth "an intelligent American gentleman, who has won a name throughout the civilised world, by our side at this exhibition, and who has visited the slave-states often, and seen the developments of slavery in every phase, and he declared to us that both the description pictorial, and description oral were as characteristic and resemblant of the original scenes and of slavery, as a young cabbage of full-blown rose."

120 D. Miller, *Dark Eden*, 122–23, 175.

121 David Reynolds, quoted in Bruce McConachie, *Melodramatic Formations*, 143. According to McConachie, the "dark adventure" form was utilized in popular panoramas as well as fiction, 135–45.

122 Wimbush, "Introduction: Reading Darkness," 21, 28; emphasis added.

123 Ibid., 18.

124 Leslie A. Fiedler, *Love and Death*, 29; Goddu, *Gothic America*, 4.

125 Robert D. Hume, "Gothic vs. Romantic," 284–85.

126 At the same time, however, the dangers of reading black antislavery discourse through the lens of the Gothic are numerous and distinct. See Goddu, *Gothic America*, 134. Certainly, the *Herald* editor's histrionic description of *the Mirror* as a mythical "sea-serpent surpassing and fire and brimstone-smacking exhibition" demonstrates how Gothic tropes and imagery potentially lend themselves to vacuous ahistoricism. The challenge, Goddu asserts, is for the slave narrative to "re-write the conventions of gothic fiction for its own factual ends," to, in effect, revise the genre by utilizing it to "rematerialize history while resisting its possible dematerializing effects" (135–38, 8, 21).

127 In this way, we might consider how the panorama may have produced a style of reversed luminism. The 1850s and 1860s aesthetic technique of luminism in landscape painting emphasized "clarity of light" and a long horizontal format intended to evoke the sublime and the "mystical effects of diffused light, giving a dreamily poetic atmosphere"; Patton, *Oxford History*, 83–84. Similarly, in the world of antebellum landscape art, Angela Miller argues, the "viewer's aesthetic experience re-enacted the actual experience of standing before the landscape of nature itself, preparing to move physically through it"; *Empire of the Eye*, 149.

Unlike "[m]uch antebellum landscape [which] visually insisted that the viewer belonged in the landscape, as part of it," the panorama's swamp creates spectatorial and epistemological obstacles for the viewer.

128 "Panorama of Slavery," *Wolverhampton & Staffordshire Herald*, March 17, 1852. Kara Walker expresses an interest in the cycloramic form because of its ability to create "a very heavy, monolithic, black presence—a curving black wall—in the gallery space, so that the viewer is aware of being contained in a black space"; interview with Lawrence Rinder.

129 Foucault, *Discipline and Punish*, 200; emphasis added.

130 Ibid., 208.

131 Meisel, *Realizations*, 62;. Wolff, "Passing Beyond," 31; A. Miller, "Panorama," 46.

132 D. Miller, *Dark Eden*, 179.

133 Ibid., 190–99; Cassuto, *Inhuman Race*, 124.

134 Cassuto, *Inhuman Race*, 83, 124; Hegel, *Philosophy of History*, 93–99.

135 *London Times*, July 30, 1852. Presumably forced to work with a smaller cadre of stage partners, Brown became even more of a one-man show while in England. Roberts did not accompany Brown to England, but J. C. A. Smith did. The mysterious fallout between the two former business partners is well known, although the specific details of their conflict remain a mystery. See Ripley, *Black Abolitionist Papers*, 293–201. Ruggles provides the most detailed account of Brown's and Smith's partnership and fallout. See Ruggles, *The Unboxing of Henry Brown*, especially 132–37.

136 Joanna Brooks, "Balm in Gilead." See also Joanna Brooks, *American Lazarus*.

137 Still, *Underground Railroad*, 70; Brown, *Narrative of the Life* (1851), 57. The misspelling of "hymn" yields a salient pun regarding Brown's "rebirth" from the box. See also Brown's 1849 version of this incident without the text of the song (*Narrative*, 63).

138 Al Raboteau has suggested to me that Psalm 40 resembles other passages calling for faith in times of trial. See Jonah 2:1–10 and Psalm 22. In these scriptures as in Psalm 40, the speaker looks to divine sources for deliverance. For examples of lament psalms ending in reversals, see Psalm 69 and Psalm 22; Claus Westermann, *Praise and Lament in the Psalms*; Patrick D. Miller, *Interpreting the Psalms*; Newman, introduction, *Narrative of the Life of Henry Box Brown*, xxiii. Newman suggests that Brown "sings, in anthem form, the first song" xxiii. For reasons that will become apparent below, I am inclined to believe that even if we were to read Brown's hymn as a truncation of the original psalm, the process of revision itself is crucial to understanding his use of song as escape.

139 Brown's use of Psalm 40 aligns him with other classical biblical escapees, like those of Psalms 56 and 57. For more on the enslaved's identification with Old Testament heroes in struggle, see L. W. Levine, *Black Culture*, 50; Arthur Jones, *Wade in the Water*, 48. My thanks to Sue Anne Morrow for her helpful thoughts about Psalm 40.

140 The 1840 antislavery hymnal *Freedom's Lyre* includes a version of Psalm 40 by

the influential nineteenth-century hymnist Isaac Watts. Watts's version of the psalm is included in the "Thanksgiving and Praise" section of the text and comprises only three stanzas: "I waited meekly for the Lord, / He bow'd to hear my cry: / He saw me resting on his word, and brought deliv'rance nigh. / Firm on a rock—he made me stand, / And taught my cheerful tongue, / To praise the wonders of his hand, / In new and thankful song. / I'll spread his works of grace abroad; / The saints with joy shall hear, / And sinners learn to make my God / Their only hope and fear.' " Hatfield, *Freedom's Lyre*, 256. Spencer argues that the "thanksgiving and praise psalms adapted by Watts and Hatfield, represent the eschaton of abolition—the Jubilee," *Stealing*, 59.

141  *Narrative of the Life* (1851), 62–63.

142  Wood, "All Right!" 80–81; Brown, 83; Mellonee Burnim, "Biblical Inspiration, Cultural Affirmation," 609–13.

143  Burnim, "Biblical Inspiration," 606.

144  Eileen Southern, *The Music of Black Americans*, 86, 185–88.

145  John Lovell, *Black Song*, 119, 223; the term "sacred ballad" is Lovell's; Lovell, 119; L. W. Levine, *Black Culture*, 39.

146  L. W. Levine, *Black Culture*, 32–33. In both the 1849 and 1851 versions of his *Narrative*, Brown describes the story of a fellow "colored man" working at the tobacco factory who endures a whipping for being in "the habit of singing religious songs quite often." Singing registers as a form of transgression and disturbance in both autobiographies; *Narrative* (1849), 43–44; Brown, *Narrative of the Life* (1851), 24–25.

147  Newman, introduction, *Narrative of the Life of Henry Box Brown*, xxiii; Elin Diamond, introduction, *Performance and Cultural Politics*; Thomas Briedenthal sermon, July 27, 2003, Princeton University Chapel; Lindon Barrett, *Blackness and Value*, *Seeing Double*, 57. In delivering Brown to himself, the "Hymn of Thanksgiving" ushers in a new Brown at multiple stages of his career. It appears first in the 1849 version of his narrative as the closing lines to Charles Stearns's notorious preface and as the penultimate lyrical interlude in the 1851 version of the text. In both cases, the song creates a bridge, delivering readers to Brown's primary story in the former and transitioning him into a free world populated by various antislavery friends in the latter. In the 1851 *Narrative*, Brown is immediately "taken by the hand and welcomed to the houses" of abolitionist "friends" and benefactors such as "Mr. J. Miller, Mr. McKim, Mr. And Mrs. Motte, Mr. And Mrs. Davis and many others," 59.

148  Spencer, *Stealing*, 35–59. Garrison was one of the first to spearhead collecting and publishing "fugitive poetical effusions" in songbook form (ibid., 36). The Anglo group the Hutchinson Family Singers are perhaps the most well-known abolitionist and social reform singing group of the antebellum era. See P. Gabrielle Foreman, *Dark Sentiment*. Spencer lists William Wells Brown, James Moses Horton, and Joshua McCarter Simpson as among the few black composers of abolitionist hymns. Wells Brown, Frederick Douglass, Harriet Tubman,

and Sojourner Truth are among the handful of black activists who were known for performing antislavery songs. Joshua McCarter Simpson is believed to be the only African American to have published a pamphlet of antislavery songs in 1852; Spencer, ibid., 46–47. For other examples of antislavery songs, see William Wells Brown, *The Anti-Slavery Harp*.

149 *National Anti-Slavery Standard*, January 31, 1850, and February 7, 1850. Samuel May introduced J. C. A. Smith as "James Boxer Smith" at the Syracuse Anti-Slavery Convention in 1850 (*National Anti-Slavery Standard*, January 31, 1850).

150 Wood, "All Right!," 84. See also Newman, introduction, *Narrative of the Life of Henry Box Brown*, xxiii–xxvi.

151 Wolff, "Passing Beyond," 24, 27.

152 Frederick Douglass, *Narrative of the Life of Frederick Douglass*, 107; T. A. Waters, *The Encyclopedia of Magic and Magicians*, 228.

153 *Leeds Mercury*, May 24, 1851.

154 *The Liberator*, May 31, 1850.

155 The link between these disparate forms of cultural work is even more striking when one considers how Brown had utilized his early boxing appearances to raise funds in order to ship his panorama from the States to England. The *London Daily News* reported on November 6, 1850, that Brown and Smith had "landed on [English] shores almost penniless. They contrived to get their panorama on board the vessel with them, but they are unable to release it, unless they receive assistance from some benevolent friends of the colored race." R. D. Webb notes on November 12, 1850, that Brown had "arrived in England with a panorama of slavery but without money to pay his passage. So that by the last accounts his panorama was in pledge in Liverpool." "R. D. Webb Letter to Mrs. Chapman," MS.A.9.2.25, 42 in Boston Public Library, Rare Books and Manuscript Reading Room. Thanks to Stuart Walker, the rare book curator, for his assistance with this transcription. Brown and J. C. A. Smith's boxing routine appears to have been fueled largely by a need to generate money to pay for shipping the display. Ripley reports that, once in the United Kingdom, the two men "lectured, sang, and sold lithographs" to generate shipping funds; *Black Abolitionist Papers*, 298 n. 2. In a wry metaphorical twist, then, Brown was placed in the position of having to re-create his escape in order to "free" his story; yet again he was forced to commodify the spectacle of his flight in order to recuperate the representation of that flight in the panorama. See Ripley, ibid.

156 Goddu, *Gothic America*, 20.

157 Karen Beckman, *Vanishing Women*, 8.

158 Kent, "Spectacular History," 17.

159 Beckman, *Vanishing Women*, 19; Ruth Brandon, *The Life and Many Deaths of Harry Houdini*, 171.

160 Waters, *Encyclopedia of Magic*, 42; Henry Hay, *Cyclopedia of Magic*, 203–12; Brandon, *Harry Houdini*, 153.

161 Geoffrey Lamb, *Victorian Magic*, 53–54; Ricky Jay, *Learned Pigs and Fireproof Women*; James Cook, *The Arts of Deception*. Houdini would later break the connections between mesmerism and magic. The Davenports mixed spiritualism hoaxes with escape tricks, Lamb, *Victorian Magic*, 53, 54, 76. Beyond the Davenports, American magic show acts continued to evolve in the late 1840s and early 1850s. Between 1849 and 1850, for instance, Boston alone hosted multiple magician acts at music halls and theatres throughout the city at precisely the moment when Box Brown would have been touring the northeast; H. J. Moulton, *History of Magic in Boston*, 36–37; Simon During, *Modern Enchantments*, 107.

162 Brandon, *Harry Houdini*, 162; Kenneth Silverman, *Houdini!*, 42.

163 Brown, *Narrative of the Life* (1851), 54.

164 Brandon, *Harry Houdini*, 165. See also J. Brooks, *American Lazarus*.

165 J. Brooks, *American Lazarus*. Reilly reveals how abolitionist visual media circulated images of the slave ship as a way to protest the dehumanizing effects of the slave trade; "Art of the Antislavery Movement," 62. Live burial operates as a major trope in other slave narratives such as Charles Ball's 1858 narrative, which documents his experience inside of a living tomb on his master's estate. See Ball, *Fifty Years in Chains*; Kari J. Winter, *Subjects of Slavery, Agents of Change*.

166 Brandon, *Harry Houdini*, 59, 152.

167 Ibid., 153.

168 Silverman, *Houdini!*, 39.

169 Brandon, *Harry Houdini*, 166. Gates, foreword, *Narrative of the Life* (1851), x.

170 Fisch, " 'Negrophilism,' " 30.

171 *West London Observer*, March 12, 1859; Fisch, " 'Negrophilism,' " 31. For more on Chadwick, see Ruggles, *The Unboxing of Henry Brown*. However, Lamb reveals that "conjurers of the [Victorian] period freely awarded themselves professorships and doctorates"; *Victorian Magic*, 88. Brandon cites A. J. Davis and other spiritualists as having claimed a certain kind of popular science known as "magnetizing"; see Ruth Brandon, *The Spiritualists*, 12.

172 The *West London Observer* for March 19, 1859, reports that Mrs. Brown's "descriptive introduction of the many pictures is very well written, and are delivered in a manner highly creditable to her, and very charming to her audience.

173 The newspaper reports that these "experiments" were "excellent and very successful."

174 Audrey Fisch, *American Slaves in Victorian England*, 82–83. Called by indigent peoples the "rebellion," the Indian Mutiny commenced on May 10, 1857, when English officers of three regiments were shot. Delhi was consequently recaptured from the English.

175 See, for instance, the infamous and litigious conflict with J. C. A. Smith in which Smith hinted at Brown's duplicity. In a letter to Gerrit Smith, J. C. A. Smith described the breach in their partnership and the fiscal controversy between the two men; Ripley, *Black Abolitionist Papers*, 293–99. Smith describes Brown as

having "behaved very bad sence [*sic*] he have been here—and indeed his Character is that bad I am ashamed to tell it for he drinks, smoke, gamble, sware and do many other things too Bad—to think off [*sic*]." J. C. A. Smith, Letter from J. C. A. Smith to Gerrit Smith, August 6, 1851, in Ripley, ibid., 296.

176 Fisch, *American Slaves*, 83.

177 Fisch, " 'Negrophilism,' " 31. Pease and Pease note that Charles Remond lectured on Indian slavery in the British Isles during his 1840–42 tour. This perhaps could have set a precedence for black abolitionist engagement with Indian social politics and oppression; see *They Who Would Be Free*, 56.

178 R. Laurence Moore, *In Search of White Crows*, 77. He points out that Garrison "would take an interest in spiritualism" as his reformist principles evolved in the 1840s, 74. Moore also points out that Gerrit Smith "believed in spirit communication and professed that the spiritualists he encountered were also reformers." See also Ann Braude, *Radical Spirits*; Barbara Goldsmith, *Other Powers*.

179 Ripley, *Black Abolitionist Papers*, 298. For more on Gerrit Smith's connections to J. C. A. Smith, see Ripley, ibid., 293–98.

180 Moore, *In Search of White Crows*, 77.

181 Ibid. Moore stresses, however, that spiritualism and abolitionism did not "share the common ground of similar philosophies. In fact, it was just the opposite." While Garrisonian abolitionists held "very literal beliefs of Christian millennialism. . . . No spiritualist seemed to fear, as Garrison once did, that a society permitting slavery was in danger of going to Hell" (78).

182 Brandon, *The Spiritualists*, 13, 12; Moore, *In Search of White Crows*, 70.

183 Henry Box Brown, *Narrative of the Life* (1851), first English edition. Future references to this edition will be cited parenthetically.

184 Olney, " 'I Was Born,' " 173. Ruggles speculates that Brown may have, in fact, been illiterate, making it impossible for him to have literally "authored" this text. We might, however, leave open the possibility for creative forms of collaborative production in relation to this second text. See Ruggles, *The Unboxing of Henry Brown*, 128–29.

185 This image is included in the Manchester-issued version of the narrative that I have obtained; however, Newman's U.S. publication of this text does not include the print image opposite its title page. Bernard Reilly lists this print as a lithograph which was probably first published in Boston in 1850. See "The Resurrection of Henry Box Brown at Philadelphia," in Reilly, *American Political Prints, 1766–1876*, 332–33. Reilly identifies Frederick Douglass as one of the figures portrayed in the print and "holding a claw hammer" to aid in the unboxing (333). Still lists the men present at the actual event as "J.M. McKim, Professor C.D. Cleveland, Lewis Thompson," and himself (*Underground Railroad*, 69). See also Ruggles, *The Unboxing of Henry Brown*.

186 Brown, *Travels*, 108.

187 Olney, " 'I Was Born,' " 161.

188 See Still, *Underground Railroad*, 69.

189 Brown, *Narrative of the Life* (1851), v–vi.

190 Stepto, "I Rose," 227.

191 Still, *Underground Railroad*, 71–3.

192 Hartman, *Scenes of Subjection*, 35.

193 *West London Oberver* and *Cardiff Times*, as quoted in Ruggles, *The Unboxing of Henry Brown*, 151.

194 Ruggles, *The Unboxing of Henry Brown*, 145. Indeed, even Wells Brown would eventually express his distaste for his one-time colleague's extravagant aesthetics, calling him at one point "a very foolish fellow" who dared to wear "a gold ring on nearly every finger" and whose ruffled outfits, "green dress coat and white hat" resembled that of "a well dressed monkey." Wells Brown, as quoted in ibid., 145.

195 *Cardiff Times*, as quoted in Ruggles, *The Unboxing of Henry Brown*, 158.

196 Ruggles, *The Unboxing of Henry Brown*, 159.

197 Ruggles has unearthed the marvelous late-nineteenth-century "return" of Box Brown and family to the States. He notes, however, that "no information about what became of [the Browns] after 1878 has been found." Ibid., 161–69.

## 3. "The Deeds Done in My Body"

1 Halttunen, *Confidence Men and Painted Women*; James W. Cooke, *The Arts of Deception*; Susan Gillman, *Dark Twins*. In 1858, white audiences attacked Truth on the grounds that she was a man masquerading as a female orator; William Hayward, Boston *Liberator*, October 15, 1858. For more on this incident, see below. Called "Millie-Christine," the Carolina twins were born into slavery in 1851, the daughters of Jacob and Monemia McKoy, and were "exhibited" by Barnum as well as a number of other show business entrepreneurs in the United States and England. In one particularly extraordinary episode, the twins endured a well-publicized custody trial while in England. One description of the incident alleges that the twins' handlers had "influenced" more than one "colored woman" to falsely "testify upon oath that she was [their] mother" in exchange for "a rich reward." See *History and Medical Description of the Two-Headed Girl*, 7–8. See also Joanne Martell, *Fearfully and Wonderfully Made*. Some have also questioned the intent and purposes of Tabbs Gross, the Cincinnati black man and entertainment promoter (called by some "the nation's black P. T. Barnum") who waged a court battle to gain guardianship of the musical prodigy Thomas Greene Wiggins ("Blind Tom"). Before he was two, Wiggins was purchased by Georgia's Bethune family, who subsequently exploited his precocious musical talents for profit. In what was a historic move, in 1865 Gross sought unsuccessfully to sue the Bethunes for custody of Wiggins. A former slave himself, Gross weathered the Bethune attorney's orchestrated attacks on his character as he attempted to wrest Wiggins from the control of a pro-Confederate family. Nevertheless, questions remain regarding the extent to which Gross in part pursued "Blind Tom" in order to obtain a cut of the profit in the revenue

from his performances. See Geneva Handy Southall, *The Continuing Enslavement of Blind Tom*, 50. See also Southall, *Blind Tom*, 45–69. Barbara Schmidt claims that Gross was "sometimes described as the nation's black P. T. Barnum"; see Schmidt, "Archangels Unaware," at http://www.twainquotes.com/arch angels.html. Ironically, the Arkansas lawyer and political journalist Tabbs Gross (formerly of Cincinnati) was dubbed " 'an imposter and an enemy to his race' " in 1869 when he controversially extended "an olive branch to the Democratic party of Arkansas" in what was seemingly more of a maverick approach to Reconstruction coalition building than a self-serving act of political accommodation. See Diane Neal, "Seduction, Accommodation, or Realism?," 57–64. A remarkable late-nineteenth and early-twentieth-century example of such a figure would be that of Joseph Howard Lee, alias "Bata Kindai Amgoza Ibn Lo Bagola." The African American Lee developed a successful transatlantic career by fraudulently marketing himself as "a black Jew from the southern Sahelian region of West Africa." See David Killingray's and Willie Henderson's illuminating article "Bata Kindai Amgoza ibn LoBagola and the Making of an African Savage's Own Story," 228–65. I am of course suggesting here that, while the "classic" racial passing narrative, particularly of the post-Reconstruction era, provides well-worn examples of African American protagonists who dabbled in identity "hoax," the stories of black historical figures who played high-stakes games with diverse forms of fraudulence are less familiar to many.

2   *The Reporter* claims that some of these individuals had incorporated the use of panoramas into their lectures and appearances; see "Coloured Lecturers—Caution," *The Anti-Slavery Reporter*, March 1, 1854, vol. 2, third series, 60. An article published several months later gives a detailed account of "the negro impostor" Reuben Nixon, who may have used the alias "Hill" in circulating a panorama and fugitive slave narrative; see "The Impostor Reuben Nixon," *Anti-Slavery Reporter*, third series, vol. 2, July 1854, 164–65. See also J. C. A. Smith's letter to the editor of the *Anti-Slavery Reporter* in which he critiques the publication for its irresponsible reporting and for its failure to promote the presence of legitimate black abolitionist activism: *Anti-Slavery Reporter*, March 13, 1854, in Ripley, *Black Abolitionist Papers*, 383–86. Smith wrote extensively of Brown's alleged moral dissipation in England; J. C. A. Smith to Gerrit Smith, August 6, 1851, in Ripley, *Black Abolitionist Papers*, 293–301. Jeffrey Ruggles provides the most detailed account of Brown's and Smith's partnership and fallout. See Jeffrey Ruggles, *The Unboxing of Henry Brown*, especially 132–37.

3   Following her marriage to Alexander Menken in 1856, Adah Isaacs Menken gained some local notoriety as an up-and-coming actress in and around the New Orleans area. From June 1858 through September 1859, she enjoyed success in Cincinnati, where she lived with her husband, wrote poetry for such publications as the *American Israelite*, and acted on the stage in a variety of roles. Renee M. Sentilles, *Performing Menken*, 22–49. Future references to Sentilles's text will be cited parenthetically as Sentilles, *Performing Menken*, unless otherwise noted.

4 Menken circulated multiple and competing narratives about her lineage. She became Ada Isaacs Menken in 1856 when she married the theatre manager Menken
and later added the "h." She briefly assumed the surname Heenan when she
married the pugilist John Carmel Heenan in 1860, signing her name publicly as
such. Her first published biographical sketch suggests that she was born the
daughter of Dr. Josiah Campbell of New Orleans; *New York Illustrated News*,
March 17, 1860. The 1888 introduction to her posthumously published collection
of poetry, *Infelicia*, insists that her "baptismal name was Adelaide McCord" (iii).
While performing in England in 1865, she began to assume several variations of
the name Dolores; Sentilles, *Performing Menken*, 126; Allen F. Lesser, *Enchanting
Rebel*, 247. See also "Adah Isaacs Menken to Gus," December 19, 1863, Adah Isaacs
Menken, ALS file, Harvard Theatre Collection, hereafter cited as AIM, ALS, HTC.
The name Ada Theodore surfaces in George L. Barclay's 1868 Menken biography,
*The Life and Remarkable Career of Adah Isaacs Menken*. In a posthumously
published autobiographical sketch, she claimed to have been born Marie Rachel
Adelaide de Vere Spenser; see Adah Isaacs Menken, "Some Notes of Her Life in
Her Own Hand," *New York Times*, September 6, 1868, 8.

5 Sentilles, *Performing Menken*, 258–86. Theatre critic and Menken acquaintance
William Winter's notoriously scathing review of Menken's Broadway *Mazeppa*
performances remains the most hyperbolic example of patronizing, anti-Menken
backlash; see Winter, "Theaters, Mazeppa at the Broadway Theatre," *New York
Tribune*, May 1, 1866. Elizabeth Cady Stanton only warmed to Menken's work
in the wake of her death and the publication of her collection of poetry; Stanton, "Adah Isaacs Menken," in Gregory Eiselein, ed., *Infelicia and Other Writings*,
245–46.

6 Lesser, *Enchanting Rebel*; Lesser, "Adah Isaacs Menken," 143; Lesser, *Weave a
Wreath of Laurel*.

7 Sentilles, *Performing Menken*, 11; Martin Favor, *Authentic Blackness*; Valerie A.
Smith, *Not Just Race*.

8 In a stroke of imaginative genius and skilled research artistry, Sentilles poses a
fascinating theory about the possibility that Menken may have been one of three
young girls growing up near one another and perhaps playing alongside one
another in the streets of 1850s New Orleans; see *Performing Menken*, 280–82.

9 Judith Halberstam, *Female Masculinity*; Eva Saks, "Representing Miscegenation
Law," 36–69; Cheryl Harris, "Whiteness as Property," 276–91.

10 Harryette Mullen, "Optic White," 80.

11 Joan R. Sherman, introduction, *Collected Black Women's Poetry*, ed. Joan R.
Sherman, 1:xxix–xxxvi; Kathleen Thompson, "Adah Isaacs Menken."

12 At present, we must take Sentilles's word that Barclay did indeed author this
anecdote. The Menken-Newell union was notoriously turbulent. Legend has it
that Menken initially abandoned Newell on their wedding night in 1862 over a
conflict about her career as an actress. She was said to have departed by climbing
out a window of his New Jersey home, only later reconciling with him; Lesser,

*Enchanting Rebel*, 92; Sentilles, *Performing Menken*, 163. Menken's unhappiness in her marriage to Newell is well documented. In an 1864 letter sent from San Francisco to an unnamed recipient, she cautions, "If you have a sister . . . never permit her to marry a 'Gentleman.' That means every sorrow of her existence. . . . suffice it to say that I married a 'gentleman.' Perhaps you do not know what these words mean as I do. It means a far superior being to either you or me. It is a being who lives in a realm far above us, and who occasionally condescends to tell us what. Low, wicked and lost creatures we are. No matter. Steer clear of 'Gentlemen' "; AIM, unmarked clipping file, HTC. Later that year and following their separation, Menken articulated a deep fear and distrust of Newell in letters that she wrote to doting confidante Ed James while in England; see, e.g., Adah Isaacs Menken to Ed James, December 19, 1864, AIM, ALS, HTC. Newell's own career was unstable and ultimately tragic. He died destitute and alone while boarding with his sister-in-law in 1901; "Robert H. Newell Dead," AIM, unmarked clipping file, HTC; "Orpheus C. Kerr, His Recent Death in Brooklyn and the True Facts of His Career," July 1901, AIM, unmarked clipping file, HTC.

13 Sentilles, *Performing Menken*, 275. The full quote reads: "I cannot feel with Abolitionism. It is more loathsome and disgusting to me than Catullus is to you. John Brown was a maniac. The North has heaped insult after insult upon the South, and it is time the latter turned. Oh, were I a man—a soldier—I'd march into the very midst of the battle, and, with voice of thunder and hands of iron, I'd shatter and cast down every chain that binds the glowing heart of the proud South to the pale, sneering sister who would crush her to the dust. . . . I love my country—the South. Oh, that, like Judith, I could go to the tent of this black Holfernes, and save my people!" Newell concludes, "It is certain, however, that her parentage was radically Southern enough to justify her in declaring" this; September 1860, in Robert Henry Newell, "Adah Isaacs Menken," publication unknown, included in the scrapbook "Biography of Adah Isaacs Menken. Extra Illustrated," found in Hay Library, Brown University, Providence, Rhode Island.

14 Joseph Roach, *Cities of the Dead*, 235. See also John Blassingame, *Black New Orleans, 1860–1880*; Virginia R. Dominguez, *White by Definition*; Arnold Hirsch and Joseph Logsdon, *Creole New Orleans*; Letter to Ed James, December 1862, AIM, ALS, HTC; Adah Isaacs Menken, "Pro Patria," in Eiselein, ed., *Infelicia and Other Writings*, 97–102.

15 Daphne A. Brooks, "Lady Menken's Secret."

16 Hortense Spillers, "Mama's Baby, Papa's Maybe."

17 John S. Kendall, " 'The World's Delight' "; Arna Bontemps and Jack Conroy, *They Seek a City*, 98. A 1965 *Negro Digest* article proclaiming Menken to be a "Negro Beauty" seems to have been culled largely from Kendall and Noel Gerson's ambiguous research. See Gerson, *Naked Lady*; Walter Monfried, "The Negro Beauty Who Bewitched Two Continents," 86–90. In 1961 the composer Norman Dello Joio mounted a libretto which claimed to be loosely based on Menken's life and which "rechristened" her "Ninnette La Fond . . . an octoroon who passes for

white" and is "loved by a wealthy young Southerner who pursues her as her career takes her to New York and eventually Paris." See Alan Rich, "Opera: 'Blood Moon' Song," *New York Times*, September 20, 1961, found in Adah Isaacs Menken file, Billy Rose Theatre Collection, New York Public Library for the Performing Arts; Adah Isaacs Menken, "Infelicia," in Sherman, ed., *Collected Black Women's Poetry*; Kathleen Thompson, "Adah Isaacs Menken"; Daphne A. Brooks, " 'The Deeds Done in My Body' "; Sentilles, *Performing Menken*, 274.

18 Bontemps and Conroy, *They Seek a City*, 107.

19 Blassingame, *Black New Orleans*, 201. Menken cites New Orleans as one of several childhood hometowns in her "Notes of My Life," believed by many to be a highly fictitious biographical sketch; Adah Isaacs Menken, "Some Notes of her life in her own Hand," *New York Times*, September 6, 1868. Virginia R. Dominguez, *White by Definition*, 122. Dominguez argues that many thought of Creole identity as a product of region (124).

20 Dominguez, *White by Definition*, 132–33. Hirsch and Logsdon add that "by 1860, fear and discouragement ran deeply through the entire black community of New Orleans, as the fragile rights and freedoms of those who were free or slave, creole or American vanished in the decade before the Civil War"; see *Creole New Orleans*, 209.

21 "Ada Isaacs Menken, the Wife of John C. Heenan," *New York Illustrated News*, March 17, 1860, 273–74. In his own research, Kendall identifies Menken as Philomene Croi Theodore, born in 1839 to Auguste Theodore, a mulatto registered as a "free man of color," and his French Creole wife Magdaleine Jean Louis Janneaux, but critics such as John Cofran and Sentilles have disputed these claims. See Kendall, " 'The World's Delight,' " 846–68; also see John Cofran, "The Identity of Adah Isaacs Menken"; Sentilles, *Performing Menken*, 274–86. In terms of Menken's ties to New Orleans, we know at the very least that she and Alexander lived and worked in the city briefly in late 1856 following their marriage; Sentilles, *Performing Menken*, 26. While we have no actual proof that the couple was there outside these years, Sentilles has pointed out to me, in a conversation in December 2003, that Menken's allusions to New Orleans culture seem to suggest her ties to that region. Menken wrote obliquely of the region in an essay published in 1858 in the New Orleans *Daily Delta*, "Mid-night in New-Orleans"; it is included in Eiselein, ed., *Infelicia and Other Writings*, 168–73; Sentilles, *Performing Menken*, 149.

22 See the *New York Illustrated News*, March 31, 1860, for a description of the Menkens in New Orleans. John S. Kendall, *The Golden Age of New Orleans Theatre*, 372–73; "Ada Isaacs Menken, The Wife of John C. Heenan, the Benecia Boy (Continued)," *New York Illustrated News*, March 31, 1860, 311. Dominguez points out that in 1857 New Orleans, marriages between whites and "free-colored" people were "on the rise"; *White by Definition*, 26.

23 Hirsch and Logsdon contend in *Creole New Orleans* (195) that passing was less

common in New Orleans and that "a good number of New Orleans free people of color chose another path" from assimilation. Many, they maintain, engaged in a form of "creole radicalism . . . to challenge American racial conceptions and the imposition of Jim Crow. It was no accident that Homer Plessy came from New Orleans." Dominguez, *White by Definition*, 9. For more on the culture of passing, see Gayle Wald, *Crossing the Line*.

24 In her dissertation on Menken, Sentilles considers both Jewish and African-American cultural politics within the broader fabric of multicultural New Orleans as an added backdrop to Menken's past in that city; see "Performing Menken."

25 Brody, *Impossible Purities*, 7.

26 At the same time, I should point out that my intent in reading for the coded ways in which blackness erupted in relation to Menken is by no means a gesture intending to circumscribe her identifications. Such a move would clearly serve to undermine the larger point that I am trying to make about the production of racial metaphors in generic and cultural spaces. As a black feminist scholar who is particularly concerned with the ways that the backs of women of color continue to persist as roadways to power for others, I am primarily concerned with how blackness and how black female sexuality in particular recede into the background of cultural consciousness—even as it washes over the bodies of "white-looking" women like Menken. My thinking here is greatly influenced by the work of Jennifer Brody, who reminds us that "the 'black' woman becomes an object that enables the 'white' to perform femininity properly and with impunity" in Victorian culture. Brody, *Impossible Purities*, 38.

27 Barclay claims that Menken told the captivity story to his "friend," the actor William Wallis; see *Life and Career*, 29. The character may have been based on the historical figure "Eagle Eye" who encountered white homesteaders in Idaho during the 1860s and led the initial movement to maintain peaceful relations between the Weiser Indians and white homesteaders. Relations between Eagle Eye's Weiser Indians, white settlers, and Idaho officials were eventually strained by the Snake War of 1866–88 and a number of conflicts in the 1870s. See Hank Corless, *The Weiser Indians*. Chief Eagle Eye also surfaces as a character in an 1862 equestrian production of *Eagle Eye* in which Menken starred at the New Bowery on September 22, 1862. The playbill lists Menken as having played for the first time Otahontas, or the Eagle Eye, a young Chief of the Delawares. Otahontas/Eagle Eye is said to die in the third act, "a noble Indian." See AIM, Productions Clipping File (hereafter PCF), HTC.

28 George Lipsitz, *The Possessive Investment in Whiteness*; Valerie Smith, "Reading the Intersection of Race and Gender," 43–45.

29 Barclay, *Life and Career*, 21–22. All future references to this text will be cited parenthetically. The *New York Illustrated News* published a version of this text which is even crasser and includes numerous racist caricatures. In this version of

the tale, Adah is protected from a "Mr. Big Injun" by "Mrs. Big Injun," from whom she receives protection and "every attention, and all advances from Indian lovers were strictly prohibited"; see the issue of March 24, 1860, 291.

30 This coalition between Menken and Laulerack works to contest some European narratives that pit light and dark women against one another. See Kim Hall, *Things of Darkness*, 178–87. On the other hand, the literary precedence for this frontier Menken persona is, of course, found in Catharine Maria Sedgwick's *Hope Leslie* (1827) in which the heroine rescues an Indian woman from prison. As Nina Baym has pointed out, in "the crisis of a Sedgwick novel the heroine must usually prove her principles by carrying out an act of rescue that is both morally correct and physically daring; see Baym, "The Rise of the Woman Author," 293. See also other examples of frontier adventures published in the popular American press during the 1860s, such as the serialized "The Wooden Walls: Adventures of John Mainbrace," *Spirit of the Times*, March 1863, vol. 8, 33–34. Most assume this narrative to be largely fictional. No historical documents corroborate Menken's whereabouts in Texas before 1854. A marriage certificate from that year "tells us that before she married Menken, she had married W. H. Kneass, signing herself as 'Adda Theodore' "; Sentilles, *Performing Menken*, 24. Not surprisingly, this has not stopped several texts from claiming Menken as a born and bred Texan. See, for instance, Pamela Lynn Palmer, "Adah Isaacs Menken," in which the captivity narrative is repeated.

31 Sentilles observes that the "story of Laulerack demonstrates the importance of exoticism in Menken's celebrity." She also points out that there is no material suggesting that she had ties to the Native American community beyond the scope of this tale; see *Performing Menken*, 130–31.

32 Brody, *Impossible Purities*, 43–44.

33 Adah Isaacs Menken, "Some Notes of Her Life in Her Own Hand." Lesser claims that Daly had held the materials for six years in anticipation of turning them into a book but the project never materialized; see Lesser, *Enchanting Rebel*, 246–47. Much of the information in the text, such as Menken's claim that her father was "Richard Irving Spenser, a young American student, whose father so nobly defended Spenser Ford in South Carolina during the Revolutionary War," has been proven inaccurate by recent biographers.

34 In 1860, Menken made frequent allusions to the death of her "mother" in her published poetry; see "Our Mother," in Eiselein, ed., *Infelicia and Other Writings*, 153.

35 Susan Gillman, *Dark Twins*. Gillman points out that past biographical studies of Twain have sought to draw a correlation between his fiction's preoccupation with "proliferating doubles" and "the overlapping series of masks that constitutes the writer's invented personae—funny man, satirist, public performance/reformer—and to situate these roles in the context of his life and times" (2).

36 Adah Isaacs Menken, "Swimming against the Current," in Eiselein, ed., *Infelicia and Other Writings*, 176–79. Mankowitz maintains that "Menken gave an occa-

sional thought to the shamefully neglected Southern genius whose work she respected so highly"; see *Mazeppa*, 89. While living in Ohio, Menken gave a dramatic reading of Poe's "The Raven"; Mankowitz, *Mazeppa*, 58. She later reportedly read Poe alongside Shakespeare during an appearance at New York's Broadway Hall. Menken reproduced reviews of the latter reading in a letter to Ed James, May 20, 1862, AIM, ALS, HTC. Sherman speculates that Menken "may have borrowed from Poe the brooding shadow of death," demons, and "melancholy" but that her fundamental influence was seemingly Whitman's free-verse style, his "frank, deficient self-revelations" and "the focus on the 'me, myself'" in what Menken called her "wild soul-poems"; see Sherman, introduction, *Collected Black Women's Poetry*, xxxv.

37 Toni Morrison, *Playing in the Dark*, 37.

38 Joan Dayan, "Amorous Bondage," 260–61. To the narrator, Ligeia "came and departed as a shadow"; Poe, "Ligeia," 169–71. Thus Dayan reads her as "the site for a crisis of racial identity. . . . That Ligeia would not tell her lover about her family, or ever reveal her 'paternal name' makes this lady sound as if she might well be Poe's rendition of the favorite fiction of white readers: the 'tragic mulatta' or 'octoroon mistress'" (260).

39 When Ligeia's imminent return is prefigured in the final pages of the text with "four large drops of a ruby-colored fluid," transforming blond Rowena into raven-haired Ligeia, Poe's text with the scarlet drops of seeming blood prefigures the impending racial hysteria embedded in the Jim Crow "one-drop" rule. Ligiea's blood "contaminates" Rowena, turns her into something and some one else an/other.

40 Light and dark children are, of course, familiar images in slave narratives from the same period as well. Consider Harriet Jacobs's tale of two antebellum girls in her 1861 *Incidents in the Life of a Slave Girl*. In grand euphemistic terms, Jacobs describes seeing "two beautiful children playing together. One was a fair white child; the other was her slave, and also her sister. . . . I foresaw the inevitable blight that would be changed to sighs. The fair child grew up to be a still fairer woman. . . . How had those years dealt with her slave sister, the little playmate of her childhood? . . . She drank the cup of sin, shame, and misery, whereof her persecuted race are compelled to drink," 29.

41 Poe, "Ligeia," 168.

42 Newell, "Biography of Adah Isaacs Menken," Hay Library, Brown University.

43 Ibid. Aligning her with the white father would work consistently with Newell's seeming attempts to distance Menken from black identity politics in this text. It would also serve to affirm his knee-jerk argument about Menken's having lacked "true" womanly traits as a result of identifying disproportionately with the father figure.

44 Spillers, "Mama's Baby, Papa's Maybe." Considering Menken's ties to New Orleans, it is also worth taking note of that city's history of the "quadroon fancy girl balls," a public and celebrated confluence of slavery and prostitution which

trafficked in captive women who were passed from the patriarchal tyranny of slavery into that of gentrified concubinage. "Fancy girl auctions" and "quadroon balls" conjured up the false veneer of property and class mobilization for women who were in fact property themselves. Hence Menken's efforts to ascend into the sphere of wealth and social mobility represent an alternative to the potential route that a black Menken might have been forced to take. For more on the "fancy girl" auctions, see Roach, *Cities of the Dead*, 211–17. For more on the New Orleans "quadroon" and "octoroon" balls, see Sentilles, "Performing Menken," 65–70.

45  The *Illustrated News* article also includes allusions to Menken's having a "slave" named Lorenzo (March 24, 1860). See Brody, *Impossible Purities*, 44.

46  Unmarked clipping from March 24, 1860; portfolio in the Player's Collection, clipping file, Billy Rose Theatre Collection, New York Public Library for the Performing Arts.

47  See HTC for examples of the cartes-de-visite of Menken and Dumas. The most famous poem written in response to the Menken-Dumas affair mocked "L'Oncle Tom avec Miss Ada"; Falk, *The Naked Lady*, 206. Mark Twain wrote a particularly patronizing and racist account of Menken's relationship with Dumas in the *Daily Alta*. Warily he remarks that "I begin to regard Menken's conduct as questionable"; see Sentilles, *Performing Menken*, 243–46; "The Menken," *Daily Alta*, June 16, 1867. For more on Menken and Dumas, see Falk, 182–215 (British edition). See also Adah Isaacs Menken file, manuscript 100, box 282, UCLA Special Collections, for French responses to Menken in Paris. Sentilles contends that regardless of "her own personal history, Menken's relationship with Dumas surely brought her into contact with the New Orleans quadroon poets who had expatriated to Paris." *Performing Menken*, 243.

48  Falk, *Naked Lady*, 216. Falk describes the "stunt" as having elicited a massive response from the French theatre-going public. He relates the incident in a series of racist binarisms: "How, they asked, could anyone replace a beautiful white woman by a negress as ugly as the New Guinea or Senegambia type, who probably had no other professors of dramatic art than the apes whose lectures she had attended in the coconut forests?"; see 190–91. Anne Fausto Sterling argues that the enormous and long-running fascination with the body of Sarah Bartmann in England and France reflected how colonialist expansion's "discovery" of the " 'wild woman' raised troubling questions about the status of European women" and necessitated attempts among European scientists "to differentiate the 'savage' land/woman from the civilized female of Europe"; see "The Comparative Anatomy," 22. Clearly, Menken operates as an ironic pawn of this sort of effort, even as her liminal body represents the transgression of the very racial borders which the French public here seems so gleefully invested in rectifying.

49  Sentilles describes a fascinating 1868 article from the "Boston *Illustrated News*" which compares Menken to "a beautiful quadroon girl from Savannah" who is

"one of the leading women of the demi-monde in Paris." See "A Dusky Beauty—Menken Outstripped," *Boston Illustrated News*, July 14, 1868, p. 11, c. 1, cited in *Performing Menken*, 135.

50 In December 1862, Menken was briefly arrested by the Union army following a performance in Maryland on suspicion of serving as a spy for the Confederate army. For more on this incident, see Sentilles, *Performing Menken*, 166–71. See also Menken's letter to Ed James wherein she describes the incident and proclaims to have portraits of Davis, Van Dorn, and Bragg on her "large looking glass"; December 1862, AIM, ALS, HTC. Aside from the description of her "faithful slave named Lorenzo" in the *New York Illustrated News* article from March 24, 1860, several biographies corroborate the existence of Menken's having had an African American servant named Minnie who adopted the surname Menken and traveled with her employer to Europe; see Mankowitz, *Mazeppa*, 127. No one has researched the history of Minnie Menken. See Newell, "Biography of Adah Isaacs Menken," Hay Library, Brown University. Menken was also the author of the pro-Unionist poem, "Pro Patria." The "quadroon" anecdote surfaces in Mankowitz, *Mazeppa*, 174.

51 Harryette Mullen, " 'Indelicate Subjects,' " 5.

52 Painter, "Sojourner Truth," 13. Of late, there has been an explosion of fine new work in the field of alternative and unconventional biographical studies. See, for instance, Painter, *Sojourner Truth*; Farah Jasmine Griffin, *If You Can't Be Free*; Jean M. Humez, *Harriet Tubman*; Scot French, *The Rebellious Slave*. See also Gayle Wald's forthcoming biography of Sister Rosetta Tharpe (*Music in the Air*) and Camille Forbes's forthcoming biography of Bert Williams.

53 Painter, "Sojourner Truth," 9. Jean Fagan Yellin, *Women and Sisters*, 81–87; Painter, "Sojourner Truth," 8–12; Sojourner Truth, *Narrative of Sojourner Truth*, 125–27.

54 Charles T. Davis and Henry Louis Gates Jr., "Introduction: The Language of Slavery," xxiii; Margaret Homans, " 'Racial Composition'. "

55 Deborah McDowell, "Recycling," 253; Valerie Smith, "Black Feminist Theory," 45; Margaret Homans, " 'Women of Color,' " 87; Patricia Williams, *The Alchemy of Race*, 201; Ann duCille, "The Occult of True Blackwomanhood," 70.

56 Carla Peterson, foreword, *Eccentric Bodies*, xi–xii.

57 Carla Peterson, *"Doers of the Word,"* 29.

58 Painter, *Sojourner Truth*, 139.

59 William Hayward, Boston *Liberator*, October 15, 1858. See Dorothy Sterling, ed., *We Are Your Sisters*, 151–53.

60 Peterson, foreword, *Eccentric Bodies*, 29; Gage, "Reminiscences," 1962; Mullen, "Indelicate Subject," 3; Judith Butler, *Gender Trouble*, 25; Elin Diamond, "Mimesis," 371.

61 Diamond, "Mimesis," 371.

62 Marx as quoted in Lesser, *Enchanting Rebel*, 170; Falk, *Naked Lady*, 27, 142. Falk

claims that Marx "became acquainted" with Menken "during a visit to London in the winter of 1865" (142). For more on Marx's relationship with Menken, see Mankowitz, *Mazeppa*, 237.

63 Mullen, "Optic Whiteness," 77. We might go a step further and recognize the precedents that Menken established for other racially "free-floating" women of the theatre. Vaudeville performers such as the Whitman Sisters perhaps owe much to the spirit and hubris of Menken's professional tactics inasmuch as they were known to have first "passed" for white and later used their liminality as a way "to go back and forth between black and white identities, while remaining popular with both white and black audiences"; see Nadine George-Graves, *The Royalty of Negro Vaudeville*, 68. See also Herman Gray, *Cultural Moves*.

64 Amy Robinson, "It Takes One to Know One," 723; Robinson, "Forms of Appearance of Value"; Gayle Wald, *Crossing the Line*.

65 Mankowitz, *Mazeppa*, 174; Brody, *Impossible Purities*, 16.

66 Mark Twain, "The Menken—Written Especially for Gentlemen," 79; *San Francisco Theatre Research* (San Francisco: Federal Writers Project, WPA, 1938), vol. 5, 67; George D. Lyman, *The Saga of the Comstock Lode*, 270. Twain's analysis of Menken's performance here closely resembles Dickens's equally disconcerted description of legendary African dancer and minstrel performer Juba; see Dickens, *American Notes*; Lott, *Love and Theft*, 115–16. Several historians have argued that Twain was eventually won over by Menken's talent and later went on to champion her work during her west coast stint; Lyman, 275–76. Others have contested the sincerity of Twain's loyalty to Menken; Sentilles, *Performing Menken*, 196–97. See also Samuel Clemens to Pamela A. Moffet, March 18, 1864, Mark Twain Collection, Bancroft Library, University of California, Berkeley.

67 For an early and favorable review of Menken's New York stage work, see unmarked clipping from March 24, 1860, AIM Portfolio in The Player's Collection, Billy Rose Theatre Collection, New York Public Library for the Performing Arts. Murdoch was said to have had to prompt the actress on her lines throughout the performance. Mankowitz, *Mazeppa*, 6; Gerson, *Queen*, 115; Falk, *Naked Lady*, 54; Lesser, *Enchanting Rebel*, 75. Her controversial one-time lover, the poet Algernon Charles Swinburne, wrote of her that "she does not appear really to have been a very good actress"; see Swinburne, *Adah Isaacs Menken*, vi; Elizabeth Reitz Mullenix, *Wearing the Breeches*, 263.

68 Robert C. Allen, *Horrible Prettiness*, 125. References to this text hereafter cited parenthetically.

69 Unmarked clipping, Adah Isaacs Menken file, Gabrielle Enthoven Theatre Collection, Victoria & Albert Museum, London; *Illustrated Police News* clipping, December 20, 1879, AIM, ALS, HTC.

70 William Winter, *New York Daily Tribune*, May 1, 1866. Sentilles calls Winter's review "the worst review Menken ever received"; see *Performing Menken*, 223–24. See also Mullenix, *Wearing the Breeches*, 263.

71 *San Francisco Theatre Research*, 5:481; Winter, *New York Daily Tribune*, May 1, 1866; Lesser, *Enchanting Rebel*, 174–75.

72 Henry Milner, *Mazeppa*, 2–7. See also Byron, *Mazeppa*; the *Mazeppa* playbill, August 2, 1863, Adah Isaacs Menken clipping file, San Francisco Performing Arts Library (hereafter SFPAL); George R. MacMinn, *The Theater of the Golden Era in California*, 216–17.

73 Edward Said, *Orientalism*, 118–77.

74 Falk, *Naked Lady*, 93; Constance Rourke, *Troupers of the Gold Coast*, 176. Critics point out that "Charollotte Crampton, an accomplished and versatile actress (1816–75), not content with acting Richard III, Iago, Shylock, Hamlet, was the first woman to play Mazeppa with her trained horses, Alexander and Black Eagle, at the Chatham Theatre, New York, Jan. 3, 1859. Other women followed her example"; see *Mazeppa*, PCF, HTC. Crampton was said to have relied on a dummy to ride the horse across the stage, however, making Menken the first woman to make Cassimer's treacherous journey on horseback each night. Menken's success in the part led to a slew of actresses attempting the role. See Menken, Letter to Ed James, August 21, 1864, AIM, ALS, HTC.

75 Gerson, *Queen*, 36. Smith was the manager of Astley's ampitheatre in London in the fall of 1864.

76 Falk, *Naked Lady*, 53. See Mankowitz, *Mazeppa*, 18–19. A 1959 episode of the western television series *Bonanza*, "Magnificent Adah," brought to life the confusion and titillation of a Menken performance in Virginia City. During that performance, the Cartwright brothers sit wide-eyed in the raucous audience and struggle to discern whether Menken (played by the actress Ruth Roman) "is or isn't" nude on stage. My thanks to the 1997 W. E. B. DuBois Institute Colloquium for bringing this episode to my attention.

77 For more on Menken's mediation of highbrow and lowbrow theatre culture, see Sentilles, *Performing Menken*. See also Lawrence Levine, *Highbrow/Lowbrow*; *San Francisco Theatre Research*, 5:57; Tracy Davis, "The Actress," 106; *The Era* as quoted in Mankowitz, *Mazeppa*, 135; Tracy Davis, "Spectacle," 323, 326; Davis, *Actresses as Working Women*, 105–36. Future references to Davis's works will be cited parenthetically and by title. Mullenix points out that the attacks on Menken's costume may have been unwarranted; *Wearing the Breeches*, 89.

78 Claudia Johnson, *American Actress*, 3–36; Mary Ryan, *Women in Public*, 1–8; Sander Gilman, "Black Bodies," 256.

79 Peterson, *Doers*, 20.

80 H. B. Farnie as quoted in Falk, *Naked Lady*, 86; Menken letter as quoted in Mankowitz, *Mazeppa*, 131. See also Adah Isaacs Menken file, Gabrielle Enthoven Theatre Collection, Victoria & Albert Museum, London. English playbills of the 1864 tour of *Mazeppa* differed from their American counterparts in that they announced that the actress would be in "classic dress"; see *Mazeppa* playbill,

Mazeppa file, v&a Museum; Falk, *Naked Lady*, 64; Charles Warren Stoddard, "La Belle Menken," 479.

81 Mark Twain, "The Menken—Written Especially for Gentlemen," 78; Joy Kasson, "Narratives of the Female Body," 178, 182; Roach, *Cities of the Dead*, 220; Brody, *Impossible Purities*, 67–71.

82 Sentilles's *Performing Menken* provides excellent examples of female audience members' reactions to Menken performances (182–83). See Florence Fane, "Florence Fane in San Francisco: About Poor Cassimer," *Golden Era*, September 27, 1863; *New York Clipper*, May 12, 1866, 38. There is no reason to suspect that Menken's audiences were not often mixed-gender—particularly by the time she reached enormous mainstream success in San Francisco, on Broadway, and in London and Paris. However, my concern here is for the way that Menken's performance was filtered through the lens of patriarchy and ways of looking which attempted to keep certain kinds of bodies "open" and available for male-dominated (sexual) business.

83 Faye E. Dudden, *Women*, 164; Mankowitz, *Mazeppa*, 231–38.

84 Dudden, *Women*, 4. Dudden's characterization of writing as a "disembodied" art form overlooks a vast array of landmark feminist works, particularly by French scholars, which consider the site of writing as inextricably linked to the (female) body. See, for instance, Luce Irigaray, *Speculum of the Other Woman*.

85 Simon Press and Joy Reynolds, *The Sex Revolts*, 229–331; Sentilles, "Performing Menken," 27.

86 Anonymous, "Mazeppa Review," Adah Isaacs Menken clipping file, Gabrielle Enthoven Theatre Collection, Victoria & Albert Museum, London. Other critics came to her defense as well. The always supportive *Golden Era* of San Francisco pointed out the hypocrisy of "very many ladies who are fond of circuses and all gymnastic exhibitions, and who attend them regularly" but who "find much fault with 'Mazeppa' and come down on the Menken like hawks on a sparrow-bird"; see "Things," *Golden Era*, August 30, 1863, Astley's Theatre, 1769–1880 (microfilm), htc.

87 Tessa Ardenne, "Tessa Ardenne," *Golden Era*, March 20, 1864.

88 *Golden Era*, March 20, 1864.

89 Menken, Letter to Daly, July 18, 1862, aim, als, htc; *Spirit of the Times*, June 14, 1862, found in Billy Rose Theatre Collection, New York Public Library for the Performing Arts. For more on her tour itinerary, see Sentilles, *Performing Menken*, 152.

90 Mullenix, *Wearing the Breeches*, 89, 264; Allen, *Horrible Prettiness*, 107.

91 See *Mazeppa*.

92 Falk, *Naked Lady*, 57.

93 *Mazeppa* playbill, *Mazeppa* production file, sfpal.

94 The original Milner script for Mazeppa calls for the hero's horseback ride to be set against a "Moving Panorama of the Course of Dneiper River—a tremendous storm of thunder and lightening, hail and rain." See Milner, *Mazeppa*, 2.1.4. See also undated *Mazeppa* playbill, *Mazeppa* production file, htc. In the 1830s,

*Mazeppa* was the most performed panorama at Astley's ampitheatre. See Richard Altick, *The Shows of London*, 176.

95 See also Dudden, *Women*, 142–43.

96 Tessa Ardenne, "Tessa Ardenne," *Golden Era*, March 20, 1864; Sentilles, *Performing Menken*, 175.

97 "Adah Isaacs Menken," *Golden Era*, August 8, 1863; "Dramatic and Musical," *Golden Era*, September 13, 1863; "The Debut of Menken," *Daily Alta*, August 25, 1863. *Mazeppa's* initial San Francisco run lasted a total of sixteen nights and earned Menken the unprecedented salary of $500 per performance; "Dramatic and Musical," *Golden Era*, September 13, 1863.

98 Jennifer Terry as cited in Noreen Barnes-McLain, "Bohemian on Horseback," 71.

99 *Mazeppa* playbill, Adah Isaacs Menken, *Mazeppa* clipping file, Gabrielle Enthoven Theatre Collection, Victoria & Albert Museum, London. The handwritten notes resemble in tone those found on a program for *Uncle Tom's Cabin* at the Princess Theatre; see playbill, n.d., *Uncle Tom's Cabin* clipping file, Gabrielle Enthoven Theatre Collection.

100 Sentilles, *Performing Menken*, 200. Boucicault had reportedly "just failed" in mounting a production at Astley's prior to Menken's arrival in the fall of 1864. See unmarked clipping file, AIM. Portfolio Playbook Collection, Billy Rose Theatre Collection, New York Public Library for the Performing Arts.

101 Frank Mayo was just one of several local actors who were said to have had a following of their own in the lively world of antebellum San Francisco theatre. Mayo performed the role of "Pete, an Old Slave" alongside Sophie Edwin's Zoe in the San Francisco production of *The Octoroon* in April 1864. See "Amusements," *Golden Era*, April 3, 1864. Sophie Edwin and Frank Mayo appeared alongside Menken in the August 1863 run of *Mazeppa* in San Francisco. See San Francisco *Mazeppa* playbills, 1863, *Mazeppa*/Menken file, SFPAL. See also *Mazeppa* advertisement, *Daily Alta*, August 28, 1863. Frank Mayo appeared alongside Menken in the September 1863 production of *The French Spy*. See play advertisement, *Daily Alta Californian*, September 25, 1863. Sophie Edwin appeared alongside Menken in the April 1864 production of *Black Ey'd Susan*. See "Black Eyed Susan," *Golden Era*, April 24, 1864. For more information on the San Francisco productions of *Mazeppa*, *The French Spy*, and *The Octoroon*, see play files, SFPAL. See also Sophie Edwin and Frank Mayo in the Hartley chronological clipping files, SFPAL. Mankowitz notes that Maguire lined up San Francisco's most famous actors to work with Menken, but he neglects to mention Edwin. See Mankowitz, *Mazeppa*, 101.

102 "Zoe, The Octoroon," *Golden Era*, April 24, 1864. The poem is signed and dated "E.L.M., April 20, 1861, and could be a reprint. See also "Saving The Octoroon," *Punch*, December 24, 1861; "Black Ey'd Susan," *Golden Era*, April 24, 1864.

103 "The Debut of Menken," *Daily Alta California*, August 25, 1863; Berson, "San Francisco Stage," 57; "Adah Isaacs Menken: The Female Sensationalist of the 19th-Century," unmarked clipping in Newell, Adah Isaacs Menken Scrapbook,

John Hay Library, Brown University; T. C. Davis, *Actresses*, 114. See also Elin Diamond, *Unmaking Mimesis*, 73; Kendall, " 'World's Delight,' " 855.

104  Garber, *Vested Interests*; Judith Butler, *Bodies that Matter*, 172.

105  Sentilles, *Performing Menken*, 110; Brody, *Impossible Purities*, 9.

106  Said, *Orientalism*, 118–77; William Dimond, *The Aethiop*; Heidi Holder, "Melodram, Realism and Empire on the British Stage"; Judith Halberstam, *Female Masculinity*, 252. Menken famously donned men's attire while socializing and gambling offstage during her time in San Francisco. See photograph, Adah Isaacs Menken file, SFPAL. See also Barnes-McLain's queer reading of Menken's offstage drag attire, "Bohemian," 69–77. Sentilles, *Performing Menken*, 166–99.

107  Marjorie Garber, *Vested Interests*, 125; Laurence Senelick, "Boys and Girls," 83.

108  *Mazeppa*, Astley Theatre playbill, n.d., Gabrielle Enthoven Theatre Collection, Victoria & Albert Museum, London. The playbill declares that these lines "were previously published in California" but greatly resemble Byron's poem. See also *San Francisco Theatre Research*, 5:64.

109  Mullenix, *Wearing the Breeches*, 17; Allen, *Horrible Prettiness*, 128.

110  *Pioneer Westerns Playbills* in Adah Isaacs Menken file, SFPAL.

111  "The Debut of Menken," *Daily Alta Californian*, August 25, 1863. See also "Things," *Golden Era*, August 30, 1863. In a letter to Ed James sent from San Francisco, Menken indicates having purchased and trained one of her horses; January 13, 1864, AIM, ALS, HTC.

112  Letter to Gus Daly, AIM, ALS, HTC, July 18, 1862; *San Francisco Theatre Research*, 5:63. The WPA contends that horsemanship in California was "a second language, and the subtleties of Mazeppa's ride, possibly overlooked in the East, here provoked comment and appreciation," *San Francisco Theatre Research*, 5:65.

113  Halberstam, *Female Masculinities*, 58–59. See Byron, *Mazeppa*, especially stanzas XI–XIV, 25–33.

114  Sentilles, *Performing Menken*, 182–84; "Dramatic and Musical," *Golden Era*, September 13, 1863; Senelick, "Boys and Girls," 84.

115  Florence Fane, "About Poor Cassimer," *Golden Era*, September 27, 1863; Sentilles, *Performing Menken*, 182–84.

116  Letter to Gus Daly, July 18, 1862, AIM, ALS, HTC; Charles Warren Stoddard, "La Belle Menken," *National Magazine*, February 1905, 479. The speaker most likely is incorrect in his recollection of having seen Menken in *Jack Sheppard* in 1855; AIM, unmarked clipping, clipping file, HTC.

117  "Dramatic & Musical," *Golden Era*, September 13, 1863; Sentilles, *Performing Menken*, 182; Roach, *Cities of the Dead*, 36–41.

118  Tessa Ardenne, "Tessa Ardenne," *Golden Era*, March 20, 1864. The reference here could be to *Macbeth* 2.2.50–53: "The sleeping and the dead / Are but as pictures; 'tis the eye of childhood / That fears a painted devil." An English critic makes a similar reference to Box Brown's panorama as well; see "Panorama of Slavery," March 17, 1852, *Wolverhampton & Staffordshire Herald*. It could also, however, be a more immediate reference to Samuel Butler's *Canterbury Sketches* (1863):

"Nature will not bow to you, neither will you mend matters by patting her on the back and telling her that she is not so black as she is painted." Each of these texts could very well be derived from the proverbial statement " The devil is not so black as he is painted." My thanks to Sarah Meer and Richard Yarborough for assisting me with these references.

119 *Rookwood* (or *Rockwood*) was an equestrian drama in which Menken played "the dual part of Jack Palmer and Dick Turpin"; see *Variety & Sensation* (found in SFPAL), 90. Alternately titled *Dick Turpin*, the production received poor reviews during its San Francisco run. "Things," *Golden Era*, January 3, 1864. *Eagle Eye* was performed on September 22, 1862, at the New Bowery Theatre in New York City; *Eagle Eye* playbill, AIM, PCF, HTC. The production shares the same name with that of Menken's captor in her frontier tale. From the playbill's synopsis of the narrative, the play appears to bear little resemblance to Menken's narrative but may have shared similarities with early-nineteenth-century popular melodramas such as John Augustus Stone's *Metamora; or the Last of the Wampanoags* (1829).

120 *San Francisco Theatre Research*, 4:67; "Dramatic & Musical," *Golden Era*, September 13, 1863.

121 White, *Stories*, 119–22. See William Moncrieff, *Tom and Jerry*, 3.3.62 to 3.6.72, Rare Books, Firestone Library, Princeton University; Moncrieff, *Tom and Jerry*, 2.3.8, Playbooks Collection, TC023, Box 90, Rare Books, Princeton University. Menken was billed as performing "the Crib scene from Tom and Jerry" on the same bill as noted the "first and only appearance of Miss Annie Josephs," her professed "sister," Bowery Theatre playbill, March 23, 1860, AIM, PCF, HTC. For more on Annie Josephs and her possible connections to Menken, see Sentilles, *Performing Menken*, 281. Shane White contends that the play "probably affected the behavior of young white males; it certainly influenced the language with which newspapers recounted this behavior" and the public's perception of "the lower orders" of early-nineteenth-century city life; see *Stories*, 120. William Brown's all-black African Company boldly adapted Tom and Jerry, resituating the play in Charleston, South Carolina, and adding a slave market scene; see Marvin McAllister, *White People Do Not Know How to Behave*, 115–22. McAllister reveals that the original roles of African Sal and Dusty Bob were performed in blackface, 119. John Brougham's American version of *Tom and Jerry* became popular in the States in the 1850s as well but notably excises the blackface characters; see Brougham, *Life in New York*, found in Playbooks Collection, Box 19, Rare Books, Firestone Library, Princeton University.

122 *Joan of Arc* playbill, New Bowery Theatre, New York City, June 11, 1862, AIM, PCF, HTC; *The Whistler* playbill, New Bowery Theatre, New York City, June 13, 1862, AIM, PCF, HTC. Menken also performed *Tom and Jerry or Life in London* on June 13, 1862, with *The Whistler*. A playbill announces that "Miss Adah" will "play Corinthian Tom and others. In the 3rd Act Mr. Cornell and Mr. Conklin will give a display of the manly art, aided by Miss Adah." The original text of

*Tom and Jerry* includes several blackface-inspired caricatures, including "African Sal." See Moncrieff, *Tom and Jerry*, 3.3.62–66. Moncrieff's play describes Corinthian Tom as a "London sportsman"; see Moncrieff, *Tom and Jerry*, 9. See *The Whistler* or *Fate of the Lily of Leonard's* playbill, AIM, PCF, HTC. See also *A Day in Paris*, New Bowery Theatre playbill, June 14, 1862, AIM, PCF, HTC. Shane White discusses the fascinating case of the African Company's 1823 adaptation of *Tom and Jerry*; *Stories,* 119–24; see *The Child of the Sun* playbill, Astley's Theatre, AIM, PCF (n.d.), HTC. The list of "slaves" on *The Child of the Sun* playbill resembles that of *Eagle Eye's*. While John Brougham was well known for writing burlesques, Allen argues that even "his send-ups of Indian plays struck at the larger issue of their hypocritical romantic representation of Native Americans"; see *Horrible Prettiness*, 104. Even so, one of his most successful burlesque plays, *Metamora* (1847), relies on grotesque images of bloodthirsty "savages" in its representation of Native American character; see John Brougham, *Metamora*. See also John Brougham, *Po-Ca-Hon-Tas*; Mankowitz, *Mazeppa*, 146; David Grimsted, *Melodrama Unveiled*, 237–38; Sentilles, *Performing Menken*, 217–18.

123 A June 13, 1862, playbill for the New Bowery Theatre promotes Menken's "life like imitations" of famous players. See AIM, PCF, HTC. Menken performed in the play based on the life of the famed actress Lola Montez, whom she claims to have met shortly before Montez's death. See playbill for *Sixteen String Jack*, June 12, 1862, New Bowery Theatre, AIM, PCF, HTC. See also Sentilles, *Performing Menken*, 8–10. Menken also performed "Lola Montez" in San Francisco to strong reviews. See *Golden Era*, September 27, 1863. The WPA observes that "there was a kind of brutal humor in this burlesque, for Lola had just died." *San Francisco Theatre Research*, 5:66.

124 *The Whistler* playbill, September 27, 1862, AIM, PCF, HTC; *Sixteen String Jack* playbill, June 12, 1862, AIM, PCF, HTC. See also *The Whistler* at the Howard Athenaeum playbill, July 7, 1862, Papers of Adah Isaacs Menken, Manuscript Reading Room, Library of Congress, Washington.

125 George Taylor, "John Baldwin Buckstone," 3. Taylor points out that playwright J. B. Buckstone specialized in writing melodramas told "from the point of view of lower-class victims," 3. *Jack Sheppard* was first performed in 1839 at the Adelphi Theatre in England with Mrs. Keely in the lead and was conceived as a dramatization of a Harrison Ainsworth crime novel. Taylor suggests that "Sheppardism" may have had ties to working-class contempt for authority in its narrative of a young thief. In England, Lord Chamberlain banned the play until 1880 on the grounds that it had a malevolent influence on young people. See Taylor, introduction to *Trilby and Other Plays*, xvi–xvii. For more on the tradition of Jack Sheppard as a breeches role, see unmarked clipping, *Jack Sheppard*, PCF, HTC. Another unmarked clipping offers a detailed profile of Jack Sheppard's historical character as "a sprightly young dare devil with whom one hesitates to say how many landies are in love." The article adds that "he was but

eighteen when he began his notorious career and but twenty-two when, after several successful escapes from Newgate, one of which he effected after forcing six great doors, he was hung at Tyburn, Nov. 18, 1724, before 200,000 specta-tors." Unmarked clipping, *Jack Sheppard*, PCF, HTC.

126 Unmarked clipping, *Jack Sheppard*, PCF, HTC.

127 See J. B. Buckstone, *Jack Sheppard*, 4.5.87. Act 4.3 features the padlock scene. The play reaches a distinct climax at the beginning of Act 4.5 during Jack's mono-logue in which he declares his freedom and brags of his escape. Menken per-formed this role as early as July 1858 while in Dayton, Ohio, during what turned out to be a particularly controversial engagement. See Sentilles, *Performing Menken*, 44.

128 J. T. Haines, *The French spy*, Rare Books, Firestone Library, Princeton Univer-sity. All future references to this text will be cited parenthetically unless other-wise noted. *The French Spy* appears to have been included in Menken's reper-toire at least as early as 1860. See unmarked clipping, AIM Portfolio in the Player's Collection, Billy Rose Theatre Collection, New York Public Library for the Performing Arts. In San Francisco, *The French Spy* opened on the heels of the first run of *Mazeppa* in September 1863. Menken performed the play in various other parts of the country as well. "Dramatic and Musical," *Golden Era*, September 13, 1863.

129 "Adah Isaacs Menken. The Artist—Her Triumphal Career in California," *Golden Era*, April 17, 1864; "Dramatic and Musical," *Golden Era*, September 13, 1863.

130 Menken's *French Spy* costuming seems to resemble that worn by the original Mathilde, Madame Celeste. See AIM photograph, Dance Collection, New York City Performing Arts Library. See also "Madame Celeste as the French Spy" il-lustration, Special Collections, New York City Performing Arts Library. Haines's drama fixates on the confluence of sexual violation and imperial combat. In act 2.1, Achmet declares that the French threaten to impose "base conditions" onto his people and request that they "deliver up to them 500 of our most beautiful maidens" (15). Subsequently ordering his own dancing girls to engage in what the stage directions describe as "an emblematical ballet," Achmet makes plain his investment in female sexuality as a symbol of wealth and a prized booty in military conflict. *The French Spy* was originally produced in Paris in 1830 and performed by Mademoiselle Celeste in the title role, and thus was originally staged for the pleasures of a French audience perhaps searching to " 'reproduce itself in Algeria' "; David Prochaska as quoted in Said, *Culture and Imperialism*, 171. An 1870 Boston Museum promptbook, however, suggests that adjustments were made in the play to reaffirm the imperialistic benevolence of the United States as well. In this particular version, Colonel Bernelle is renamed "Delancey" and given a crucial line regarding America's political allegiances and invest-ments in European colonialism. In act 2 he exclaims to Achmet, "the Americans are too faithful friends in peace—too generous foes in war; even to join with Tyrants, or the enslaves of mankind!" See "Promptbook for *The French Spy*," the

property of the Boston Museum, June 1870, found in Rare Books, Firestone Library, Princeton University. For more on the culture of empire and theatre, see Heidi Holder, "Melodrama, Realism and Empire," 129–49; Michael Hays, "Representing Empire"; Said, *Culture and Imperialism*, especially 62–185.

131 Unmarked clipping, Adah Isaacs Menken file, Billy Rose Theatre Collection, New York Public Library for the Performing Arts; "Maguire's Opera House," *Golden Era*, September 27, 1863.

132 J. S. Bratton, "British Heroism and the Structure of Melodrama," 33, 42–43. As Jesse Lemisch reminds, Jack Tar was an inherently "double-faceted" character, as "young and optimistic" as he was a "non-conformist," a "rebel," and an "extreme individualist"; see *Jack Tar vs. John Bull*, 8. Jerrold, "Preface," *Black-Ey'd Susan*, vii–viii; Douglas Jerrold, *Black-Ey'd Susan*, Rare Book Reading Room, British Library, London, England. The play was first performed with T. P. Cooke in the lead role at the Surrey Theatre on June 8, 1829. Playwright J. B. Buckstone also appeared in this production. See *Black-Ey'd Susan* production file, HTC.

133 Bratton, "British Heroism," 36–38. The script calls for William to kneel while "all aboard appear to join in prayer with him." He embraces the Union Jack. See Jerrold, *Black Ey'd Susan*, 3.5.48; Bratton, 40, 22–23.

134 "Adah Isaacs Menken. The Artist—Her Triumphal Career in California," *Golden Era*, April 17, 1864. This production of *Black-Ey'd Susan* featured Sophie Edwin in the title role and Frank Mayo as Quid. Other Menken productions of the play featured the actress Josephine Fiddes as Susan. Fiddes performed alongside Menken in a July 22, 1865, production of the play. See Letter from Josephine Fiddes, June 28, 1909, unmarked clipping, Papers of Adah Isaacs Menken, Manuscript Reading Room, Library of Congress. See also playbill, July 22, 1865, unmarked clipping in Papers of Adah Isaacs Menken, Manuscript Reading Room, Library of Congress.

135 "Black Eyed Susan," *Golden Era*, April 24, 1864.

136 Ibid., emphasis added.

137 Bratton, "British Heroism," 40–41; Stoddard, "La Belle Menken," 481.

138 In 1822, William Wilberforce and Thomas Fowell Buxton established an anti-slavery society in Great Britain and led the English abolitionist movement which culminated in 1834 with the British empire's abolition of slavery; Peter Fryer, *Staying Power*, 203. See also Michael Booth, "Soldiers of the Queen," 6–7.

139 Jerrold, *Black Eyed Susan*, 2.3.35–36. It is important to note that different versions of *Black Ey'd Susan* which featured new scenes and characters were apparently edited and performed in both England and America throughout the nineteenth century. For instance, actor Roy Redgrave authored a different version of the play with a first act that was reportedly "entirely new." See "A New 'Black-Eye'd Susan," unmarked clipping, *Black-Ey'd Susan* production file, HTC. A two-act version of the play published in Chicago includes these same lines in act 1, scene 6. Douglas Jerrold, *Black Ey'd Susan*, 19–20, Playbooks Collection,

Box 69, Rare Books, Firestone Library, Princeton University. A version that was edited by Wayne Olwine and performed at the Boston Theatre collapses the play into two acts and excises many scenes from the earlier text. See Wayne Olwine, ed., *Black Ey'd Susan*, Playbooks Collection, Box 69, Rare Books, Firestone Library, Princeton University. Questions remain as to which version Menken may have performed. American actor, stage director, and theatre manager William Seymour (1855–1933), for instance, authored a promptbook of the play that features Jerrold's 1829 text as well as handwritten annotations. In his promptbook, Seymour preserves the "black bumboat-woman" narrative and adds additional text describing a "picanny" as a "nigger baby." See William Seymour, *Black Eyed Susan* promptbook, Playbooks Collection, Box 69, Rare Books, Firestone Library, Princeton University. William Seymour would have been a child at the time of Menken's performances in the play. However, his access to the original script and his interest in embellishing some of the more flagrantly spectacular scenes suggests that this version remained in circulation during Menken's era and may have been a text with which she was engaged. For more on William Seymour, see *Dictionary of American Biography*, 13.

140 Jerrold, preface, *Black Ey'd Susan*, vii.

141 See *The Unprotected Female* playbill reproduction, Adah Isaacs Menken file, SFPAL. See also *The Whistler or Fate of the Lily of St. Leonard's*, June 13, 1862, New Bowery Theatre playbill, AIM, PCF, HTC. Allen argues that early burlesque produced speech with a "threatening electrical charge"; *Horrible Prettiness*, xii. Also see "Maguire's Opera House," *Golden Era*, September 27, 1863. In *The Unprotected Female*, Menken performed "The Captain with His Whiskers Gave a Sly Wink at Me," a song made popular by San Francisco friend and upstart actress Lotta Crabtree; *San Francisco Theatre Research*, 5:67–68. Constance Rourke observes that "for many in her audiences her voice transcended every other impression"; see *Troupers*, 177.

142 *Three Fast Women* playbill, December 3, 1861, Adah Isaacs Menken file, Billy Rose Theatre Collection, New York Public Library for the Performing Arts. This version of the play was subtitled "The Female Robinson Crusoes." The WPA claims that this production was adapted from an English piece and "transformed into a satire of local conditions." *San Francisco Theatre Research*, 5:76–77. *Three Fast Women*, June 9, 10, 1862, New Bowery Theatre, AIM, PCF, HTC. She performed the production in January 1864 in San Francisco. See Adah Isaacs Menken file, SFPAL; *Variety and Sensation*, 90, found in SFPAL. See also *The San Francisco Stage Gagey*, June 24, 1864, clipping transcription as found in the Adah Isaacs Menken file, SFPAL. Early 1860s news clippings report that Menken performed "Protean pieces" during her initial months in New York theatre. See unmarked clipping from March 24, 1860 in AIM file, Portfolio in the Player's Collection, Billy Rose Theatre Collection, New York Public Library for the Performing Arts.

143 *San Francisco Theatre Research*, 5:67, 78.

144 The list of Menken's *Three Fast Women* roles appears consistent in New York City playbills and San Francisco theatre reviews of her show; however, it is possible that these characters changed according to regional context. Mankowitz lists six roles in this production as opposed to nine; see *Mazeppa*, 104. Eric Lott makes plain the connections between the "Young Mose" icon and minstrelsy; see *Love and Theft*, 81–85, 208. Mocking the uptown gentry, the young Mose(s) of the city clambered onto the Bowery stage and beyond beginning in the 1840s and typified the shifting tide of popular American theater. With "a brusque manner, peculiar lingo, and extravagant costume," the young Mose character, Lott argues, "exemplified the first U.S. working-class subculture—the volunteer fireman bent on class travesty," 81. For more on 1840s evolution of Mose iconography, see Lott, 81–85. See also David R. Roediger, *The Wages of Whiteness*, 99–100; Sean Wilentz, *Chants Democratic*, 300–301; Mullenix, *Wearing the Breeches*, 252, 343, note 45.

145 Blackface minstrelsy appears to have been a consistent staple of *Three Fast Women*. See *Three Fast Women* playbill, Billy Rose Theatre Collection, New York Public Library for the Performing Arts. See also *Variety and Sensation*, 90, found in SFPAL.

146 *Three Fast Women* playbill, Billy Rose Theatre Collection, New York Public Library for the Performing Arts; *San Francisco Theatre Research*, 5:76–77. For more on the local cast, see also playbill clipping, Maguire's Opera House, January 22, 1864, SFPAL; Frank W. Sweet, *A History of The Minstrel Show*, 14; Mankowitz, *Mazeppa*, 106. The WPA provides a lengthy list of the names of the local San Francisco performers in *Three Fast Women*. See *San Francisco Theatre Research*, 5:77.

147 Lotta Crabtree, a San Francisco actress whom Menken befriended and mentored and who now remains a legend in her own right, is one of the few other female entertainers to find success in minstrelsy. A number of white women worked as dancers in the mid-to-late extravaganza versions of minstrel productions but very rarely did they perform in blackface. For more on Lotta Crabtree, see Johnson, *American Actress*, 161–72; *Golden Era*, April 24, 1864. On the presence of women in minstrels, see Robert Toll, *Blacking Up*. For a description of Bones's standard attire, see Sweet, *History*, 11–12; Lesser, *Enchanting Rebel*, 114; Mullenix, *Wearing the Breeches*, 250; Dudden, *Women*, 118.

148 *Eagle Eye* remains a little-discussed piece in Menken's repertoire, yet it may have been one of the early plays in which Menken worked on developing her performances of American racial caricature. *Eagle Eye* clearly sought to capitalize on the "noble American Indian" melodrama craze of the 1830s and 1840s; see Allen, *Horrible Prettiness*, 103–4. In the title role, she played the stock caricature of the "noble Indian" savage who "stands triumphant" in the face of death. The play also seems to have consisted of a full range of racial types including a role listed as "a nigger" played by an actor named "Mr. Beane." See *Eagle Eye* playbill, September 22, 1862, AIM, PCF, HTC; *San Francisco Theatre Research*, 5:75.

149 Annemarie Bean, "Transgressing the Gender Divide," 255–56. By the late nine-teenth century and the early twentieth, black female performers began appear-ing in the context of minstrel formats, in shows such as *The Creole Burlesque Show* (1890) and in all-black vaudeville reviews such as the Whitman Sisters' company. See Thomas L. Riis, *Just before Jazz*, 12; Nadine George-Graves, *The Royalty of Negro Vaudeville*, 64–65. Jayna Brown, *Babylon Girls*.

150 Lott, *Love and Theft*, 159–68; Bean, "Transgressing," 248–49. The "prima donna" female impersonator in minstrelsy was, Bean argues, "a highly stylized and costumed near-white woman" who evolved "out of the darkened shell of the wench" in late minstrelsy, 248–49.

151 A correspondent for *The Anti-Slavery Reporter* claimed to have found evidence that Nixon may have been using the alias "Hill" and circulating a story that he was a house servant from Baltimore. See *Anti-Slavery Reporter*, July 1, 1854, 165. J. C. A. Smith alludes to Box Brown's having deserted his wife and children in slavery and having gotten "into his head to get a wife or something worse" in the UK. See Letter from J. C. A. Smith to Gerrit Smith, August 6, 1851, in Ripley, ed., *Black Abolitionist Papers*, 297.

152 Hortense Spillers, "A Hateful Passion, A Lost Love," 95.

## 4. Alien/Nation

1 "The Real Cake-Walk by Real Coons," *The Tatler*, May 13, 1903, 246A, in the Gabrielle Enthoven Theatre Collection, Victoria & Albert Museum, London. Future references to this collection will be cited parenthetically as GEC. See "Review," *New York Clipper*, May 20, 1903, as cited in Henry T. Sampson, *The Ghost Walks*, 296; Jeffrey P. Green, "*In Dahomey*," 24; hereafter cited as Green, "*In Dahomey*."

2 Nina Auerbach, *Private Theatricals*, 55–83; Edwin M. Eigner, *The Dickens Pan-tomime*, 41.

3 Jesse A. Shipp, Will Marion Cook, and Paul Laurence Dunbar, *In Dahomey*, in Hatch and Shine, eds., *Black Theatre USA*, 82; "The Script of *In Dahomey*," in Thomas Riis, ed., *The Music and Scripts of In Dahomey*, lxvii. There are at least two extant scripts of *In Dahomey*, and numerous versions of the pro-duction were performed on tour in the United States and the United Kingdom in the early 1900s; Riis, "*In Dahomey* in Text and Performance," in *Music and Scripts*, xvii. Below I make use of both Hatch and Shine's version of the Ameri-can libretto published in 1902 and registered with the Library of Congress as well as Riis's annotated edition of the American script and the revised Brit-ish script which was registered with Lord Chamberlain's office in London in 1903; Riis, "*In Dahomey*," xxxvi. Hereafter the 1902 libretto will be cited paren-thetically as ID1.

4 Unmarked clipping, the Billy Rose Theatre Collection, New York Public Library for the Performing Arts. Future references to this collection will be cited paren-thetically as BRT, unless otherwise noted. Ann Charters, *Nobody*, 70.

5 Mary Louis Pratt, *Imperial Eyes*, 39; Michael Hays, "Representing Empire," 144; Pratt, *Imperial Eyes*, 61.

6 Riis, *Music and Scripts*, xx.

7 Unmarked clipping, Harvard Theatre Collection, Houghton Library, Harvard University, Cambridge, Mass. Future references to this file will be cited as HTC unless otherwise noted. See John Graziano, "Sentimental Songs, Rags, and Transformations," 215–17; Green, "*In Dahomey*," 24.

8 Renato Rosaldo, *Culture and Truth*, 69; Ali Behdad, *Belated Travelers*, 6.

9 Rosaldo, *Culture and Truth*, 70; *When We Were Kings*, dir. Leon Gast, with Muhammad Ali and George Foreman, Gramercy, 1996; Auerbach, *Private Theatricals*, 14.

10 Anne McClintock, *Imperial Leather*, 40–42; Riis, *Music and Scripts*, xx. See also Richard F. Burton, *A Mission to Gelele, King of Dahome, and Wanderings in West Africa*.

11 In a radio interview, Riis alludes to *In Dahomey*'s "busy-ness" ("Fresh Air: American Popular Song Series"); Riis, *Music and Scripts*, xxix.

12 See Henry T. Sampson, *Blacks in Blackface*, 131. See also Allen Woll, *Black Musical Theatre*, 46; and David Krasner, *Resistance, Parody and Double Consciousness*, 19. Future references to Krasner's text will be cited parenthetically as Krasner, *Resistance*, unless otherwise noted.

13 Eric Sundquist, *To Wake the Nations*, 580; Riis, *Music and Scripts*, xviii; Allen Woll, *Dictionary of the Black Theatre*, 86.

14 Green, "*In Dahomey*," 32–33; Sampson, "Williams and Walker's *In Dahomey* Co.," 294–96. "Sensing a crisis," conductor Will Marion Cook was said to have cued the musicians to play the anthem; Eric Ledell Smith, *Bert Williams*, 69.

15 Sylvester Russell, "Williams and Walker's *In Dahomey* Company," *The Freeman*, September 26, 1902, in Sampson, *Ghost Walks*, 268–69 and 290–92.

16 W. E. B. Du Bois, *The Souls of Black Folk*; James Weldon Johnson, *Black Manhattan*, 90–92; Robert C. Toll, *Blacking Up*, 217; Sampson, *Blacks in Blackface*; Tom Fletcher, *100 Years of the Negro in Show Business*.

17 See William Wells Brown, *Clotel, or The President's Daughter*; Charles Chesnutt, *The Marrow of Tradition*.

18 Shane White, *Stories of Freedom in Black New York*; Marvin McCallister, *White People*.

19 Toll, *Blacking Up*, 227.

20 See "Richards and Pringle's Georgia Minstrels," *Commercial Appeal*, in Sampson, *Ghost Walks*, 265–66. See also Toll, *Blacking Up*; Sampson, *Blacks in Blackface*.

21 Toll, *Blacking Up*, 223, 195–96.

22 Ibid., 195–99, 211–16.

23 Ibid., 199, 201–5, 235.

24 Sam Dennison, *Scandalize My Name*; James Dorman, "Shaping the Popular Image." Sylvester Russell openly protested coon song popularity and the repugnance of songs such as "Carve dat Nigger"; see Sampson, *Ghost Walks*, 326.

25 Dorman, "Shaping the Popular Image," notes that Williams and Walker "were not only performers of 'coon' material but prolific writers of the material as well" (469 n. 26).

26 Thomas L. Riis, *Just before Jazz*, 5–6; Sandra Richards, "Bert Williams," 15; Malcolm X, "The Ballot or the Bullet," in Henry Louis Gates Jr. and Nelly McKay, eds., *Norton Anthology of African-American Literature*, 93.

27 Sonnet Retman demonstrates the myriad ways in which Schuyler's narrative exposes how "the color line defines race relations by promoting surveillance and observation and prohibiting contact"; Retman, " 'In the Face of American Standardizations.' " See Riis, *Music and Scripts*, xxiii.

28 George Walker, "The Real 'Coon,' " i–ii.

29 Ibid., i; Retman, "In the Face," 6–14.

30 Walker, "The Real 'Coon,' " 224.

31 Ibid.; Mia Bay, *The White Image in the Black Mind*. For more on black theatregoers and spectators in the nineteenth century, see McCallister, *White People*; Camille Forbes, *Performed Fictions*, 5.

32 Toll, *Blacking Up*, 28; Lott, *Love and Theft*; W. T. Lhaman, *Raising Cain*; McAllister, *White People*, especially 160, 171–76.

33 George Walker, "Bert and Me and Them"; James Weldon Johnson, *Black Manhattan*, 105; Sundquist, *To Wake the Nations*, 293; Walker, "Two Real Coons," 224.

34 J. W. Johnson, *Black Manhattan*, 107; Riis, *Music and Scripts*, xxxii.

35 Forbes, *Performed Fictions*, 27. See also Smith, *Bert Williams*; Charters, *Nobody*; and Riis, *Music and Scripts*, xxiv–xxv.

36 Marva Griffin Carter, "Removing the 'Minstrel Mask' in the Musicals of Will Marion Cook," 206–20; Riis, *Jazz*, 40–43. This was not, however, a process that came to Cook without great angst. A famous anecdote involving Cook and his mother's reactions to his theatre endeavors illustrates the composer's struggle to reconcile his parents' grand Reconstruction-era expectations with the realities of his postbellum career. Cook's mother was said to have cried while he rehearsed his coon song hit "Who Dat Say Chicken in Dis Crowd," claiming that she sent him "all over the world to study and become a great musician, and you return such 'a nigger!' "; Carter, "Removing," 207; Duke Ellington, *Music Is My Mistress*, 97; Samuel Floyd, *The Power of Black Music*; Maurice Peress, "Fresh Air: American Popular Song Series," May 18, 2000, NPR Radio; Green, "In Dahomey," 26–29.

37 R. C. Murray, "Williams and Walker, Comedians," *Colored American Magazine* (1906), 498; Riis, *Music and Scripts*, xxii. This production team also included the composer and lyricist Alex Rogers and the white vaudeville promoters Hurtig and Seamon, who posted $15,000 for the production of the show and who ultimately made a threefold profit from the production. Riis, *Music and Scripts*, xxi.

38 Mitchell was married to Will Marion Cook, Williams to Bert Williams, and Overton Walker to George Walker; Riis, *Just before Jazz*; Richard Newman, " 'The Brightest Star' "; Sylvester Russell, "Williams and Walker's *In Dahomey* Com-

pany," *The Freeman*, September 6, 1902, in Sampson, *Ghost Walks*, 269. See also Aida Overton Walker, "Opportunities the Stage Offers Intelligent and Talented Women," *New York Age*, December 24, 1908. For a discussion of queer politics in postbellum black women's narratives, see Siobhan Somerville, "Passing through the Closet."

39 Allen Woll, *Black Musical Theatre*, xiv; Harry Jackson, "Williams and Walker's *In Dahomey*," *The Freeman*, February 24, 1903, in Sampson, *Ghost Walks*, 288; Smith, *Bert Williams*, 55. See also Thomas Riis, *More than Just Minstrel Shows*, 5. The local New York press apparently gave ample coverage to the race conflict resulting from the New York Theatre's segregation policies; Smith, *Bert Williams*, 55. *In Dahomey* ran for fifty-three performances on Broadway before embarking on its transatlantic tour. In 1904 Sylvester Russell wrote a blistering letter of protest to the *Indianapolis Freeman* regarding the New York Theatre's segregated seating policy; see Russell, Letter to Elwood C. Knox from Sylvester Russell, *Indianapolis Freeman*, April 11, 1904, in Sampson, *Ghost Walks*, 292.

40 Jackson, "Review of *In Dahomey*," in Sampson, *Ghost Walks*, 288; Forbes, *Performed Fictions*, 2–5. The New York press alleged that Williams and Walker supported the New York Theatre's segregation practices. Nevertheless, Walker would write in his 1908 *New York Age* article that "we want our folks to like us. Not for the sake of the box office, but because over and behind all the money and prestige which move Williams and Walker, is a love for the race"; Walker, "Bert and Me"; Riis, *Music and Scripts*, xxi. See also Riis, *More than Just Minstrel Shows*, 5.

41 Helen Armstead-Johnson, "Themes and Values," 134; J. W. Johnson, *Black Manhattan*, 111–25; Charters, *Nobody*, 93–94; George Walker, "The Real 'Coon,' " i. In addition to Williams and Walker, other Frogs members included black Manhattanites and theatre artists James Reese Europe, Alex Rogers, Tom Brown, J. Rosamond Johnson, Jesse Shipp, and Cecil Mack.

42 Peter Revell, *Paul Laurence Dunbar*, 94–97; Carter, "Removing," 207–9; Riis, *Music and Scripts*, xxiii.

43 Revell, *Paul Laurence Dunbar*, 106; Addison Gayle as quoted in Carter, "Removing," 208; Brent Edwards, "Feminism, Collaboration, and the Poetics of Diaspora"; Dunbar, *In His Own Voice*, ed. Herbert Woodward Martin and Ronald Primeau, general introduction, xix, xxi. Dunbar borrowed mechanisms from the eighteenth-century English comedy of manners to write the play *Herrick, An Imaginative Comedy in Three Acts*. See Dunbar, "*Herrick*," in *In His Own Voice*, 17–83.

44 Dunbar would in fact publicly articulate a deep moral ambivalence toward the world of New York black theatre in his novel *Sport of the Gods*, published the same year as *In Dahomey*'s 1902 premiere. Cook and Dunbar each worked on separate musical projects that manifest some thematic and textual similarities to *In Dahomey*. Cook's *Cannibal King* carried the seeds of certain *In Dahomey* plot twists. See Sampson, *Ghost Walks*, 233. Likewise, their 1899 "operetto" *Jes Lak White Fo'ks* would anticipate the more polished and developed *In Dahomey*; Riis,

*Music and Scripts*, xviii. Dunbar collaborated on the lyrics for *In Dahomey* with Cook between 1901 and 1902; Riis, *Music and Scripts*, xxii.

45  George Walker, "The Real 'Coon,'" i; Robert Rydell, "Darkest Africa," 140–42; Green, "*In Dahomey*," 27–28.

46  Walker, "The Real 'Coon,'" i–ii.

47  Ibid., emphasis added.

48  Brecht, "Alienation Effects in Chinese Acting," "Short Description of a New Technique of Acting Which Produces Alienation Effect," and "A Short Organum for the Theatre," all in Willett, *Brecht on Theatre*.

49  Nell Painter, *Standing at Armageddon*, 141–69; Amy Kaplan and Donald Pease, eds., *Cultures of United States Imperialism*.

50  Rydell, "Darkest Africa," 135–55; Green, *Black Edwardians*; Riis, *More than Just Minstrel Shows*, 7.

51  Riis, *Just before Jazz*, 11–14, 151–55; Robert Allen, *Horrible Prettiness*, 17–18; Riis, *Music and Scripts*, xiii–xiv.

52  Riis, *Music and Scripts*, xiv–xvi; Leroi Jones, "The Changing Same," in *The Leroi Jones (Amiri Baraka) Reader*, 186–209.

53  Dorman, "Shaping the Popular Image," 462.

54  Riis, *Music and Scripts*, xiv.

55  Ibid., xiv. In this version of the production, the characters Rareback and Shylock fantasize about erecting a "broadway in the jungle" in a song number of the same name; see ID1, 72. The Hatch and Shine edition of the script uses the name "Punkerton"; however, all other allusions to this character (including the Riis script) use the name Pinkerton. I have chosen to use the latter here. Also, in the version that I examine here, the script calls for Cicero Lightfoot, president of the Colonization Society, to become "disgusted with Dahomey" and to "announc[e] his return to America" in act 3, scene 1; see ID1, 83. The British version of the script submitted to Lord Chamberlain's office includes an extended third act in which the characters arrive in Dahomey as "colonists" and weather varying levels of conflict with the King of Dahomey before deciding to return to Florida. See Thomas L. Riis, "British Script," *Music and Scripts*, lxviii–lxxii; Woll, *Black Musical Theatre*, 86; Krasner, *Resistance*, 54.

56  The Shakespearean allusion embedded in Shylock Homestead's name should not be overlooked here as well. *In Dahomey* was not immune to the trend of expressing familiar forms of xenophobic discontent in its plot. In the case of the Shylock reference, the allusion carries a potentially insidious double-meaning. An icon of anti-Semitic literary caricature, Shylock emerges in *In Dahomey* early on as an architect of swindling schemes. His rapaciousness further aligns him with classic coon song images of black hustling thieves as well. Thus Shylock reinforces the dual stereotypes of Jewish and black miscreants. On the coon song hustler, see Dorman, "Shaping the Popular Image," 456.

57  Forbes, *Performed Fictions*, 73; see also Mabel Rowland, *Bert Williams*, 46. Russell

called Walker's monologue "the talk of his life" even in the production's earliest incarnation; see Sylvester Russell, "Williams and Walker's *In Dahomey* Company," in Sampson, *Ghost Walks*, 268. Williams often sang "Jonah Man" at the end of this scene; Riis, *Music and Scripts*, xli.

58 Riis, *Music and Scripts*, xxvi; Jacqui Malone, *Steppin' on the Blues*, 66; Riis, *Just before Jazz*, 19. One should certainly note the political ambiguity of Straight's language in the context of shifting Egyptological debates regarding "European" versus "African" beauty aesthetics. Rife with malapropisms and puns, Straight's speech may signify on the politics of racial beauty. Given the popularity of associating Cleopatra iconography with Egyptology and ancient African history during this period, one could easily read for the ambiguity of "transforming" an individual of African descent into a "Cleopatra" figure. To both affirm and deny any claims of "blackness" in relation to classical figures such as Apollo and Cleopatra would have had shifting political currencies in nineteenth-century culture. Hence one could read the product's promise to create a black individual's "transformation" into a "Greek goddess" as a coded gesture which affirms a move toward some recuperated, essentialized blackness; see Susan Gillman, "Pauline Hopkins and the Occult," 64–65. For more on Egyptology and ancient African history, see Dickson Bruce, "Ancient Africa and the Early Black American Historians," 678–99. For more on Western imaging of Cleopatra in the nineteenth century, see Lucy Hughes-Hallett, *Cleopatra*.

59 Kobena Mercer, *Welcome to the Jungle*, 101, 102.

60 Shane White and Graham White, *Stylin'*, 154.

61 Mercer, *Welcome*, 115, emphasis his; Noliwe Rooks, *Hair Raising*; Ingrid Banks, *Hair Matters*.

62 Thomas F. Gossett, *Race*, 69.

63 Wilson J. Moses, *The Golden Age of Black Nationalism*, 23; Kevin Gaines, *Uplifting the Race*, especially 179–208.

64 Immanuel Geiss, *The Pan-African Movement*, 83; Mercer, *Welcome*, 111.

65 See also *Compact Edition of the Oxford English Dictionary*, 1:901; Gossett, *Uncle Tom's*, especially 54–83; Sander Gilman, *Difference and Pathology*, 61–62; Michael Pickering, "Mock Blacks and Racial Mockery"; Sarah Meer, *Uncle Tom Mania*.

66 Sampson, *Ghost Walks*, 294–96; *In Dahomey* clippings folder, HTC.

67 Pratt, *Imperial Eyes*, 33.

68 Brecht, "Alienation Effects in Chinese Acting"; Dorman, "Shaping the Popular Image," 454, emphasis his; Sylvester Russell, *Indianapolis Freeman* commentary, April 15, 1904, in Sampson, *Ghost Walks*, 317; Russell, "Williams and Walker's *In Dahomey* Company," in Sampson, *Ghost Walks*, 330.

69 *London Times* as quoted in Eric Smith, *Bert Williams*, 64. Critics used the "not so black" formulation in reviews of Box Brown's and Menken's performances; see chapters 2 and 3; Smith, *Bert Williams*, 60–61.

70 Pickering, "Mock Blacks," 191; Peter Frye, *Staying Power*. In November 1903 the

*Indianapolis Freeman* published a letter written by Charles H. Moore, who traveled with the Williams and Walker troupe in Great Britain. Moore's letter outlined the racism that the company encountered on tour, and he declared: "I am pessimistic as regards the future of the black man in England"; see Charles Moore letter, *Indianapolis Freeman*, in Sampson, *Ghost Walks*, 308; Green, "*In Dahomey*," 24–25, 37–38. Green also speculates that there were perhaps occasional groups of "rowdies making audible their racist views" in the gallery seats during some *In Dahomey* performances (24–25).

71 Behdad, *Belated Travelers*, 13.

72 Green, "*In Dahomey*," 31–32.

73 See "Written, Composed, and Played by Coloured Coons: A Chat with the Composer of '*In Dahomey*,'" *The Tatler*, May 20, 1903, found in GEC; Torgovnick, *Gone Primitive*, 9.

74 Bert Williams, "Fun in the Land of J. Bull."

75 Sylvester Russell, "Williams and Walker's *In Dahomey* Co. on Broadway," *Indianapolis Freeman*, April 4, 1903, in Sampson, *Ghost Walks*, 291.

76 Walker was also something of a mentor to a number of other black actors of the period, including the Whitman Sisters, who hailed from Kansas as well; Nadine George-Graves, *The Royalty of Negro Vaudeville*, 16; Bracey and Meier, eds., *Black Nationalism in America*, 235; Krasner, *Resistance*, 41–74.

77 Armstead Johnson, "Themes and Values," 136; Eddie Glaude, *Exodus!* 8–9.

78 Glaude, *Exodus!* 15. The "hustler" mentality of *In Dahomey*'s characters would surely align them with the archetypal Anglo-American spirit that Walter McDougall describes in *Freedom Just Around the Corner*.

79 The British version of the script which continues act 3, scene 3, through a revised act 3 features added dialogue between the Syndicate members who together decide to sail for Dahomey. The three express some of the most pronounced hostility toward the ruler of Dahomey in act 3. See British script, in Riis, *Music and Scripts*, lxviii–lxx.

80 Du Bois, *The Souls of Black Folk*; Sterling Stuckey, *The Ideological Origins of Black Nationalism*, 23.

81 Woll, *Black Musical Theatre*, 40. See also the original *Variety* clipping located in BRT.

82 Stuckey, *Ideological*, 11.

83 The script describes Moses as "a calcium artist," a potential reference to "the man who puts a solution of calamine on his skin to make it appear white" (ID1, 67–68). A Moses who whitens up would certainly add emphasis to his character's reactionary interest in "kick[ing] the stuffin' out of dem [Indians] and put them on a reservation" (ID1, 68). Again however, names signify on multiple meanings in *In Dahomey*. The biblical implications of Moses's name clearly suggest his leadership potential to carry his people out of bondage. The script shortens his name to "Mose" throughout, a potential reference to nineteenth-century Bowery

boy "Mose," the heroic figure of the labor class. For more on 1840s evolution of the Mose iconography, see Lott, *Love and Theft*, 81–85; David R. Roediger, *The Wages of Whiteness*, 99–100; Sean Wilentz, *Chants Democratic*, 300–301.

84  Bruce, "Ancient Africa," 694; Alexander Crummell, "Hope for Africa," 284–91; Wilson J. Moses, *Alexander Crummell*. See also Kwame Anthony Appiah, *In My Father's House*, 3–27; Mia Bay, *White Image*, 97–100; Moses, *Golden Age*, 26; Kevin Gaines, "Black Americans' Racial Uplift," 437.

85  Geiss, *Pan-African*, 82; Painter, "Prosperity," in *Standing on Armageddon*, 170–215.

86  Riis, *Just before Jazz*, 123. Catlin's "Chinese act in *In Dahomey* and Abyssinia" was said to have influenced other black musical entertainers who worked in ethnic humor; Riis, *Just before Jazz*, 183. For other examples of Asian racial caricature in black musical theatre, see, for instance, "Programme: Black Patti Troubadours at the Los Angeles Theatre," in Sampson, *Ghost Walks*, 242–43. See also Black Patti Troubadours, "Life in the Philippines," in *Ghost Walks*, 299. On Me Sing's exit from the scene, Shipp's script calls for the "Song of the Colonization Society." With no extant lyrics or music for this song, it is impossible to consider whether the number either amplified or undercut the scene before it. However, the focus on colonization here presents an interesting juxtaposition to the construction of Me Sing and his subservience to the black characters in the scene. See ID1, 71; Gisele L. Fong, " 'These People Come in Vast Numbers,' " 13; Ronald Takaki, *Iron Cages*; Painter, *Standing at Armageddon*, 1–35, 141–69.

87  Fong, "These People Come," 14. African colonization was not without its vociferous opponents, particularly in African American communities from 1816 forward when the controversial American Colonization Society first made inroads in the movement to transport free blacks back to Africa. Roundly rejected by early-nineteenth-century African Americans who recognized the organization as a plot to divest them of their right to American liberties, the antebellum colonization movement never fully advanced; see Bay, *White Image*, 22–26. Black emigration outside the context of the colonization movement was also a subject garnering much attention and debate among African Americans in the early nineteenth century; Glaude, *Exodus!*, 115–17.

88  Martin and Primeau, "Introduction," xx–xxi. Called "the Trust" or "the Syndicate," Charles Frohman, Al Hayman, Marc Klaw, Abraham Erlanger, J. Frederick Zimmerman, and Samuel Nixon had a controlling "interest in a large number of theaters throughout the country" in the late nineteenth and early twentieth century; see Riis, *Just before Jazz*, 18; Smith, *Bert Williams*, 54–55; James Haskins, *Black Theatre in America*, 42.

89  Stuart Hall, "New Ethnicities," 448, emphasis his; Henry Louis Gates Jr., "The Trope of a New Negro"; Stuart Hall, "What Is This 'Black' in Black Popular Culture?" 32.

90  Krasner, *Resistance*, 111; Jacqueline Jones, *Labor of Love, Labor of Sorrow*, 155;

Alferdteen Harrison, ed., *Black Exodus*; Farah Jasmine Griffin, *"Who Set You Flowin'?"* 13–47.

91 Bracey and Meier, *Black Nationalism*, 156–60; Krasner, *Resistance*, 72.

92 Forbes, *Performed Fictions*, 83–89.

93 White and White, *Stylin'*, 136. Elements of marching songs such as the Civil War song "Marching through Georgia" were incorporated into *In Dahomey*; see Riis, *Music and Scripts*, lxvi n. 16; Griffin, *Flowin'*, 177.

94 "Fresh Air: American Popular Song Series," May 18, 2000, NPR Radio.

95 This formulation refers to a number often performed immediately following Cicero's discovery of gold in the musical. Strewn with racial epithets and caricatures, it is, nonetheless, significant in its affirmation of an alternative nation-state which offers each individual authority as the title suggests (ID1, 81). The song surfaces as "Every Niggah Is a King" in *Jes Lak White Folks*. During the spring in which *In Dahomey* returned to Broadway, Sylvester Russell wrote that the "Negro race has no objections to the word 'coon' and no objections to the word 'darky.' We care nothing for the words black, colored, or Negro, but we do object to the word 'nigger' "; see Russell, in Sampson, *Ghost Walks*, 317.

96 James Clifford, "Traveling Cultures," 101.

97 Anna Deavere Smith, introduction, *Fires in the Mirror*, xxxiv, xli.

98 See Moses, *Golden Age*, 17; Martin Delaney as quoted in Stuckey, *Ideological*, 26.

99 See ID1, 83 note; Riis, *Music and Scripts*, xx.

100 Rowland, *Bert Williams*, 45; Riis, *Music and Scripts*, xx; Rydell, "Darkest Africa," 138.

101 In a grotesque reproduction of Anglo imperialism, Rare, Shy, and the Syndicate morph into callous colonizers who cause "endless trouble" and who stir the ire of the King of Dahomey, who threatens their execution and who "intends to keep his colonists within the limits of territory granted them," as one messenger assures; Riis, *Music and Scripts*, lxix. What could be read as a purely mimetic scene of imperialism, though, is challenged by the resolve of Cicero, Shy, Rare, and company to return to Florida and vacate their colonizing positions.

102 Riis, *More than Just Minstrels*, 51–52; Smith, *Bert Williams*, 64–65; Martin and Primeau, "Introduction to the Dramatic Pieces," 10. A kind of discursive cousin to Williams and Walker's Pan-Africanist musical, *Jes Lak White Fo'ks* included several numbers from *In Dahomey* and featured a similar plot involving Pompous Johnsing's quest for wealth and his effort to engage in diplomatic relations with an African prince in order to marry his daughter into royalty. Both productions mock the social aspirations of Anglo-Americans who, as one of Dunbar's characters explains it, "go to Europe, and by 'n by" marry dukes (11); *The Era* as quoted in Green, "*In Dahomey*," 34.

103 Photograph of George Walker. The Yale Collection of American Literature, Beinecke Rare Book and Manuscript Library, lists this image as being from *In Dahomey*.

104 Unmarked photograph, Schomburg Library Photo Collection, New York City Public Library. It is worth noting that cataloguing complexities have caused a number of photos from early black musicals to be misfiled. In many cases, photographs of Williams and Walker's performances have been labeled according to more than one production, making it all the more difficult to reconstruct a consistent visual history of these shows through photography. This particular shot of George Walker could be that of the performer in *In Dahomey*, rather than *Abyssinia*.

105 For allusions to Box Brown's jewelry, see *London Times*, July 30, 1852; "The 'Nigger' Panorama," *Wolverhampton & Staffordshire Herald*, March 24, 1852.

106 Amy Robinson, "It Takes One to Know One," 727.

107 Moe Meyer, "Introduction: Reclaiming the Discourse of Camp," in Meyer, ed., *The Politics and Poetics of Camp*, 7. Future references to Meyer's introduction will be cited parenthetically as Meyer, introduction.

108 Chuck Kleinhans, "Taking Out the Trash," 189; Robinson, "It Takes One to Know One," 730; Hall, "What Is This 'Black' in Black Popular Culture?" 27.

109 He added that Williams as well "would not then look out of place as an eccentric masquerader"; Russell, "Williams and Walker's *In Dahomey* Company," in Sampson, *Ghost Walks*, 268.

110 See Marjorie Garber, *Vested Interests*, 275.

111 Sylvester Russell, "Williams and Walker's *In Dahomey* Co. on Broadway," in Sampson, *Ghost Walks*, 290; Sandra Richards, "Bert Williams," 16; Rhonda Garelick, *Rising Star*, 3–5; Susan Sontag, "Notes on 'Camp,'" 289; Sampson, *Blacks in Blackface*, 82.

112 Lott, *Love and Theft*, 34; Krasner, *Resistance*, 50; J. W. Johnson, *Black Manhattan*, 126–28; Russell, "Williams and Walker's *In Dahomey* Co. on Broadway," in Sampson, *Ghost Walks*, 291.

113 J. W. Johnson, *Black Manhattan*, 107.

114 "Actor Lady," ID1, 73–74; Riis, *Music and Scripts*, xxiii, xl; "Leader of the Colored Aristocracy," ID1, 80.

115 *London Times* as quoted in Green, "*In Dahomey*," 25.

116 Following the onset of her husband's struggle with paresis in 1908, Overton Walker's "drag" routines would become more pronounced and poignantly meaningful. The actress famously assumed Walker's role in the musical *Bandanna Land*, donning "a straw hat, plaid four-button suit," "spats," and "white gloves" and sang his signature song in the show, "Bon Bon Buddy"; see Charters, *Nobody*, 96–97. Walker died of paresis, a late stage of syphilis, on January 6, 1911, at the age of thirty-eight. Overton Walker would continue this performance in the wake of his passing. See "Aida Overton Walker & Co.," San Francisco Orpheum Theatre playbill, May 12, 1912, Aida Overton Walker file, SFPAL.

117 Critics have debated when and whether "Vassar Girl" was actually sung by Overton Walker in the musical; see ID1, 73 n. 13. See also Riis, *Music and Scripts*, lv. "The Colored Girl from Vassar" appears as a number in *Jes Lak White Fo'ks*, 137.

Minstrelsy promoted the image of greedy, garishly ostentatious black women; see Toll, *Blacking Up*, and "Social Commentary," 102; Dorman, "Shaping the Popular Image," 461–63; Dennison, *Scandalize*, 404–9. Dunbar imagined his own actress heroine in *Sport of the Gods* as succumbing to the immorality and avarice of theatre culture. Abbie Mitchell's performances of Cook's "Brown-Skin Baby Mine," called by Riis a "sentimental love song," also amplified and rewrote black female romantic desire in ways that intervened in coon song images of black women; see IDI, 85; Riis, *Just before Jazz*, 95–96. The closest Walker came to performing the more traditional role of the coon song gold-digger was in the interpolated number "A Rich Coon's Babe," incidentally the production's only song written by a female composer, Clare Kummer; see Riis, *Music and Scripts*, 135–38. Kummer's composition was interpolated into the London production; Riis, *Music and Scripts*, xli. Kummer was, in fact, the grand-niece of Harriet Beecher Stowe; Newman, "Brighest Star," 70.

118 Said, *Culture and Imperialism*, 30. See Garber, *Vested Interests*, 274.

119 Kevin Shillington, *History of Africa*, 192–93, 309. Shillington notes that King Agaja initially tried with little luck to prevent the exportation of captives, favoring instead internal slave trading and external trade that emphasized material goods (193). See Boniface I. Obichere, *West African States and European Expansion*, 159; Sundquist, *To Wake the Nations*, 551–63; Wilson Moses, ed., *Classic Black Nationalism*.

120 With words by Frank Williams and music by J. Leubrie Hill, "My Dahomian Queen" also provides the unlikely occasion to forge anti-imperialist alliances with other indigenous peoples and to disrupt the anti-Asian sentiment embedded in Me-Sing's characterization. The song's allusion to "Kai-o-ka-lo-nian," the deposed and exiled Queen of Hawaii, reveals the extent to which the musical's composers and performers were in dialogue with contemporary global and political events. Later versions of show numbers included allusions to cultural politics in the Philippines. The American invasion of the Philippines coincided with the American tour of *In Dahomey*. See Smith, *Bert Williams*, 78; "My Dahomian Queen," IDI, 82–83. E. P. Moran and Paul Laurence Dunbar wrote the lyrics to "Evah Dahkey Is a King" while John H. Cook composed the music; see "Evah Dahkey Is a King," in Riis, *Music and Scripts*, 47–54. Walker sang the interpolated number "My Castle on the Nile" in London performances of *In Dahomey*. With lyrics by James Weldon Johnson and Bob Cole and music by Rosamond Johnson, "Nile" alluded lyrically and musically to Verdi's opera *Aida*; Riis, *Music and Scripts*, xxxix.

121 See David Glassberg, *American Historical Pageantry*, appendix; Sundquist, *To Wake the Nations*, 563–81; David Krasner, *A Beautiful Pageant*.

122 White and White, *Stylin'*, 137–38.

123 Riis, *Music and Scripts*, xxxiii.

124 Primeau and Martin, "Introduction to the Dramatic Pieces," 11.

125 Pickering, "Mock Blacks," 200; Guy Debord, *Society of the Spectacle*, 24.

126 Peter Jackson and Jan Penrose, introduction, *Constructions of Race, Place and Nation*, 6.

127 Michael McCarthy, *Dark Continent*, 15, 29; Torgovnick, *Gone Primitive*, 3–41.

128 Peggy Phelan, *Unmarked*; Robert Eric Livingston, "Decolonizing the Theatre," 185; Valerie Smith, "The Documentary Impulse."

129 Said, *Culture and Imperialism*, 12; Geiss, *Pan-African Movement*, 94; Krasner, *Resistance*, 108; Armstead-Johnson, "Themes," 133.

130 The name "Lightfoot" itself may have been meant to reference the contemporary black actor James E. Lightfoot. The character may have also been an allusion to the broad panoramic adventures of William Moncrieff's *Tom and Jerry* and that play's dancing "Mr. and Miss Lightfoot"; see William Moncrieff, *Tom and Jerry Or, Life in London*, 3.3.65. The 1898 Dunbar and Cook number "Returned: Empty and So Silent Now the Old Cabin Stands," a nostalgia-laden composition, appears to be a song that the character Cicero might have sung in various versions of the musical; Dunbar, "Musical and Lyrical Fragments," *In His Own Voice*, 159; Riis, *Music and Scripts*, 131–34; Riis, *Just before Jazz*, 102.

131 Benedict Anderson, *Imagined Communities*. 6, emphasis his; Fernando de Toro, *Theatre Semiotics*. See Krasner, *Resistance*, 108; Green, "*In Dahomey*," 24; J. Ellen Gainor, introduction, *Imperialism and Theatre*, xiv.

132 Brenda Dixon Gottschild, *Digging*, 116; Rowland, *Bert Williams*, 60; Green, "*In Dahomey*," 23. The English press reported that letters had been sent to the management requesting the dance. Subsequently, at some English performances an actual cakewalk was conducted with the audience. Likewise, some of the cast members were invited to perform the dance in the "homes of the rich—for the smart society"; Green, "*In Dahomey*," 35. Cook, Mitchell, and other principals were said to have "argued heatedly" about the incorporation of the cakewalk and "Swing Along" into the show; Riis, *Music and Scripts*, xl. The *Telegraph* reported the addition of "a Negro minuet entitled 'That's how the Cake-Walk's Done'" for the one hundred fiftieth performance of the show at the Shaftesbury Theatre, September 17, 1903, as quoted in Sampson, *Ghost Walks*, 307; Smith, *Bert Williams*, 70. See Hatch and Shine, 1D1, 83 note; Sampson, *Ghost Walks*, 240.

133 Sundquist, *To Wake the Nations*, 277. Future references to Sundquist's text will be cited parenthetically as Sundquist, *To Wake the Nations*. See Fletcher, *One Hundred Years*, 103–05; Malone, *Steppin'*, 57–62.

134 Fletcher, *One Hundred Years*, 103.

135 Amiri Baraka [Leroi Jones], *Blues People*, 86; David Krasner, "Rewriting the Body," 72; Gottschild, *Digging*, 114–17.

136 Krasner, "Rewriting the Body," 71, and *Resistance*.

137 See Krasner, "Rewriting the Body," 84; Homi Bhabha, *The Location of Culture*; Krasner, "Rewriting the Body," 73.

138 Du Bois, *Souls*, 3. See Krasner, "Rewriting the Body," 82.

139 Krasner, "Rewriting the Body," 72–73.

140 Judith Butler, *Gender Trouble*.

141 Randy Martin, *Critical Moves*, 6; Linda Hutcheon as quoted in Meyer, *Camp*, 9.

142 Meyer, introduction, 15.

143 Malone, *Steppin'*, 72–73.

144 Ibid., 138.

145 Riis, *Music and Scripts*, xxxiii–xxxiv; Will Cook, "Swing Along," in Riis, *Music and Scripts*, 155–162; Brecht, "Alienation Effects in Chinese Acting," 207; Riis, *Just before Jazz*, 93, xxix. In a letter to his son, Cook once wrote that he "felt as if 'Swing Along' was exactly what we were to do—no obstacles—nothing could stop us," as quoted in Marva Griffin Carter, "Removing," 211.

146 Toll, *Blacking Up*, 247. Katrina Hazzard-Gordon demonstrates how "Emancipation Day" celebrations in the post-Reconstruction era served as a central arena for the development of modern African American dance traditions; *Jookin', African American*, 70–73. See also White and White, *Stylin'*, 133–35. "Emancipation Day" also appears in the overture to *In Dahomey*.

147 Krasner, "Rewriting the Body," 70; Kleinhans, "Taking Out," 188.

148 Michael Hays, "Representing Empire," 136; Pickering, "Mock Blacks," 213.

149 Anderson, *Imagined Communities*, 141–42, 145.

150 Dorman, "Shaping the Popular Image," 458, 469 n. 34. One critic remarked in his review of *In Dahomey*, "Judaism's dream of a return to the Promised Land is not half so real as the pathetic desire of thousands of negroes in America to have a land and a nation of their own" (BRT).

151 Geiss, *Pan-African*, 192; Appiah, *In My Father's House*, 28–46.

152 Charters, *Nobody*, 76.

153 Sampson, *Ghost Walks*, 80.

154 Auerbach, *Private Theatricals*, 50–51.

155 Sampson, *Ghost Walks*, 296–98; Smith, *Bert Williams*, 71–73.

## 5. Divas and Diasporic Consciousness

1 Iola, "The Model Woman: A Picture of the Typical Southern Girl," *New York Freeman*, February 18, 1888; Patricia Schechter, *Ida B. Wells-Barnett*, 48–51.

2 Schechter, *Ida B. Wells-Barnett*, 9, 185. Schechter reveals how Wells, while living in Memphis, "had performed public readings, organized and acted in a dramatic club, and even been scouted by New York talent agents. The northern press had already noted her ambition to be a 'full-fledged journalist, a physician, or an actress,'" 20.

3 Iola, "The Model Woman"; Schechter, *Ida B. Wells-Barnett*, 55; Shakespeare, *As You Like It*, 2.7.139.

4 Ida B. Wells, *Southern Horrors and Other Writings*, 15. See also Schechter, *Ida B. Wells-Barnett*, 18–19. For more on the black women's club movement, see Hazel Carby, *Reconstructing Womanhood*; Claudia Tate, *Domestic Allegories of Political Desire*; Nicole King, " 'A Colored Woman in Another Country Pleading for Justice in Her Own' "; P. Gabrielle Foreman, *Dark Sentiment*.

5 Paul Laurence Dunbar, *The Sport of the Gods*, 71, 74.

6 Sylvester Russell, "Williams and Walker's In Dahomey Co. on Broadway," *The Freeman*, April 4, 1903, in Henry T. Sampson, ed., *Ghost Walks*, 290–91; Russell, "Williams and Walker's *In Dahomey* Co.," *The Freeman*, October 1, 1904, in Sampson, *Ghost Walks*, 328–29; James Weldon Johnson, *Black Manhattan*, 107; Richard Newman, "'The Brightest Star'"; Jo Tanner, *Dusky Maidens*, 35–52.

7 Newman, "'Brightest Star,'" 56–57.

8 Aida Overton Walker, "Colored Men and Women on the American Stage," 574.

9 Aida Overton Walker, "Opportunities the Stage Offers Intelligent and Talented Women."

10 Bernard L. Peterson, *Profiles of African American Stage Performers and Theatre People, 1816–1960*, 125; Daphne A. Brooks, "Pauline Hopkins."

11 Pauline Hopkins, *Of One Blood*, 531.

12 Eileen Southern, introduction, *African American Theatre*, xxiii–xxvi.

13 See Pauline Hopkins, *Peculiar Sam*, 50–65; Southern, introduction, *African American Theatre*, xx–xxv.

14 Pauline Hopkins, *Peculiar Sam*, 105. Future references to this text will be cited parenthetically.

15 Southern, introduction, *African American Theatre*, xxiv–xxvi. For more on Sam Lucas, see Henry T. Sampson, *Blacks in Blackface*.

16 Hopkins's stage directions call for Juno to circle Jim while threatening him (116). In the play's postwar act 4, Juno pulls out her pistol and threatens Jim once more before the characters discover that he has reformed (122).

17 Southern, introduction, *African American Theatre*, xxiv–xxv; Errol Hill, "The Hyers Sisters."

18 See Hazel Carby, introduction, *The Magazine Novels of Pauline Hopkins*, by Pauline Hopkins, xxix–l; Richard Yarborough, introduction, *Contending Forces*, by Pauline Hopkins, xxvii–xlviii; Carby, *Reconstructing Womanhood*, 121–62; Jane Campbell, *Mythic Black Fiction*; Henry Louis Gates Jr., "The Trope of a New Negro"; Carol Allen, *Black Women Intellectuals*, 29–30.

19 Carby, introduction, *The Magazine Novels of Pauline Hopkins*, xlv; C. Allen, *Black Women Intellectuals*; Sundquist, *To Wake the Nations*, 569–74; Hanna Wallinger, "Voyage into the Heart of Africa," 203–14; John Gruesser, "Pauline Hopkins's *Of One Blood*"; Susan Gillman, "Pauline Hopkins and the Occult."

20 Cynthia Schrager, "Both Sides of the Veil." See also Susan Gillman, *Blood Talk*.

21 Thomas J. Otten, "Pauline Hopkins," 244. See also Schrager, "Pauline Hopkins and William James," in John Cullen Gruesser, ed., *The Unruly Voice: Rediscovering Pauline Elizabeth Hopkins*, 182–90 (future references to this text will be cited parenthetically as Schrager, "Pauline Hopkins"); Gillman, "Pauline Hopkins and the Occult," 73, 72; Schrager, "Pauline Hopkins," 189.

22 Kevin Gaines, "Black Americans' Racial Uplift Ideology as 'Civilizing Mission,'" 193–94; Claudia Tate, *Domestic Allegories of Political Desire*, 206–8; Elizabeth Ammons, *Conflicting Stories*, 81–85; Jennie Kassanoff, "'Fate Has Linked Us

Together,' " 173; Ammons, *Conflicting Stories*, 83. See also Debra Bernardi, "Narratives of Domestic Imperialism," 220.

23 C. Allen, *Black Women Intellectuals*, 42.

24 Dana Luciano, "Passing Shadows," 165.

25 Otten, "Pauline Hopkins," especially 227–44. See also Schrager, "Pauline Hopkins," 182–90.

26 Andrew Ward, *Dark Midnight*, 22–25, 100; hereafter cited parenthetically as Ward, *Dark Midnight*.

27 See "Index of Musical Numbers," in *Peculiar Sam*, ed. Eileen Southern, xxxiv–xxxv. See J. B. T. Marsh, *The Story of the Jubilee Singers*, "Index to Music," 123–24. See also Ward, *Dark Midnight*.

28 W. E. B. Du Bois, *The Souls of Black Folk*.

29 Doug Seroff, "Fisk Jubilee Singers" and "The Fisk Jubilee Singers in Britain," in Lynn Abbott and Doug Seroff, *Out of Sight: The Rise of African American Popular Music, 1889–1895*, 42–54; Louis D. Silveri, "Singing Tours," 112.

30 P. Gabrielle Foreman, " 'Reading Aright,' " 329.

31 Ibid., 331.

32 Ibid., 330.

33 Paul Allen Anderson, *Deep River*, 18. See also Mellonee Burnim, "Biblical Inspiration, Cultural Affirmation," 608.

34 Paul Gilroy, *The Black Atlantic*, 89.

35 Colin Brown as quoted in Silveri, "Singing Tours," 113.

36 Burnim, "Biblical Inspiration," 608. See also Samuel Floyd, *The Power of Black Music*, 61; Colin Brown as quoted in Silveri, "Singing Tours," 113; Ward, *Dark Midnight*, 110.

37 Jon Cruz, *Culture on the Margins*, 22.

38 Ibid., 168, 4, 130.

39 Anderson, *Deep River*, 18.

40 Gilroy, *Black Atlantic*, 90; Marsh, *The Story of the Jubilee Singers*, 121. See also Ward, *Dark Midnight*, 185.

41 Anderson, *Deep River*, 22.

42 Gilroy, *Black Atlantic*, 88.

43 Seroff, "Fisk Jubilee Singers," 44–45; Ward, *Dark Midnight*, 213.

44 Sheppard as quoted in Ward, *Dark Midnight*, 110; Floyd, *Power of Black Music*, 10.

45 Silveri, "Singing Tours," 107.

46 Anderson, *Deep River*, 37–44. See also Du Bois, *Souls*, 186–203.

47 John Lovell, *Black Song*, 327.

48 Luciano, "Passing Shadows," 163–64; Du Bois, *Souls*, 179; Gilroy, *Black Atlantic*, 111–45; Sundquist, *To Wake the Nations*, 525–39; Anderson, *Deep River*, 13–57.

49 Cruz, *Culture on the Margins*, 4, 31.

50 Ibid., 129–30; Eileen Southern, *The Music of Black Americans*, 228.

51 C. Allen, *Black Women Intellectuals*, 44; Joseph Roach, *Cities of the Dead*, 36–41.

52 Lovell, *Black Song*, 196.

53  John W. Work, *American Negro Songs*, 27; Ward, *Dark Midnight*, 403.

54  Robert O'Meally, liner notes, *Norton Anthology of African American Literature Audio Companion Disc*.

55  Lovell, *Black Song*, 327.

56  Cruz, *Culture on the Margins*, 129; Marsh, *The Story of the Jubilee Singers*, 142–43; Southern, *Music of Black Americans*, 215.

57  "Go Down, Moses," stanzas 1–3; Marsh, *The Story of the Jubilee Singers*, 142.

58  Lovell, *Black Song*, 327.

59  Ibid., 414.

60  C. Allen, *Black Women Intellectuals*, 27.

61  Katherine Bassard, *Spiritual Interrogations*, 134–39.

62  Kassanoff, "'Fate Has Linked Us,'" 173; Schrager, "Pauline Hopkins," 191; Ammons, *Conflicting Stories*, 83; Luciano, "Passing Shadows," 177.

63  I borrow this formulation from Sharon Holland's lively critical reinterpretation of Parliament Funkadelic's "One Nation under a Groove"; see Holland, *Raising the Dead*, 41–67.

64  Anderson, *Deep River*; Cruz, *Culture on the Margins*. Eileen Southern and Rosalyn Story are two of the few scholars who have done extensive work on early black female musical artists.

65  Arthur LaBrew, *The Black Swan*, 30; Rosalyn M. Story, *And So I Sing*, 21.

66  Eric Lott, *Love and Theft*, 235–56; LaBrew, *Black Swan*, 22–45.

67  Carla Peterson, *Doers of the Word*, 122–24; Letter to Miss Greenfield from E.S.M., in LaBrew, *Black Swan*, 38; LaBrew, *Black Swan*, 34, 39; Story, *And So I Sing*, 22. See also Elizabeth Taylor Greenfield Clippings, Reviews, and Memoirs, Special Collections, Schomburg Center for Research in Black Culture, New York City Public Library. Susan McClary, *Feminine Endings*, 11; Story, *And So I Sing*, 22; LaBrew, *Black Swan*, 23, 41.

68  Sam Dennison, *Scandalize My Name*; James Dorman, "Shaping the Popular Image"; Hortense Spillers, "Interstices," 155; McClary, *Feminine Endings*, 37, 35–79.

69  Story, *And So I Sing*, 33; Errol Hill, "Hyers Sisters." See Programmes, The Hyers Sisters, Billy Rose Theatre Collection, New York Public Library for the Performing Arts. The third act of *Out of Bondage* imagines four of its characters as moving "from the Cotton Field to the Opera" and earning their way as professional vocalists before yielding the stage to the Sisters' concert repertoire; Joseph Bradford, *Out of Bondage*, 3–116. See Hill, "Hyers Sisters," 119. Hill argues that the "Sisters and other members of their troupe merely supported Ms. Hopkins in getting her play staged" (125).

70  Southern argues that Hopkins would probably have seen *Out of Bondage* during its 1877 Boston run and maybe even later when the Hyers Sisters Combination toured the Boston suburbs in the 1880s; see introduction, *African American Theatre*, xxiii; Southern, *Music of Black Americans*, 244–47; Story, *And So I Sing*, 20–36.

71  Southern, *Music of Black Americans*, 246–47; Story, *And So I Sing*, 6, 19. For more reviews of Black Patti, see Sampson, *Ghost Walks*, 426.

72  McClary, *Feminine Endings*, 53–79; Lindon Barrett, *Blackness and Value*, 78–79; Spillers, "Interstices," 167.

73  Southern, *Music of Black Americans*, 302.

74  Gustavas Pike, *The Jubilee Singers and Their Campaign for Twenty Thousand Dollars*. See also Pike, *The Singing Campaign for Ten Thousand Pounds*; Marsh, *The Story of the Jubilee Singers*.

75  On Maggie Porter, see Marsh, *The Story of the Jubilee Singers*, 105–6. On Ella Sheppard, see Marsh, *The Story of the Jubilee Singers*, 103–5; Ward, *Dark Midnight*, 71–72. On Mabel Lewis, see Marsh, *The Story of the Jubilee Singers*, 114–15; Ward, *Dark Midnight*, 192–93. The similarities between Mabel Lewis's biography and both Dianthe and Hopkins's *Contending Forces* heroine Sappho Clarke are strikingly apparent.

76  Barrett, *Blackness and Value*, 55–93; "The Hyers Sisters Company"; *The Inter-Ocean*; Sampson, *Ghost Walks*, 58.

77  Spillers, "Interstices," 165.

78  Schrager, "Pauline Hopkins," 192.

79  Earl Lewis, "To Turn as on a Pivot," 767, 783.

80  C. Allen, *Black Women Intellectuals*, 20.

81  Sundquist, *To Wake the Nations*, 570–72.

82  Story, *And So I Sing*, xiv–xv. For a contemporary discussion of the diva figure, see Jordan Brown, "Lauryn Hill." See also "Platinum," a series written and directed by John Ridley (United Paramount Network, 2003).

83  Hill, "Hyers Sisters," 120–22; Southern, *Music of Black Americans*, 246–47. Later in her career, Jones performed in productions that presented variations on the African princess theme. See, for instance, the review of "A Trip to Africa," February 26, 1910, in Sampson, *Ghost Walks*, 506. Not all these images of diaspora-traversing ingenues were unambiguously committed to uplift. One unmarked clipping describes a performance in which "Miss Jones . . . in gorgeous raiments . . . steps forth in the jungles of Africa, among the half breeds, and is acclaimed the princess"; see S. Jones clipping file, Billy Rose Theatre Collection, New York Public Library for the Performing Arts.

84  See also Marsh, *The Story of the Jubilee Singers*, 107. The Jubilees performed *Esther, the Beautiful Queen* at the Greenlaw Opera House in Memphis in June 1871. Ward, *Dark Midnight*, 90, 118.

85  George Du Maurier, *Trilby*; Hopkins, *Of One Blood*, 456, 461; Wilkie Collins, *The Woman in White*; Allen, *Black Women Intellectuals*, 41; Nina Auerbach, *Woman and the Demon*, 35, 38 (future references to this text will be cited as Auerbach, *Woman and the Demon*); Edith Hamilton, *Mythology*, 31–32. For a contemporary example of "moon" imagery, black female desire, and the politics of (twentieth-century) change, see Tony Kushner, *Caroline or, Change*.

86  Elin Diamond, *Unmaking Mimesis*, 5; Janet Wolff, "Reinstating Corporeality," 89;

Deborah Horvitz, "Hysteria and Trauma in Pauline Hopkins' *Of One Blood*," 251. See also Luciano, "Passing Shadows"; and Ammons, *Conflicting Stories*.

87 Unlike Little Eva, whose death chamber and body are "shrouded in white napkins," and unlike Zoe, the protagonist of Dion Boucicault's drama *The Octoroon*, Dianthe, by being carried back to Africa, becomes "blacker" figuratively in her death. See Harriet Beecher Stowe, *Uncle Tom's Cabin*, 412–28; and Dion Boucicault, *The Octoroon*.

88 Auerbach, *Woman and the Demon*, 40–41. This potency and "metamorphic energy" residing in the trance state is, of course, not merely characteristic of Victorian heroines (Auerbach, *Woman and the Demon*, 43). See Joy Driskell Baklanoff, "The Celebration of a Feast: Music, Dance, and Possession Trance in the Black Primitive Baptist Footwashing Ritual," 381–94.

89 Tate, *Domestic Allegories*, 208; Judith Walkowitz, *City of Dreadful Delight*, 177; Gabrielle Foreman, *Dark Sentiment*.

90 Kassanoff, "Fate Has Linked Us," 173.

91 R. Laurence Moore, *In Search of White Crows*, 106; Richard Brodhead, "Veiled Ladies," 276, 279. See also Walkowitz, *City of Dreadful Delight*, 176–77. For background on Harriet Wilson's work as the "colored medium," see P. Gabrielle Foreman and Reginald Pitts, introduction to *Our Nig* by Harriet Wilson.

92 Joseph Roach, *Cities of the Dead*, 208; Lynn Wardley, "Relic, Fetish, Femmage," 204; George Lipsitz, *Time Passages*.

93 Moore, *In Search of White Crows*, 106; Carby, *Reconstructing Womanhood*, 160; Schrager, "Pauline Hopkins," 193–95; Ammons, *Conflicting Stories*, 81–85.

94 Du Bois, *Souls*, 3; Schrager, "Both Sides of the Veil," 568, 575; Sundquist, *To Wake the Nations*, 574; Kassanoff, "Fate," 173–76.

95 Sundquist, *To Wake the Nations*, 572; Walkowitz, *City of Dreadful Delight*, 176; Brodhead, "Veiled Ladies," 287.

96 *Ghost Walks*, 120–21; Newman, " 'Brightest Star.' "

97 Unsourced clipping, Williams and Walker file, Billy Rose Theatre Collection, New York Public Library for the Performing Arts (future references to this collection will be cited parenthetically as BRT); "Special Cable to New York American," June 23, 1903, in Sampson, *Ghost Walks*, 297. See also Sylvester Russell, "Williams and Walker's *In Dahomey* Co.," October 1, 1904, in Sampson, *Ghost Walks*, 327–30; Russell, "Williams and Walker's *Abyssinia* Co. at the Park Theatre, Indianapolis," October 27, 1906, in Sampson, *Ghost Walks*, 376–78; Newman, " 'Brightest Star,' " 60.

98 See Thomas Riis, *Music and Scripts*, lv; Vincent Bryan and H. Von Tizler, "Vassar Girl," in Hatch and Shine, *In Dahomey*, *Black Theatre USA*, 74. For more on "Vassar Girl," see chapter 4. Vincent Bryan and H. Von Tizler, "I Wants to Be an Actor Lady," in Riis, *Music and Scripts*, 68–70; Riis, *Music and Scripts*, xl. Minstrelsy promoted the image of greedy, garishly ostentatious black women; see Robert Toll, "Social Commentary," 102; Dorman, "Shaping the Popular Image," 461–63; Dennison, *Scandalize*, 404–9.

99  Shipp, Cook, and Dunbar, *In Dahomey*, 74; Story, *And So I Sing*, xiv; David
    Krassner, "Rewriting the Body," 76.

100 "Mrs. Aida Overton Walker comment on the lack of love scenes in Negro musical
    plays," *Indianapolis Freeman*, October 6, 1906, in Sampson, *Ghost Walks*, 371–72;
    Eric Ledell Smith, *Bert Williams*, 158–60; Aida Overton Walker, "Colored Men
    and Women on the American Stage," 574. See Sampson, *Ghost Walks*, June 3,
    1908, 428. For more on Walker's benefit work, see Smith, *Bert Williams*, 165–66.

101 Eric Ledell Smith, "Aida Overton Walker," 37; Edward Said, *Culture and Imperi-
    alism*, 132, 125; Smith, *Bert Williams*, 98; Newman, " 'Brightest Star,' " 63.

102 Unsourced clipping, BRT. For more on Walker's work as an understudy to her
    husband, see BRT. See also Smith, *Bert Williams*, 94, 111; Ann Charters, *Nobody*.

103 Jeanie Forte, "Focus on the Body."

104 Contemporaries such as Alain Locke chastised Tanner for failing to purpose-
    fully politicize his work. Locke found Tanner disappointing for "not us[ing] his
    international prestige to take the lead" in "a specifically African American
    school of art"; Dewey F. Mosby, *Across Continents and Cultures*, 5. Others cri-
    tiqued him for avoiding biblical scenes "in which Ethiopians actually or pre-
    sumably figured"; Mosby, *Across Continents*, 60. Yet no one, it seems, took
    notice of the ideological politics evidenced in the painter's *Salome*. Finished in
    the wake of Du Bois's *Souls*, his *Salome* seems to mark the inevitable segue to the
    dreamlike promised lands of his "Near Eastern Scene" landscape portraits;
    Mosby, *Across Continents*, 5.

105 Richard Powell, ed., *Rhapsodies in Black*, 18. Warrick-Fuller was a friend and
    coworker of Pauline Hopkins. See Nellie Y. McKay, introduction, *The Unruly
    Voice*, 8.

106 Schrager, "Veil," 554; Du Bois, *Souls*, 159–60.

107 For more on "Salomania," see Elizabeth Kendall, *Where She Danced*, 75; Susan
    Glenn, *Feminine Spectacle*. See also Tom Fletcher, *100 Years*, 181–82; James Has-
    kins, *Black Dance in America*, 30–31; Evelyn Brooks Higginbotham, "African
    American Women's History and the Metalanguage of Race," 262; Darlene Clark
    Hine, "Rape and the Inner Lives of Black Women in the Middle West."

108 See Helen Grace Zagona, *The Legend of Salome*; Susan Glenn, *Female Spectacle*,
    106–7. See also Toni Bentley, *Sisters of Salome*, 22.

109 Oscar Wilde, *Salome*; Bentley, *Sisters*, 26, 28; Kendall, *Golden Age*, 74–75; Glenn,
    *Female Spectacle*, 98; Zagona, *Legend*, 127.

110 Zagona, *Legend*, 132.

111 Glenn, *Female Spectacle*, 109–11.

112 Higginbotham, "African American Women's History," 266.

113 Walker's Salome debut in *Bandanna Land* was first reviewed by Lester Walton in
    the August 27, 1908, edition of the *New York Age*. See Glenn, *Female Spectacle*,
    114; David Krasner, *A Beautiful Pageant*, 55–70; "Spirit of the Dance," *New York
    Age*, December 24, 1908.

114 Smith, *Bert Williams*, 94. See also *Bandanna Land*, Clipping File, Harvard The-

atre Collection, Houghton Library, Harvard University; Glenn, *Female Spectacle*, 114.

115 George Walker, *New York Age*, September 3, 1908; Newman, " 'Brightest Star,' " 64; Glenn, *Female Spectacle*, 114; Sampson, *Ghost Walks*; Black Patti Troubadours Clipping file, BRT, New York Public Library; Glenn, *Female Spectacle*, 117.

116 Walker, "Bert and Me," *New York Age*, December 24, 1908; Glenn, *Female Spectacle*, 118; Krasner, *A Beautiful Pageant*, 66–67.

117 Brodhead, "Veiled Ladies," 275; Elaine Showalter, *Sexual Anarchy*, 144–45, 148; Marjorie Garber, *Vested Interests*, 338.

118 Bentley, *Sisters*, 36–37; Amy Koritz, "Dancing the Orient for England."

119 Malek Alloula, *The Colonial Harem*, 106, 7, 13, emphasis his.

120 Unsourced clipping, BRT.

121 Newman, " 'Brightest Star,' " 64.

122 Susan Leigh Foster, "Pygmalion's No-Body and the Body of Dance," 145, 132; Krasner, *A Beautiful Pageant*, 68.

123 Lester Walton, "Salome," *New York Age*, August 27, 1908.

124 Wolff, "Reinstating," 95–96; Susan Leigh Foster, "Dancing Bodies," 245–46.

125 Forte, "Focus," 254; Foster, "Pygmalion," 137.

126 Alloula, *Colonial Harem*, 145; Gillian Brown, *Domestic Individualism*, 122.

127 Schrager, "Veil," 568; Rhonda K. Garelick, "Electric Salome," 90, 92.

128 Garber, *Vested Interests*, 339; Foucault, *The History of Sexuality: An Introduction*, vol. 1, 71; Thulani Davis, "Black Artists and the Next Millennium."

129 Krasner, *A Beautiful Pageant*, 65; Evelyn Hammonds, "Toward a Genealogy of Black Female Sexuality," 171–77. See also Spillers, "Interstices"; Hammonds, "Black (W)holes and the Geometry of Black Female Sexuality."

130 Madhu DuBey, *Black Women Novelists and the Nationalist Aesthetic*, 5, 4.

131 Higginbotham, "African American Women's History," 271; Walker, "Colored Men and Women," 574.

132 Bentley, *Sisters*, 35, 38.

133 Françoise Meltzer, *Salome and the Dance of Writing*, 46; Hammonds, "Black (W)holes," 316; Barret, *Blackness and Value*, 88.

## Epilogue

1 Nellie Y. McKay, introduction, *The Unruly Voice*, ed. John Cullen Gruess, 7–8. Pushed out perhaps by Booker T. Washington's politically accommodationist staff of supporters, Hopkins would continue to publish her unique and multifaceted fiction and journalism in two brief spurts before almost entirely disappearing from the public eye after 1916. Employed as a stenographer at the Massachusetts Institute of Technology, Hopkins died accidentally as a result of a house fire in her Cambridge, Massachusetts, home in 1930.

2 2004 Tony Awards program, June 6, 2004, CBS.

3 Ibid.; Jesse McKinley, "Rashad Breaks Barrier as Leading Actress."

4 For more on Carol Channing, see Channing, *Just Lucky I Guess*. Channing notes

that her father, George Channing, was of African American descent. In many ways, the show marked the high point of what was already a remarkable season for black women in the New York theatre world. In addition to the aforementioned Broadway productions, the African American playwright Lynn Nottage's ambitious *Intimate Apparel*, which starred Viola Davis and followed the trials and travails of a turn-of-the-century black seamstress, played to sold-out audiences off-Broadway. Also, the hip-hop–informed performance artist and poet Sarah Jones continued her successful one-woman performance of *bridge and tunnel*, a play produced, in part, by Jones fan Meryl Streep.

5 Jesse McKinley and Jason Zinoman, "Tony Awards Finish Up with a Fuzzy Surprise."
6 David Cote, "Avenue Q."
7 "Avenue Q advertisement," *Time Out New York*, June 3–10, 2004, 145.
8 Adam Feldman, "Divalution."
9 2004 Tony Awards program, June 6, 2004, CBS.

# BIBLIOGRAPHY

## Newspapers

The Anti-Slavery Reporter
Boston Evening Transcript
Boston Liberator
The Colored American Magazine
Daily Alta California
Golden Era
The Leeds Mercury
The Liberator
The London Daily News
London Times
National Anti-Slavery Standard
New York Age
New York Clipper
New York Freeman
New York Herald
New York Illustrated News
New York Times
The North Star
Preston Guardian & Advertiser
Providence Daily Journal
Punch
Spirit of the Times
The Tatler
West London Observer
Wolverhampton & Staffordshire Herald

## Archives and Collections

Bancroft Library, University of California, Berkeley
Beinecke Rare Book and Manuscript Library, Yale University, New Haven, Connecticut

Billy Rose Theatre Collection, New York Public Library for the Performing Arts, New York

Book Arts and Special Collections, San Francisco Public Library, San Francisco

Gabrielle Enthoven Theatre Collection, Victoria and Albert Museum, London

Harvard Theatre Collection, Houghton Library, Harvard University, Cambridge, Massachusetts

John Hay Library, Brown University, Providence, Rhode Island

Lord Chamberlain Play Collection, Manuscript Reading Room, British Library, London

Manuscript Reading Room, Library of Congress, Washington

Rare Books and Manuscript Reading Room, Boston Public Library, Boston

Rhodes House Library, Oxford University, Oxford

San Francisco Performing Arts Library, San Francisco

Schomburg Library and Center for Research in Black Culture, New York Public Library, New York

Smithsonian Institution, Washington

Special Collections, Firestone Library, Princeton University, Princeton, New Jersey

Special Collections, University Research Library, University of California, Los Angeles

## Primary Sources

Aiken, G. L. *Uncle Tom's Cabin: or, Life Among the Lowly, a Domestic Drama in 6 Acts, as Performed in the Principal English and American Theatres*. New York: S. French, [185?].

Aldridge, Ira. "The Black Doctor." 1847. In *Black Theatre USA: Plays by African Americans, 1847 to Today*, edited by James V. Hatch and Ted Shine. New York: Free Press, 1996. 3–24.

Armistead, W. *A Tribute for the Negro: Being a Vindication of the Moral, Intellectual, and Religious Capabilities of the Coloured Portion of Mankind*. Manchester, England: William Irwin Publishers, 1848.

Ball, Charles. *Fifty Years in Chains, or, The Life of an American Slave*. New York: H. Dayton, 1858.

Ball, J. P. "Ball's Splendid Mammoth Pictorial Tour of the United States." In *J. P. Ball, Daguerrean and Studio Photographer*, edited by Deborah Willis. New York: Garland Publishing, 1993. 237–301.

Banvard, John. *Description of Banvard's Panorama of the Mississippi & Missouri Rivers, Extensively Known as the "Three-Mile Painting," Exhibiting A View of Country Over 3000 Miles in Length, Extending from the Mouth of the Yellow Stone to the City of New Orleans, Being by Far the Largest Picture Ever Executed By Man*. London: W. J. Golbourn, 1848.

Barclay, George L. *The Life and Career of Adah Isaacs Menken, the Celebrated Actress*. Philadelphia: Barclay & Co., 1868.

Bibb, Henry. "Narrative of the Life and Adventures of Henry Bibb, an American

Slave." 1849. In *Puttin' on Ole Massa: The Slave Narratives of Henry Bibb, William Wells Brown, and Solomon Northup*, edited by Gilbert Osofsky. New York: Harper & Row, 1969. 51–172.

Boucicault, Dion. *The Octoroon*. 1859. Salem, N.H.: Ayer, 1987.

——. *The Octoroon*. 1859. *Selected Plays of Dion Boucicault*. Edited by Andrew Parkin. Washington: Colin Smythe; Catholic University of America Press, 1987. 135–90.

Braddon, Mary Elizabeth. *Lady Audley's Secret*. 1862. Introduction by David Skilton. New York: Oxford University Press, 1987.

——. *The Octoroon*. New York: Optimus Printing, [186?].

Bradford, Joseph. *Out of Bondage: A Dramatization Written for the Hyers Sisters*. In *African American Theatre: Out of Bondage and Peculiar Sam; or, The Underground Railroad*, edited by Eileen Southern. New York: Garland Publishing, 1994. 1–116.

Brougham, John. *Dred: A Tale of the Dismal Swamp*. New York: Samuel French, 1856?

——. *Life in New York, or, Tom and Jerry on a Visit: A Comic Drama in Two Acts*. New York: Samuel French, 1856.

——. "Metamora; or, the Last of the Pollywogs." 1847. In *Staging the Nation: Plays from the American Theater, 1787–1909*, edited by Don Wilmeth. Boston: Bedford Books, 1998.

——. *Po-ca-hon-tas, or, The Gentle Savage: In Two Acts*. New York: Samuel French & Son, 1878.

Brown, Henry Box. *Mirror of Slavery*. Boston, Mass., 1850.

——. *Narrative of Henry Box Brown, Who Escaped from Slavery Enclosed in a Box 3 feet Long and 2 Wide. By Charles Stearns*. Boston: Brown & Stearns, 1849.

——. *Narrative of the Life of Henry Box Brown: Written by Himself*. Manchester, England: Lee and Glynn, 1851.

——. *Narrative of the Life of Henry Box Brown: Written by Himself*. 1851. Introduction by Richard Newman. New York: Oxford University Press, 2002.

Brown, William Wells. *The American Fugitive in Europe: Sketches of Places and People Abroad*. Boston: J. P. Jewett, 1855.

——. *The Anti-Slavery Harp: A Collection of Songs for Anti-Slavery Meetings*. Boston: B. Marsh, 1848.

——. "A Description of William Wells Brown's Original Panoramic Views of the Scenes in the Life of an American Slave, from His Birth in Slavery to His Death or His Escape to His First Home of Freedom on British Soil." In *The Black Abolitionist Papers*, edited by C. Peter Ripley et al. Vol. 1: *The British Isles, 1830–1865*. Chapel Hill, N.C.: University of North Carolina Press, 1985. 191–224.

——. *Clotel, or, The President's Daughter*. 1853. Introduction by Joan E. Cashin. Armonk, N.Y.: M. E. Sharpe, 1996.

——. "The Escape; Or, a Leap For Freedom." 1858. In *Black Theatre USA: Plays by African Americans, 1847 to Today*, edited by James V. Hatch and Ted Shine. New York: Free Press, 1996. 35–60.

——. *Three Years in Europe: or, Places I have Seen and People I Have Met. By W. Wells*

*Brown, a Fugitive Slave. With a Memoir of the Author by William Farmer*. London: Charles Gilpin, 1852.

———. *The Travels of William Wells Brown: The Narrative of William Wells Brown, A Fugitive Slave, and The American Fugitive in Europe, Sketches of Places and People Abroad*. 1848. Edited by Paul Jefferson. New York: M. Weiner, 1991.

Bryan, Vincent, and H. Von Tizler. "I Wants to Be an Actor Lady." In *The Music and Scripts of In Dahomey*, edited by Thomas L. Riis. Madison, Wisc.: A-R Editions, Inc., for the American Musicological Society, 1996. 68–70.

———. "Vassar Girl." In *Black Theatre USA: Plays by African-Americans 1847 to Today*, edited by James V. Hatch and Ted Shine. New York: Free Press, 1996. 74–75.

Buckstone, J. B. "Jack Sheppard." In *Trilby and Other Plays*, edited by George Taylor. New York: Oxford University Press, 1996. 6–83.

———. *Jack Sheppard: A Drama in Four Acts*. New York: Samuel French, 1853.

Burton, Richard F. *A Mission to Gelele, King of Dahome*. London: Tylston and Edwards, 1893.

———. *Wanderings in West Africa*. 1863. New York: Dover, 1991.

Byron, George Gordon. *Mazeppa*. In *Lord Byron: Selected Poems*. London: Penguin, 1996.

Carlyle, Thomas. "Occasional Discourse on the Nigger Question." *Latter-Day Pamphlets*. London, 1858.

Carr, Comyns. "Dr. Jekyll and Mr. Hyde." 1910. Lord Chamberlain Play Collection. Manuscript Reading Room, British Library. London.

Channing, Carol. *Just Lucky I Guess: Memoir of Sorts*. New York: Simon & Schuster, 2002.

Channing, William Ellery. "On Abolitionists and Integration." In *Racial Thought in America: From the Puritans to Abraham Lincoln*, edited by Louis Ruchames. New York: Grosset & Dunlap, 1969.

Chesnutt, Charles. *The Conjure Woman and Other Conjure Tales*. Edited by Richard H. Brodhead. Durham, N.C.: Duke University Press, 1993.

———. *The Marrow of Tradition*. 1901. New York: Penguin Books, 1993.

Collins, Wilkie. *Black and White*. 1869. *MS 53075*. Lord Chamberlain Play Collection. Manuscript Reading Room, British Library. London.

———. *The Woman in White*. 1860. New York: Bantam Books, 1985.

*The Complete Repertoire of the Songs, Ballads and Plantation Melodies*. London: Hopwood & Crew, 1870.

Cook, Will. "Swing Along." In *The Music and Scripts of In Dahomey*, edited by Thomas L. Riis. Madison, Wisc.: A-R Editions, Inc. for the American Musicological Society, 1996. 155–62.

Cooper, Anna Julia. *A Voice from the South by a Black Woman from the South*. 1892. Introduction by Mary Helen Washington. New York: Oxford University Press, 1988.

Craft, William. *Running a Thousand Miles for Freedom; or, The Escape of William and Ellen Craft from Slavery*. 1860. Edited by Arna Bontemps. Boston: Beacon Press, 1969. 269–331.

Crummell, Alexander. "Hope for Africa." *The Future of Africa: Being Addresses, Sermons, Etc., Etc., Delivered in the Republic of Liberia.* 1862. New York: Negro Universities Press. 284–91.

Delany, Martin R. *Blake or The Huts of America.* Boston: Beacon Press, 1970.

——. *Condition, Elevation, Emigration, and Destiny of the Colored People of the United States.* 1852. New York: Arno Press, 1968.

Dickens, Charles. *American Notes.* 1842. Introduction by Christopher Hitchens. New York: Modern Library, 1996.

Dimond, William. *The Aethiop: or, The Child of the Desert: A Romantic Play, in Three Acts.* New York: Samuel French, [185?].

Donne, W. B. *Cora, or the Octoroon Slave of Louisiana Drama.* 1861. Lord Chamberlain Play Collection. Manuscript Reading Room, British Library. London.

Douglass, Frederick. *My Bondage and My Freedom.* 1855. Introduction by Philip S. Foner. New York: Dover Publications, 1969.

——. *Narrative of the Life of Frederick Douglass, An American Slave.* 1846. Introduction by Houston A. Baker Jr. New York: Penguin Books, 1982.

——. *The Nature, Character and History of the Anti-Slavery Movement, a Glasgow Lecture.* London: Anti-Slavery Society, 1855.

——. "What to the Slave is the Fourth of July? An Address Delivered on July 5, 1852 in Rochester New York." *The Frederick Douglass Papers,* edited by John Blassingame. Vol. 2: 1847–1854. New Haven, Conn.: Yale University Press, 1982. 359–87.

Du Bois, W. E. B. *The Souls of Black Folk.* 1903. New York: Bantam Books, 1989.

Du Maurier, George. *Trilby.* 1894. Introduction by Leonee Ormond. London: Everyman, 1994.

Dunbar, Paul Laurence. "Evah Dahkey is a King." In *The Music and Scripts of In Dahomey,* edited by Thomas L. Riis. Madison, Wisc.: A-R Editions, Inc. for the American Musicological Society, 1996. 47–54.

——. "*Herrick*: An Imaginative Comedy in Three Acts." In *In His Own Voice: The Dramatic and Other Uncollected Works of Paul Laurence Dunbar,* edited by Herbert Woodward Martin and Ronald Primeau. Athens: Ohio University Press, 2002. 17–83.

——. "Jes Lak White Fo'ks: A One Act Negro Operetto." In *In His Own Voice: The Dramatic and Other Uncollected Works of Paul Laurence Dunbar,* edited by Herbert Woodward Martin and Ronald Primeau. Athens: Ohio University Press, 2002. 133–44.

——. *The Sport of the Gods.* 1902. Salem, N.H.: Ayer Co., 1984.

Ellington, Duke. *Music Is My Mistress.* Garden City, N.Y.: Doubleday, 1973.

Ellison, Ralph. *Invisible Man.* 1952. New York: Vintage, 1982.

Engle, Gary. D., ed. *This Grotesque Essence: Plays from the American Minstrel Stage.* Baton Rouge: Louisiana State University Press, 1978.

Equiano, Olaudah. "The Interesting Narrative of the Life of Olaudah Equiano, or Gustavus Vassa, the African." 1789. In *The Classic Slave Narratives,* edited by Henry Louis Gates Jr. New York: New American Library, 1987. 1–182.

Foster, Frances S., ed. *A Brighter Coming Day: A Frances Ellen Watkins Harper Reader*. New York: City University of New York, 1990.

Gage, Frances. "Reminiscences by Frances D. Gage of Sojourner Truth, for May 28–9, 1851." In *The Heath Anthology of American Literature*, edited by Paul Lauter et al. Lexington, Mass.: D. C. Heath, 1990.

Gast, Leon, dir. *When We Were Kings*. Gramercy, 1996.

Haines, J. T. *The French Spy; or, The Siege of Constantina. A Military Drama, in Three Acts. Partly from the French*. New York: S. French, 1856.

Harper, Frances Ellen Watkins. *Iola Leroy, or, Shadows Uplifted*. 1892. Introduction by Hazel V. Carby. Boston: Beacon Press, 1987.

Hatfield, Edwin F. *Freedom's Lyre*. New York: S. W. Benedict, 1840.

Hawthorne, Nathaniel H. *The Blithedale Romance*. 1852. New York: Penguin Books, 1983.

Hazelwood, C. H. *Lady Audley's Secret: An Original Version of Miss Braddon's Popular Novel in Two Acts*. London: Thomas Hailes Lacy, 1863.

*History and Medical Description of the Two-Headed Girl*. 1869. Stratford, Conn.: Alton Vexierbild, 1976.

Hopkins, Pauline E. *Contending Forces: A Romance Illustrative of Negro Life North and South*. 1900. Introduction by Richard Yarborough. New York: Oxford University Press, 1988.

———. *Of One Blood. Or, The Hidden Self*. 1902–1903. In *The Magazine Novels of Pauline Hopkins*. Introduction by Hazel V. Carby. New York: Oxford University Press, 1988. 439–621.

———. *Peculiar Sam, Or, The Underground Railroad*. 1879. In *The Roots of African American Drama: An Anthology of Early Plays, 1858–1938*, edited by Leo Hamalian and James V. Hatch. Detroit: Wayne State University Press, 1991. 100–123.

*The Interpreter's Bible*. New York: Abingdon Press, 1999.

Jacobs, Harriet. *Incidents in the Life of a Slave Girl*. 1861. Introduction by Jean Fagan Yellin. Cambridge, Mass.: Harvard University Press, 1987.

James, Edwin. *Biography of Adah Isaacs Menken, with Selections from Infelicia*. New York: Edwin James, [1881?].

James, Henry. *The Beast in the Jungle*. London: Dover Publications, 1993.

Jerrold, Douglas. *Black-Ey'd Susan*. London: Thomas Richardson, 1829.

Johnson, James Weldon. *Black Manhattan*. 1930. New York: Da Capo Press, 1991.

Johnson, James Weldon, Bob Cole, and Rosamond Johnson. "My Castle on the Nile." In *The Music and Scripts of In Dahomey*, edited by Thomas L. Riis. Madison, Wisc.: A-R Editions, Inc. for the American Musicological Society, 1996.

Longfellow, Henry W. *Poems on Slavery*. Cambridge, Mass.: J. Owen, 1842.

Marsh, J. B. T. *The Story of the Jubilee Singers, with Their Songs*. New York: S. W. Green's Son, 1880.

Mattison, Hiram. *Louisa Picquet, the Octoroon: Or Inside Views of Southern Domestic Life*. 1861. In *Collected Black Women's Narratives*, edited by Anthony G. Barthelemy. New York: Oxford University Press, 1988. 90–150.

——. *Spirit Rapping Unveiled! An Exposé of the Origin, History, Theology and Philoso-phy of Certain Alleged Communications from the Spirit World, by Means of "Spirit Rapping," "Medium Writing," "Physical Demonstrations," etc.: with illustrations*. New York: Mason Brothers, 1853.

*Mazeppa; or, The Wild Horse of the Ukraine. A Romance*. London: E. Lloyd, 1850.

Menken, Adah Isaacs. *Infelicia*. Philadelphia: J. B. Lippincott, 1888.

——. "Infelicia." 1868. In *Collected Black Women's Poetry*, edited by Joan R. Sherman. Vol. 1. New York: Oxford University Press, 1988. 217–341.

——. "Mid-night in New Orleans." In *Infelicia and Other Writings*, edited by Gregory Eiselein. Peterborough, Ontario: Broadview Press, 2002. 168–73.

——. "Our Mother." In *Infelicia and Other Writings*, edited by Gregory Eiselein. Peterborough, Ontario: Broadview Press, 2002. 153.

——. "Pro Patria." In *Infelicia and Other Writings*, edited by Gregory Eiselein. Peter-borough, Ontario: Broadview Press, 2002. 97–102.

——. "Some Notes of Her Life in Her Own Hand." *New York Times*, September 6, 1868.

——. "Swimming Against the Current." In *Infelicia and Other Writings*, edited by Gregory Eiselein. Peterborough, Ontario: Broadview Press, 2002. 176–79.

Milner, Henry M. *Mazeppa, or the Wild Horse of Tartary, A Romantic Drama in Two Acts*. New York: G. Purkess, [183?].

Mitchell, O., ed. *Francis and Day's Nigger Dramas and Stump Speeches for Amateur Minstrels, Etc*. London: Francis Bros. & Day, 1888.

Molin, Sven Eric, and Robin Goodefellowe, eds. *Dion Boucicault, The Shaugraun: A Document. Life, Letters, and Selected Works*. Newark, Del.: Proscenium Press, 1979.

Moncrieff, William T. *Tom and Jerry: or, Life in London: an Operatic Extravaganza, in Three Acts by W. T. Moncrieff*. London: Thomas Richardson, 1828.

——. *Tom and Jerry; or, Life in London, A Burletta of Fun, Frolic, and Flash in Two Acts*. London: Samuel French, 1825.

Moore, George. "Mummer-Worship." *Impressions and Opinions*. London: David Nutt Publishing, 1891. 153–80.

Mott, Lucretia. *Slavery and "the Woman Question"; Lucretia Mott's Diary of Her Visit to Great Britain to Attend the World's Anti-Slavery Convention of 1840*. Haverford, Pa.: Friends' Historical Association, 1952.

Nell, William Cooper. *The Colored Patriots of the American Revolution with Sketches of Several Distinguished Colored Persons: to Which is Added a Brief Survey of the Condition and Prospects of Colored Americans*. Boston: R. F. Wallcut, 1855.

Newell, Robert Henry. "Biography of Adah Isaacs Menken. Extra Illustrated." Hay Library, Brown University, Providence, R.I.

Northup, Solomon. *Twelve Years a Slave: Narrative of Solomon Northrup, a Citizen of New York, Kidnapped in Washington City in 1841, and Rescued in 1853, from a Cotton Plantation Near the Red River, in Louisiana*. 1853. Edited by Sue Eakin and Joseph Logsdon. Baton Rouge: Louisiana State University Press, 1992.

Nyby, Christian, dir. "Magnificent Adah." *Bonanza*, 1959. Videocassette. Republic Entertainment Video, 1998.

Olwine, Wayne, ed. *Black-Eyed Susan*. Boston: William V. Spencer, 1855.

Palmer, T. A. *East Lynne: A Domestic Drama in a Prologue and Four Acts: Adapted from Mrs. Wood's Novel*. London: S. French, 1874.

Pike, Gustavas D. *The Jubilee Singers and Their Campaign for Twenty Thousand Dollars*. Boston: Lee and Shepard, 1873; New York, 1874.

———. *The Singing Campaign for Ten Thousand Pounds; or The Jubilee Singers in Great Britain*. New York: American Missionary Association, 1875.

Poe, Edgar Allan. "Ligeia." 1838. In *Tales of Mystery and Imagination*, edited by Graham Clarke. London: Everyman, 1993. 169–88.

———. *Narrative of A. Gordon Pym*. 1837. New York: Penguin Books, 1999.

Rawson, M. A., ed. *Hymns for Anti-Slavery Prayer Meetings*. London: Anti-Slavery Society, 1838.

*Revised Standard Version Bible*. Iowa Falls: Riverside Books & Bible House, 1952.

Ridley, John, dir. "Platinum." United Paramount Network, 2003.

Riis, Thomas L., ed. *The Music and Scripts of In Dahomey*. Madison, Wisc.: A-R Editions, Inc. for the American Musicological Society, 1996.

Robertson, T. W. *Caste: An Original Comedy in Three Acts, as First Produced Saturday, April 6th, 1867, at the Prince of Wales Theatre, London*. New York: Robert M. De Witt, 1867.

Robeson, Paul. "Go Down, Moses." *Norton Anthology of African American Literature Audio Companion*. New York: W. W. Norton, 1965.

Shipp, Jesse A., Will Marion Cook, and Paul Laurence Dunbar. "In Dahomey, a Negro Musical Comedy." 1902. In *Black Theatre USA: Plays by African Americans*, edited by James V. Hatch and Ted Shine. New York: Free Press, 1996. 65–85.

Stanton, Elizabeth Cady. "Adah Isaacs Menken." In *Infelicia and Other Writings*, edited by Gregory Eiselein. Peterborough, Ontario: Broadview Press, 2002. 245–46.

Stearns, Charles. Preface. *Narrative of Henry Box Brown, Who Escaped from Slavery Enclosed in a Box—3 Feet Long and 2 Wide by Charles Stearns*. Boston: Brown and Stearns, 1849.

Stevenson, Robert Louis. *The Strange Case of Dr. Jekyll and Mr. Hyde*. 1885. New York: Penguin Books, 1979.

Stewart, Maria W. *Maria W. Stewart, America's First Black Woman Political Writer: Essays and Speeches*. Edited by Marilyn Richardson. Bloomington: Indiana University Press, 1987.

Stowe, Harriet Beecher. *Dred; A Tale of the Great Dismal Swamp*. 1856. Introduction by Robert S. Levine. New York: Penguin Books, 2000.

———. *Uncle Tom's Cabin: or, Life Among the Lowly*. 1852. Introduction by Ann Douglas. New York: Penguin Books, 1981.

*The Strange Case of Hyde and Seekyll*. 1886. Lord Chamberlain Play Collection. Manuscript Reading Room, British Library. London.

Sullivan, Thomas R. *Dr. Jekyll and Mr. Hyde*. Promptbook for the Mansfield production Mansfield Costume Collection. Smithsonian Institution, Washington.

Swinburne, Charles Algernon. *Adah Isaacs Menken: A Fragment of Autobiography*. London: Printed for private circulation only, 1917.

Truth, Sojourner. "Address to the First Annual Meeting of the American Equal Rights Association." In *The Heath Anthology of American Literature*, edited by Paul Lauter et al. Lexington, Mass.: D. C. Heath, 1990.

——. *Narrative of Sojourner Truth, by Sojourner Truth*. 1850. Ed. Margaret Washington. New York: Vintage, 1991.

Twain, Mark. "The Menken—Written Especially for Gentlemen." In *Mark Twain of the Enterprise: Newspaper Articles & Other Documents, 1862–1864*, edited by Henry Nash Smith. Berkeley: University of California Press, 1957.

——. *Pudd'nhead Wilson and Those Extraordinary Twins*. 1894. Introduction by Malcolm Bradbury. New York: Penguin Books, 1969.

*Uncle Tom's Cabin*. 1878. Lord Chamberlain Play Collection. Manuscript Reading Room, British Library. London.

*Uncle Tom's Cabin in England, or A Proof that Black's White: An Echo to the American "Uncle Tom."* New York: A. D. Failing, 1852.

Walker, Aida Overton. "Colored Men and Women on the Stage." *Colored American Magazine* (1905).

——. "Opportunities the Stage Offers Intelligent and Talented Women." *New York Age*, December 24, 1908.

Walker, George. "Bert and Me and Them." *New York Age*, December 24, 1908.

——. "The Real 'Coon' on the American Stage." *Theatre Magazine* (supplement), August 1906.

Warner, Samuel. "Authentic and Impartial Narrative of the Tragical Scene." 1831. In *The Southampton Slave Revolt of 1831*, edited by Henry Irving Tragle. Amherst: University of Massachusetts Press, 1971. 280–300.

Weld, Theodore. "American Slavery As It Is." 1839. In *Black Protest: History, Documents, and Analyses*, edited by Joanne Grant. New York: Fawcett, 1968. 72–75.

Wells, Ida B. *Southern Horrors and Other Writings: The Anti-lynching Campaign of Ida B. Wells, 1892–1900*. Edited by Jacqueline Jones Royster. New York: St. Martin's Press, 1997.

Wells-Barnett, Ida B. *Crusade for Justice: The Autobiography of Ida B. Wells*. Edited by Alfreda M. Duster. Chicago: University of Chicago Press, 1970.

Whitman, Walt. *Leaves of Grass: Authoritative Texts, Prefaces, Whitman on His Art, Criticism*. Edited by Sculley Bradley and Harold W. Blodgett. New York: W. W. Norton, 1973.

Wilde, Oscar. *Salome: A Tragedy in One Act*. 1894. Translated by Alfred Douglas. New York: Dover Publications, 1967.

Williams, Bert. "Fun in the Land of J. Bull." *The Green Book Album*. July 1909. Billy Rose Theatre Collection. New York Public Library of Performing Arts.

Wood, Mrs. Henry. *East Lynne.* 1877. Introduction by Sally Mitchell. New Brunswick, N.J.: Rutgers University Press, 1984.

Work, John W. *American Negro Songs: A Comprehensive Collection of 230 Folk Songs, Religious and Secular.* New York: Howell, 1940.

## Secondary Sources

Abbott, Lynn, and Doug Seroff. *Out of Sight: The Rise of African American Popular Music, 1889–1895.* Jackson: University Press of Mississippi, 2003.

Adams, Rachel. *Sideshow USA: Freaks and the American Cultural Imagination.* Chicago: University of Chicago Press, 2001.

Allen, Carol. *Black Women Intellectuals: Strategies of Nation, Family, and Neighborhood in the Works of Pauline Hopkins, Jessie Fauset, and Marita Bonner.* New York: Garland Publishing, 1998.

Allen, Robert C. *Horrible Prettiness: Burlesque and American Culture.* Chapel Hill, N.C.: University of North Carolina Press, 1991.

Alloula, Malek. *The Colonial Harem.* Translated by Myrna Godzich and Wlad Godzich. Minneapolis: University of Minnesota Press, 1986.

Altick, Richard D. *The Shows of London.* Cambridge, Mass.: Harvard University Press, 1978.

American Council of Learned Societies. *Dictionary of American Biography.* Vols. 1–20. New York: Charles Scribner's Sons, 1937.

Ammons, Elizabeth. *Conflicting Stories: American Women Writers at the Turn into the Twentieth Century.* New York: Oxford University Press, 1991.

Anderson, Benedict. *Imagined Communities: Reflections on the Origin and Spread of Nationalism.* London: Verso, 1991.

Anderson, Paul Allen. *Deep River: Music and Memory in Harlem Renaissance Thought.* Durham, N.C.: Duke University Press, 2001.

Andrews, William L. *To Tell a Free Story: the First Century of Afro-American Autobiography, 1760–1865.* Urbana: University of Illinois Press, 1986.

Appiah, Anthony. *In My Father's House: Africa in the Philosophy of Culture.* New York: Oxford University Press, 1992.

Aptheker, Herbert. "Maroons within the Present Limits of the United States." In *Maroon Societies: Rebel Slave Communities in the Americas,* edited by Richard Price. New York: Anchor Press, 1973.

Armstead-Johnson, Helen. "Themes and Values in Afro-American Librettos and Book Musicals, 1898–1930." In *Musical Theatre in America: Papers and Proceedings of the Conference on the Musical Theatre in America,* edited by Glenn Loney. Westport, Conn.: Greenwood Press, 1984. 133–42.

Artaud, Antonin. *The Theater and Its Double.* New York: Grove Press, 1958.

Auerbach, Nina. *Woman and the Demon: the Life of a Victorian Myth.* Cambridge, Mass.: Harvard University Press, 1982.

——. *Ellen Terry, Player in Her Time.* New York: W. W. Norton, 1987.

———. *Private Theatricals: The Lives of the Victorians.* Cambridge, Mass.: Harvard University Press, 1990.

Austin, Allan D. "More Black Panoramas: An Addendum." *The Massachusetts Review* 37.4 (Winter 1996): 636–39.

Bailey, David, and Richard Powell, eds. *Rhapsodies in Black: Art of the Harlem Renaissance.* Berkeley: University of California Press, 1997.

———. "Scene . . . Not Heard." In *Reading Rodney King: Reading Urban Uprising,* edited by Robert Gooding-Williams. New York: Routledge, 1993. 38–48.

Baklanoff, Joy Driskell. "The Celebration of a Feast: Music, Dance and Possession Trance in the Black Primitive Baptist Footwashing Ritual." *Ethnomusicology* 31.3 (autumn 1987): 381–94.

Banks, Ingrid. *Hair Matters: Beauty, Power, and Black Women's Consciousness.* New York: New York University Press, 2000.

Baraka, Amiri. "The Changing Same (R&B and New Black Music)." 1966. In *The Leroi Jones/Amiri Baraka Reader,* edited by William J. Harris and Amiri Baraka. New York: Thunder's Mouth Press, 1991. 186–209.

Barnes-McLain, Noreen. "Bohemian on Horseback: Adah Isaacs Menken." In *Passing Performances: Queer Readings of Leading Players in American Theater History,* edited by Robert A. Schanke and Kim Marra. Ann Arbor: University of Michigan Press, 1998. 63–79.

Barrett, Lindon. *Blackness and Value: Seeing Double.* New York: Cambridge University Press, 1999.

Bassard, Katherine C. *Spiritual Interrogations: Culture, Gender, and Community in Early African American Women's Writing.* Princeton, N.J.: Princeton University Press, 1999.

Bay, Mia. *The White Image in the Black Mind: African-American Ideas about White People, 1830–1925.* New York: Oxford University Press, 2000.

Baym, Nina. "The Rise of the Woman Author." In *Columbia Literary History of the United States,* edited by Emory Elliott et al. New York: Columbia University Press, 1987. 289–305.

Bean, Annemarie. "Transgressing the Gender Divide: The Female Impersonator in Nineteenth-Century Blackface Minstrelsy." In *Inside the Minstrel Mask: Readings in Nineteenth-Century Blackface Minstrelsy,* edited by Annemarie Bean, James V. Hatch, and Brooks McNamara. Hanover, N.H.: Wesleyan University Press, 1996. 245–56.

Beckman, Karen R. *Vanishing Women: Magic, Film, and Feminism.* Durham, N.C.: Duke University Press, 2003.

Behdad, Ali. *Belated Travelers: Orientalism in the Age of Colonial Dissolution.* Durham, N.C.: Duke University Press, 1994.

Bell, Howard H. "National Negro Conventions of the Middle 1840's: Moral Suasion vs. Political Action." In *Blacks in the Abolitionist Movement,* edited by John H. Bracey Jr., August Meier, and Elliott Rudwick. Belmont, Calif.: Wadsworth Publishing, 1971. 123–33.

Benjamin, Walter. *Reflections: Essays, Aphorisms, Autobiographical Writings*. New York: Harcourt Brace Jovanovich, 1978.

Bennett, Michael, and Vanessa D. Dickerson, eds. *Recovering the Black Female Body: Self-Representation by African American Women*. New Brunswick, N.J.: Rutgers University Press, 2001.

Bentley, Toni. *Sisters of Salome*. New Haven, Conn.: Yale University Press, 2002.

Bernardi, Debra. "Narratives of Domestic Imperialism: The African-American Home in the Colored American Magazine and in the Novels of Pauline Hopkins, 1900–1903." In *Separate Spheres No More: Gender Convergence in American Literature, 1830–1930*, edited by Monika M. Elbert. Tuscaloosa: University of Alabama Press, 2000. 203–24.

Berson, Misha. "The San Francisco Stage: From Gold Rush to Golden Spike, 1849–1869." *San Francisco Performing Arts Library and Museum Journal*, no. 2. 1989.

Bhabha, Homi K. *Nation and Narration*. London: Routledge, 1990.

——. *The Location of Culture*. London: Routledge, 1994.

Blackett, R. J. M. *Building An Antislavery Wall: Black Americans in the Atlantic abolitionist movement, 1830–1860*. Ithaca, N.Y.: Cornell University Press, 1989.

Blassingame, John W. *Black New Orleans, 1860–1880*. Chicago: University of Chicago Press, 1973.

——. *Slave Testimony: Two Centuries of Letters, Speeches, Interviews, and Autobiographies*. Baton Rouge: Louisiana State University Press, 1977.

Bontemps, Arna W., and Jack Conroy. *They Seek a City*. Garden City, N.Y.: Doubleday, Doran and Co., 1945.

Booth, Michael. R. *Victorian Spectacular Theatre: 1850–1910*. Boston: Routledge & Kegan Paul, 1981.

Booth, Michael. "Soldiers of the Queen: Drury Lane Imperialism." In *Melodrama: The Cultural Emergence of a Genre*, edited by Michael Hays and Anastasia Nikolopoulou. Basingstake: Macmillan, 1999. 3–20.

Bracey, John H. Jr., and August Meier, eds. *Black Nationalism in America*. Indianapolis: Bobbs-Merrill Co. Inc., 1970.

Brandon, Ruth. *The Life and Many Deaths of Harry Houdini*. London: Secker & Warburg, 1993.

——. *The Spiritualists: The Passion for the Occult in the Nineteenth and Twentieth Centuries*. New York: A. A. Knopf, 1983.

Brantlinger, Patrick. "What Is 'Sensational' about the 'Sensation Novel'?" *Nineteenth-Century Fiction* 37.1 (June 1982): 1–28.

Bratton, J. S. "British Heroism and the Structure of Melodrama." In *Acts of Supremacy: the British Empire and the Stage, 1790–1930*, edited by J. S. Bratton et al. Manchester, England: University of Manchester Press, 1991. 18–61.

Braude, Ann. *Radical Spirits: Spiritualism and Women's Rights in Nineteenth-Century America*. Boston: Beacon Press, 1989.

Brecht, Bertolt. *Brecht on Theatre; the Development of an Aesthetic*. Ed. John Willett. New York: Hill and Wang, 1992.

Brodhead, Richard. "Veiled Ladies: Toward a History of Antebellum Entertainment." *American Literary History* 1.2 (summer 1989): 273–94.

Brody, Jennifer D. *Impossible Purities: Blackness, Femininity, and Victorian Culture.* Durham, N.C.: Duke University Press, 1998.

Brooks, Daphne A. " 'The Deeds Done in My Body': Black Feminist Theory, Performance, and the Truth about Adah Isaacs Menken." In *Recovering the Black Female Body: Self-Representations by African-American Women,* edited by Michael Bennett and Vanessa D. Dickerson. New Brunswick, N.J.: Rutgers University Press, 2001. 41–70.

——. "Lady Menken's Secret: Adah Isaacs Menken, Actress Biographies, and the Race for Sensation." *Legacy: A Journal of American Women Writers* 15.1 (1998): 68–77.

——. "Pauline Hopkins." In *African-American Writers, Revised Edition,* edited by Valerie Smith. New York: Charles Scribner & Sons, 2000. 349–366.

Brooks, Joanna. *American Lazarus: Religion and the Rise of African-American and Native American Literature.* New York: Oxford University Press, 2003.

——. "Balm in Gilead: Spiritual Narrative and African-American Autobiography." Princeton University, Princeton, N.J. February 2005.

Brooks, Peter. *The Melodramatic Imagination: Balzac, Henry James, Melodrama, and the Mode of Excess.* New Haven, Conn.: Yale University Press, 1976.

Brown, Gillian. *Domestic Individualism: Imagining Self in Nineteenth-Century America.* Berkeley: University of California Press, 1990.

Brown, Jayna. *Babylon Girls: Race Mimicry, Black Chorus Line Dancers, and the Modern Body.* Durham, N.C.: Duke University press, forthcoming.

Brown, Jordan. "Lauryn Hill: Soul and Steel." *The New Crisis* 106.2 (March–April 1999): 16–20.

Bruce, Dickson. "Ancient Africa and the Early Black American Historians, 1883–1915." *American Quarterly* 36.5 (Winter 1984): 684–99.

——. *Black American Writing from the Nadir: The Evolution of a Literary Tradition, 1877–1915.* Baton Rouge: Louisiana State University Press, 1989.

Buck-Morss, Susan. *The Dialectics of Seeing: Walter Benjamin and the Arcades Project.* Cambridge, Mass.: MIT Press, 1989.

Burnim, Mellonee. "Biblical Inspiration, Cultural Affirmation: The African American Gift of Song." In *African Americans and the Bible: Sacred Text and Social Textures,* edited by Vincent L. Wimbush. New York: Continuum, 2000. 603–15.

Butler, Jon. "The Dark Ages of American Occultism, 1760–1848." In *The Occult in America: New Historical Perspectives,* edited by Howard Kerr and Charles L. Crow. Urbana: University of Illinois Press, 1983. 58–78.

——. *Gender Trouble: Feminism and the Subversion of Identity.* New York: Routledge, 1990.

Butler, Judith. *Bodies that Matter: On the Discursive Limits of "Sex."* New York: Routledge, 1993.

Campbell, Jane. *Mythic Black Fiction: The Transformation of History.* Knoxville: University of Tennessee Press, 1986.

Carby, Hazel V. Introduction. *The Magazine Novels of Pauline Hopkins*. New York: Oxford University Press, 1988. xxix–l.

———. "It Just Be's Dat Way Sometime." In *Unequal Sisters: A Multicultural Reader in U.S. Women's History,* edited by Ellen Carol DuBois and Vicki L. Ruiz. New York: Routledge, 1990. 238–49.

———. "On the Threshold of the Woman's Era: Lynching, Empire and Sexuality in Black Feminist Theory." *Critical Inquiry* 12.1 (Autumn 1985): 262–77.

———. *Reconstructing Womanhood: The Emergence of the Afro-American Woman Novelist*. New York: Oxford University Press, 1987.

Carroll, Brett E. *Spiritualism in Antebellum America*. Bloomington: Indiana University Press, 1997.

Carter, Marva Griffin. "Removing the 'Minstrel Mask' in the Musicals of Will Marion Cook." *Musical Quarterly* 84.2 (summer 2000): 206–20.

Cassuto, Leonard. *The Inhuman Race: The Racial Grotesque in American Literature and Culture*. New York: Columbia University Press, 1996.

Castle, Terry. "Phantasmagoria: Spectral Technology and the Metaphoric of Modern Reverie." *Critical Inquiry* 15.1 (autumn 1988): 26–61.

Castronovo, Russ. *Necro Citizenship: Death, Eroticism, and the Public Sphere in the Nineteenth-Century United States*. Durham, N.C.: Duke University Press, 2001.

Charters, Ann. *Nobody: The Story of Bert Williams*. New York: Macmillan, 1970.

Christian, Barbara. *Black Women Novelists: The Development of a Tradition, 1892–1976*. Westport, Conn.: Greenwood Press, 1980.

Clifford, James. "Traveling Cultures." In *Cultural Studies,* edited by Cary Nelson, Lawrence Grossberg, and Paula Treichler. New York: Routledge, 1992.

Cofran, John. "The Identity of Adah Isaacs Menken: A Theatrical Mystery Solved." *Theatre Survey* 31.1 (May 1990): 47–54.

Cook, James. *The Arts of Deception: Playing with Fraud in the Age of Barnum*. Cambridge, Mass.: Harvard University Press, 2001.

Corless, Hank. *The Weiser Indians: Shoshoni Peacemakers*. Salt Lake City: University of Utah Press, 1990.

Cote, David. "Avenue Q." *Time Out New York,* June 3–10, 2004, 147.

Cruz, Jon. *Culture on the Margins: The Black Spiritual and the Rise of American Cultural Interpretation*. Princeton, N.J.: Princeton University Press, 1999.

Cutter, Martha J. "Sliding Significations: Passing as a Narrative and Textual Strategy in Nella Larsen's Fiction." In *Passing and the Fictions of Identity,* edited by Elaine K. Ginsberg. Durham, N.C.: Duke University Press, 1996. 75–100.

Cvetkovich, Ann. *Mixed Feelings: Feminism, Mass Culture, and Victorian Sensationalism*. New Brunswick, N.J.: Rutgers University Press, 1992.

Danahay, Martin A., and Alex Chisholm, eds. *Jekyll and Hyde Dramatized*. Jefferson, N.C.: McFarland, 2004.

Davis, Charles T., and Henry Louis Gates. "Introduction: The Language of Slavery." In *The Slave's Narrative,* edited by Charles T. Davis and Henry Louis Gates Jr. New York: Oxford University Press, 1985. xi–xxxiv.

Davis, David Brion. *The Problem of Slavery in the Age of Revolution, 1770–1823.* Ithaca, N.Y.: Cornell University Press, 1975.

Davis, Thulani. "Black Artists and the Next Millennium." I'll Make Me A World: A Century of African-American Art, Artists, and Communities, Blackside Conference and Forum, Colonnade Plaza Hotel, Boston, Mass., May 1997.

Davis, Tracy C. *Actresses as Working Women: Their Social Identity in Victorian Culture.* New York: Routledge, 1991.

———. "The Actress in Victorian Pornography." In *Victorian Scandals: Representations of Gender and Class,* edited by Kristine Ottesen Garrigan. Athens: Ohio University Press, 1992. 99–133.

———. "The Spectacle of Absent Costume: Nudity on the Victorian Stage." *New Theatre Quarterly* 5.20 (Nov. 1989): 321–33.

Davison, Helen. "Minstrelsy and the Turn of the Century." *Black America Onstage.* Austria: Armstead-Johnson Foundation, 1982.

Dayan, Joan. "Amorous Bondage: Poe, Ladies, and Slaves." *American Literature* 66.2 (June 1984): 239–73.

Debord, Guy. *The Society of the Spectacle.* Detroit: Black and Red, 1983.

Degen, John A. "How to End *The Octoroon.*" *Educational Theatre Journal* 27.2 (May 1975): 170–78.

Dennison, Sam. *Scandalize My Name: Black Imagery in American Popular Music.* New York: Garland Publishing, 1982.

Diamond, Elin. Introduction. *Performance and Cultural Politics,* edited by Elin Diamond. New York: Routledge, 1996. 1–12.

———. "Mimesis, Mimicry, and the 'True-Real.'" In *Acting Out: Feminist Performances,* edited by Lynda Hart and Peggy Phelan. Ann Arbor: University of Michigan Press, 1993. 363–82.

———. *Unmaking Mimesis: Essays on Feminism and Theater.* London: Routledge, 1997.

Dickson, Samuel. *Tales of San Francisco: Comprising San Francisco is Your Home, San Francisco Kaleidoscope, and The Streets of San Francisco.* Stanford, Calif.: Stanford University Press, 1957.

Domínguez, Virginia R. *White by Definition: Social Classification in Creole Louisiana.* New Brunswick, N.J.: Rutgers University Press, 1986.

Donohue, Joseph. "Women in the Victorian Theatre: Images, Illusions, Realities." In *Gender in Performance: The Presentation of Difference in the Performing Arts,* edited by Laurence Senelick. Hanover, N.H.: University Press of New England, 1992. 117–40.

Dorman, James. "Shaping the Popular Image of Post-Reconstruction American Blacks: The 'Coon Song' Phenomenon of the Gilded Age." *American Quarterly* 40.4 (December 1988): 450–71.

Dubey, Madhu. *Black Women Novelists and the Nationalist Aesthetic.* Bloomington: Indiana University Press, 1994.

duCille, Ann. "The Occult of True Blackwomanhood: Critical Demeanor and Black Feminist Studies." In *The Second Signs Reader: Feminist Scholarship, 1983–1996,* edited by Ruth-Ellen B. Joeres and Barbara Laslett. Chicago: University of Chicago Press, 1996. 70–108.

Dudden, Faye E. *Women in the American Theatre: Actresses and Audiences, 1790–1870*. New Haven, Conn.: Yale University Press, 1994.

During, Simon. *Modern Enchantments: The Cultural Power of Secular Magic*. Cambridge, Mass.: Harvard University Press, 2002.

Edwards, Brent. "Feminism, Collaboration and the Poetics of Diaspora." Women and Religion in the African Diaspora Conference, Princeton University, Princeton, N.J., April 2004.

Eigner, Edwin. *The Dickens Pantomime*. Berkeley: University of California Press, 1989.

Engle, Gary D. *This Grotesque Essence: Plays from the American Minstrel Stage*. Baton Rouge: Louisiana State University Press, 1978.

Engle, Ron, and Tice L. Miller. *The American Stage: Social and Economic Issues from the Colonial Period to the Present*. New York: Cambridge University Press, 1993.

Erdman, Harley. "Caught in the 'Eye of the Eternal': Justice, Race, and the Camera, From *The Octoroon* to Rodney King." *Theatre Journal* 45.3 (October 1993): 333–48.

Ernest, John. "Fugitive Performances." MELUS 2000 International Conference, Orleans, France, June 2000.

———. "The Reconstruction of Whiteness: William Wells Brown's *The Escape; or, A Leap for Freedom*." *PMLA* 113.5 (October 1998): 1108–121.

Ewen, David. *Complete Book of the American Musical Theater*. New York: Henry Holt, 1958.

Falk, Bernard. *The Naked Lady; or, Storm over Adah*. London: Hutchinson, 1934.

Faulkner, Seldon. "The 'Octoroon' War." *Educational Theatre Journal* 15.1 (March 1963): 33–38.

Fausto-Sterling, Anne. "The Comparative Anatomy of 'Hottentot' Women in Europe, 1815–1817." In *Deviant Bodies: Critical Perspectives on Difference in Science and Popular Culture*, edited by Jennifer Terry and Jaqueline Urla. Bloomington: Indiana University Press, 1995. 19–48.

Favor, J. Martin. *Authentic Blackness: The Folk in the New Negro Renaissance*. Durham, N.C.: Duke University Press, 1999.

Feldman, Adam. "Divalution: Every Night is Ladies' Night on Broadway, Thanks to a Cluster of New Stars Who Are Revitalizing the Diva Tradition." *Time Out New York*, June 3–10, 2004, 15–18.

Fiedler, Leslie A. *Love and Death in the American Novel*. New York: Stein and Day, 1966.

Fisch, Audrey A. *American Slaves in Victorian England: Abolitionist Politics in Popular Literature and Culture*. New York: Cambridge University Press, 2000.

———. " 'Exhibiting Uncle Tom in Some Shape or Other': The Commodification and Reception of *Uncle Tom's Cabin* in England." *Nineteenth Century Contexts* 17.2 (1993): 145–58.

———. "'Negrophilism' and British Nationalism: The Spectacle of the Black American Abolitionist." *Victorian Review* 19.2 (winter 1993): 20–47.

———. "Repetitious Accounts So Piteous and So Harrowing." *Journal of Victorian Culture* 1.1 (spring 1996): 16–34.

Fisher, Judith. "The 'Sensation Scene' in Charles Dickens and Dion Boucicault." In *Dramatic Dickens,* edited by Carol Hanbery MacKay. London: Macmillan, 1989. 152–67.

Fletcher, Thomas. *One Hundred Years of the Negro in Show Business.* New York: Da Capo Press, 1984.

Floyd, Samuel A. *The Power of Black Music: Interpreting its History from Africa to the United States.* New York: Oxford University Press, 1995.

Foner, Eric. *Reconstruction: America's Unfinished Revolution, 1863–1877.* New York: Harper & Row, 1988.

Fong, Gisele L. "'These people come in vast numbers . . . to do us a grievous wrong': African American Attitudes of Chinese in a Multi-Racial City, San Francisco, 1850–1880." Unpublished paper, 1996.

Forbes, Camille. "Performed Fictions: The Onstage and Offstage Lives of Bert Williams." Unpublished manuscript, 2002.

Foreman, P. Gabrielle. *Dark Sentiment: Reading Black Women in the Nineteenth Century.* Forthcoming.

———. "Reading Aright: White Slavery, Black Referents, and the Strategy of Histo-textuality in *Iola Leroy.*" *Yale Journal of Criticism* 10.2 (1997): 327–54.

———. "'This Promiscuous Housekeeping': Death, Transgression, and Homoeroticism in *Uncle Tom's Cabin.*" *Representations* 43 (summer 1993): 51–72.

———. "'Who's Your Mama?': 'White' Mulatta Genealogies, Early Photography, and Anti-Passing Narratives of Slavery and Freedom." *American Literary History* 14.3 (fall 2002): 505–39.

Foreman, P. Gabrielle, and Reginald Pitts. Introduction to *Our Nig,* by Harriet E. Wilson. New York: Penguin Books, 2005. xxiii–l.

Fornell, Earl Wesley. *The Unhappy Medium: Spiritualism and the Life of Margaret Fox.* Austin: University of Texas Press, 1964.

Forte, Jeanie. "Focus on the Body: Pain, Praxis, and Pleasure in Feminist Performance." *Critical Theory and Performance.* Ann Arbor: University of Michigan, 1992. 248–62.

Foster, Frances S. *Witnessing Slavery: The Development of Ante-Bellum Slave Narratives.* Westport, Conn.: Greenwood Press, 1979.

Foster, Susan Leigh. "Dancing Bodies." In *Meaning in Motion: New Cultural Studies of Dance,* edited by Jane C. Desmond. Durham, N.C.: Duke University Press, 1997. 235–57.

———. "Pygmalion's No-Body and the Body of Dance." In *Performance and Cultural Politics,* edited by Elin Diamond. New York: Routledge, 1996. 133–56.

Foucault, Michel. *Discipline and Punish: The Birth of the Prison.* New York: Vintage Books, 1995.

——. *The History of Sexuality: An Introduction*. Vol. 1. New York: Vintage Books, 1988.

——. "Nietzsche, Genealogy, History." In *Language, Counter-Memory, Practice: Selected Essays and Interviews*, edited by Donald Bouchard. Ithaca, N.Y.: Cornell University Press, 1977. 139–64.

Fredrickson, George M. *The Black Image in the White Mind: The Debate on Afro-American Character and Destiny, 1817–1914*. Hanover, N.H.: Wesleyan University Press, 1987.

French, Scot. *The Rebellious Slave: Nat Turner in American Memory*. Boston: Houghton Mifflin, 2004.

Frow, Gerald. *Oh, Yes It Is!: A History of Pantomime*. London: British Broadcasting Corporation, 1985.

Fryer, Peter. *Staying Power: Black People in Britain since 1504*. Atlantic Highlands, N.J.: Humanities Press, 1984.

Gaines, Kevin K. "Black Americans' Racial Uplift Ideology as 'Civilizing Mission': Pauline E. Hopkins on Race and Imperialism." In *Cultures of United States Imperialism*, edited by Amy Kaplan and Donald E. Pease. Durham, N.C.: Duke University Press, 1993. 433–55.

——. *Uplifting the Race: Black Leadership, Politics, and Culture in the Twentieth Century*. Chapel Hill, N.C.: University of North Carolina Press, 1996.

Garber, Marjorie B. *Vested Interests: Cross-Dressing and Cultural Anxiety*. New York: Routledge, 1992.

Garelick, Rhonda K. "Electric Salome: Loie Fuller and the Exposition Universelle of 1900." In *Imperialism and Theatre: Essays on World Theatre, Drama, and Performance*, edited by J. Ellen Gainor. London: Routledge, 1995. 85–103.

——. *Rising Star: Dandyism, Gender, and Performance in the Fin de Siècle*. Princeton, N.J.: Princeton University Press, 1998.

Gatens, Moira. *Imaginary Bodies: Ethics, Power, and Corporeality*. London: Routledge, 1996.

Gates, Henry Louis Jr. "The Trope of a New Negro and the Reconstruction of the Image of the Black." In *The New American Studies: Essays from Representations*, edited by Philip K. Fisher. Berkeley: University of California Press, 1991. 319–45.

Geduld, Harold M., ed. *The Definitive Dr. Jekyll and Mr. Hyde Companion*. New York: Garland Publishing, 1983.

Geiss, Immanuel. *The Pan-African Movement: A History of Pan-Africanism in America, Europe and Africa*. New York: Africana Publishing, 1968.

Genovese, Eugene. *From Rebellion to Revolution: Afro-American Slave Revolts in the Making of the Modern World*. Baton Rouge: Louisiana State University Press, 1979.

George-Graves, Nadine. *The Royalty of Negro Vaudeville: The Whitman Sisters and the Negotiation of Race, Gender and Class in African American Theatre, 1900–1940*. New York: St. Martin's Press, 2000.

Gerson, Noel B. *Queen of the Plaza: A Biography of Adah Isaacs Menken*. New York: Funk & Wagnalls Co., 1964.

Giddings, Paula. *When and Where I Enter: The Impact of Black Women on Race and Sex in America.* New York: W. Morrow, 1984.

Gienapp, William E. "Abolitionism and the Nature of Antebellum Reform." In *Courage and Conscience: Black and White Abolitionists in Boston,* edited by Donald M. Jacobs. Bloomington: Indiana University Press, 1993. 21–46.

Gilbert, Sandra M., and Susan Gubar. *The Madwoman in the Attic: The Woman Writer and Nineteenth-Century Literary Imagination.* New Haven, Conn.: Yale University Press, 1984.

Gillman, Susan K. *Blood Talk: American Race Melodrama and the Culture of the Occult.* Chicago: University of Chicago Press, 2003.

——. *Dark Twins: Imposture and Identity in Mark Twain's America.* Chicago: University of Chicago Press, 1989.

——. "Pauline Hopkins and the Occult: African-American Revisions of the Nineteenth-Century Sciences." *American Literary History* 8.1 (spring 1996): 57–82.

Gilman, Sander L. "Black Bodies, White Bodies: Toward an Iconography of Female Sexuality in Late Nineteenth-Century Art, Medicine and Literature." In *Race, Writing and Difference,* edited by Henry Louis Gates Jr. Chicago: University of Chicago Press, 1986. 223–61.

——. *Difference and Pathology: Stereotypes of Sexuality, Race, and Madness.* Ithaca, N.Y.: Cornell University Press, 1985.

——. " '. . . to be real': The Dissident Forms of Black Expressive Culture." In *Let's Get it On: The Politics of Black Performance,* edited by Catherine Ugwu. Seattle: Bay Press, 1995. 12–33.

Gilroy, Paul. The *Black Atlantic: Modernity and Double Consciousness.* Cambridge, Mass.: Harvard University Press, 1993.

Ginsberg, Elaine K. Introduction. *Passing and the Fictions of Identity,* edited by Elaine K. Ginsberg. Durham, N.C.: Duke University Press, 1996. 1–18.

Glassberg, David. *American Historical Pageantry: The Uses of Tradition in the Early Twentieth Century.* Chapel Hill, N.C.: University of North Carolina Press, 1990.

Glaude, Eddie S. *Exodus! Religion, Race, and Nation in Early Nineteenth-Century Black America.* Chicago: University of Chicago Press, 2000.

Glenn, Susan A. *Female Spectacle: The Theatrical Roots of Modern Feminism.* Cambridge, Mass.: Harvard University Press, 2000.

Goddu, Teresa A. *Gothic America: Narrative, History, and Nation.* New York: Columbia University Press, 1997.

Goldsby, Jacqueline. "The High and Low Tech of It: The Meaning of Lynching and the Death of Emmett Till." *Yale Journal of Criticism* 9.2 (fall 1996): 245–82.

Goldsmith, Barbara. *Other Powers: The Age of Suffrage, Spiritualism, and the Scandalous Victoria Woodhull.* New York: A. A. Knopf, 1998.

Gorman, Herbert S. *The Incredible Marquis: Alexandre Dumas.* New York: Farrar & Rinehart, 1929.

Gossett, Thomas F. *Uncle Tom's Cabin and American Culture.* Dallas: Southern Methodist University Press, 1985.

Gottschild, Brenda Dixon. *Digging the Africanist Presence in American Performance: Dance and Other Contexts.* Westport, Conn.: Greenwood Press, 1996.

Graziano, John. "Sentimental Songs, Rags, and Transformations: The Emergence of the Black Musical, 1895–1910." In *Musical Theatre in America: Papers and Proceedings of the Conference on the Musical Theatre in America,* edited by Glenn Loney. Westport, Conn.: Greenwood Press, 1984. 211–32.

Green, Jeffrey P. *Black Edwardians: Black People in Britain, 1901–1914.* London: Frank Cass, 1998.

——. "*In Dahomey* in London in 1903." *The Black Perspective in Music* 11.1 (spring 1983): 22–40.

Greenblatt, Stephen. "Resonance and Wonder." In *Exhibiting Cultures: The Poetics and Politics of Museum Display,* edited by Ivan Karp and Steven D. Lavine. Washington: Smithsonian Institution Press, 1991. 42–56.

Greenfield, Bruce R. *Narrating Discovery: The Romantic Explorer in American Literature, 1790–1855.* New York: Columbia University Press, 1992.

Griffin, Farah Jasmine. *If You Can't Be Free, Be a Mystery: In Search of Billie Holiday.* New York: Free Press, 2001.

——. "*Who Set You Flowin'?*" *The African-American Migration Narrative.* New York: Oxford University Press, 1995.

Grimsted, David. *Melodrama Unveiled: American Theatre and Culture, 1800–1850.* Berkeley: University of California Press, 1987.

Groneman, Carol. "Nymphomania: The Historical Construction of Female Sexuality." In *Deviant Bodies: Critical Perspectives on Difference in Science and Popular Culture,* edited by Jennifer Terry and Jacqueline Urla. Bloomington: Indiana University Press, 1995. 219–50.

Grover, Katherine. *The Fugitive's Gibraltar: Escaping Slaves and Abolitionism in New Bedford, Massachusetts.* Amherst: University of Massachusetts Press, 2001.

Gruesser, John C. "Pauline Hopkins's *Of One Blood*: Creating an Afrocentric Fantasy for a Black Middle Class Audience." In *Modes of the Fantastic: Selected Essays from the Twelfth International Conference on the Fantastic in the Arts,* edited by Robert A. Latham and Robert A. Collins. Westport, Conn.: Greenwood Press, 1995. 74–83.

Guarneri, Carl G. *The Utopian Alternative: Fourierism in Nineteenth-Century America.* Ithaca, N.Y.: Cornell University Press, 1991.

Gunning, Sandra. *Race, Rape, and Lynching: The Red Record of American Literature, 1890–1912.* New York: Oxford University Press, 1996.

Halberstam, Judith. *Female Masculinity.* Durham, N.C.: Duke University Press, 1998.

——. *Skin Shows: Gothic Horror and the Technology of Monsters.* Durham, N.C.: Duke University Press, 1995.

Hall, Jacquelyn Dowd. "The Mind that Burns in Each Body: Women, Rape and Racial Violence." In *Powers of Desire: The Politics of Sexuality,* edited by Ann Snitow, Christine Stansell, and Sharon Thompson. New York: Monthly Review Press, 1983. 328–49.

Hall, Kim F. *Things of Darkness: Economies of Race and Gender in Early Modern England*. Ithaca, N.Y.: Cornell University Press, 1995.

Hall, Stuart. "New Ethnicities." In *Stuart Hall: Critical Dialogues in Cultural Studies*, edited by David Morley and Kuan-Hsing Chen. New York: Routledge, 1996. 441–49.

———. "What Is This 'Black' in Black Popular Culture?" In *Black Popular Culture*, edited by Gina Dent. Seattle: Bay Press, 1992. 21–33.

Halttunen, Karen. *Confidence Men and Painted Women: A Study of Middle Class Culture in America, 1830–1870*. New Haven, Conn.: Yale University Press, 1982.

Hamilton, Edith. *Mythology: Timeless Tales of Gods and Heroes*. New York: Mentor, 1969.

Hammonds, Evelynn. "Black (W)holes and the Geometry of Black Female Sexuality." In *Skin Deep, Spirit Strong: The Black Female Body in American Culture*, edited by Kimberly Wallace-Sanders. Ann Arbor: University of Michigan Press, 2002. 301–20.

———. "Toward a Genealogy of Black Female Sexuality: The Problematic of Silence." In *Feminist Genealogies, Colonial Legacies, Democratic Futures*, edited by M. Jacqui Alexander and Chandra Talpade Mohanty. New York: Routledge, 1997.

Harris, Cheryl. "Whiteness as Property." In *Critical Race Theory: The Key Writings that Formed the Movement*, edited by Kimberlé Crenshaw. New York: New Press, 1995. 276–91.

Harrison, Alferdteen, ed. *Black Exodus: The Great Migration from the American South*. Jackson: University Press of Mississippi, 1991.

Harrison, J. F. C. *The Second Coming: Popular Millenarianism, 1780–1850*. London: Routledge & Kegan Paul, 1979.

Hartman, Saidiya V. *Scenes of Subjection: Terror, Slavery, and Self-Making in Nineteenth-Century America*. New York: Oxford University Press, 1997.

Haskins, James. *Black Dance in America: A History through its People*. New York: Thomas Y. Crowell, 1990.

———. *Black Theatre in America*. New York: Thomas Y. Crowell, 1983.

Hay, Henry. *Cyclopedia of Magic*. New York: Dover Publications, 1949.

Hays, Michael. "Representing Empire: Class, Culture, and the Popular Theatre in the Nineteenth Century." In *Imperialism and Theatre: Essays on World Theatre, Drama and Performance*, edited by J. Ellen Gainor. London: Routledge, 1995. 132–47.

Haywood, Charles. *Negro Minstrelsy and Shakespearean Burlesque*. Hatbor, Penn.: Folklore Assoc., 1966.

Hazzard-Gordon, Katrina. *Jookin': The Rise of Social Dance Formations in African-American Culture*. Philadelphia: Temple University Press, 1990.

Heath, Stephen. "Psychopathia Sexualis: Stevenson's *Strange Case*." *Critical Quarterly* 28.1–2 (1986): 93–108.

Hedin, Raymond. "Strategies of Form in the American Slave Narrative." In *The Art of*

*Slave Narrative: Original Essays in Criticism and Theory,* edited by John Sekora and Darwin T. Turner. Macomb: Western Illinois University Press, 1982. 25–35.

Hegel, G. W. F. *Introduction to the Philosophy of History with an Appendix from the Philosophy of Right.* Translated by Leo Rauch. Indianapolis: Hackett Publishing, 1988.

Hewitt, Nancy A. *Women's Activism and Social Change: Rochester, New York, 1822–1872.* Ithaca, N.Y.: Cornell University Press, 1984.

Hibbert, H. G. *A Playgoer's Memories.* London: G. Richards, 1920.

Higginbotham, Evelyn Brooks. "African-American Women's History and the Metalanguage of Race." *Signs* 17.2 (winter 1992): 251–74.

Hill, Errol. "The Hyers Sisters: Pioneers in Black Musical Comedy." In *The American Stage: Social and Economic Issues from the Colonial Period to the Present,* edited by Ron Engle and Tice L. Miller. New York: Cambridge University Press, 1993. 115–30.

——. *Shakespeare in Sable: A History of Black Shakespearean Actors.* Amherst: University of Massachusetts Press, 1984.

——. *The Theatre of Black Americans: A Collection of Critical Essays.* Englewood Cliffs, N.J.: Prentice-Hall, 1980.

Hine, Darlene Clark. "Rape and the Inner Lives of Black Women in the Middle West: Preliminary Thoughts on the Culture of Dissemblance." *Signs* 14.4 (summer 1989): 912–20.

Hirsch, Arnold R., and Joseph Logsdon. *Creole New Orleans: Race and Americanization.* Baton Rouge: Louisiana State University Press, 1992.

Holder, Heidi. "Melodrama, Realism and Empire on the British Stage." In *Acts of Supremacy: the British Empire and the Stage, 1790–1930,* edited by J. S. Bratton, et al. Manchester, England: University of Manchester Press, 1991. 129–49.

Holland, Sharon P. *Raising the Dead: Readings of Death and (Black) Subjectivity.* Durham, N.C.: Duke University Press, 2000.

Homans, Margaret. " 'Racial Composition': Metaphor and the Body in the Writing of Race." In *Female Subjects in Black and White: Race, Psychoanalysis, Feminism,* edited by Elizabeth Abel, Barbara Christian, and Helene Moglen. Berkeley: University of California Press, 1997. 77–101.

——. " 'Women of Color': Writers and Feminist Theory." *New Literary History* 25.1 (winter 1994): 73–94.

Horvitz, Deborah. "Hysteria and Trauma in Pauline Hopkins' *Of One Blood; Or, The Hidden Self.*" *African-American Review* 33.2 (summer 1999): 245–60.

Hughes-Hallett, Lucy. *Cleopatra: Histories, Dreams and Distortions.* New York: Harper Perennial, 1990.

Hughes, Winifred. *The Maniac in the Cellar: Sensation Novels of the 1860s.* Princeton, N.J.: Princeton University Press, 1980.

Hume, Robert D. "Gothic versus Romantic: A Revaluation of the Gothic Novel." *PMLA* 84.2 (March 1969): 282–90.

Humez, Jean M. *Harriet Tubman: The Life and the Life Stories.* Madison: University of Wisconsin Press, 2003.

Irigaray, Luce. *Speculum of the Other Woman*. Translated by Gillian C. Gill. Ithaca, N.Y.: Cornell University Press, 1985.

Jackson, Peter, and Jan Penrose. *Constructions of Race, Place and Nation*. London: UCL Press, 1993.

Jay, Ricky. *Learned Pigs and Fireproof Women*. New York: Villard Books, 1987.

Jefferson, Paul. Introduction. *The Travels of William Wells Brown by William Wells Brown*. New York: Markus Wiener Publishing, 1991. 1–20.

Johnson, Claudia D. *American Actress: Perspective on the Nineteenth Century*. Chicago: Nelson-Hall, 1984.

Jones, Arthur C. *Wade in the Water: The Wisdom of the Spirituals*. Maryknoll, N.Y.: Orbis Books, 1993.

Jones, Jacqueline. *Labor of Love, Labor of Sorrow: Black Women, Work, and the Family from Slavery to the Present*. New York: Basic Books, 1985.

Jones, Leroi. *Blues People: Negro Music in White America*. New York: W. Morrow, 1963.

Jordan, Winthrop. *White over Black: American Attitudes toward the Negro, 1550–1812*. Chapel Hill, N.C.: Institute of Early American History and Culture, University of North Carolina Press, 1968.

Kaplan, Amy, and Donald Pease, eds. *Cultures of United States Imperialism*. Durham, N.C.: Duke University Press, 1993.

Kaplan, Sidney. *The Black Presence in the Era of the American Revolution 1770–1800*. Greenwich, Conn.: New York Graphic Society, 1978.

——. "*The Octoroon*: Early History of the Drama of Miscegenation." *Journal of Negro Education* 20.4 (autumn 1951): 547–57.

Kassanoff, Jennie. " 'Fate Has Linked Us Together': Blood, Gender, and the Politics of Representation in Pauline Hopkins's *Of One Blood*." In *The Unruly Voice: Rediscovering Pauline Elizabeth Hopkins*, edited by John Cullen Gruesser. Urbana: University of Illinois Press, 1996. 158–81.

Kasson, Joy. "Narratives of the Female Body: The Greek Slave." In *The Culture of Sentiment: Race, Gender and Sentimentality in Nineteenth Century America*, edited by Shirley Samuels. New York: Oxford University Press, 1992.

Kawash, Samira. "The Autobiography of an Ex-Colored Man: (Passing for) Black Passing for White." In *Passing and the Fictions of Identity*, edited by Elaine K. Ginsberg. Durham, N.C.: Duke University Press, 1996. 59–74.

Kelley, Robin. *Freedom Dreams: The Black Radical Imagination*. Boston: Beacon Press, 2002.

Kendall, Elizabeth. *Where She Danced*. New York: A. A. Knopf, 1979.

Kendall, John S. *The Golden Age of New Orleans Theatre*. Baton Rouge: Louisiana State University Press, 1952.

——. "The World's Delight: The Story of Adah Isaacs Menken." *Louisiana Historical Quarterly* 21.3 (July 1938): 846–68.

Kent, Christopher. "Spectacular History as an Ocular Discipline." *Wide Angle* 18.3 (July 1996): 1–21.

Kerr, Howard. *Mediums, and Spirit-Rappers, and Roaring Radicals; Spiritualism in American Literature, 1850–1900*. Urbana: University of Illinois Press, 1972.

Ketner, Joseph D. *The Emergence of the African-American Artist: Robert S. Duncanson, 1821–1872*. Columbia: University of Missouri Press, 1993.

Killingray, David, and Willie Henderson. "Bata Kindai Amgoza ibn LoBagola and the Making of an African Savage's Own Story." In *Africans on Stage: Studies in Ethnological Show Business*, edited by Bernth Lindfors. Bloomington: Indiana University Press, 1999. 228–65.

King, Nicole. "'A Colored Woman in Another Country Pleading for Justice in Her Own': Ida B. Wells in Great Britain." In *Black Victorians/Black Victoriana*, edited by Gretchen Holbrook Gerzina. New Brunswick, N.J.: Rutgers University Press, 2003. 88–109.

Kleinhans, Chuck. "Taking Out the Trash: Camp and the Politics of Parody." In *The Politics and Poetics of Camp*, edited by Moe Meyer. New York: Routledge, 1994. 182–201.

Koritz, Amy. "Dancing the Orient for England: Maud Allan's *The Vision of Salome*." In *Meaning in Motion: New Cultural Studies of Dance*, edited by Jane C. Desmond. Durham, N.C.: Duke University Press, 1997. 133–52.

Kosok, Heinz. "Dion Boucicault's 'American' Plays: Considerations on Defining National Literatures in English." In *Literature and the Art of Creation: Essays and Poems in Honour of A. Norman Jeffries*, edited by Robert Welch and Suheil Badi Bushrui. Totowa, N.J.: Barnes and Noble Books, 1988. 81–97.

Krasner, David. *A Beautiful Pageant: African American Theatre, Drama, and Performance in the Harlem Renaissance, 1910–1927*. New York: Palgrave Macmillan, 2002.

——. *Resistance, Parody, and Double Consciousness in African American Theatre, 1895–1910*. New York: St. Martin's Press, 1997.

——. "Rewriting the Body: Aida Overton Walker and the Social Formation of Cakewalking." *Theatre Survey* 37.2 (November 1996): 67–92.

LaBrew, Arthur. *The Black Swan: Elizabeth T. Greenfield, Songstress*. Detroit: Arthur R. LaBrew, 1969.

Lamb, Geoffrey. *Victorian Magic*. London: Routledge & Kegan Paul, 1976.

Lemisch, Jesse. *Jack Tar vs. John Bull: The Role of New York's Seamen in Precipitating the Revolution*. New York: Garland Publishing, 1997.

Lesser, Allen F. "Adah Isaacs Menken: A Daughter of Israel." *American Jewish Historical Society* 34 (1937): 143–47.

——. *Enchanting Rebel: The Secret of Adah Isaacs Menken*. New York: Jewish Book Guild, 1947.

——. *Weave a Wreath of Laurel: The Lives of Four Jewish Contributors to American Civilization*. New York: Coven Press, 1938.

Levine, Lawrence W. *Black Culture and Black Consciousness: Afro-American Thought from Slavery to Freedom*. New York: Oxford University Press, 1977.

——. *Highbrow/Lowbrow: The Emergence of Cultural Hierarchy in America.* Cambridge, Mass.: Harvard University Press, 1988.

Levine, Robert. Introduction to *Dred: A Tale of the Great Dismal Swamp,* by Harriet Beecher Stowe. New York: Penguin Books, 2000. ix–xxx.

Lewis, Earl. "To Turn as on a Pivot: Writing African-Americans into a History of Overlapping Diasporas." *American Historical Review* 100.3 (June 1995): 765–87.

Lhamon, W. T. *Raising Cain: Blackface Performance from Jim Crow to Hip Hop.* Cambridge, Mass.: Harvard University Press, 1998.

Lipsitz, George. *The Possessive Investment in Whiteness: How White People Profit from Identity Politics.* Philadelphia: Temple University Press, 1998.

——. *Time Passages: Collective Memory and American Popular Culture.* Minneapolis: University of Minnesota Press, 1990.

Livingston, Robert E. "Decolonizing the Theatre: Césaire, Serreau and the Drama of Negritude." In *Imperialism and Theatre: Essays on World Theatre, Drama and Performance,* edited by J. Ellen Gainor. London: Routledge, 1995. 182–98.

Lloyd, Alan. *The Great Prize Fight.* New York: Coward, McCann & Geoghegan, 1977.

Loesberg, Jonathan. "The Ideology of Narrative Form in Sensation Fiction." *Representations* 13 (winter 1986): 115–38.

Loewenberg, Bert James, and Ruth Bogin. *Black Women in Nineteenth-Century American Life: Their Words, Their Thoughts, Their Feelings.* University Park: Pennsylvania State University Press, 1976.

Looby, Christopher. "George Thompson's 'Romance of the Real': Transgression and Taboo in American Sensation Fiction." *American Literature* 65.4 (December 1993): 651–72.

Lorimer, Douglas A. *Colour Class, and the Victorians: English Attitudes to the Negro in the Mid-Nineteenth Century.* Leicester, England: Leicester University Press, 1978.

Lott, Eric. *Love and Theft: Blackface Minstrelsy and the American Working Class.* New York: Oxford University Press, 1993.

——. "White Like Me: Racial Cross-Dressing and the Construction of American Whiteness." In *Cultures of United States Imperialism,* edited by Amy Kaplan and Donald E. Pease. Durham, N.C.: Duke University Press, 1993. 474–95.

Lovell, John. *Black Song: The Forge and the Flame; The Story of How the Afro-American Spiritual Was Hammered Out.* New York: Macmillan, 1972.

Luciano, Dana. "Passing Shadows: Melancholic Nationality and Black Critical Publicity in Pauline E. Hopkins's *Of One Blood.*" In *Loss: The Politics of Mourning,* edited by David L. Eng and David Kazanjian. Berkeley: University of California Press, 2003. 148–87.

Lyman, George D. *The Saga of the Comstock Lode: Boom Days in Virginia City.* New York: Charles Scribner & Sons, 1934.

MacKenzie, John M. *Imperialism and Popular Culture.* Dover, N.H.: Manchester University Press, 1986.

——. *Propaganda and Empire: The Manipulation of British Public Opinion, 1880–1960.* Manchester, England: Manchester University Press, 1984.

MacMinn, George R. *The Theater of the Golden Era in California*. Caldwell, Idaho: Caxton Printers, 1941.

Mahar, William J. "Ethiopian Skits and Sketches: Contents and Contexts of Blackface Minstrelsy, 1840–1890." In *Inside the Minstrel Mask: Readings in Nineteenth-Century Blackface Minstrelsy*, edited by Annemarie Bean, James V. Hatch, and Brooks McNamara. Hanover, N.H.: Wesleyan University Press, 1996. 179–220.

Malcolm X. "The Ballot or the Bullet." In *The Norton Anthology of African-American Literature*, edited by Henry Louis Gates Jr. and Nellie Y. McKay. New York: W. W. Norton, 1997. 90–101.

Malone, Jacqui. *Steppin' on the Blues: The Visible Rhythms of African American Dance*. Urbana: University of Illinois Press, 1996.

Mankowitz, Wolf. *Mazeppa, the Lives, Loves, and Legends of Adah Isaacs Menken: A Biographical Quest*. New York: Stein and Day, 1982.

Marcus, George E. " 'What Did He Reckon Would Become of the Other Half if He Killed His Half?' Doubled, Divided and Crossed Selves in Pudd'nhead Wilson: Or, Mark Twain as Cultural Critic in His Own Times and Ours." In *Pudd'nhead Wilson: Race, Conflict and Culture*, edited by Susan Gillman and Forrest G. Robinson. Durham, N.C.: Duke University Press, 1990. 190–210.

Martell, Joanne. *Fearfully and Wonderfully Made*. Winston-Salem, N.C.: John F. Blair, 2000.

Martin, Herbert Woodward, and Ronald Primeau. "Introduction to the Dramatic Pieces." *In His Own Voice: The Dramatic and Other Uncollected Works of Paul Laurence Dunbar*. Athens: Ohio University Press, 2002. 3–16.

Martin, Randy. *Critical Moves: Dance Studies in Theory and Politics*. Durham, N.C.: Duke University Press, 1998.

Matlaw, Myron. "Preface to *The Black Crook*." In *The Black Crook, and Other Nineteenth-Century American Plays*, edited by Myron Matlaw. New York: E. P. Dutton, 1967. 319–22.

Mayer, Henry. *All On Fire: William Lloyd Garrison and the Abolition of Slavery*. New York: St. Martin's Press, 1998.

McAllister, Marvin E. *White People Do Not Know How to Behave at Entertainments Designed for Ladies and Gentlemen of Colour: William Brown's African and American Theater*. Chapel Hill, N.C.: University of North Carolina Press, 2003.

McCarthy, Michael. *Dark Continent: Africa as Seen by Americans*. Westport, Conn.: Greenwood Press, 1983.

McCaskill, Barbara. Introduction. *Running A Thousand Miles for Freedom: The Escape of William and Ellen Craft from Slavery*, by William Craft and Ellen Craft. Athens: University of Georgia Press, 1999. vii–xxv.

McClary, Susan. *Feminine Endings: Music, Gender, and Sexuality*. Minneapolis: University of Minnesota Press, 2002.

McClintock, Anne. *Imperial Leather: Race, Gender, and Sexuality in the Colonial Conquest*. New York: Routledge, 1995.

McConachie, Bruce A. *Melodramatic Formations: American Theatre and Society, 1820–1870*. Iowa City: University of Iowa Press, 1992.

McDougall, Walter A. *Freedom Just Around the Corner: A New American History, 1585–1828*. New York: HarperCollins, 2004.

McDowell, Deborah E. "Recycling: Race, Gender, and the Practice of Theory." In *Studies in Historical Change*, edited by Ralph Cohen. Charlottesville: University of Virginia Press, 1992. 246–63.

McElroy, Guy C. *Facing History: The Black Image in American Art, 1710–1940*. San Francisco: Bedford Arts Publishers, 1990.

McFeely, William S. *Frederick Douglass*. New York: W. W. Norton, 1991.

McKay, Nellie Y. Introduction. *The Unruly Voice: Rediscovering Pauline Elizabeth Hopkins*, edited by John Cullen Gruesser. Urbana: University of Illinois Press, 1996. 1–20.

McKinley, Jesse. "Rashad Breaks Barrier as Leading Actress." *New York Times*, June 7, 2004: E5.

McKinley, Jesse, and Jason Zinoman. "Tony Awards Finish Up with a Fuzzy Surprise: Puppet Musical Wins Big, as Does 'My Own Wife.'" *New York Times*, June 7, 2004, E1.

Meer, Sarah. *Uncle Tom Mania: Slavery, Minstrelsy, and Transatlantic Culture in the 1850s*. Athens: University of Georgia Press, 2005.

Meese, Elizabeth A., and Alice Parker. *The Difference Within: Feminism and Critical Theory*. Philadelphia: John Benjamins Publishing, 1989.

Meier, August, and Elliott Rudwick. "The Role of Blacks in the Abolitionist Movement." In *Blacks in the Abolitionist Movement*, edited by John H. Bracey Jr., August Meier, and Elliott Rudwick. Belmont, Calif.: Wadsworth Publishing, 1971. 108–22.

Meisel, Martin. *Realizations: Narrative, Pictorial, and Theatrical Arts in Nineteenth-Century England*. Princeton, N.J.: Princeton University Press, 1983.

Meltzer, Françoise. *Salome and the Dance of Writing: Portraits of Mimesis in Literature*. Chicago: University of Chicago Press, 1987.

Mercer, Kobena. *Welcome to the Jungle: New Positions in Black Cultural Studies*. New York: Routledge, 1994.

Meyer, Moe. "Introduction: Reclaiming the Discourse of Camp." In *The Politics and Poetics of Camp*, edited by Moe Meyer. New York: Routledge, 1994. 1–22.

Miller, Angela. *The Empire of the Eye: Landscape Representation and American Cultural Politics, 1825–1875*. Ithaca, N.Y.: Cornell University Press, 1993.

——. "The Panorama, the Cinema and the Emergence of the Spectacular." *Wide Angle* 18.2 (April 1996): 35–69.

Miller, David C. *Dark Eden: The Swamp in Nineteenth-Century American Culture*. New York: Cambridge University Press, 1989.

Miller, Patrick D. *Interpreting the Psalms*. Philadelphia: Fortress Press, 1986.

Mitchell, Angelyn. *Within the Circle: An Anthology of African American Literary Criticism from the Harlem Renaissance to the Present*. Durham, N.C.: Duke University Press, 1994.

Miyoshi, Masao. "The Divided Self." In *The Definitive Dr. Jekyll and Mr. Hyde Companion*, edited by Harry M. Geduld. New York: Garland Publishing, 1983.

Monfried, Walter. "The Negro Beauty Who Bewitched Two Continents." *Negro Digest* 14 (1965): 86–90.

Moon, Michael, and Cathy N. Davidson. *Subjects and Citizens: Nation, Race, and Gender from Oroonoko to Anita Hill*. Durham, N.C.: Duke University Press, 1995.

Moore, R. Laurence. *In Search of White Crows: Spiritualism, Parapsychology, and American Culture*. New York: Oxford University Press, 1977.

Morrison, Toni. *Playing in the Dark: Whiteness and the Literary Imagination*. Cambridge, Mass.: Harvard University Press, 1992.

Mosby, Dewey F. *Across Continents and Cultures: The Art and Life of Henry Ossawa Tanner*. Kansas City: Nelson-Atkins Museum of Art, 1995.

Moses, Wilson J. *Alexander Crummell: A Study of Civilization and Discontent*. New York: Oxford University Press, 1989.

———, ed. *Classic Black Nationalism: From the American Revolution to Marcus Garvey*. New York: New York University Press, 1996.

———. *The Golden Age of Black Nationalism, 1850–1925*. New York: Oxford University Press, 1988.

Moten, Fred. *In the Break: The Aesthetics of the Black Radical Tradition*. Minneapolis: University of Minnesota Press, 2003.

Moulton, H. J. *History of Magic in Boston, 1792–1915*. Glenwood, Ill.: Meyerbrooks, 1983.

Mullen, Harryette. "Indelicate Subjects: African American Women's Subjugated Subjectivity." *Sub/versions: Feminist Studies*. Santa Cruz: University of California Press, 1991.

———. "Optic White: Blackness and the Production of Whiteness." *Diacritics* 24.2 (summer–autumn 1994): 71–89.

———. "Runaway Tongue: Resistant Orality in *Uncle Tom's Cabin, Our Nig, Incidents in the Life of a Slave Girl*, and *Beloved*." In *The Culture of Sentiment: Race, Gender and Sentimentality in Nineteenth Century America*, edited by Shirley Samuels. New York: Oxford University Press, 1992. 244–64.

Mullenix, Elizabeth Reitz. *Wearing the Breeches: Gender on the Antebellum Stage*. New York: St. Martin's Press, 2000.

Nathan, Hans. *Dan Emmett and the Rise of Early Negro Minstrelsy*. Norman: University of Oklahoma Press, 1962.

Neal, Diane. "Seduction, Accommodation, or Realism? Tabbs Gross and the Arkansas Freeman." *Arkansas Historical Quarterly* 48.1 (spring 1989): 57–64.

Newbury, Michael. "Eaten Alive: Slavery and Celebrity in Antebellum America." *ELH* 61.1 (spring 1994): 159–87.

Newman, Richard. "The Brightest Star: Aida Overton Walker in the Age of Ragtime and Cakewalk." In *Words Like Freedom: Essays on African-American Culture and History*. West Cornwall, Conn.: Locust Hill Press, 1996. 55–76.

——. Introduction. *Narrative of the Life of Henry Box Brown*. New York: Oxford University Press, 2002. xi–xxxiii.

——. *Words like Freedom: Essays on African-American Culture and History*. West Cornwall, Conn.: Locust Hill Press, 1996.

Northcott, Richard. *Adah Isaacs Menken: An Illustrated Biography*. London: Press Printers, 1921.

Nye, Russell B. *The Unembarrassed Muse: The Popular Arts in America*. New York: Dial Press, 1970.

Obichere, Boniface I. *West African States and European Expansion: The Dahomey-Niger Hinterland, 1885–1898*. New Haven, Conn.: Yale University Press, 1971.

Olney, James. " 'I Was Born': Slave Narratives, Their Status as Autobiography and as Literature." In *The Slave's Narrative*, edited by Charles T. Davis and Henry Louis Gates Jr. New York: Oxford University Press, 1985. 148–74.

O'Meally, Robert. Liner Notes. *Norton Anthology of African American Literature Audio Companion Disc*. Paul Robeson. "Go Down, Moses." Performed by Paul Robeson in 1965. *Norton Anthology of African American Literature Audio Companion*. Track #1.

Osgood, Nancy. "Josiah Wolcott: Artist and Associationist." *Old-Time New England Quarterly* (1998).

Otten, Thomas J. "Pauline Hopkins and the Hidden Self of Race." *ELH* 59.1 (spring 1992): 227–56.

Owen, Alex. *The Darkened Room: Women, Power, and Spiritualism in Late Nineteenth Century England*. Philadelphia: University of Pennsylvania Press, 1990.

Painter, Nell. I. *Sojourner Truth: A Life, A Symbol*. New York: W. W. Norton, 1996.

——. "Sojourner Truth in Life and Memory: Writing the Biography of an American Exotic." *Gender and History* 2.1 (1990): 3–16.

——. *Standing at Armageddon: The United States, 1877–1919*. New York: W. W. Norton, 1987.

Palmer, Pamela L. "Adah Isaacs Menken: From Texas to Paris." In *Legendary Ladies of Texas*, edited by Francis E. Abernathy. Nocodoches: University of North Texas, 1994. 85–94.

Parkin, Andrew. Introduction. *Selected Plays of Dion Boucicault*. Edited by Andrew Parkin. New York: Catholic University of America Press, 1987. 7–22.

Parks, Suzan-Lori. "For Posterior's Sake: Interview with Una Chaudhuri." *The Program of the Public Theatre* 2.2 (1996).

Patterson, Orlando. *Slavery and Social Death: A Comparative Study*. Cambridge, Mass.: Harvard University Press, 1982.

Patton, Sharon F. *The Oxford History of African-American Art*. New York: Oxford University Press, 1998.

Paulin, Diana. "Representing Forbidden Desire: Interracial Unions, Surrogacy and Performance." *Theatre Journal* 49.4 (December 1997): 417–39.

Pease, Jane H., and William H. Pease. *They Who Would be Free: Blacks' Search for Freedom, 1830–1861*. New York: Atheneum, 1974.

Peterson, Bernard L. *Profiles of African American Stage Performers and Theatre People, 1816–1960*. Westport, Conn.: Greenwood Press, 2001.

Peterson, Carla L. *"Doers of the Word": African-American Women Speakers and Writers in the North (1830–1880)*. New York: Oxford University Press, 1995.

———. "Foreword: Eccentric Bodies." In *Recovering the Black Female Body: Self Representations by African American Women,* edited by Michael Bennett and Vanessa D. Dickerson. New Brunswick, N.J.: Rutgers University Press, 2001. ix–xvi.

Phelan, Peggy. *Unmarked: the Politics of Performance*. New York: Routledge, 1993.

Pickering, Michael. "Mock Blacks and Racial Mockery: The 'Nigger' Minstrel and British Imperialism." In *Acts of Supremacy: The British Empire and the Stage, 1790–1930*, edited by J. S. Bratton et al. Manchester, England: Manchester University Press, 1991. 179–236.

Pinkston, C. Alex. "The Stage Premiere of Dr. Jekyll and Mr. Hyde." *Nineteenth Century Theatre* 14.1–2 (1986): 21–43.

Pratt, Mary Louise. *Imperial Eyes: Travel Writing and Transculturation*. New York: Routledge, 1992.

Price, Richard. *Maroon Societies: Rebel Slave Communities in the Americas*. Garden City, N.Y.: Anchor Press, 1973.

Quarles, Benjamin. *Black Abolitionists*. New York: Oxford University Press, 1969.

Rauch, Leo. Translator's Introduction. *Introduction to The Philosophy of History with an Appendix from The Philosophy of Right,* by G. W. F. Hegel. Indianapolis: Hackett Publishing Company, 1988. vii–xii.

Reilly, Bernard F. *American Political Prints, 1766–1876: A Catalog of the Collection in the Library of Congress*. Boston, Mass.: G. K. Hall, 1991.

———. "The Art of the Antislavery Movement." In *Courage and Conscience: Black and White Abolitionists in Boston,* edited by Donald M. Jacobs. Bloomington: Indiana University Press, 1993. 47–74.

Retman, Sonnet. " 'In the Face of American Standardizations': The Mechanics of Race and Reproduction in Fiction by Schuyler, Hughes and Larsen." Unpublished paper, 2000.

Revell, Peter. *Paul Laurence Dunbar*. Boston: Twayne Publishers, 1979.

Reynolds, Harry. *Minstrel Memories: The Story of Burnt Cork Minstrelsy in Great Britain from 1836 to 1927*. London: A. Rivers, 1928.

Reynolds, Simon, and Joy Press. *The Sex Revolts: Gender, Rebellion, and Rock'n'Roll.* Cambridge, Mass.: Harvard University Press, 1995.

Richards, Sandra. "Bert Williams: The Man and the Mask." *Mime, Mask & Marionette* 1.1 (spring 1978): 7–24.

Riis, Thomas L. *Just before Jazz: Black Musical Theater in New York, 1890–1915*. Washington: Smithsonian Institution Press, 1989.

———. *More than Just Minstrel Shows: The Rise of Black Musical Theatre at the Turn of the Century*. New York: Institute for Studies in American Music, 1992.

Ripley, C. Peter. Introduction. *The Black Abolitionist Papers*. Edited by C. Peter Ripley et al. Vol. 1: *The British Isles, 1830–1865*. Chapel Hill, N.C.: University of North Carolina Press, 1985. 3–35.

Roach, Joseph R. *Cities of the Dead: Circum-Atlantic Performance*. New York: Columbia University Press, 1996.

Robinson, Amy. "Forms of Appearance of Value: Homer Plessy and the Politics of Privacy." In *Performance and Cultural Politics*, edited by Elin Diamond. New York: Routledge, 1996. 237–61.

——. "It Takes One to Know One: Passing and Communities of Common Interest." *Critical Inquiry* 20.4 (summer 1994): 715–36.

Roediger, David R. *The Wages of Whiteness: Race and the Making of the American Working Class*. New York: Verso, 1991.

Rogin, Michael. *Blackface, White Noise: Jewish Immigrants in the Hollywood Melting Pot*. Berkeley: University of California Press, 1996.

Rooks, Noliwe M. *Hair Raising: Beauty, Culture, and African American Women*. New Brunswick, N.J.: Rutgers University Press, 1996.

Rosaldo, Renato. *Culture and Truth: The Remaking of Social Analysis*. Boston: Beacon Press, 1989.

Rourke, Constance. *Troupers of the Gold Coast; or, The Rise of Lotta Crabtree*. New York: Harcourt, 1928.

Rowell, George. *The Victorian Theatre: A Survey*. New York: Oxford University Press, 1956.

Rowland, Mabel. *Bert Williams, Son of Laughter: A Symposium of Tribute to the Man and to His Work*. New York: English Crafters, 1923.

Ruggles, Jeffrey. "Go and Get a Box: Henry Brown's Escape from Slavery, 1849." *Virginia Cavalcade* 48.2 (1999): 84–95.

——. *The Unboxing of Henry Brown*. Richmond, Va.: Library of Virginia, 2003.

Ryan, Mary P. *Women in Public: Between Banners to Ballots, 1825–1880*. Baltimore: Johns Hopkins University Press, 1990.

Rydell, Robert. "Darkest Africa: African Shows at America's World's Fairs, 1893–1940." In *Africans On Stage: Studies in Ethnological Show Business*, edited by Bernth Lindfors. Bloomington: Indiana University Press, 1999. 135–55.

Said, Edward W. *Culture and Imperialism*. New York: A. A. Knopf, 1993.

——. *Orientalism*. New York: Vintage, 1979.

Saks, Eva. "Representing Miscegenation Law." *Raritan* 8.2 (1988): 39–69.

Sale, Margaret M. *The Slumbering Volcano: American Slave Ship Revolts and the Production of Rebellious Masculinity*. Durham, N.C.: Duke University Press, 1997.

Sampson, Henry T. *Blacks in Black and White: A Source Book on Black Films*. Metuchen, N.J.: Scarecrow Press, 1980.

——. *The Ghost Walks: A Chronological History of Blacks in Show Business, 1865–1910*. Metuchen, N.J.: Scarecrow Press, 1988.

Sánchez-Eppler, Karen. "Bodily Bonds: The Intersecting Rhetorics of Feminism and Abolition." In *The New American Studies: Essays from Representations*, edited by Phillip K. Fisher. Berkeley: University of California Press, 1991.

———. *Touching Liberty: Abolition, Feminism, and the Politics of the Body*. Berkeley: University of California Press, 1993.

Saxton, Andrew. *The Rise and Fall of the White Republic: Class Politics and Mass Culture in Nineteenth Century America*. New York: Verso, 1990.

Schechter, Patricia A. *Ida B. Wells-Barnett and American Reform, 1880–1930*. Chapel Hill, N.C.: University of North Carolina Press, 2001.

Schrager, Cynthia D. "Both Sides of the Veil: Race, Science, and Mysticism in W. E. B. Du Bois." *American Quarterly* 48.4 (December 1996): 551–86.

———. "Pauline Hopkins and William James: The New Psychology and the Politics of Race." In *The Unruly Voice: Rediscovering Pauline Elizabeth Hopkins*, edited by John Cullen Gruesser. Urbana: University of Illinois Press, 1996. 182–210.

Scott, James C. *Domination and the Arts of Resistance: Hidden Transcripts*. New Haven, Conn.: Yale University Press, 1990.

Sedgwick, Eve K. *Between Men: English Literature and Male Homosocial Desire*. New York: Columbia University Press, 1985.

Sekora, John, and Darwin T. Turner. *The Art of Slave Narrative: Original Essays in Criticism and Theory*. Macomb: Western Illinois University, 1982.

Seltzer, Mark. *Bodies and Machines*. New York: Routledge, 1992.

Senelick, Laurence. "Boys and Girls Together: Subcultural Origins of Glamour Drag and Male Impersonation on the Nineteenth-Century Stage." In *Crossing the Stage: Controversies on Cross-Dressing*, edited by Lesley Ferris. New York: Routledge, 1993. 80–95.

Sentilles, Renee M. *Performing Menken: Adah Isaacs Menken and the Birth of American Celebrity*. New York: Cambridge University Press, 2003.

———. "Performing Menken: Adah Isaacs Menken's American Odyssey." Ph.D. diss., University of Michigan, 1997.

Seroff, Doug. "The Fisk Jubilee Singers in Britain." In *Under the Imperial Carpet: Essays in Black History, 1780–1950*, edited by Rainer Lotz and Ian Pegg. Crawley, England: Rabbit Press, 1986. 42–54.

Shaw, Nate. *All God's Dangers: The Life of Nate Shaw*. Edited by Theodore Rosengarten. New York: A. A. Knopf, 1974.

Sherman, Joan R. Introduction. *Collected Black Women's Poetry*. Vol. 1. Edited by Joan R. Sherman. New York: Oxford University Press, 1988. xxix–xxxvi.

Shillington, Kevin. *History of Africa*. New York: St. Martin's Press, 1989.

Showalter, Elaine, ed. "Feminist Criticism in the Wilderness." In *The New Feminist Criticism: Essays on Women, Literature, and Theory*. New York: Pantheon, 1985.

———. *Sexual Anarchy: Gender and Culture at the Fin de Siècle*. New York: Viking, 1990.

Silveri, Louis D. "The Singing Tours of the Fisk Jubilee Singers: 1871–1874." In *Feel the Spirit: Studies in Nineteenth-Century Afro-American Music*, edited by George R. Keck and Sherrill V. Martin. New York: Greenwood Press, 1988. 105–16.

Silverman, Kenneth. *Houdini! The Career of Ehrich Weiss: American Self-Liberator, Europe's Eclipsing Sensation, World's Handcuff King and Prison Breaker*. New York: HarperCollins, 1996.

Smith, Anna Deavere. Introduction. *Fires in the Mirror.* New York: Anchor Books, 1993. xxiii–xlv.

Smith, Eric Ledell. *Bert Williams: A Biography of the Pioneer Black Comedian.* Jefferson, N.C.: McFarland, 1992.

Smith, Valerie A. "Black Feminist Theory and the Representation of the 'Other.'" In *Changing Our Own Words: Essays on Criticism, Theory, and Writing by Black Women,* edited by Cheryl A. Wall. New Brunswick, N.J.: Rutgers University Press, 1990. 38–57.

——. "The Documentary Impulse in Contemporary U.S. African-American Film." In *Black Popular Culture: A Project,* edited by Gina Dent. Seattle: Bay Press, 1992. 56–64.

——. "Loopholes of Retreat: Architecture and Ideology in Harriet Jacobs' *Incidents in the Life of a Slave Girl.*" In *Reading Black, Reading Feminist: A Critical Anthology,* edited by Henry Louis Gates Jr. New York: Meridian Books, 1990. 212–26.

——. *Not Just Race, Not Just Gender: Black Feminist Readings.* New York: Routledge, 1998.

——. "Reading the Intersection of Race and Gender in Narratives of Passing." *Diacritics* 24.2 (summer 1994): 43–57.

——. *Self-Discovery and Authority in Afro-American Narrative.* Cambridge, Mass.: Harvard University Press, 1987.

Smitherman, Geneva. *Talkin and Testifyin: The Language of Black America.* Detroit: Wayne State University Press, 1985.

Smith-Rosenberg, Carroll. *Disorderly Conduct: Visions of Gender in Victorian America.* New York: A. A. Knopf, 1985.

Somerville, Siobhan. "Passing through the Closet in Pauline E. Hopkins's *Contending Forces.*" In *No More Separate Spheres!: A Next Wave American Studies Reader,* edited by Cathy N. Davidson, Ruth DeVarney, and Jessamyn Hatcher. Durham, N.C.: Duke University Press, 2002. 209–35.

Sontag, Susan. "Notes on 'Camp.'" 1964. *Against Interpretation, and Other Essays.* New York: Farrar, Straus & Giroux, 1966. 275–92.

Southall, Geneva Handy. *Blind Tom: The Post-Civil War Enslavement of a Black Musical Genius.* Minneapolis: Challenge Productions, 1979.

——. *The Continuing Enslavement of Blind Tom: The Black Pianist-Composer.* Minneapolis: Challenge Productions, 1983.

Southern, Eileen. Introduction. *African American Theatre: Out of Bondage and Peculiar Sam; or, The Underground Railroad,* edited by Eileen Southern. New York: Garland Publishing, 1994. xiii–xxix.

——. *The Music of Black Americans: A History.* New York: W. W. Norton, 1997.

Spencer, Suzette. "Stealing A Way: African Diaspora Maroon Poetics." Ph.D. diss., University of California, Berkeley, 2002.

Spillers, Hortense. "A Hateful Passion, A Lost Love: Three Women's Fiction." *Black, White, and in Color: Essays on American Literature and Culture.* Chicago: University of Chicago Press, 2003. 93–118.

——. "Interstices: A Small Drama of Words." *Black, White, and in Color: Essays on American Literature and Culture*. Chicago: University of Chicago, 2003. 152–75.

——. "Mama's Baby, Papa's Maybe: An American Grammar Book." In *African American Literary Theory: A Reader,* edited by Winston Napier. New York: New York University Press, 2000. 257–79.

——. "Notes on an Alternative Model—Neither/Nor." In *The Difference Within: Feminism and Critical Theory,* edited by Elizabeth Meese and Alice Parker. Philadelphia: John Benjamins Publishing, 1989. 165–88.

Stallybrass, Peter, and Allon White. *The Politics and Poetics of Transgression*. Ithaca, N.Y.: Cornell University Press, 1986.

Stepto, Robert Burns. "I Rose and Found My Voice: Narration, Authentication and Authorial Control in Four Slave Narratives." In *The Slave's Narrative,* edited by Charles T. Davis and Henry Louis Gates Jr. New York: Oxford University Press, 1985. 225–41.

Sterling, Dorothy. *We Are Your Sisters: Black Women in the Nineteenth Century*. New York: W. W. Norton, 1984.

Stevens, Charles E. *Anthony Burns: A History*. New York: Arno Press, 1969.

Stewart, James Brewer. *Holy Warriors: The Abolitionists and American Slavery*. New York: Hill and Wang, 1976.

Still, William. *The Underground Railroad*. Chicago: Johnson Publishing, 1970.

Stoddard, Charles Warren. "La Belle Menken." *National Magazine,* February 1905.

Story, Rosalyn M. *And So I Sing: African-American Divas of Opera and Concert*. New York: Warner Books, 1990.

Straub, Kristina. *Sexual Suspects: Eighteenth-Century Players and Sexual Ideology*. Princeton, N.J.: Princeton University Press, 1992.

Stuckey, Sterling. *The Ideological Origins of Black Nationalism*. Boston: Beacon Press, 1972.

——. *Slave Culture: Nationalist Theory and the Foundations of Black America*. New York: Oxford University Press, 1987.

Sundquist, Eric J. *To Wake the Nations: Race in the Making of American Literature*. Cambridge, Mass.: Belknap Press of Harvard University Press, 1993.

Sweet, Frank. *A History of the Minstrel Show*. Palm Coast, Fla.: Backintyme, 2000.

Takaki, Ronald T. *Iron Cages: Race and Culture in Nineteenth-Century America*. New York: A. A. Knopf, 1979.

Tanner, Jo A. *Dusky Maidens: The Odyssey of the Early Black Dramatic Actress*. Westport, Conn.: Greenwood Press, 1993.

Tate, Claudia. *Domestic Allegories of Political Desire: The Black Heroine's Text at the Turn of the Century*. New York: Oxford University Press, 1992.

Taylor, Clare. *British and American Abolitionists: An Episode in Transatlantic Understanding*. Edinburgh, Scotland: Edinburgh University Press, 1974.

Taylor, Diana. *The Archive and the Repertoire: Performing Cultural Memory in the Americas*. Durham, N.C.: Duke University Press, 2003.

Taylor, George. "John Baldwin Buckstone." In *Trilby and Other Plays*, edited by George Taylor. New York: Oxford University Press, 1996. 3–5.

Terry, Jennifer, and Jacqueline Urla. *Deviant Bodies: Critical Perspectives on Difference in Science and Popular Culture*. Bloomington: Indiana University Press, 1995.

Thompson, Kathleen. "Adah Isaacs Menken." In *Black Women in America: An Historical Encyclopedia*, edited by Darlene Clark Hine. Vol. 2. Brooklyn: Carlson, 1993. 782.

Thomson, Rosemarie Garland. *Freakery: Cultural Spectacles of the Extraordinary Body*. New York: New York University Press, 1996.

Toll, Robert C. *Blacking Up: The Minstrel Show in Nineteenth Century America*. New York: Oxford University Press, 1974.

——. "Social Commentary." In *Inside the Minstrel Mask: Readings in Nineteenth-Century Blackface Minstrelsy*, edited by Annemarie Bean, James V. Hatch, and Brooks McNamara. Hanover, N.H.: Wesleyan University Press, 1996. 86–109.

Torgovnick, Marianna. *Gone Primitive: Savage Intellects, Modern Lives*. Chicago: University of Chicago Press, 1990.

Van Deburg, William L. *Slavery and Race in American Popular Culture*. Madison: University of Wisconsin Press, 1984.

Wald, Gayle F. *Crossing the Line: Racial Passing in Twentieth-Century U.S. Literature and Culture*. Durham, N.C.: Duke University Press, 2000.

——. *Music in the Air: A Life of Rosetta Tharpe*. Boston: Beacon, forthcoming.

Walker, Kara. "Interview with Lawrence Rinder." *The CCAC Institute Publication* Capp Street Project. Oakland, Calif. April 3, 1999.

Walkowitz, Judith R. *City of Dreadful Delight: Narratives of Sexual Danger in Late-Victorian London*. Chicago: University of Chicago, 1992.

Wallace-Sanders, Kimberly. *Skin Deep, Spirit Strong: The Black Female Body in American Culture*. Ann Arbor: University of Michigan Press, 2002.

Wallinger, Hannah. "Voyage into the Heart of Africa." In *The Black Imagination and the Middle Passage*, edited by Maria Diedrich, Henry Louis Gates Jr., and Carl Pedersen. New York: Oxford University Press, 1999. 203–14.

Walsh, Townsend. *The Career of Dion Boucicault*. New York: B. Blom, 1967.

Ward, Andrew. *Dark Midnight When I Rise: The Story of the Jubilee Singers, Who Introduced the World to the Music of Black America*. New York: Farrar, Straus & Giroux, 2000.

Wardley, Lynn. "Relic, Fetish, Femmage: The Aesthetics of Sentiment in the Work of Stowe." In *The Culture of Sentiment: Race, Gender and Sentimentality in Nineteenth Century America*, edited by Shirley Samuels. New York: Oxford University Press, 1992.

Waters, T. A. *The Encyclopedia of Magic and Magicians*. New York: Facts on File, 1988.

Weisberg, Barbara. *Talking to the Dead: Kate and Maggie Fox and the Rise of Spiritualism*. San Francisco: Harper SanFrancisco, 2004.

Westermann, Claus. *Praise and Lament in the Psalms*. Atlanta: J. Knox Press, 1981.

Wexman, Virginia Wright. "Horrors of the Body: Hollywood's Discourse on Beauty and Rouben Mamoulian's Dr. Jekyll and Mr. Hyde." In *Dr. Jekyll and Mr. Hyde after One Hundred Years,* edited by William Veeder and Gordon Hirsch. Chicago: University of Chicago Press, 1988. 283–307.

White, Shane. *Stories of Freedom in Black New York.* Cambridge, Mass.: Harvard University Press, 2002.

White, Shane, and Graham J. White. *Stylin': African American Expressive Culture from Its Beginnings to the Zoot Suit.* Ithaca, N.Y.: Cornell University Press, 1998.

Wiegman, Robyn. *American Anatomies: Theorizing Race and Gender.* Durham, N.C.: Duke University Press, 1995.

——. "The Anatomy of Lynching." *Journal of the History of Sexuality* 3.3 (January 1993): 445–67.

Wilentz, Sean. *Chants Democratic: New York City and the Rise of the American Working Class, 1788–1850.* New York: Oxford University Press, 1984.

Williams, Linda. *Playing the Race Card: Melodramas of Black and White from Uncle Tom to O. J. Simpson.* Princeton, N.J.: Princeton University Press, 2001.

Williams, Patricia J. *The Alchemy of Race and Rights.* Cambridge, Mass.: Harvard University Press, 1991.

Williamson, Joel. *New People: Miscegenation and Mulattoes in the United States.* New York: New York University Press, 1984.

Willis, Deborah, and Carla Williams. *The Black Female Body: A Photographic History.* Philadelphia: Temple University Press, 2002.

Willis, Deborah, and Carla Williams, eds. *Picturing Us: African American Identity in Photography.* New York: New Press, 1994.

Wilstach, Paul. *Richard Mansfield: The Man and the Actor.* New York: Charles Scribner & Sons, 1908.

Wimbush, Vincent L. "Introduction: Reading Darkness, Reading Scriptures." In *African Americans and the Bible: Sacred Text and Social Textures,* edited by Vincent L. Wimbush. New York: Continuum, 2000. 1–43.

Winter, Kari J. *Subjects of Slavery, Agents of Change: Women and Power in Gothic Novels and Slave Narratives, 1790–1865.* Athens: University of Georgia Press, 1992.

Winter, William. *The Life and Art of Richard Mansfield.* New York: Moffat, Yard, and Company, 1910.

Wolff, Cynthia Griffin. "Passing beyond the Middle Passage: Henry 'Box' Brown's Translations of Slavery." *Massachusetts Review* 37.1 (1996): 23–44.

Wolff, Janet. "Reinstating Corporeality: Feminism and Body Politics." In *Meaning in Motion: New Cultural Studies of Dance,* edited by Jane C. Desmond. Durham, N.C.: Duke University Press, 1997. 81–99.

Wolff, Robert L. *Sensational Victorian: The Life and Fiction of Mary Elizabeth Braddon.* New York: Garland Publishing, 1979.

Woll, Allen L. *Black Musical Theatre: From Coontown to Dreamgirls.* Baton Rouge: Louisiana State University Press, 1989.

——. *Dictionary of the Black Theatre: Broadway, Off-Broadway, and Selected Harlem Theatre*. Westport, Conn.: Greenwood Press, 1983.

Wood, Marcus. " 'All Right!' The Narrative of Henry Box Brown as a Test Case for the Racial Prescription of Rhetoric and Semiotics." *Proceedings of the American Antiquarian Society* 107.1 (April 1997): 65–104.

——. *Blind Memory: Visual Representations of Slavery in England and America, 1780–1865*. New York: Routledge, 2002.

Woodward, C. Vann. *The Strange Career of Jim Crow*. New York: Oxford University Press, 1955.

Yarborough, Richard. "Strategies of Black Characterization in *Uncle Tom's Cabin* and the Early Afro-American Novel." In *New Essays on Uncle Tom's Cabin,* edited by Eric J. Sundquist. New York: Cambridge University Press, 1986. 45–84.

——. Introduction. *Contending Forces: A Romance Illustrative of Negro Life North and South,* by Pauline E. Hopkins. New York: Oxford University Press, 1988. xxvii–xlviii.

Yee, Shirley J. *Black Women Abolitionists: A Study in Activism, 1828–1860*. Knoxville: University of Tennessee Press, 1992.

Yellin, Jean Fagan. Introduction. *Incidents in the Life of a Slave Girl,* by Harriet Jacobs. Cambridge, Mass.: Harvard University Press, 1987. xiii–xxxiv.

——. *Women and Sisters: The Antislavery Feminists in American Culture*. New Haven, Conn.: Yale University Press, 1989.

Zagona, Helen Grace. *The Legend of Salome and the Principle of Art for Art's Sake*. Geneva: Droz, 1960.

# INDEX

antislavery (*continued*)
370 n.148. *See also* abolitionism; Box
Brown, Henry
archives, controversies within, 9–10,
404 n.104
Ardenne, Tessa, 185–86
Asian racial caricature, 245–46, 402
n.86, 405 n.120
audience: abolitionism and, 74, 76, 91,
94–96, 113, 120, 123, 362 n.48, 367
n.119; black spectators and, 217, 298–
99, 302–3, 398 n.39, 398 n.40; desire
and, 182–84; (dis)belief and, 167–68;
gender and, 19, 159–60, 161, 182–84,
203, 324, 386 n.82; Jim Crow and, 297,
302–3; narrative strategies and, 72–73,
74, 108, 110, 159–60, 368 n.119; participation of, 90, 96, 110, 364 n.75, 406
n.132; performer's relationship to, 10,
72–73, 218, 224, 253, 298–99, 301;
racial phantasmagoria and, 15, 39, 43,
60–61, 175–76; segregation and, 302–
3, 398 nn.39–40, 400 n.58; voyeurism
of, 53; whiteness and, 19, 72, 112, 298–
300, 303, 304, 305
Auerbach, Nina, 23
authenticity: actor and performance, 65;
authorship and, 73–74; black abolitionists and, 66, 78; blackness and, 135,
139, 238; black performance and, 217,
222, 234, 238, 257–58, 262–63, 279, 280,
337–38; Box Brown and, 95, 97, 126,
128, 129–30, 368 n.119; class mobility
and, 262–63; corporeal performance
and, 337; culture and, 299, 300–301;
fugitive slaves and, 66; minstrelsy and,
63; *Mirror of Slavery* and, 95–97, 128;
panoramas and, 82, 368 n.119; pantomime and, 23; race and, 65, 95, 135,
139, 217, 222, 232; racial identity and,
139, 241–42, 267–68; skin color and,
229–32, 238, 330; slave narratives and,
97, 126, 128, 129–30, 368 n.119

authorship: authenticity, 73–74; Box
Brown and, 69, 111, 364 n.79, 373
n.184; race and, 20; slave narratives
and, 69, 73–74
autonomy: culture of performance
and, 23
*Avenue Q* (Lopez and Marx), 344–45

Ball, Charles, 372 n.165
Ball, James Presley, 85, 361 n.48
*Bandanna Land* (Williams and Walker
Company), 233–34, 328, 332–33, 413
n.113
Banvard, John, 80, 86, 92, 364 n.78
Barclay, George L., 138–41, 145, 376 n.4,
379 n.27
Barrett, Lindon, 117, 315
Bartmann, Sarah, 154, 382 n.48
Bassard, Katherine, 309
Bata Kindai Amgoza Ibn Lo Bagola (aka
Joseph Howard Lee), 374 n.1
Batson, Flora, 314
Bay, Mia, 217
Bean, Annemarie, 395 n.150
Beckman, Karen, 121
Bedman, Henry, 128
Bell, John, 169
Benjamin, Walter, 89
Bentley, Toni, 342
Bibb, Henry, 67, 90, 106
black abolitionists: cultural production
and, 67–69; panoramas and, 68–69,
81–84, 93–94, 361 n.48; reformists
and, 78–79, 85–86. *See also* Box
Brown, Henry
*Black Crook, The,* 24–25
*Black Doctor, The,* 352 n.44
*Black Ey'd Susan* (Jerrold), 178–79, 189,
194–96, 198, 200, 387 n.101, 392 n. 139
blackface: Bert Williams and, 233–34,
240; blackness and, 2, 29, 98, 185–86,
233–34, 235–38, 240; black performers
and, 63, 65, 217, 220, 232, 233–34, 240,

Mankowitz, Wolf, 167, 380 n.36, 387
n.101, 394 n.144
Mansfield, Richard, 51–52, 58–65, 356
n.129
Marsh, J. B. T., 300, 307, 316
Martin, Herbert Woodward and Ronald
Primeau, 246
Martin, Randy, 273
Marx, Adrien, 161, 163, 383 n. 62
Maskelyne, J. N., 121
masquerade: corporeal, 4, 26, 235–36;
drag and, 179–81, 190–91, 256–57,
262–63; gender and, 374 n.1; as
impersonation, 254, 256; minstrel
performance and, 2, 27, 33–34; pan-
tomime and, 207–8; skin color and,
33–34, 39–40, 180–81, 231–32, 276;
subversive, 327; women and, 374 n.1
Mattison, Hiram, 14–15, 17–21, 22–23,
31, 32, 351 n.16
May, Samuel, 362 n.56, 371 n.149
Mayo, Frank, 387 n.101
*Mazeppa*, 11, 134, 152, 154, 165–70, 172,
173–78, 179–85, 356 n.124, 376 n.5, 384
n.70, 387 n.97, 387 n.101
McAllister, Marvin, 389 n.121
McClary, Susan, 312
McClintock, Anne, 210
McConachie, Bruce, 368 n.121
McDonald, Audra, 343
McDougall, Walter, 401 n.78
McDowell, Deborah, 158
McIntosh, Hattie, 219
McKim, James Miller, 127–28
McKoy Twins (Millie-Christine), 131,
374 n.1
Meer, Sarah, 365 n.94, 388 n.118
melodrama, 30–31, 33, 36–38, 108–9,
125–26. *See also* sensation melodrama
Melville, Herman, 107
Menken, Adah Isaacs, 131–206; Annie
Josephs and, 389 n.121; audience and,
386 n.82; authenticity and, 135, 139,

155–56, 171–72, 176–77, 185; blackface
and, 185–86, 203–4, 394 n.145; blackness and, 135–37, 139–40, 143, 147, 149,
151, 154, 156, 204, 377 n.17, 379 n.26; as
breeches actress, 174, 180, 183, 184,
191–92, 196–97, 203–4; California
years, 176–84; captivity narrative, 144,
379 n.27, 380 n. 30, 380 n.31; as coon
songs and, 404 n.117; corporeal performance and, 155–56, 160–63, 164–
66, 167–73; costume and, 180–82, 187,
193, 385 n.77, 385 n.80, 391 n.130; Creole identity and, 139, 140–42, 378
n.20; cross-dressing and, 134, 180,
191–93, 258; drag and, 388 n.106;
Dumas and, 382 n.47; early history, 4,
11, 132–36, 138–39, 376 n.4, 376 n.8,
378 n.21, 380 nn.33–34; eccentricity
and, 158; Elizabeth Cady Stanton and,
376 n.5; English sailor narrative, 194–
96, 198, 199; escape themes, 190–91;
gender identity and, 176–77, 183–84,
191–93, 195–96, 203–4; homoeroticism and, 145, 192, 197, 201; horsemanship, 166–67, 173–74, 182–84, 195,
385 n.74, 386 n.94, 388 n.111; images
of, 133, 162, 171, 177, 187, 191, 192, 200,
205; impersonations and, 189; *Infelicia*, 376 n.4; Jack Tar character, 194,
195, 197, 392 n.132; literary influences
on, 148–49, 380 n.36, 382 n.47, 384
n.66; "Lola Montez," 390 n.123; marriages, 138–39, 142, 173, 178, 375 n.3,
376 n.12, 380 n.30; Marx and, 161, 163,
383 n.62, 383 n. 62; masculinities and,
195–96, 198–99; minstrelsy and, 177–
78; miscegenation and, 152, 177; Murdoch and, 164–65; Newell biography,
138–39, 149, 150, 173, 376 n.12, 376 n.13,
381 n.43; New Orleans and, 141, 142–
43, 147, 150–51, 375 n.3, 376 n.4, 376
n.8, 378 n.39; nudity and, 161–63, 167–
70, 385 n.74; *Octoroon* production,

Nottage, Lynn, 414 n.4
*Nubian Slave, The* (Green), 84

Obichere, Boniface, 264
*Octoroon, The* (Bell), 169
*Octoroon, The* (Boucicault), 30–48; abolitionism and, 34; alternative endings, 354 n.83; American version, 33, 34–35, 41, 42; Bell sculpture, 169; blackness and, 38–42; British production, 34, 43–48; compared to *Dr. Jekyll and Mr. Hyde*, 21–22, 51–52; critical reviews of, 34–35, 39, 41, 43, 45–46; English nationalism and, 47–48; gender and, 29–30, 41–42; morality and, 36–38, 45; *New York Herald* review, 354 n.75; racial identity within, 34–38; racial order and, 32–34; racial transfiguration and, 29–30, 38–42; slavery and, 34, 39–40, 47; transatlantic bodies and, 41; whiteness and, 38–42
*Octoroon, The* (Braddon), 44–45
*Of One Blood, Or, the Hidden Self* (Hopkins), 289–326; audience and, 298–303, 304–5; black womanhood and, 308–9, 317–18, 321, 322–26; class mobility and, 298, 310–11, 315–16; diasporic consciousness and, 319–26; divas, 320–21; ethnosympathy and, 299, 305–6; Fisk Jubilee Singers and, 292–303, 315–16; gender and, 309–14, 319, 322; "Go Down, Moses," 303–9; historical performance and, 292, 295–97, 295–98; new psychology and, 293; sacred song and, 299–300; spiritualism and, 321–26; subjectivity/artistry in, 300–301
Olney, James, 72, 74, 126, 367 n.114
Olwine, Wayne, 392 n.139
O'Meally, Robert, 307
opacity: as aesthetic device, 110–11, 159–60, 337, 340–41, 350 n.13; blackness and, 8, 101, 108, 110–11, 137–38, 165–

66, 341, 350 n.13; defined, 8–9; resistance and contestation and, 8, 74, 101–2, 106–8, 350 n.13; self-invention and, 159–60, 161, 165–66, 173, 350 n.13; social mobility and, 342; terror and, 109–10; the Veil and, 160–61, 165–66, 173, 336–37. *See also* visibility and invisibility
Osgood, Nancy, 85, 363 n.63
*Out of Bondage* (Bradford), 410 n.70

pain: freedom and, 74, 122; racialized, 36, 37–38, 74, 122, 169, 352 n.44; terror and, 110
Painter, Nell, 157, 383 n.52
Pan-Africanism, 242–43, 250, 264, 268, 291, 293, 328, 329, 403 n.102
*Panorama of a Whaling Voyage* (Russell and Purrington), 85
*Panorama of the Mississippi and Missouri Rivers* (Banvard), 92
panoramas: Africa and, 90; antislavery, 47–48, 68, 78–79, 81–84, 86, 93–94, 361 n.48, 363 n.63; authenticity and, 82, 368 n.119; black abolitionists and, 81–84, 93–94; blackface and, 83–84, 98–99; blackness and, 92; cycloramas, 358 n.9, 362 n.49, 369 n.128; fugitive slaves and, 91, 360 n.37, 368 n.119; imperialism and, 47–48, 82–83; landscape painting and, 78, 79–81, 361 n.48, 362 n.60, 368 n.127; minstrelsy and, 86; moving panoramas, 79–84, 361 n.45, 363 n.62, 364 n.75; mythic history and, 88–93; nationalism and, 47–48, 94; New England reform and, 85–86; panopticon devices and, 111; *Panorama of a Whaling City* (Russell and Purrington), 85; *Panorama of the Mississippi and Missouri Rivers* (Banvard), 92; *Paris by Night,* 78; river imagery in, 80–81, 88–89, 92; sacred song and, 102–3; veracity and, 82. See

also *Mirror of Slavery, The* (Box Brown)

pantomimes, 23–24, 27, 207–8, 352 n.34, 361 n.45

*Paris by Night,* 78, 360 n.35

parody, 24, 203–4, 246, 256, 271–74, 278, 355 n.104

passing narratives, 131–32, 140–41, 143, 146, 169, 192, 262, 290, 374 n.1, 378 n.23, 383 n.62, 395 n.150; New Orleans and, 378 nn.22–23. *See also* Menken, Adah Isaacs; "Vassar Girl" (von Tizler and Bryan)

Patton, Sharon, 93

Pease, Jane H., 361 n.48, 373 n.177

Pease, William H., 361 n.48, 373 n.177

*Peculiar Sam, or, The Underground Railroad* (Hopkins), 12–13, 285, 287–89, 295, 314, 408 n.16

peristrephic movement, 79, 81–82, 94. *See also* moving panoramas

Peterson, Carla, 6, 158, 169, 312

phantasmagoria shows, 15, 23–24, 30, 31

Picquet, Louisa, 19–20

Pinkins, Tonya, 344, 345–46, 348

Pinkston, C. Alex, Jr., 59, 60, 61, 63, 64, 356 n.124

Pitts, Reginald, 351 n.6

pleasure: black womanhood and, 301, 314–15, 341, 349 n.7; dandyism and, 258, 260; performance and, 283, 284, 301, 314–15; spectatorship and, 209

*Plessy v. Ferguson* (1896), 51, 326, 378 n.23

Poe, Edgar Allen, 16, 106, 107, 148–49, 354 n.81, 367 n.113, 380 n.36, 381 n.38

Porter, Maggie, 294, 315–17, 320

Post, Amy and Isaac, 16

Post, Isaac, 16

Powell, Richard, 329

Powers, Hiram, 169

Pratt, Mary Louise, 45, 208

Primeau, Ronald, 246

Prochaska, David, 391 n.130

psalms: escape and deliverance and, 369 n.138; "Hymn of Thanksgiving" and, 103, 112–17, 369 nn.138–40, 370 n.147; lament psalms, 102; Psalm 40, 102–3, 112–13, 115, 116, 366 n.107, 369 n.138, 369 n.140

public culture: blackness and, 156, 159, 233, 235, 246, 260–61; corporeal performance and, 8, 50–51, 53–54, 68, 69, 117, 120, 135, 265, 342; dandyism and, 260–61; racialization and, 160, 163, 168–69; racialized female mythologies and, 137–38, 143–44, 146, 154–55, 156, 160, 313

*Pudd'nhead Wilson* (Twain), 51

Purrington, Caleb, 85

*Quack Doctor, The,* 28, 216, 352 n.44

queer interventions, 55, 197, 256–57, 273–74

Raboteau, Al, 369 n.138

racial categorization: binaries, 37; enslavement and, 19; Eurocolonialism and, 45; hair and, 229–30, 233–34; hierarchies, 57; loss and, 34; mulattas/mulattos, 18–21, 49; in *The Octoroon* (Boucicault), 32–34; purity and, 34; racial ambiguity, 18–19, 54–55, 169; skin color, 229–32; slave narratives and, 381 n.40; surveillance and, 20; white supremacy and, 57

racial identity: authenticity and, 139, 241–42; back-to-Africa musicals and, 211–12, 215, 221, 241–42; blackness and, 139–41; burnt cork performance and, 186, 199, 224, 235; class mobility and; Creoles and, 141–42; cross-dressing and, 258; dandyism and, 60, 97, 100, 235–36, 258–61, 260–63; impersonation and, 199; interracial marriage

racial identity (*continued*)
and, 142; Jim Crow and, 52, 381 n.39;
loss and, 34, 234, 304–6, 311–12;
nudity and, 171–72; psychological terror of, 148; visibility and, 335–36. *See
also* Menken, Adah Isaacs
racialization: deviance and, 53–55; in *Dr.
Jekyll and Mr. Hyde,* 53–56; Gothic
monstrosity and, 50–51, 54–55, 65,
149; masculinities and, 195–96, 198–
99; nudity and, 171–72; sexual difference and, 55
racialized masculinities, 198–99, 203–4
racial monstrosity, 49, 50–51, 54, 56, 57,
65, 149
racial phantasmagoria, 21, 35–37, 39,
148–49, 186; audience and, 15, 39, 43,
60–61, 175–76; blackface and, 27; in *In
Dahomey,* 209, 228–33; in *Dr. Jekyll
and Mr. Hyde,* 50–51, 55–58, 60–65;
essentialism and, 400 n.58; phantasmagoria shows, 15, 23–24, 30, 31;
women and, 41–42, 154
*Raisin in the Sun* (Hansberry), 343–44
Rashad, Phylicia, 343–44
Redgrave, Roy, 392 n.139
reformists: apocalyptic melodramas
and, 108–9, 125–26; black abolitionists and, 78–79, 85–86; fugitive slaves
and, 358 n.8; histotexuality and, 296–
97, 298; New England, 85–86; spiritualism and, 124–26, 373 n.178; utopian, 363 n.63
Reilly, Bernard F., 71, 93–94, 372 n.165,
373 n.185
Remond, Charles, 373 n.177
Remond, Charles Lennox, 361 n.48
resistance politics: collective resistance,
286; fugitive slaves and, 91–92; gaze
and, 53, 76, 91, 93, 103, 107–8, 253, 304,
337, 338, 350 n.16; opacity and, 8, 74,
101–2, 106–8, 350 n.13; performance
and, 130, 215–16, 224, 231; psychologi-

cal space and, 271, 288, 325, 331; sacred
song and, 303–9; spiritualism and,
284, 292, 323, 324–25; swamp iconog-
raphy and, 106, 107–8
Retman, Sonnet, 397 n.27
Reynolds, David, 108
Reynolds, Harry, 65
Rice, T. D., 217
Richards, Sandra, 215
Ricketson, Joseph, Jr., 84, 362 n.58
Riis, Thomas, 225–26, 249, 250–51, 276,
395 n.3, 396 n.11, 399 n.55, 402 n.86,
403 n.101, 404 n.117
Ripley, C. Peter, 359 n.13, 361 n.48, 371
n.155
Roach, Joseph, 29, 34, 38, 39, 40, 41, 323
Roberts, Benjamin F., 84, 369 n.135
Robertson, Agnes, 31, 35, 39, 41–42, 52
Robinson, America, 294, 315–16
Robinson, Amy, 163, 254–55
*Robinson Crusoe* (burlesque), 225
Rogers, Alex, 219, 252, 397 n.37
Rogin, Michael, 22
*Rookwood,* 389 n.119
Rose, Anika Noni, 343
Ross, Albert, 243
Rourke, Constance, 393 n.141
Rowell, George, 47
Rowland, Mabel, 269
Ruggles, Jeffrey, 84, 130, 363 n.66, 365
n.89, 369 n.135, 373 n.184, 374 n.197
Russell, Benjamin, 85
Russell, Sylvester, 212, 226, 239, 257–58,
260, 282, 396 n.24, 398 n.39, 403 n.95
Rutling, Thomas, 294

sacred songs, 102–3, 115, 117–18, 303–9,
369 n.140, 370 nn.146–48
Said, Edward, 268
Saks, Eva, 34, 49
*Salome, the Dance of the Seven Veils,* 12,
286, 293, 329–32, 334–42, 413 n.104,
413 n.113

Walker, Eliza, 294

Walker, George, 4, 215, 216–19, 221, 235, 236, 237, 397 n.25, 404 n.116. See also *In Dahomey* (Williams and Walker Company)

Walker, Kara, 358 n.9, 362 n.49, 369 n.128

Walker, Rachel, 314

Walker, Stuart, 371 n.155

Walton, Lester, 338–39, 413 n.113

Warner, Samuel, 104–5, 106, 107, 367 n.111

Warrick Fuller, Meta, 329–30, 335, 413 n.105

Watts, Isaac, 369 n.140

Webb, R. D., 1–3, 360 n.37, 371 n.155

Wells, Ida B., 57, 281–82, 407 n.2

Wells Brown, William, 1, 66, 77–78, 81, 102, 127, 213, 360 n.37, 362 n.56, 370 n.148

White, George, 294, 299, 319, 320

White, Shane, 389 n.121

whiteface, 352 n.37

whiteness: audience and, 19, 72, 112, 298–300, 303, 304, 305; blackface and, 25–26; blackness and, 19–20, 55, 148–49, 354 n.81; black womenhood and, 379 n.26; class power and, 57; enslavement and, 19; Jim Crow and, 52, 58, 213, 297, 302–3, 378 n.23, 381 n.39; masculinities and, 195–96, 198–99, 203–4; minstrel performance and, 28–29; miscegenation and, 49; nudity and, 168–69; *Octoroon, The* (Boucicault), 38–42; racial ambiguity of, 19–20; slavery and, 41–42; social mobility and, 381 n.44; stability of, 136

white supremacy: Civil War and, 48, 58, 214, 252; class hierarchies and, 57; mulattas/mulattos and, 49; racial categorization and, 57; sexual identity and, 57; terror and, 51, 57, 107, 162, 185

Whitman, Walt, 148, 380 n.36

Whitman Sisters, 384 n.63, 395 n.149, 401 n.76

Whittier, John Greenleaf, 306

Wiegman, Robin, 57

Wiggins, Thomas Greene (Blind Tom), 374 n.1

Wilberforce, William, 392 n.139

Wilde, Oscar, 331, 342

Williams, Bert, 4, 218, 227–28, 236, 237, 248, 333–34, 397 n.24, 399 n.47. See also *In Dahomey* (Williams and Walker Company)

Williams, Carla, 7

Williams, Frank, 405 n.120

Williams, Linda, 30, 37

Williams, Lottie, 219

Williams, Patricia, 158

Williams and Walker Company, 218–26, 233–34, 240. See also *Abyssinia* (Williams and Walker Company); *Bandanna Land* (Williams and Walker Company); *In Dahomey* (Williams and Walker Company)

Williamson, Joel, 49, 351 n.16

Willis, Deborah, 7

Wilson, Harriet, 288, 351 n.6, 412 n.91

Wilstach, Paul, 64–65

Wimbush, Vincent, 109

*Winona* (Hopkins), 289

Winter, William, 59–60, 65, 165, 356 n.124, 376 n.5, 384 n.70

Wolcott, Josiah, 85–86, 363 nn.62–63

Wolff, Cynthia, 81, 90

Woll, Allen, 243

women: blackface and, 137, 186, 199, 202, 312, 394 n.145, 394 n. 147; blackness and, 38; burlesque and, 24, 164, 168, 199–200, 332, 395 n.149; class mobility and, 137–38, 189, 261, 262, 281–82, 285–86, 327, 381 n.45; comedy performances, 326–27; contemporary theatre culture and, 343–48; coon songs and, 262, 333, 397 n.36, 404 n.117;

divas and, 324–26; masquerade and, 374 n.1; minstrel performance and, 352 n.35, 394 n.145, 394 n.147, 395 n.149, 395 n.150, 404 n.117; race and, 11, 38, 41–42, 143–45; representation in *Dr. Jekyll and Mr. Hyde,* 59–60; spiritualism and, 18; survival literature and, 45; vaudeville and, 330

Wood, Marcus, 91, 103, 129, 366 n.107

Work, John W., 307

World Fair (Chicago, 1893), 336

World Fair (Paris, 1900), 340

Wright, Henry, 120

Yarborough, Richard, 285, 336, 365 n.94, 388 n.118

Zagona, Helen Grace, 331

Zimmerman, J. Frederick, 402 n.88

"Zoe, The Octoroon," 387 n.102

Daphne A. Brooks is an associate professor of African
American Studies and English at Princeton University.

———

A version of the middle section of chapter 3 appeared as
" 'The Deeds Done in My Body': Black Feminist Theory, '
Performance, and the Truth about Adah Isaacs Menken," in
*Recovering the Body: Self Representations by African American
Women Writers*, ed. Michael Bennett and Vanessa Dickerson
(New Brunswick, N.J.: Rutgers University Press, 2000), 41–70.
Grateful acknowledgment is made to Rutgers University Press
for permission to reprint this previously published work.

———

Library of Congress Cataloging-in-Publication Data
Brooks, Daphne.
Bodies in dissent : spectacular performances of race and
freedom, 1850–1910 / Daphne A. Brooks.
p. cm.
Includes bibliographical references and index.
ISBN 0-8223-3710-x (cloth : alk. paper)
ISBN 0-8223-3772-3 (pbk. : alk. paper)
1. African Americans in the performing arts. 2. African
American theater—History—19th century. 3. African
American theater—History—20th century. 4. Brown, Henry
Box, b. 1816. 5. Hopkins, Pauline E. (Pauline Elizabeth)—
Criticism and interpretation. I. Title.
PN2270.A35B77 2006
791.089'96073—dc22 2006001662